MUSIC THERAPY

Second Edition

MUSIC THERAPY

AN INTRODUCTION

By

JACQUELINE SCHMIDT PETERS
MMT, MT-BC

Charles C Thomas
PUBLISHER • LTD.
SPRINGFIELD • ILLINOIS • U.S.A.

Published and Distributed Throughout the World by

CHARLES C THOMAS • PUBLISHER, LTD.
2600 South First Street
Springfield, Illinois 62704

© 2000 *and* 1987 by CHARLES C THOMAS • PUBLISHER, LTD.

ISBN 0-398-07042-3 (cloth)
ISBN 0-398-07043-1 (paper)

Library of Congress Catalog Card Number: 99-088599

First Edition, 1987
Second Edition, 2000

With THOMAS BOOKS *careful attention is given to all details of manufacturing and design. It is the Publisher's desire to present books that are satisfactory as to their physical qualities and artistic possibilities and appropriate for their particular use.* THOMAS BOOKS *will be true to those laws of quality that assure a good name and good will.*

Printed in the United States of America
JL-R-3

Library of Congress Cataloging-in-Publication Data

Peters, Jacqueline Schmidt.
    Music therapy: an introduction / by Jacqueline Schmidt Peters. – 2nd ed.
        p. cm.
Includes bibliographic references (p.) and indexes.
ISBN 0-398-07042-3 (cloth) – ISBN 0-398-07043-1 (pbk.)
1. Music therapy. I. Title.

ML 3920 .P383 2000
615.8'5154–dc21   99-088599

To the glory of God,
who gave us music and the ability to use it to help others,
and to the memory of
Leo C. Muskatevc (1917–1998),
who, by his instruction and mentorship, profoundly
influenced my life as a music therapist.

PREFACE

SINCE THE FIRST edition of *Music Therapy: An Introduction* was published in 1987, the field of music therapy has continued to develop, and a wealth of new research and clinical literature has been published. For this second edition, I have extensively reviewed the music therapy literature since 1985 to update and expand the information contained in the first edition, particularly with regard to clinical practices in music therapy. The chapters dealing with definitions of and guiding principles for music therapy also reflect developments in my own thinking and perspectives, based on reading, research, and clinical work.

Like the first edition, this revision aims to provide an overview of basic information regarding (1) a definition of music therapy; (2) the skills, knowledges, and attitudes that are needed to become a competent professional music therapist; (3) the historical development of the music therapy profession; (4) general principles and procedures that guide music therapy practice; and (5) major areas of music therapy clinical practice. Due to the many new developments in music therapy practice during the past decade, the clinical practice section (Part III) has been extensively revised and greatly expanded, with each population or area of music therapy clinical practice being given its own chapter. This second edition also tries to include more information on adult clients whom music therapists may serve in each disability area. Readers may choose to read the entire text to get an idea of the broad scope of music therapy and its history, processes, and practices, or they may choose to focus on topics of particular interest. Thus, this book will be useful both to those who want to know about the field of music therapy as a whole and whose who are only interested in an overview of particular topics.

The book is divided into three major sections. Part I presents a definition of music therapy (Chapter One) and discusses the music therapist's education and training (Chapter Two). Part II gives the historical background for music therapy, both from the perspective of the use of music in healing practices from ancient times to the present (Chapter Three) and from that of the development of the modern music therapy profession (Chapter Four). The concepts and historical overview presented in these sections provide a foundation that will enhance the reader's understanding of the clinical examples and applications presented in the final and most extensive section of the book. Part III begins with a discussion of general guidelines for the use of music in therapy (Chapters Five and Six), followed by specific examples of music therapy clinical practices with various client populations (Chapters Seven through Twenty-one). This final section concludes with an overview of several "schools" of music therapy practice (Chapter Twenty-two) and a discussion of the importance of research to the practicing clinician (Chapter Twenty-three). Some of the specific information that the reader should be able to gain from this text are enumerated in the introductions to each part of the book. Each chapter concludes with a summary, questions to help the reader reflect upon or apply the information, and suggestions for further reading. All references are contained in a separate section at the end of the book.

Those readers who are familiar with the first edition of this text will note several differences in this second edition. First, the definition of music therapy has been revised and expanded to place more emphasis on the interactional nature of the music therapy process and the importance of individualized assessment. The discussion of general guidelines for practice has also been expanded, particularly with regard to some reasons *why* music is useful for therapeutic purposes. Thus, theoretical principles and practical planning considerations now are treated in separate chapters. As mentioned above, each clinical population is now discussed in its own chapter, and more examples of music therapy interventions are given. The information on music therapy with geriatric clients has been greatly expanded, and now includes sections on the well elderly, those who are semi-independent, those who are chronically ill and cared for at home, and those who have Alzheimer's disease, as well as those in nursing homes. In addition, this second edition has several new clinical sections: music therapy and medical treatment, music therapy in physical rehabilitation programs, music therapy to promote health and well-being in the general population, and a separate chapter on music therapy for individuals who have autism. Throughout the book, there is a greater use of subheadings, which hopefully will make the outline of each chapter more apparent to the reader.

Since it is an *introduction* to music therapy, this book is directed primarily toward an audience that has little or no knowledge of the field of music therapy: students in introductory music therapy courses; professionals in related disciplines who desire a basic knowledge of the scope of music therapy, including some of the research on which music therapy is based, but who have neither the time nor the inclination to search through many sources; individuals who are contemplating a career in music therapy; those in the general public who want to find out more about the field; and the like. However, because of its copious references and wealth of suggestions for music therapy clinical work with various populations, this book may also be useful to some practicing music therapists: those who are looking for a summary of research related to music therapy and a certain population; those who are searching for additional clinical techniques they might use in their practice; those who desire a current overview of music therapy practice and research; or those who are contemplating working with a different client population.

The purpose of this text is to give the reader an idea of the entire scope of music therapy in the United States; therefore, it presents an overview of several basic topics and key concepts, rather than treating any one area in great depth. In keeping with the survey nature of the project, only brief examples of music therapy treatment procedures, rather than complete case histories, are presented. Therefore, when this text is used in an introductory music therapy course, the instructor may wish to use journal articles, case studies, and experiential activities to supplement and exemplify the material included in this book. In addition, those who use this text should be aware that its construction was guided by the philosophy that introductory courses in music therapy should primarily emphasize the *use of music* as an integral part of the treatment process, since using music and music-based experiences as their primary treatment modality is what sets music therapists apart from other therapists. To be sure, an understanding of client problems and needs and an awareness of the dynamics of the client-therapist relationship are also important to the successful practice of music therapy, and these topics are mentioned briefly in this text. However, a detailed explanation and exploration of these topics is left for more advanced courses.

This book also tries to provide the reader with a beginning list of sources for additional information on the topics surveyed. Therefore, all information presented is well-referenced, and suggestions for further reading have been provided at the end of each chapter. These sources (as well as the references they cite) should provide the reader with a good starting point for finding more detailed information on a particular topic of interest. Due to the survey nature of this project, many references listed refer to reviews or compilations of literature related to a particular topic rather than to numerous individual studies (although many individual studies are also referenced). In addition, a conscious choice has been made to cite secondary rather than primary sources in some instances, in the hope of providing references that might be most accessible (in libraries, etc.) to the average reader who desires more information or elaboration on a particular topic.

Since this book compiles information from many sources in its attempt to provide an overview of the field of music therapy, I especially want to thank all of those whose names are listed in the reference section for taking the time and making the effort to publish their findings and add to the body of knowledge of the field of music therapy. All of us interested in the field of music therapy appreciate your work! In addition, I would like to thank the many colleagues and friends who encouraged me to keep going through the tough times and complete this revision. Your support was invaluable! Finally, a special measure of thanks to my husband, Randy, and my daughters, Elizabeth and Sarah, for all their patience, love, and support as I spent time at the computer instead of with them. This project never would have been completed without their cooperation, and they have my deepest love and appreciation. Above all, my gratitude to Him who created both human beings and music and gave us the wonderful gift of being able to use music to make a difference in people's lives. For His guidance throughout life and His grace in giving me the strength and ability to complete this project, all praise, honor, thanks, and glory be to God through our Lord and Savior, Jesus Christ.

J.S.P.

CONTENTS

MUSIC THERAPY

PART I

MUSIC THERAPY AND THE MUSIC THERAPIST

IN THE FIRST section of this book, the reader is provided with some initial answers to some basic questions: What is music therapy? What does the music therapist do? What kinds of training and education does the music therapist receive? What kinds of skills and knowledges does the music therapist possess?

The information presented in Part I helps to provide a frame of reference for the material in subsequent sections. In Chapter One, a definition of music therapy is presented and discussed. In Chapter Two, attention is focused on the process of becoming a music therapist. After discussing the knowledges, skills, and attitudes that are important to the professional music therapist, the chapter gives a general overview of music therapy education and training programs in the United States and describes the professional credentials that are commonly held by music therapists in the United States.

After completing Part I, the reader should have gained the knowledge and information needed to perform the following tasks:

1. Give a brief description or definition of music therapy.

2. List the key elements that must be present for an activity or experience to be music therapy.

3. List knowledges, skills, and attitudes that are important to the professional music therapist.

4. List major areas of study and experience included in a music therapy curriculum.

5. List and briefly explain the professional credentials that are commonly held by music therapists in the United States.

Chapter One

A DEFINITION OF MUSIC THERAPY

MUSIC THERAPY has been an organized professional discipline in the United States since 1950. It is recognized by the Joint Commission on Accreditation of Health Care Organizations as one of the creative arts therapies, is listed as a related service in The Education for All Handicapped Children Act (Public Law 94-142), and was even given special recognition by a hearing before the U.S. Senate Special Committee on Aging on August 1, 1991 (Special Committee on Aging, 1992). Yet, although public awareness of music therapy has increased to the point where two thirds of the people in a recent survey had at least *heard* of music therapy (Furman, Adamek, & Furman, 1991), many people are still not sure exactly what music therapy is. If you stood on a street corner and asked people to define music therapy, you probably would get a lot of quizzical looks and a wide variety of verbal responses:

"*What* kind of therapy?"
"I think I read something about that somewhere . . ."
"Making sick music sound better?"
"Using music to help people feel good."
"Teaching music to people in institutions."
"Playing music to relax and reduce stress."
"Music *what*?"

Even if they may have some vague idea that music therapy uses music to help people in some way, members of the general public often do not realize that music therapy is a distinct professional discipline that has a large body of research and stringent educational and training requirements.

While music therapy has been defined in many ways, most definitions recognize "the significance of music and sound in achieving a broad variety of nonmusical goals in the areas of mental and physical health" (Moreno et al., 1990, p. 43). The American Music Therapy Association (AMTA) broadly defines music therapy as "the use of music in the accomplishment of therapeutic aims: the restoration, maintenance, and improvement of mental and physical health" (AMTA, 1998, p. xii). More specifically, **music therapy may be defined as a planned, goal-directed process of interaction and intervention, based on assessment and evaluation of individual clients' specific needs, strengths, and weaknesses, in which music or music-based experiences** (e.g., singing, playing musical instruments, moving or listening to music, creating or discussing songs and music) **are specifically prescribed to be used by specially trained personnel** (i.e., music therapists or those they train and supervise) **to influence positive changes in an individual's condition, skills, thoughts, feelings, or behaviors**. This definition contains several key elements that help differentiate music therapy, a scientifically-based, allied health profession, from new age music healers and mass-marketed music healing solutions (Summer, 1995; Summer & Summer, 1996) or from the general beneficial effects some individuals may experience when they participate in certain types of music experiences. For music-based experience to be true music therapy, all of the following components must be present.

MUSIC THERAPY IS A PROCESS

Music therapy is a *process*, something that takes place over time and involves growth, change, and development. Music therapy demands a commitment of time and energy from both the client and the therapist; it is not a simple, instant cure or a magical panacea. The clinical process of music therapy gradually produces an unfolding of growth toward desired outcomes (Aigen, 1995a).

Music therapy . . . is not an isolated therapeutic intervention or a single musical experience leading to a spontaneous or sudden cure. For the client, therapy is a gradual change process leading to a desired state; for the therapist, it is a systematic sequence of interventions leading to specific changes in the client. (Bruscia, 1989a, p. 48)

The process of music therapy may include various musical, creative, artistic, therapeutic, developmental, educational, interpersonal, behavioral, and scientific components as music therapist and client interact over time in both musical and nonmusical areas. More specific information on these is covered in Part III of this book.

MUSIC THERAPY IS PLANNED AND GOAL-DIRECTED, BASED ON INDIVIDUAL ASSESSMENT

Music therapy is not just any process involving musical experiences. A series of random experiences involving music that somehow help a person feel better are *not* music therapy. Rather, music therapy is a planned process that involves a carefully thought-out sequence of steps and procedures. First, the music therapist observes and assesses the client to determine problems and areas of needs as well as his or her strengths and responses to or preferences for various musical stimuli or musical experiences. Based on the information from this assessment, the music therapist sets specific goals and objectives in one or more of the client's areas of need (with the input of the client when possible). These goals and objectives give direction to the therapeutic process (Hanser, 1987). They specify what changes must occur in the client's condition, thoughts, feelings, or behaviors to indicate improvement in the targeted physical, mental, social, or emotional functioning areas. The music therapist has the same kinds of goals for clients that other members of the treatment team do (e.g., improving motor, social, cognitive, communication, behavioral, or emotional skills/functioning). The difference lies in the treatment modality: The music therapist uses music and music-based experiences to help clients reach their therapeutic goals.

Once the client has been assessed and evaluated and individual therapeutic goals have been formulated, the music therapist designs a series of specific music- and/or rhythm-based experiences that will help the client reach these goals and objectives. This music therapy treatment plan is then implemented over a designated period of time. After this period, the music therapist evaluates client progress to see if goals and objectives have been met or if revisions in treatment approaches are indicated. More specific information on assessment, goal-setting, and the process of planning music therapy intervention strategies is presented in the Chapter Six.

MUSIC THERAPY INVOLVES INTERACTION AND INTERVENTION

Music therapy is not a solitary pursuit; it involves interaction between and among three main entities: the music therapist, the client, and the music. In music therapy, as in any therapeutic or helping encounter, a supportive, success-oriented atmos- phere and a caring, trusting relationship are of vital importance. As Hanser (1987) emphasized:

One of the most significant ingredients in any successful therapeutic program is the establishment of a caring relationship between therapist and client. Without it, even the most effective techniques may be utterly useless. (p. 46)

While the music therapist and client will undoubtedly interact through words and actions apart from music at times, the primary interactions in music therapy occur through and within music activities and experiences. In the musical relationship that develops within music therapy sessions, client and therapist meet on the common ground of expression in sound. Through their listening, singing, playing, creating, moving, discussing, and responding emotionally to music, they interact in unique ways that go beyond the constraints and limits of verbal expression.

> The musical relationship is a very subtle and intimate way of connecting with another person's emotional and spiritual life, yet it leaves the therapy couple free and impersonal at the mental and physical levels. It is a sensitive and wonderful phenomenon, worthy of a great deal of study. (Priestley, 1985, p. 226)

The interaction of the music therapy process takes place because of a need for some kind of inter-

vention: the client desires to make a change in some area of his or her life and is seeking the assistance of the music therapist in making this change. Therefore, the music therapist has the responsibility to introduce some elements into the relationship or process that will move the client toward positive change and growth in his or her current area of need. In order to find appropriate intervention strategies, the music therapist must assess the client in both musical and nonmusical areas to determine the client's particular strengths, weaknesses, interests, and areas of need. Using both the special knowledge gained from the individual assessment of the client and the more general knowledge of various music experiences and their effects on human beings gained from his or her training and experience, the music therapist then plans a specific series of steps to interact purposefully with the client in and through various carefully chosen music experiences (i.e., music therapy interventions) to facilitate improvement in particular conditions, skills, thoughts, feelings, or behaviors of the client. In the relational, goal-directed process of music therapy interactions, "music is used intentionally to bring about a positive change, and the choice of music and activities is governed by this intent" (Birkenshaw-Fleming, 1993, p. vi).

MUSIC THERAPY USES MUSIC OR MUSIC-BASED EXPERIENCES

"Music therapy to be music therapy requires musical involvement" (Muskatevc, 1967, p. 138). Music is the primary tool of the music therapist, the vehicle through which he or she establishes contact with the client and the structure or modality through which the client develops skills to reach therapeutic goals. "What makes music therapy different from every other form of therapy is its reliance on music. Thus, at the core of every session is a musical experience of some kind" (Bruscia, 1991a, p. 5).

Although musical involvement is a necessary component of music therapy, clients need not be accomplished musicians to partake in or benefit from music therapy experiences. Music is a pervasive phenomenon in cultures and societies throughout the world (see Chapter Five), and most human beings are capable of experiencing music in basic ways by

listening to music, feeling its vibrations, singing, moving to music, playing simple instruments, or responding emotionally to music. Music therapists are trained to design music experiences in which people with little or no musical training can participate with some degree of success.

As they formulate activities for use in therapy, music therapists make use of their knowledge of the basic capabilities every human being possesses to make or respond to music as well as the information they have gained about the client's musical preferences and capabilities from their assessment. The music used in music therapy may be pre-composed (either selected from works of other composers or specially written by the music therapist) or improvised by the therapist and/or client. It may be in any style or form and may be conveyed or responded to through singing, listening, playing instruments, moving to music, or any combination of musical media, depending on the needs and capabilities of the client. Musical experiences used for therapy may be active, requiring the client or clients to sing, play, move to, improvise, create, or make music in some way, or they may be receptive, achieving their effect by the client or clients listening to, taking in, or receiving the music (Bruscia, 1989a).

Music therapy interventions may utilize many different kinds of music (e.g., popular, classical, country, rock, vocal, instrumental) and music-based experiences (e.g., singing, playing musical instruments, moving or listening to music, creating or discussing songs and music). No one type of music or music experience is inherently more useful than another for therapeutic purposes. In choosing appropriate music experiences and activities for use in therapy, music therapists consider all possible modes of musical experience and expression and all possible styles or genres of music. Client needs, capabilities, responses, and preferences (as indicated by the assessment) help determine the most appropriate selection of music experiences and materials for use in therapy with an individual client or group of clients. (For more information on planning music therapy intervention strategies, see Chapter Six.)

Since clients are directly involved with music and music materials in music therapy sessions, many clients develop certain musical skills as they move through the music therapy process. However, it is important to realize that the music therapist is not concerned with the development of these musical skills and behaviors for their own sake, as the music educator might be. Rather, the music therapist is concerned with how these musical skills and behaviors can be used to help the clients improve their level of physical, mental, social, or emotional functioning and facilitate the development of nonmusical skills (e.g., motor control and coordination, physical comfort, perceptual skills, cognitive or academic skills, behavior patterns, appropriate emotional expression, communication skills, problem-solving skills, interpersonal skills). "Music therapy contains many elements of recreational music and music education, but healing is its primary aim" (Birkenshaw-Fleming, 1993, p. vi). Therefore, even when music therapy interventions use activities that involve the teaching and learning of musical skills or behaviors, their primary focus is still on using these musical skills and behaviors to improve client functioning in nonmusical areas. In this way, clients develop skills through music activity that help them reach their therapeutic goals.

MUSIC THERAPY IS SPECIFICALLY PRESCRIBED

Music therapists often work directly with other professionals (e.g., physicians, psychiatrists, social workers, physical therapists, special educators) on medical or educational treatment teams. When they work in teams, these specialists meet together and decide how to coordinate their services in a way that will best help the client meet certain therapeutic goals. Musical therapy services, just like the services of other professionals, are prescribed as a specific part of the client's treatment plan. In medical settings, the prescriptive order for music therapy is signed by the physician in charge, just as an order for medication or physical therapy would be. In nonmedical settings, music therapy services may be requested formally by people like the client's caseworker, psychologist, teacher, or parents, or

music therapy services may be written into the client's treatment plan by the general consensus of the professional team. When music therapists work in private practice, the music therapist and the individual client (and/or the client's family members) work together in determining the goals for therapy and establish some sort of contract stipulating the goals and objectives, methods to be used, duration of treatment, and responsibilities of each party. In all settings, the important point to remember is that music therapy is not an all-encompassing, "hit-or-miss" diversion, but a specific corrective agent prescribed to help influence positive changes in a targeted condition, skill, thought, feeling, or behavior of an individual client.

MUSIC THERAPY IS IMPLEMENTED BY
SPECIALLY TRAINED PERSONNEL

People certainly may experience some benefits by listening to relaxing music on their own or by banging on a drum or playing a piano to let off steam, but this is not music therapy. It also takes a music therapist – a person who is specially trained to select music and structure music experiences for maximum therapeutic benefit and who knows how to use music to establish and guide a dynamic, therapeutic relationship – to transform music activity into music *therapy*. Music activities can at times have therapeutic benefits without the direction of a music therapist, but these at best occur only haphazardly or accidentally. Under the direction of a trained music therapist, however, music and music-based experiences become potent therapeutic tools that can predictably and efficiently influence positive changes in an individual's condition, skills, thoughts, feelings, or behaviors. Music therapists are highly trained professionals, who have skills and knowledge in a variety of areas, including music, human behavior, human abilities and disabilities, and the influence of music on human beings. Those who pass an examination given by the Certification Board for Music Therapists receive the credential "music therapist-board certified" (MT-BC). (More detailed information on music therapy education, training, and credentialling is presented in Chapter Two.)

In planning music therapy intervention strategies, the music therapist carefully selects the music or music activity to be used with a particular client, based on the therapist's knowledge of the effects of music on human behavior and the particular client's strengths, weaknesses, and therapeutic goals. Although the outward appearance of music experiences may change only slightly from client to client, the way these experiences are used and the purposes they serve may vary considerably (Barnard, 1953; Farnan & Johnson, 1988b). It takes the skills of a trained music therapist to adapt and structure music experiences to fit the unique needs, personality, preferences, and response patterns of each individual client, so that each may achieve the maximum possible therapeutic benefit. The music therapist also knows how to use the context of music experiences to establish a nurturing, growth-promoting relationship with the clients that will facilitate the achievement of therapeutic goals. The music therapist always keeps the client's goals in mind, structuring music therapy interventions and guiding interactions within music experiences to help the client gain skills that will help him or her reach those goals. Thus, the skills and guidance of the music therapist play a vital role in transforming music activity into music therapy.

Sometimes, music therapists may assess clients, establish goals, and plan music therapy treatment programs for clients and then train others (e.g., individual clients, family members, teachers, other professionals, or paraprofessionals) to carry out these programs on a daily basis. In these instances, it is important for the music therapist to meet regularly with the person implementing the program to evaluate client progress, make any necessary changes or revisions to the treatment program, and offer suggestions for more effective implementation.

MUSIC THERAPY IS DIRECTED TOWARD MEETING
THE SPECIFIC NEEDS OF INDIVIDUAL CLIENTS

Mass-marketed music healing cures or music self-help programs are not music therapy. Music therapy interventions are directed to meet the specific, unique needs of individual clients and are specially formulated to correspond to the individual client's unique preferences, personality, capabilities, and response patterns. Music therapy services exist to serve individual clients who need to improve some aspect of their physical, mental, social, and/or emotional functioning. Without clients who can benefit from what it has to offer, there would be no reason for music therapy. As Sears (1968) pointed out:

> Of most importance in any therapeutic situation is the person receiving the therapy. Only through the individual's behavior, and changes therein, can the success of the therapeutic endeavor be seen. (p. 31)

Music therapy techniques have been used effectively in both group and individual settings with clients of all ages who have a wide variety of needs or disabilities. In the United States, music therapy services first became widely available in adult psychiatric settings and in mental retardation centers. Now, music therapists use their special skills to help clients in a wide variety of treatment settings, including "hospitals, clinics, day care facilities, schools, community mental health centers, substance abuse facilities, nursing homes, hospices, rehabilitation centers, correctional facilities, and private practice" (AMTA, 1998, p. xii). In addition to being used in a remedial, rehabilitative, habilitative, medical, psychological, or educational way to help clients who have various physical, mental, emotional, social, learning, or behavioral problems, music therapy also may be used as preventive medicine to help reduce stress, increase coping skills, and promote or maintain physical, mental, and emotional health in the general population or certain "at risk" groups (Beckett, 1990; Bonny, 1986; Gfeller, 1988; Giles, Cogan, & Cox, 1991; Goldman, 1988; Itoh & Lee, 1989; Luetje, 1989; Staum, 1993). Chapters Seven through Twenty-one provide specific information on how music therapy services can help various client populations.

SUMMARY

Music therapy may be defined as a planned, goal-directed process of interaction and intervention, based on assessment and evaluation of individual clients' specific needs, strengths, and weaknesses, in which music or music-based experiences are specifically prescribed to be used by specially trained personnel to influence positive changes in an individual's condition, skills, thoughts, feelings, or behaviors. According to this definition, for an experience to be music therapy, it must (1) involve a process, (2) be planned and goal-directed, based on individual assessment, (3) involve interaction and intervention, (4) use music or music-based experiences, (5) be specifically prescribed, (6) be implemented by specially trained personnel (i.e., music therapists or those they train and supervise), and (7) be directed toward meeting the specific needs of individual clients.

Although musical involvement is a necessary component of music therapy, clients need not be accomplished musicians to partake in or benefit from music therapy experiences. And, while individuals may develop certain musical skills during their involvement in the music therapy process, the primary aim of music therapy is not to develop musical skills and behaviors but to utilize the learning and expressive experiences of music to help clients improve their skills in nonmusical areas, resulting in improved physical, mental, social, and/or emotional functioning.

QUESTIONS FOR THOUGHT AND DISCUSSION

Determine whether or not each of the following examples represents a music therapy situation. If an example does represent a music therapy situation, identify the elements that make it music therapy. If it does not, identify the missing element(s).

1. Tina has low self-esteem and very little self-confidence. One day she told her social worker that she would like to be able to play the piano. The social worker talked to a music therapist who worked at a local recreation center. The music therapist, the social worker, and Tina met together and decided that learning to play the piano and preparing a song to perform at one of the recreation center's programs might be a good way to help Tina develop more confidence in herself and increase her self-esteem. The music therapist plans to give Tina piano lessons two times a week so that Tina will be able to play a simple duet with the therapist for the center's winter program and a simple piano solo for the center's spring program.

2. Ken is a client at a residential facility for multiply handicapped children. Because he seems to enjoy listening to popular songs, his parents bought him a radio to keep in his room at the center. Ken often listens to the radio when he is in his room, and the music usually seems to make him calm and happy.

3. John has trouble relaxing after driving home in rush-hour traffic following a hard day at work. His friend Bill mentioned that he used to have the same problem, but he had found something that helped. Bill now plays relaxing music on the tape player in his car while he drives home and then listens to slow, quiet, soothing music on his stereo when he gets home. Bill suggests that John try this, too. John does, and he begins to feel much better and more relaxed.

4. A special education teacher has been working with her class of mentally retarded children on learning colors and numbers. Since her students enjoy music, the teacher asked the music therapist who worked for the school district to show her some music activities that would help the students learn and practice their colors and numbers. The music therapist lent the teacher some educational records and a xylophone with colored bars and told her how to use these materials to teach and reinforce color and number concepts. (HINT: Remember, the music therapist is directing the teacher as to how to use the materials and activities.)

5. David had been attending a special school for orthopedically handicapped children until he was "mainstreamed" in junior high. David signed up for beginning band at the junior high school and is now learning to play the baritone horn. He has band four times a week and private lessons with the band director once a week. David hopes to learn to play well enough to be able to play a solo for the spring contest.

SUGGESTIONS FOR FURTHER READING

Barnard, R. I. (1953). The philosophy and theory of music therapy as an adjuvant therapy. In E. G. Gilliland (Ed.), *Music therapy 1952* (pp. 45-49). Lawrence, KS: Allen Press.

Bruscia, K. E. (1989). *Defining music therapy.* Spring City, PA: Spring House Books.

Bruscia, K. E. (Ed.) (1991). *Case studies in music therapy.* Phoenixville, PA: Barcelona Publishers.

Dolan, M. C. (1973). Music therapy: An explanation. *Journal of Music Therapy, 10*(4), 172-176.

Gaston, E. T. (1954). Functions of the music therapist. In M. Bing (Ed.), *Music therapy 1953* (pp. 28-29). Lawrence, KS: Allen Press.

Gaston, E. T. (1968). Foreword. In E. T. Gaston (Ed.), *Music in therapy* (pp. v-vii). New York: Macmillan.

Graham, R. M. (1974, Fall). The education of the music therapist. *College Music Symposium, 14,* 50-59.

Hanser, S. B. (1987). *Music therapist's handbook.* St. Louis: Warren H. Green.

Lathom, W. (1981). *The role of the music therapist in the education of severely and profoundly handicapped children and youth.* Lawrence, KS: National Association for Music Therapy.

Muskatevc, L. C. (1961). The role of music therapy in the clinical setting. In E. H. Schneider (Ed.), *Music therapy 1960* (pp. 41-43). Lawrence, KS: Allen Press.

Unkefer, R. F. (1961). The music therapist. In E. H. Schneider (Ed.), *Music therapy 1960* (pp. 27-31). Lawrence, KS: Allen Press.

Chapter Two

THE EDUCATION AND TRAINING
OF THE MUSIC THERAPIST

PERSONAL QUALITIES OF VALUE TO THE ASPIRING MUSIC THERAPIST

S EVERAL PERSONAL qualities or characteristics will be beneficial to an individual who desires to become a professional music therapist (AMTA, n.d.; Gibbons, 1989; Sandbank, 1989b). The practice of music therapy is very demanding, both physically and mentally. Therefore, good physical health, energy, and stamina, as well as good mental health and emotional stability are very important to the aspiring music therapist. Other valuable skills and attributes include creativity, good coping skills, a high level of frustration tolerance, self-confidence, intelligence, good judgment, common sense, the ability to think clearly and quickly, imagination, flexibility, and an openness to new and innovative ideas and/or solutions.

Since the practice of music therapy involves establishing caring and helping professional relationships with people of many ages and ability levels, the aspiring music therapist should have a genuine interest in and desire to help people and work on developing good personal interaction skills. Qualities such as empathy and sincerity, patience, tact, and understanding, as well as the ability to relate to people of various abilities on their level, are also very valuable. In addition, music therapists need good observation and problem-solving skills and proficiency in both written and oral communication.

Music therapists are not only therapists but also musicians. Music is their primary mode of therapeutic interaction – the language through which they reach and relate to their clients. Therefore, the aspiring music therapist should have a strong interest and general background in music as well as the interest, commitment, and ability to develop strong musical skills. In addition, he or she should possess a genuine love for music, feel that music is an essential part of his or her being, and believe that music can be used to reach and help people.

Since music therapists often find themselves working in situations in which there are no other professional music therapists readily available for feedback and consultation, the aspiring music therapist would do well to develop an intrinsic sense of self-worth and motivation, a high level of self-confidence, an ability to objectively and fairly evaluate his or her own work, and an ability to work competently and efficiently without a high degree of supervision or praise from others. In addition, the ability to be a self-starter and to have the perseverance to independently carry tasks through to completion will be of great value in future music therapy work, both in researching problems and in developing and implementing treatment plans. The individual will also benefit from developing the ability to make connections and apply previous learning and experience intelligently in new situations and from learning how to integrate multidisciplinary knowledge and apply it in creative ways to a given situation. These basic personal qualities, attributes, attitudes, and characteristics all will help provide a solid foundation on which to build the unique professional knowledges, skills, and attitudes that the aspiring music therapist will acquire in the course of his or her formal professional education and training.

THE COMPONENTS OF PROFESSIONAL PREPARATION

The process of preparing to be a professional music therapist involves more than acquiring theoretical concepts in the classroom. Music therapy training also includes the practical aspects of learning to apply these concepts in clinical fieldwork and research. Both the classroom and practical learning experiences involved in music therapy training help the music therapy student develop certain professional attitudes. Thus, the training that a music therapist receives is "a unique type of preparation taking place in the classroom, laboratory and clinic that integrates several kinds of learning experiences, all directed toward producing a professional person" (Purtilo, 1978, p. 3). During the course of their formal education and training, then, music therapy students acquire a number of special knowledges, skills, and attitudes that combine to help them become competent professional music therapists.

Knowledges (Basic Theoretical Concepts)

What does a person need to *know* to become a competent professional music therapist? To help answer this question, it may be useful to remember that a music therapist is a person who uses music to help clients of many ages and with many different types of disabilities reach therapeutic goals. Thus, music therapists might be thought of as generalists who work with and through a special medium (i.e., music) (Michel, 1985). In order to use music to help people, then, music therapy students must first acquire general and specific background knowledge and information (1) about music and all of its various aspects, (2) about people (including both normal and abnormal functioning), and (3) about how music influences people. They usually obtain much of this information through coursework in classroom situations.

Since the use of music as their primary therapeutic modality is what sets music therapists apart from other therapists, individuals who wish to become music therapists must have an in-depth knowledge of music and all of its many aspects. In the United States, most music therapy educational programs are currently part of university schools of music, and aspiring music therapists must be accepted as music majors by the university. Music history and music theory courses that are part of university music curricula give music therapy students more knowledge and understanding of their special tool, music. In music theory classes, they learn more about the elements of music and how they can be manipulated and arranged to create different effects, knowledges that will be useful as they later learn to select and create music for therapeutic purposes. In music history courses, they learn about many of the various forms, styles, and genres of music. Since music therapists will need to establish contact with clients from varying cultural backgrounds in their clinical work, it is important for their coursework to include basic information on various world music genres and ethnic and popular musics in addition to Western art music (Moreno, 1988; Prickett, 1989).

Because they will be working with people in a helping profession, music therapy students must acquire basic understandings of standard treatment methods for human problems as well as general knowledge of human beings and the way they communicate and interact with one another. Courses in the biological and natural sciences furnish a foundation for understanding the human body and the forces that act upon it, while behavioral science courses (e.g., psychology, sociology, anthropology) provide a basis for understanding the behaviors, needs, and interactions of people. Courses in abnormal psychology and exceptionalities provide background knowledge for understanding the unique needs of individuals who have various disabilities or handicapping conditions.

Since music therapists deal with people and music not as isolated entities but as interacting phenomena, they must also know how people acquire musical skills (music learning and musical development) and how people perceive, respond to, and are influenced by various musical phenomena. Knowledge in these areas is often obtained through studies in music psychology and the influence of music on human behavior. In professional courses on music therapy principles and practices, students are exposed to readings, resource materials, case studies, and research that illustrate the breadth and depth of the field of music therapy and the many ways that music can be used to help people reach therapeutic goals.

In this way, music therapy educators strive to provide the background knowledge necessary "to help *every* student meet the *widest* possible range of client needs which he or she may encounter in a variety of clinical settings" (Bruscia, 1989b, pp. 84-85).

Skills

What does a person need to be able to *do* to be a competent professional music therapist? In answering this question, one must take into account the "dual nature" of the music therapist. Music therapists are both musicians and therapists; therefore, they must acquire technical skills in both music and therapy as well as skills in the use of music in therapy. Skill learning, a process that involves the practical application of theoretical concepts, most often takes place in performance situations and in laboratory and clinical settings. Experiences may include instruction and rehearsal of specific techniques or skills, role-play simulations, and supervised clinical field work or practicum experiences. These experiential learning activities are a very important part of the music therapist's education and training, for an individual must be able to apply theoretical concepts in practical ways and must develop skills in working effectively with people in order to be an effective music therapy clinician (Bruscia, 1989b; Tims, 1989).

Since music is what distinguishes music therapists from all other therapists, music therapists should have highly developed technical and interpretive skills in at least one musical performance medium. Music is the "language" music therapists use in establishing contact and communication with their clients; therefore, music therapists must learn to be fluent and expressive in this language. In addition to being a fluent and competent performer on his or her major instrument, it is important the aspiring music therapist develop functional skills on a number of instruments, be able to perform artistically and sensitively in a variety of musical styles and genres, and "be able to project himself or herself musically" (Boxill, 1985, p. 89). As music therapy students gain technical musical performance skills in applied music studies, they are also developing important secondary skills (e.g., leadership, nonverbal interaction, musicianship, confidence) which can be transferred to and used in clinical settings (Cohen,

Hadsell, & Williams, 1997).

During the course of their music therapy training, individuals develop a number of specific musical skills, including keyboard, guitar, and vocal skills, the ability to arrange, compose, and improvise simple songs and accompaniments, proficiency in playing a variety of melodic and percussive non-symphonic instruments, and conducting skills. They also learn to select music materials that are appropriate to an individual's background, age level, and skill level, and gain skills in adapting materials as necessary to correspond to the special needs and capabilities of individual clients. In addition, aspiring music therapists learn to communicate musically in many different idioms and styles of music with freedom and confidence, and to improvise, compose, or arrange music for clinical and therapeutic purposes. They will begin to develop a repertoire of specific music materials, activities, and strategies that can be useful in various clinical situations and with different client populations.

To become effective *therapists*, music therapy students must learn to relate effectively to and communicate effectively with both other professionals and various clients who have wide ranges of functioning levels. To become effective *music* therapists, they must also learn how to use and structure music experiences to develop therapeutic relationships, promote growth, enhance communication, and bring about desired changes in behavior. Much of music therapy students' practical training involves learning how to assess clients, design treatment plans, and implement and evaluate music therapy sessions. In conjunction with this, students develop skills in written and oral communication as they learn how to communicate information about client progress and music therapy treatment strategies to clients, other treatment team members, and/or the client's family. As they work with groups and individuals, music therapy students also learn group management skills and behavior control strategies that employ both musical and nonmusical elements.

Finally, music therapy students develop skills in research. Through actual participation in research projects and activities, they learn how to formulate hypotheses, how to collect and analyze data in a way that will help determine whether or not their hypotheses are acceptable, and how to report research findings promptly and accurately. They also learn how to read, interpret, and critique research reports and how to apply research findings to clinical practice. The importance of research skills to professional music therapy clinicians is discussed in detail in Chapter Twenty-three.

Attitudes

Attitudes are the beliefs or dispositions one holds. They help determine how a person responds or reacts to various people, situations, or events. "Attitudes form a kind of 'bent,' an inclination to react in a certain, predictable way when certain stimuli are presented" (Michel, 1985, p. 85). Attitudes may be fostered and developed through experience, discussion, exposure to certain standards or ideas, and observation of competent role models. Some attitudes may be rooted in deeply held personal convictions and may be very resistant to change. What particular *beliefs* or *attitudes*, then, does music therapy education and training try to instill, and how do these help one function optimally as a professional music therapist?

According to Michel (1985), "a primary attitude would be one of willingness, or even of eagerness, to learn and accept the responsibilities of one's profession" (p. 100). Coupled with this attitude would be the development of a belief in the importance and efficacy of one's chosen profession. Music therapy students will develop an attitude of respect for and confidence in the profession of music therapy as they see the therapeutic power of music demonstrated in clinical situations, in controlled research studies, and in their own lives. They will learn professional responsibilities as music therapy ethics and standards of practice are discussed and analyzed in the classroom and observed and experienced in the clinic. In addition, both the American Music Therapy Association (AMTA, 1998) and Certification Board for Music Therapists (CBMT, 1998a) have established standards of professional practice and ethical conduct by which their members and certificants are to abide.

Since music therapy is an allied health field, music therapists also adhere to a general code of ethics followed by all health professionals (Michel, 1976, 1985). Basic to this code is an attitude of concern for all human beings and a willingness to assist anyone in distress. Professional ethics also mandate certain standards of behavior for relationships with clients, other professionals, and the community. For example, professional music therapists should respect a client's right to privacy and exercise care in maintaining confidentiality. Music therapists see their clients as people first, not as objects or diseases or conditions, and treat them as individual human beings with potential for wellness and growth. "Every action of a music therapist must demonstrate respect for the client and accord the client every dignity due to a fellow human being, no matter what the client's presenting problem or situation" (Prickett, 1989, p. 100). Music therapists also act with integrity toward their colleagues in music therapy and other professions and should strive to maintain harmonious relationships. Moreover, professional music therapists should make every effort to ensure that public information materials give an accurate and complete picture of professional services and facilities. Professional music therapists should also respect the social and moral expectations of the community at all times.

Two additional attitudes of importance to professional music therapists are related to the areas of continuing education and research First, it is vital that music therapists be willing to take responsibility for continual self-assessment and be committed to seeking ongoing opportunities for continuing their own learning and professional growth (Gibbons, 1989; Michel, 1985). This may involve continuing to avail themselves of opportunities to continue to grow and develop musically as well as in other professional areas. Secondly, it is important for music therapists to develop an open-minded, "scientific attitude" (Michel, 1985, p. 100) toward the world and themselves. This scientific or research attitude involves a willingness to question and rigorously test new evidence and a willingness to accept change and to change one's concepts in the face of new evidence. (The importance of the research attitude to music therapy professionals is discussed further in Chapter Twenty-three.)

Finally, aspiring music therapists will benefit from developing the attitude of looking at everything with a therapist's eye (Muskatevc, 1967). This process involves being open to learning from every encounter, perpetually asking, "What does this mean to me as a Music Therapist?" (Muskatevc, 1967, p.

139). As they approach all people and situations with attitudes of humility and respect, as they continually search to make connections and take time to stop and listen, as they are open to learning from everything and everyone, aspiring music therapists will gain many valuable insights that will help them be better persons as well as better professional music therapists.

MUSIC THERAPY DEGREE PROGRAMS

In the United States, standards for music therapy education and training programs are set by the professional music therapy association. Prior to 1998, the United States had two professional music therapy associations, the National Association for Music Therapy [NAMT] and the American Association for Music Therapy [AAMT]. Both the NAMT and the AAMT had established standards for music therapy degree programs, as well as for equivalency programs and alternate route certifications (AAMT, 1993; NAMT, 1994a, 1994b). Basic music therapy degree programs approved by the AAMT or the NAMT provided for entry-level music therapy training to be completed at the bachelor's level and included at least four years of academic coursework, pre-internship field experience, and an extended clinical internship (AAMT, 1993; Maranto & Bruscia, 1987; NAMT, 1994b). AAMT programs were totally competency-based, with AAMT specifying the competencies in music foundations, clinical foundations, and music therapy that were essential to entry-level music therapy practice and each school designing a curriculum to enable students to acquire those competencies (AAMT, 1993; Bruscia, Hesser, & Boxill, 1981). NAMT programs operated under a course/competency-based system, with the NAMT outlining a curriculum of 127 semester hours (190 quarter hours) that specified minimum percentages for coursework in areas considered essential to the practice of music therapy (45% music; 16% music therapy; 16% behavioral /health /natural sciences; 22% general education; 5% electives) as well as listing competencies to be acquired in music therapy degree programs (NAMT, 1994b). While both associations required clinical internships, internships in AAMT programs were slightly shorter (a minimum of 900 clock hours as compared with NAMT's minimum of 1040 hours for internship) and more flexible. In addition, in AAMT programs, the academic institution was accountable to the AAMT for the quality of the internship, while in NAMT programs, the internship site and the clinical training director were accountable to the NAMT for the quality of the program (Maranto & Bruscia, 1987).

In 1998, NAMT and AAMT merged to form the American Music Therapy Association [AMTA], which now is the sole body for setting standards for music therapy degree programs in the United States. As of June 1, 1998, 69 colleges and universities offered degree programs approved by the AMTA, with 23 of these offering graduate as well as undergraduate programs (AMTA, 1998). For the most current information on AMTA-approved schools and internship sites, the reader should consult the AMTA web site (www.musictherapy.org).

As part of the unification agreement, the AMTA embraced "both of the educational and clinical training models that are currently approved by AAMT and NAMT" (AMTA, 1998, p. xxxviii). In addition, AMTA formed a Commission on Education and Clinical Training to make recommendations for future paradigms for music therapy education and training. In its draft report, this Commission made recommendations for association standards to cover three levels of education (bachelor's, master's, and doctoral study), with each level reflecting "different levels of competence and professional designation" (Crowe & Bruscia, 1999, p. 8). The Commission sees AMTA's role as insuring the quality of music therapy education and training by establishing outcome-specific (i.e., competency-based), flexible standards that will be continually responsive to new developments in the field (Bruscia et al., 1998; Crowe & Bruscia, 1999).

While the Commission has published a draft report and made initial recommendations (Bruscia et al., 1998; Crowe & Bruscia, 1999), its work is still in progress at this writing. The interested reader should contact AMTA for the most current information.

Undergraduate Degree Programs

In the United States, entry-level skills and competencies for music therapy practice are gained at the bachelor's level. Baccalaureate degree programs in music therapy include at least four years of academic coursework in music therapy; music; psychology; behavioral, biological, and social sciences; abnormal conditions or disabilities; and general studies. Concurrently with their academic coursework, students are involved in various supervised clinical field experiences, culminating with an in-depth internship. Here students experience the practical application of knowledge learned in the classroom, as they observe and assist music therapy professionals and then learn to assess clients' needs and independently design, implement, document, and evaluate music therapy treatment plans. Thus, "education and clinical training are not separate processes, but rather reflect a continuum of learning experiences at the undergraduate level" (Crowe & Bruscia, 1999, p. 9). Upon completion of a bachelor's degree in music therapy, individuals are eligible to take a standardized national examination offered by the independent Certification Board for Music Therapists [CBMT] which leads to the professional credential "Music Therapist-Board Certified" [MT-BC]. (For more information, see the section on "Professional Credentials for Music Therapists" later in this chapter.)

Master's Degree Programs

As the field of music therapy continually expands, "the need for graduate degrees becomes more pronounced, not only to train higher level clinicians but also to prepare them for jobs as educators, supervisors, and administrators" (Bruscia, 1986, p. 58). According to a survey of music therapy educators conducted by Maranto and Bruscia (1988), the attainment of advanced competencies in clinical skills, assessment skills, research skills, and supervisory skills are of primary importance in a master's degree program. Persons who have completed a bachelor's degree or equivalency program in music therapy and an approved internship or who have received alternate certification/registration are eligible to apply for admission to graduate programs in music therapy. Coursework at the master's degree level may include music therapy seminar, practicum, and research courses as well as work in supportive areas. Since graduate programs focus on more specific and in-depth learning, the content and orientation of master's degree programs in music therapy may vary greatly from school to school.

In its draft report of recommendations, the AMTA Commission on Education and Clinical Training viewed master's degree programs in music therapy as being designed to meet two educational objectives:

1) to provide advanced competence in entry level areas (i.e., breadth and depth of knowledge and skill in music foundations, clinical foundations, and music therapy); 2) to provide basic competence in any advanced topic or specialization in music therapy. (Crowe & Bruscia, 1999, p. 8)

Advanced topics or specializations studied in master's degrees programs might include theory development, research, supervision, college teaching, clinical administration, or in-depth study of and training in particular areas of practice, client populations, or clinical approaches.

Doctoral Study

While some academic institutions offer advanced doctoral studies with a concentration in music therapy, as of the early to mid-1990s, there were "no PhD or EdD programs solely in music therapy" (Maranto, 1993b, p. 618). Doctoral study may concentrate on research skills (experimental, historical, philosophical, and/or descriptive research), university teaching skills, advanced music therapy theory, and/or clinical specialization and advanced clinical skills (Maranto & Bruscia, 1988). Doctoral programs are often tailored to individual interests (Gibbons, 1989) and usually include a research component and require the completion of a dissertation.

The AMTA Commission on Education and Clinical Training has made initial recommendations for specific doctoral degree programs in music therapy (Bruscia et al., 1998; Crowe & Bruscia, 1999). According to these recommendations, doctoral degree programs in music therapy have two educational objectives:

1) to provide advanced competence in research (or theory development) along with college teaching and supervision; and 2) to provide advanced competence in any specialization area in music therapy. (Crowe & Bruscia, 1999, p. 9)

As the field of music therapy continues to develop, specific doctoral programs in music therapy are likely to increase. The interested reader is urged to contact AMTA for current information on doctoral degree programs in music therapy.

PROFESSIONAL CREDENTIALS FOR MUSIC THERAPISTS

When individuals have completed their bachelor's level training in music therapy, they are eligible to apply for a professional credential in music therapy. Credentials help assure the public and the employer that the individual holding the credential has received certain training and is capable of performing at a specified level of quality and competence. Professional credentialing for music therapists in the United States takes place at the national level, under the direction of the Certification Board for Music Therapists [CBMT]. CBMT is an independent certifying agency, fully accredited by the National Commission for Certifying Agencies (CBMT, 1991, 1992, 1997, 1998b). It was incorporated in 1983 as an autonomous certifying body for music therapists, independent from the professional membership association (at that time, NAMT and AAMT). Its function is to set rules and regulations for obtaining and maintaining a specific, voluntary credential; the music therapists certified by the CBMT may or may not be members of a professional music therapy membership association (CBMT, 1992). (See Chapter Four for more information on CBMT).

Since 1985, CBMT has granted the credential "Music Therapist-Board Certified" [MT-BC] to any music therapist who "has met specific educational and clinical training requirements for eligibility and has passed the Board Certification Exam" (CBMT, 1998b, p. 4). This exam provides a national objective standard to demonstrate competence in the knowledge, skills, and abilities needed for current entry-level music therapy practice. It consists of multiple choice questions covering the broad areas of music therapy foundations and principles, related clinical theories and techniques, music, and professional role and responsibilities (CBMT, 1991). To maintain board-certified status, MT-BCs must demonstrate continuing competence in music therapy practice by participating in the CBMT's recertification program, which involves ongoing continuing education or additional examinations related to current music therapy practice. MT-BCs must apply for recertification every five years (CBMT, 1991, 1997, 1998b). As of 1997, there were over 2,200 music therapists who held the MT-BC credential (CBMT, 1997).

Since all music therapy credentialling responsibilities in the United States were yielded to CBMT on January 1, 1998, as part of the unification agreement between NAMT and AAMT (AMTA, 1998), CBMT is currently the only credentialling agency for music therapists in the United States, and the MT-BC is the only music therapy credential now awarded. The MT-BC is recognized by American Music Therapy Association [AMTA] as *the* entry-level credential required to practice music therapy (AMTA, 1998).

Prior to their unification on January 1, 1998, the National Association for Music Therapy [NAMT] and the American Association for Music Therapy [AAMT] both awarded various music therapy credentials to individuals they considered to be qualified music therapists. "Registered Music Therapist" [RMT], the oldest music therapy credential in the United States, is a title that the NAMT granted from 1956–1997 to persons who had successfully completed both an NAMT-approved academic program and an NAMT-approved clinical training program. Once the individual's records had been reviewed and approved by the NAMT Registration Committee, that individual's name was added to the National Registry list maintained by the NAMT. Individuals could also apply for registration through alternate routes under special circumstances

(NAMT, 1994b). The advent of the AAMT in 1971 spawned the creation of other music therapy credentials. Through 1997, the AAMT granted the title "Certified Music Therapist" [CMT] to persons who had successfully completed AAMT-approved baccalaureate degree or equivalency programs and internships in music therapy (AAMT, 1993). Alternate route certification mechanisms were also available from the AAMT. From 1989–1997, the AAMT offered an additional credential, the title of "Advanced Certified Music Therapist" [ACMT], to music therapists who had advanced experience and training. Advanced certification required a master's degree in music therapy or a closely related field, at least 100 contact hours in continuing education, and extensive experience in music therapy (AAMT, 1993). (See Chapter Four for more information on NAMT and AAMT.)

So that qualified music therapists were not left without credentials when all credentialling responsibilities were yielded to the CBMT with the unification of AAMT and NAMT, the National Music Therapy Registry [NMTR] was formed in 1998 to serve the needs of those music therapists who held a valid credential from the former AAMT or NAMT but who were not board certified (i.e., not MT-BCs). The NMTR is "a separate and distinct organization with its own Board of Directors and staff" (AMTA, 1998, p. xviii). For a yearly maintenance fee, those music therapists who held the professional designation of RMT, CMT, or ACMT prior to January 1, 1998, can be listed on a professional registry maintained by the NMTR. According to the Unification Agreement, the NMTR will continue to maintain a listing of those with current RMT, CMT, or ACMT credentials until the year 2020. Music therapists who become board certified (i.e., receive the MT-BC credential from CBMT by passing the national board certification exam) cease to use their RMT, CMT, or ACMT title and are no longer listed on the Registry (AMTA, 1998).

SUMMARY

Personal qualities that may be beneficial to an individual who desires to become a professional music therapist include good physical and mental health, energy, stamina, emotional stability, self-confidence, good judgment, common sense, the ability to think clearly and quickly, a genuine interest in others, good skills in communication and personal interaction, a love for music and an ability to express one's self musically, perseverance, creativity, flexibility, and the ability to apply and integrate knowledge and experience gained from a wide variety of sources. These basic personal attributes, attitudes, and characteristics all will help provide a solid foundation on which to build the unique professional knowledges, skills, and attitudes that the aspiring music therapist will acquire in the course of his or her formal professional education and training.

Preparation for any profession involves the acquisition of certain theoretical concepts (knowledges), skills, and attitudes. The discipline of music therapy is concerned with music, with people, and with the interaction between music and people. Therefore, as part of their professional preparation, music therapy students must acquire basic knowledges in the areas of (1) music, (2) the physical and psychological characteristics, needs, and behaviors of people, and (3) the influence of music on people. An equally important part of music therapy professional preparation takes place outside the classroom in performance, laboratory, and clinical settings, where students develop and practice skills in music performance, therapeutic interaction, music therapy intervention, and research. Throughout the course of their professional training, music therapy students also develop certain attitudes and learn standards of professional conduct that equip them for optimum functioning as professional music therapists.

In the United States, standards for music therapy education and training programs are set by the professional music therapy association. Prior to 1998, the United States had two professional music therapy associations, the National Association for Music Therapy [NAMT] and the American Association for Music Therapy [AAMT], which both had specific standards for music therapy degree programs, equivalency programs, and alternate route certifications.

In 1998, NAMT and AAMT unified and formed the American Music Therapy Association [AMTA], which now is the sole body for setting standards for music therapy education and clinical training programs in the United States. The AMTA Commission on Education and Clinical Training is currently making recommendations for association standards to cover three levels of music therapy education: bachelor's, master's, and doctoral study.

In the United States, entry-level skills and competencies for music therapy practice are gained at the bachelor's level. Baccalaureate degree programs in music therapy include at least four years of academic coursework in music therapy, music, psychology, behavioral, biological, and social sciences, abnormal conditions or disabilities, and general studies. Concurrently with their academic coursework, students are involved in various supervised clinical field experiences, culminating with an in-depth internship. Upon completion of a bachelor's degree in music therapy, individuals are eligible to take a standardized national examination offered by the independent Certification Board for Music Therapists [CBMT] which leads to the professional credential "Music Therapist-Board Certified" [MT-BC].

Master's degree programs and doctoral study in music therapy focus on more specialized or advanced topics. Advanced topics or specializations studied in master's degrees programs might include theory development, research, supervision, college teaching, clinical administration, or in-depth study of and training in particular areas of practice, client populations, or clinical approaches. Doctoral study may concentrate on research skills, advanced music therapy theory, skills in college teaching and supervision, and/or clinical specializations and advanced clinical skills.

Professional credentials help assure the public and the employer that the individual holding the credential has received certain training and is capable of performing at a specified level of quality and competence. Professional credentialing for music therapists in the United States takes place at the national level, under the direction of the Certification Board for Music Therapists [CBMT]. CBMT is currently the only credentialling agency for music therapists in the United States, and the MT-BC is the only music therapy credential now awarded. The MT-BC is recognized by American Music Therapy Association [AMTA] as *the* entry-level credential required to practice music therapy.

Prior to their unification as the American Music Therapy Association [AMTA] on January 1, 1998, the National Association for Music Therapy [NAMT] awarded the title "Registered Music Therapist" to persons who had successfully completed both an NAMT-approved academic program and an NAMT-approved clinical training program, while the American Association for Music Therapy [AAMT] granted the title "Certified Music Therapist" [CMT] to persons who had successfully completed AAMT-approved programs. From 1989–1997, the AAMT offered an additional credential, the title of "Advanced Certified Music Therapist" [ACMT], to music therapists who had advanced experience and training. So that qualified music therapists who held current professional designation of RMT, CMT, or ACMT prior to January 1, 1998, were not left without credentials when all credentialling responsibilities were yielded to the CBMT with the unification of AAMT and NAMT, the National Music Therapy Registry [NMTR] was formed in 1998. The NMTR is a separate organization from AMTA or CBMT. Its primary function, which will continue until the year 2020, is to maintain a listing of those non-board-certified music therapists who hold valid RMT, CMT, or ACMT credential.

QUESTIONS FOR THOUGHT AND DISCUSSION

1. What are some personal qualities or characteristics that will benefit the aspiring music therapist? Why or how will these be important in his or her professional work?

2. What are some of the knowledges, skills, and attitudes that are important to professional music therapists?

3. How do "musician" skills and knowledges and "therapist" skills and knowledges interact in the delivery of music therapy services?

4. Why are standards for music therapy education and training and professional credentials for music therapists important? What organizations are currently responsible for these functions in the United States? How do they carry out their tasks?

5. Consider the "Music Therapist's Creed" written by Michel (1963):

I believe in Music Therapy because I believe in music as an effective, communicative, therapeutic tool, and as an important and necessary part of every man's life. I believe in Music Therapy because I believe in therapy – that is,

I believe that sick people can and should be helped. I believe in Music Therapy because I believe that the "essence of life" is in what contributions I can make to it, and that may chosen profession provides me with a unique and wonderful means for making such contributions. (p. 204)

What does this creed say about the purpose of music therapy? What does it say about the responsibilities and attitudes of the music therapist? How do the sentiments expressed in this creed compare with your own attitudes and beliefs toward music therapy?

SUGGESTIONS FOR FURTHER READING

American Music Therapy Association [AMTA]. (n.d.). *Music therapy as a career* [brochure]. Silver Spring, MD: Author.

Bruscia, K. E. (1986). Advanced competencies in music therapy. *Music Therapy, 6A*(1), 57-67.

Bruscia, K. E. (1989). The content of music therapy education at undergraduate and graduate levels. *Music Therapy Perspectives, 7*, 83-87.

Bruscia, K. E., Hesser, B., & Boxill, E. H. (1981) Essential competencies for the practice of music therapy. *Music Therapy, 7*(1), 43-49.

Certification Board for Music Therapists [CBMT]. (1991). *Recertification manual.* Tucson, AZ: Author.

Certification Board for Music Therapists [CBMT]. (1997). *CBMT: The certification board for music therapists* [brochure]. Richmond, VA: Author.

Certification Board for Music Therapists [CBMT]. (1998). *Your music therapist is certified by the certification board for music therapists* [brochure]. Richmond, VA: Author.

Maranto, C. D., & Bruscia, K. E. (Eds.). (1987). *Perspectives on music therapy education and training.* Philadelphia: Temple University, Esther Boyer College of Music.

Maranto, C. D., & Bruscia, K. E. (1988). *Methods of teaching and training the music therapist.* Philadelphia: Temple University, Esther Boyer College of Music.

Michel, D. E. (1985). The professional music therapist: Responsibilities and attitudes. In D. E. Michel, *Music therapy: An introduction, including music in special education* (2nd ed.) (pp. 98-111). Springfield, IL: Charles C Thomas.

Purtilo, R. (1978). The health professional. In R. Purtilo, *Health professional interaction* (2nd ed.) (pp. 1-37). Philadelphia: W. B. Saunders.

Sandbank, G. (1989). The right personality for the music therapist. In R. R. Pratt (Ed.), *Music therapy and music in special education: The international state of the art II* (ISME Edition Number Four) (pp. 87-93). St. Louis: MMB Music.

Tims, F. (1989). Experiential learning in the music therapy curriculum. *Music Therapy Perspectives, 7*, 91–92.

SOURCES FOR ADDITIONAL INFORMATION*

American Music Therapy Association [AMTA], 8455 Colesville Rd., Suite 1000, Silver Spring, MD 20910, (301) 589-3300, FAX (301) 589-5175, email: info@music-therapy.org, Web: http://www.musictherapy.org

Certification Board for Music Therapist [CBMT], 589 Southlake Blvd., Richmond, VA 23236, 1-800-765-CBMT, FAX (804-379-9354), email: info@cbmt.com, Web: http://www.cbmt.com

National Music Therapy Registry [NMTR], P.O. Box 13623, Silver Spring, MD 20910-3623, (301) 562-9330

*Contact information current as of February, 2000.

PART II

MUSIC THERAPY THROUGH THE AGES

WHAT ARE THE roots of music therapy? Is the idea of using music for healing purposes something new, or has music been used in connection with healing for a long time? Where can foreshadowings of modern music therapy practice be seen throughout history? How did the modern, scientific profession of music therapy develop in the United States? In Part II, these questions are answered as historical summaries of the uses of music in healing and the development of the modern music therapy profession are presented.

Although music therapy has become an organized, scientific discipline only in relatively recent times, music has been used to promote health and combat disease almost since the dawn of civilization. In Chapter Three, a general overview of the use of music in connection with healing practices is presented, beginning with the rituals of primitive tribes and continuing through the centuries to the present-day uses of music with the general public for stress reduction, general wellness, and enhanced creativity and cooperation. Chapter Four overviews the development of music therapy as an organized, scientifically-based professional discipline in the twentieth century. Much of the chapter focuses on the people and events that led to the eventual formation of the first professional music therapy organization in the United States, the National Association for Music Therapy, in 1950. Organizational developments since that time, such as the formation of the American Association for Music Therapy in 1971, the incorporation of the Certification Board for Music Therapists in 1983, the recent unification of professional music therapy associations in the United States that resulted in the formation of the American Music

Therapy Association in 1998, and the increasing international scope of music therapy, are also briefly discussed. In addition, summaries of current treatment settings, job satisfaction and employment trends, and the changing roles of professional music therapists are presented.

After completing Part II, the reader should have gained the knowledge and information needed to complete the following tasks:

1. List several examples of ways music has been used to promote health at various times in history.

2. Trace the steps that led to the formation of a national professional music therapy organization in the United States.

3. Describe the function of the Certification Board for Music Therapists.

4. Name the only professional membership organization for music therapists that currently exists in the United States. Briefly describe how it came into being and summarize its mission.

5. List several types of treatment settings and populations in which and with whom music therapy is currently used.

6 Identify some employment trends and discuss the changing roles of music therapy professional.

7. Name several other countries that have professional music therapy organizations.

19

Chapter Three

A HISTORICAL OVERVIEW OF THE USE
OF MUSIC TO PROMOTE HEALTH

THE CONNECTION between music and healing goes back a long way, almost to the dawn of time, and continues to spiral throughout history to the present day. To be sure, attitudes and practices regarding music and healing throughout history were always closely connected to the prevailing beliefs and practices of that time and culture. Nevertheless, echoes of various aspects of contemporary music therapy principles and practices can be seen in some of the approaches and techniques of music healers throughout history. Thus, music therapists draw on a long tradition of music healing practices as they seek to use music or music-based experiences in a planned, prescribed, goal-directed process of interaction and intervention, based on assessment and evaluation of individual clients' specific needs, strengths, and weaknesses, to influence positive changes in an individual's condition, skills, thoughts, feelings, or behaviors.

PRIMITIVE AND ANCIENT CULTURES

In most primitive and ancient civilizations, the promotion of physical and psychological health and well-being were functions of religion, and medicine was closely tied to religious rituals. Music was also an important part of both medical and religious practices. According to Boxberger (1962), "the close relationship of music to temple rituals indicates why it was so intimately bound up with medical practices in the cultures of ancient people" (p. 138). Anthropologists and ethnomusicologists have found that music and religion are still integrally tied to the healing practices of many of these cultures today (Nettl, 1956).

African and American Indian Tribes

Connections between music, religion, and healing were very evident in many primitive tribal civilizations in Africa, where the *shaman* (i.e., witch doctor or medicine man) functioned as the tribe's chief musician, medicine man, and priest. The shaman used special songs, rhythms, musical instruments (especially drums, bells, and rattles), dances, and dramas in conjunction with magic or religious rituals to draw out or drive away illness and disease. Singing was often an indispensable part of the healing process. For example, the !Kung Bushman shaman used song both to awaken his healing powers and to focus that power on treating the patient's disease (Weldin & Eagle, 1991). In other African tribes, shamans or medicine men would play special instruments believed to have healing powers (e.g., a magic drum or harp) over the afflicted part of a patient (e.g., his or her stomach) to effect a cure (Feder & Feder, 1981).

American Indian medicine men also used songs and music as specific tools of healing, even having specific songs to treat specific ailments (Apel, 1972; Winn, Crowe, & Moreno, 1989). Many medicine men or shamans of the American Southwest, Mexico, and Central America believed the power for healing a particular illness or disease resided in a particular song. Their belief in the healing power of specific songs was so great that "without the knowledge of the proper song, a shaman would not attempt a treatment" (Winn, Crowe, & Moreno, 1989, p. 68). The Navaho Indians, for example, used "sings" as their healing ceremonies, employing special combinations of song, dance, and sand paintings in particular patterns to cure specific illnesses (Feder & Feder, 1981; Kenny, 1982; Weldin & Eagle, 1991). For the Navaho, an important part of medicine was their belief that "the magic of the music will bring healing" (Kenny, 1982, p. 77). Among the Walla Walla Indians, patients as well as medicine men used healing songs, as the sick were directed to play an active role in seeking their cure by singing for several hours a day (Weldin & Eagle, 1991).

In addition to songs, drums and rhythms played an important part in the healing practices of many shamans and medicine men from primitive tribes and cultures of the Americas, Africa, and Asia (Hamel, 1976/1979; Winn, Crowe, & Moreno, 1989). Shamans often used specific drum signals to contact the gods or spirits and establish communication between beings on earth and those in the sky and/or the underworld. Shamans also used drum rhythms, bells, chants, and special costumes and dances in healing rituals to help the patient reach a trance-like altered state of consciousness that facilitated crisis resolution and healing (Hamel, 1976/1979; Kovach, 1985).

> To the shaman, then, the act of therapy involves going beyond the seen reality of consciousness and into another level of awareness. . . . It is in this process of traveling to another dimension that one finds the earliest examples of music therapy as shamans enlisted the drumbeat for thousands of years in order to elicit the altered or shamanic state of consciousness. (Winn, Crowe, & Moreno, 1989, p. 67)

Ancient Hebrews

From the evidence recorded in the Bible, it can be seen that music also played an important part in the life of the ancient Hebrews. When the Lord wanted the Hebrew people to be sure to remember special events, He instructed Moses to teach the people a song that told of those events to serve as a memory aid for them (Deuteronomy 31:19). Much music was included in the religious rites of the Hebrews; in fact, the temple establishment included 288 full-time musicians whose job it was to prophesy and help people reach their God, their source of strength and healing, through music (I Chronicles 25:1-8). The Hebrews also recognized that music could have calming effects on people in daily life: When an evil spirit troubled King Saul, his servants sent for a man, David, who was a skillful harp player, to calm and refresh Saul and make him well through playing harp music (I Samuel 16:14-23).

Egypt and Babylonia

Music, religious rituals, and healing practices were also intertwined in the cultures of ancient Egypt and Babylonia. The Babylonian priest-physicians used clappers and rattles to exorcise evil spirits, and chanting was an important part of temple healing practices (Apel, 1972; Weldin & Eagle, 1991). In Egypt, the connection between music, religion, and healing was so great that their priests also were required to become both musicians and physicians (Weldin & Eagle, 1991). Egyptian priest-physicians considered music to be "the physic of the soul" (Feder & Feder, 1981, p. 3) and used hymns and incantations to cure sickness and suffering. The earliest medical papyri record special chant therapies used for these purposes. Egyptians also believed music cast spells, that sounds symbolized other entities, and that each note had a particular magical force to summon the gods (Boxberger, 1962). In addition, the Egyptians used songs for functional purposes: They had special work songs composed and organized for the particular tasks associated with sowing seed, harvesting, weaving, carrying stones from quarries, etc. "The Egyptians realized that concerted singing facilitated labour, just as martial music encouraged the soldier as he set forth to war" (Scott, 1958).

China and India

Ancient Asian cultures, too, believed in the healing powers of music and used it as an integral part of religious and health-promoting rituals. In China, as early as the second century B.C., "there were elaborate discourses on music in relation to the human spirit and on the use of music to inculcate moderation" (Apel, 1972, p. 156). Cosmological connotations of pitches became an important part of Chinese musical thought and practice, and the emotions associated with various modes (i.e., systems of organizing pitches, comparable to our scales) regulated their use in musical drama. The priests of ancient India valued music for its mantra-mystic qualities (Scott, 1958). They discovered that certain sequences of notes produced meditative states, and they experimented and subtly refined these to achieve *Samadhi*, a superconscious trance. The Hindus believed that this music-induced, mystical, metaphysical state of consciousness helped them achieve oneness with the universe and promoted healthiness of body, mind, and spirit and a purer state of inner awareness. Already before the second century B.C., the *Samaveda* told of links between man, music, and the cosmos (Apel, 1972; Hamel, 1976/1979). Strict adherence to correct performance of the *Veda* chant was essential, for the ancient Hindus believed that any mistake in intonation or enunciation would upset the balance of the universe (Apel, 1972). Beginning with the second century A.D., intricate systems of pitch organization known as *ragas* were developed. Each *raga* was believed to promote distinct moods or psychological temperaments (rasas), ranging from erotic longing to humorous to sad to fury to bravery to fear to disgust to amazement to peace, tranquility, and relaxation (Hamel, 1976/1979). Hindu thinkers prescribed ways in which the ragas should be used in drama and in music instruction and performance for maximum spiritual psychological benefit (Apel, 1972; Hamel, 1976/1979).

GREEK AND ROMAN CULTURES

The close association between music and healing that existed in ancient Greece is personified in the Greek god, Apollo, who was both the god of music and the god of medicine. The Greeks believed that disease was the result of disharmony in a person's being. Music, with its ethical and moral power, could be used to bring a person's being back into a state of harmony and order and thus promote health. According to the Greek doctrine of *ethos*, music was a potent force interlocked with the system of nature that could affect an individual's will, character, and conduct (Grout, 1973). Different types of music affected human thought and conduct in different ways: Some types of music, such as those played on the lyre and related to the poetic forms of the ode and the epic, had calming and uplifting effects, while other types of music, such as those played on the aulos and related to the poetic forms of the dithyramb and the drama, "tended to produce excitement and enthusiasm" (Grout, 1973, p. 9).

Since the Greeks found that different types of music and different modes had fairly predictable effects on human conduct and emotions, they began to apply music systematically as both curative and preventative medicine. Pythagoras's belief that a specially prescribed use of music could benefit one's health led him to investigate the physical qualities of sound and develop the foundation for today's tonal system (Munro & Mount, 1978). In addition, Pythagorus explored clinical applications of music, using dance and music to treat patients who were mentally ill and introducing treatments in which "musical medicine" was central in promoting order and proportions necessary for health (Feder & Feder, 1981). The Greeks also used musical and dramatic performances to effect a cathartic purge of the emotions, something they felt was essential to mental health (Alvin, 1975).

Much of the Greek therapeutic use of music focused on listening to music to restore lost balance and promote health. Greek physicians cautioned against the indiscriminate use of music in treating madness or mental illness, noting that music could cause harm instead of good if it was not applied in the correct way (Feder & Feder, 1981). In addition, the Greek philosophers Plato and Aristotle often spoke of the beneficial effects of music and its importance to the health of the whole person, advocating the carefully controlled use of music and rhythm to restore persons to health and to promote the development of healthy and ethical citizens (Alvin, 1975; Boxberger, 1962; Grout, 1973; Pratt, 1989; Schullian & Schoen, 1948). According to Alvin (1975):

> If Hippocrates is called the father of medicine, we may recognize Plato and Aristotle as the forerunners of music therapy, which is the controlled use of music. (p. 38)

The Romans adopted the Greek philosophy regarding the beneficial moral, ethical, medicinal, and healing influences of music. For example, they believed that music could cure snakebites, combat pestilence, and aid in curing insomnia. The physician Aeslepiades treated insanity with harmonious sounds and calmed recalcitrant mobs by a change in music or by playing a certain kind of music (Boxberger, 1962). Lucretius recommended that flute music be played after meals to aid digestion and also noted the influence music could have on a person's mind, emotions, and behavior. Theophrastus, a disciple of Aristotle, made note of the somatic effects of flute music (Pratt, 1989). Celsus, who was known as a master artist in medicine, recommended that music, cymbals, and sounds be used to dispel the melancholy thoughts associated with certain types of mental illness. Insanity was also treated with organ music by Zenocrates and with flute music and vocal exercises by Caelius Aurelianus. Aristedes Quintilianus wrote that music could apply the proper therapeutics to the abnormal emotions of psychotic states and gradually, by means of an unconscious purging, restore those emotions to a more normal state (Schullian & Schoen, 1948). For Aristedes, the controlled use of music was essentially a form of psychotherapy. Consequently, he maintained that music, like medicine, had preventative as well as curative powers.

THE MIDDLE AGES

Boethius, an influential authority on music in the early Middle Ages, strongly emphasized the influence of music on a person's character and moral and ethical behavior. Like the Greeks, Boethius regarded music as "a corollary of arithmetic, thus exemplifying in sounds the fundamental principles of order and harmony that prevail throughout the universe" (Grout, 1973, p. 23). *Musica humana*, one of the three-fold divisions of music proposed by Boethius, showed how this order and harmony was exemplified in the human body and soul. Boethius believed music could influence human character and morals and have either beneficial or detrimental effects on the health and harmony of body and soul. Because of this, music became an important element in the education of the young during the Middle Ages, holding a place in the four higher subjects in the medieval educational system (Grout, 1973).

The Christian Church was the predominant influence on life in the Western world during the Middle Ages. Musical practices, like all other areas of life, were regulated by the Church. Certain forms of music were regarded as unsuitable, for they had pagan associations and would be detrimental to moral and ethical behavior (Grout, 1973). Music was to be the servant of religion, opening the mind to Christian teachings and disposing it to holy thoughts. According to the prevalent theology of the day, disease was a punishment for sin. Consequently, religion and religious music played an important part in the medical practices of the Middle Ages: Special hymns were used as remedies for colds and other maladies; music was composed to honor saints who supposedly protected people from illness; and court composers wrote special music to help and cheer people of high rank who became ill (Boxberger, 1962).

During the Middles Ages, a peculiar malady known as *tarantism* arose particularly prevalent in Italy (Alvin, 1975; Boxberger, 1962; Feder & Feder, 1981; Schullian & Schoen, 1948). This disease, believed to be caused by the sting of the tarantula, was characterized by alternating fits of frenzy and complete inertia. Whether this was a nervous disorder or, as some suspect, a persistence of pagan orgies and ecstatic dances which were now at odds with the prevailing Christian society, the fact remains that treatment and catharsis were achieved only through music and dancing. In order to effect a cure, musicians had to be able to match their music to the symptoms (dancing, violent, sleeping, or melancholy) of the patient. The curative *tarantellas* would mirror the tempi and movements appropriate to the particular type of spider that had bitten and taken possession of the afflicted individual and then change to show the return of the patient's identity and the fight against the spider's possession. Thus, through a treatment process based on specially organized music and dance that was specific to the patient and his or her individual manifestation of symptoms, the tarantism would eventually be cured (Alvin, 1975; Feder & Feder, 1981).

During the Middle Ages, the Greek and Roman traditions of philosophy, music, and medicine were preserved in the Arab culture, which was at its height in the eighth and ninth centuries (Feder & Feder, 1981; Pratt, 1989). Works of Greek physicians and philosophers were translated into Arabic, and the idea that musical regularity was related to universal order and relations was an integral part of Arab thought. In hospitals in Cairo, music was played on the wards, with human voices or stringed instruments being selected with regard to the proper proportion of the universal order (Feder & Feder, 1981). Ibn Hindu, an eleventh century physician and theorist, discussed the psychic effects and therapeutic applications of the Arabian musical modes and felt that doctors should study music in order to be well rounded (Pratt, 1989). The Sufi masters, the mystics of Islamic society, also advocated the healing powers of music, speaking of music as being "life and health, a reflection of the grand scheme, divine itself" (Kenny, 1982, p. 76). With the Crusades, Islamic and Arabic influences began to impact Europe, and Europeans began to rediscover Greek ideas, largely as they had been preserved and interpreted by Arabic scholars (Feder & Feder, 1981; Pratt, 1989).

THE RENAISSANCE

During the Renaissance, both musicians and physicians looked back to the classical Greek period for inspiration. The Greek view of health as a state of harmony and of disease as a state of disharmony again prevailed, replacing the medieval view that disease was a punishment for sin. The Greek theory of the four humors, or elements, which must be in balance for a state of health, became "a point of contact for music and medicine, functioning in both medical and musical theory" (Boxberger, 1962, p. 152). Just as medical theorists had derived the four humors of the human body (black bile, phlegm, blood, and yellow bile) and their corresponding temperaments (melancholic, phlegmatic, sanguine, and choleric) from the four elements that constituted the world according to Empedoclean theory (earth, water, air, and fire), so now did music theorists pair four musical elements (bass, tenor, alto, and soprano) with the Empedoclean cosmic elements. The four music modes commonly used at this time (Mixolydian, Dorian, Lydian, and Phrygian) were also related to the four musical elements and their corresponding temperaments (see Table I). For people living during the Renaissance, harmony or health in music, in the body, and in the cosmos was present only when there was a proper balance of the four elements (Boxberger, 1962; Schullian & Schoen, 1948). Application of the proper type of music could help restore balance and health in body and spirit.

The close connection between music and medicine at the time of the Renaissance is also illustrated by the writings of Zarlino, a sixteenth century music theorist and composer. Zarlino felt that music was indispensible to the practice of medicine, for a knowledge of music enabled a physician both to prescribe the proper proportion of the elements needed to restore health and to have the skill necessary to judge the rhythm of the human pulse correctly (Schullian & Schoen, 1948). Zarlino credited music with many beneficial effects, including those of mitigating pain, restoring hearing to the deaf, healing vermin bites, curing insanity and the habit of drunkenness, and chasing away pestilence. In addition, Zarlino strongly believed that each of the different modes used in music could serve to arouse or abate particular passions and affections

Table I
RELATIONSHIPS BETWEEN THE COSMIC, HUMAN,
AND MUSICAL SPHERES DURING
THE RENAISSANCE

Cosmic	Human			Musical	
Element	"Humor"	Source	Temperament	Element	Mode
fire	yellow bile	liver	choleric	soprano	Phrygian
air	blood	heart	sanguine	alto	Lydian
water	phlegm	brain	phlegmatic	tenor	Dorian
earth	black bile	spleen	melancholic	bass	Mixolydian

(i.e., moods, emotions, or feelings).

During the Renaissance, music also became more unified with medicine "as Renaissance man attempted to integrate all areas of knowledge" (Weldin & Eagle, 1991, p. 14). Renaissance physicians believed that music could have powerful effects on human psychological states, and it was common and accepted medical practice at this time to use music as preventative medicine. For example, Tommaso del Garbo, in giving medical advice on how to avoid the plague, stressed the importance of a happy state of mind and the desirability of listening to music (Schullian & Schoen, 1948). Music was believed to have beneficial emotional effects that would help people resist disease, something that was of vital importance during this era of widespread plagues. Ambroise Pare, a surgeon of the time, also used music to ease pain and relieve symptoms of gout and sciatica (Feder & Feder, 1981; Weldin & Eagle, 1991).

THE BAROQUE ERA

During the Baroque Era, the period of time from the seventeenth century to the mid-eighteenth century, a general philosophical orientation in medicine toward the theory of the four humors and an emphasis in musical composition on the ability of music to arouse affections and passions continued to provide a common meeting ground for music and medicine. The belief in the power of music to affect the character, affections, passions, mind, and body of human beings became codified by German music theorists in the *Figurenlehre,* or doctrine of figures (Grout, 1973). "If there is any common thread that unites the great variety of music that we call baroque, then, it is an underlying faith in music's power, indeed its obligation, to move the affections" (Palisca, 1968, pp. 4-5). The strength of popular belief in the curative powers of music is further evidenced by the numerous references to the therapeutic effects of music made by the writers of this time, such as Shakespeare and Spencer (Boxberger, 1962).

Music continued to retain its importance as a medical cure for royalty during this period. For example, in 1737, the Queen of Spain engaged the services of the famous Italian singer, Farinelli, to rouse King Philip V from his acute melancholia. Farinelli's efforts had such a beneficial effect that he was subsequently employed as a personal singer to the king, and he sang every night to keep King Philip in good spirits (Alvin, 1975).

Physicians continued to write about the curative effects of music on various physical maladies and diseases during the Baroque Era. However, from the seventeenth century onward, they also began to write more specifically about the psychological effects of music. For example, Burton, in his 1621 classic, *The Anatomy of Melancholy*, devoted an entire chapter to the use of music as a remedy (Rogers, 1918). Louis Roger, an eighteenth century French physician, wrote a serious treatise based on carefully observed case histories, and advocated music as therapy to give order to minds craving structure and to stimulate

the nervous system through sympathetic vibration, helping them "throw off the thickened and foreign humors" (Feder & Feder, 1981, p. 11). Roger also wrote of the effects of music on the human body and emphasized the need for careful scientific observation and experimentation to substantiate the salutary effects of music. In his review of seventeenth and eighteenth century treatises on music and medicine, Carapetyan (Schullian & Schoen, 1948) noted that music received much serious consideration from the physicians of the time: "A number of these writers reject the well-known legends and strive to establish a more plausible and scientific place for music in the cure of psychopathic cases and of nervous disorders" (p. 146).

THE MID-EIGHTEENTH CENTURY THROUGH THE NINETEENTH CENTURY

Although the broad claims made for the therapeutic power of music were beginning to be examined more critically during the last half of the eighteenth century and the early nineteenth century, there was still some affinity between music and medicine during this period. Throughout the nineteenth century, many physicians remained convinced that music could play an important role in treating mental and emotional illnesses (Pratt, 1989). Since many of the more traditional forms of medical treatment available in the nineteenth century were often life-threatening, the therapeutic use of music also offered an attractive, more humane, alternative approach to treatment (Davis, 1987). As knowledge and understanding of human physiology increased during the nineteenth century, several physicians also began to investigate the effects of music on physical parameters such as blood pressure, pulse rate, respiration, and digestion, and circulated specialized scientific reports on the physiological influences of music (Weldin & Eagle, 1991). In addition, some musician-scientists of the time, such as Hermann von Hemholtz and Hector Berlioz, investigated and wrote of the effects of music and sound on human behavior and the power of music to relieve stress and cure illness (Weldin & Eagle, 1991).

Late in the eighteenth century, the therapeutic effects of music received public attention as the press in the United States began to write stories dealing

with music as an adjunct to medical practice, especially to influence mental and emotional conditions (Heller, 1987). A 1789 article in *Columbian Magazine*, "Music Physically Considered," asserted the influence of the mind upon the body and developed the case for using music as a therapeutic agent, especially to treat depression. The anonymous author also noted that "proper application of music as therapy requires a skilled and knowledgeable person to make decisions about what kind of music and how much of it should be used" (Heller, 1987, p. 37). Seven years later, an article in the *New York Weekly Magazine* reported on the cure of a fever by music.

Early in the nineteenth century, medical and psychiatric journals in the United States also began to carry reports advocating music as a viable alternative treatment for various mental and physical disorders (Davis, 1987; Heller, 1987). The physician/ psychiatrist Benjamin Rush, who was a professor at the University of Pennsylvania at the time, was a strong advocate of the use of music in the treatment of mental disease. He included the therapeutic use of music in one of his sophisticated courses in psychiatry (Davis, 1987) and likely encouraged his students to research the topic (Davis & Gfeller, 1992). In 1804, Edwin Atlee's dissertation proposed that music was especially useful in treating mental disorders because of its unique capacity "to focus one's attention on healthy thoughts" (Heller, 1987, p. 39). Two years later, Samuel Matthews' dissertation, *On the Effects of Music in Curing and Palliating Diseases*, outlined the therapeutic uses of music in the treatment of both mental and physical illnesses. Matthews noted the ability of music to counteract pain as well as to influence moods and emotional states. He anticipated later principles of music therapy practice by recognizing the importance of the client's musical background, training, and preferences in selecting music for therapeutic purposes and by recommending that, in treating mental disorders, therapists first use music that matches the patient's mood and then gradually change the music to move the patient to the desired mood. This latter recommendation is now generally known as the *iso principle*. Heller (1987) noted that Matthews was also the first to advocate *in print* that music therapy be used in existing institutions.

Around the beginning of the nineteenth century, Pinel and other French physicians were using music to treat mental and nervous diseases such as hysteria (Rogers, 1918). In 1846, Chomet presented his treatise, *The Influence of Music on Health and Life*, to the Paris Academy of Sciences, "a fact which shows the interest of a learned body in the subject" (Alvin, 1975, p. 48). In an 1874 article entitled "Music as Medicine," Whittaker brought Chomet's ideas to the attention of physicians in the United States (Davis, 1987). This led to an increased interest in the therapeutic use of music, especially as a viable treatment for psychiatric disorders. In 1878, a New York newspaper and the *Virginia Medical Monthly* reported on a series of experiments testing the reactions of mentally ill patients at Blackwell's Island to live vocal and instrumental music. The patients responded so favorably to experimental music treatment of live concerts and individual sessions that the New York City Charities Commissioner and the hospital's medical director supported additional experimentation on the use of music to alleviate suffering among the destitute mentally ill (Davis, 1987). Later in the century, George Adler Blumer, a leading reformer in the treatment of the mentally ill, advocated the use of music therapy to treat the mentally ill in his article "Music in its Relation to the Mind" that appeared in the *American Journal of Insanity* in 1892. Blumer recognized music's therapeutic value without making extravagant claims for its power, basing his argument

on European, British, and American scientific publications and his own observations. As Chief Executive Officer of Utica State Hospital, Blumer also hired musicians to perform for the patients and "may have been the first person to establish and ongoing music therapy program in an American hospital" (Davis, 1987, p. 84). The neurologist Corning, another physician of this time who was interested in the psychological effects of music, used music extensively in private practice as a contribution to emotional therapy for his patients. In 1899, he published a paper discussing the physiological and psychological constructs that provided a rationale for treating mental illness with aural and visual stimuli and describing his controlled experiments to treat mental and nervous diseases and positively influence his patients' feelings. Corning's premise was that music could be used to suppress the bad dreams of his patients, thus cleansing the mind and enabling patients to function more effectively during their waking hours (Davis, 1987).

The therapeutic use of music was also being introduced in London hospitals in the late nineteenth century (Davis, 1989). In 1891, the Reverend Frederick Kill Harford founded the Guild of St. Cecilia, an organization that provided on-call musicians to London hospitals to perform live sedative music to help dispel anxiety, reduce pain, and induce sleep in the hospitalized patients. Harford emphasized that the Guild would work closely with the medical profession, dispensing its musical tranquilizer only upon the request of a physician, and also stressed that the musicians should be remunerated for their services. The use of music boxes and phonographs was recommended to help continue treatments between the musicians' visits. Members of the Guild also conducted experiments to determine for what mental and physical ailments music was most effective. They achieved some success in soothing patients, eliciting speech in some depressed patients, reducing fevers, calming delirium associated with high fever, and sedating patients with certain nervous disorders. Experiments with both stimulative and sedative music showed that, while most patients felt they benefitted more from sedative music, some were interested in stimulative music. Davis (1989) noted that Harford was "astute in his observation that differences in personality, age, and sex were important variables to consider when choosing appropriate music for patients" (p. 20). The Guild of St. Cecilia enjoyed the endorsement of Florence Nightingale and Queen Victoria's physician, Sir Richard Quain, and also was the first British organization dedicated to providing quality music therapy services to a significant number of hospitalized people and to scientifically testing the influence of music on people with physical and mental illnesses (Davis, 1989). At the close of the nineteenth century, in 1899, the British physician Davison reported on the beneficial effects of music on hospital wards, citing cases in which music reduced or eliminated pain and fever and cured insomnia. Davison also noted the importance of matching the patient's mood when first applying the music treatment, and theorized that music achieved its effects by influencing the body directly, replacing the painful vibrations of disease and causing the body to vibrate synchronously with the pleasant vibrations of the music (Pratt, 1989).

During the nineteenth century, institutions and schools for individuals who were blind, deaf, or physically handicapped also began to use music as an important part of their therapeutic activity programs (Darrow & Heller, 1985; Heller, 1987; Solomon, 1980). One of the first uses of music as adaptive therapy came in 1832 when Lowell Mason organized a music program at the Perkins School for the Blind. In the 1840s, music and rhythm programs were instituted at schools and asylums for the deaf and included in model curricula for deaf education. Music therapy programs were also developed in special schools for children who had physical handi-caps. In addition, a series of articles in a popular magazine of the time helped inform the general public of the health benefits of music, particularly noting the benefits of music and singing instruction as vehicles for molding character, promoting the internalization of good moral values, motivating the better feelings of one's nature, soothing discordant persons, guarding against consumption, strengthening the lungs, and curing indigestion (Koza, 1990).

From the preceding examples, it is evident that several physicians, psychiatrists, social reformers, and educators did advocate and seek to demonstrate the therapeutic value of music during the late eighteenth and nineteenth centuries. However, as Boxberger (1962) noted, the use of music as therapy at this time seemed to be restricted to specific cases rather than incorporated in the general theory and philosophy of medical treatment. During this time period, then, the fields of music and medicine also began to diverge somewhat, as technology increased and as music developed as a performing art while medicine developed as a specialized science. Nevertheless, those isolated instances of therapeutic applications of music in specific clinical cases and the beginning of more scientific research into the influence of music on human physiology and on various mental and physical ailments kept interest in the potential palliative, salutary, and adaptive applications of music alive (Heller, 1987) and provided "the necessary link for a continuation of the use of music in medicine into the Twentieth Century" (Weldin & Eagle, 1991, p. 17).

THE TWENTIETH CENTURY

Although "the traditional close association between music and medical practice was largely forgotten in the technological explosion of the twentieth century" (Munro & Mount, 1978, p. 1029), some scientific investigations into the therapeutic benefits of music did continue to occur around the turn of the century. For example, laboratory experiments with both human and animal subjects demonstrated that changes in various physical functions were related to different types of music (Taylor, 1981). Several musicians in the New York area (e.g. Eva Vescilius, Margaret Anderton, Isa Maud Ilsen, and Harriet Ayer Seymour) also promoted the therapeutic use of music throughout the early to middle part of the twentieth century by conducting experiments, providing music in hospitals, giving lectures and teaching courses on music therapy, and forming organizations advocating the use of music therapy. (More information on these early twentieth century organizations is given in Chapter Four, which traces the development of music therapy as an organized profession in the United States.) In the 1920s and 1930s, scientific studies into the psychological effects of and psychological responses to music began to increase, as the field of music psychology began to develop under the pioneering efforts of psychologists James Mursell, Max Schoen, and Carl Seashore (Weldin & Eagle, 1991). During the 1940s and 1950s, researchers also investigated the effects of music on physiological responses, while continuing to research the influence of music on mood changes and general mental health. According to Feder and Feder (1981), "such studies persuaded the Veterans Administration to develop comprehensive music therapy programs at all VA hospitals" (p. 116) during this time period.

The advent of the phonograph also led to a renewed interest in the use of music in hospital settings around the turn of the century (Boxberger, 1963). Recorded music was used as a diversion, as an aid to inducing sleep, to calm fears associated with medical operations, and as an aid to anesthesia and analgesia (Taylor, 1981). Although music therapy was not widely accepted by the medical community in the early part of the twentieth century, some physicians did continue to promote and endorse the therapeutic use of music in the operating room, recovery areas, on adult and children's wards, and with orthopedic patients (Davis & Gfeller, 1992). During World War I, music activities were prescribed as exercises for joints and muscles to aid military patients in recovering the use of wounded limbs (Tyson, 1981). During the inter-war period and World War II, music received increasing use both as a general psychological stimulus in the total hospital environment and as an adjunct to psychiatric treatment (Tyson, 1981). The musician Willem Van de Wall, who worked in hospitals in New York and Pennsylvania, and the psychiatrist and composer Ira Altshuler, who worked at Wayne County General Hospital in Eloise, Michigan, developed significant music therapy programs in mental hospitals and prisons during this period (Boxberger, 1963; Collins, 1982; Davis & Gfeller, 1992). Van de Wall also published important books on music therapy with the support of grants from the Russell Sage Foundation, including the comprehensive *Music in Institutions* (1936). (More information on these men and their work is given in Chapter Four.)

Some special education settings also continued to show an interest in adaptive uses of music throughout the twentieth century. For example, schools and institutions for individuals with hearing impairments used music to improve residual hearing function and facilitate speech development (Solomon, 1980). As music therapy developed into an organized professional discipline in the years following World War II (see Chapter Four), the therapeutic use of music came to be applied to clients having a wide variety of disorders and conditions (see Chapters Seven to Twenty-one). In recent years, the use of music as preventative medicine and as a strengthener of health and character seems to be making a resurgence in the United States. Corporations such as MUZAK have made a business out of supplying background music to influence and regulate people's moods and behaviors in offices, businesses, industries, and many other commercial and public environments (Radocy & Boyle, 1988). The therapeutic use of music is finding its way into the board rooms and wellness programs of businesses, hospitals, and major corporations as employers recognize the need to reduce stress, alleviate staff burnout, and promote wellness, and seek innovative and effective ways to encourage teamwork and enhance creativity (Clark & Ficken, 1988; McCarthy, 1992; Weitz, 1993). In addition, as the holistic health movement focuses public attention on the interconnection of body, mind, and spirit, chants and "sound healing" practices that have their roots in Eastern countries and philosophies are being used as tools for healing, wholeness, relaxation, and consciousness expansion in the Western world as well (Bonny & Savary, 1973, 1990; Crowe & Scovel, 1996; Halpern, 1978; Hamel, 1976/1979; Trevisan, 1978). (For more information on holistic uses of music therapy, see Chapter Twenty-one.)

Since the late 1970s, leading medical doctors have exhibited a renewed interest in the role of music in medical treatment, and scientific studies in the field of music and medicine have steadily increased (Bartlett, Kaufman, & Smeltekopp, 1993; Harvey, 1991; Maranto, 1991; Pratt, 1989; Taylor, 1988, 1997). The early 1980s saw the development of several professional organizations related to the use of music in medicine and healing, among them the International Society for Music in Medicine, Biology of Music Making, Inc., and the International Association of Music for the Handicapped (Taylor, 1988). In a related development connecting music and medicine, "a substantial number of physicians have begun to specialize in the treatment of 'musiogenic' physical disorders, or therapy for musicians" (Taylor, 1988, p. 91).

In recent years, there has also been an increased interest in using music for the health and good of society in general. For example, the organization Music Therapists for Peace was founded in 1988. The members of this worldwide movement sponsor various projects and activities, with the aim of "making more conscious use of the possibilities of music to promote healing and unite people" (Moreno, 1992, p. 87). During the 1991 Persian Gulf War, the Israeli government also made use of the power of music to help its citizens cope with the crisis (Brodsky, 1991). The Israeli Broadcasting Authority specifically structured its programming in the days before the crisis by playing songs stressing strength and national unity and giving specific instructions for safety and defense preparations in parodies of popular tunes. Then, on the first night of the attack, as people waited in their sealed-off gas-proof rooms, soothing, nostalgic music was broadcast to help reduce fear and anxiety. During the war, only Hebrew songs were broadcast, and special children's music was played in the evening to help the children cope with the stress and trauma of the situation. In these ways, "through mass communication, the power of music was used to assist the entire population in developing more adaptive coping methods, which included instilling feelings of nation-al unity and establishing support systems" (Brodsky, 1991, p. 99).

Recently, there has also been an increasing interest in achieving healing by applying music vibrations directly to the body. Several experiments have shown that the process of applying carefully selected music and vibrational frequencies to the body through special speakers in tables or chairs or through music-electro-acupuncture techniques has been successful in reducing arthritic pain, decreasing muscle rigidity, decreasing insomnia, and aiding the recovery of muscle function in stroke victims (Chesky & Michel, 1991; Shi-jing, Hui-ju, Guo, & Maranto, 1991; Skille, 1989). Noting the renewed interest by the medical profession in researching the effects of music in healing and the worldwide concern with increased quality of life for individuals with various handicaps or disabilities, Pratt (1989) summarized developments in music and healing in the latter part of the twentieth century in this way:

> There are signs that physicians and musicians are seeking out each other. . . . Throughout the world, there is an awakening, a renascence of dialogue between the arts of medicine and music. . . . The conversation they began so long ago has been renewed, this time with new vigor, more information, and the camaraderie of old friends. (p. 10)

SUMMARY

The use of music in connection with healing practices goes back to the shaman and medicine man of primitive tribes and to the ancient Hebrew, Egyptian, Chinese, and Hindu civilizations. The Greeks were among the first to advocate a controlled use of music to produce health, good character, and high moral standards. From the time of the Greeks to the dawn of the scientific age in medicine in the late eighteenth century, music was incorporated in the general theory and philosophy of medical treatment and was often prescribed as a cure for various physical and psychological ailments.

During the nineteenth century, however, as technological advances began to emerge and as music developed as a performing art and medicine developed as specialized science, the traditional close association between music and medicine seemed largely to be forgotten. Although the use of music was no longer a part of general medical treatment philosophy at this time, isolated reports of the therapeutic use of music in special cases did continue to occur, along with some preliminary scientific research into the effects of music on hospitalized patients. At this time, music also began to be used in therapeutic treatment and adaptive activities programs for individuals with visual, hearing, or physical impairments.

Although the explosion of technology of the twentieth century in many ways undermined the historical close association of music and medicine, some connections were maintained as scientific principles began to be used to study the therapeutic effects of music. Several musicians, physicians, psychiatrists, and psychologists continued to advocate using music for healing purposes, and various organizations and institutional programs for music therapy were formed. The field of music psychology also began to develop in the early twentieth century, and scientific investigations into the psychological and physical effects of music were conducted with increasing frequency.

As music therapy developed into an organized profession in the years following World War II, the therapeutic used of music was applied to individuals who had a wide range of disabilities and disorders.

Recently, public interest in the use of music as preventative medicine and as a means of strengthening health and character seems to be making a resurgence. In addition, the fields of music and medicine show signs of increased convergence as more and more medical professionals have a renewed interest in researching the effects of music in healing and as people all over the world become concerned with increased quality of life for individuals with various handicaps or disabilities. Since the late 1970s, scientific studies in the field of music and medicine have steadily increased, and several international organizations advocating the use of music to promote health have been formed.

QUESTIONS FOR THOUGHT AND DISCUSSION

1. How did the effectiveness of music as a cure at various times in history relate to the prevailing philosophy of the time?

2. What does faith or trust in a cure or method of treatment have to do with the effectiveness or power of that cure? Must one believe a healing power is present in a particular music experience in order to receive therapeutic benefits from that music experience?

3. Are there any theories, philosophies, or techniques that seem to be prevalent throughout the history of the use of music to promote health? If so, what are they and why so you think they seem to keep resurfacing?

4. What connections can you see between some of the ideas contained in the contemporary definition of music therapy presented in Chapter One of this book and the ways music has been used to promote health throughout history? In what practices and philosophies throughout history do you see echoes of the ideas that using music for therapeutic or healing purposes (1) involves a process, (2) is planned and goal-directed, based on individual assessment, (3) involves interaction and intervention, (4) relies primarily on music or music-based experiences, (5) is specifically prescribed, (6) is implemented by specially trained personnel, or (7) is directed toward meeting the specific needs of individual clients?

SUGGESTIONS FURTHER READING

Alvin, J. (1975). Music in healing. In J. Alvin, *Music therapy* (pp. 21-60). New York: Basic Books.

Boxberger, R. (1962). Historical bases for the use of music in therapy. In E. H. Schneider (Ed.), *Music therapy 1961* (pp. 125-166). Lawrence, KS: Allen Press.

Davis, W. B. (1987). Music therapy in 19th century America. *Journal of Music Therapy, 24*(2), 76-87.

Davis, W. B. (1989). Music therapy in Victorian England: Frederick Kill Harford and the Guild of St. Cecilia. *Music Therapy Perspectives, 7*, 17-22.

Davis, W. B., & Gfeller, K. E. (1992). Music therapy: An historical perspective. In W. B. Davis, K. E. Gfeller, & M. H. Thaut, *An introduction to music therapy: Theory and practice* (pp. 16-37). Dubuque, IA: Wm. C. Brown.

Hamel, P. M. (1979). *Through music to the self* (P. Lemesurier, Trans.). Boulder, CO: Shambala. (Original work published 1976)

Heller, G. N. (1987). Ideas, initiatives, and implementations: Music therapy in America, 1789-1848. *Journal of Music Therapy, 24*(1), 35-46.

Pratt, R. R. (1989). A brief history of music and medicine. In M. H. M. Lee (Ed.), *Rehabilitation, music and human well-being* (pp. 1-12). St. Louis: MMB Music.

Schullian, D. M., & Schoen, M. (Eds.). (1948). *Music and medicine.* New York: Henry Schuman.

Solomon, A. L. (1980). Music in special education before 1930: Hearing and speech development. *Journal of Research in Music Education, 28*(4), 236-242.

Taylor, D. C. (1981). Music in general hospital treatment from 1900-1950. *Journal of Music Therapy. 18*(2), 62-73.

Taylor, D. B. (1988). Therapeutic musicians or musical physicians: The future is at stake. *Music Therapy Perspectives, 5,* 86-93.

Trevisan, L. A. (1978). A comparative study of scientific and spiritualistic perspectives of wholistic healing (via music and massage). In A. L. Nowicki and L. A. Tevisan, *Beyond the sound: A technical and philosophical approach to music therapy* (Rev. ed.) (pp. vii-xxii). Porterville & Santa Barbara, CA: Nowicki/Trevisan.

Weldin, C., & Eagle, C. T. (1991). An historical overview of music medicine. In C. D. Maranto (Ed.), *Applications of music in medicine* (pp. 7-27). Washington, D.C.: National Association for Music Therapy.

Chapter Four

THE DEVELOPMENT OF MUSIC THERAPY
AS AN ORGANIZED PROFESSION

LTHOUGH THE therapeutic benefits of music have been recognized since primitive times, it was not until the mid-twentieth century that music therapy emerged as an organized professional discipline. As Unkefer (1961) pointed out, the development of music therapy as a profession is related more closely to the development of activity therapy than to historical support for the therapeutic effects of music. Boxberger (1963) concluded that, although historical precedents for the use of music in healing may have influenced musicians to experiment with the use of music activities in treatment, "it was the need to make music applicable to the scientific aspects of medicine in the twentieth century that initiated the drive toward an organization based on common goals and purposes" (p. 133).

EARLY TWENTIETH CENTURY ATTEMPTS AT ORGANIZATION

In the early twentieth century, a renewed interest in the use of music in hospitals led to a more vigorous promotion of the clinical practice of music therapy and the development of specific courses of training for music therapists (Boxberger, 1963; Taylor, 1981). During this time, three women, Eva Augusta Vescelius (activity span, 1900-1917), Isa Maud Ilsen (activity span, 1905–1930), and Harriet Ayer Seymour (activity span, 1915–1944), founded organizations designed to promote the practice of music therapy and help train music therapy practitioners (Davis, 1993). Although none of these resulted in a sustained national music therapy movement in the first half of the twentieth century, the efforts of these pioneers achieved the recognition of music therapy as a viable form of treatment by organizations such as the American Red Cross and the United States Army (Davis & Gfeller, 1992) and "provided the impetus for the continued growth and development of music therapy during the second half of the twentieth century" (Davis, 1993, p. 43).

Eva Vescelius and the National Therapeutic Society of New York

Early in the twentieth century, Eva Augusta Vescelius, a trained professional singer who sometimes performed concerts in hospitals and asylums, became interested in "mental therapy" and the use of music in healing. She developed a personal theory of music therapy, first conducting experiments at home to perfect her theories and then applying the therapeutic use of music to patients in hospitals or mental institutions (Davis, 1993). She also actively promoted music therapy through various lectures, writings, and demonstrations (Davis, 1993; Davis & Gfeller, 1992). Vescelius (1918) asserted that the cures affected by music were "based on the law of harmonious rhythmic vibration" (p. 379). Thus, it was essential to use appropriate musical selections in therapeutic work and to have harmony between musician-therapist who transmitted the music and the patient receiving the music. To that end,

Vescelius developed a system for classifying musical selections as to types and uses, suggested specific music prescriptions for various ailments, and offered a course in "musico-therapy" to give musicians training as therapists before they worked with patients (Davis, 1993; Davis & Gfeller, 1992; Vescelius, 1918). Those who worked for and with her also had to be very competent musicians, as individual artistry would be reflected in and affect the healing potential of the music. Thus, Vescelius recognized the importance of both musical skills and therapist skills for those who would use music in healing.

In an attempt to organize the work of music therapists and promote the use of music therapy, Vescelius founded the National Therapeutic Society of New York City in 1903 and served as its president until her death in 1917. She also published the first American music therapy journal, *Music and Health*, in 1913; however, the periodical only lasted for three issues. Nevertheless, Vescelius strongly influenced many individuals who continued to pursue and promote the use of music therapy in the early twentieth century (Boxberger, 1963) and also espoused some ideas which are still used in music therapy training and practice today.

Early University Courses in Music Therapy

In 1919, the first university courses in music therapy were offered at Columbia University in New York City. These classes were taught by Margaret Anderton, a pianist who had provided music therapy to Canadian soldiers during World War I . Anderton's courses were aimed at preparing musicians to work in hospitals, providing information on psychological and physical reactions to music and training on practical ways of using music to help patients with neuro-psychiatric problems or orthopedic injuries (Davis & Gfeller, 1992; Taylor, 1981; Weldin & Eagle, 1991). Isa Maud Ilsen and Willem Van de Wall, two other early music therapy pioneers, also taught courses on music and health at Columbia University in the early decades of the twentieth century (Davis & Gfeller, 1992).

Isa Maud Ilsen and the National Association for Music in Hospitals

Isa Maud Ilsen became interested in the therapeutic use of music while attending nursing school in 1905 (Davis, 1993) Ilsen used music therapy to treat people with mental illnesses, mental retardation, and terminal illnesses and advocated using music in factories to help humanize working conditions. She worked with injured soldiers in Canada and the United States during World War I, using music to alleviate pain and help in the rehabilitation of those with corrective or reconstructive needs (Davis, 1993; Davis & Gfeller, 1992). Ilsen briefly served as a lecturer in "musico-therapy" with Margaret Anderton at Columbia University in 1919. She also had extensive experience as administrator, working for the American Red Cross as Director of Hospital Music in Reconstruction Hospitals in 1918 and later serving as Associate Secretary for the Department of Hospital Services, New York Tuberculosis and Health Association. In both these positions, Ilsen advocated the therapeutic use of music for her patients and also worked as a clinician to provide these services. Seeing the need for an organization that would train people to use music in hospitals and that would bring properly prepared programs of music into hospitals as a supplement to medical treatment, Ilsen founded the National Association for Music in Hospitals in 1926 (Davis, 1993; Davis & Gfeller, 1992; Graham, 1974). This organization solicited medical professionals' support for the therapeutic use of music in hospitals and encouraged philanthropists to raise funds that were used to train music therapists and transport them to local hospitals and institutions.

Ilsen established several specific rules of conduct for using music in hospitals and emphasized that those who used music in hospitals should make sure that the music was appropriate to the needs of the situation as well as to the needs of the patients. According to Ilsen, music was to serve as an adjunct to treatment; therefore, it should never interfere with hospital routines and procedures (Boxberger, 1963). Ilsen insisted on the use of qualified, trained professionals to conduct music therapy services with patients and believed that a variety of music should be used. She also believed it was important that the musicians be able to relate to clients and staff. As Davis (1993) noted, several of Ilsen's rules and ideas are still relevant to contemporary music therapy practice.

Harriet Ayer Seymour and the National Foundation for Music Therapy

Another active advocate of music therapy in the first half of the twentieth century, Harriet Ayer Seymour, was acquainted with the writings of Eva Vescelius and had direct experience working with hospitalized veterans during World War I. In 1920, Seymour published a guide to the therapeutic use of music, entitled *What Music Can Do for You*, and she later taught courses and workshops in the New York City area on the therapeutic use of music (Boxberger, 1963; Davis, 1993, 1996; Davis & Gfeller, 1992). During the 1930s, Seymour became active in bringing live music to New York hospitals and prisons in connection with the Federal Music Project of the Works Project Administration (WPA). In connection with this work, she became involved with experiments striving to classify songs on the basis of their psychological and physiological effects. In the early 1940s, she worked with sick children and adults in New York City, becoming an especially strong advocate for the use of music in the care of sick children (Davis, 1996).

Seymour founded the National Foundation for Music Therapy in 1941. As president of this organization until her death in 1944, she presented lectures and classes to train music therapists, emphasizing the use of music therapy with sick or injured World War II veterans. Seymour reportedly trained over 500 "musical doctors" to work in New York City hospitals during the short existence of her organization (Davis, 1993). Seymour's treatment philosophy incorporated the use of music and constructive thought (i.e., positive thinking) and prescribed the use of particular styles of music, or certain styles of music coupled with mental imagery, for various disorders, including heart ailments, paralysis, and depression. She included the use of folk music and marches in her treatments. In training music therapists, Seymour looked for people who could play music with good tone and rhythm, who were sensitive to the reactions of the patients, and who "had a desire to become a 'channel' for the healing properties of music" (Davis, 1993, p. 43). Some of these same qualities are still important to people who desire to become music therapists today (see Chapter Two). Just prior to her death, Seymour published a text, *An Instruction Course in the Use and Practice of Music Therapy*, that gave information on appropriate ways to use music as therapy for various client populations. This was the first published practical handbook for the clinical practice of music therapy (Davis, 1996).

THE DEVELOPMENT OF MUSIC THERAPY PROGRAMS IN INSTITUTIONS

While the activities and organizations of Vescelius, Ilsen, and Seymour were concentrated in the New York City area, interest in music therapy was also present in other parts of the United States during the first half of the twentieth century. Even though music therapy received only limited support and acceptance from the medical community, reports of music therapy activity in institutions continued to increase (Davis & Gfeller, 1992; Taylor, 1981). For example, some physicians and researchers promoted the use of music in operating rooms, and, by 1929, Duke University was using music extensively, giving every patient access to radio reception by way of speakers or earphones located throughout the hospital. During

this time period, significant music therapy programs were also developed in various institutions in New York, Pennsylvania, and Michigan by the musician/therapist, Willem Van de Wall, and the psychiatrist/musician/composer, Ira Altshuler.

Willem Van de Wall

Willem Van de Wall, considered by many to be one of the key early organizers and innovators in music therapy in the United States, contributed much to the development of music therapy programs in mental hospitals and prisons in the years between

World War I and World War II (Boxberger, 1963; Clair & Heller, 1989; Davis & Gfeller, 1992). His several writings give many ideas for the use of music with patients who have mental disorders, with prisoners, and with children with varying degrees of mentally deficiencies, as well as describing ways to use music for pain relief, to promote aesthetic satisfaction, relaxation, emotional expression, and stress reduction in adults, and to increase efficient production in industrial settings (Clair & Heller, 1989). Van de Wall had a career as a professional harpist with the Metropolitan Opera House, the New York Symphony, and the Marine Band. After World War I, he began to work with music in the treatment of mental illness. His program at Central Islip State Hospital in New York attracted the attention of the Russell Sage Foundation, which subsequently supported his work. In 1923, Van de Wall began his tenure at Pennsylvania's Allentown State Hospital for Mental Diseases, where he established the first comprehensive institutional music therapy program in the United States (Boxberger, 1963; Davis & Gfeller, 1992; Graham, 1974; Wheeler & Golden, 1987). The components of this program, which became a prototype for music therapy programs across the United States, are summarized in Van de Wall's (1936) monumental work, *Music in Institutions*.

Van de Wall believed that the most therapeutic music was that which the patient preferred, with the racial, cultural, and social history of the particular patient also being important variables. In a 1923 article, he advocated the use of music in the general hospital to "overcome apathy, provide moments of emotional unity, and promote the healing process" (Clair & Heller, 1989, p. 169), also noting that music was cost-effective medicine as it could serve many patients simultaneously and made the hospital environment more appealing to patients and their families. Van de Wall theorized that music was an effective therapy with patients suffering from mental illnesses because of its structure and organization, its power as a sensory stimulant, its ability to awaken emotions and provide a means of appropriate emotional expression, its ability to elicit memories, and, most importantly, because it provided a way for patients to actively participate in their treatment. As will be seen in Part III of this text, some of these same ideas still form the basis for much of music therapy practice today. Van de Wall's 1946 book,

Music in Hospitals, summarizes his ideas on music therapy formed from his research and experience, and contains sections on the functions of music, the organization of hospitals, practical suggestions for implementing hospital music programs, and suggestions for the education and training of hospital musicians. Clair and Heller (1989) call this work Van de Wall's legacy and a fitting culmination to his career, noting that "it contains a concise summary of the best information on music therapy available at that time, as well as the seeds of present and future ideas on those topics" (p. 176).

Ira Altshuler

In 1938, another significant institutional music therapy program was founded at Wayne County General Hospital in Eloise, Michigan, by Dr. Ira M. Altshuler (Collins, 1982). Altshuler received his medical training in Switzerland and completed his training in neuropsychiatry at Harvard Medical School in 1927 and 1928. He was also a musician and composer who had specific theories about the way music acted upon psychiatric patients and wrote musical compositions for his clinical work and research in music therapy at Eloise. Altshuler's (1948) essay, "A Psychiatrist's Experience with Music as a Therapeutic Agent," summarized his work and theories. He advocated a strong relationship between psychiatry and music and stressed the importance of research on music and the relationship between man and music (Pratt, 1989).

One of Altshuler's most significant contributions to the field of music therapy was his development of the "iso" principle, something that still plays a major role in music therapy clinical practice today. According to Altshuler's (1948) "iso" principle, music therapists must first use music that matches the mood, activity level, or condition of the patients, before gradually changing the music to effect a change in these areas. Altshuler also theorized that music was effective in helping patients with severe mental disturbances because music bypassed cerebral interpretive relays and appealed directly to the seat of aesthetic reactions, which he believed was located in the thalamus. Altshuler's ideas and his program at Eloise received much attention through his writings and lectures to both musicians and psychiatrists in the late 1930s through the 1950s and had a great impact on the early development of music therapy in psychiatric institutions (Collins, 1982).

THE SUSTAINED MOVE TOWARD PROFESSIONAL ORGANIZATION FOLLOWING WAR II

During the course of their efforts to care for large numbers of soldiers wounded in World War II, physicians discovered that music could not only boost the morale of their patients but also facilitate their recovery. The physician George Ainlay supported the use of music in military hospitals and was largely responsible for having the U.S. Army and War Department develop and publish various music materials (Pratt, 1989; Weldin & Eagle, 1991). In 1943, music became part of the Army's Reconditioning Program, which was designed to help the wounded return to active duty or civilian life (Rorke, 1996; Tyson, 1981). In this model program, goal-directed, specifically prescribed music activities involving active participation (e.g., singing, playing instruments, making instruments, writing song parodies, calisthenics to music), passive participation (e.g., listening to music and discussing music applications) or audioreception (listening only, to live or recorded music) were used (a) to facilitate exercise, (b) as postoperative exercises for patients with orthopedic or lung impairments, (c) as educational activities, (d) for resocialization, or (e) to assist in neuropsychiatric treatment (Rorke, 1996). Music continued to be used as part of the treatment program in 122 Veteran's Administration Hospitals during the post-war years (1946–1950). This use of music to help hospitalized veterans greatly stimulated the general use of music in hospitals and state institutions, leading to a marked increase in the employment of hospital musicians during the mid to late 1940s (Schneider, Unkefer, & Gaston, 1968).

Most of the musicians who worked in Veterans Administration Hospitals and state institutions during the 1940s were volunteers or part-time staff members with little professional training or status (Davis & Gfeller, 1992). Requests from hospitals to train these musicians in basic clinical techniques precipitated the development of college-degree programs in music therapy. The first curriculum specifically designed to train music therapists was established in 1944 at what is now Michigan State University, and the first didactic and laboratory course was taught in 1946 at the University of Kansas (Schneider, Unkefer, & Gaston, 1968). E. Thayer Gaston, then chairman of the Music Education Department at the University of Kansas, was "perhaps the most influential figure in American music therapy during this time and for the next 20 years" (Maranto, 1993b, p. 608). In addition to initiating music therapy training programs at the undergraduate and graduate levels at the University of Kansas, Gaston also encouraged much research in the field, wrote and lectured extensively in support of the use of music in therapy, and established the first music therapy internship training site in collaboration with the renowned Menninger Clinic in Topeka, Kansas (Davis & Gfeller, 1992; R. Johnson, 1981). Because of his leadership in scientific thought, research, and training in music therapy and education in the United States, E. Thayer Gaston is often referred to as the "father of music therapy" (R. Johnson, 1981, p. 279).

During the late 1940s, music therapy training programs were also initiated at institutions such as Chicago Musical College, the College of the Pacific in Stockton, California, and Alverno College in Milwaukee, Wisconsin, and some music therapy courses were taught at the Boston School of Occupational Therapy (Boxberger, 1963; Davis & Gfeller, 1992). This trend toward providing increased training for music therapists (or hospital musicians) did much to promote the growth of music therapy as a recognized professional discipline and helped provide the impetus for the formation of a national organization specific to the field of music therapy (Davis & Gfeller, 1992; Lathom, 1980).

In the 1940s, three professional music associations – the Music Teachers National Association (MTNA), the National Music Council (NMC), and the Music Educators National Conference (MENC) – were particularly influential in establishing communication among people working with therapeutic or functional music (Boxberger, 1963). During the early years of the decade, MTNA heard special reports on music therapy projects (Altshuler, 1940) and established special committees on Music in Psychotherapy, Music in Industry, and Music Therapy. Persons who were instrumental in establishing some of the first music therapy college programs were among the members of these committees. In 1945, based on the results of a 1944 survey that showed the need for medical testing of the effects of music and for standard curricular programs to train qualified personnel (Van de Wall, 1944), NMC formed a Committee on the Use of Music in Hospitals to work with musicians and psychiatrists in exploring the possibilities for adequately training workers for the use of music in therapy. Also in 1945, the councils of MENC recommended that the use of music in hospitals (i.e., any music performance presented at a hospital) be differentiated from the use of music in therapy and that definite steps be taken toward licensing people who practiced and taught music therapy. In addition, MENC formed a Special Committee on Functional Music, whose members began to emphasize the need for controlled research in music therapy and for some kind of publication for the field (Gaston, 1947).

During 1948 and 1949, regional meetings of music therapists, hospital musicians, and others active in the field were held in Massachusetts, Kansas, and Illinois. At some of these meetings, plans for forming a national organization specifically for music therapy were discussed, but no definite progress was made. Meanwhile, MTNA's Committee on Music Therapy continued to present informational sessions on music therapy at various meetings. At MTNA's annual meeting in Cleveland, Ohio, February 28 to March 2, 1950, a special sectional meeting for the purpose of developing a national organization for music therapy was held. At this time, Ray Green was elected chairman of the organizational committee. On June 1, 1950, when reporting to an annual meeting of NMC in his capacity as Chairman of NMC's Committee on the use of Music in Hospitals, Green announced that a meeting would be held the following day to form an organization in the field of hospital music (Boxberger, 1963).

THE NATIONAL ASSOCIATION FOR MUSIC THERAPY

The organizational meeting that marked the beginning of the National Association for Music Therapy [NAMT], the first enduring professional music therapy organization in the United States, was held on June 2, 1950, in New York City. Ray Green was elected as the first president, and one standing committee, the Research Committee, was established (Boxberger, 1963). According to its constitution, the Association's purpose was

> the progressive development of the use of music to accomplish therapeutic aims and the advancement of training, education, and research in the music therapy profession. (NAMT, 1994a, p. xix)

Since its inception in 1950 to its unification with the American Association in 1998, NAMT has continued to serve this purpose by developing and periodically reviewing standards for college course requirements, establishing criteria for the certification and registration of music therapists, establishing standards for clinical practice and ethical conduct, and encouraging research and publication among members of the profession. In 1956, NAMT established the first professional credential in the United States, the title of Registered Music Therapist [RMT], in conjunction with the accrediting agency, the National Association for Schools of Music [NASM] (Boxberger, 1963; Davis & Gfeller, 1992). This title signified that the individual had met all music therapy educational and clinical training standards established by NAMT and NASM. NAMT has also published a number of professional publications. From 1951–1962, NAMT published annual books of proceedings (e.g., *Music Therapy 1951*) and a Bulletin that came out three times a year. In 1964, NAMT began to publish a quarterly research journal, the *Journal of Music Therapy*, as well as a bimonthly member newsletter. Since 1982, NAMT has also published *Music Therapy Perspectives*, a more clinically- and practically-oriented journal.

For many years, NAMT's national office was located in Lawrence, Kansas. In 1982, it relocated in Washington, D.C., later moving to Silver Spring, Maryland, a Washington, D.C. suburb. On January, 1, 1998, NAMT joined with the American Association for Music Therapy (see below) to form the American Music Therapy Association [AMTA], which is currently the only professional music therapy association in the United States (see below).

NAMT's governance structure was carried over into this new organization, which continues to have its offices in Silver Spring, Maryland (AMTA, 1998).

THE AMERICAN ASSOCIATION FOR MUSIC THERAPY

In 1971, a group of music therapists in the New York City area who had philosophical differences with the NAMT over the structure of clinical and educational training programs and a desire for more flexible internship sites in the New York City area met at New York University in New York City and established a second professional organization for music therapists in the United States (Maranto, 1993b; Tyson, 1981; Wheeler & Golden, 1987). Initially called the Urban Federation for Music Therapists, this group changed its name to the American Association for Music Therapy [AAMT] in 1975 to reflect the broadening scope of the organization beyond the New York City area and the urban northeast (Wheeler & Golden, 1987).

Although the AMTA offered more flexibility in its educational and clinical training programs, following a competency-based rather than a course-based approach (see Chapter Two), the purposes of the AAMT remained very similar to those of the NAMT. The AAMT dedicated itself to

- improving the quality of life through the use of music in therapy

- establishing standards of professional competence
- implementing these standards through certification of individuals and approval of university curricula
- promoting and disseminating research through professional publications
- fostering community awareness and public education in regard to the goals and applications of music therapy
- developing employment opportunities
- developing continuing education curricula reflective of new trends in the field. (AAMT, 1993, p. 1)

From 1981–1997, the AAMT published an annual professional journal, *Music Therapy*, which included clinical as well as research reports. It also published a quarterly member newsletter and the *Music Therapy International Report* (formerly *The International Newsletter of Music Therapy*). On January 1, 1998, AAMT joined with NAMT to form the American Music Therapy Association [AMTA], which is currently the only professional music therapy association in the United States (see below).

THE CERTIFICATION BOARD FOR MUSIC THERAPISTS

In the early 1980s, professional music therapists began to feel a need for a process that would give more objectivity and credibility to certification procedures for music therapists and hopefully "have a positive effect on employment practices and reimbursement possibilities" (Certification Board for Music Therapists, 1983, p. 6). The Certification Board for Music Therapists [CBMT], an independent certifying agency for music therapists established with the support of music therapists from NAMT and AAMT under the guidelines of the National Commission on Health Certifying Agencies

[NCHCA], was incorporated in 1983. CBMT received full NCHCA accreditation in 1986. In contrast to NAMT, AAMT, or AMTA, which were or are professional membership associations, CBMT is a *certifying agency*. Its function is to set rules and regulations for obtaining and maintaining a specific, voluntary credential (CBMT, 1992). Simply stated,

The mission of the Certification Board for Music Therapists is to evaluate individuals who wish to enter, continue and/or advance in their discipline through a certification process, and to issue the credential of MT-BC to individuals who demonstrate the required level of competence. (CBMT, 1997, p. 1)

The structure of CBMT includes (1) a Board of Directors that establishes policy for certification and recertification in accordance with the National Commission for Certifying Agencies, (2) an Exam Committee that develops the CBMT Certification Exam in conjunction with the testing firm, Applied Measurement Professionals, (3) a Continuing Education Committee that administers and monitors continuing education programs and records of MT-BCs, and (4) a Job Analysis Committee that conducts a survey of practicing music therapists every five years to determine tasks, skills, and knowledges necessary for current entry level practice of music therapy. These results are used to generate content for the CBMT exam, assuring it continues to measure competence for *current* practice (CBMT, 1997).

CBMT has administered a standardized national certification exam for music therapists since 1985. Upon passing this exam, individuals receive the professional credential Music Therapist-Board Certified [MT-BC]. As of 1997, there were over 2,200 music therapists who held the MT-BC credential (CBMT, 1997). (See Chapter Two for additional information on the CBMT exam and music therapy credentials.)

In 1988, CBMT implemented a recertification program (CBMT, 1992). To maintain their board-certified status, MT-BCs must apply for recertification every five years. In order to be recertified, MT-BCs must demonstrate continuing competence in music therapy practice by participating in ongoing continuing education or by taking additional examinations (CBMT, 1991, 1997, 1998b).

THE AMERICAN MUSIC THERAPY ASSOCIATION

In 1994, the leadership and governing bodies of the AAMT and the NAMT began discussing the possible unification of the two groups and the formation of one professional association for music therapists in the United States (Aigen, 1994; Hunter, 1994). During the spring of 1996, the members of the AAMT and the NAMT voted overwhelmingly in favor of unification, and the new, unified American Music Therapy Association [AMTA] came into being on January 1, 1998 ("Introducing the American Music Therapy Association," 1998). With unification, AMTA became and is now the only music therapy professional membership association in the United States. In its first year of existence, AMTA had 3,611 members as of May 15, 1998 (AMTA, 1998).

The mission of AMTA is "to increase public awareness of the benefits of music therapy and to increase access to quality music therapy services in a rapidly changing world" (AMTA, 1998, p. xii). AMTA publishes a quarterly research-oriented journal, the *Journal of Music Therapy*; a semiannual, practice-oriented journal, *Music Therapy Perspectives*; a quarterly newsletter, *Music Therapy Matters*; and numerous brochures, monographs, and informational publications. AMTA also maintains a website (www.musictherapy.org) that provides information for music therapists and the general public. While AMTA still continues to establish training and competency standards for music therapists, as did the former AAMT and NAMT, all credentialling responsibilities have now been yielded to the independent Certification Board for Music Therapists [CBMT]. (Information on CBMT and music therapy credentialling is presented above and in Chapter Two.)

AMTA's governance structure, taken from the former NAMT, is modeled after the structure of the U.S. government and includes an Executive Board, an Assembly of Delegates (the legislative and policy-making body) which has proportionate representation from each region, an Appeals and Judicial Review Board, an Ethics Board, and various standing councils and committees related to (a) training and development and (b) professional practices and services (AMTA, 1998). The National Office is headed by the Executive Director, who is an employee of the Association. Annual national conferences are held in the fall, and regional conferences are held in the spring of each year. AMTA is now the United States' "primary organizational agency for the advancement of education, clinical practice, research, and ethical standards in the music therapy profession" (AMTA, 1998, p. xxxi).

CURRENT TREATMENT SETTINGS AND ROLES OF PROFESSIONAL MUSIC THERAPISTS

Where Music Therapy Is Used

When music therapy first became an organized profession in 1950, most music therapists worked in adult psychiatric settings. As the value of music in the treatment of children with various handicaps was recognized, music therapists also began to find increasing employment opportunities in institutions serving individuals with mental retardation (Lathom, 1980). Surveys conducted in 1978 (Braswell, Maranto, & Decuir, 1979a) and 1980 (Lathom, 1982) found that most music therapists were still employed by psychiatric facilities at that time, with mental retardation facilities again employing the second greatest number. More recent surveys (AMTA, 1998; Braswell, Decuir, & Jacobs, 1989; NAMT, 1994a; Taylor, 1987a) have shown that, while psychiatric and mental health settings continue to be the most common work settings for music therapists, the types of treatment settings in which music therapists work have greatly expanded as new applications of music therapy services continually develop. Music therapists currently are working in almost 80 different types of settings (AMTA, 1998), including adult day care centers, community mental health centers, special education programs, hospice care, substance abuse programs, oncology treatment centers, correctional institutions, nursing homes, physical rehabilitation centers, psychiatric hospitals, medical hospitals, retirement facilities, day care programs, community centers and recreational programs, senior centers, programs for the developmentally disabled, group homes and halfway houses, outpatient clinics, schools, and private studios or clinics.

In the 1970s, some music therapists began to work independently and contract their services to individuals or agencies (Henry, Knoll, & Anderson, 1982; Michel, 1981). Lathom (1982) reported that 4.1 percent of the 466 music therapists responding to her 1980 survey worked in private practice. As health care paradigms change and the trends in the workplace as a whole move more toward self-employment and contract workers, non-traditional job opportunities, such as private practice, contractual arrangements, and independent consultant services, also continue to offer expanding, viable employment opportunities for music therapists (O'Brien & Goldstein, 1985; Oliver, 1989; Reuer, 1996). Recent surveys have demonstrated how the trend toward self-employment and private practice in music therapy continues to rise. In 1994, 193 (7%) of the music therapists responding to a survey were self-employed or in private practice (NAMT, 1994a); by 1998, the number of music therapists in private practice had increased to 445 (11%) (AMTA, 1998).

In recent years, as the fields of music and medicine are once again converging (see Chapter Three), music therapists have also begun to find more employment opportunities in medical, physical rehabilitation, and general hospital settings (AMTA, 1998; Crowe, 1985; Maranto, 1991; Michel, 1981; Standley, 1996b). (See Chapters Seventeen and Eighteen for specific information on music therapy in medical and rehabilitation settings.) With attention focused on music therapy and the elderly in a hearing by the U. S. Senate Special Committee on Aging in August of 1991 and the passage of the Older Americans Act of 1992 , elderly populations, too, are now emerging as a major recipient of music therapy services (NAMT, 1994a; AMTA, 1998). (See Chapter Nineteen for specific information on music therapy with the elderly.) In addition, music therapists are beginning to explore job opportunities in wellness programs, expanding beyond traditional healing and educational institutional roles to helping people in everyday circumstances deal more effectively with life and live a life of "richer quality and deeper meaning" (Broucek, 1987, p. 58). (See Chapter Twenty-one for specific information on the use music therapy to promote health and well-being in the general population.)

Job Satisfaction and Employment Trends

A survey by Braswell, Decuir, & Jacobs (1989) found that most music therapists report being very satisfied to fairly satisfied with their jobs. Aspects that were rated most positively included "independence in work, importance of the job, challenge of the job, opportunity to learn, immediate supervisor, job security, staff relations, and professional respect" (p. 16). The outlook for continued job development in music therapy also appears positive: In 1997, "in most work settings, there were nearly twice as many new jobs as jobs lost" (AMTA, 1998, p. 200). A recent survey showed jobs in the aging sector, mental-health-related facilities, and physical rehabilitation to be major growth areas for music therapy, with the development of private practices in music therapy also continuing to rise (AMTA, 1998). Geographically, the most new music therapy jobs were developed in the Great Lakes and Mid-Atlantic regions. (These areas currently also have the greatest number of music therapists.)

Salaries for music therapists vary greatly depending on population served, work setting, region of the country, job title, and years of experience. For 1997, average salaries were highest in the New England, Western, and Mid-Atlantic regions (AMTA, 1998), with average salaries across the country ranging from $28,118 in the South Central region to $35,556 in New England. The average salary for a professional with 1 to 5 years of experience was $27,004, while professional music therapists with 16 to 20 years experience had an average salary of $36,980. Salaries also varied by work setting, with the highest average salaries being found in universities and colleges (i.e., music therapy professors), correctional facilities, wellness programs, oncology programs, and Veteran's Administration hospitals. Music therapy jobs have a wide salary range, with salaries from $13,000 to $90,000 being reported (AMTA, 1998). A recent analysis of salary trends by AMTA staff members concluded that, although the lowest salaries for music therapists are still very low, "both the low and high range of salaries appear to be rising" (AMTA, 1998, p. 202).

Changing Roles of Music Therapy Professionals

When music therapy first began to be recognized as a professional discipline in the late 1940s and early 1950s, music therapists were generally looked upon as technicians. They were considered to be adjunctive to other therapy specialists, and they usually worked under many layers of supervision (Michel, 1981, 1985). Since that time, however, music therapists have been achieving more and more recognition as independent, responsible allied health professionals. In the 1960s and 1970s, that recognition was facilitated by an increased research base in music therapy and an increased orientation to measurable data in music therapy practice (Michel, 1981, 1985). The passage of Public Law 94-142, the Education for All Handicapped Children Act, in 1975, also led to increased recognition of music therapists as independent, competent professionals and to expanded employment opportunities in special education and public school settings (Gfeller, 1992e; Michel, 1985). By the late 1970s, many music therapists were serving as supervisors or primary therapists. McGinty (1980) found that over 61 percent of the music therapists surveyed had responsibility for supervising other personnel and that 46.5 percent were regarded as the primary therapist for some clients. 94 percent of the respondents were responsible, either solely or in conjunction with a team, for setting up and evaluating client treatment plans. In addition, 89 percent had free access to confidential data on their clients, while another 3.9 percent had access with some limitations. According to McGinty, this access to confidential information indicated that music therapists were viewed as people who were responsible and had integrity.

As the trend in health care in general has been to move away from large institutional settings, so music therapists, too, have begun to work more and more in community and special education settings. Michel (1976) predicted that "the future of music therapy definitely lies in the mainstream of health-related services rather than in traditional institutions" (p. 117). A few years later, Henry, Knoll, and Anderson (1982) observed that "non-traditional job opportunities such as self-employment, contractual arrangements, and consultant services" (p. 2) were definitely increasing in popularity as employment alternatives for music therapists. A recent survey by the American Music Therapy Association (1998) found that the development of private practices by music therapists continues to be a rising trend. In Chapters Seven to Twenty-one of this text, it will become readily apparent that music therapists currently use their professional skills to serve clients with a wide range of disabilities in a wide variety of both traditional and non-traditional treatment settings.

As our society begins to focus more and more on preventive medicine and health maintenance, music therapists may find a place for their skills in holistic health centers, adult education settings, and stress-reduction clinics. As people become more aware of the dangers of noise pollution, music therapists might also take on the role of designing healthy sonic environments for the home and other settings. The planners of space stations recognize the benefits music can have for promising a healthy stimulus environment (Clearwater, 1985); perhaps music therapists will some day hold important positions in the National Aeronautics and Space Administration! In moving into the mainstream of health-related services, music therapists may well expand their role to help "normal" individuals as well as those with disabilities improve their condition, skills, thoughts, feelings, or behaviors through the use of specifically prescribed, goal-directed music and music-based experiences. (Some information on current uses of music therapy in wellness and holistic health programs is presented in Chapter Twenty-one).

MUSIC THERAPY IN OTHER COUNTRIES

Probably the most widespread use of music therapy outside the United States developed in England, where the British Society for Music Therapy (first called the Society for Music Therapy and Remedial Music) was established in 1958 under the leadership of Juliette Alvin. During the 1960s and 1970s, music therapy developed in an organized way in several other European countries, including the Netherlands, the Scandinavian countries, East and West Germany, Austria, France, Switzerland, Yugoslavia, and Belgium (Michel, 1985). In North America, a strong interest in music therapy also developed in Canada, and the Canadian Association of Music Therapy was established in 1974. In yet another part of the world, Australia has been reporting developments in music therapy since the 1960s (Michel, 1985). The Australian Music Therapy Association was founded in 1975, with Ruth Bright as president. In the Far East, Japan was one of the first countries to embrace modern music therapy practices, with the first developments occurring after World War II (Maranto, 1993a). Several professional organizations developed during the 1970s and 1980s, and a formal music therapy training program, the Nippon Institute of Music Therapy, was established in 1988. Modern music therapy practices also developed in China during the 1980s and 1990s (Maranto, 1993a). In addition, students from countries in the Far East have also been coming to the United States to receive music therapy training (Michel, 1985).

At the present time, music therapy is practiced in almost 40 countries across the globe (Maranto, 1993a; Moreno et al., 1990). Active associations and training programs are found in South America (Argentina, Brazil), North America (Canada, U.S.A.), Europe (Austria, Denmark, England, Finland, France, Germany, Italy, the Netherlands, Norway, Spain, Sweden), the Mid East (Israel), Australia, the Far East (Japan, People's Republic of China), and South Africa. Clinical practices are also taking place in many other countries around the world, including Uruguay, Colombia, Chile, Mexico, Puerto Rico, Greece, Slovenia, Switzerland, Iceland, Portugal, Ireland, Scotland, Poland, Belgium, Korea, India, and countries of the former Soviet Union.

The first World Congress of Music Therapy was held in France in 1974. Subsequent world congresses of music therapy have been held in several cities around the world, approximately every two to three years (Maranto, 1993a). The growing need for international communication and cooperation within the profession of music therapy led to the formation of the World Federation of Music Therapy in 1985. The World Federation, which in 1993 included 32 associations from 13 countries, "seeks to promote and support the development of music therapy on an international level" (Maranto, 1993a, p. 679). The

1993 World Congress of Music Therapy was held in Spain and included presentations on music therapy from thirty different countries (Moreno, 1993), while the 1996 World Congress of Music Therapy, held in Hamburg, Germany, included over 240 diverse presentations with first-time representation from China, Hungary, Taiwan, Korea, Venezuela, Bulgaria, Poland, and the former East Germany (Moreno, 1996). To help promote international communication within the profession, an international computer network for music therapy is being developed by Pieter van den Berk of the Netherlands (Maranto, 1993a) and plans are underway for the creation of an international journal of music therapy, sponsored by the World Federation of Music Therapy (Moreno, 1993).

SUMMARY

In the first decades of the twentieth century, music therapy was vigorously promoted by several individuals, most notably by Eva Vescelius, Isa Maud Ilsen, and Harriet Ayer Seymour. Various organizations and clinical training programs for music therapy were established, especially in the New York City area, but none developed into a lasting national movement. Reports of music therapy activity in institutions continued to increase, however, and significant music therapy programs were developed in New York, Pennsylvania, and Michigan during the 1920s and 1930s by the music therapy pioneers Willem Van de Wall and Ira Altshuler. During the 1940s, music was used in the treatment of hospitalized veterans and was recognized as part of the Army's Reconditioning Program. As a result of this increased use of music in hospitals, college courses and degree programs in music therapy began to develop to train "hospital musicians" in basic clinical techniques. E. Thayer Gaston, chairman of the Music Education Department at the University of Kansas, was a leader in scientific thought, research, and training in music therapy in the United States during the 1940s, 1950s, and 1960s, and is often referred to as the "father of music therapy."

In response to the need for developing standards for training individuals to use music therapeutically in hospital and institutional settings, the National Association for Music Therapy [NAMT] was founded on June 2, 1950. Its purpose was to develop the therapeutic use of music and to advance training, education, and research in music therapy. NAMT was the first enduring national professional music therapy organization in the United States, being in continuous existence from 1950 until 1998, when it joined with the American Association for Music Therapy to form the new, unified American Music Therapy Association [AMTA].

In 1971, a group of music therapists in the New York City area established a second professional organization for music therapists in the United States. Initially called the Urban Federation for Music Therapists, this group changed its name to the American Association for Music Therapy [AAMT] in 1975. Its membership was concentrated mainly in the northeastern United States. On January 1, 1998, AAMT joined with NAMT to form the new, unified American Music Therapy Association [AMTA].

In 1983, an independent certifying agency for music therapists, the Certification Board for Music Therapists [CBMT], was incorporated. Its function is to set rules and regulations for obtaining and maintaining a specific, voluntary credential, that of Music Therapist-Board Certified [MT-BC]. The CBMT administers a national certification examination and recertification program for music therapists. MT-BCs must apply for recertification every five years.

In 1994, the leadership and governing bodies of the AAMT and the NAMT began discussing the possible unification of the two groups and the formation of one professional association for music therapists in the United States. During the spring of 1996, the members of the AAMT and the NAMT voted overwhelmingly in favor of unification, and the new, unified American Music Therapy Association [AMTA] came into being on January 1, 1998. AMTA is now the *only* music therapy professional membership association in the United States. Its mission is "to increase public awareness of the benefits of music therapy and to increase access to quality music therapy services in a rapidly changing world"

(AMTA, 1998, p. xii). Publications include a quarterly research-oriented journal, the *Journal of Music Therapy*; a semiannual, practice-oriented journal, *Music Therapy Perspectives*; a quarterly newsletter, *Music Therapy Matters*; and numerous brochures, monographs, and informational publications.

Music therapy is currently used in a wide variety of treatment settings, including psychiatric hospitals, mental retardation centers, hospitals and schools for the physically disabled, community mental health centers, day care centers, special education facilities, geriatric care centers, special service centers, substance abuse treatment centers, and general hospitals. Music therapists are also receiving increasing recognition as independent, responsible allied health professionals. Some music therapists have established private practices, while others are regarded as the primary therapist for clients in certain treatment settings. Music therapists continue to create more areas of application for music therapy as they move beyond traditional institutional settings into the mainstream of health-related services.

The profession of music therapy has also developed in an organized way in countries other than the United States. Music therapy is now practiced in almost 40 countries around the world, and global awareness of music therapy and music therapy organizations and training programs in other countries are continuing to expand. World Congresses of Music Therapy have been held periodically since 1974, and the World Federation of Music Therapy was formed in 1985.

QUESTIONS FOR THOUGHT AND DISCUSSION

1. How and where was music therapy promoted and practiced in the United States in the first half of the twentieth century? What impact did these early promoters and practitioners have on the development and growth of music therapy in the United States?

2. How did musicians and professional music associations interact with medical and hospital personnel in the early to mid 1940s? How did these interactions pave the way for a closer association between the fields of music and medicine?

3. What factors precipitated the development of an organization to regulate practice and training in music therapy?

4. What are the current certifying and professional associations for music therapists in the United States? What are the functions of each, and how do these serve music therapists, employers, and consumers/clients?

5. How has the role of the professional music therapist changed since music therapy first emerged as an organized professional discipline in the 1950s?

6. What are some current employment trends in the field of music therapy? How do you think these will change in the future? What clinical and employment opportunities do you see developing for music therapists?

7. In what other parts of the world is music therapy practiced? How do you think the continued expansion of the global awareness and practice of music therapy will influence the development and practice of the field in the United States?

SUGGESTIONS FOR FURTHER READING

American Association for Music Therapy [AAMT]. (1993). *Introducing the American Association for Music Therapy* [brochure]. Valley Forge, PA: Author.

American Music Therapy Association [AMTA]. (1998). *AMTA member sourcebook 1998*. Silver Spring, MD: Author.

Boxberger, R. (1963). A historical study of the National Association for Music Therapy. In E. H. Schneider (Ed.) *Music therapy 1962* (pp. 133-197). Lawrence, KS: Allen Press.

Certification Board for Music Therapists [CBMT]. (1997). *CBMT: The certification board for music therapists* [brochure]. Richmond, VA: Author.

Certification Board for Music Therapists [CBMT]. (1998). *Your music therapist is certified by the certification board for music therapists* [brochure]. Richmond, VA: Author.

Clair, A. A., & Heller, G. N. (1989). Willem Van de Wall (1887-1953): Organizer and innovator in music education and music therapy. *Journal of Research in Music Education, 37*(3), 165-178.

Davis, W. B. (1993). Keeping the dream alive: Profiles of three early twentieth century music therapists. *Journal of Music Therapy, 30*(1), 34-45.

Davis, W. B. (1996). An instruction course in the use and practice of musical therapy: the first handbook of music therapy clinical practice. *Journal of Music Therapy, 33*(1), 34-49.

Davis, W. B., & Gfeller, K. E. (1992). Music therapy: An historical perspective. In W. B. Davis, K. E. Gfeller, & M. H. Thaut, *An introduction to music therapy: Theory and practice* (pp. 16-37). Dubuque, IA: Wm. C. Brown.

Gfeller, K. (1992). The profession in a larger context. In W. B. Davis, K. E. Gfeller, & M. H. Thaut, *An introduction to music therapy: Theory and practice* (pp. 352–360). Dubuque, IA: Wm. C. Brown.

Maranto, C. D. (Ed.) (1993). *Music therapy: International perspectives.* Pipersville, PA: Jeffrey Books.

Maranto, C. D. (1993). Music therapy in the United States of America. In C. D. Maranto (Ed.), *Music therapy: international perspectives* (pp. 605-662). Pipersville, PA: Jeffrey Books.

Michel, D. E. (1985). Developments in other countries. In D. E. Michel, *Music therapy: An introduction, including music in special education* (2nd ed.) (pp. 103-110). Springfield, IL: Charles C Thomas.

Michel, D. E. (1985). Recent historical perspectives. In D. E. Michel, *Music therapy: An introduction, including music in special education* (2nd ed.) (pp. 8-14). Springfield, IL: Charles C Thomas.

Moreno, J., Brotons, M., Hairston, M., Hawley, T., Kiel, H., Michel, D., & Rohrbacher, M. (1990). International music therapy: A global perspective. *Music Therapy Perspectives, 8*, 41-46.

Reuer, B. (1996). Posturing for a changing world: Consulting as a career option. *Music Therapy Perspectives, 14*(1), 16-20.

Rorke, M. A. (1996). Music and the wounded of World War II. *Journal of Music Therapy, 33*(3), 189-207.

Schneider, E. H., Unkefer, R. F., & Gaston, E. T. (1968). Introduction. In E. T. Gaston (Ed.), *Music in therapy* (pp. 1-4). New York: Macmillan.

Tyson, F. (1981). Music therapy in hospitals. In F. Tyson, *Psychiatric music therapy: Origins and development* (pp. 7-12). New York: Fred Weidner & Sons Printers.

Van de Wall, W. (1936). *Music in institutions.* New York: Russell Sage Foundation.

Wheeler, B. L., & Golden, S. (1987). NAMT and its Mid-Atlantic region: Changing together. *Music Therapy Perspectives, 4*, 56-63.

SOURCES FOR ADDITIONAL INFORMATION

American Music Therapy Association [AMTA], 8455 Colesville Rd., Suite 1000, Silver Spring, MD 20910, (301) 589-3300, FAX (301) 589-5175, email: info@music therapy.org, Web: http://www.music therapy.org

Certification Board for Music Therapists [CBMT], 506 E. Lancaster Ave., Suite 102, Downington, PA 19335, 1-800-765-CBMT, email: info@cbmt.com, Web: http://www.cbmt.com

*Contact information current as of February, 2000.

PART III

CURRENT CLINICAL PRACTICES
IN MUSIC THERAPY

HOW DOES ONE *do* music therapy? Are there any general guiding principles for theory and practice? What is involved in planning, implementing, and evaluating music therapy intervention strategies? In what specific ways can music and music-based experiences be used to benefit clients who have various disabilities? Are there different "schools" of music therapy techniques or approaches? Is research important to the practicing music therapy clinician? In Part III, these questions and others are discussed as more detailed information on the clinical practice of music therapy is presented.

The first two chapters in this section provide some general guidelines for the use of music in therapy. Chapter Five provides a theoretical foundation, discussing some reasons why music is useful as treatment modality and presenting three basic principles that often guide the use of music and music-based experiences in therapy. Chapter Six gives more practical information, discussing the basic stages in the delivery of music therapy services and providing examples of music therapy experiences that may be used to address general goal areas. Chapters Seven through Twenty-one, then, give detailed information on music therapy interventions and practices with specific client populations. Each of these chapters contains (a) a definition of the particular population or disability, (b) descriptions of common characteristics, problems, and needs of individuals in that particular client group, (c) a listing of settings for service delivery, (d) examples of how music is used in therapy to benefit individuals in that client population, including common music therapy

goals and approaches, and (e) special considerations and tips for success applicable to the particular client population. Short case study problems are included in the "Questions for Thought and Discussion" sections of each chapter to help the reader begin applying the information to specific clinical situations. Copious references and extensive suggestions for further reading are provided for readers who might desire more detailed information on music therapy practices and approaches with specific types of clientele. In addition, these readers may wish to consult bibliographic sources (e.g., Eagle, 1976, 1978, 1982; Eagle & Miniter, 1984) or music therapy web sites (e.g., www.musictherapy.org) and databases (e.g., CAIRSS for Music [http://galaxy.einet.net/hytelnet/FUL064.html] or MuSICA [http://www.musica.uci.edu]) available through the Internet.

The use of music in therapy involves a wide range of procedures and techniques. Chapter Twenty-two overviews several "schools" of music therapy practice in an attempt to give the reader a basic understanding of some of the more common approaches to music therapy treatment that are currently used in the United States. Some of these approaches are centered around particular music techniques, while others adapt music education approaches and methodologies to clinical use. Still others are based on specific educational, psychotherapeutic, or medical models and theories. The pros and cons of choosing to adhere to one particular system or approach are also discussed.

Although a "research attitude" may sound like something that belongs in the laboratory rather that in the clinic, it is, in fact, an attitude that is of vital importance to effective clinical practice. Chapter Twenty-three focuses on the value of research to music therapy clinicians, both as they use the research of others and do research for themselves. Parallels are drawn between the approach the clinician takes in developing, implementing, and evaluating the effectiveness of a treatment plan and the steps the researcher follows in devising, conducting, and evaluating experiments. The importance of reporting clinical findings is also emphasized.

After completing Part III, the reader should have gained the knowledge and information needed to perform the following tasks:

1. Give several reasons why music is useful as a treatment modality.

2. Use Gaston's three guiding principles and/or Sear's three basic classifications to explain general ways music is used in therapy.

3. List and briefly describe the basic stages in the delivery of music therapy services.

4. Give examples of music experiences that might be used to help improve (a) behavioral skills (e.g., attending skills, compliance), (b) sensory skills, (c) motor skills, (d) language and communication skills, (e) emotional learning and emotional expression, (f) interpersonal (social) skills, (g) self-help/survival skills, and (h) academic/cognitive skills.

5. Describe music therapy goals and treatment procedures applicable to clients who have (a) mental retardation, (b) learning disabilities, (c) hearing impairments, (d) visual impairments, (e) orthopedic impairments, (f) communication disorders, (g) autism, (h) mental or behavioral disorders or severe emotional disturbances, or (i) severe and profound multiple disabilities.

6. Describe music therapy goals and treatment procedures used (a) in medical treatment settings, (b) in physical rehabilitation programs, (c) with individuals who are elderly, (d) with individuals who are terminally ill, and (e) to promote health and well-being in the general population.

7. Describe several different "schools" of music therapy.

8. Explain why research is important to the field of music therapy and to the music therapy clinician.

9. Describe methods and benefits of using and doing research in the clinical setting.

Chapter Five

GENERAL GUIDELINES FOR THE THERAPEUTIC USE OF MUSIC, PART I THEORETICAL PRINCIPLES

WHY MUSIC IS USEFUL AS A TREATMENT MODALITY

As IS EVIDENT from the information presented in Chapter Three, music has been used in connection with healing practices for many centuries. Contrary to ancient myths, music has no magical qualities that give it a special healing power. However, there are certain aspects of the physical components of music and of the human uses of and reactions to music that make music particularly useful as a therapeutic treatment modality. These various aspects and effects of music, together with its cultural meanings and uses, help one understand some of the processes that underlie both the use of music in therapy and the influences of music on human behavior (Abeles & Chung, 1996; Bartlett, 1996; Gaston, 1968a; Gfeller, 1992a; Hodges, 1996; Hodges & Haack, 1996; Merriam, 1964; Radocy & Boyle, 1988).

Music Is a Universal, Essential Part of Human Behavior

Anthropologists and ethnomusicologists tell us that music can be found in all cultures, both primitive and civilized (Blacking, 1973; Dowling & Harwood, 1986; Hodges & Haack, 1996; Merriam, 1964; Nettl, 1956). As Spintge (1991) noted, "there is no human civilization that has not experienced and produced music" (p. 59). Scientific anthropological and ethnomusicological studies of cultures throughout the world continue to show that "musical behavior is a human invariant" (Hodges & Haack, 1996, p. 495) and that "music, like love, is one of the most universal of human experiences" (Whitwell, 1993, p. 46). Sociological, psychological, and biological evidence, too, point to the prominent, all-inclusive place and influence music has in and on human behavior and experience (Hodges & Haack, 1996).

Even in our complex societies today, people are avid music consumers, spending a great amount of time and money on concert tickets, electronic music systems, recorded music and music videos, etc. Hardly a day goes by where one does not hear some kind of music: as part of a commercial, during a television program or movie, from a radio or tape or compact disc player, from a multimedia computer program, while waiting on hold on the telephone, as a background in stores or restaurants, from children singing at play, from cars passing by with their radios playing loudly, etc. Music is also associated with government and civic ceremonies, sporting events, and religious services as well as many of our formal and informal gatherings. In addition, it is frequently used as background sound to break monotony, mask unwanted sounds, establish certain moods, stimulate conversations during parties, alleviate a feeling of aloneness, or to help "humanize" impersonal environments (Hodges & Haack, 1996; Radocy & Boyle, 1988).

Music has been a part of most people's lives from

the time they are born, when their mothers sang them to sleep with a lullaby or engaged them in play with sing-song speech and musical rhymes. Usually, music continues to be a prevalent art form for the rest of their lives (Gfeller, 1992a), whether they participate mainly as listeners and consumers or also actively engage in making music at a professional or an amateur level (e.g., singing in church or community groups). Although they may not always agree on the particular forms it should take, music is something that is used and valued by people of all walks of life. As Hesser (1995) observed:

> We all recognize the power of music in our lives. . . . We may not understand intellectually exactly what it is about music that moves us so deeply, but we still spend a great deal of time listening to and making music. (p. 45)

Research and clinical experience have also shown that even individuals who have severe physical, mental, or emotional disabilities can respond to and participate successfully in musical experiences (see Chapters Seven to Twenty).

Gaston (1968a), the father of modern music therapy, considered music to be a defining behavior of human beings, something that was vital to their nature and its expression:

> Music is the essence of humanness, not only because man creates it, but because he creates his relationship to it. . . . Music is an essential and necessary function of man. It influences his behavior and condition and has done so for thousands of years. (p. 15)

His lifetime of ethnomusicological research led Blacking (1973) to concur: "Music, like language and possibly religion, is a species-specific trait of man" (p. 7). The physician and medical researcher Lewis Thomas (1974) also found that: "The need to make music, and to listen to it, is universally expressed by human beings. . . . It is, like speech, a dominant aspect of human biology" (p. 23).

In their study of human behavior, psychologists have recently proposed several theories of multiple intelligences (Hodges & Haack, 1996). Howard Gardner's (1983) theory includes musical intelligence as one of the basic types of human intellectual competence. Thus, Gardner considers musical intelligence to be one of the important and valuable ways of human knowing. Current research on music and the brain is also demonstrating that music is an essential, biologically based aspect of human behavior. For examples, studies have shown that music has definite effects on neural processes, that human beings have a biological affinity for melodic patterns, that even infants recognize and respond to music, and that human beings are born with certain brain cells that respond to musical sounds (Hodges, 1996; Taylor, 1997; Whitwell, 1993). After reviewing recent neuromusical research, Hodges (1996) concluded:

> All human beings are born with a musical brain. . . . We all have neurological and bodily mechanisms that allow us to be aware of and responsive to the music of the surrounding culture. . . . Given proper instruction and reinforcement, nearly everyone can improve musical skills. (p. 258)

Since it is such a pervasive, essential aspect of human behavior, music is something that is universally accessible to people of all cultures and age groups. Thus, it has great potential for use as a medium to facilitate growth and healing with individuals of many varying ability and age levels. (See Chapters Seven to Twenty-one for specific examples.)

Music Is Composed of Real Physical Structures, Ordered in Time

"All music has its basis in the physical world. . . . All involve the same starting point – vibrations have been initiated in some object(s)" (Hedden, 1980a, p. 37). Music is made up of real physical structures, vibrations, which can be felt, heard, measured, and graphed. Different frequencies, different wave forms, different intensities, and different durations of these vibrations produce various pitches, tone qualities, loudness levels, and rhythms (Hedden, 1980b). Music, like other aspects of the physical world, is something we perceive through our senses. "All the senses bring to us aspects of reality. To hear a chord of music is no less real that to smell a rose, to see a sunset, to taste an apple, or to feel the impact of striking a wall" (Gaston, 1968a, p. 24).

From the time of Pythagorus, people have noted that the overtone series of musical tones and vibrations is connected to natural, physical structures. Thus, by participating in musical experiences, an individual becomes intimately connected with nature and the natural laws of the universe: "In everything the musician does he is at one with a natural law of physics – the overtone series" (Whitwell, 1993, p. 143). In recent years, findings and theories from modern physics and quantum mechanics, which tell us that the basic substance of the universe is patterned vibration, have led some music therapy philosophers and theorists to suggest that some of the power of music in therapy lies in the fact that music, which can be thought of as special patterns of vibrations moving through time, is congruent with the basic stuff of the universe (Eagle, 1991). Truly, "the elements of music are in all of life" (Priestley, 1985, p. 245).

Another special aspect of the structure of music is that it is ordered in time and exists only through experiencing it in time.

> Except for relatively minute deviations, music (whether an entire piece or merely a measure or phrase in repeated practice) cannot be inter-rupted without losing its intent. . . . The music must be carried through in its time order. (Sears, 1968, p. 35)

The elements of rhythm, form, and structure in music are related to this time-ordered nature. Music unfolds in and through time even as life and individuals develop in and through time. The rhythms, forms, and structures in music can be used to mirror, stimulate, enhance, or help sustain rhythmic and organizational processes within individuals and among group members. In its time order, too, then, music has connections to basic aspects of life and human development.

Music Affects the Whole Person

Music is a multisensory and multidimensional experience that affects people physically, cognitively, and emotionally. Music is often perceived and experienced consciously, but it can also be perceived and experienced on levels that do not involve conscious mental processes. "Music is a very complex stimulus, influencing conscious brain functions as well as autonomic and unconscious cerebral processes effectively and in different ways" (Spintge, 1991, p. 61). Music has impact upon the whole person, in all of his or her functioning domains. As Boxill (1985) noted, "music contacts the human being on primordial to intricate physiological levels, on basic to dynamic psychological levels, and on simple to complicated cerebral levels" (p. 18). For purposes of research and for ease of discussion, the effects of music on each of these domains or levels is often treated separately; however, it is important to remember that music affects people in all these ways simultaneously, even though one aspect may be more dominant at a given time.

Music Affects Physical Responses

Although responses will vary somewhat from individual to individual based on each individual's preferences and previous experiences with music, research has shown that music does have definite effects on a person's physiological responses (Bartlett, 1996; Radocy & Boyle, 1988; Taylor, 1997). Individual musical elements (e.g., rhythm, timbre) as well as distinctive combinations of musical elements in particular musical compositions can be used to influence and affect physical responses. For example, rhythmic stimuli can enhance timing and readiness in gait training and physical fitness activities, help sustain muscular effort, and affect respiration and relaxation responses (Gfeller, 1992a; Miller, 1979). Research has also shown that music with different amounts of rhythmic activity and different degrees of percussive or sustained sounds (stimulative vs. sedative music) has different effects on several physiological responses, including heart and pulse rates, blood pressure, respiration, skin conductivity, muscular tension and motor activity, motor/postural responses, finger or peripheral skin temperature, stomach contractions, brain waves, and biochemical responses (e.g., changes in levels of various hormones related to stress or immune system function) (Bartlett, 1996; Edwards et al., 1991; Radocy & Boyle, 1988). Bartlett (1996) provides several tables summarizing studies that have been conducted in these areas over the past 120 years. While the exact nature and extent of music's influence did vary from study to study, at least partially because of various definition and measurement difficulties and uncontrollable confounding variables, the majority of the studies reviewed by Bartlett did show that music and sound stimuli do influence bodily systems and physiological responses.

In recent years, there has been a resurgence of interest in the way music and specific tones and frequencies affect various organs, tissues, and bones, all the way down to the cellular level, and the implications this might have for the use of music in healing (Crowe & Scovel, 1996; Goldman, 1988; Halpern, 1978; Marcus, 1995). Several experiments have shown that the process of applying carefully selected music and vibrational frequencies to the body through special speakers in tables or chairs or through music-electro-acupuncture techniques has been successful in reducing arthritic pain, decreasing muscle rigidity, decreasing insomnia, and aiding the recovery of muscle function in stroke victims (Chesky & Michel, 1991; Shi-jing, Hui-ju, Guo, & Maranto, 1991; Skille, 1989; Wigram, 1995). (See Chapter Twenty-two for more information on Vibroacoustic Therapy.)

Music Affects Cognitive and Emotional Responses

Research has demonstrated that music can have definite effects on a person's brain function and cognitive processes (Hodges & Haack, 1996; Radocy & Boyle, 1988; Taylor, 1997). For example, music can assist a person in organizing and remembering information. As advertisers well know, product names and information are recalled more readily when they are presented as part of a catchy tune. A market has also developed in the educational field for songs that help students learn and retain information such as math and geography facts, spelling words, health and safety rules, and the like (Kimbo Educational, 1995). Through music, information can be presented in a unique and appealing manner. Since music is the language of the brain's right hemisphere (Whitwell, 1993), it may also provide an additional pathway to the brain and be especially

useful to those who have more difficulty processing verbal information more commonly processed in the left hemisphere. [See discussions of music therapy with communication disorders and stroke victims in Chapters Twelve and Eighteen.] In addition, music may help to provide a link or "bridge of understanding" (Whitwell, 1993, p. 30) between the two hemispheres of the brain and stimulate fuller brain function. As the composer Franz Liszt observed,

> Music is the intermediary which places emotion in harmony with intelligence; enabling us to enjoy and love that which intelligence enables us to become acquainted with. The Greeks . . . well understood the subtle connecting link provided by music between the perceptible and the impalpable – between that which is understood and that which is felt. (cited in Whitwell, 1993, p. 30)

At an even more basic level, music can influence the very structure and organization of brain function. Bharucha (cited in Whitwell, 1993), a researcher at Dartmouth, has found that exposure to music causes neural networks in the brain to organize themselves in certain ways. Music influences both conscious and unconscious mental processes (Spintge, 1991) and can affect different areas of the brain, "stimulating a variety of responses from the release of endorphins to the synchronization of the left and right hemispheres" (Goldman, 1988, p. 29). Music can also induce different states of consciousness (Bonny & Savary, 1973, 1990) and lead listeners to new levels of awareness. Music integrates diverse psychic processes and may serve to unite an individual's inner and outer worlds (Aigen, 1991). In the mid-1990s, well-publicized research on the "Mozart effect" by psychologist Frances Rauscher and neurologist Gordon Shaw from the University of California at Irvine demonstrated that listening to certain types of music (e.g., Mozart) or taking music lessons could enhance spatial reasoning abilities, suggesting a causal link between music and spatial intelligence (Knox, 1994; "Music Education Linked," 1994).

Different types of music also have varying effects on listeners' moods and emotional (affective) responses (Abeles, 1980; Abeles & Chung, 1996; Radocy & Boyle, 1988). For example, certain music may be relaxing to an individual, while other music may make a person feel happy or sad, and still other music make evoke feelings of anger or frustration. While some general effects of music with certain characteristics that will be true for many people may be predicted, it is important to remember that how any particular individual will react to a particular piece of music is determined to a large extent by that individual's previous experience with music.

> The influence of music on humans is not exclusively mechanical. It is psychic, emotional, sensorial, social, and spiritual as well. All of these aspects are interrelated and self-managed and model our appreciation and inner experience of music. If this influence were specifically mechanical, we would all experience identical sensations while listening to a specific musical work, which is definitely not the case. (Deschenes, 1990, p. 87)

Music can both excite or arouse emotions in a listener and represent or mimic various emotional responses (Dowling & Harwood, 1986). Associations that a listener makes with a certain piece of music, any imagery evoked by the music, reactions to lyrics and word meaning, reactions to various instruments or combinations of instruments, individual interests and values, attitudes, cultural or stylistic preferences, and environmental factors may all influence a person's affective responses to any given piece of music at any given time.

Music Facilitates Mind-Body Connections

In recent years, the western world has taken a renewed interest in holistic healing processes, looking at the ways in which the mind and body are connected and influence each other in achieving and maintaining health. Because it acts on *both* the mind and the body and affects *all* aspects of a person – physical, mental, emotional, and spiritual – *simultaneously*, music can help us cross the mind-body barrier and facilitate truly holistic methods of healing (Clynes, 1991; Goldman, 1988). (More detailed information on this subject is presented in Chapters Seventeen and Twenty-one of this text.) Much of the therapeutic power and potential of music may lie in

the fact that music directly influences the entire person , "entraining autonomic functions, stimulating the senses, probing the emotions, presenting ideas, and inspiring the spirit" (Bruscia, 1995c, p. 182).

Music Affects Interpersonal Interactions

Just as music affects various processes and domains within an individual, so music also affects interactions between and among individuals. As Gaston (1968a) noted, "music, by its very nature, draws people together for intimate, yet ordered, function" (p. 27). Moreover, once music has stimulated interaction among people, it also acts as a powerful reinforcer, encouraging people to maintain enjoyable and productive interactions (Maultsby, 1977).

Many social, civic, and ceremonial occasions are accompanied by music, for music often serves to put people at ease, encourages them to participate in the group activity, or helps them invest in common group goals or beliefs (Gaston, 1968a; Merriam, 1964; Radocy & Boyle, 1988; Sears, 1968). In addition, communal music-making can be an expression of social solidarity and a symbol of cultural identity (Dowling & Harwood, 1986).

> Since the dawn of time, one of the primary functions of music has been as communal activity. People have always gathered together to make music as a group experience, sharing the joyous spirit and life energy inherent in the creation of music. (Goldman, 1988, p. 31)

This unifying and communal aspect of music activity continues to be evident in societies today: People from all walks of life come together to listen to concerts, to listen or dance to live or recorded music at parties and other social gatherings, to sing or play instruments together in formally organized choirs and instrumental groups, to sing or play instruments informally with friends for fun, to sing patriotic or religious songs or participate in songs or dances or music that are in some way special to their group or heritage. Music still functions as a signal for people to gather together, as a rallying point to draw individuals together in support of a common cause, and as a means of unifying group members' individual efforts, as everyone moves to the same beat and their actions become synchronized and coordinated (Merriam, 1964; Radocy & Boyle, 1988).

Music affects the way people relate to one another by adding emotional impact, rhythmic energy and organization, and a subtle yet compelling motivation and encouragement to join in the group activity. Music and rhythm provide common bonds that organize and energize interactions, making it easier for people to work together and somehow encouraging them to interact more freely with one another (Gaston, 1968a). As they participate in music experiences together, individuals form a special type of society. Through music activity, they find new ways to explore and understand relationships and to express themselves to and with the group.

> Playing music in a group provides an opportunity to explore and more deeply understand relationships in the community, and the changing dynamics of groups as they grow and develop. It is also a chance for each individual to explore his uniqueness in relations to the community. At times, we can feel the oneness of all group members when we make music and dance together. This consonance can be supportive and healing. (Hesser, 1995, p. 49)

This ability of music to affect and facilitate group interactions has important implications for the use of music in therapy, for "the chief aim of therapy is to enable the individual to function at his best in society" (Gaston, 1968a, p. 27) and "if we always deal with the difficulties of life in isolation, and never relate ourselves to the whole, any solution or cure is likely to be merely an illusion, and short-lived" (Kenny, 1982, p. 36).

Music may also enhance both the quantity and emotional depth of verbal interactions and facilitate the expression of highly emotional material between individuals and within groups (Gaston, 1968a; Merriam, 1964; Prueter & Mezzano, 1973; Radocy & Boyle, 1988; Sears, 1968). In addition, music can serve as an acceptable outlet for expressing displeasure and frustration with various situations (e.g., protest songs), or it can serve to convey or express group feelings in a powerful way. Musical vehicles such as theme songs may also affect group relationships by helping to give a group a particular

identity, thereby increasing the cohesiveness of individual group members.

So, then, just as music affects the whole individual – physically, mentally, emotionally, and spiritually – it also affects all these aspects of group interactions. Music and rhythm can provide the physical structure to coordinate and sustain group activity. Music can motivate people to participate or join with a group, and music can provide a vehicle for expressing common ideas, feelings, and philosophies. Music can also set a tone or mood that will affect group moods or activity levels even as it affects the individuals within the group. Through its ability to structure and organize and its ability to convey and influence ideas and feelings, music can have powerful effects on interpersonal interactions. Since all persons, even those with severe disabilities, respond to music, these positive effects of music on interpersonal interactions can be important tools for establishing or reestablishing contact and positive interactions with individuals who are withdrawn from society and/or reality (Gaston, 1968a; Sears, 1968).

Music Is a Unique Form of Communication

The specially patterned sounds of music, which are derived from tender emotions and are given meaning by the culture in which they are found (Gaston, 1968a), serve as a very unique form of communication. Of course, the words of songs usually express some idea, feeling, story, or message. However, as Gaston (1968a) noted, music's ability to communicate *nonverbally* is far more significant: "It is the *wordless* meaning of music that provides its potency and value" (p. 23).

This nonverbal communicative aspect of music, which adds emotional depth to human expression and provides a vehicle to speak for the experiential, feeling side of us (Whitwell, 1993), can be of vital importance to therapy, for music may be able to communicate and help establish a relationship where words alone have failed. Even before we talk about it or in any way analyze it, "music speaks directly to us; music allows us to 'gaze into the inmost Essence of ourselves'" (Whitwell, 1993, p. 65). For people who are unable to use words or for those who hide behind words, music experiences may provide a way to reach issues and achieve insight and growth through nonverbal processes (e.g., by playing or improvising with simple rhythm instruments in a therapy group, or by using a recorded song to express feelings they are unable to express verbally). Since music speaks directly to the emotions, it can be very useful in breaking through intellectual defenses and facilitating the expression of emotionally charged or fearful issues. Music is something that is difficult to ignore, for it is a powerful form of multisensory stimulation that touches the depths of our being and experience. Therefore, music used in therapy may often bring out responses that are more honest and personally revealing than those elicited by purely verbal means:

> Music therapy shares with the romantic mythology its skepticism against the language and the intellectual control of reality. Musical improvisation is thought of as more honest than language. Music may express what is feared or hidden by language and intellect. (Ruud, 1995, p. 105)

Music, then, assists us in expressing those parts of ourselves and our experiences that cannot be touched or fully expressed by words alone.

Music also is a powerful communication tool because of its ability to convey symbolic meaning (Gfeller, 1992a; Kenny, 1982). Through the music they make and its symbolic representations, people may uniquely communicate some aspects of their experience they cannot put into words. For example, in relating the story of a patient's inability to explain verbally the feelings or meanings that his chant and drumbeat expressed, Kenny (1982) observed:

> He has already told me what it meant by singing and drumming. His music was a symbolic representation of some aspect of his experience – pure and simple. It was also self-contained and complete. It had already gone beyond words. It was an expression of clarity and communication. Everyone in the group had been moved. (p. 58)

Music may express both specific cultural values and universal, archetypal ideas and myths (Gaston, 1968a; Gfeller, 1992a; Kenny, 1982; Merriam, 1964; Radocy & Boyle, 1988). Through music and the ceremonies associated with it, societies pass on

various aspects of their culture (Gaston, 1968a; Hodges & Haack, 1996; Kenny, 1982; Merriam, 1964; Nettl, 1956). Music also connects individuals with basic human emotions and archetypal patterns and themes that have been present throughout history (Gaston, 1968a; Kenny, 1982; Whitwell, 1993). While allowing people to express their most individual and intimate feelings and longings, music at the same time connects these with the universal feelings and longings of human beings of other times and places.

Music may stimulate various types of imagery and fantasy and be useful in retrieving old memories or revealing new perceptions, helping people to communicate with events and ideas from times past or to communicate with previously untouched aspects of themselves (Bonny & Savary, 1973, 1990; Kenny, 1982). When utilizing these communicative properties of music, however, it is important to remember that musical meaning and expression are usually tied to the traditions and practices of the culture in which they are found (Gaston, 1968a; Gfeller, 1992a; Hodges & Haack, 1996; Merriam, 1964; Radocy & Boyle, 1988). Even as different cultures have different languages and speech patterns, so different cultures use different scale patterns and instruments in their music. In addition, "musical symbols differ from culture to culture" (Gfeller, 1992a, p. 50). Therefore, a person from one culture may find it extremely difficult to organize, interpret, understand, or communicate with the music of another culture. The degree to which a particular piece of music or type of musical expression communicates to or for a person is dependent somewhat on the degree to which that person understands or is familiar with that particular type or style of musical expression. This has important implications as one considers what music may be effective for therapy: "If patients are to be reached, the music employed must be that which they understand, at least to some extent" (Gaston, 1968a, p. 22).

Music Is Integrally Connected to the Emotions

Much of the communicative power of music that was discussed in the previous section is related to the fact that music is integrally connected to the emotions, both through cultural convention and practice (Merriam, 1964) and through common biological and neurological arousal and processing sites (e.g., limbic system, right brain hemisphere) (Hodges, 1980, 1996; Taylor, 1997; Thaut, 1989a; Whitwell, 1993). Music can both excite or arouse emotions in a listener and symbolically represent various emotional responses of the listener (Dowling & Harwood, 1986). As Langer (1966) observed, while people express ideas primarily through language, they express emotions primarily through music.

Throughout history, people often have demonstrated and experienced the connection between music and emotion, as they have used music to express strong feelings, such as joy or sorrow, patriotism or discontent, or as they have become calmed or agitated or otherwise moved by different types of music. In fact, the use of music for emotional expression heads Merriam's (1964) list of ten major functions of music that are common to most cultures. Many theories for this propensity of human beings to use music to express emotions have been proposed. Gfeller (1992a, pp. 46-49) provides an excellent summary of various referentialist and expressionalist viewpoints, while Whitwell (1993) presents an extensive overview of biological and neurological explanations. Whatever the explanation – whether emotional expression and perception in music are the result of external associations (referentialist view), are inherent in the structure of the music itself (expressionalist view), are the result of biological and neurological mechanisms, or are perhaps due to some combination of all of these – it can be seen that music does both influence a person's emotions and provide an important vehicle for human emotional expression and understanding.

Music has the ability not only to move or express the specific emotions of a particular individual but also to convey basic human feelings in a manner that is perceived similarly by most human beings (Clynes, 1977, 1982, 1991; Whitwell, 1993). This connection between music and the expression of the essence of universal emotions is basic to an understanding of how music can be used as a language of emotions among human beings in general, while still having its own unique meaning to a specific individual. Consider Whitwell's (1993) explanation of what happens when a generally "sad" piece of music, such as Tchaikovsky's Symphony No. 6, is performed:

What travels through space and communicates to the listener is not a *specific* form of sadness, but a quintessence of emotion, the essence of emotion in its purest and most concentrated form. . . . Each listener in the concert hall takes in this quintessence of sadness through his senses (in this case, his ears), sifts this form of the emotion through the experiential data-bank of his right hemisphere, where this emotion (and this music) takes on a personal definition when it interfaces with that listener's own personal understanding of that emotion. In this way we hear music both generally and personally. (p. 55).

Thus, music connects us with the basic emotions of all humankind, while at the same time giving us a unique way of accessing and expressing our own personal emotional experiences and identities.

The integral link between emotions and music offers many possibilities for the therapeutic use of music. For clients who are struggling to cope with overwhelming emotions or for those who have difficulty expressing emotions verbally, music may offer "a less threatening or alternative way to share emotions" (Gfeller, 1992a, p. 50) and may provide a way to help express those feelings which are too deep for words alone (Gaston, 1968a). Seeing and experiencing universal emotions through music may also help individuals feel less alone and more connected to the rest of society and humanity as they realize that others have shared the same fears and feelings (Kenny, 1982). In this way, sounds and music that complement or mirror a client's feelings can provide some degree of comfort and reassurance. Conversely, music experiences that portray feelings or attitudes foreign to the client may give the client a vehicle for experiencing new feelings or for experiencing feelings and attitudes in new or alternative ways. Because of its link to the emotions, music also can provide a stimulus that taps into those emotional and affective components of a person that may motivate, facilitate, support, and sustain positive growth and change:

The unique contribution of musical experience in the addition of affective/motivational qualities which provide positive affective tone to each behavior experience, and, thus, tune, attenuate, modulate, and positively bias a client's perceptual process towards therapeutic change. (Thaut, 1989a, p. 58)

The integral connection between music and the emotions, therefore, may be considered to be a primary factor underlying the usefulness of music as a therapeutic treatment modality.

Music Is an Aesthetic and Creative Experience

Music is an *aesthetic* experience, one that both evokes aesthetic responses and provides a vehicle for creative expression of beauty, meaning, and order (Gaston, 1968a; Radocy & Boyle, 1988). It is the aesthetic qualities of music that play a major role in transforming sound into music; these qualities also help establish our affinity for various sounds and are instrumental in determining the power and effects of music (Aigen, 1995a; Summer, 1995). When individuals become involved in aesthetic experiences, every aspect of their being – physical, mental, and emotional processes – are stimulated and integrated (Nagler, 1995). Music is an aesthetic experience that can reach an individuals' "inner core of humanness" (Nagler, 1995, p. 79), regardless of their age, life experience, or functioning level (Boxill, 1985; Nordoff & Robbins, 1977), and give insight into and influence their lifeworld.

Many music experiences also involve *creative* processes. People can create music as they sing, play instruments, write songs, orchestrate, or improvise. In addition, people create their relationship to music as they find personal meaning in listening, performance, or creative experience. Through these creative processes and experiences, music allows people to participate with their whole being – intellect, imagination, and emotions – in creating order out of disorder and form out of chaos as they "struggle to bring into existence new kinds of being that give harmony and integration" (May, 1975, p. 169).

The need for aesthetic experiences and expression are fundamental to human existence; human beings in all cultures search for and try to express beauty and meaning in life (Gaston, 1968a; Gfeller, 1992a; Kenny, 1982; Merriam, 1964; Radocy & Boyle, 1988;

Spencer, 1978). Creativity, a process by which something new is brought into being and given form and expression, is also a basic human drive or instinct (Jung, 1956; May, 1975). As all cultures have recognized, music offers one vehicle through which desires for beauty, order, and meaning can be satisfied and through which creative instincts can be channeled towards constructive ends (Gaston, 1968a; Hodges & Haack, 1996; Merriam, 1964; Radocy & Boyle, 1988). Researchers have found that most people, regardless of their degree of musical sophistication or training, respond aesthetically to music in fairly similar ways (Abeles, 1980; Abeles & Chung, 1996; Madsen et al., 1993; Radocy & Boyle, 1988). As an aesthetic and creative art form, music contributes to the quality of life for *all* individuals in a society, whatever their age or degree of health, and helps them to experience, explore, express, and celebrate the nobler aspects of life (Boxill, 1985; Gaston, 1968a; Gfeller, 1992a; Nordoff & Robbins, 1977).

Aesthetic and creative experiences also give individuals a better capacity to cope with and find meaning in life, thus improving their total health and life satisfaction (Aigen, 1995a; Edelman, 1978; *The Healing Role of the Arts*, 1978; May, 1975; Spencer, 1978).

> The processes that represent the furtherance and development of life, on the biological, social, and emotional level, necessarily contain aesthetic features. The aesthetic is essential to our healthful embrace of life. (Aigen, 1995a, p. 242)

Aesthetic and creative experiences in music, then, have the potential to be both curative and preventative, both enjoyable and rehabilitative, both artistic and therapeutic (Edelman, 1978; Kenny, 1982; Spencer, 1978). Through aesthetic and creative experiences, emotional energy is not only released but also be channeled productively and used for growth, nondestructive self-expression, and increased self-awareness (Aigen, 1995a; Kenny, 1982). Creative and aesthetic involvement, realized through some form of experience with music or the other arts, can give joy, relieve feelings of disappointment and failure, offer new ideas and new ways of experiencing, provide a safe structure within which to explore new possibilities, give order and meaning to life, provide forms to express intimate feelings, and help people find ways to adapt to their environment and relate constructively to their internal and external worlds (Edelman, 1978; *The Healing Role of the Arts*, 1978; Kenny, 1982; Salas, 1990; Spencer, 1978).

The aesthetic qualities and creative processes involved in a music experience add much to music's usefulness and uniqueness as a therapeutic tool (Aigen, 1995a; Gaston, 1968a; Kenny, 1992; Nagler, 1995; Summer, 1995). Because of human beings' basic need for aesthetic experience, their innate capacity to respond aesthetically, and their drive to be creative, even people who are not musically trained or sophisticated can experience therapeutic benefits from music that provides quality aesthetic experiences. Aesthetically pleasing and stimulating music experiences and materials are vital aspects of music therapy processes, for the aesthetic helps provide integration and meaning and connections to the basic processes of life and nature, and, in some cases, may even serve as a direct vehicle for healing (Aigen, 1995a; *The Healing Role of the Arts*, 1978; Nordoff & Robbins, 1971a, 1971b, 1977; Salas, 1990). Moreover, many of the components of aesthetic experience, such as high levels of integration and meaning, enhanced personality development, increased cognitive functioning, and improved social interaction, are strongly related to many clinical goals (Aigen, 1995a).

Kenny (1982) observed that "even though music may not be the natural vehicle for everyone's creativity, it can be an experimental ground in which to try out creative processes and apply them through a powerful medium" (pp. 79-80). Involvement in creative music experiences helps provide individuals with links to order and purpose, to form and organization. These experiences can be vital to clients who are striving to make sense of a chaotic and disordered life, who are trying to find meaning for their lives, or who are searching for better ways of functioning in and relating to the world (May, 1975). Creative experiences in the arts may also open the door to other people and other treatments by giving the clients successful, positive, hope-filled experiences (*The Healing Role of the Arts*, 1978). In addition, successful participation in meaningful creative and aesthetic experiences also promotes increased

feelings of self-worth and facilitates self-actualization (Gaston, 1968a; Maslow, 1968; May, 1975; Nordoff & Robbins, 1977). The aesthetic and creative aspects of music, therefore, have great potential for use as tools that facilitate growth and healing, enhance integration and insight, bring meaning and order, increase self-esteem, and generally contribute to a better quality of life for many clients in music therapy.

Music Provides a Source of Enjoyment and Gratification

Music is a fun, normal experience, something that is part of everyday life. Throughout history, societies of all types have used music for enjoyment and entertainment (Blacking, 1973; Hodges & Haack, 1996; Merriam, 1964; Radocy & Boyle, 1988). These aspects of music cannot be discounted in considering its potential for therapeutic effectiveness, for, as we have seen above, the positive affective qualities that music adds to an experience may be very important factors in motivating clients to engage in processes that will lead them to therapeutic change (*The Healing Role of the Arts*, 1978; Thaut, 1989a). In speaking of the unique factors that music therapy brings to treatment, Lathom (1981b) noted:

> There is no pain with music, as there may be with other aspects of rehabilitation, and the child can feel successful and capable if appropriate activities are selected. Music activities are fun and the person associated with them is greeted with pleasure. (p. 22)

Thus, the sense of fun and enjoyment that are inherent in many music experiences can be instrumental in helping clients begin to relate to others in positive ways. In addition, as clients participate successfully in fun, non-threatening music experiences, they begin to gain a sense of gratification and pride in their accomplishments, which increases their feelings of self-worth and competence (Gaston, 1968a; Lathom, 1981b; Sears, 1968).

Since music is something that is highly valued by and pervasive in society in general, it can also be something that will help "normalize" the environment of hospital, special education, or other treatment settings. Through music, people may be able to relate to some aspects of their lives outside the treatment setting or find new ways of relating to others who do not share their disabilities. Music may also be useful in providing a necessary diversion from the more stressful or painful aspects of treatment or therapy. As Gfeller (1992a) noted, although the use of music for entertainment, diversional, or recreational purposes may somehow seem less noble or important, these types of music experiences, too, have their place, both in society and in various treatment settings, and "can even contribute to emotional and physical well-being" (p. 54). Thus, the fact that music is a source of entertainment and pleasure highly valued by society in general also contributes to its potential usefulness as a treatment modality. Since music experiences are seen as something "fun," they can often motivate reluctant clients to participate in treatment, help establish contact and relationships where other methods have failed, and help make clients more receptive to other forms of treatment.

HOW MUSIC IS USED IN THERAPY

According to Gaston (1968b), the father of modern music therapy, three basic principles "form much of the foundation of music therapy . . . [and] are a primary source of direction in music therapy" (p. v). These are:

1. The use of music and music experiences to establish or reestablish interpersonal relationships

2. The use of music and music experiences to bring about self-esteem through self-actualization

3. The use of the unique potential of rhythm to energize and bring order.

Although he used a different sequence, Sears's (1968) explanation of music therapy processes included that same triad of social relations, self relations, and general order or structure:

> The three classifications that underlie the constructs and processes of music therapy are (1) experience with structure, (2) experience in self-organization, and (3) experience in relating to others. (p. 31).

The ideas embodied in Gaston's (1968b) guiding principles for the use of music in therapy and Sears's (1968) classifications of processes in music therapy have much to say about the general ways music is used to accomplish therapeutic purposes. In fact, many of the current clinical practices in music therapy today still stem from these basic concepts (Feder & Feder, 1981; Gfeller, 1987a). This will become increasingly evident in the discussions of music therapy practices with specific client populations found in later chapters.

Music Experiences Attract Attention and Provide Order and Structure

In some models of healing and human development, persons are seen as moving on a continuum from chaos and disorder to an eventual state of transcendent wholeness and health with one's self and with the whole universe (Crowe, 1991). Some clients seen by music therapists have various severe physical, mental, or emotional impairments that cause them to function at the low end of this continuum. These clients may have difficulty perceiving or making sense of their internal and external worlds and may be unable to control and organize their behavior or respond to stimuli in appropriate or meaningful ways. At times they may seem totally unaware of or oblivious to their surroundings. These clients often benefit greatly from music therapy interventions that "emphasize awareness of and response to the order and structure of music" (Crowe, 1991, p. 114). Music can help attract and sustain attention, elicit and organize response, and provide an example of ways to make beauty and order out of chaos. The music therapist carefully selects, structures, and manipulates various musical elements and personal and environmental factors in ways that will assist the client in moving closer to a state of health (Bruscia, 1989a; Gfeller, 1987a). Particular useful at this level are those qualities of music which evoke basic sensory, rhythmic, and affective responses.

Music is a powerful form of sensory stimulation, a multisensory experience. Music consists of sounds which can be heard (auditory stimulation) and vibrations which can be felt (tactile stimulation). Live performances of music may also add visual stimulation, while moving to music can add kinesthetic and proprioceptive stimulation to the experience. Therefore, music an often attract a person's attention by providing stimulation that is almost impossible to ignore.

In addition, music experiences also offer the individual a chance to respond through auditory, visual, tactile, and kinesthetic channels: by looking to the music source, by turning toward or reaching out to the music source, by moving to the music, by vocalizing with the music, by manipulating musical instruments to make sounds, etc. As a stimulus, music can provide multisensory input; as a response, music offers opportunities for multisensory output. A client who has difficulty perceiving, organizing, or responding through one sensory mode may be able to be stimulated by or respond through another sensory mode.

"Music is structured reality" (Gaston, 1968a, p. 24), a real event that takes place in time and demands a moment-by-moment commitment from the individual (Sears, 1968). There are certain qualities inherent in music itself that demand, permit, evoke, and provoke specific physical, psychological, and affective behaviors (Abeles, 1980; Abeles & Chung, 1996; Bartlett, 1996; Hodges, 1980, 1996; Hodges & Haack, 1996; Radocy & Boyle, 1988; Sears, 1968). The ability of music to touch an individual on all of these levels increases the likelihood that music will be able to break into the individual's world or awareness in at least one of these areas. Furthermore, after the rhythms, sounds, and melodies attract an individual's attention, the time-ordered structure and experience of music help hold that attention, providing an environment or structure in which growth and learning can occur. The order and structure of music, especially as contained in its rhythm and form, may also assist an individual in organizing his or her perceptions and responses.

For the child [or adult] whose world is often a confusing chaos, the order of music is a welcome structured experience in which the child [or adult] may feel free from confusion and safe in the ability to predict the activity and the person associated with the music. (Lathom, 1981b, p. 23)

Music Experiences Provide Self-Knowledge, Self-Expression, and Self-Gratification

Before people can relate successfully and appropriately to those around them, they must be comfortable with themselves as individuals. Music can provide a means of self-expression and opportunities for enhancement of feelings of self-worth (Sears, 1968). As an avenue of both verbal and nonverbal communication, music can function as a vehicle for expression of moods, attitudes, and feelings. Music activities are also very adaptable and can allow for success at many different levels of achievement. Achieving success and competency in music activities can enhance an individual's sense of self-esteem (Gaston, 1968a; Lathom, 1981b; Sears, 1968), especially since music is something that is usually valued by society. Music experiences that involve song lyric analysis, song writing, improvisation, or guided imagery can also help individuals explore alternative viewpoints or possibilities for action in relatively safe and non-threatening ways. In addition, music experiences can assist individuals in achieving new perspectives on the ways they view themselves and can help them see new possibilities for response, growth and development (Bonny & Savary, 1990; Crowe, 1991).

Music Experiences Promote Positive Relationships with Others

For individuals to function in society, they must be able to relate successfully and appropriately to those around them. Music activities often occur as group activities. "Music, by its very nature, draws people together for intimate, yet ordered, function" (Gaston, 1968a, p. 27). Music activities involving two or more people provide individuals with a non-threatening atmosphere in which to learn to relate to others. Because it is a positive, enjoyable activity and because of its inherent persuasive and communicative powers, music may often provide the motivation needed for individuals to join in the group and interact with others (Gaston, 1968a; Lathom, 1981b; Sears, 1968). As they participate in group vocal, instrumental, movement-to-music, improvisation, composition, and music-based discussion experiences, group members can see what types of actions lead to success or failure and can learn to relate to others in productive ways while participating in fun and enjoyable activities. Music experiences may also make destructive or ineffective patterns of relating to others apparent in ways that are much more potent than verbal, intellectual analysis.

The sounds produced mirror the group dynamics and issues and concerns of the individuals involved. The musical event makes

these processes overt and obvious so that they can be explored and discussed. (Crowe, 1991, p. 115)

Group music experiences, then, can help individuals see the necessity for change in the ways they relate to others while simultaneously providing a vehicle in which to explore and practice more productive and effective methods of interaction. Music can both support clients while they question their current behavior patterns and belief systems and can assist them in adopting and owning more effective and productive ones. Thus, through participation in carefully structured therapeutic group music activities, individuals can gain insights and skills that will help them relate more successfully, appropriately, and responsibly toward others.

SUMMARY

Contrary to ancient myths, music has no magical qualities that give it a special healing power. However, there are certain aspects of the physical components of music and of the human uses of and reactions to music that make music particularly useful as a therapeutic treatment modality:

1. Music is a universal human behavior; it is found in all cultures, both primitive and civilized. Some philosophers, theorists, and researchers believe this is the case because human beings have a biological predisposition toward and need for music.

2. Music is something that is based in the physical world; it is composed of real physical structures that can be perceived by a person's senses. In addition, the structure of music is linked to time order: Music always unfolds and exists only through experiencing it in time.

3. Music is a phenomenon that affects the whole person; it affects physical, cognitive, and emotional responses as well as mind-body connections and interactions.

4. Music affects interactions between and among individuals. It can motivate, structure, and

organize activity and interactions; convey or influence ideas; and influence group moods and activity levels.

5. Music is a unique form of both verbal and nonverbal communication. It speaks directly to and for the emotions, helping individuals express those parts of themselves and their experiences that cannot be fully expressed by words alone. Music also conveys symbolic meanings and communicates universal, archetypal ideas and myths. It may stimulate imagery and fantasy that helps individuals communicate with events or ideas from their past or with previously untouched aspects of themselves.

6. Music is integrally connected to the emotions, both through cultural convention and practice and through common biological and neurological arousal and processing sites (e.g., limbic system, right brain hemisphere). Music connects individuals with the basic emotions of all humankind, while at the same time giving them a unique way of accessing and expressing their own personal emotional experiences and identities. Because of its link to the emotions, music also can provide a stimulus that taps into those emotional

and affective components of a person that may motivate, facilitate, support, and sustain positive growth and change.

7. Music is an aesthetic and creative experience. As such, it can stimulate and integrate all aspects of a person's being and provide a means through which creative instincts can be channeled toward constructive ends. Aesthetic and creative experiences also give individuals a better capacity to cope with and find meaning in life, thus improving their total health and life satisfaction.

8. Music provides a source of enjoyment and gratification. Since music is something that is generally considered to be "fun" and is valued by society, it can help motivate participation, enhance self-esteem, promote positive interactions, and normalize treatment environments.

All these factors impact music's potential for use as a therapeutic tool.

Gaston's (1968b) principles and Sears's (1968) classifications of music therapy processes still provide much of the foundation for the current clinical practices in music therapy. According to these principles and classifications, music is used in therapy in three main ways: (1) to attract attention and provide order and structure; (2) to provide an impetus or vehicle for self-knowledge, self-expression, and self-gratification; and (3) to promote positive relationships with others by providing insights, skills, and experiences that will help individuals relate more successfully, appropriately, and responsibly toward those around them.

QUESTIONS FOR THOUGHT AND DISCUSSION

1. What are some aspects of music that make it useful as a treatment modality? How or why do these impact its therapeutic effectiveness?

2. Describe three general ways music may be used in therapy. How do Gaston's guiding principles and Sears's classifications of processes relate to these?

3. How do music experiences attract attention and provide order and structure? What types of clients might benefit from this type of music therapy experience?

4. How do music experiences help individuals increase self-knowledge, self-expression, or self-gratification? What types of clients might benefit from this type of music therapy experience?

5. How do music experiences help individuals increase their skills and abilities to relate more successfully, appropriately, and responsibly toward those around them? What types of clients might benefit from this type of music therapy experience?

FURTHER READING

Blacking, J. (1973). *How musical is man?* Seattle: University of Washington Press.

Campbell, D. (Ed.) (1991). *Music: Physician for times to come.* Wheaton, IL: Quest Books.

Dowling, W. J., & Harwood, D. L. (1986). *Music cognition.* Orlando, FL: Academic Press.

Gaston, E. T. (1968). Foreword. In E. T. Gaston (Ed.), *Music in therapy* (pp. v-vii). New York: Macmillan.

Gaston, E. T. (1968). Man and music. In E. T. Gaston (Ed), *Music in therapy* (pp. 7-29). New York: Macmillan.

Gfeller, K. (1987). Music therapy theory and practice as reflected in research literature. *Journal of Music Therapy, 25*(1), 28-43.

Gfeller, K. (1992). Music: A human phenomenon. In W. B. Davis, K. E. Gfeller, & M. H. Thaut, *An introduction to music therapy: Theory and practice* (pp. 38-64). Dubuque, IA: Wm. C. Brown.

The Healing Role of the Arts (Working papers – The Rockefeller Foundation). (1978). New York: The Rockefeller Foundation.

Hodges, D. A. (Ed.) (1996). *Handbook of music psychology* (2nd ed.). San Antonio, TX: Institute for Music

Research Press, The University of Texas at San Antonio.

Kenny, C. B. (Ed.) (1995). *Listening, playing, creating: Essays on the power of sound.* Albany, NY: State University of New York Press.

Lathom, W. (1981). Aspects of music therapy that are unique on the treatment and education team.

In W. Lathom, *The role of them music therapist in the education of severely and profoundly handicapped children and youth* (pp. 21-24). Lawrence, KS: National Association for Music Therapy.

Nagler, J. C. (1995). Toward the aesthetic lifeworld. *Music Therapy, 13*(1), 75-91.

Radocy, R. E., & Boyle, J. D. (1988). *Psychological foundations of musical behavior* (2nd ed.). Springfield, IL: Charles C Thomas.

Sears, W. W. (1958). Processes in music therapy. In E. T. Gaston (Ed.), *Music in therapy* (pp. 30-44). New York: Macmillan.

Thaut, M. H. (1989). Music therapy, affect modulation, and therapeutic change: Toward an integrative model. *Music Therapy Perspectives, 7,* 55-62.

Chapter Six

GENERAL GUIDELINES FOR THE THERAPEUTIC USE OF MUSIC, PART II: PRACTICAL PLANNING

CHAPTER FIVE discussed some aspects of music that make it useful as a therapeutic treatment modality and described three general ways music is used in therapy. Chapter Six now focuses on the actual process a music therapist goes through in determining what a client needs and in planning, implementing, and evaluating music therapy intervention strategies. In addition, examples of various types of music experiences that may be useful in helping clients gain skills in several general areas are presented. Taken together, Chapters Five and Six provide fundamental background knowledge for the more specific information on music therapy practices with various client populations that will be presented in the next several chapters.

BASIC STAGES IN THE DELIVERY OF MUSIC THERAPY SERVICES

As Chapter One explained, music therapy is not a haphazard process where some kind of music is played in the hope that it will help people feel better. Music therapy is a planned, goal-directed process of interaction and intervention, based on assessment and evaluation of individual clients' specific needs, strengths, and weaknesses, in which music or music-based experiences are specifically prescribed to be used by specially trained personnel (i.e., music therapists or those they train and supervise) to influence positive changes in an individual's condition, skills, thoughts, feelings, or behaviors. Music therapists, therefore, must engage in specific procedures that will help them (1) determine the client's strengths, weaknesses, and area(s) of needs, (2) decide what types of music experiences will be most beneficial to the client, and (3) find ways of evaluating whether or not the client is making progress as a result of the music therapy treatment.

The music therapy treatment process begins when a music therapist accepts a client for music therapy services based on some kind of referral (AMTA, 1998; Davis, 1992c; Maranto, 1993b). Referrals may come from many sources, including members of the interdisciplinary treatment team, other professionals, other music therapists, the client's family members, parents, guardians, or advocates, or requests for treatment may be initiated by the potential clients themselves. Once the music therapist decides to accept a client for treatment, the music therapist then must plan, implement, and evaluate a music therapy treatment program for that client. This process usually includes several general stages (AMTA, 1998; Davis, 1992c; Hanser, 1987; Maranto, 1993b): (1) assessing the client to determine strengths, weaknesses, problems, and areas of need, (2) setting goals and objectives, (3) planning music-based intervention strategies to help the client reach these goals and objectives, (4) implementing treatment procedures,

(5) documenting responses, and (6) evaluating the results. All of these steps are integral to helping a music therapist carry out successful music therapy treatment interventions.

Assessment

Before music therapists can plan appropriate music therapy intervention strategies to help a client, they must know in what area(s) that client needs help. Therefore, the first step in planning effective music therapy intervention strategies involves the process of determining the client's individual strengths and weaknesses, including the client's particular problems or area(s) of need. This process is generally known as assessment. It is completed prior to treatment and gives a broad overview and analysis of the client's level of functioning in many areas. This information helps provide a direction for treatment and recommended services or treatment modalities (AMTA, 1998; Davis, 1992c; Hanser, 1987; Lathom, 1981b; Maranto, 1993b).

During the assessment process, the music therapist seeks to gather as much background information about the client as possible. This knowledge about the client's strengths, weaknesses, skills, and abilities can be obtained in a number of ways: (1) by reviewing the client's developmental, personal, social, and medical history; (2) by interviewing the client or the client's family members, caregivers, or guardians; (3) by observing the client in various situations; (4) by discussing the client's needs with other members of the treatment team; and (5) by engaging or observing the client participating in music experiences that give some indication of the client's responses to and preferences for various types of music experiences and music materials as well as the client's level of motor, social, auditory, communication, and musical skills (AMTA, 1998; Bruscia, 1991a; Davis, 1992c; Hanser, 1987; Lathom, 1981b; Maranto, 1993b). The music therapist needs background information in *both* musical and nonmusical areas to design a music therapy treatment program that will be meaningful to the client, appropriate to the client's chronological age, functioning level, and cultural background, and relevant to the client's needs.

The tools and activities used for assessment will vary with the orientation and training of the person doing the assessment, the particular disability, needs, or functioning level of the client being assessed, and the type of information being sought. Music therapists often gain much useful nonmusical information about a client from the assessments given by other professionals. In addition, however, music therapists will want to assess a client's specific responses, interactions, skills, and preferences with regard to music and the many different types of modalities, media, activities, instruments, idioms, styles, moods, and qualities available in music experiences. Clients may respond differently in music settings than they do in other treatment settings, and different skills, responses, and aspects of their personality may become apparent through their interaction with music materials (Boxill, 1985; Bruscia, 1987, 1991a; Davis, 1992c; Hanser, 1987; Isenberg-Grzeda, 1988). Since music reaches the brain in different ways than many other assessment tools, may bypass intellectual filters, and has many inherent motivating and gratifying aspects, music may also be useful in assessing clients who are considered to be "untestable" with other assessment tools or methods (Isenberg-Grzeda, 1988). However, it is important that the music therapist assess and be aware of the client's level of musical development, especially when working with children, for different phases of musical development have specific associated auditory, vocal/tonal, and rhythmic behaviors, and what is appropriate for one stage of development may not necessarily be appropriate for another (Briggs, 1991).

Often, music therapists develop clinical assessment tools specifically for their population or setting to help them gain the type of information they need in an efficient manner. Several sources, including Boxill (1985), Davis (1992c), Hanser (1987), and Isenberg-Grzeda (1988), as well as general references on assessment development or samples of various assessments, may be helpful to the reader desiring more information in this area. As will be seen in the later chapters of this book, some music therapy assessment tools have been developed for various client populations and for various music therapy techniques, but reliability and validity have not been established for most of these (Davis, 1992c; Maranto 1993b).

Setting Goals and Objectives

After assessing the client to obtain a clear picture of the client's strengths, needs, preferences, and overall level of functioning, the music therapist has the necessary information to set appropriate and realistic therapeutic goals and objectives for that client. Therapeutic goals and objectives state what the client is to accomplish or what changes in behavior the client will show if the therapeutic intervention strategies are successful. Goals and objectives give direction, purpose, and focus to music therapy treatment procedures. The specific expectations set forth in the goals and objectives also help the music therapist know whether or not the client is receiving any benefit from music therapy treatment.

Usually, goals are broad statements of desired outcomes in a certain area, while objectives are more specific and involve operationally defined steps and definite time frames for achievement (AMTA, 1998; Davis, 1992c; Hanser, 1987). Consider the analogy of standing on a river bank and trying to reach the other side. The river bank on which you are currently standing represents the current level of functioning of the client, as determined from the assessment. The opposite river bank represents the goal, the final state of improved functioning you hope the client will reach. The objectives, then, might be thought of as the stepping stones that will help the client reach the goals – the specific behaviors or skills the client will need to develop in order to achieve the goal.

Goals usually indicate the desire for improvement or maintenance of skills in a broad division of a general skill area in which the client has a problem or weakness. Goals sometimes are expressed as infinitive phrases rather than as complete statements:

"To increase positive interactions with other group members."
"To improve receptive language skills."
"To increase reality orientation."
"To maintain range of motion in upper extremities."
"To increase ability to express feelings accurately and appropriately."
"To increase functional motor skills."

After defining this broad treatment focus, the music therapist breaks it down into a series of short-term objectives, each of which relate to the goal and define a specific step, skill, or behavior needed to achieve the goal. By clearly defining expectations in terms of observable outcomes, objectives help the therapist measure and evaluate the changes that take place (or fail to take place) throughout the course of therapy. Each objective delineates (1) a specific *behavior* the client must show (what the client will do to demonstrate competency in the defined area; e.g., "look to speaker"; "wait to be called upon before speaking"; "address group members by name"; "grasp and hold maraca"; "sing at same tempo and volume as rest of group"), (2) the *criterion* for successful performance (the level of proficiency the client must demonstrate to demonstrate mastery, usually expressed quantitatively as number of times, length of time, or percent; e.g., "4 out of 5 times"; "each time"; "for two minutes"; "within 3 seconds"; "at least three times each session"; "for four consecutive sessions"), (3) any important *conditions* or *qualifiers* for the performance of the task (prompts or restrictions which will be part of the setting or procedure; e.g., "with one physical prompt"; "independently"; "given a list of five song titles"; "without gestural cues"); and (4) a *time frame* or termination date (the targeted date for achievement of the objective; e.g., "within six months"; "during the next two weeks"; "by the end of ten sessions"). [Note: Often, more cues or prompts are given in the initial stages of treatment, while a client's skills are just emerging. The degree of independence required for performance increases throughout the course of therapy as the client gains skills; this is reflected in the conditions or qualifiers section of the objective.] Including all these elements (behavior, criterion, qualifiers or conditions, and time frame) in the objective at times may make the process of constructing objectives a difficult and time-consuming one (Davis, 1992c), but a well-written, operationally defined objective is essential to providing a direction for therapeutic treatment and a means of measuring and evaluating client progress.

Planning Music-Based Intervention Strategies

Music is the main tool of the music therapist, the thing that differentiates music therapy from other therapies. Therefore, in planning treatment interventions, the music therapist must develop specific procedures that use music and music materials to help the client reach the therapeutic goals and objectives. In order to do this, the music therapist must consider several factors, including (a) how music will function to help the client meet the goals and objectives; (b) what types of music experiences and musical materials will be used; (c) if the intervention procedures will incorporate any specific therapeutic or educational strategies; and (d) any environmental or structural factors that may affect the activity or the client's response. Above all, however, the music therapist must always keep in mind how these factors relate both to the individual client's needs, strengths, preferences, age, cultural background, skills, and capabilities and to the objective to be accomplished. In planning music-based intervention strategies, one must never forget the purpose for which they are being designed (goal/objective) or the unique individual qualities of the client with whom they will be used. "The initial selection of music for therapy must reflect the clients' interests, preferences, and background as well as the nonmusical therapeutic objectives" (Prickett, 1989, p. 98).

Determining the Function of Music

Music experiences selected for use in music therapy treatment programs are designed so that something in their content or process stimulates or provides a means of reward for the client to progress toward the established therapeutic goal (Prickett, 1989). Duerksen (1978) has identified five general ways in which music activities can be used to help clients gain the nonmusical skills they need to reach therapeutic goals:

1. Music as a carrier of information.

2. Music as a reinforcer.

3. Music as a background for learning.

4. Music as a physical structure for the learning activity.

5. Music as a reflection of skills or processes to be

learned. (cited in Lathom, 1981a, p. 160)

All the various learning and expressive experiences of music – singing, playing musical instruments, creating or composing music, moving to music, discussing music – can be used therapeutically in one or more of these ways. For example, special songs may be written to include information (e.g., facts, sequences of events in a task) that relate to skills a client is trying to master (Kramer, 1978; Wolfe & Hom, 1993; Wolfe & Stambaugh, 1993). Songs and music games can also help teach various academic and social skills. In addition, song lyrics, instrumental improvisations, and movement-to-music experiences can provide safe, nonthreatening frameworks in which to express and discuss emotionally laden material.

Since music is something that is pleasurable to most people, various music activities and experiences, such as listening to preferred music, singing, dancing, or playing musical instruments, can also serve as powerful reinforcers of skills and behaviors (Bellamy & Sontag, 1973; Dorow, 1976; Jorgenson, 1974; Metzler, 1974; Michel, 1971; Reid et al., 1975; Saperston et al., 1980; Saperston, 1989; Underhill & Harris, 1974; Wilson, 1976; Wolfe, 1980). Maultsby (1977) suggested that music is such a powerful reinforcer of new learning because of its connection with the satisfaction of basic survival needs, as parents throughout the world often sing as they give their babies food, water, and shelter. According to Lathom (1981b), music is especially effective as a reinforcer "because it can be started immediately after the desired response and it does not produce satiation, as does food or other reinforcers" (p. 21).

Music can also be used therapeutically as a background for learning. By masking unwanted sounds, helping break monotony, or helping to establish a specific mood, carefully selected background music can facilitate learning, improve task performance, increase verbal interaction, enhance performance on some spatial and numerical processing tasks, and provide a pleasant environment for other activities (Miller & Schyb, 1989; Radocy & Boyle, 1988; Wolfe & Stambaugh, 1993). In addition, music can structure the time frame of an activity, as when a specific motor action is "choreographed" to particular music. The rhythmic structure provided by music can facilitate improvement in physical rhythmic activities, such as respiration, gait training, range of motion, and relaxation (Miller, 1979). Finally, the way in which the client interacts with the music materials, the music therapist, and other individuals in the music therapy session often serves as a reflection of how well the client is progressing toward the therapeutic goal or of at what level the client is functioning. For example, Rider (1978, 1981) has shown that musical perception tasks may be used to assess levels of cognitive functioning.

Selecting Musical Materials and Types of Music Experiences

In the process of designing music therapy intervention strategies and selecting appropriate types of music and music experiences to accomplish certain goals and objectives, music therapists make use of their knowledge of the general functions and effects of various types of music and music experiences. This general knowledge, however, always must be tempered by the specific knowledge of the individual client's actual reactions to and preferences for various musical stimuli, which the music therapist gained in the client's assessment. Just as physicians take into account individual variables and reactions and do not prescribe uniform courses of treatment or dosages of medication for all patients with the same condition, music therapists take into account individual variables when determining what music or types of music experiences will be used for music therapy treatment interventions with a particular client (Summer, 1995). While generalizations and precategorized music or music activities certainly can serve as starting points in looking for music experiences that are suitable to reach certain objectives or achieve certain effects, appropriateness for an individual client must still be verified by checking that individual's responses or reactions (Hadsell, 1989). On the other hand, while the client's preferences and requests do greatly influence the selection and design of musical materials used in music therapy interventions, "it is also important to realize that the client's preferences may be a manifestation of his/her problem, and therefore in need of modification or expansion" (Bruscia, 1991a, p. 10).

As music therapists determine which music experiences to use with individual clients to achieve specific purposes, they have many aspects to consider. For example, there are many modes of music activity or ways of interacting with music, including listening to music, moving to music, singing/chanting/humming, playing musical instruments, creating music (improvising or composing), discussing music, and notating music (Boxill, 1985; Bruscia, 1987; Standley, 1991a). These activities may be used alone on in combination with one another (e.g., sing and move, sing and play instruments, listen and notate, etc.), and experiences may include both passive and active participation. There are also many musical media that can be used by the therapist and/or clients, including voice, guitar, piano or keyboard, autoharp, rhythm instruments, band or orchestral instruments, electronic instruments, records, audio or video tapes, compact discs, and computer programs. These various media, too, may be used alone on in combination with others. In addition, the therapist might present music in one mode or medium (e.g., sing), while the client may respond in another mode or with another medium (e.g., by moving or playing instruments). Some music therapy intervention strategies might also have therapist and client interacting or performing together using various modes of musical activity or types of musical media.

At a more basic level, the music therapist must consider the effect of various elements of music (e.g., rhythm, tempo, pitch, melody, harmony, texture, timbre, dynamics, song text [if applicable]) and different ways of manipulating them (amount of novelty, redundancy, complexity, etc.). Obviously, myriad possible combinations exist, making a wide range of idioms, styles, and moods of music available for use in therapy. Again, the therapist's knowledge of the general effects of music, coupled with his or her knowledge and observation of the individual client's specific preferences, interests, needs, and capabilities, will be primary factors in selecting the specific type, style, mood, or aspect of music used for therapeutic intervention. In addition, if the music is to be paired with a learning task, the music therapist will want to carefully monitor the complexity of the rhythms, melody, lyrics, and/or accompaniment. Generally, the more repetitive the words, rhythms, notes, and chords, the simpler the learning task will be (Standley, 1991a). Finally, the music therapist should always monitor the age appropriateness of musical selections, materials, and activities being considered for use with clients. Activities, experiences, and materials should be appropriate to the chronological age of the individual client being served.

Music therapists often must be very creative to fit the demands and focus of music activities to a client's individual needs, abilities, and interests. Not every client is interested in the same type of music, the same instrument, or the same song, nor does every client possess the same degree of motor coordination, communication and social skills, or intellectual ability. Therefore, in planning music therapy intervention strategies, music therapists must consider each client individually and strive to design activities that will engage the client's interest and utilize the client's strengths as well as ameliorate the client's weaknesses. For example, a client who does not have the psychomotor coordination needed to finger chords on a guitar might still be able to play simple guitar accompaniments if the open strings of the guitar were tuned to a major chord (Cassity, 1977). According to Tyson (1959), the ability to adapt musical concepts and materials to each client's level of understanding and capacity to respond is a most important factor in developing effective therapeutic relationship with clients. And, as Bruscia (1991) observed, "the subtle and wonderful thing about music therapy is that, in actuality, every musical experience can be adapted to meet a broad spectrum of client needs" (p. 9).

Incorporating Specific Therapeutic or Educational Strategies

In order to develop a coordinated treatment approach with other members of the professional team, music therapists often incorporate specific therapeutic, educational, or psychological theories or approaches into their music therapy intervention strategies. For example, music therapists working in settings that emphasize cognitive approaches will structure their presentation strategies differently than music therapists who work in settings emphasizing a strong behavior modification approach. It is important for the client and consistency of treatment

that the music therapist's approach be consistent with that of the rest of the treatment team and with the general therapeutic milieu of the institution or facility (AMTA, 1998; Isenberg-Grzeda, 1988; F. Johnson, 1981). Therefore, music therapists must be knowledgeable of the techniques, philosophies, and approaches used by the other professionals with whom they work and find ways of incorporating or complementing those strategies and approaches in any music therapy treatment interventions they design. (More information on the way music therapy treatment approaches have been related to some specific psychotherapeutic or educational models and theories is presented in Chapter Twenty-two of this book.)

Considering Environmental and Structural Factors

As music therapists plan music-based intervention strategies, they want to create activities and experiences that are appropriately challenging to the client (Aigen, 1995a; James, 1987). Within a success-oriented environment, music therapists strive to provide therapeutic music experiences in which the demands do not exceed the capabilities of the client but which at the same time provide enough challenge to be engaging and move the client toward productive growth. While clients may need immediate success experiences in the initial stages of therapy, gratification can become more delayed and activities may become more challenging as the clients gain competence in performance and develop increased confidence in themselves and their abilities. As clients occasionally fail and learn to try again, they begin to develop coping skills needed to face the realities and challenges of daily life. However, "while some failure indicates that a client is being challenged, constant and repeated failure indicates poor assessment on the part of the therapist" (James, 1987, p. 33).

Including an appropriate amount of structure in activities is essential to helping clients attain therapeutic goals and objectives (Hadsell, 1993). References to the amount of structure needed for a client to successfully perform a task may even be included as a condition or qualifier portion of the objective (see above). In addition to the music variables considered above, several other aspects of the environment can also be controlled to help eliminate behavior problems and provide clear expectations and necessary cues for desired responses. These include (1) *time* (general organization of session, length of activities, time between activities, organization of transitions, time spent waiting for turns); (2) *physical space* and *equipment* (room arrangement, number of visual or auditory distractions, type and placement of equipment used in session, storage or placement of equipment not being used); (3) *choices* (number and complexity of options); (4) *materials* (color, spacing, texture, amount of information, number of materials used in the session, therapist- or client-selected or -provided, placement and manner of presentation, appropriateness for age and developmental level and physical capabilities); (5) *instructions* (appropriateness of language, speed, form, complexity to client's functioning level); and (6) *presentation of activities* (sequencing and pacing, number and timing of cues, complexity and amount of information, age-appropriateness, adequate task analysis, variations) (Hadsell, 1993).

Often, clients develop new skills and behaviors through successive steps of approximation. Thus, more structure, assistance, cues, and prompts may be needed in the initial stages of therapy or in the client's first encounters with a certain type of music experience or medium. Structure can be reduced and cues or assistance faded as the client's skills emerge and develop (Hadsell, 1993; Hanser, 1987). The type and amount of structure needed varies from client to client, from environment to environment, from task to task, and from one stage of therapy to another; thus, the therapist must carefully monitor the client's responses and adjust accordingly (Hadsell, 1993). Carefully analyzing the various aspects of external structure can both facilitate the performance of an individual client and make the same activity "appropriate for many clients if its structure is varied to meet their individual needs" (Hadsell, 1993, p. 64).

Implementing Treatment Procedures

Once strategies for music therapy intervention and treatment have been devised, they must be implemented to see whether they will, in fact, help the client progress toward the established therapeutic goal. Continuous observation and evaluation of the client's responses, both to the music therapy activities themselves and to the music therapist's methods of implementing these activities, are very important factors in developing effective music therapy intervention strategies. No matter how wonderful a procedure or activity may look on paper, if the client cannot or will not respond to it, some form of modification is necessary. Therefore, while the music therapist strives to deliver services according to the written program plan (AMTA, 1998), the implementation phase of treatment also allows for adjustments in procedures, materials, and approaches as necessary to help the client achieve the highest possible level of functioning and the maximum therapeutic benefit. Thus, the implementation phase of therapy involves both science and art, both convention and spontaneity (Bruscia, 1989a; Kenny, 1982). "It is the rare case that proceeds according to plan without any deviation whatsoever" (Hanser, 1987, p. 141).

The music therapist, therefore, while attending to the predetermined treatment plan, must also continuously observe what is happening within the process. Paying close attention to the client's smallest responses, the music therapist continuously shapes and molds the therapeutic encounter, using his or her best clinical judgment to adjust components as necessary to meet the client's immediate needs. Even in this process of spontaneous adaptation – the "art" of doing music therapy – the music therapist always is mindful of the client's goals and objectives, the reason and purpose behind the therapeutic encounter (Hanser, 1987). "Virtually everything the skilled therapist does is therapeutically purposeful, engaging clients in active participation in their own growth" (Boxill, 1985, p. 179).

Documentation and Data Collection

In order to maintain a record of client progress and response to treatment, music therapists must have some format for collecting data on the client's responses and for documenting the client's progress. These procedures help provide a chronological account of the client's treatment, help monitor effectiveness and efficiency of treatment, provide for quality assurance and accountability, and provide communication links to all those involved with the client's care (Davis, 1992c; Hanser, 1987). Usually, music therapists are required to document a client's referral to music therapy, assessment, placement, program plan, and ongoing progress in music therapy (AMTA, 1998). Reporting formats may vary greatly from one setting to another, dependent in part upon state, federal, and facility regulations. Generally, however, music therapists have some method of collecting data on the targeted client behaviors and some manner of periodically reporting client progress. All documentation is "written in an objective, professional style based on observable client responses" (AMTA, 1998, p. xliii).

In collecting data to see if a client is making progress in therapy, the therapist focuses on changes in the specific behavior outlined in the client's therapeutic objective. A baseline measurement indicates the client's level of behavior before treatment and serves as a reference point by which to gauge progress (Davis, 1992c; Hanser, 1987). Even if clients do not reach the established criterion level for successful completion of the objective within the projected time frame, they may still be making some progress toward the objective as compared with their initial level of performance.

A summary of a client's initial proficiency levels is usually given in the music therapy assessment. During the implementation phase of treatment, the music therapist regularly collects data on the frequency or duration of the targeted behaviors specified in the objective. Data may be charted in many ways, using formats such as tables, graphs, or written progress notes. Video and audio recordings may also be useful tools for tracking and recording data and progress in music therapy; however, the music therapist must be sure to obtain client consent for these recordings. The behavior and criterion sections of the objective will help the therapist determine what sort of data collection strategies to employ, for, in order to be useful in evaluating the effectiveness of music therapy treatment, the data must relate to the objective or purpose for treatment. Analysis of the data collected on the client's observed responses during the implementation of music therapy treatment intervention helps the music therapist determine the relative success or failure of that course of treatment. This, along with recommendations for future treatment, is duly

documented in periodic progress reports.

All music therapy documentation becomes part of the client's file and, like any professional documentation, is to remain confidential unless proper authorization is given for release (AMTA, 1998; Davis, 1992c). In accordance with the standards of professional ethics, the music therapist also keeps *all* client information – written, pictorial, audio, or verbal – confidential and does not share it outside the treatment team without proper release from the client or his/her responsible party. This principle of confidentiality helps protect the client's right to privacy.

Evaluation and Termination

As has been noted above, the music therapist continually observes and evaluates the client's responses during the course of treatment and adapts or revises the details of procedures accordingly. However, more formal evaluation of the entire program occurs at scheduled intervals to determine how successful the treatment interventions are in helping the client reach the specified goals and objectives. In this overall evaluation, the music therapist may also report secondary outcomes of therapy and make recommendations for future action. The evaluation process helps the music therapist, client (if applicable), and treatment team (if applicable) decide whether the treatment program should be continued in a similar fashion, revised in some way, or terminated.

Sometimes the evaluation schedule is specified in the time frame section of the objective or the targeted completion date for the objective listed in the client's treatment plan. Schedules for periodic evaluation and review of client treatment plans may also be specified by facility procedures or by state or federal regulations. Whatever the case, it is important that the music therapy treatment program be evaluated regularly to determine whether, in fact, the client is benefitting from services. Analysis of the data collected in therapy sessions and comparison of the client's current level of functioning to his or her initial level of functioning will help the therapist, client, and treatment team make this determination.

Music therapy services may be discontinued for several reasons (AMTA, 1998; Davis, 1992c). Music therapy treatment is terminated when the client has met the stated goals and objectives for treatment, when the client fails to benefit from services, or when the treatment team feels the client has received the maximum possible benefit from the services. Music therapy services may also be terminated if the client can no longer be scheduled or is the client is discharged from the facility. Termination of music therapy services may be initiated by either client or therapist, by mutual consent, or by external factors related to personal, time, financial, or agency-related considerations (McGuire & Smeltekop, 1994a, 1994b).

At the time of termination, the music therapist prepares a discharge report. This report usually contains a summary and evaluation of the entire music therapy treatment process, including goals and objectives set, any progress made, and the client's level of functioning at the time of termination. Often, recommendations and suggestions for follow-up treatment or integration of community services are also be given. Whenever possible, a discharge or termination plan should be developed in sufficient time to allow for coordination of services and ensure a smooth transition for the client.

The process of terminating a significant therapeutic relationship also may bring up strong feelings and personal issues for both client and therapist. It is important that adequate notice of the impending termination be given whenever possible and that the persons involved be allowed time to review and evaluate the course of treatment, to express feelings, to project into the future, and to say good-bye (McGuire & Smeltekop, 1994b). Activities involving these processes can be incorporated into the final music therapy sessions to facilitate a successful termination for both client and therapist (McGuire & Smeltekop, 1994a, 1994b).

INDIVIDUAL VS. GROUP TREATMENT

When devising a music therapy treatment plan for a particular client, a music therapist must consider whether that client's needs can be met best in an individual setting, a group setting, or some combination of group and individual treatment (Hanser, 1987). Sometimes, the setting or facility will dictate the treatment option; at other times, the amount of time or space the therapist has available for group or individual sessions will be limited or fixed in some way. Music therapists must at times make difficult decisions about how a limited number of resources can be distributed most effectively to meet the needs of a large number of potential clients. Considerations such as what other types of services the client is receiving, how favorably the client responds to various treatment modalities, the long-term prognosis or placement options for the client, the client's ability to function in a group setting, etc., may all affect the treatment team's and/or music therapist's decision to recommend group or individual treatment in music therapy. Each type of treatment has certain advantages, and either one or some combination of both may be appropriate at various times for clients served in music therapy.

In individual music therapy treatment, there is a one-to-one relationship between therapist and client. This provides unique opportunities for initial explorations of a client's individual skills, preferences, and problems and allows for a concentrated focus on the needs and development of that particular client at all times during the course of treatment (Boxill, 1985; Hanser, 1987; Nordoff & Robbins, 1971b). Individual treatment affords a more intensive and in-depth experience to both client and therapist. Although most clients could probably benefit from this type of concentrated treatment effort, the reality of staffing situations in most facilities usually precludes this possibility. Therefore, "referrals for one-to-one therapy depend on the needs of each client relative to those of others" (Boxill, 1985, p. 92).

For clients who lack the impulse control necessary for appropriate group behavior or who must be isolated for certain medical conditions or who cannot or will not come to group setting for any of a number of reasons, one-to-one treatment may be the only viable alternative, at least for the initial course of therapy. Also, individual treatment may be the usual setting of choice for therapists of a particular theoretical orientation (e.g., psychoanalytic, guided imagery and music, some types of improvisational music therapy). [See Chapter Twenty-two for more information on various schools of music therapy practice.]

Group music therapy obviously allows more clients to receive music therapy services at one time; thus, if it is successful, group treatment is more cost-effective than individual treatment (Hanser, 1987). In addition, group settings have several therapeutic advantages (Boxill, 1985; Gaston, 1968a; Hanser, 1987). For example, clients in music therapy groups with peers can learn and practice appropriate ways of relating to and interacting with others, skills that they will need to function effectively and successfully in the real world. Moreover, group treatment provides the benefits of support, insights, and encouragement from other group members. In some groups, members may also model appropriate behaviors or responses for one another and, in so doing, learn from one another.

Since music is usually perceived as a fun, enjoyable experience that has inherent motivating and socializing qualities (see Chapter Five) and since music experiences can be structured to meet a wide variety of needs simultaneously (Boxill, 1985; Bruscia, 1991a; Gaston, 1968a; Hanser, 1987; Nordoff & Robbins, 1971b; Sears, 1968), as well as because of budgetary or time considerations, music therapists frequently provide group treatment. In some settings, music therapy often is used as the first group experience for many clients. As music therapists work in group treatment, they must be aware of the basic principles of group development and note how these apply to their work in music therapy groups (Sandness, 1991). In addition, music therapists working in group settings must become adept at individualizing approaches, taking into account the capabilities and needs of a particular group member and encouraging his or her active participation, while simultaneously attending to all group members and keeping in mind the needs, goals, and objectives of the group as a whole (Boxill, 1985; Farnan & Johnson, 1988b; Hanser, 1987; Krout, 1987). Hanser (1987, pp. 90-93) provides several excellent suggestions for individualizing treatment within music therapy groups.

EXAMPLES OF MUSIC EXPERIENCES USEFUL IN ADDRESSING GENERAL GOAL AREAS

As Chapter One noted, the therapeutic goals that music therapists have for clients are the same kinds of goals other members of the treatment team have for those clients: improving motor skills, communication skills, academic or cognitive skills, social skills, etc. The difference lies in the treatment modality: Music therapists use music and music-based experiences to help their clients reach these goals. The final section of this chapter gives general examples of music experiences that music therapists might use to help clients improve their skills in several general goal areas, such as behavioral, sensory, motor, communication, emotional (affective), interpersonal (social), self-help/survival, and academic or cognitive skills. Descriptions and examples of various music activities and experiences which are useful in addressing these areas are drawn from sources such as Cassity & Cassity (1991, 1994a), Eagle (1982), Lathom (1981a, 1981b), Nocera (1979), Schulberg (1981), and Standley (1991a), as well as the author's own experience. The discussion in this section is purposely kept on a very broad and general level; specific examples and applications of music therapy experiences to the unique needs, capabilities, goals, and characteristics of client groups with various disabilities will be presented in the Chapters Seven through Twenty-one.

Individual Behavioral Skills (Attending and Compliance)

Since music provides a powerful form of multi-sensory stimulation that is almost impossible to ignore (see Chapter Five), music experiences can be very useful in attracting the attention of clients who seem oblivious to most of the world around them. Improvisatory exploration of various music media is often useful in finding sounds, styles, or idioms that will attract the attention and interest of these clients (Alvin, 1978; Nordoff & Robbins, 1977). The time-ordered structure of music also helps clients attend to tasks presented in a musical format for longer periods of time. At first, the client may only be able to attend for a few seconds. Through the course of therapy, the music therapist may gradually increase the length of songs and music experiences, with the rhythm and form of the music assisting the client to attend and participate for longer and longer periods of time. Action songs, singing activities, and individual or group instrumental performance activities can all be increased in length and difficulty, gradually requiring clients to attend and remain on task for more extended periods of time. Music activities that require clients to wait to sing or play an instrument or move until a specific point in the music can also help clients develop the impulse control necessary to achieve that desired result. The musical structure provides a stimulus that attracts and holds their attention and orders and cues their responses.

In some situations, structured relaxation exercises to music may help clients develop skills necessary to control impulsive, violent, or destructive behavior, while various vocal, instrumental, or movement-to-music improvisation exercises may be useful in channeling restless or agitated behavior into more structured and productive forms. In more formal music situations, such as individual lessons or group ensembles, clients may also learn to increase their frustration tolerance and develop skills necessary to see tasks through to completion as they practice and rehearse to develop the required degree of proficiency. Moreover, the rewards of music performance provide increased self-esteem and positive recognition by others.

Sensory Skills

Music is a multisensory experience that may include auditory, visual, tactile, and kinesthetic components. Therefore, music experiences can be structured to help clients increase their perception and discrimination skills in many sensory areas. Music experiences related to increasing auditory perception skills may include activities such as: (1) indicating by word or gesture when sounds start and stop; (2) identifying the location of hidden sound sources; (3) using words or gestures to indicate contrasts of loud-soft or fast-slow; (4) singing or playing instruments loud or soft or fast or slow as directed; (5) moving, playing, or clapping with the beat of the music; (6) imitating rhythm patterns;

(7) using words or gestures to indicate whether pitches are the same, higher, or lower; (8) identifying instruments by their sound; and (9) playing instruments in the sequence played by the leader. Activities used to develop visual perception skills include: (1) instrumental activities that require clients to play musical instruments on a visual cue from a conductor; (2) locating specific notes or symbols in musical scores; (3) musical games that require clients to imitate movements demonstrated by another person; (4) playing color-coded instruments; (5) identifying colors, shapes, or objects as requested by song lyrics; (6) sorting individual resonator bells from biggest to smallest to arrange them in scale order; and (7) creating and playing from musical scores which use colors, pictures, shapes, or letters to represent certain instruments, sounds, pitches, chords, or rhythm patterns. By involving clients in touching and holding and manipulating musical instruments made of various materials or by having clients touch or feel different textured objects during relaxing background music or by having clients activate switches covered with different textures to turn on recordings of preferred music, music therapists may also help clients increase their tolerance for tactile stimulation. The prospect of producing a musical sound may do much to motivate a client who is very tactilely defensive to reach out and touch and explore objects in the environment.

Motor Skills

Many music experiences, such as those that involve playing instruments or moving to music, require some degree of motor skill for their performance. For clients who lack motor control and coordination, music may provide the motivation needed to engage in or sustain various movement or exercise activities or it may give the structure needed to help clients coordinate movement patterns. Music carefully selected for its relaxing or stimulating qualities or for its rhythmic and melodic structure that mirrors the patterns of the required movement can facilitate range of motion exercises, gait training, and the performance or other exercise routines (see Chapter Eleven). Music may also help lessen pain perception so that clients with painful conditions such as arthritis will engage in prescribed movement activities. Other music experiences and activities that may help clients improve their motor control and coordination skills include (1) performing locomotor movements (walking, running, jumping, etc.) to a steady or rhythmic beat; (2) performing non-locomotor movements (bending, swaying, rocking, etc.) to the beat of the music; (3) performing actions described by song lyrics; (4) learning and performing dances and movement games; (5) playing musical instruments that require different kinds of arm, hand, and finger movements; (6) conducting music in various beat patterns; (7) grasping, holding, and releasing musical instruments or various objects or props as required by musical songs or games; and (8) participating in marching bands, drum corps, or drill teams.

Language and Communication Skills

The area of language and communication skills includes both receptive (processing and responding to language) and expressive (speaking or signing) components, as well as pre-speech skills (see Chapter Twelve). Music experiences that are useful in helping clients develop receptive language skills include: (1) picking up or pointing to objects or pictures as requested by song lyrics; (2) responding to commands to stop, start, look, touch, etc., contained in songs or musical games; (3) performing actions or playing instruments as directed by song lyrics; and (4) following directions to play instruments or perform dance movements in a certain sequence. Activities such as (1) playing simple wind instruments like kazoos, whistles, and recorders to help develop the breath and muscle control needed for speech or (2) singing vowel sounds or simple syllables in imitation of the therapist may be useful in helping clients develop pre-speech skills. Higher level expressive language skills may be developed through experiences that include (1) singing or signing or using a communication board to provide specific words in a song; (2) singing or signing phrases, choruses, verses, or entire songs; (3) singing or chanting original answers in questions and answer or fill-in-the-blank songs; (4) adding new words or verses to existing songs; and (5) writing original song lyrics.

Emotional Learning and Emotional Expression

Since music is the language of the emotions (see Chapter Five), music experiences can be an important vehicle for facilitating emotional learning and providing appropriate, socially acceptable means of emotional expression. As they participate in structured music experiences, individuals can be guided to experience, identify, and express various emotions and moods. In addition, they can learn to perceive the emotional communications of others and increase their ability to control, adjust, and adapt their own emotional behaviors and responses (Thaut, 1989a). Music activities and experiences that may be useful in helping clients gain skills in these areas include: (1) choosing words to describe moods or feelings expressed by certain songs, improvisations, or instrumental compositions; (2) selecting songs to express specified feelings; (3) moving to music or playing musical instruments to express feelings nonverbally; (4) writing lists or drawing pictures to describe feelings that emerge when listening to music; (5) singing or performing songs with certain emotional themes; (6) discussing song lyrics or improvisations dealing with emotions or emotionally-charged situations; (7) contributing words or phrases to a group song about a specified emotion; and (8) writing songs to express one's own feelings.

Interpersonal (Social) Skills

When they participate in small or large group music experiences, clients have many opportunities to develop and practice various interpersonal or social interaction skills. These may include behaviors like establishing and maintaining eye contact, being aware of other group members, interacting appropriately with others, working cooperatively with others, complying with stated rules and limits, taking turns, sharing, exchanging roles of leader and follower, showing respect for others and their property, giving and accepting constructive feedback, and listening attentively to others. Music activities and experiences that may be useful in helping clients gain skills in these areas include: (1) songs or chants that require clients to name themselves or other group members; (2) group songs, dances, or instrumental activities that require clients to play, sing, or move together with one or more other group members; (3) rondo form chants and songs that alternate group and individual responses; (4) songs and games that require clients to take turns suggesting movements or rhythms and imitating the movements or rhythms suggested by other group members; (5) writing group songs or developing group improvisations according to specified guidelines; (6) taking turns playing solos on instruments; (7) taking turns conducting group vocal or instrumental performances; (8) discussing song lyrics with others; (9) choosing songs for the group to listen to and listening quietly and attentively to everyone's selection; (10) working together on group shows, music videos, or other performance projects; (11) evaluating performances and giving constructive suggestions for improvement; and (12) incorporating the constructive suggestions of others in revising composition projects or refining performance techniques.

Self-Help/Survival Skills

Some clients may need help in learning basic self-help or survival skills. Special songs that teach the sequence of steps needed to perform various tasks like dressing or washing hands may be useful in this area (Kramer, 1978). Specially designed song lyrics and musical games also may be used to help clients practice identifying things like items of clothing or safety and survival signs or to help them learn and rehearse safety rules. In addition, participating in performance groups or in special musical shows or productions may give some clients the incentive needed to take pride in their appearance and practice good grooming and personal hygiene skills.

Academic or Cognitive Skills

Academic concepts, such as letters, colors, numbers, spatial direction and position, and time, can be learned and reinforced in music activities that require clients to read graphic, letters, or color-coded musical scores, participate in special musical games or dances, or learn songs explaining the concepts in their lyrics. Cognitive skills, such as reality orientation, long- and short-term memory, sequencing skills, problem-solving skills, organizational skills, and the like, can also be learned, practiced, or reinforced through participation in various types of music experiences. Music activities useful in these areas include: (1) experiential, structured instrumental activities, such as playing instruments in rhythm or with the proper chords or at the proper time; (2) singing or playing or listening to and discussing songs referring to some aspects of person, place, or time; (3) recalling song titles or lyrics; (4) learning songs or accompaniments by rote and then performing them from memory; (5) composition or music analysis activities or lyric substitution song writing activities; (6) directed listening activities; (7) discussion of lyrics dealing with problem solving methods; (8) following along on a song sheet, chord chart, song map, or musical score; (9) playing, singing, or chanting ostinato accompaniment patterns; (10) recalling items mentioned by song lyrics in the proper sequence; (11) learning and performing specific dance or movement-to-music routines or relaxation to music exercises; (12) learning and recalling fingering patterns or positions needed to play notes or chords on various instruments; and (13) learning and remembering the sequence of steps needed to operate tape players, compact disc players, etc., or learning and remembering how to find one's preferred music on the radio or in a tape library.

SUMMARY

Once music therapists decide to accept a client for treatment, they then must determine just how music therapy services will be delivered to that client. This process usually includes several basic stages: (1) assessment, (2) setting goals and objectives, (3) planning music-based intervention strategies, (4) implementing treatment procedures, (5) documentation and data collection, and (6) evaluation and termination. As music therapists design music-based intervention strategies, they consider several factors, including (a) how music will function to help the client meet the goals and objectives; (b) what types of music experiences and musical materials will be used; (c) if the intervention procedures will incorporate any specific therapeutic or educational strategies; and (d) any environmental or structural factors that may affect the activity or the client's response. Above all, however, music therapists must always keep in mind how these factors relate both to the individual client's needs, strengths, preferences, age, cultural background, skills, and capabilities and to the objective to be accomplished. In planning music-based intervention strategies, one must never forget the purpose for which they are being designed (objective) or the unique individual qualities of the client with whom they will be used.

When devising a music therapy treatment plan for a particular client, music therapists must consider whether that client's needs can be met best in an individual setting, a group setting, or some combination of group and individual treatment. Both individual and group treatment have certain unique

therapeutic advantages. For example, individual treatment allows for a concentrated focus on the needs and development of a particular client, thus providing a more intensive and in-depth experience for both therapist and client. Group treatment allows more clients to receive music therapy services and gives clients the opportunity to practice skills in relating to others, as well as providing the benefits of the support, insights, and encouragement of other group members. Either individual or group treatment or some combination of both may be appropriate at various times for clients served in music therapy.

Many different types of music experiences may be used to help clients gain skills in many different goal areas. The last section of this chapter provided several brief general descriptions and examples of various music activities and experiences that might be used to help clients improve behavioral, sensory, motor, communication, emotional (affective), interpersonal (social), self-help/survival, and academic or cognitive skills.

QUESTIONS FOR THOUGHT AND DISCUSSION

1. What are the basic stages in the delivery of music therapy services? How is each stage important to successful music therapy treatment?

2. What is involved in the assessment process? What type of information is gathered and in what ways? How does this information impact other stages of the music therapy treatment process?

3. What is the difference between a goal and an objective? Why do music therapists establish therapeutic goals and objectives for their clients? How do goals and objectives impact other stages of the music therapy treatment process?

4. What four factors do music therapists consider as they design music-based intervention strategies? How/why are these important? In considering these factors, what must the music therapist always keep in mind? Why?

5. How does treatment implementation involve both science and art, both convention and

spontaneity?

6. Why is it important for music therapists to collect data and document client progress?

7. What is involved in the evaluation of music therapy services? Why is evaluation important?

8. What factors may be involved in deciding whether to treat a client in a group or individual setting? What are some advantages/disadvantages of each type of treatment? What are some examples of times when one may be more appropriate than the other?

9. How do the general goal areas and related music experiences listed in the last section of this chapter relate to Gaston's (1968a) three guiding principles and Sears's (1968) three classifications discussed in Chapter Five?

10. Review the general examples of music activities and experiences which may be useful in help

clients develop various behavioral, sensory, motor, communication, emotional (affective), interpersonal (social), self-help/survival, and academic or cognitive skills. For each goal area, describe some ways the process or content of the sample music experiences relates to the therapeutic goal area or desired behavioral response. What are some other music experiences that might be used to help clients develop skills in these areas?

SUGGESTIONS FOR FURTHER READING

Alley, J. M. (1979). Music in the IEP: Therapy/education. *Journal of Music Therapy, 16*(3), 111-127.

American Music Therapy Association [AMTA]. (1998). Standards of clinical practice. In *AMTA Member Sourcebook 1998* (pp. xli-l). Silver Spring, MD: Author.

Cassity, M. D., & Cassity, J. E. (1994). *Multimodal psychiatric music therapy for adults, adolescents, and children.* St. Louis: MMB Music.

Davis, W. B. (1992). The music therapy treatment process. In W. B. Davis, K. E. Gfeller, & M. H. Thaut, *An introduction to music therapy: Theory and practice* (pp. 287-301). Dubuque, IA: Wm. C. Brown.

Eagle, C. T., Jr. (Ed.). (1982). *Music therapy for handicapped individuals: An annotated and indexed bibliography.* Washington, D.C.: National Association for Music Therapy.

Farnan, L., & Johnson, F. (1988). *Music is for everyone: A handbook for providing music to people with special needs.* New Berlin, WI: Jenson Publications.

Hadsell, N. A. (1993). Levels of external structure in music therapy. *Music Therapy Perspectives, 11*(2), 61-65.

Hanser, S. B. (1987). *Music therapist's handbook.* St. Louis: Warren H. Green.

Lathom, W. (1981). How a music therapist determines goals and objectives. In W. Lathom, *The role of the music therapist in the education of severely and profoundly handicapped children and youth* (pp. 7-10). Lawrence, KS: National Association for Music Therapy.

Mager, R. F. (1962). *Preparing instructional objectives.* Belmont, CA: Fearson Publishers.

Mager, R. F. (1972). *Goal analysis.* Belmont, CA: Fearson Publishers.

Nocera, S. D. (1979). *Reaching the special learner through music.* Morristown, NJ: Silver Burdett.

Nowicki, A. L., & Trevisan, L. A. (1978). *Beyond the sound: A technical and philosophical approach to music therapy* (Rev. ed.). Porterville & Santa Barbara, CA: Nowicki/Trevisan.

Sandness, M. I. (1991). Developmental sequence in music therapy groups: A review of theoretical models. *Music Therapy Perspectives, 9,* 66-72.

Schulberg, C. H. (1981). *The music therapy sourcebook: A collection of activities categorized and analyzed.* New York: Human Sciences Press.

Standley, J. (1991). *Music techniques in therapy, counseling, and special education.* St. Louis: MMB Music.

Steele, A. L. (1977). Directive teaching and the music therapist as consultant. *Journal of Music Therapy, 14*(1), 17-26.

Zinar, R. (1987). *Music activities for special children.* West Nyack, NY: Parker Publishing.

Chapter Seven

MUSIC THERAPY FOR INDIVIDUALS WHO HAVE MENTAL RETARDATION

DEFINITION

MENTAL RETARDATION has been defined and described in various ways and with many different terms throughout the years. Currently, definitions focus on three key factors: (1) significantly subaverage general intellectual functioning, (2) deficits in adaptive behavior, and (3) onset of symptoms occurring during the developmental period. According to the American Association on Mental Retardation [AAMR] (1992),

> *Mental retardation* refers to substantial limitations in present functioning. It is characterized by significantly subaverage intellectual functioning, existing concurrently with related limitations in two or more of the following applicable adaptive skill areas: communication, self-care, home living, social skills, community use, self-direction, health and safety, functional academics, leisure, and work. Mental retardation manifests before age 18. (p. 1)

The American Psychiatric Association [APA] (1994) describes mental retardation in this way:

> This disorder is characterized by significantly subaverage intellectual functioning (an IQ of approximately 70 or below) with onset before 18 years and concurrent deficits or impairments in adaptive functioning. (p. 37)

Although these definitions and their associated classification systems (see below) reflect the concerns and emphases of each association to some degree, they do show general agreement that mental retardation is not defined solely by deficits in intellectual functioning but also includes concurrent limitations or deficits in more than one adaptive skill area. Thus, subaverage intellectual functioning is a necessary but not a sufficient condition for a diagnosis of mental retardation. In addition, although mental retardation may be a lifelong condition, its symptoms must first be manifested during the *developmental period*. The developmental period is that time during which individuals mature and grow to adulthood, usually considered to be any time from birth to eighteen years of age.

Intellectual functioning is usually measured by one or more standardized tests and reported in terms of an intelligence quotient (IQ) score. Individuals are considered to have significantly subaverage intellectual functioning when their IQ scores are 70-75 or below (AAMR, 1992; APA, 1994). This represents a score of approximately two standard deviations below the mean, allowing for a measurement error of five points. If persons have mental retardation, they manifest limits or impairments in adaptive functioning concurrently with these intellectual limitations.

Adaptive functioning refers to how well individuals cope with the common demands of life and how well they function independently, based on the expectations for an average individual of their age and sociocultural group. Adaptive functioning includes the areas of communication, self-care, home living, social or interpersonal skills, use of community resources, self-direction, health, safety, functional academics, leisure, and work or vocational skills (AAMR, 1992; APA, 1994). In persons with mental retardation, adaptive skill limits occur in two or more of these areas and are primarily related to their limited intellectual functioning, not to other circumstances (e.g., sensory limits, cultural or language diversity). Often, adaptive functioning limits, rather than low IQ, are the presenting symptoms in individuals with mental retardation (APA, 1994).

Related Terminology

Since mental retardation manifests itself during the developmental period, individuals with this condition are sometimes called "developmentally disabled" or "developmentally delayed." The term developmental disability, however, is a more general term, and may include individuals with other conditions, such as autism, cerebral palsy, epilepsy, and other neurological impairments, who may or may not also have mental retardation (Boxill, 1985). According to Public Law 95-682, the Developmental Disabilities Bill of Rights Act (1978):

> A *developmental disability* is attributable to a mental or physical impairment that begins before age 22 and is likely to continue indefinitely and that results in substantial functional limitation in *three* or more areas of major life activity. (AAMR, 1992, p. 13)

DSM-IV (APA, 1994) also includes the category of "pervasive developmental disorders," for specific disorders (e.g., autism, Rett syndrome, Asperger's disorder) that are characterized by severe and pervasive impairments in multiple areas of development, including deficits in reciprocal social interaction and communication and the presence of stereotypic behaviors, interests, or activities. Although about 75%–80% of the individuals who have pervasive developmental disorders also have mental retardation (APA, 1994), individuals with these disorders will not necessarily also have

intellectual or cognitive deficits.

Typically, particularly in educational settings, the broader label of developmental delay is used during preschool years with a diagnosis of mental retardation, if appropriate, being made after age five (AAMR, 1992). A child with a developmental delay shows a significant variation from normal development in cognitive, physical, communication, or socio-emotional development or in adaptive or self-help skills, as determined by appropriate diagnostic instruments or procedures administered by an interdisciplinary team (ECIC, 1992). Not every child who is developmentally delayed is or ever will be classified as mentally retarded; deficits occurring in other areas do not necessarily impact cognitive or intellectual functioning. In a sense, *mental retardation* is a much more specific term than *developmental disability*, because, in individuals with mental retardation, their limits in adaptive functioning are necessarily related primarily to their intellectual limitations and not some other organic or environmental factors (AAMR, 1992).

Down syndrome, also known as trisomy 21 and formally called mongolism, is one of the congenital conditions that is characterized by some degree of mental retardation. Individuals with Down syndrome also have characteristic physical features, including small, flattened skulls, short flat-bridged noses, wide-set eyes, and short, broad hands and feet (Miller & Keane, 1978). Down syndrome is associated with a defect on the twenty-first chromosome.

Causes

Mental retardation may be caused by organic (biological) factors, environmental factors, or a combination of the two. Only about 25% of the cases can be traced to specific biological causes (Furman & Furman, 1996). Sometimes, mental retardation occurs because of prenatal factors, such as chromosomal disorders, various syndrome disorders, inborn metabolic errors, developmental defects in brain formation, or influences of malnutrition, drugs or toxins, maternal diseases, or irradiation during pregnancy. Other cases are caused by perinatal factors, such as placental insufficiency, abnormal labor or delivery, neonatal hemorrhages, seizures, respiratory disorders, infections, head trauma, metabolic, or nutritional disorders. Still other cases are due to postnatal causes, such as head injuries, various infections, demyelinating disorders, degenerative syndromes or disorders, seizure disorders, toxic or metabolic disorders, malnutrition, or environmental deprivation due to psychosocial disadvantage, child abuse or neglect, or chronic social/sensory deprivation (AAMR, 1992). In about 30%–40% of the cases, no clear etiology or cause for the mental retardation can be determined, even with extensive evaluation and testing (APA, 1994). Since mental retardation has so many different causes, some view it as "a final common pathway of various pathological processes that affect the functioning of the central nervous system" (APA, 1994, p. 39).

Classification Systems

Throughout the years, various classification systems have been developed in an attempt to help clarify degrees of mental retardation. Many of these systems rely primarily on IQ measurements to assign a level or degree of severity to the disability. However, a new classification recently developed by the American Association on Mental Retardation [AAMR] (1992) specifically avoids reliance on IQ scores to assign levels of disability. Instead, it emphasizes the person's functioning level and the intensity and type of support systems needed to help that person function as independently and productively as possible within his or her community. Since both types of classification systems are encountered in various settings, each is briefly described in the following paragraphs.

Physicians and psychiatrists frequently classify individuals who have mental retardation according to a system based on the severity of intellectual deficit. In such classification systems, persons with IQ levels of 50-55 to approximately 70 are said to have **mild mental retardation**, those with IQ levels ranging from 35-40 to 50-55 are considered to have **moderate mental retardation**, those with IQ levels ranging from 20-25 to 35-40 are classified as having **severe mental retardation**, and those with IQ levels below 20 or 25 are diagnosed with **profound mental retardation** (APA, 1994). Persons who fall into these subclassifications of mental retardation have certain typical developmental characteristics

(Sarason & Sarason, 1984; APA, 1994). Individuals who have mild mental retardation (about 80%–85% of the entire population of persons with mental retardation) can develop some communication, elementary academic, and basic social skills and have minimally impaired sensorimotor functions. Those who have moderate mental retardation (10%–12% of those with mental retardation) can talk and learn to communicate, have fair motor development, can learn self-help skills, and can be managed with moderate supervision. They usually have poor social awareness, but this can be improved somewhat with training. Although they are unlikely to progress beyond a second-grade level in academic skills, they may benefit from vocational training. Persons who have severe mental retardation (3%–4% of those with mental retardation) have poor motor development, minimal speech, and few communication skills. As they grow older, some can master simple pre-academic skills and may be able to perform simple tasks under close supervision. Some can adapt well to life in the community in supervised living arrangements, if they have no associated problems that require specialized nursing care. Those individuals who have profound mental retardation (1%–2% of those with mental retardation) have minimal functioning capacities in all or most sensorimotor areas. With intensive training over a long period of time, they may gain very limited self-help skills. Most, however, will need constant supervision and nursing care.

Historically, many educators have used a slightly different classification system, which groups individuals with mental retardation by educational potential into the following four groups (Hewett & Forness, 1974):

1. **Slow learners**, or **borderline retarded** children, are usually capable of marginal success in school and often go on to become self-supporting, socially adjusted adults. Their IQs generally fall in the 75-85 range.

2. **Educable mentally retarded** (EMR) children progress at a developmental rate that is approximately one-half to three-fourths that of average children. EMR children are usually not ready for reading, math, and writing skills at age six.

However, progressing at a much slower rate than that of average children, EMR children eventually can be expected to attain anywhere from a second-grade to a sixth-grade skills level. Their IQs tend to fall in the 50-75 range. As adults, most will be capable of working as semi-skilled or unskilled laborers.

3. **Trainable mentally retarded** (TMR) children develop at a rate approximately one-fourth to one-half that of average children. Their IQs generally fall within the 25-50 range, and many have physical or sensory impairments in addition to their retardation. When they are given special training, many TMR children can learn self-help skills, elementary language skills, and common safety rules, but most are incapable of achieving any but the most rudimentary first-grade academic skills. As adults, some may be capable of employment in sheltered workshop situations.

4. **Profoundly retarded** children usually have multiple problems, which may include motor impairments, developmental aphasia, sensory impairments, seizures, and bizarre behaviors (Nocera, 1979). Their IQs are generally below 25. These children often require total supervision, protection, and care; therefore, they may be institutionalized early in life. Some can learn to walk and feed themselves, but many are nonambulatory and bedridden (Smith & Neisworth, 1975). Although they may vocalize, profoundly retarded individuals rarely develop intelligible speech (Clausman, 1980).

In recent years, many professionals who work in the field of mental retardation have begun to use a new classification system, the 1992 AAMR *Definition, Classification, and Systems of Supports* (AAMR, 1992). In viewing mental retardation not as a *trait* to be measured but as a *state* in which functioning is impaired in certain specific ways, this system departs significantly from previous classification systems. The result is a classification system for mental retardation in which the person's *level of functioning* is the critical measure; thus, the classification is focused on an individual's adaptive behavior and level of support systems needed, not severity of intellectual impairment (IQ scores).

Rather than requiring subclassification into four levels of a person's mental retardation (mild, moderate, severe, and profound), the system subclassifies the intensities and pattern of supports systems into four levels (intermittent, limited, extensive, and pervasive). (AAMR, 1992, p. x)

In the 1992 AAMR classification system, terms such as *mildly, moderately, severely,* or *profoundly* retarded are no longer used. Instead, the single code of mental retardation is used if the person meets the three criteria of age of onset, significantly subaverage abilities in intellectual functioning, and limitations in two or more adaptive skill areas. For purposes of classifying severity of impairment, the person's strengths and weaknesses are described in reference to psychological, physical, and environmental dimensions and a profile is developed of needed levels of supports (intermittent, limited, extensive, or pervasive) across the four basic dimensions of intellectual functioning and adaptive skills (Dimension I), psychological and emotional concern (Dimension II), physical/health/etiology concerns (Dimension III), and environmental considerations (Dimension IV).

Thus, a diagnosis might well be "a person with mental retardation who needs limited supports in communication and social skills." Another sample diagnosis might be "a person with mental retardation with extensive supports needed in the areas of social skills and self-direction." Such descriptions are more functional, relevant, and oriented to service delivery and outcomes than the labeling system currently in use. (AAMR, 1992, p. 34)

The 1992 AAMR classification system provides a more functional description of an individual's capabilities and adaptive behavior and his or her needs for specific intensities of support within the various adaptive skill areas and the three other dimensions of psychological/emotional considerations, physical/health/etiology considerations, and environmental considerations. This system recognizes that individuals with mental retardation may have strengths in some adaptive or personal capabilities (e.g., good health and strong social skills but difficulty in communication, or good at functional math but not functional reading) in spite of limitations in two or more adaptive skill areas. It also underscores the importance of appropriate supports over sustained periods to help improve the general life functioning of persons with mental retardation. The classification process acknowledges that "numerous variations in adaptive skill functioning are possible across individuals diagnosed as having mental retardation and even within a single individual over time" (AAMR, 1992, p. 113).

The focus on individual needs in the 1992 AAMR classification system moves away from the historical conception of mental retardation as representing global deficits and directs service delivery toward individual planning and functional supports. The recognition that limitations in some adaptive skill areas may be juxtaposed with strengths in other areas highlights the *capabilities* of individuals with mental retardation and facilitates the planning of intervention strategies that are targeted and functional

and that will help individuals be integrated into the community as fully as possible in spite of the significant limitations that may result from their mental retardation. This shift of focus and emphasis from previous classification systems is resulting in many changes in service delivery, particularly in the area of adult services. The paradigm shift engendered by the 1992 AAMR classification system represents the third phase in evolution of services for individuals who have mental retardation, from the former phases of institutionalization and segregation (Phase 1; prevalent well into the twentieth century) and deinstitutionalization and community development (Phase 2; beginning in the 1970s) to a functional supports model. As they adopt this new definition and classification system for individuals with mental retardation, "delivery systems must reorient their roles from being providers of program services to being providers and facilitators of individual supports." (AAMR, 1992, p. 146)

COMMON CHARACTERISTICS, PROBLEMS, AND NEEDS OF CLIENTS

As with any population, those individuals who have mental retardation are a very heterogeneous group. Any individual client will have a unique combination of abilities, needs, personality traits, strengths, and weaknesses that will impact his or her treatment program and functioning level; therefore, it is unwise to attempt to predict a particular person's skill levels or ceiling of abilities based on broad generalizations about a certain population. However, an awareness of some of those characteristics, problems, and needs which may be common to many clients who have a diagnosis of mental retardation will be beneficial both to the therapist who desires to work with this population and to the reader who is trying to understand how music therapy intervention strategies may benefit this population.

Individuals with mental retardation generally have fundamental difficulties in learning and performing various skills of daily living. Because of their mental retardation, they have substantial limits in three specific areas: conceptual intelligence, practical intelligence, and social intelligence (AAMR,

1992). *Conceptual intelligence* relates to a person's ability to learn and use academic skills and knowledge and to understand and interpret abstract thoughts and ideas. This type of intelligence is what is generally measured on IQ tests. It also impacts adaptive skill areas, such as safety skills, functional academics, and work. *Practical intelligence* is concerned with an individual's ability to independently manage ordinary activities of daily living. This type of intelligence is central to the adaptive skill areas of self-care, sensorimotor skills, safety skills, functional academics, work, leisure, self-direction, and use of community resources. *Social intelligence* includes the ability to understand social expectations and the behaviors of others and the ability to judge how to conduct one's self appropriately in social situations. This type of intelligence is important to adaptive skill areas of social or interpersonal skills, communication, work, leisure, home living, and use of community resources. Because of significant limitations in the area of social intelligence, individuals with mental retardation may have difficulty understanding appropriate or expected social behaviors or be unable to infer or interpret personal and situational cues. They may also lack social insight into the motivation and personal characteristics of others and may have significant limitations in their ability to show good judgment in their interpersonal interactions. In addition, limits in social intelligence may inhibit their ability to communicate their own thoughts and feelings in problem-solving situations or in social situations where some kind of conflict exists. Thus, it becomes apparent that many of the adaptive skill limitations found in individuals with mental retardation may be related very closely to their substantial limitations in conceptual, practical, and social intelligence (AAMR, 1992).

There are no particular personality patterns, behaviors, or physical features that are uniquely associated with the general condition of mental retardation (APA, 1994). Many individuals do, however, have delayed development of motor skills (resulting in poor motor control and coordination, poor balance, poor spatial perception, and/or a poor body image). Several also have delays or deficits in language skills and need assistance developing functional communication. Often, individuals with mental retardation also need intensive training to develop self-help skills (e.g., feeding, dressing, personal hygiene). Other common problems include low self-esteem, poor frustration tolerance, poor impulse control, short attention span, poor social skills, difficulty making independent choices, and an inability to structure leisure time. Of course, when mental retardation is part of a specific syndrome, that syndrome's particular physical features (e.g., in Down syndrome) or behavioral symptoms (e.g., the intractable self-injurious behavior of Lesch-Nyhan syndrome) will be present. Also, generally speaking, the more severe the mental retardation, the greater the likelihood that other conditions, such as seizures or other neurological impairments, neuromuscular difficulties, visual or auditory impairments, or cardio-

vascular conditions, will be associated with it (APA, 1994). Individuals who have severe or profound mental retardation often have multiple handicaps or disabilities which cause them to need extensive or pervasive support services. (For more information on severe, multiple disabilities, see Chapter Sixteen).

Because of their impairments in general intellectual functioning, individuals with mental retardation have certain special learning needs. These include "(1) a slower rate of presentation, (2) more repetition, (3) smaller amounts of new material, and (4) concrete experiences" (Atterbury, 1986, p. 35). As these individuals grow older, most will need special training in functional living skills, basic work skills, and responsible social behaviors. They may also need assistance in identifying and accessing support services that will enable them to continue to improve their functioning level and help them become more independent, productive, and integrated into their community.

Recent research has indicated that individuals with mental retardation demonstrate better skill generalization and retention when skills are taught as integrated parts of functional routines, rather than in isolation (AAMR, 1992). As people with mental retardation move from more restrictive institutional placements to less restrictive living options, they often make significant improvements in their adaptive skills and their behavioral characteristics. Being included in integrated educational and community settings beside peers without mental retardation can be beneficial for many individuals with mental retardation. These peers can provide powerful models for language, behavior, dress, and social skills. Integrated and inclusive settings provide opportunities for both planned and spontaneous peer-to-peer instruction that usually is not possible in separate schools and community groups where all the individuals have disabilities (AAMR, 1992).

SETTINGS FOR SERVICE DELIVERY

Until fairly recent times, persons with mental retardation were institutionalized and segregated from the mainstream of society and were thought to be unable to learn to care for themselves or become independent in any areas (AAMR, 1992; Furman &

Furman, 1988). In the second half of the twentieth century, there came to be an increasing recognition "that with special education programs these people can improve their daily living skills as well as their abilities to plan and make good judgments" (Furman

& Furman, 1988, p. 285). With this change in attitude came an increased advocacy for the rights of individuals with mental retardation. Changes in legislation and educational practices and a movement toward deinstitutionalization in the 1970s and 1980s greatly expanded educational, vocational, and community living options for both children and adults. Many children who used to be institutionalized now receive support services in their homes and schools, and many adults now live in semi-independent living situations in group homes or apartments within the community at large and work in sheltered workshops or are employed in various community jobs that fit their skill capabilities. With the paradigm shift engendered by the 1992 AAMR classification, most systems of service delivery are moving to a functional supports model that maximizes habilitation goals related to health (physical, psychological, and/or functional wellness) and fosters "characteristics of a satisfying life (choice, competence, respects, community presence, and participation in the environment" (AAMR, 1992, p. 115).

> The expectation today is that supportive services are provided to promote the acquisition of adaptive skills which will prepare individuals to live in the community within the limits of their handicapping conditions. . . . Most retarded citizens live in homes, group homes or apartments with a prescribed level of assistance. (Furman & Furman, 1996, p. 129)

The institutionalized population now consists mainly of adults who are severely or profoundly impaired and who have major treatment and support needs, usually including multiple handicaps or disabilities (Furman & Furman, 1996).

Before age 21, most individuals with mental retardation receive educational, training, and support services through the special education programs of their local school districts. The Individuals with Disabilities Act (IDEA) (Public Law 101-476), the 1990 revision of the 1975 Education for All Handicapped Children Act (Public Law 94-142) assures a free, appropriate public education to all children, ages 3–21, who have disabilities, including those with mental retardation. This law, as well as the Technology-Related Assistance for Individuals with

Disabilities Act (Public Law 100-407), also provide for assistive technology devices and services that may be needed by the individual (Adamek, 1996; Johnson, 1996). Incentives for early intervention programs to address the needs of children from birth through age 2 who have handicaps or disabilities are provided by Public Law 99-457 of 1986 (Adamek, 1996; Humpal, 1990). Therefore, early intervention services usually begin at birth or during the first two years of life. Children may come to an early intervention center to receive treatment, or professionals from early intervention programs may provide treatment in the child's home or day care setting. During these years, Individualized Family Service Plans (IFSPs) are written to address the needs of the child and family. When they are 3 years old, individuals usually are referred to special education programs in their local school district. After initial assessment and identification of the individual's unique areas of ability and disability, Individualized Educational Programs (IEPs) are written to guide instruction and programming. IEPs set educational/habilitative goals matched to the individual's specific profile of functioning. They also provide for appropriate support services, placement in the least restrictive environment, and an annual evaluation of student progress in the program. Recent trends in special education have placed great emphasis on "inclusion" practices, providing for individuals receiving special education services to be educated with their "normal" peers to the greatest extent possible. For example, a student may be sent to a resource room for help or training in specific areas with a special education teacher or specific therapist for short segments of the day, while being mainstreamed or included in a regular classroom for as much of the day as possible, perhaps with the assistance of an aide when necessary. For junior high and high school students with mental retardation, Individualized Transitional Programs (ITPs) often complement IEPs and guide the transition from schools and education to community services and work.

Music therapists may work as employees of or consultants to school districts or early intervention programs (Humpal, 1990; Wilson, 1996). When IEP assessments find that music therapy can provide a unique means of helping students achieve their educational objectives, music therapists may be called upon to provide traditional direct services, work with students in self-contained classes, work with students in inclusive classes, provide direct in-home services to students who are confined to their homes for medical reasons, provide consultation services to facilitate classroom instruction, inclusion, or music education, and/or provide staff development workshops (Wilson, 1996). Music therapy is usually classified as a related service in special education settings. Some music therapists also work with children and adolescents who have mental retardation in other settings, such as private studios or clinics, the client's home, community programs, day care programs, private programs for individuals who have developmental disabilities, or special schools and institutions.

After age 21, individuals may receive support services through a variety of agencies in a variety of settings, such as group homes, sheltered or specially structured work environments, day treatment programs for individuals who have developmental disabilities, community facilities, state schools, or special training centers. Some individuals also receive services in their own homes. Music therapists may work in any of these programs or settings as full-time or part-time employees, or they may provide services on a contractual or consultive basis. Furman and Furman (1996) predict that, as medical and technological advances increase life expectancy for individuals with mental retardation, programs focusing on elderly clients with mental retardation will become more numerous. In addition, programs that focus on developing music skills may become an important means of providing individuals with "appropriate and dignified leisure time activities which are immediately usable in the community" (p. 291).

In a recent survey of populations served by music therapists in which respondents were permitted to list as many categories as appropriate (AMTA, 1998), 580 of 1,620 music therapists responding said they worked with individuals who were developmentally disabled. (The survey did not list a separate category for mental retardation.)

HOW MUSIC IS USED IN THERAPY

In her review of music therapy literature related to mental retardation, Reynolds (1982) showed that "the use of music as a treatment mode for mentally retarded individuals has changed in focus and scope as the field of music therapy has grown to meet the needs of this population" (p. 43). In the 1950s, typical goals in music therapy programs for mentally retarded clients included social adjustment, increased concentration, improved muscular coordination, self-control, emotional stability, and motivation and satisfaction of achievement (Brewer, 1955; Gilliland, 1959). In the 1960s, music therapy goals tended to focus on socialization, strengthening of defenses, impulse control, intrusion on fantasy, sensory stimulation, and gratification (Lathom, 1968). In the late 1960s and the 1970s, when behavior modification techniques began to receive a prominent place in education and training programs for the mentally retarded, music therapy goals "began to emphasize overt behavior rather than the former emphasis on psychoanalytical goals" (Reynolds, 1982, p. 45). Several studies conducted during this period demonstrated that music could be used effectively as a reinforcer of desired behaviors (Bellamy & Sontag, 1973; Dileo, 1975; Dorow, 1976; Johnson & Phillips, 1971; Jorgenson, 1974; Metzler, 1974; Remington, Foxen, & Hogg, 1977; Saperston et al., 1980; Steele, 1968; Underhill & Harris, 1974; Walker, 1972). Johnson and Zinner (1974) also demonstrated that behaviors and concepts learned in music therapy sessions could be maintained and generalized to other aspects of the environment. In their surveys of music therapy research in the field of mental retardation, Furman and Furman (1988, 1996) found that contingent music was still the most frequently used music therapy procedure documented in music therapy studies involving clients with mental retardation.

In the late 1970s and early 1980s, more educational and training programs began to be developed for individuals who were severely and profoundly retarded, and music therapists began to develop intervention strategies geared specifically to the needs of this population (Carter, 1982; Gonzales, 1981; Lathom, 1981b; Miorin & Covault, 1979; Nordoff & Robbins, 1977; Saperston et al., 1980; see also Chapter Sixteen). These music therapy techniques helped elicit and develop responses that enabled these individuals to become more aware of and responsive to people and objects in their environment, thus contributing to the growth and development of individuals who otherwise might show little progress in a clinical or educational setting (Furman & Furman, 1988; Lathom, 1981b; Madsen, 1981; Nordoff & Robbins, 1977). As more and more clients have become mainstreamed or included in music groups with their "normal" peers, music therapists have also investigated and developed various techniques to facilitate the inclusion or normalization process (Atterbury, 1990; Birkenshaw-Fleming, 1993; Boxill, 1989; Furman & Furman, 1988; Gunsberg, 1988, 1991; Hughes et al., 1990; Humpal, 1991; Humpal & Dimmick, 1995; Jellison & Duke, 1994; Jellison & Flowers, 1991; Krout, 1986a; Zinar, 1987). Similarly, with the move toward deinstitutionalization and the introduction of a new classification system for mental retardation (AAMR, 1992) that emphasizes adaptive functioning, music therapy programs, too, have increasingly emphasized the development of functional skills that can be useful in community settings (Coates, 1987; DiGiammarino, 1990, 1994; Furman & Furman, 1988, 1996). Programs and services focusing on early intervention and the elderly client with mental retardation are also increasing as medical and technological advances continue and as legislation mandates and provides funding for services (Furman & Furman, 1988, 1996; Humpal, 1990). In addition, music therapy has been found to be a very effective intervention for increasing and maintaining communication responses, motor functioning, cognitive skills, and social and affective responses in individuals with Rett Syndrome (Hadsell & Coleman, 1988; International Rett Syndrome Association, 1987; Wesecky, 1986; Wylie, 1996). Furman and Furman (1996) provide an excellent survey and summary of the literature on music therapy and mental retardation published from 1970-1995.

Many different types of music experiences (e.g., singing, listening, moving to music, playing musical instruments, creating music, discussing music, and reading music notation) can be structured to help individuals who have mental retardation reach nonmusical, therapeutic goals. Music experiences and activities can be used (a) as *reinforcers* to increase or maintain desired behaviors, (b) to *structure* or serve as a vehicle for presenting the material or skill to be learned, and (c) to *stimulate* the production and development of desired social, perceptual motor, or academic skills and behaviors (Madsen, 1981). Various music therapy techniques and experiences can help individuals with mental retardation or other developmental disabilities improve their skills in many areas, including (1) communication skills, (2) academic, cognitive, or vocational skills, (3) motor skills, (4) social and emotional skills, (5) self-help or independent living skills, and (6) leisure skills (Boxill, 1985; Carter, 1982; Coates, 1987; Davis, 1992b; DiGiammarino, 1990, 1994; Furman & Furman, 1988, 1996; Grant, 1989). While the next sections of this chapter will look at each of these areas individually to discuss particular music therapy strategies often used to improve specific developmental and adaptive skills, it is important to remember that, in practice, all of these areas overlap and influence one another. In fact, one of the strengths and unique aspects of the discipline of music therapy is that it can address skills in many areas and on many levels of development simultaneously (Grant, 1989; Lathom, 1981b), thus facilitating the growth of the whole person in an integrated fashion.

Music Therapy Strategies to Improve Communication Skills

The ability to communicate greatly influences an individual's ability to function in society. Individuals with mental retardation have varying degrees of impairment in communication abilities. Some may have no functional speech and may need to develop ways of communicating nonverbally, with basic sign language or simple communication boards. (See Chapter Twelve for more information on these and other alternative and augmentive communication devices.) Others may have difficulty with awareness of or attention to auditory stimuli (auditory perception) or in interpreting and responding to communications from others (receptive language). Still others may need alternative ways to learn to develop and expand their functional verbal communication skills (expressive language). Various music therapy strategies can help in many of these areas.

For those individuals who need help in developing *auditory perception skills* that are necessary to attend to and understand spoken language, music therapists might use music experiences that require the client to locate, track, identify, and discriminate among sound sources (Grant, 1989). Simple sound exploration activities, using musical instruments, vocal sounds, and body sounds (e.g., clapping, tapping, tongue clicking) can stimulate the initial auditory awareness and attention necessary to language development (Boxill, 1985; Monti, 1985; Nordoff & Robbins, 1971a, 1977). "Since sound constitutes the first environment of the infant, it appears that a return to this environment stimulates awareness of reality and growth" (Monti, 1985). Later, simple music activities employing matching, sequencing, and echo techniques can be used to develop auditory memory and sequencing skills (Grant, 1989).

Songs, movement-to-music activities, dances, and instrumental activities that require clients to follow directions or point to certain things named in the song can be used to help clients develop *receptive language skills* (Grant, 1989). Spencer (1988) found that movement activities were generally more effective than instrumental activities in developing the ability to follow directions in adolescents and young adults with mental retardation; however, at least 16 to 20 treatment sessions were needed to make a significant change. Of course, a particular client's individual preferences and skills must always be considered when planning what approaches to try with that client.

In the area of *expressive language*, various musical experiences and techniques can be used to elicit, stimulate, and increase an individual's vocalizations. These include vibroacoustic therapy (Skille, 1989), soft instrumental background music (Cunningham, 1986), and various vocal exploration and imitation exercises (Boxill, 1985; Grant, 1989; Nordoff & Robbins, 1977). Research has also shown that singing activities involving singing alone or in conjunction with actions, picture cards, or concept learning, can be useful in encouraging spontaneous speech and increasing expressive language skills in preschool children with mental retardation or developmental disabilities (Hoskins, 1988). In addition, music therapy experiences can be structured so as to gradually increase an individual's expressive communication, first requiring him or her to supply one, then two, three, or more words within the context of a musical activity. Reading recognition and comprehension skills may also be increased in words that are presented in songs or with other musical activities. For example, pairing the words "walk," "run," and "hop" with descriptive music may help clients learn to associate printed words with their corresponding actions.

Music Therapy Strategies to Improve Academic, Cognitive, and Vocational Skills

Prior to learning any academic or vocational skills, individuals must have both the motivation to participate in the experience and certain behaviors, such as eye contact, the ability to discriminate and focus on specific auditory, visual, or tactile cues and stimuli, sufficient attention span, and the ability to follow directions, that will enable them to engage in learning experiences. Music therapy experiences can help clients develop skills in all of these areas (Davis, 1992b; Lathom, 1981a, 1981b; Nocera, 1979). For example, unique musical sounds and rhythms can attract attention and elicit eye contact. Attention span can be gradually lengthened as the duration of songs or musical experiences are increased and as individuals are asked to wait longer and longer to have their turn to play an instrument or give a specific response within the context of the music activity. Various songs and musical games requiring clients to point to, match, or identify certain sounds, pictures, or objects can also help individuals learn to attend to and discriminate among different auditory, visual, or tactile stimuli. In addition, songs or musical games that incorporate specific commands or directions in the lyrics are effective in helping individuals learn to attend to and follow directions. The interest of musical sounds and rhythms, the pleasure of making music, and the gratification gained by participating in musical experiences often motivate even the most unresponsive clients to attend, respond, and participate.

Once individuals have learned to attend to the learning situation, many academic skills and concepts, such as colors, shapes, numbers, body part identification, clothing identification, directionality, time and space concepts, etc., can be presented and practiced through various song lyrics, action songs, musical games, dances, or musical instrument activities (Boxill, 1985; Lathom, 1981a, 1981b; Nocera, 1979). For example, song lyrics can be written to describe or express certain concepts, or action songs, musical games, or dances can require individuals to point to or match or identify colors or numbers or shapes or body parts. Using colors, shapes, or numbers to correspond to various musical sounds or pitches on charts for song or ensemble playing can also give clients practice in identifying and recognizing colors, shapes, and numbers. When material is presented in a musical context, the melody and rhythm of the music help provide the structure necessary to help individuals with mental retardation learn, process, and retain certain concepts. In addition, the natural repetition inherent in the structure of music gives clients needed multiple presentations of information without the boredom of tedious drill.

Researchers have also found that musical perception tasks can be used to assess that level of cognitive development in individuals with mental retardation as well as in nonhandicapped children (Jones, 1986; Rider, 1978, 1981). Music intervention strategies employing a controlled increase in musical complexity then can be used to enhance cognitive development in individuals with mental retardation by helping them move through the tasks associated with different stages of cognitive development. Some research also indicates that exposure to certain types of stimulating music and rhythmic drum beats for a period of 15–20 minutes prior to academic instruction can increase muscle tone in hypotonic children with Down syndrome, leading to greater physical alertness and enhancing intellectual responsiveness to the learning tasks (Sekeles, 1989).

Music therapists frequently use contingent music experiences, involving both active (e.g., instrument playing, dancing) and passive (e.g., listening) responses, to facilitate skill learning among individuals who have mental retardation (Furman & Furman, 1988, 1996). These strategies are often very effective in increasing many different pre-academic and academic skills (Dorow, 1976; Holloway, 1980; Saperston et al., 1980; Underhill & Harris, 1974). However, it is important to note that the reinforcing properties of music vary not only with individual reinforcement history but also with the degree of mental retardation. Although some individuals who

have more severe levels of involvement do respond positively to contingent music programs (Walker, 1972), those with greater degrees of impairment usually have the least consistent responses to contingent music (Furman & Furman, 1988).

In addition to facilitating the development of attending behaviors and the learning of certain procedures and tasks, music may also be used to help structure the general work or learning environment. There is some evidence that certain types of background music have significant positive effects on the work behavior of adults with mental retardation on sorting tasks in a vocational training environment (Groeneweg et al., 1988). However, other studies have shown that easy listening music and distracting noises have no effect on the productivity of workers with mental retardation (Wentworth, 1991). Not all types of background music will have equally beneficial effects for all clients or for all tasks; clients' responses must be carefully observed and monitored for each situation. What is beneficial or reinforcing in one situation may not be so in another.

Music Therapy Strategies to Improve Motor Skills

The development of functional motor skills can be very important in helping individuals learn to interact with and learn from their environment (Boxill, 1985). Individuals with mental retardation may have delays in motor development or have various concurrent motor or nervous system difficulties that make voluntary control and coordination of movement difficult or impossible (Davis, 1992b). Motor skills allow individuals to explore the environment and provide the foundation for much other learning. They are also an integral part of the performance of many activities of daily living (feeding, bathing, dressing, etc.). Therefore, the process of developing and refining motor skills for learning and functional activities is often an important part of therapeutic programs for individuals who have mental retardation. Because of its direct physical effects and its time-ordered structure (see Chapter Five), music can be an important tool both for stimulating motor responses and for facilitating the development of motor control and coordination.

Many types of music experiences, including action songs, dances and movement-to-music activities, and the exploration and use of musical instruments, can be used to stimulate and develop motor responses (Boxill, 1985; Grant, 1989; Lathom, 1981a, 1981b; Nocera, 1979). Movement-to-music experiences may be active or passive: individuals may be required to perform activities independently or may be guided through normal movement patterns by the therapist, with assistance gradually being faded as the individual's skills emerge and develop. Passive range of motion or movement-to-music activities can play vital roles in maintaining joint mobility and range of motion in individuals who have limited independent mobility. Careful attention to the structure, mood, and physical and psychoemotional effects of the music that accompanies the exercises can enhance individuals' receptiveness and responsiveness to passive and active range of motion exercises.

Certain types of music also stimulate active movement and help individuals coordinate and control their actions. For example, Sekeles (1989) found that stimulating drum beats, stimulating music improvised by the music therapist, and recordings of music from ecstatic healing rituals could help elicit spontaneous motor responses and increase muscle tone in hypotonic children with Down syndrome, leading to greater physical alertness and enhancing responses to posture and motor control exercises. Various motor activities, such as ball tossing, block stacking, exercise patterns, etc., can also be structured by or choreographed to rhythmic music or song lyrics, leading to increased fluidity and coordination of movement. Both gross and fine motor movements can be incorporated in dances, musical games, or action songs, depending upon the needs of the individual client. In addition, music activities can be structured to include various motor skills individuals need to practice, thus reinforcing the development of these skills (Holloway, 1980).

Musical instruments can provide clients with many enjoyable opportunities for developing and refining motor skills. According to Grant (1989), the rhythmic structure of music provides a unique means of programming the input, cognitive processing, and output process of perceptual motor function, while active participation in playing various musical instruments gives many possibilities for developing and practicing specific movement patterns. The

motions required to play various instruments can help clients develop and refine skills in reaching, grasping, releasing, arm extension, eye-hand coordination, finger movements, and coordination of bilateral or unilateral movements (Boxill, 1985; Grant, 1989; Lathom, 1981a, 1981b; Nocera, 1979). Experiences in playing musical instruments can also promote appropriate hand usage in individuals with Rett Syndrome (Hadsell & Coleman, 1988; Wylie, 1996). Instrumental activities may be structured to require very gross or very fine motor movements, depending on the needs of the individual. For example, a hand drum may be sounded by a slap or tap (Hadsell & Coleman, 1988) for those individuals with limited motor skills or may be played with intricate finger patterns for those who are developing fine motor skills (Sekeles, 1989). As an individual's skills increase, the music therapist gradually increases the difficulty of the movement required to play the instrument. For example, an autoharp may be positioned farther away from an individual, so that individual will have to extend his or her arms more to strum the instrument. Or an individual may be challenged to play a rhythmic pattern faster or be given a part that has faster notes or more chord changes. With various adaptations, even those individuals with limited motor skills can participate in playing musical instruments (Clark & Chadwick, 1979; Rudenberg, 1982). More information on specific music therapy procedures used to develop motor skills and adaptations for various levels of motor ability is found in Chapter Eleven.

Music Therapy Strategies to Improve Social and Emotional Skills

In working with clients who have mental retardation, music therapists frequently target the areas of improving social skills and eliminating inappropriate or self-stimulatory behaviors (Furman & Furman, 1988, 1996). The adaptive limitations associated with mental retardation often include significant limits in social intelligence (AAMR, 1992); therefore, individuals who have mental retardation often need help in acquiring and practicing appropriate social behaviors (Davis, 1992b). Group music experiences using songs, movement-to-music, and instrumental activities can all be structured to incorporate social skills such as parallel or cooperative play, appropriate greetings, sharing, taking turns, listening to others, and group awareness and cooperation (Boxill, 1985; Grant, 1989; Krout, 1986a; Lathom, 1981a, 1981b; Nocera, 1979). By playing instruments or dancing or singing together, individuals learn to work together, listen to each other, follow a group leader, and wait for their turn to sing, move, or play. The repetition and order of music help the clients predict what is coming, thus increasing their comfort level and helping them become more confident of their ability to participate with the group. Clients who participate in performing groups, such as bell choirs, bands, drum corps, and singing groups, also learn to improve self-discipline, impulse control, and social skills. In addition, these activities provide the group members with experiences that bring gratification and increase self-esteem. Since music activities are adaptable to different ability levels within a group (e.g., less coordination is needed to strike a bass drum than to strike the correct bar of a xylophone), group music activities can provide opportunities for clients of many different ability levels to work together and achieve success.

Music groups and improvised musical play experiences can also provide fun and nonthreatening opportunities for individuals with mental retardation to associate and interact with their nondisabled peers (Boxill, 1989; Gunsberg, 1988, 1991; Hughes et al., 1990; Humpal, 1990, 1991; Monti, 1985). By using specific strategies, music therapists can facilitate the development of interaction between disabled and non-disabled individuals. For example, Humpal (1991) found that, for early childhood groups, parachute games and hoop or elastic rope dances to music were most effective in fostering interaction, while creative movement to music and line dancing were least effective. Music experiences using rhythm instruments, bean bags, circle activities, or partner dances were all moderately effective in promoting interaction.

Some individuals with mental retardation may be very impulsive, lack emotional stability, or exhibit inappropriate behaviors, such as aggressiveness, talking out of turn, getting out of their seats without permission, or verbal or physical abuse. In many cases, programs of contingent music activities can effectively increase appropriate social behaviors and eliminate inappropriate behaviors (Furman &

Furman, 1988, 1996; Krout, 1986a; Madsen, 1981). Songs and improvisational activities dealing with various emotions and feelings may also be useful in helping clients learn how to express emotions in appropriate and socially acceptable ways. In addition, song lyrics can be written to help clients learn and remember appropriate ways to express various emotions, such as anger.

Saperston (1989) developed a special individualized music-based relaxation training technique to help individuals with mental retardation control or eliminate inappropriate behaviors. In this program, various music experiences, including songs, chanting, and recorded or improvised music that elicits physiological responses associated with relaxation, or combinations of different musical elements are used as reinforcers, structural prompts, or eliciting stimuli of desired behaviors to help clients circumvent behavior problems. Pujol (1994) also found that pentatonic music was useful in increasing deep inhalations and relaxation responses in individuals who were severely or profoundly impaired.

Music therapists have also successfully used music in conjunction with intensive play techniques to decrease inappropriate or self-abusive behaviors, establish social rapport, and increase adaptive responses in clients who had severe or profound impairments (Carter, 1982; Gonzales, 1981; Miorin & Covault, 1979). In this process, music, close body contact, and physical stimulation are used to establish rapport between the therapist and the client. Once rapport is established, the therapist continues to use these elements to evoke and develop positive responses, such as eye contact, appropriate affect, cooperative interaction, initiation of sounds, facial expressions, and purposeful motor actions, in the client. Other music therapists use improvisational music, based on the client's movements and vocalizations, to elicit and develop adaptive responses and appropriate interactions with clients who are severely or profoundly impaired (Boxill, 1985; Nordoff & Robbins, 1977; Pfeifer, 1982).

Music Therapy Strategies to Improve Self-Help and Independent Living Skills

Because of the limits in practical intelligence that

occur with mental retardation, individuals often need support or specially structured programs to help them achieve the greatest degree of independence possible in self-help and self-care skills (AAMR, 1992). Music can assist in many of these areas, providing the structure, motivation, or reinforcement for appropriate skill development (Boxill, 1985, 1989; Furman & Furman, 1988, 1996; Lathom, 1981a, 1981b). For example, pleasurable music activities can provide effective positive reinforcement for self-care skills (Garwood, 1988). In other cases, song lyrics may provide the necessary cues and structure to help clients learn and remember the sequence of steps needed for various dressing or personal hygiene routines (Kramer, 1978). Other clients may be motivated to adhere to acceptable standards of personal hygiene and learn to take pride in their appearance to maintain their membership in a musical performance group. Increased motor skill coordination and independence developed in music experiences may also be transferred to functional areas like personal mobility, holding eating or grooming utensils, etc.

Music Therapy Strategies to Improve Leisure Skills

A final area where music therapy can be of great benefit to individuals who have mental retardation is that of developing meaningful and satisfying leisure time activities. As individuals with mental retardation are integrated more and more into the community, they must find ways of occupying their hours of free time, when they are not involved in specific work or training programs. Music therapists can help these individuals gain functional leisure and music performance skills that will help them enjoy and participate in many different types of music activities in their free time, either alone or with others, at their residence or in community settings (Coates, 1987; Davis, 1992b; DiGiammarino, 1990, 1994; Furman & Furman, 1996).

Persons with mental retardation can learn to access and enjoy many music activities independently if they are given appropriately structured training which leads to generalization of skills to other settings and in the presence of people other than the trainer (Coates, 1987; DiGiammarino, 1990, 1994).

Functional music leisure skills may include items such as learning to operate a record player, compact disc player, or tape player, learning to tune the radio to one's preferred stations, learning appropriate concert etiquette, learning to select and borrow or purchase recordings and tapes, learning to purchase concert tickets, becoming a member of a community chorus or band, attending and participating in community dances, and learning to play musical instruments. Most individuals *without* mental retardation develop several of these skills incidentally through everyday experiences at home or in the community. "Individuals with mental retardation, however, may need direct instruction in skills which will help them access music independently during leisure time" (DiGiammarino, 1994, p. 19). It is here the skills of the music therapist become important, for the music therapist knows not only how to use, access, and teach various types of music skills but also how to structure and sequence training so that it can be assimilated and understood by persons with mental retardation. For example, the music therapist might employ certain types of special notation or symbolic representations or cueing techniques to teach music performance skills, such as piano performance (Velasquez, 1991). Other music therapists are beginning to use personal computers and special applications of music education software to help clients with mental retardation uncover and develop musical talent. For example, Spitzer (1989) has used computers to help an individual with Down syndrome improve his singing range and accuracy so he was better able to join in singing groups. Individuals with mild retardation who had difficulty with traditional notation were also able to play and create melodies and spend many enjoyable hours in this way because of computer programs. This success with music and the computer also enhanced their motivation and level of concentration, "thereby allowing them to feel better about themselves in general" (Spitzer, 1989).

As the clients gain functional music listening and performance skills, they are equipped with more tools that will help them be integrated successfully into the community. Although initial treatment may require many prompts and much interaction between the music therapist and the client, independent functioning by the client within the community setting is always the ultimate goal (Coates, 1987;

DiGiammarino, 1990, 1994). "Leisure programming should include instruction in functional music skills for persons with mental retardation so that they may be able to access and enjoy music independently and at will throughout their lives" (DiGiammarino, 1990, p. 219).

SPECIAL CONSIDERATIONS AND TIPS FOR SUCCESS

Music activities used with individuals who have mental retardation should be clear, direct, concrete, and incorporate multisensory experiences as much as possible (Atterbury, 1990; Birkenshaw-Fleming, 1993; Boxill, 1985; Nocera, 1979; Zinar, 1987). Material must often be presented at a slower rate and in smaller steps, and language and demonstrations used must be simple and concrete enough for the individual to understand. Gestures and verbal or physical prompts may be used initially to help clients achieve the desired responses, and then faded as the clients' skills emerge and develop. Group leaders may need to specifically direct the client's attention to important features of the lesson or experience and review and summarize these clearly before going on to the next point. Color-coding or adaptive notation may be useful in helping clients to perform skills independently. Electronic instruments or computer programs may also help unlock an individual's musical talent and independent performance abilities (Birkenshaw-Fleming, 1993; Farnan, 1993; Spitzer, 1989).

When planning and selecting materials, it is important to consider the clients' chronological age as well as their level of intellectual and adaptive development. Songs and instruments used should be age-appropriate and have universal appeal (Atterbury, 1990; Birkenshaw-Fleming, 1993; Boxill, 1985; Nocera, 1979; Zinar, 1987). If clients are to be integrated in school or community settings, it is important that they are exposed to the same types of vocal, instrumental, and listening experiences as their nondisabled peers (Jellison & Flowers, 1991).

Songs that have simple text and lots of repetition are generally most successful with clients who have mental retardation. Concrete representation of song content and use of familiar vocabulary will also facilitate participation (Atterbury, 1986). It is important that the range of the song's melody correspond to the clients' singing range, which is generally lower and narrower than that of their nondisabled peers (Furman & Furman, 1988, 1996;

Larson, 1977; Zinar, 1987). It is also important to make sure that the accompaniment is not distracting and that it serves to enhance the meaning of any song lyrics (Birkenshaw-Fleming, 1993; Boxill, 1985; Nordoff & Robbins, 1971a; Zinar, 1987). Different types of accompaniment may also positively or negatively influence vocal responses, especially among clients who are severely or profoundly impaired (Wylie, 1983).

When structuring music experiences, it is important to find ways to actively involve the clients in making music, responding to music, and creating music (Birkenshaw-Fleming, 1993; Boxill, 1985; Nordoff & Robbins, 1971a, 1971b). Adaptations of instruments may be necessary, or the therapist may need to find ways to build the musical experience around the clients' movements or simple vocal responses, but with sensitivity and creativity on the part of the music therapist, most clients can become actively engaged in the music experience. Of course, activities should be structured to provide clients with success experiences, but it is also important to provide the client with some degree of challenge. Although praise should be given for even the smallest accomplishments, praise should never be given falsely or indiscriminately. It is also very important to be specific when praising clients so that they know what they are doing right and where they still need to improve.

As individuals with mental retardation are integrated more and more into the community, functional skills that can be generalized to community use must receive an increasing emphasis (Coates, 1987; DiGiammarino, 1990, 1994; Furman & Furman, 1988, 1996). It is important for the music therapist to remember that, although initial treatment may require many prompts and much interaction between the music therapist and the client, independent functioning by the client within the community setting is always the ultimate goal. Teaching methods and therapeutic strategies should promote generalized skill use in normalized environments used by the individual: home, school, leisure, community, and work (AAMR, 1992). Research also indicates that individuals with mental retardation demonstrate better skill generalization and retention when skills are taught as integrated parts of functional routines, rather than in isolation. "Rather than simply scheduled for instruction in discrete blocks of time, basic motor, language, and social skills are taught as they occur or are needed, naturally *embedded* within routine activities" (AAMR, 1992, p. 131). Music therapy can be especially effective as a means of integrated instruction because music experiences naturally include all of these areas.

In preparing individuals with mental retardation to participate with their non-disabled peers in mainstreamed, inclusive, or community settings, it is important to pay special attention to the specific social behaviors that will be required by that situation (Jellison & Duke, 1994; Krout, 1986a). Jellison and Duke (1994) found that social behavior was rated as more important than music skills by teachers who were considering integrating individuals with mental retardation into inclusive music settings. When conducting music therapy activities in an integrated or mainstreamed setting, it is also important to train other staff in the use of appropriate teaching techniques that will facilitate learning and integration within a music setting (Hughes et al., 1990).

Music therapists who work with individuals in programs for the mentally retarded or developmentally disabled may occasionally come across individuals who have a unique condition known as Williams syndrome. Although most individuals who have this chromosomal disorder have mild to moderate mental retardation, they also have some mental strengths, including strong verbal abilities and a great appreciation of and talent for music, with a good memory for songs, melodies, and lyrics (Lenhoff, 1998; Stambaugh, 1996). Generally, individuals with Williams syndrome learn better in one-to-one learning situations than in group classes, learn better through hearing and imitating than through written music notation, and, because of motor limitations, have the most success with voice, keyboard, and drums (Lenhoff, 1998). In working with these individuals, it is important to (a) match instruments to the physical characteristics of the students; (b) use short sentences and frequently address students by name to help maintain attention; and (c) anticipate escalating frustration and help students remove themselves from the situation or find alternate activities (Stambaugh, 1996).

SUMMARY

Current definitions of mental retardation focus on three key factors: (1) significantly subaverage general intellectual functioning, (2) deficits in adaptive behavior, and (3) onset of symptoms occurring during the developmental period (ages 0-18). Thus, subaverage intellectual functioning is a necessary but not sufficient condition for a diagnosis of mental retardation; a person with mental retardation must also exhibit concurrent limitations or deficits in two or more adaptive skill areas. These adaptive skill areas include the domains of communication, self-care, home living, social or interpersonal skills, use of community resources, self-direction, health, safety, functional academics, leisure, and work or vocational skills.

Mental retardation may be caused by a variety of factors, including chromosomal or metabolic disorders or alterations, infections, toxins, problems during pregnancy or delivery, and trauma or infections or lead poisoning occurring during childhood. Environmental factors, such as deprivation of nurturance or of stimulation, may also be predisposing factors in some cases of mental retardation.

Various classification systems have been developed in an attempt to clarify the concept of mental retardation and the degree of individual impairment. Some systems classify individuals based on the severity of their intellectual impairment and rely primarily on IQ measurements to assign a level or degree of severity to the disability. In recent years, many professionals who work in the field of mental retardation have begun to use a new classification system developed by the American Association on Mental Retardation (AAMR, 1992). This system specifically avoids reliance on IQ scores to assign levels of disability, instead emphasizing the person's functioning level and the intensity and type of support systems needed to help that person function as independently and productively as possible within his or her community.

Individuals who have mental retardation have fundamental difficulties in learning and performing various skills of daily living. Because of their mental retardation, they have substantial limits in conceptual, practical, and social intelligence. Individuals who have mental retardation may also have delays in the development of motor, language, and/or communication skills. Other problems may include rigid behavior patterns, difficulty making independent choices, low self-esteem, low frustration tolerance, poor impulse control, short attention span, poor social skills, and an inability to structure leisure time. Generally speaking, the more severe the mental retardation, the greater the likelihood that other conditions, such as seizures or other neurological impairments, neuromuscular difficulties, visual or auditory impairments, or cardiovascular conditions, will be associated with it. Individuals who have severe or profound mental retardation often have multiple handicaps or disabilities which cause them to need extensive or pervasive support services.

Many different types of music activities and experiences, including singing, listening, moving to music, playing musical instruments, creating music, discussing music, and reading music notation, can have therapeutic benefits for individuals who have mental retardation. Music experiences and activities can be used (a) as *reinforcers* to increase or maintain desired behaviors, (b) to *structure* or serve as a vehicle for presenting the material or skill to be learned, and (c) to *stimulate* the production and development of desired social, perceptual motor, or academic skills

and behaviors (Madsen, 1981). Various music therapy techniques and experiences can help individuals with mental retardation or other developmental disabilities improve their skills in many areas, including (1) *communication* skills, (2) *academic, cognitive, or vocational* skills, (3) *motor* skills, (4) *social and emotional* skills, (5) *self-help or independent living* skills, and (6) *leisure* skills. One of the strengths and unique aspects of the discipline of music therapy is that it can address skills in many areas and on many levels of development simultaneously, thus facilitating the growth of the whole person in an integrated fashion.

When developing therapeutic intervention strategies for persons with mental retardation, it is important to present information in a clear, direct, concrete manner, incorporating multisensory experiences whenever possible. Material often must be presented at a slower rate and in smaller steps, and language and demonstrations used must be simple and concrete enough for the individual to understand. When selecting materials for use in music therapy session, it is important to consider the clients' chronological age and level of social development as well as their level of intellectual functioning. It is important for music therapists to remember that, although initial treatment may require many prompts and much interaction between the music therapist and the client, independent functioning by the client within the community setting is always the ultimate goal. Teaching methods and therapeutic strategies should promote generalized skill use in normalized environments frequented by the individual: home, school, leisure, community, and work.

QUESTIONS FOR THOUGHT AND DISCUSSION

1. Discuss the major differences between the 1992 AAMR classification system and the other systems of classification for mental retardation described in this chapter. What impact do these have for the provision of music therapy services?

2. Describe several characteristics, problems, and needs which may be common to many individuals who are mentally retarded. How do these special characteristics, problems, and needs impact the

structure or methodology of music therapy treatment approaches?

3. Describe various ways that music therapy techniques and experiences can help individuals with mental retardation improve their skills in the general areas of (1) communication skills, (2) academic, cognitive, or vocational skills, (3) motor skills, (4) social and emotional skills, (5) self-help or independent living skills, and (6) leisure skills.

Do techniques and approaches vary according to the individual's level of impairment? If so, how?

4. List several special considerations that may be important to remember when developing therapeutic intervention strategies for persons with mental retardation. Why are these important? What are their implications for the structure of music therapy intervention strategies?

5. For the situations described below, (a) define the problem or areas of need for the client or group of clients, (b) describe one or more of the goals you might pursue in music therapy sessions with the client(s), (c) describe music activities you might use to help the client(s) meet those goals, (d) tell how the music activities you described relate to the goals and needs of the client(s), and (e) mention any special considerations you might want to take into account when working with the client(s).

Situation 1:

Mark is a three-year old boy with mental retardation due to Down syndrome. Mark has been referred to you for music therapy. He can use a spoon to feed himself soft foods (although he still spills a lot) and can drink from a plastic cup without assistance. He can pull off his shirt, shoes,

and socks, but he needs help putting them back on. Mark can stand alone, but he walks with an unsteady gait. His mother says that he sometimes flaps his arms and bounces up and down to music from a radio or record as if he were dancing. Mark can imitate sounds, and he is just beginning to say "Ma" consistently. He recognizes familiar people and shows preferences for some people over others.

Situation 2:

You have been contracted to provide weekly music therapy sessions for a group of 10–12 older teenagers and young adults who have mental retardation. Most have limited perceptual motor skills, short attention spans, limited communication skills, and limited means of personal expression. Some need work on impulse control. Many have needs in the areas of increasing their awareness of and attention to people, objects, and events in their environment and/or of improving functional skills that will enable them to initiate responses and interact cooperatively and positively with others in group situations. Other programming for these individuals emphasizes functional living skills, attention span, and appropriate social behaviors.

SUGGESTIONS FOR FURTHER READING

Alvin, J. (1976). *Music for the handicapped child* (2nd ed.). London: Oxford University Press.

American Association on Mental Retardation [AAMR]. (1992). *Mental retardation: Definition, classification, and systems of support (9th ed.).* Washington, D.C.: Author.

Atterbury, B. W. (1990). *Mainstreaming exceptional learners in music.* Englewood Cliffs, NJ: Prentice-Hall.

Bailey, P. (1973). *They can make music.* London: Oxford University Press.

Beal, M. R., & Gilbert, J. P. (1982). *Music curriculum guidelines for moderately retarded adolescents.* Springfield, IL: Charles C Thomas.

Boxill, E. H. (1985). *Music therapy for the developmentally disabled.* Rockville, MD: Aspen Systems.

Boxill, E. H. (1989). *Music therapy for living: The principle of normalization embodied in music therapy.* St. Louis: MMB Music.

Carter, S. A. (1982). *Music therapy for handicapped children:*

Mentally retarded. Washington, D.C.: National Association for Music Therapy.

Cypret, D. (1975). Music with the mentally retarded. In R. M. Graham (Compiler), *Music for the exceptional child* (pp. 85-96). Reston, VA: Music Educators National Conference.

Davis, W. B. (1992). Music therapy for mentally retarded children and adults. In W. B. Davis, K. E. Gfeller, & M. H. Thaut, *An introduction to music therapy: Theory and practice* (pp. 67-92). Dubuque, IA: Wm. C. Brown.

DiGiammarino, M. (1994). Functional music leisure skills for individuals with mental retardation. *Music Therapy Perspectives, 12*(1), 15-19.

Dobbs, J. B. (1972). *Music and the slow learner* (4th ed.). London: Oxford University Press.

Farnan, L., & Johnson, F. (1988). *Everyone can move: Music and activities that promote movement and motor development.* New Berlin, WI: Jenson Publications.

Farnan, L., & Johnson, F. (1988). *Music is for everyone: A handbook for providing music to people with special needs.* New Berlin, WI: Jenson Publications.

Furman, C. E., & Furman, A. G. (1988). Music therapy research with mental retardation: Analysis and clinical implications. In C. E. Furman (Ed.), *Effectiveness of music therapy procedures: Documentation or research and clinical practice* (pp. 285-299). Washington, D. C.: National Association for Music Therapy.

Furman, C. E., & Furman, A. G. (1996). Uses of music therapy with people having mental retardation: An update of a previous analysis. In C. E. Furman (Ed.), *Effectiveness of music therapy procedures: Documentation of research and clinical practice* (2nd ed.) (pp. 279-296). Silver Spring, MD: National Association for Music Therapy.

Grant, R. E. (1989). Music therapy guidelines for developmentally disabled children. *Music Therapy Perspectives, 6,* 18-22.

Hadsell, N. A., & Coleman, K. A. (1988). Rett syndrome: A challenge for music therapists. *Music Therapy Perspectives, 5,* 52-56.

Howery, B. I. (1968). Part II. Music therapy for mentally retarded children and adults. In E. T. Gaston (Ed.) *Music in therapy* (pp. 45-95). New York: Macmillan.

Humpal, M. E. (1990). Early intervention: The implications for music therapy. *Music Therapy Perspectives, 8,* 30-35.

Krout, R. (1986). *Music therapy in special education: Developing and maintaining social skills necessary for mainstreaming.* St. Louis: MMB Music.

Lenhoff, H. M. (1998). Insights into the musical potential of cognitively impaired people diagnosed with Williams syndrome. *Music Therapy Perspectives, 16*(1), 33-36.

Madsen, C. K. (1981). *Music therapy: A behavioral guide for the mentally retarded.* Lawrence, KS: National Association for Music Therapy.

Nocera, S. D. (1979) *Reaching the special learner through music.* Morristown, NJ: Silver Burdett.

Nordoff, P., & Robbins, C. (1971). *Music therapy in special education.* New York: John Day.

Nordoff, P., & Robbins, C. (1971). *Therapy in music for handicapped children.* London: Victor Gollancz Ltd.

Nowicki, A. L., & Trevisan, L. A. (1978). *Beyond the sound: A technical and philosophical approach to music therapy* (Rev. Ed.). Porterville & Santa Barbara, CA: Nowicki/Trevisan.

Scoggins, R. T., Jr. (1975). Music at the costal center. In R. M. Graham (Compiler), *Music for the exceptional child* (pp. 99-110). Reston, Va: Music Educators National Conference.

Standley, J. (1991). *Music techniques in therapy, counseling, and special education.* St. Louis: MMB Music.

Ward, D. (1976). *Hearts and hands and voices: Music in the education of slow learners.* London: Oxford University Press.

Zinar, R. (1987). *Music activities for special children.* West Nyack, NY: Parker Publishing.

Chapter Eight

MUSIC THERAPY FOR INDIVIDUALS WHO HAVE
LEARNING DISABILITIES

DEFINITION

SOME PEOPLE display an educationally significant discrepancy between their estimated intellectual potential and their actual academic performance that cannot be explained in terms of physical, sensory, intellectual, or experiential problems. These individuals are usually classified as having some sort of learning disability. Learning disabilities are sometimes called invisible or hidden handicaps (NIMH, 1993); there are no physical signs and the people who have them usually have average or above average general intelligence. However, individuals with learning disabilities have some brain processing malfunction that negatively affects the manner in which they select, retain, or process information (Gladfelter, 1996). For example, individuals with learning disabilities may have impaired abilities to interpret what they see or hear, or they may have difficulties linking information from different parts of the brain. Learning disabilities are manifested in many different ways, as specific difficulties in written or spoken language, attention, coordination, or self-control. They often impede the individual's ability to do schoolwork or to read, write, or do math (NIMH, 1993). While attention deficit disorder (ADD) or attention-deficit-hyperactivity disorder (ADHD) may often accompany learning disorders, these disorders are not in and of themselves considered to be learning disorders (APA, 1994; NIMH, 1993). See Chapter Fourteen for information on ADD and ADHD.

The term *learning disability* or *learning disorder* is not used to describe a single condition; rather, it is a broad umbrella term used for classification purposes to cover a wide variety of specific learning problems that have in common processing or learning difficulties in some specific area while development in other areas is average or above average (APA, 1994; Atterbury, 1990; Birkenshaw-Fleming, 1993; Gfeller, 1992b; Gladfelter, 1996; Hamill et al., 1981; Mercer, 1987; NIMH, 1993; Welsbacher, 1975; Zinar, 1987). Any two individuals classified as learning disabled will likely have many differences both in the type of deficits in perceptive, integrative, or expressive processes which impair learning and in the academic areas affected. Because of the great diversity of problems that may be associated with this condition, professionals have found it difficult to develop a single, succinct definition of learning disabilities.

School settings often use the definition of learning disabilities developed by the United States Office of Education in 1977, found in Public Law 94-142 (the Education for All Handicapped Children Act):

Specific learning disability means a disorder in one or more of the basic psychological processes involved in understanding or in using language, spoken or written, which may manifest itself in an imperfect ability to listen, think, speak, read, write, spell, or to do mathematical calculations. The term includes such conditions as perceptual handicaps, brain injury, minimal brain dysfunction, dyslexia, and developmental aphasia. The term does not include children who have learning problems which are primarily the result of visual, hearing, or motor handicaps, of mental retardation, of emotional disturbance, or of environmental, cultural, or economic disadvantage. (*Federal Register*, 1977, p. 42478)

However, many professionals prefer the definition that was prepared by the National Joint Committee for Learning Disabilities in 1981, which stresses a physiological, central nervous system basis for the disability, notes the uniqueness of the manifestation in each individual, and recognizes that learning disabilities exist in individuals of all ages (Gfeller, 1992b; Mercer, 1987):

"Learning disabilities" is a generic term that refers to a heterogeneous group of disorders manifested by significant difficulties in acquisition and use of listening, speaking, reading, writing, reasoning, or mathematical abilities. The disorders are intrinsic to the individual and presumed to be due to central nervous system dysfunction. Even though a learning disability may occur concomitantly with other handicapping conditions (e.g., sensory impairments, mental retardation, social and emotional disturbance) or environmental influences (e.g., cultural differences, insufficient/inappropriate instruction, psychogenic factors), it is not the direct result of those conditions or influences. (Hamill et al., 1981, p. 336)

The American Psychiatric Association also defined learning disorders in the fourth edition of its *Diagnostic and Statistical Manual of Mental Disorders [DSM-IV]*. According to the APA (1994),

Learning Disorders are diagnosed when the individual's achievement on individually administered, standardized tests in reading, mathematics, or written expression is substantially below that expected for age, schooling, and level of intelligence. The learning problems significantly interfere with academic achievement or activities of daily living that require reading, mathematical, or writing skills. . . . If a sensory deficit is present, the learning difficulties must be in excess of those usually associated with the deficit.

Learning Disorders may persist into adulthood. (pp. 46-47).

DSM-IV provides separate codes for reading disorder, mathematics disorder, disorders of written expression, and learning disorders not otherwise specified; however, an individual may have more than one learning disorder. Learning disorders are differentiated from normal variations in academic achievement and from academic difficulties due to lack of opportunity, poor teaching, or cultural factors. The primary diagnostic criteria for learning disorders are (1) that demonstrated reading, mathematical, and/or written expression abilities are *substantially* below that expected for the individual's chronological age, measured intelligence, and age-appropriate education, (2) that these difficulties in reading, mathematical, and/or written expression abilities *significantly* interfere with areas of academic achievement or daily living requiring these abilities, and (3) that, if sensory deficits are present, the difficulties in reading, mathematical, and/or written expression abilities *exceed* those difficulties usually associated with the sensory deficit (APA, 1994).

It is important to remember that learning disabilities are disorders in psychological processing, not in general intellectual functioning, and usually affect only specific, limited areas of learning or development (APA, 1994; Atterbury, 1990; NIMH, 1993). Individuals who have a learning disability have some dysfunction in the way they learn, but their basic capacity to learn remains intact.

Various terms may be used by medical, psychological, and educational professionals to identify specific types of learning disabilities (Clayton & Morrison, 1992). For example, *developmental reading disorder* is the term used to describe a condition in which all learning skills except reading (silent and oral) develop at normal rate. *Dyslexia* is another term used to describe impairments in reading ability: Individuals with dyslexia have difficulties with spelling, reading, and writing, and may have trouble with reversals or left to right orientation. In *developmental arithmetic disorder (dyscalculia)*, all learning skills except math develop at normal rate, while in *developmental expressive writing disorder*, all learning skills except expressive writing develop at a normal rate. Other terms that may be used in the broad classification of learning disabilities include *sequencing disorder* (reversing the order of numbers and words; mix-ups happen in speech and writing), *tracking disorder* (difficulty following objects; also causes difficulty staying on same line when reading), *fine motor skills disorder* or *dysgraphia* (difficulty with writing and small muscle tasks), *auditory figure-ground* or *discrimination disorder* (difficulty separating out competing sounds), *visual figure-ground disorder* (difficulty separating out visual stimuli to attend to), *visual closure disorder* (difficulty completing incomplete visual image), *auditory closure disorder* (listener unable to hear every word said and unable to fill in gaps), *alexia* or *visual aphasia* or *word-blindness disorder* (confusion in letter recognition or symbol decoding [especially d, b and p, q] beyond normal developmental stages; involves reading of letters), *agraphia* or *dysgraphia* (confusion in letter recognition or symbol decoding [especially d, b and p, q] beyond normal developmental stages; involves writing of letters), *perseveration disorder* (difficulty stopping a task when it is completed; trouble switching from one concept or task to next), or *left to right orientation disorder* (tendency to confuse right and left).

Developmental speech and language disorders, such as *developmental articulation disorder* (difficulty in articulation skills; may substitute or omit certain speech sounds), *developmental expressive language disorder* (difficulty in oral communication; may be mute, have difficulty learning new words, have a small vocabulary, or omit, substitute, or overgeneralize words), *developmental receptive disorder* (difficulty in ability to understand others' speech), or *cluttering disorder* (speech is hurried, drops letters or syllables), are sometimes included in the classification or discussion of learning disorders (Clayton & Morrison, 1992; NIMH, 1993), as various receptive and expressive language difficulties may be related to specific neural processing problems and the resultant difficulties understanding certain aspects of speech may lead to academic difficulties. Other sources (APA, 1994; *Federal Register*, 1977) have a separate category or classification for communication disorders that includes developmental speech and language disorders. In this text, developmental speech and language disorders will be discussed separately in Chapter Twelve. As mentioned earlier, attention deficit disorder (ADD) and attention-deficit-hyperactivity disorder (ADHD), although often associated with learning disorders, are not learning disorders in and of themselves (APA, 1994; NIMH, 1993), and will be discussed separately in Chapter Fourteen of this text.

CAUSES

The exact causes of learning disabilities have not been firmly established at this time, and, since learning disabilities manifest themselves in so many different ways, they may have a variety of causes (APA, 1994; Gfeller, 1992b; Mercer, 1987; NIMH, 1993). Current theories suggest that learning disabilities are the result of neurological processing dysfunctions caused by subtle disturbances in brain structures and functions. Recent research also seems to indicate that "most learning disabilities do not stem from a single area of the brain, but from difficulties in bringing together information from various brain regions" (NIMH, 1993, p. 10). Contributing causes to these subtle disturbances in brain dysfunction may include (1) disruptions in fetal brain development occurring after the brain cells are becoming specialized and moving into place, resulting in errors in cell makeup, location, or connections; (2) genetic factors or heredity influences; (3) effects of maternal tobacco, alcohol, or other drug use during pregnancy on fetal brain development; (4) complications, trauma, or infections during pregnancy or delivery that may disrupt or alter fetal brain development; (5) environmental influences, such as toxins (e.g., cadmium and lead), allergic reactions to foods or additives, or radiation or chemotherapy treatment at an early age; and (6) acquired trauma after birth (Mercer, 1987; NIMH, 1993). Although the impact of some of these factors can be diminished through medical intervention or nutritional and environmental changes, most conditions classified as learning disabilities cannot be cured, but rather must be managed (Gfeller, 1992b; NIMH, 1993). Learning disabilities usually are not outgrown, but most people adapt to them and live fulfilling lives "not by being cured, but by developing their personal strengths" (NIMH, 1993, p. 28).

COMMON CHARACTERISTICS, PROBLEMS, AND NEEDS OF CLIENTS

As with any population, those individuals who have learning disabilities are a very heterogeneous group. Any individual client will have a unique combination of abilities, needs, personality traits, strengths, and weaknesses that will impact his or her treatment program and functioning level; therefore, it is unwise to attempt to predict a particular person's skill levels or ceiling of abilities based on broad generalizations about a certain population. Since the developmental patterns and subsequent behaviors of clients with learning disabilities are so unique to each individual, it is especially difficult to make many generalizations about this condition. In addition, learning disabilities is an umbrella term used for classification purposes to include a wide variety of specific learning problems. Each particular type of learning problem included under this general term has its own peculiar manifestations which may or may not impact other areas. However, there are some general characteristics, problems, and needs that may be found in many individuals who have some kind of learning disability, and an awareness of these may be beneficial both to the therapist who desires to work with this population and to the reader who is trying to understand how music therapy intervention strategies may benefit these individuals.

Most individuals who have learning disabilities have normal, near normal, or above average intelligence; however, they frequently have difficulty with intellectual achievement in school because of perceptual problems that make it difficult for them to select, retain, or process certain types of incoming sensory data (Atterbury, 1990; Berry & Kirk, 1980; Birkenshaw-Fleming, 1993; Clayton & Morrison, 1992; Gladfelter, 1996; Hibben, 1991; Mercer, 1987; NIMH, 1993; Zinar, 1987). These individuals often have jagged learning profiles, excelling in some areas but lagging far behind in others. Because developmental skills in reading, writing, speaking, listening, and math often overlap, individuals may also experience difficulties in more than one of these areas (NIMH, 1993).

Individuals who have learning disabilities may experience problems in (1) input (receiving information), (2) integration (processing information), and/or (3) output (expressing responses) (Atterbury, 1990). They may feel bombarded by sights and sounds, unable to focus their attention. They may try to read or add, but be unable to make sense of the letters or numbers. They may have important ideas or needs to express, but be unable to communicate them. These experiences can lead to a cycle of failure, frustration, and lowered self-esteem (NIMH, 1993), which may lead to additional social and emotional problems or maladaptive behaviors (Berry & Kirk, 1980; Mercer, 1987; Smith & Neisworth, 1975). Determining in what area or areas a particular individual's problems lie will help provide a framework for understanding that individual's particular strengths and weaknesses and suggest strategies for maximizing strengths and working around weaknesses.

The difficulties with information processing common to individuals with learning disabilities may manifest themselves in several ways (APA, 1994; Atterbury, 1990; Berry & Kirk, 1980; Birkenshaw-Fleming, 1993; Clayton & Morrison, 1992; Hibben, 1991; Mercer, 1987; NIMH, 1993; Nocera, 1979; Smith & Neisworth, 1975; Zinar, 1987). Some of the more common behaviors and characteristics associated with various types of learning disabilities include difficulties in selective attention (attending to or isolating visual and auditory information), sequencing, or symbol recognition; difficulties with spatial relationships, quantity perception, or time perception; difficulties in performing perceptual motor skills; difficulties in integrating visual and auditory input or output; difficulties in verbal expression or in understanding others; difficulties in mental organization, strategies, and pattern recognition; problems with memory or conceptual thinking; and general orientation and laterality problems. Other associated features may include hyperactivity, emotional lability, impulsivity, poor social skills, difficulty listening to others or accepting authority, difficulty helping others or cooperating with others, difficulty expressing feelings or ideas, negative self-attitude or low self-esteem, demoralization, and feelings of failure, stress, and frustration. Although it is certainly true that not all or even most of these behaviors and characteristics will be found in every individual classified as having a learning disability, it is important to recognize that any of these factors may be present and may contribute in some way to the individual's various academic or learning difficulties. Careful observation and testing are vital to determine in what areas a particular client's deficits lie, so programs of training and intervention can be matched to his or her particular needs.

Learning disabilities are usually first diagnosed during the school years, as teachers notice a child's persistent difficulties in reading, writing, or arithmetic which seem out of character for his or her level of ability and intelligence. After visual or hearing problems and inadequate instruction or opportunity are ruled out as causes for the child's difficulties, specific tests are used to pinpoint the exact nature of the individual's skill gaps. The impact of learning disabilities can be greatly reduced by appropriate educational plans and medical and psychosocial support systems (Gfeller, 1992b; NIMH, 1993). Since learning disabilities can affect the individual and his or her family in many ways, support and specific plans for controlling or working around the learning disability may be needed in educational, medical, social, emotional, and practical areas.

Although learning disabilities are usually thought of in association with children, these disorders may be found in adults, too (APA, 1994; Berman, 1982; Gfeller, 1992b; Mercer, 1987; NIMH, 1993; Schulman, 1986). Many adults who have mild forms of learning disabilities, such as mild dyslexia, have grown up without needed help. Consequently, they now may take twice as long as an average person to master certain tasks. Problems associated with learning disabilities may cause adults to have difficulties in the areas of employment, higher education, leisure activities, and social relationships (APA, 1994; Dworkis, 1994; Mercer, 1987; NIMH, 1993; Schulman, 1986). Fortunately, the existence of learning disabilities in adults is increasingly being recognized, and, once a learning disability has been diagnosed, many special aids can be used to help remediate or bypass the problem. In addition, self-help sessions specialized college programs are now available for adults with learning disabilities (Berman, 1982; NIMH, 1993; Schulman, 1986). Equal employment opportunities for individuals with learning disabilities are also mandated by the Americans with Disabilities Act of 1990, and state departments of vocational rehabilitation have many programs available to assist adults with learning disabilities in receiving training, counseling, and special equipment to help them sidestep their disability (NIMH, 1993).

Learning disabilities are not a disease, but are the result of deficits in some aspect of information processing. They may be single or overlapping; they may affect only part of a person's routine or impact several aspects of school or work, family life, or social and leisure activities. Although learning disabilities usually cannot be cured, with proper identification of problem areas, appropriately structured programs of training and education, and adequate social, emotional, medical, and practical support, their effects on a person's life can be greatly diminished. Adults as well as children can benefit from appropriate programs specially designed to help them maximize their strengths and work around their areas of weakness. Most people, given appropriate supports and opportunities, can learn to adapt and lead fulfilling and productive lives.

SETTINGS FOR SERVICE DELIVERY

Individuals who have learning disabilities may receive special programs to help meet their specific learning needs in a variety of settings (NIMH, 1993). The Individuals with Disabilities Act (IDEA) (Public Law 101-476), the 1990 revision of the 1975 Education for All Handicapped Children Act (Public Law 94-142) assures a free, appropriate public education to all children, ages 3-21, who have disabilities, including those who are diagnosed with learning disabilities. This law, as well as the

Technology-Related Assistance for Individuals with Disabilities Act (Public Law 100-407), also provide for assistive technology devices and services that may be needed by the individual (Adamek, 1996; Johnson, 1996). Special education services are delivered according to the same general procedure outlined in Chapter Seven: After initial referral, assessment, and identification of the disability, Individualized Educational Programs (IEPs) are written to guide instruction. The goals in IEPs are matched to the individual's specific strengths and weaknesses. IEPs also provide for appropriate support services in areas of need, placement in the least restrictive environment, and an annual evaluation of student progress in the program. When IEP assessments find that music therapy can provide a unique means of helping students achieve their educational objectives, music therapists may be called upon to provide traditional direct services, work with students in self-contained classes, work with students in inclusive classes, provide direct in-home services to students who are confined to their homes for medical reasons, provide consultation services to facilitate classroom instruction, inclusion, or music education, and/or provide staff development workshops (Wilson, 1996). Music therapy is usually classified as a related service in special education settings.

Students who have learning disabilities are usually included with their normal peers in a regular classroom for as much of the day as possible, attending special education classes or therapy sessions for several hours a week as needed. Students with severe learning disabilities may need instruction in separate all-day classrooms or in special schools for the learning disabled. Some parents chose to go outside the public school system, arranging for their child to work with trained tutors or therapists after school.

Programs to assist adults with learning disabilities continue to increase as the lifelong nature of most learning disabilities continues to become more evident. Colleges and universities often have special programs that may include specific testing to determine areas of need and the development of strategies to help students maximize strengths while working around their areas of deficits. Special programs and help are available in many forms, and may include alternate provisions such as providing recorded books and lectures, allowing the student to tape record rather than write reports, or allowing the student to take tests orally or in rooms free from distraction. The American Council on Education provides a national clearing house on resources for postsecondary education for people with learning disabilities (NIMH, 1993).

Individuals with learning disabilities are also served by state departments of vocational rehabilitation (NIMH, 1993). These agencies can refer adults to counseling, health care, and high school equivalence programs. They can also help individuals with learning disabilities identify their areas of aptitude and assist in arranging for job training that sidesteps the individual's disabilities. In addition, these agencies can help individuals find special equipment (e.g., a special computer that reads books aloud) that makes it possible for them to receive training, retain jobs, or live independently.

Music therapists may work with both children and adults who have learning disabilities. They deliver services to these clients in many different settings, including public schools, private schools or clinics, music studios, or community programs. Music therapists may provide direct or consultant services and work with clients as individuals or in groups. In a recent survey of populations served by music therapists (AMTA, 1998), 338 of 1,620 music therapists responding said they worked with individuals who had learning disabilities.

HOW MUSIC IS USED IN THERAPY

Since learning disabilities have so many different manifestations, music therapy intervention strategies must be structured to take into account the unique strengths, weaknesses, and needs of each client. Some approaches and techniques that are very effective with certain clients who have learning disabilities will be totally ineffective with other clients labeled as learning disabled: "There is no standard method or approach deemed effective for all students with learning disabilities" (Gfeller, 1992b, p. 201). Music therapy intervention strategies for clients with learning disabilities may incorporate strict behavioral approaches or more client-centered or developmental approaches. Experiences may include various modes of music involvement, such as singing, listening, playing instruments, moving to music, notating music, reading music, and creating music, used alone or in combination. Specific music education approaches, such as Orff-Schulwerk and Dalcroze eurhythmics, have also been adapted for use in therapy with individuals who have learning disabilities (Hibben, 1991). See Chapter Twenty-two for more information on Orff and Dalcroze approaches.

Various music therapy experiences may help individuals with learning disabilities improve their functioning in one or more of several different areas, both with regard to developing strengths and working around the weaknesses associated with their specific learning disability and with regard to associated problems such as low self-esteem, poor behavior control, poor social skills, attention deficits, poor listening skills, and low frustration tolerance. Some music experiences can provide an alternate means of receiving, processing, or rehearsing information as well as affording alternate modes of expressing responses. Music may also help an individual focus his or her attention and provide the motivation to concentrate on or practice difficult movements, exercises, or concepts. For some individuals, music may be used as part of a behavioral program employing operant conditioning procedures to provide unique rewards or reinforcements for academic learning or behavior control. In addition, the very structure of music experiences can facilitate behavior control and promote group cooperation, while success in music activities can lead to increased feelings of self-worth and self-esteem. In general, music therapy programs and intervention strategies for individuals with learning disabilities focus on one or more of the following areas (Atterbury, 1990; Birkenshaw-Fleming, 1993; Gfeller, 1984, 1992b; Gladfelter, 1996; Hanser, 1987; Hibben, 1991; Nocera, 1979; Phipps, 1975; Rink, 1989; Sandbank, 1989a; Steele, 1984; Welsbacher, 1975; Zinar, 1987): (1) developing behavior control and increasing attention span; (2) improving visual and auditory skills, including perception, discrimination, memory, sequencing, and integration; (3) improving motor control and coordination; (4) supporting academic learning; (5) improving

communication skills; (6) promoting social and emotional growth and development; and (7) supporting music education and assisting in leisure skill development.

Music Therapy Experiences Help Develop Behavior Control and Increase Attention Span

The area of behavior management often becomes a primary focus in early music therapy sessions with individuals who have learning disabilities, for behavior control is necessary in order for learning and skill development to occur. The strong attention-attracting qualities of music, combined with its order and structure and its ability to function as a powerful reinforcer (Lathom, 1981b), can make music therapy sessions an ideal setting for developing impulse control and increasing on-task behavior in clients with learning disabilities. For example, since music is often an enjoyable activity, various individual or group music experiences (e.g., listening to preferred music, taking music lessons, being able to participate in a music group) can be used within behavioral programs employing operant conditioning procedures to provide unique rewards or reinforcements for behavior control (Gfeller, 1992b). Through careful assessment, the music therapist can determine just what type of music activities or experiences are motivating or reinforcing to a particular individual, and then use these in devising a contingent music program to reinforce the desired response. It is important to specify exactly what behaviors or responses are to be reinforced, and it is also essential that the student clearly understand what specific behavior (e.g., remaining quiet until called upon in-seat behavior or both) is required to earn the music reward.

Music therapists frequently structure their treatment programs so that the difficulty level and amount of structure in the music task complements the level of attention and behavioral control expected at each stage of the music therapy process (Hibben, 1991; Steele, 1984). For example, in early stages of the program, experiences are highly structured and geared for instant success, with all decisions being made by the therapist. As they develop skills in attending and impulse control, clients are given more opportunities to work independently or with partners and to make some decisions about activities. They may also have to practice or rehearse music tasks before achieving success. In later stages, individuals are given more creative freedom in developing musical performances and may work in teams and make group decisions, with the therapist providing only indirect supervision. Thus, music experiences that are carefully structured to demand increased levels of attention and independence can help individuals learn to control and manage their own behavior by providing (1) a novel stimulus to attract attention, (2) structure and boundaries for activity, (3) reinforcement for cooperative, attentive behaviors, and (4) a pleasurable, successful experience.

As individuals learn to gain more control over impulsive behaviors, they can more readily focus on selected tasks and activities that will help them gain skills in many areas. Initially, techniques like singing instead of speaking commands, using props (puppets, pictures, hoops, scarves) to complement songs or movements, and making use of instruments like drums and metallophones may help attract the attention of individuals with learning disabilities and help them tune into the song or activity (Birkenshaw-Fleming, 1993). The music therapist starts with short experiences, gradually increasing the length of the experience as the individual's ability to attend increases. By presenting materials in a highly structured manner, with clear objectives and careful step-by-step directions, and by having different modes of sensory input and response readily available, the therapist can increase the successful participation of individuals who have learning disabilities (Atterbury, 1990; Birkenshaw-Fleming, 1993; Nocera, 1979; Zinar, 1987).

Many different types of music experiences may be used to help individuals with learning disabilities increase their attention spans. For example, music listening activities that require clients to attend to, order, and remember auditory stimuli can help develop listening skills and concentration abilities. Music therapists can help clients focus their attention by asking them to listen for specific things in songs or recordings. Initial experiences are kept very short so that they stay within the clients' limited attention spans. Later, activities are gradually lengthened as

the clients' listening and attending skills increase.

Instrumental activities that require clients to wait for their turn to play an instrument or to play only at a certain point in the song also help develop attention span. Again, the individual will be asked to wait only a short time at first, with the waiting time gradually being increased as self-control and attention span develop. For example, a client might first be asked to wait until one other person has played the drum with a song before he takes his turn. Later, that client might be asked to wait for three or four others to play before getting his turn. Or, the individual might be given the cymbal part to play in an ensemble, but have to follow a chart or conductor to play only at specified times.

Performing actions to songs can also help clients focus on activities and increase attention to a specified task. If a song has a spot for a particular loud clap or certain rhythmic pattern (e.g., hands clapping together like the snap of an alligator's jaws or the rhythmic clapping pattern of the children's song "B-I-N-G-O"), the client must also listen to others so he or she will perform the action with the rest of the group at the appropriate time. This takes self-control and attention to task, but most will recognize how much better the song sounds when everyone performs the action together. Tape recording performances may assist individuals in monitoring their performance and finding ways to improve it.

Music Therapy Experiences Improve Auditory and Visual Skills

Since music is an auditory phenomenon, it would seem natural to use music to help individuals improve their auditory perception and discrimination skills. Individuals with learning disabilities that involve deficits in auditory perception or processing need to learn what to listen for, how to listen for it, and how to attach meaning to what they hear (Phipps, 1975). Those who have difficulties with auditory memory and sequencing skills may also have problems remembering the series of tones in a melody or the sequences of words for the lyrics of the songs or be confused by the many simultaneous sounds in music (Welsbacher, 1975; Zinar, 1987). The music therapist can help the individuals with deficits in auditory perception improve their skills by using experiences that direct their attention to specific sounds or sound characteristics. Visual aids and motor activities may facilitate learning. For example, individuals might be asked to bend low when they hear low pitches and stretch high when they hear high pitches. They might also move their hands or bodies up and down to indicate the rise and fall of pitches in a familiar melody or trace the contour of a notated melody with their finger or pencil. Music therapists also use activities employing contrasts in volume, tempo, timbre, and pitch level to help clients develop auditory awareness and auditory discrimination skills. In addition, songs and musical games that associate sounds with actions, commands, or objects can be used to help clients learn to perceive and respond to auditory cues. For example, the music therapist might have clients play a game where they are asked to turn around when they hear a bell, walk when they hear a drumbeat, tiptoe when they hear a maraca, etc. Rhythm pattern echo activities are also useful in developing auditory discrimination and auditory memory, but it is important to realize that motor coordination problems may limit the ability of some individuals with learning disabilities to perform rhythmic patterns (Gilbert, 1983). Adding spoken rhythmic syllables or words to the rhythmic patterns may help some individuals with learning disabilities reproduce the rhythmic patterns more easily (Atterbury, 1983a; Zinar, 1987). In addition, singing can improve auditory awareness and enhance memory training (Gladfelter, 1996).

With regard to visual perception, it is important to remember that individuals with specific learning disabilities that result in problems in distinguishing letters and numbers may also have difficulty distinguishing musical symbols. These individuals need special instructional methods that include multisensory activities and mnemonic devices to assist them in making sense of the visual symbols (Zinar, 1987). Since learning symbols in music means not only learning a written sign but also learning to clap, sing, play, hear, and move in response to the symbol, music experiences may be particularly well-suited to the type of multisensory instruction that will assist these individuals in refining their visual perception abilities by learning through complementary aural and motor activities that increase attention and aid learning by taking advantage of

abilities they do have (Zinar, 1987). Specific techniques may include special instruction in distinguishing notes and rests using mnemonic devices or aural and movement aids, using chants when practicing writing symbols, giving aural as well as visual instructions or examples, and showing symbols in different ways (e.g., felt or plastic models that can be manipulated). As individuals learn to correctly distinguish and identify letters, numbers, notations, and other symbols within the context of music experience, they simultaneously improve their visual perception, discrimination, and memory skills (Gladfelter, 1996). Learning behaviors in music experiences that parallel skills needed in other areas may also help individuals master skills and then transfer them to other areas. For example, visual tracking skills required to read written music and then play it on a keyboard are similar to the left-to-right eye movement used in reading words. The motivation to produce music may help the individual succeed in learning this skill in a musical context, and then transfer it to the correlated reading skill (Hanser, 1987).

Music Therapy Experiences Support Academic Learning

Music therapy activities and experiences support academic learning in many ways. Various musical activities may be structured to allow individuals who have learning disabilities another means and modality in which to practice and demonstrate skills and basic cognitive concepts such as object classification, seriation, and spatial and temporal relationships (Gfeller, 1984, 1992b). For example, Roskam (1979) found that music therapy activities requiring clients to match, sort, group, reproduce, and associate pitches, loudness levels, rhythm patterns, and tone qualities, used alone and in combination with language development activities, could help children who had learning disabilities improve their skills in the areas of verbal and non-verbal auditory awareness, reading word recognition, and spelling. Musical instruments of varied shapes and sizes can also be used to provide different representations of the concepts of large/small and square/rectangle/circle/triangle, while music of different tempos can help illustrate concepts of fast and slow (Gfeller, 1992b). In addition, songs requiring clients to hold up, point to, match, or identify various shapes, colors, numbers, etc., can help clients practice these skills. Instruments or pitches on a xylophone or piano can also be given color, letter, number, or shape codes which the clients must match to a chart to play a certain tune.

Music, especially in the form of songs or rhythmic chants, can be used as a carrier of information to help individuals with learning disabilities learn and retain certain academic information like grammar rules and multiplication tables (Gfeller, 1983, 1992b; Gladfelter, 1996; Zinar, 1987). Shehan (1981) also found that the combination of auditory and visual modes enhanced short-term memory of word pairs for children who had learning disabilities. These results may indicate that music activities employing visual aids could help some individuals with learning disabilities learn to synthesize and integrate stimuli from two sensory modalities. Activities that require clients to connect visual symbols with the auditory stimulus of music have the additional benefit of giving clients opportunities to gain facility in decoding symbols and in using symbols to process information. To maximize the benefits of music as a carrier of academic information, the music therapist will (1) structure the information that is to be learned into well organized units to facilitate recall through "chunking", (2) pair the information with a familiar melody to assist memory processes and facilitate recall, and (3) use the novel presentation of information in musical jingles or rhythmic chants to increase motivation and attending (Gfeller, 1983, 1992b). It is also very important to coordinate and design plans and strategies in close consultation with the special education staff, for "a well-coordinated plan of action is an essential component of a successful special education program" (Gfeller, 1992b, p. 203).

Music experiences can also be used to reinforce academic learning and reward the completion of academic tasks. Students who have short attention spans and poor ability to concentrate and focus on tasks (Gfeller, 1992b) may be motivated to complete academic tasks accurately if this behavior is rewarded by a preferred music activity (e.g., listening to preferred music, taking music lessons, being able to participate in a music group). Through careful assessment, the music therapist can determine just what type of music activities or experiences are motivating or reinforcing to a particular individual. When using music in this way, therapists must specify exactly what responses are to be reinforced. For example, reinforcing in-seat behavior will not necessarily increase the quality of academic work. Therefore, if music is to be use to improve academic outcomes, the music reward must be linked clearly to these outcomes, and not just to good behavior (Gfeller, 1992b).

Music Therapy Experiences Improve Communication Skills

Some individuals who have learning disabilities have communication difficulties that may result from problems in understanding or processing auditory or visual information or from difficulties in oral and/or written expression. For many of these individuals, music can provide a nonthreatening or less threatening means of communication and speech and language development (Birkenshaw-Fleming, 1993; Gladfelter, 1996; Phipps, 1975; Zinar, 1987). Choruses and glee clubs can be a very valuable part of programs for individuals with learning disabilities, for singing "assists in the sequencing of verbal ideas, reinforces sight vocabulary, enhances pronunciation, modifies speech behaviors, improves auditory awareness, and involves memory training" (Gladfelter, 1996, p. 187). Songs, rhythmic chants, and musical games can all be used to help develop vocal fluidity, increase vocabulary, and improve enunciation. Learning to play simple wind instruments like recorders or harmonicas may also help individuals develop increased oral muscular coordination necessary for clear speech, while composition and improvisation experiences may help individuals gain confidence in their expressive skills. In addition, successful participation in verbal (e.g., singing, chanting, lyric writing) and nonverbal (e.g., instrumental performance or improvisation, creative movement to music) expressive experiences of music can do much to bolster self-confidence and enhance self-esteem. For more information on music therapy techniques and strategies used to develop language and communication skills, see Chapter Twelve.

Music Therapy Experiences Promote Social and Emotional Growth and Development

Researchers have found that individuals with learning disabilities often have poorer social skills than do their nondisabled peers (Gresham & Reschly, 1986). Behaviors such as not listening to others, not accepting authority, not helping or cooperating with others, not expressing feelings, or using an inappropriate tone of voice often lead to poor teacher and peer acceptance (Atterbury, 1990). A constant cycle of failure and frustration in academic work can also give individuals with learning disabilities feeling of low self-worth and low self-esteem.

Well-structured music groups can give all individuals, learning disabled and nondisabled alike, a chance to successfully participate in positive musical experiences. The focus on cognitive demands present in most classes can be replaced by direct experiences with affective material as the class becomes involved in producing and processing musical events (Atterbury, 1990). Structured music groups also create motivating environments in which individuals see appropriate behavior modeled by the therapist and learn to integrate these behaviors into their interactions with one another (Gfeller, 1992b; Gladfelter, 1996; Hibben, 1991; Steele, 1984). In addition, music therapy groups can provide a framework in which individuals can integrate abilities and skills they work on separately in other classes or therapies and give the individuals an opportunity to practice and use these skills in a normal, social setting (Sandbank, 1989a).

Various music therapy experiences incorporating listening, movement, improvisation, lyric analysis, composition, and song writing activities can be used to help individuals who have difficulty with emotional expression learn to experience and express emotions appropriately. These experiences can also be structured to afford opportunities to practice group cooperation and problem-solving skills (Gfeller, 1984, 1992b; Hibben, 1991). For example, Gladfelter (1996) used chorus and instrumental ensemble experiences to help students with learning disabilities develop social skills, learn to function successfully as part of a large group, develop poise and self-confidence, develop the skills needed to cooperate with others in producing a pleasing musical product, and increase self-esteem through successful experiences. As Nocera (1979) observed, these social and emotional benefits of music experiences can be of utmost value to individuals who have learning disabilities and even serve to enhance their success in other areas:

A good attitude, motivation, self-control, and ego strength are prerequisites to benefitting from remedial academic programs. Music can be the preliminary experience that develops these fundamental requirements for learning. (p. 239)

Music Therapy Can Support Music Education and Help Develop Leisure Skills

In public school settings, students with learning disabilities are often mainstreamed or included with their same-aged peers in regular music classes (Atterbury, 1990; Gfeller, 1992b). However, because of the processing and perceptual difficulties associated with their particular learning disability, these students may need special adaptations or compensatory teaching strategies so they can benefit from and participate successfully in music instruction or classroom music activities. Music therapists, who are trained in working with the special needs of students with specific learning disabilities as well as in music techniques, may work with music educators to help them adapt activities or instructional methods to the unique learning needs of these students (Atterbury, 1990; Birkenshaw-Fleming, 1993; Gfeller, 1992b; Gladfelter, 1996; Nocera, 1979; Phipps, 1975; Welsbacher, 1975; Zinar, 1987). For example, some students will need special aids to help them focus on the appropriate material, while others may need extra time or practice to be able to perform rhythm patterns. Those who have reading or language problems may need special adaptations when reading from songbooks or workbooks or when receiving instructions from the teacher. In some situations, students with learning disabilities may receive special instruction from music therapists to help them develop skills necessary to succeed in mainstreamed or inclusive settings (Gfeller, 1992b; Krout, 1986a).

As more and more adults are learning to play musical instruments, music therapists can also provide valuable assistance to studio teachers or music store instructors who may find themselves working with adults who have learning disabilities. Music therapists might conceivably work with college or vocational programs that serve adults with learning disabilities and develop a private practice to provide adaptive music instruction to these clients. Learning to play a musical instrument can enhance a person's self-esteem and self-confidence and also provide an enjoyable leisure activity which can be useful both for stress reduction and as a means of personal expression. In addition, developing an interest or skill in music can lead to new opportunities to interact with others through concerts, music appreciation or adult enrichment classes, community performance groups, and the like.

SPECIAL CONSIDERATIONS AND TIPS FOR SUCCESS

Individuals who have learning disabilities usually function best within an organized, structured environment. The music therapist should always remember to plan activities in such a way that distractions are minimized. Moreover, "consistency, firmness, warmth, and acceptance on the part of the teacher [or therapist] play a major role in directing successful learning experiences" (Phipps, 1975, p. 130).

Individuals who have learning disabilities will benefit most from an active music program that utilizes a multisensory approach to learning, engaging several skills and senses in the process of presenting or rehearsing any one concept (Atterbury, 1990; Birkenshaw-Fleming, 1993; Gladfelter, 1996; NIMH, 1993; Zinar, 1987). By incorporating many modes of presentation and providing for many modes of responses, the music therapist will be most likely to find ways that teach to the individual's strengths and work around his or her areas of weakness. For example, individuals with difficulties in visual perception may be encouraged to use their auditory, oral, kinesthetic or tactile abilities or modes of expression, while individual who have poor auditory memory skills might benefit from visual aids or movement cues.

When giving directions, it is important to use a few carefully chosen words and to speak in short sentences. Directions should also be concrete and specific, and care must be taken to repeat them exactly the same way each time they are given. The use of simple tactile or visual aids may help reinforce concepts. One must be extremely careful when using commercially available visual aids, however, for some music books and seemingly attractive posters or charts may contain so much information that they cause visual overload for individuals who have learning disabilities. Adaptive devices, like frames, color cues, and arrows, can be used to help clients screen out extraneous information and focus in on the information they need (Atterbury, 1983b, 1990; Birkenshaw-Fleming, 1993; Gladfelter, 1996; Nocera, 1979; Zinar, 1987). In addition, specially adapted methods of instruction may help individuals with specific learning disabilities learn music skills more easily. For example, Denckla (1990) found that an individual with dyslexia learned piano more easily if the correspondence of the "music map" to the instrument was constantly emphasized and if they proceeded directly to the auditory and kinesthetic experience without worrying about naming the notes.

It is also important to remember that, because of their perceptual difficulties, individuals who have learning disabilities often need extra time to process and respond to information. Therefore, it may be necessary to adapt imitation, echo, and call-and-response activities by adding extra beats of rest or measures of instrumental accompaniment so the clients have adequate time to process the auditory information given before they are expected to respond (Atterbury, 1986). At times, it may also be necessary to be ready to provide clients with alternative modes of response (e.g., "show me" instead of "tell me"). Furthermore, some common music activities may be too "busy" for perceptually handicapped clients who have difficulty processing auditory stimuli and attending to more than one thing at a time. In order to provide successful experiences for learning disabled clients, these activities may have to be simplified by limiting the number of accompanying rhythm patterns, or limiting the number of actions requested to be performed (Atterbury, 1990; Birkenshaw-Fleming, 1993; Nocera, 1979; Zinar, 1987). It may also be beneficial to have individuals practice movement patterns separately before applying them to instruments and to practice the subskills associated with a complex skill or movement (Gilbert, 1983; Rink, 1989). In addition, the practice of adding spoken rhythmic syllables or words to rhythmic patterns may help some individuals with learning disabilities be able to reproduce rhythmic patterns more easily (Atterbury, 1983a; Zinar, 1987). Gladfelter (1996, pp. 197-199) provides many additional practical suggestions for working in a music environment with students who have learning disabilities.

When instructing individuals who have learning disabilities, "manner of presentation is as important as content" (Gfeller, 1992b, p. 202). Therefore, music therapists must be familiar with special teaching methods designed for individuals with learning disabilities and design approaches and intervention strategies in close consultation with the special education team, taking into account the unique manifestations of a specific learning disability in the particular individual (Gfeller, 1992b; Gladfelter, 1996). It is also important for the therapist to practice good social skills and desired behaviors, such as taking care of equipment, using appropriate language, treating others with respect, obeying rules, etc., so that individuals in the group will see appropriate behavior and have a good model to imitate.

SUMMARY

When individuals display an educationally significant discrepancy between their estimated intellectual potential and their actual academic performance that cannot be explained in terms of physical, sensory, intellectual, or experiential deficits or impairments, they are classified as having some sort of learning disability. The term learning disability or learning disorder is not used to describe a single condition; rather, it is a broad umbrella term used for classification purposes to cover a wide variety of specific learning problems that have in common processing or learning difficulties in some specific area while development in other areas is average or above average. Learning disabilities are sometimes called invisible or hidden handicaps; there are no physical signs and the people who have them usually have average or above average general intelligence. Individuals who have a learning disability have some dysfunction in the *way* they learn, but their basic capacity to learn remains intact.

Individuals who have learning disabilities may experience problems in any or all of the following three areas: (1) input (receiving information), (2) integration (processing information), and (3) output (expressing responses). These difficulties can lead to a cycle of failure, frustration, and lowered self-esteem, which may lead to additional social and

emotional problems or maladaptive behaviors. Although learning disabilities are usually thought of in association with children, the various processing and behavior problems associated with learning disabilities also affect adults. Learning disabilities may be single or overlapping; they may affect only part of a person's routine or impact several aspects of school or work, family life, or social and leisure activities. Although learning disabilities usually are never cured or outgrown, most people, given appropriate supports and opportunities, can learn to adapt and lead fulfilling and productive lives. Adults as well as children can benefit from appropriate programs specially designed to help them maximize their strengths and work around their areas of weakness.

Since learning disabilities have so many different manifestations, music therapy intervention strategies must be structured to take into account the specific strengths, weaknesses, and needs of each client. Various music therapy experiences may help individuals with learning disabilities improve their functioning in one or more of several different areas, both with regard to developing strengths and working around the weaknesses associated with their specific learning disability and with regard to associated problems such as low self-esteem, poor behavior control, poor social skills, attention deficits, poor listening skills, and low frustration tolerance. In general, music therapy programs and intervention strategies for individuals with learning disabilities focus on one or more of the following areas: (1) developing behavior control and increasing attention span; (2) improving auditory and visual skills; (3) improving motor control and coordination; (4) supporting academic learning; (5) improving communication skills; (6) promoting social and emotional growth and development; and (7) supporting music education and assisting in leisure skill development. Specific examples of music therapy interventions for each of these areas were provided in this chapter.

Individuals who have learning disabilities usually function best within an organized, structured environment that has minimal distractions. They often benefit most from an active music program that utilizes a multisensory approach to learning, engaging several skills and senses in the process of presenting or rehearsing any one concept. By incorporating many modes of presentation and providing for many modes of responses, the music therapist will be most likely to find ways that teach to the individual's strengths and work around his or her areas of weakness. Music therapists who work with clients who have learning disabilities should also be familiar with special teaching methods designed for individuals with learning disabilities and should design their music therapy approaches and intervention strategies in close consultation with the special education team, taking into account the unique manifestations of a specific learning disability in the particular individual.

QUESTIONS FOR THOUGHT AND DISCUSSION

1 Discuss some of the special characteristics and needs of individuals who have learning disabilities. What implications do these have for music therapy programming?

2. Why and how are music experiences useful for helping individuals who have learning disabilities reach therapeutic goals? Are some types of experiences and activities more useful than others? Which ones? Why?

3. Describe some specific music therapy experiences that might be used to help individuals who have learning disabilities (a) develop behavior control and increase attention span; (b) improve auditory and visual skills; (c) improve motor control and coordination; (d) increase and practice academic skills; (e) improve communication skills; (f) increase social skills and enhance emotional growth and development; and (g) develop music and leisure skills. What special adaptations might you have to make in choice of music, instruments, mode of expression, etc., to fit these to the unique needs and preferences of specific clients?

4. List several special considerations that may be important to remember when developing therapeutic intervention strategies for persons who have learning disabilities. Why are these important? What are their implications for the structure of music therapy intervention strategies?

5. For each of the situations listed below, (a) define the problem or areas of need for the client or group of clients, (b) describe one or more of the goals you might pursue in music therapy sessions with the client(s), (c) describe music activities you might use to help the client(s) meet those goals, (d) tell how the music activities you described relate to the goals and needs of the client(s), and (e) mention any special considerations you might want to take into account when working with the client(s).

Situation 1:

You have been asked to begin music therapy sessions for a group of eight children, ages 9-11, who are diagnosed as having specific learning disabilities. These children are easily distracted and have short attention spans. They have trouble organizing auditory perceptions due to poor auditory discrimination, memory, and sequencing skills. They also have a poor sense of spatial orientation and find it difficult to use symbols to process information.

Situation 2:

A 32-year-old man with dyslexia, poor concentration, and poor spatial awareness, and poor motor coordination has come to you inquiring about piano lessons. He says he has always wanted to learn to play the piano, but never thought he could because of his learning problems. He recently heard that music therapists know how to teach music to people with special needs, and he wants to know if you could help him, too.

SUGGESTIONS FOR FURTHER READING

Atterbury, B. W. (1990). *Mainstreaming exceptional learners in music.* Englewood Cliffs, NJ: Prentice-Hall.

Bernstorf, E. D., & Welsbacher, B. T. (1996). Helping students in the inclusive classroom. *Music Educators Journal, 82*(5), 21-29.

Birkenshaw-Fleming, L. (1993). *Music for all: Teaching music to people with special needs.* Toronto: Gordon V. Thompson.

Bruscia, K. E. (Ed.) (1991). *Case studies in music therapy.* Phoenixville, PA: Barcelona Publishers.

Gfeller, K. E. (1984). Prominent theories in learning disabilities and implications for music therapy methodology. *Music Therapy Perspectives, 2*(1), 9-13.

Gfeller, K. (1992). Music therapy in the treatment of learning disabilities. In W. B. Davis, K. E. Gfeller, & M. H. Thaut, *An introduction to music therapy: Theory and practice* (pp. 197-208). Dubuque, IA: Wm. C. Brown.

Gladfelter, N. D. (1996). Music therapy for learners with learning disabilities in a private day school. In B. L. Wilson (Ed.), *Models of music therapy interventions in school settings: From institution to inclusion* (pp. 184-199). Silver Spring, MD: National Association for Music Therapy.

National Institute of Mental Health [NIMH]. (1993). *Learning disabilities.* Washington, D.C.: U.S. Government Printing Office.

Nocera, S. D. (1979). *Reaching the special learner through music.* Morristown, NJ: Silver Burdett.

Phipps, M. F. (1975). Music education for learning disabilities. In R. M. Graham (Compiler), *Music for the exceptional child* (pp. 130-135). Reston, VA: Music Educators National Conference.

Rejto, A. (1973). Music as an aid in the remediation of learning disabilities. *Journal of Learning Disabilities, 6*(3) 286-195.

Standley, J. (1991). *Music techniques in therapy, counseling, and special education.* St. Louis: MMB Music.

Zinar, R. (1987). *Music activities for special children.* West Nyack, NY: Parker Publishing.

Chapter Nine

MUSIC THERAPY FOR INDIVIDUALS WHO HAVE HEARING IMPAIRMENTS

DEFINITIONS

HEARING IMPAIRMENT is a general or generic term that includes all the different types and severities of hearing losses. Individuals of whatever age who are deaf, deafened, hard-of-hearing, or partially hearing are all included in this population. People who are *deaf* have hearing impairments so severe that they cannot understand or process speech through their auditory sense, even with the assistance of hearing aids or fine amplification systems. For deaf individuals, the sense of hearing is nonfunctional for the ordinary purposes and activities of daily life; sounds, including speech, have no meaning or function for their day-to-day activities. For these individuals, sounds are not processed auditorily but experienced as vibrations perceived tactilely by the skin and felt in the bones and body cavities (Kapla, 1975; Zinar, 1987). When individuals acquire this degree of severe hearing impairment after they have acquired speech, they may be classified as *deafened* rather than deaf.

People are said to be *hard-of-hearing* or *partially hearing* when they have some degree of hearing loss but still have enough functional hearing to understand speech and process language through their auditory sense, with or without the aid of amplification systems. Although these individuals have some defect in their sense of hearing, they can still get enough functional meaning from sounds that they can use their auditory sense for ordinary life purposes and activities. Usually, these individuals use some type of hearing aid.

Classification of Hearing Loss

Hearing losses may range in degree and severity from very slight to very extreme. Generally, the more severe the hearing impairment, the greater impact it will have on the development of language and other communication skills (Gfeller, 1992d). However, total deafness is very rare. By most estimates, at least 90% of individuals who have hearing impairments have some sensitivity to sound and some degree of usable or residual hearing (Boothroyd, 1980; Gfeller, 1992d; Matthias, 1989; Zinar, 1987).

Hearing impairments are generally classified by degree of decibel (dB) loss as *slight* (27-40 dB loss), *mild* (41-55 dB loss), *moderate* (56-70 dB loss), *severe* (71-90 dB loss), or *profound* (greater than 90 dB loss) (Darrow & Gfeller, 1988, 1996; Darrow & Schunk, 1996; Gfeller, 1992d; Smith & Neisworth, 1975). The amount of hearing loss greatly influences the individual's ability to participate in conversation and develop or maintain language and communication skills (Darrow & Gfeller, 1988, 1996; Darrow & Schunk, 1996; Gfeller, 1992d; Lovejoy & Estridge, 1987; Zinar, 1987). For example, individuals with *mild* hearing losses can usually still understand normal conversational speech at a distance of three to five feet; however, they may miss as much as half of the conversation if they are not able to see the speaker or if the speaker's voice is soft. Individuals with mild hearing losses may also have some speech abnormalities or a limited vocabulary. While individuals who have mild losses usually only have

113

problems hearing faint or distant speech, those who have *moderate* losses often have difficulty understanding even loud speech. Individuals with moderate hearing losses also frequently wear hearing aids and are likely to have some difficulties in speech and in participating in group discussions. Individuals who have *severe* hearing losses can only hear loud speech that is within one foot of ears and usually have marked deficits in speech and language abilities. However, these individuals can still distinguish pitch, intensity, and tone color in music if the sounds are louder than 70 to 85 dB. In contrast, those persons who have *profound* hearing losses tend to be aware of vibrations more than tonal patterns and rely on vision rather than hearing as their primary means of communication.

Hearing losses may also be classified by time of onset. If an individual's hearing loss is present at birth, he or she has a *congenital* hearing loss. If the hearing loss occurs after birth, it is called an *adventitious* or *acquired* hearing loss. In addition, the relationship of the onset of hearing loss to the individual's stage of language development may be considered. If the hearing loss occurs before the individual acquires or develops speech and language skills, it is called a *prelingual* hearing loss. Hearing losses that occur after the individual acquires language are termed *postlingual* hearing losses. Generally, an individual will have greater speech and language deficits with a prelingual hearing loss than with a postlingual loss (Gfeller, 1992d).

Types of Hearing Loss

There are two main dimensions to the sense of hearing: (1) the loudness with which the sound is received, measured in dB, and (2) the clarity with which the sound is received, which is related to frequency perception and is measured in cycles per second, or Hertz (Hz). Hearing ability may be impaired along either or both of these dimensions. In the process of hearing, sound waves travel from a sound source to the listener, where they are collected by the outer ear and travel through the ear canal to the ear drum or tympanic *membrane*. The sound waves cause the tympanic membrane to vibrate and transmit the sound energy to the three small bones (*ossicles*) of the middle ear. These bones (hammer or

malleus, anvil or *incus*, and stirrup or *stapes*) carry the sound waves to the inner ear (*cochlea*), where delicate hair cells receive sensory information on the pitch or frequency and loudness or magnitude of the sound signal. The auditory nerve then carries this information to the brain, where the signals are processed and interpreted. When any part of this process is disrupted or malfunctions, some degree of hearing loss or impairment results. The term *hearing impairment* usually implies that the hearing problem is permanent, while the term *hearing loss* is a general term that may describe either a temporary or permanent condition (Lovejoy & Estridge, 1987). Depending upon which part or parts of the auditory system are affected, hearing losses may be fall into one of four categories: conductive, sensorineural, mixed, or central (Atterbury, 1990; Darrow & Gfeller, 1988, 1996; Gfeller, 1992d; Lovejoy & Estridge, 1987). Hearing losses in any of these categories may be partial or total. Severity of impairment and possibilities for remediation vary with the type and extent of the loss.

A *conductive hearing loss* occurs when there is some disease, malformation, or obstruction in the outer or middle ear that interferes with the travel of sound waves. This type of loss affects the loudness or magnitude of the sound signal reaching the inner ear and usually results in a mild to moderately severe hearing loss across all frequencies. Sometimes these losses respond to medical treatment to remove the obstruction, clear up the infection, or correct the malformation. If medical treatment is not an option, conductive hearing losses usually can be at least partially corrected by the use of hearing aids or other amplification systems.

A *sensorineural hearing loss* is caused by damage to the nerve fibers in the inner ear or by damage to the auditory nerve. Because of this damage, hearing may be faulty or nonexistent at certain frequencies. Missing frequencies cause certain words that have consonant or vowel sounds at these frequencies or other environmental sounds that contain these frequencies to be unclear or distorted. Sensorineural losses may be slight or extreme. Persons with these losses may have difficulties with high frequencies, low frequencies, or various frequencies throughout the spectrum. These types of losses are generally more severe and difficult to treat, since the inner ear and auditory nerve are less accessible and more delicate than the outer and middle ear structures. Ordinary hearing aids may be of little help in sensorineural losses, for ordinary hearing aids amplify all frequencies, not just the problem frequencies.

A *mixed hearing loss* occurs when there is some degree of defect or damage both to the outer or middle ear structures *and* to the inner ear or auditory nerve. The extent to which hearing aids or medical procedures will improve hearing in mixed losses varies from one individual to another, depending on the type and extent of the losses.

A *central hearing loss* occurs when there is damage to the brain or central nervous system. In these losses, sound waves are transmitted clearly and at adequate volume through all the ear structures; however, the individual has difficulty interpreting, understanding, or recognizing the sound because of damage or defects in some portion of his or her auditory processing centers. See Chapter Eighteen for more information on music therapy and traumatic brain injury.

CAUSES

Hearing losses may be caused by a variety of biological or environmental factors. Hearing losses that are present at birth can be caused by genetic abnormalities, viral disease or infection in the mother during pregnancy, drug or alcohol abuse by the mother during pregnancy, congenital malformations, lack of oxygen during birth, exposure to radiation or certain medication during pregnancy, severe injury or trauma during pregnancy or birth, or severe newborn jaundice due to problems like Rh incompatibility. After birth, things like serious viral infections, middle ear inflammations, accumulation of wax or fluid in the ear, foreign objects in the ear, injury or trauma, or prolonged exposure to loud noises can precipitate hearing impairments. In about half the cases of hearing loss, the exact cause is unknown (Lovejoy & Estridge, 1987).

Conductive hearing losses are most often due to infections or disease that produce middle ear inflammation or to injury or trauma from accidents or from foreign objects being inserted into the ear. Certain birth defects, such as the malformations associated with cleft lip and cleft palate that hinder the eustachian tube's ability to equalize of middle ear pressure, can also cause conductive losses (Atterbury, 1990; Lovejoy & Estridge, 1987). As many as half of all congenital sensorineural hearing losses are caused by inherited structural defects in the auditory mechanism (Lovejoy & Estridge, 1987). Other congenital causes of sensorineural losses include trauma or lack of oxygen during birth, infection in the mother during pregnancy, or drug or alcohol abuse by the mother during pregnancy. After birth,

sensorineural hearing losses may be caused by severe viral infections and injury or trauma. In addition, prolonged exposure to loud sounds, either in the environment or through headphones, is an increasingly common cause of temporary and permanent sensorineural hearing deficits (Brody, 1982; Jaret, 1991; Lovejoy & Estridge, 1987). *Presbycusis*, the gradual loss of hearing associated with the aging process, may also result in sensorineural impairments caused by deterioration of hair cells at the base of the cochlea (high frequency receptors) and degeneration of neural pathways leading from the cochlea to the cortex (Miller, 1983). Mixed hearing losses are often the result of genetic factors; they may also result from trauma, injury, or infection. Central hearing losses are most often caused by traumatic brain injuries, strokes, or brain tumors.

Estimates of the number of individuals with hearing impairments in this country range from 16 million to 22 million (Darrow & Gfeller, 1996; Matthias, 1989). According to Lovejoy and Estridge (1987), approximately one-half of one percent of the population have some sort of permanent hearing loss, and four of every five people who have a hearing impairment have problems in both ears. Conductive hearing losses are more common than sensorineural hearing losses. About 40% of individuals with hearing impairments have a mild impairment, about 20% have moderate impairments, about 20% have severe impairments, and the remaining 20% have profound impairments (Lovejoy & Estridge, 1987).

COMMON CHARACTERISTICS, PROBLEMS, AND NEEDS OF CLIENTS

As with any population, those individuals who have hearing impairments are a very heterogeneous group. Any individual client will have a unique combination of abilities, needs, personality traits, strengths, and weaknesses that will impact his or her treatment program and functioning level; therefore, it is unwise to attempt to predict a particular person's skill levels or ceiling of abilities based on broad generalizations about a certain population. However, an awareness of some of those characteristics, problems, and needs which may be common to many clients who are diagnosed with hearing impairments will be beneficial both to the therapist who desires to work with this population and to the reader who is trying to understand how music therapy intervention strategies may benefit these individuals.

Depending on the type, severity, and onset of their hearing loss, individuals who have hearing impairments have various degrees of difficulty in (a) perceiving, understanding, and interpreting speech or environmental sounds, (b) producing intelligible speech, (c) developing language skills, and (d) interacting with others in social situations. Since most individuals who have hearing impairments must live and function within a hearing society, two of their biggest needs are: (1) to learn to use whatever residual hearing they have to perceive, discriminate, and interpret sounds; and (2) to find ways to communicate with hearing individuals. Consequently, rehabilitative and educational programs for individuals with hearing impairment often stress auditory training, speech and language development, and development of skills and strategies for communication and socialization with others (Darrow, 1985; Darrow & Gfeller, 1988, 1996; Darrow & Schunk, 1996; Gfeller, 1992d; Gfeller & Bauman, 1988).

Those individuals who have early onset severe hearing problems usually need intensive training to develop speech and language skills, since they do not hear well enough to benefit from everyday language models and develop speech and language skills on their own. Generally, the greater the hearing loss, the more difficulty an individual will have with speech and language (Gfeller & Bauman, 1988). However, even individuals who have severe hearing losses can develop some speech skills, but they need intensive therapeutic training to develop proper speech rhythms, infections, and enunciations.

Because they acquire language skills at a slower rate than the average person and because poor language skills also affect performance on reading and in written tasks, individuals who have hearing impairments often lag behind their hearing peers in academic achievement. In addition, individuals who are deaf or hard-of-hearing may experience much frustration because they lack verbal skills to express their thoughts, wants, and needs. They often have a very literal interpretation of vocabulary and poor skills in grammar and syntax. Due to the great effort they must expend to discriminate and interpret auditory stimuli, individuals who have hearing impairments often have short attention spans and especially experience difficulty in concentrating on auditory activities. Because of their difficulties in communicating with others, individuals who are deaf or hard-of-hearing may also have poor social skills.

When individuals acquire hearing losses as adults, they often retain enough speech and language skills to be understood by others and can develop some ability to compensate for their hearing losses by using hearing aids and other assistive devices. For these individuals, the main problems associated with their acquired hearing losses involve (1) increasing social isolation because of difficulty hearing conversations or hearing television and radio and (2) vocational disabilities when job skills, such as the ability to use a telephone, hear instructions, or hear sounds important to work performance, are affected by the hearing loss (Gfeller, 1992d). Persons who acquire hearing losses as adults, especially in their elderly years, may need the support of family and friends to help them admit their loss and motivate or encourage them to seek out and utilize assistive devices and strategies to help them maintain their abilities to communicate and socialize (Miller, 1983).

Hearing Aids and Assistive Devices

Individuals who have hearing losses may use hearing aids or other assistive devices to enhance their residual hearing capacities (Atterbury, 1990; Boothroyd, 1980; Matthias, 1989). These devices also help individuals with hearing impairments become more aware of sounds and more perceptive of auditory cues. In addition, amplification of auditory stimuli can help individuals with moderate and severe hearing losses become more aware of their own voice. Thus, hearing aids can be important for sound and speech production as well as for speech and sound comprehension.

There are different hearing aids for different types and severities of hearing losses. Many individuals who have hearing impairments wear personal ear-level aids, which may be fitted behind or in the ear. Others use portable FM systems that include two units: The person speaking to the individual wears a unit containing a microphone and transmitter, while the individual with the hearing impairment wears a unit containing a receiver and hearing aid. Advances in technology are also giving rise to innovations such as "smart" hearing aids that help filter out background noise and cochlear implants, devices that act like an electronic inner ear to pick up sound waves and then stimulate the auditory nerve (Atterbury, 1990; Zinar, 1987). In addition, individuals with hearing impairments may use special devices that replace the usual auditory medium with visual communication, such as Teletype telephones [Telecommunications Device for the Deaf or TDD], decoders for close-captioned television programming, or flashing lights for telephone or doorbell rings (Lovejoy & Estridge, 1987; Matthias, 1989).

Alternative Communication Methods

Some sort of communication aid or alternative method of communication is essential to most individuals who have permanent hearing losses. These individuals may use one or more of a variety of methods to communicate among themselves and with the hearing world (Atterbury, 1990; Darrow & Gfeller, 1988, 1996; Darrow & Schunk, 1996; Gfeller, 1992d; Lovejoy & Estridge, 1987; Matthias, 1989).

The type of method used may vary with the degree of hearing impairment and the social or educational situation.

Individuals with less severe hearing losses can often communicate by speaking and can usually understand the speech of others by using a combination of assistance from a hearing aid, speech reading (looking carefully at the speaker's lips, body, and facial expression as well as environmental cues to pick up the basic thought of the speaker's message), and careful listening. People who emphasize the use of speech and speech reading together with amplification of residual hearing as the exclusive means of communication for individuals with hearing impairments believe in an *oral communication* philosophy.

Many individuals with more severe hearing losses, especially those whose hearing impairment had an early onset, need alternative methods to enable them to communicate to the fullest extent possible (Darrow & Gfeller, 1988, 1996; Darrow & Schunk, 1996; Gfeller, 1992d; Matthias, 1989). *Cued speech* is a method used to supplement speech reading that uses different hand shapes or movements shown at a specific place on the face to visually represent the sounds or pronunciations of the syllables being spoken. *Fingerspelling* uses a system of hand shapes and positions to represent the letters of the written alphabet. People who use fingerspelling to communicate spell out their messages letter by letter. The Rochester Method of communication uses fingerspelling in combination with spoken English as the primary mode of communication (Darrow & Gfeller, 1988).

Systems of *sign-supported speech* or *manual communication* use various combinations of hand positions and gestures, along with fingerspelling, both to send and receive messages (expressive and receptive communication). Some of these systems, such as Signed English, Signing Exact English, Seeing Essential English, and Linguistics of Visual English, follow the grammar and syntax of spoken English. American Sign Language (ASL), however, is a manually produced language that has its own syntax and grammar, which is very different from spoken English (Darrow & Gfeller, 1988, 1996; Darrow & Schunk, 1996; Gfeller, 1992d; Matthias, 1989). ASL is used by many members of the deaf community in the United States and Canada. When children with profound hearing impairments establish ASL as their first language, English is learned as a second language (Matthias, 1989).

Total communication involves the use of speech, speech reading, residual hearing, one or more forms of manual communication, and written language. These various modes of communication may be used simultaneously or chosen selectively depending on the specific situation. In the total communication philosophy, all methods that help the individual with hearing impairments acquire or understand language are used and accepted (Darrow & Gfeller, 1988, 1996; Darrow & Schunk, 1996; Gfeller, 1992d; Matthias, 1989).

Some individuals who have hearing impairments may use other alternative devices for communication, including pointing to pictures, letters, numbers, or words on specially constructed *communication boards* or using *electronic speech devices* that mechanically "speak" the words typed in by the user (Lovejoy & Estridge, 1987). More information on these devices is given in Chapter Twelve of this text.

Historically, there has been much disagreement both among educators of individuals with hearing impairments and among members of the deaf community as to which of the various systems of communication mentioned above is most beneficial. Currently, however, many experts believe that most individuals benefit from a combination of approaches (Lovejoy & Estridge, 1987). "There is increasing consensus that whatever system or method works most successfully for the individual should be used to allow the hearing-impaired person access to clear and understandable communication" (Darrow & Gfeller, 1988, p. 140).

Deaf Culture

Gfeller (1992d) noted that those who work with

persons who have significant hearing losses must also be aware of Deaf culture. When capitalized, the term *Deaf* refers primarily to an individual's affiliation with the Deaf community, a cultural alignment based not only on severity of hearing loss but also on social attitude. Individuals who are Deaf in their cultural orientation usually use American Sign Language as their primary system of communication and may seek out activities and organizations where they can socialize with other deaf people (Gfeller, 1992d). Music does have a limited role in Deaf culture, although some members of the Deaf community consider music to be of little or no importance (Darrow, 1993). "Before initiating any significant rehabilitative program with deaf children, it would be advisable to learn more about Deaf culture in order to interact appropriately and sensitively" (Gfeller, 1992d, p. 223).

People who align themselves with the Deaf community may include those who have congenital hearing losses, those who have one or more parents and/or grandparents who are deaf, and those who acquired hearing losses early in childhood and attended residential schools for the deaf (Gfeller, 1992d). On the other hand, some individuals with severe hearing impairments, especially those who acquired their losses well into adulthood or those who were raised by hearing parents and exposed primarily to an oral approach to communication, may not consider themselves to be part of the Deaf community (Gfeller, 1992d; Matthias, 1989). The degree to which an individual identifies with Deaf or hearing culture also influences that individual's perception of the role and importance. In a study by Darrow (1993), the majority of subjects who primarily identified with Deaf culture ranked music as of little or no importance, while the majority of those who identified with hearing culture considered music to be very important.

SETTINGS FOR SERVICE DELIVERY

Individuals who have hearing impairments may receive special programs to help meet their specific learning needs in a variety of settings, depending on the type, severity, and onset of their loss. Audiologists can help determine the degree and extent of the

hearing loss and suggest appropriate amplification devices or acoustical measures that will best make use of residual hearing. Speech and language pathologists and teachers specially trained to work with individuals who have hearing impairments often assist these individuals in developing communication skills, either in private clinics, public schools, or special schools and residential programs for the deaf and hearing impaired (see Chapter Twelve).

The Individuals with Disabilities Act (IDEA) (Public Law 101-476), the 1990 revision of the 1975 Education for All Handicapped Children Act (Public Law 94-142) assures a free, appropriate public education to all children, ages 3-21, who have disabilities, including those with hearing impairments. This law and the Technology-Related Assistance for Individuals with Disabilities Act (Public Law 100-407) also provide for assistive technology devices and services that may be needed by the individual (Adamek, 1996; Johnson, 1996). Incentives for early intervention programs to address the needs children birth through age 2 who have handicaps or disabilities are provided by Public Law 99-457 of 1986 (Adamek, 1996; Humpal, 1990). Special education services for students who are deaf or hard-of-hearing are delivered according to the same general procedure outlined in Chapter Seven. After initial referral, assessment and identification of the disability, Individualized Educational Programs (IEPs) are written to guide instruction. IEPs set educational and habilitative goals that reflect the individual's specific strengths and weaknesses. IEPs provide for appropriate support services in areas of need, placement in the least restrictive environment, and an annual evaluation of student progress in the program. The student is usually included with peers in a regular classroom for as much of the day as possible. When the IEP assessment finds that music therapy can provide a unique means of helping students achieve their educational objectives, music therapists may be called upon to provide traditional direct services, work with students in self-contained classes, work with students in inclusive classes, provide direct in-home services to students who are confined to their homes for medical reasons, provide consultation services to facilitate classroom instruction, inclusion, or music education, and/or provide staff development workshops (Wilson, 1996). Music therapy is usually classified as a related service in special education settings.

Those individuals who acquire hearing losses later in life may also benefit from the services of audiologists and speech and language pathologists to help them learn to adjust to their hearing aids and/or to develop effective compensatory strategies to help maintain their abilities to communicate and socialize with their peers and families. Associations for the deaf or hearing impaired may also provide valuable information on assistive communication devices or sources for assistive devices to aid in performing vocational tasks or in perceiving environmental sound cues associated with activities of daily living (e.g., flashing light instead of ring for telephone).

Music therapists may work with both children and adults who have varying degrees and types of hearing impairments. They deliver services to these clients in many different settings, including public schools, private schools or clinics, music studios, nursing homes, rehabilitation centers, or community programs. Music therapists may provide direct or consultant services and work with clients as individuals or in groups. In a recent survey of populations served by music therapists (AMTA, 1998), 299 of 1,620 music therapists responding said they worked with individuals who were hearing impaired.

HOW MUSIC IS USED IN THERAPY

Many researchers, therapists, and educators have found that music experiences and activities can be perceived and enjoyed by people who have hearing impairments, especially when accommodations are made for their auditory limitations and the auditory input is supplemented by vibrotactile and/or visual input (Bang, 1980; Buechler, 1982; Darrow, 1985, 1989, 1992; Darrow & Gfeller, 1988, 1991, 1996; Darrow & Goll, 1989; Darrow & Heller, 1985; Darrow & Schunk, 1996; Edwards, 1975; Ford, 1988; Gfeller, 1992d; Humpal & Dimmick, 1995; Kapla, 1975; Robbins & Robbins, 1980; Solomon, 1980). As with individuals who have normal hearing, individuals who have hearing impairments vary in their degrees of inborn musicality or musical aptitude (Robbins & Robbins, 1980). However, although hearing impairment may delay the development of musical skills and abilities, it does not necessarily preclude or impair their development (Darrow, 1987a).

Because music has a much wider range and variety of frequencies and a greater intensity, music is generally more accessible to individuals who have hearing impairments than are the sounds of speech (Darrow, 1989, 1991; Robbins & Robbins, 1980). Although individuals who have hearing impairments may be more attuned and sensitive to the rhythmic and vibrational aspects of the music stimuli and be inclined to process auditory stimuli through their tactile sense (Darrow, 1987a; Darrow & Goll, 1989), it is important not to limit their experience to feeling the vibrations of music (Ford, 1988). Tonal aspects of music, as well as experiences in singing, moving, listening, and playing instruments, can also be used successfully with and have potential benefits for individuals with hearing impairments (Buechler, 1982; Darrow, 1985, 1991; Darrow & Gfeller, 1991, 1996; Edwards, 1975; Ford, 1988; Robbins & Robbins, 1980; Sheldon, 1997).

Since the nineteenth century, music has been used in various ways as part of special education, training programs, or therapy for individuals who have hearing impairments (Darrow & Heller, 1985; Solomon, 1980). Today, music therapy strategies continue to benefit people who have hearing impairments, assisting in the areas of (1) assessment of auditory functioning, (2) auditory training, (3) speech production, (4) language development, and (5) social skill development (Buechler, 1982; Darrow, 1989; Darrow & Gfeller, 1988, 1996; Darrow & Schunk, 1996; Gfeller, 1992d; Michel, 1985; Robbins & Robbins, 1980). Working with speech pathologists, audiologists, and language specialists, music therapists bring an additional avenue for motivation and reinforcement of shared goal areas for clients who have hearing impairments, as they strive "to find unique and exciting ways to use music as a tool to teach speech, language, and listening skills" (Darrow, 1989, p. 65).

Music to Help Assess Auditory Functioning

As has been mentioned earlier, total hearing loss is rare. Most individuals with hearing impairments possess some degree of residual hearing. Since music has a much wider range of frequencies than speech,

musical auditory stimulation may often be more accessible than speech sounds for individuals who have hearing impairments (Darrow, 1989, 1991; Michel, 1985; Robbins & Robbins, 1980; Zinar, 1987). Therefore, music experiences may be very useful in helping to diagnose what frequency ranges are most impaired in a particular individual's hearing loss and what areas or ranges of functional hearing the individual might still possess (Michel, 1985; Robbins & Robbins, 1980). For example, Robbins and Robbins (1980) have devised a hearing perception test in which clients' responses to auditory stimuli from a drum and piano are used to give a fairly reliable estimate of functional hearing ability. May (1961) has also found that loud, low piano tones can help stimulate the residual hearing of deaf children. As they carefully note clients' responses to various ranges and timbres of musical sounds, music therapists can provide audiologists, speech-language pathologists, and other professionals with much information that will be useful in determining what residual hearing individuals possess and what types of sounds might be used to stimulate and develop their residual hearing potential.

Specially structured music activities may also be used to help individuals who may be difficult to test prepare for audiological screenings. For example, Heyer, Downs, Kalloy, and Magdinec (1986) found that music therapists could use group sessions with a piano to condition many previously untestable subjects to respond successfully to pure-tone hearing screenings by an audiologist. By working in conjunction with audiologists, music therapists can develop protocols for those hard-to-test individuals who need prior conditioning to the tones and tasks in order to be measured by audiological screenings. These protocols then could be carried out effectively and efficiently in groups by the music therapists, freeing audiologists to devote more of their time to the actual screenings (Heyer et al., 1986).

Music Therapy Strategies to Assist in Auditory Training

Auditory training programs help individuals with hearing impairments learn to make maximum use of any residual hearing they have, thus increasing their ability to become aware of, attend to, understand,

and interpret speech and environmental sounds (Darrow, 1989; Darrow & Gfeller, 1988, 1996; Darrow & Schunk, 1996; Gfeller, 1992d). Since the perception, interpretation, and performance of sound are common to both speech and music, and since the perception of music and speech involves the discrimination of many similar characteristics (e.g., sound/silence, pitch, duration, rhythm, loudness or intensity, sound quality or timbre), music activities and experiences can be a valuable supplement to auditory training programs, helping to motivate the use of residual hearing and offering another way to practice listening skills (Bang, 1980; Buechler, 1982; Darrow, 1989, 1991; Darrow & Gfeller, 1988, 1996; Darrow & Schunk, 1996; Gfeller, 1992d; Kapla, 1975; Michel, 1985; Robbins & Robbins, 1980). In addition, music activities frequently increase attention to the task while decreasing some of the tedium and boredom often associated with repeated drill and practice (Darrow, 1991).

Auditory training programs give individuals who have hearing impairments specific training and practice in developing listening skills, beginning with simple reflexive and alerting responses to sound and moving from gross discriminations to increasingly more subtle tasks. The ultimate goal is comprehension of speech to the maximum extent possible. Objectives in auditory training programs include (1) increasing attention to sound and the ability to detect the presence or absence of sound, (2) increasing ability to discriminate sounds as same or different, (3) increasing ability to recognize and identify sounds, and (4) increasing ability to understand or comprehend sounds (Darrow, 1989; Darrow & Gfeller, 1988, 1996; Darrow & Schunk, 1996). By working with audiologists and speech-language pathologists, music therapists can determine which objectives are most appropriate for individual clients. Using their knowledge of the frequency ranges, timbre characteristics, and vibrotactile qualities of various instruments and musical sound sources, music therapists then can devise specific music therapy interventions that will complement auditory training programs and motivate clients to use and develop their residual hearing abilities.

Music experiences are often very useful in the early stages of auditory training exercises, for musical sounds have a wider range of frequencies (pitches)

and intensities (loudness) than do speech sounds (Darrow, 1989; Gfeller, 1992d; Robbins & Robbins, 1980). In addition, the vibrations of music have a tactile as well as an auditory component. Even clients with severe or profound hearing impairments still may be able to perceive the vibrational patterns of music through their tactile sense. Kapla (1975) recommended that auditory training programs for the hearing impaired should use musical instruments to help the clients learn to distinguish vibrations and sensations in their environment. In this type of program, clients first would be asked to sit near a piano or bass xylophone and touch the instrument directly to feel its vibrations. When the vibrations stopped, clients were to indicate this by word or gesture. Gradually, clients would be asked to tell when vibrations stopped and started with fewer and fewer direct visual and tactile cues. Kapla also reported that clients could learn to distinguish the high and low tones of different instruments by relating vibrations to different body locations. "High tones are felt in the head cavity, medium tones in the chest, and low tones in the stomach, feet, and legs" (p. 63).

Similar structured experiences in sound awareness and detection using drums, bass tone bars, pianos, xylophones, and other musical instruments with vibrating surfaces that are easily felt are described by Bang (1980), Gfeller (1992d), and Robbins and Robbins (1980). String instruments, such as the violin, that provide vibratory as well as auditory feedback, may also be useful for auditory training (Darrow, 1991). In addition, enhancing the vibrotactile stimulation of sound sources by placing sound speakers near the individual (Buechler, 1982) or by using specially manufactured platform mattresses (Darrow, 1992; Darrow & Goll, 1989) may help individuals who have hearing impairments learn to perceive sound and distinguish various sound characteristics.

Tactile stimulation from the patterned vibrations of music can also provide cues that increase clients' ability to discriminate and reproduce rhythm patterns and to perceive pitch changes (Darrow, 1992; Darrow & Goll, 1989; Kapla, 1975; Korduba, 1975). The vibrotactile stimuli readily available from many musical sound sources can enhance auditory training experiences greatly by providing individuals who have hearing impairments with additional sensory input that is complementary or redundant to the information they can receive auditorily. "This additional support increases the amount of available information and solidifies existing concepts" (Darrow & Goll, 1989, p. 123). Korduba (1975) found that deaf third-grade students could listen to rhythms presented on a bass drum and then reproduce these rhythms on a snare drum significantly better than third-grade students with normal hearing could. Buechler (1982) hypothesized that "it is very possible that the vibrations coming from the drum provided additional tactile cues to those students who, because of their deafness, had become more receptive to tactile stimuli" (p. 13).

In summary, then, music activities used in auditory training programs usually require individuals (a) to move or signify by gestures when sounds start or stop; (b) to show differentiated responses to auditory stimuli with different levels of loudness, tempi, pitch, durations, timbres, or rhythms; (c) to show recognition or identification of specified sounds, instrument timbres, words, or phrases; or (d) to locate sound sources or follow moving sound sources (Bang, 1980; Buechler, 1982; Darrow, 1989; Darrow & Gfeller, 1988, 1996; Darrow & Schunk, 1996; Gfeller, 1992d; Kapla, 1975; Robbins & Robbins, 1980). Generally, initial activities require clients to respond to very gross distinctions, with finer and finer discriminations being required as the clients develop their ability to use their residual hearing. Buechler (1982), Darrow (1989), Darrow and Gfeller (1988, 1996), and Robbins and Robbins (1980) give several examples of specific music therapy objectives and activities that may be used to complement auditory training programs for individuals who have hearing impairments. Darrow (1989) and Darrow and Gfeller (1988, 1996) also provide information on assessments and hierarchies for auditory processing that will assist the music therapist in planning appropriate interventions for clients who have hearing impairments.

Music Therapy Strategies to Improve and Reinforce Speech Production

Individuals who have normal hearing learn to speak by hearing others speak and trying to imitate those sounds. They then receive the auditory feedback of hearing their own voices, which enables them to make adjustments in their pronunciation, inflection, or speech rhythm as necessary to better match the model. Individuals who have hearing impairments hear only distorted or partial speech models and receive distorted auditory feedback from their own speech production. Therefore, they often have some degree of speech impairment and need special intensive speech training to help them learn to use their voices and speak clearly and at a proper pitch level and with appropriate speech rhythm and inflection (Darrow, 1989; Darrow & Gfeller, 1988, 1996; Darrow & Schunk, 1996; Gfeller, 1992d). Since music and speech have many common elements, such as intonation and inflection, tempo and rate, accent and stress, and rhythm, music activities often can be very useful in encouraging vocalization and in improving and reinforcing various aspects of speech production with individuals who have hearing impairments (Bang, 1980; Buechler, 1982; Darrow, 1989, 1990; Darrow & Cohen, 1991; Darrow & Gfeller, 1988, 1996; Darrow & Schunk, 1996; Darrow & Starmer, 1986; Edwards, 1975; Gfeller, 1992d; Robbins & Robbins, 1980; Staum, 1987; Zinar, 1987). Although music therapists usually are not trained as speech therapists, music therapists can work with speech therapists to identity a client's particular areas of need for speech production and then develop specially structured music activities and experiences that will promote development in those areas and complement and reinforce the work of the speech therapists. Common treatment objectives in the area of speech production for individuals with hearing impairments include: (1) increasing free vocalization and improving vocal imitation skills; (2) increasing awareness of rhythmic patterns and improving ability to speak with natural speech rate and rhythms; (3) increasing awareness of pitch movement and improving vocal intonation and inflection, (4) increasing awareness of vocal dynamics and phrasing, (5) increasing speech fluency, (6) improving vocal quality, and (7) improving articulation skills and speech intelligibility (Bang, 1980; Buechler, 1982; Darrow, 1989; Darrow & Gfeller, 1988, 1996; Darrow & Schunk, 1996; Edwards, 1975; Gfeller, 1992d; Robbins & Robbins, 1980; Staum, 1987).

Many types of music experiences can be used to stimulate vocalization, encourage vocal play, and increase vocal awareness. Bang (1980) has found that specially constructed large wooden and metal tone resonator bars (frequency range of 64-380 Hz) are very useful in increasing sound and pitch perception and in eliciting vocal production in individuals who have hearing impairments. Others have used vocal play exercises that include the tactile perception of laryngeal vibrations to stimulate initial vocalizations in individuals who are deaf or hard-of-hearing (Buechler, 1982; Darrow & Gfeller, 1988, 1996; Robbins & Robbins, 1980). In this technique, the client touches the therapist's throat and feels the laryngeal vibrations as the therapist vocalizes, singing tones or short phrases or playfully laughing. Then, the client's hand is placed on his or her own throat and he or she is encouraged to vocalize in imitation of the therapist. When the client feels the vibrations of his or her own larynx, awareness of his or her own vocalization efforts are reinforced.

Clients who do not vocalize in imitation of the therapist may begin to vocalize when they try to produce a sound on a reed horn (Robbins & Robbins, 1980). Amplification or electronic devices that provide both tactile and visual stimulation can also encourage and cue vocal production, provide feedback to help increase awareness of vocalizations, and facilitate improvement of vocal accuracy (Buechler, 1982; Darrow & Cohen, 1991; Robbins & Robbins, 1980). In addition, some clients who have hearing impairments may find auditory stimuli more accessible and perform better on vocal reproduction tasks when a 10-band graphic equalizer is used to adjust the stimuli to accommodate the individual subject's audiogram (Darrow, 1990). Once clients have learned to vocalize freely and spontaneously, music therapists can refine skills by gradually adding more structure to vocal play exercises, using longer vocal phrases and encouraging more exact imitation.

Rhythmic programs have been an important part of speech development programs for individuals who are deaf or hearing impaired throughout the history of deaf education in this country (Darrow & Heller, 1985; Solomon, 1980). Music experiences that include rhythmic movement, rhythmic use of musical instruments, or rhythmic speech and chanting all can help increase clients' abilities to perceive rhythm patterns aurally and then reproduce them. It is possible that the visual and tactile cues received from the vibrations of instruments, movements used, or rhythmic notation, provide additional sensory input that helps individuals with hearing impairments increase their awareness of sensitivity to the rhythmic components of speech. For example, when clients who have hearing impairments use their entire body for rhythmic expression in movement-to-music activities, they often achieve a better understanding of and a refined ability to reproduce speech rhythms (Darrow, 1985; Robbins & Robbins, 1980). Some therapists and educators have found that experiences incorporating Dalcroze eurhythmics and Orff-Schulwerk techniques, with their inherent visual, imitative, and rhythmic aspects, can be used very successfully with clients who have hearing impairments (Darrow, 1985; Darrow & Gfeller, 1991; Swaiko, 1974). Speech rhythms, inflections, and patterns also can be played and experienced on percussion instruments, helping clients become more aware of and better able to produce those patterns (Bang, 1980; Buechler, 1982; Gfeller, 1992d; Robbins & Robbins, 1980). In addition, music notation can be used as a cue to represent the duration and rhythm of words and syllables, helping clients improve their awareness of speech rhythms and increase their ability to speak with natural rhythms and inflections (Staum, 1987).

Since the prosodic features of speech include many melodic elements (rhythm, intonation, rate, and stress), group and individual singing experiences, vocal exercises, and private vocal instruction can all be structured to help individuals who have hearing impairments improve their vocal intonation, inflection, pitch, volume, and quality (Darrow, 1989; Darrow & Cohen, 1991; Darrow & Starmer, 1986; Edwards, 1975; Gfeller, 1992d; Robbins & Robbins, 1980; Staum, 1987). Instrumental, movement, or vocal exercises that help clients develop proper breath support and breathing techniques may also have positive effects on clients' vocal quality and speech volume. In addition, various music activities, such as song practice using targeted words or sounds, can help clients improve or practice articulation skills (Darrow, 1989).

Many more examples of specific music therapy objectives and interventions that may be used to help individuals who have hearing impairments develop and improve various aspects of their speech production are given by Buechler (1982), Darrow (1989), Darrow and Gfeller (1988, 1996), Edwards (1975), and Robbins and Robbins (1980). Darrow

(1989) and Darrow and Gfeller (1988, 1996) also provide information on specific assessment procedures that will assist the music therapist in determining clients' particular abilities and needs in area of speech production. Additional music therapy strategies for developing speech skills are also discussed in Chapter Twelve of this text, which provides a more detailed discussion of the use of music therapy to help remediate various types of speech and language disorders.

Music Therapy Strategies to Improve and Reinforce Language Development

Individuals who have serious hearing losses often lag behind their peers in language development, for they do not have the regular exposure to everyday conversational models of language, syntax, and vocabulary from which individuals who have normal hearing learn many words and rules of language (Darrow, 1989; Darrow & Gfeller, 1988, 1996; Darrow & Schunk, 1996; Gfeller & Bauman, 1988; Gfeller, 1992d). Therefore, individuals who have hearing impairments usually need special training and intervention to help them develop and practice language skills, in whatever methods of oral and/or manual communication they choose to use. Usually, individuals who have more severe hearing losses have greater difficulty in the area of language skills (Gfeller & Bauman, 1988). Poor language skills manifest themselves in problems with vocabulary, complex sentence structure, and multiple meanings of words. Delayed development of language skills also adversely affects performance in both reading and writing, which can seriously hamper academic development. In addition, poor ability to use language to communicate with others or to receive information from others diminishes opportunities for spontaneous interactions with others, thus hampering social and emotional development (Darrow & Gfeller, 1988, 1996; Darrow & Schunk, 1996).

Music experiences, with their ability to be structured to promote small group socialization, communication, and interaction, and with their ability to provide opportunities for using written, spoken, and/or signed language in singing, song signing, and song writing activities, can provide many motivating and enjoyable opportunities for developing and practicing receptive and expressive language skills in safe, structured, socially appropriate environments (Darrow, 1987a, 1989; Darrow & Gfeller, 1988, 1996; Darrow & Schunk, 1996; Galloway & Bean, 1974; Gfeller, 1987b, 1990; Gfeller & Bauman, 1988; Knapp, 1980; Prueter & Giles, 1981; Swaiko, 1974; Warner, 1981). According to Darrow (1989), music therapists most often work with the language components of syntax and semantics, while focusing on the development of both receptive and expressive language skills. In addition, some music therapy experiences may ask clients to use various reading and writing skills. After consulting with the speech/language pathologist to help determine the individual's specific needs, current level of functioning, and best methods for language remediation, the music therapist also assesses the individual's interests and level of functioning in areas specific to the music therapy context to help determine what types of music therapy experiences might best complement the individual's language development program (Darrow & Gfeller, 1988, 1996). More specific information on assessment procedures for various components of language development is given by Darrow (1989), Darrow and Gfeller (1988, 1996), and Gfeller and Bauman (1988). For maximum facilitation of language development, music therapists should also be familiar with and at least somewhat conversant in the client's primary method of communication (speech, signing system, etc.).

Typically, language development goals in music therapy for individuals with hearing impairments focus on one or more of the following areas: (1) increasing vocabulary (including both knowledge of word meaning and appropriate use of words); (2) increasing spontaneous, topic-related interaction within a group by increasing ability to understand and functionally use rules and behaviors that affect group communication; and (3) increasing complexity and completeness of sentences used (Darrow, 1989; Darrow & Gfeller, 1988, 1996; Darrow & Schunk, 1996; Gfeller, 1992d; Gfeller & Bauman, 1988). Music therapists structure music therapy interventions and sessions to continually encourage and reinforce interaction and communication, modeling appropriate uses of language and providing opportunities for clients to (a) participate in spontaneous and solicited dialogue, (b) practice using selected vocabulary words, (c) construct and interpret sentences, and (d) practice using appropriate grammar and syntax (Darrow, 1989; Darrow & Gfeller, 1988, 1996; Darrow & Schunk, 1996). As these skills are practiced within the context of carefully structured music experiences, they will be reinforced and refined so they can be transferred to other settings.

Many different types of music experiences can be structured to help encourage and reinforce various aspects of language development for individuals who have hearing impairments. For example, action songs and movement-to-music experiences can be used to introduce words and have clients experience and demonstrate word meanings (Galloway & Bean, 1974; Gfeller, 1990), while eurhythmics programs can facilitate the development of total communication skills and enhance emotional expression (Swaiko, 1974). Targeted vocabulary words can also be included in specially designed song lyrics. Individuals can practice the words and become more proficient in their chosen mode of communication (spoken language or sign language) as they sing or sign the lyrics. In addition, they can demonstrate word comprehension by holding up or pointing to appropriate pictures, graphics, or word cards at appropriate places in the song or by following directions contained in the song lyrics (Darrow, 1989; Darrow & Gfeller, 1988, 1996; Darrow & Schunk, 1996; Gfeller, 1990, 1992d; Gfeller & Bauman, 1988; Prueter & Giles, 1981; Warner, 1981). Additional opportunities to learn and practice oral and/or manual language skills occur within the context of music therapy sessions as clients request preferred activities, respond to questions, discuss song lyrics, participate in performance groups (e.g., choirs that combine sign and song), or communicate with others in group movement or instrumental activities (Darrow, 1987a, 1989; Darrow & Gfeller, 1988, 1996; Darrow & Schunk, 1996; Gfeller, 1990, 1992d; Gfeller & Bauman, 1988; Knapp, 1980; Prueter & Giles, 1981; Warner, 1981).

Song-writing activities can also provide many unique and motivating opportunities for clients with hearing impairments to develop vocabulary, practice sentence construction and use of correct grammar and syntax, practice reading and writing skills, and use expressive language skills (Darrow, 1989; Darrow & Gfeller, 1988, 1996; Darrow & Schunk, 1996; Gfeller, 1987b, 1992d; Gfeller & Bauman, 1988). Song-writing can increase motivation and attention by providing a novel teaching method, while the lyrics and music provide a focus for thematic discussion and a structure for teaching listening, speaking, reading, and writing skills (Gfeller, 1987b). Song-writing experiences may be as simple as having the client provide one word to complete a lyric phrase or as involved as writing original lyrics for an entire song. Discussion of song lyrics, composition techniques, or group processes provide additional opportunities for increasing spontaneous, topic-related interactions.

Additional examples of specific music therapy objectives and interventions for language development with individuals who have hearing impairments can be found in Darrow (1989), Darrow and Gfeller (1988, 1996), Gfeller (1990), Gfeller and Bauman (1988), and Robbins and Robbins (1980). General music therapy strategies for developing language and communication skills are also discussed in Chapter Twelve of this text.

Music Therapy Strategies to Improve and Reinforce Social Skills

Since many of our everyday interactions with others involve communicating through the exchange of auditory information, "hearing impairment acts as a barrier to social contact" (Zinar, 1987, p. 123). Because of their distorted or absent perceptions of certain speech or environmental sounds, individuals who have hearing impairments find it difficult if not impossible to participate in incidental conversations or everyday social exchanges with others. Poor hearing and limited speech and language skills may also hamper their ability to understand instructions, ask questions, or express ideas and concerns. Moreover, individuals who have hearing impairments may have difficulty joining in many recreational, social, and leisure time activities, unless special efforts are made to include them and find ways for them to communicate and participate with others. Thus, hearing impairments can impede the development of many basic social skills, including the abilities to attend to others, share, take turns, follow directions, work cooperatively with others, and express feelings in socially acceptable ways. If individuals who have hearing impairments do not learn constructive and appropriate ways of interacting with others, they may experience social isolation and exhibit various social adjustment problems, such as immature behavior, poor emotional control, tantrums, withdrawal, inflexibility, egocentricity, or depression (Gfeller, 1992d; Zinar, 1987). Since many music experiences involve cooperative group activity and since music can often be perceived tactilely and visually as well as auditorily, music can be a useful tool for helping clients who have hearing impairments learn and practice many different levels and types of social skills, improving their ability to interact both with other individuals who have hearing impairments and with persons who have normal hearing (Bang, 1980; Buechler, 1982; Darrow, 1985, 1987a; Darrow & Gfeller, 1991; "Deaf People," 1980; Donnelly, 1991; Edwards, 1975; Folts, 1977; Gfeller, 1987b; 1992d; Michel, 1985; Robbins & Robbins, 1980; Standley, 1991a; Thomas, 1976; Zinar, 1987).

At a most basic level, an awareness of music's vibrations or the gratification experienced from playing musical instruments can lead an individual to increase his or her attention to and interaction with others. For example, once a individual becomes aware of and intrigued with the sounds or vibrations made by rhythm instruments, rhythm instruments may be used as part of a contingency system to reward and increase attention to a designated task or person (Michel, 1985) or as a means of interacting with others in structured or improvisatory duet or small ensemble experiences (Bang, 1980; Buechler, 1982; Donnelly, 1991; Robbins & Robbins, 1980; Standley, 1991a; Thomas, 1976; Zinar, 1987). In addition, dance and rhythmic movement activities can help individuals with hearing impairments improve their rhythmic perception and grace and confidence in movement while giving them opportunities to interact with others and develop social skills (Birkenshaw-Fleming, 1993; Michel, 1985; Robbins & Robbins, 1980; Swaiko, 1974; Thomas, 1976; Zinar, 1987). Structuring activities and choosing materials so that tactile or visual cues and stimulation supplement auditory input will facilitate the involvement and participation of clients who have hearing impairments. Group song-writing or lyric discussion experiences, using topics such as friendship or cooperation, can also be used to explore and develop

social skills (Gfeller, 1987b).

With special methods of instruction, even individuals who have severe hearing losses can learn to play band and orchestral instruments and participate successfully in instrumental ensembles, bands, and orchestras ("Deaf People," 1980; Edwards, 1975; Folts, 1977; Robbins & Robbins, 1980; Sheldon, 1997; Zinar, 1987). These ensemble performance experiences, as well as those involving percussion ensembles (Donnelly, 1991), musical plays (Robbins & Robbins, 1980), or song-signing and total communication choirs (Darrow, 1987a; Darrow & Gfeller, 1988, 1996; Knapp, 1980; Standley, 1991a; Zinar, 1987), can do much to increase clients' skills in working cooperatively with others. In addition, clients' self-esteem increases as they work hard to learn their parts, perform successfully, and have their accomplishment acknowledged and appreciated by others. Readers desiring more information on instrumental instruction and ensemble work with individuals who have hearing impairments are encouraged to consult Edwards (1975) and Robbins and Robbins (1980).

Since group music experiences are a normal part of human behavior and are commonly used by people in all parts of society in both formal and informal interactions (see Chapter Five), group music experiences can be used very effectively as part of mainstreaming or inclusion approaches to facilitate interaction between individuals who have hearing impairments and those with normal hearing. For example, traditional music play activities can provide a unique environment to motivate positive interactions between preschoolers with and without handicaps or disabilities (Hughes et al., 1990). Since over half of all children with hearing impairments who attend public schools attend regular music classes (Darrow & Gfeller, 1991), music education settings frequently provide opportunities for integrating children who have hearing impairments with their normal hearing peers (Atterbury, 1990; Birkenshaw-Fleming, 1993; Darrow, 1985; Darrow & Gfeller, 1991; Humpal & Dimmick, 1995; Knapp, 1980). By using their residual hearing, most individuals with hearing impairments can participate with their peers who have normal hearing in all the traditional music education experiences of singing, playing, listening, moving, and creating, especially when appropriate instructional techniques and beneficial adaptations are used (Darrow, 1985; see also "Special Considerations" section below). Generally, children with hearing impairments succeed better in movement-to-music and instrumental activities than in listening or composition activities (Darrow & Gfeller, 1991). Orff, Kodaly, and Dalcroze techniques, with their strong visual, imitative, and rhythmic components, also facilitate successful participation by and inclusion of students who are deaf or hard-of-hearing (Darrow, 1985; Darrow & Gfeller, 1991; Swaiko, 1974). In addition, song-signing experiences, either within the music classroom or as part of a formal performing organization, can provide many unique and valuable opportunities for "cross-cultural exchange" between students who have hearing impairments and those with normal hearing (Darrow, 1987a; Knapp, 1980; Standley, 1991a). Moreover, for some individuals who have hearing impairments, music experiences can provide important and unique avenues for personal achievement and increased self-esteem as well as many opportunities for enjoyable leisure time activities (Darrow & Heller, 1985; Donnelly, 1991; Gfeller, 1992d; Robbins & Robbins, 1980).

SPECIAL CONSIDERATIONS AND TIPS FOR SUCCESS

It is imperative that music therapists who work with clients who have hearing impairments consult and cooperate with the clients' speech/language pathologists and audiologists and learn to communicate in the clients' preferred mode of communication or have a qualified interpreter (Darrow, 1989; Darrow & Gfeller, 1988, 1996; Darrow & Schunk, 1996; Gfeller, 1990, 1992d; Gfeller & Bauman, 1988; Robbins & Robbins, 1980). Music therapists who want to initiate rehabilitative programs with persons who align themselves with the Deaf community are also advised "to learn more about Deaf culture in order to interact appropriately and sensitively" (Gfeller, 1992d, p. 223). Those who work with groups where individuals use both speech or speech reading and sign language must remember to talk and sign at the same time (Knapp, 1980). When planning intervention strategies and selecting music materials, music therapists must also take into account the clients' language and communication abilities and/or deficits as well as their limited hearing abilities, modifying the language level of activities as needed (Darrow, 1989; Gfeller, 1992d). By making judicious use of visual aids, tactile or visual cues, vibrotactile stimulation, movement activities, and multisensory or multimodal presentation techniques to support and emphasize auditory information, music therapists can both facilitate the clients' participation and help them better understand the concepts or skills that are being presented (Atterbury, 1990; Birkenshaw-Fleming, 1993; Darrow & Gfeller, 1988, 1991; Ford, 1988; Gfeller, 1992d; Robbins & Robbins, 1980; Zinar, 1987). Approaches and techniques such as Orff, Kodaly, and Dalcroze that utilize strong visual, imitative, and rhythmic components, have been found to be extremely useful and effective with individuals who have hearing impairments (Darrow, 1985; Darrow & Gfeller, 1991; Swaiko, 1974).

When using musical instruments with individuals who have hearing impairments, it is important to consider how the acoustical properties of the instrument (frequency range, loudness, resonance) correspond to the hearing abilities of the client who will play it (Edwards, 1975; Robbins & Robbins, 1980). For example, a client with no hearing in the upper frequencies would probably have a much more enjoyable musical experience playing a bass metallophone than playing a triangle. Since individuals with hearing impairments already have limited sound perception abilities, it is especially important to use musical instruments with the best sound quality possible (Robbins & Robbins, 1980). Instruments that have a low frequency range or large vibrotactile surfaces, as well as those that have physical appeal or those that provide greater degrees of supplementary vibratory feedback, are usually most successful (Bang, 1980; Buechler, 1982; Darrow, 1991; Darrow & Gfeller, 1991; Edwards, 1975; Robbins & Robbins, 1980). Several electronic, special amplification, and computerized devices, such as electronic instruments with built-in speakers or headphones, video learning screens or computer programs that give visual representations of sounds, or electronic pick-ups and amplifiers that can enhance the sound of acoustic instruments, may also be useful in working with clients who have hearing impairments (Birkenshaw-Fleming, 1993; Buechler, 1982).

Vocal work with individuals who have hearing impairments can sometimes be facilitated by special amplification devices, microphone headsets, computer programs, or electronic devices that give visual or tactile feedback about an individual's vocalization (Buechler, 1982; Darrow & Cohen, 1991). Kodaly hand signals can also help provide supplementary visual and kinesthetic feedback (Darrow & Cohen, 1991; Darrow & Gfeller, 1991). In addition, songs may be more accessible to individuals with hearing impairments if slightly lower keys or a range of the B below middle C to a twelfth above is used (Birkenshaw-Fleming, 1993; Ford, 1988).

Music experiences will also be more accessible to individuals who have hearing impairments when the room is arranged so that they can sit very close to the sound sources. A very high-quality sound system is also desirable. Some clients will also benefit when auditory signals are adjusted with graphic equalizers (Darrow, 1990) or when recordings that are specially arranged and acoustically mixed for easier perception by the hearing impaired are used (Market Space, 1987). In addition, music therapists should eliminate or minimize extraneous environmental sounds (e.g., buzzing lights, noise of heater or fan or air conditioner, outdoor traffic) as much as possible, using room fixtures such as draperies, carpeting, and upholstery to absorb unnecessary noise (Darrow & Schunk, 1996).

When working with clients who wear hearing aids, music therapists should understand how the hearing aids work and how they may most effectively be used in the music setting (Atterbury, 1990; Robbins & Robbins, 1980). For example, in group activities, clients who wear hearing aids "should be positioned with their hearing aids toward the group" (Darrow & Schunk, 1996, p. 209). It is also important to remember that hearing aids amplify all sounds, not just those sounds to which the clients wish to attend. Most hearing aids also have an automatic gain cutoff at the pain threshold. This may cause problems if the clients are asked to play or are seated near very loud instruments, such as drums or cymbals. Every time the drum or cymbal is struck loudly, the intensity of the sound will trigger the hearing aid's automatic cutoff mechanism and cause the aid to shut off momentarily. Because of this, the clients will perceive a series of clicks or gaps in the music.

Finally, as more and more people fall victim to noise-induced hearing damage, music therapists may consider being advocates for hearing health and the prevention of hearing impairments. Exposure to loud noises in the workplace has long been recognized as a contributing factor to hearing loss; however, permanent hearing damage can also come from prolonged exposure to loud music or noise from many other common sound sources, including powerful speakers at concerts, personal stereo headphones, customized car stereos, and television sets (Brody, 1982; Lovejoy & Estridge, 1987; Jaret, 1991). People who live or work along busy flight paths or next to busy train tracks may also suffer noise-related damage. In addition to damaging hearing acuity, noisy environments may increase stress levels, irritability, and fatigue, and possibly contribute to increased blood pressure, cardiovascular injury, ulcers, accidents, and reduced work efficiency (Jaret, 1991). High environmental noise levels may also disrupt sensory and motor skill development in infants and toddlers (Jaret, 1991). Thus, by alerting people to the dangers associated with prolonged exposure to loud sounds or noisy environments, music therapists might do much to improve the general health and well-being of the population at large as well as helping to prevent noise-induced hearing losses.

SUMMARY

Hearing impairment is a broad, general term that includes all the different types and severities of hearing losses. Persons who are deaf, deafened, hard-of-hearing, or partially hearing are all part of the population of individuals who have hearing impairments. Hearing losses may be classified by *severity* (slight to profound, depending on degree of decibel loss), *time of onset* (congenital or adventitious, prelingual or postlingual), and *type* (conductive, sensorineural, mixed, or central). Generally, individuals who have hearing losses that are more severe or have early onsets will have greater speech and language deficits.

Total deafness is very rare; the vast majority of individuals who have hearing impairments have some sensitivity to sound and some degree of residual hearing. Various types of hearing aids and amplification systems are often used to enhance whatever residual hearing individuals may have, helping them become more aware of sounds and assisting them in perceiving auditory cues. Many individuals who have permanent hearing losses may also use one or more of a variety of alternative communication methods, such as speech reading, cued speech, fingerspelling, or some system of manual communication, to help them communicate with each other or with the hearing world. Rehabilitative and educational programs for individuals with hearing impairments often stress auditory training, speech and language development, and development of skills and strategies for communication and socialization with others.

Since there are many similarities between the way speech and music are structured and perceived and since many music activities inherently promote socialization and group cooperation, specially structured music experiences can greatly enhance education and therapy programs for individuals who have hearing impairments, assisting in the areas of (1) assessment of auditory functioning, (2) auditory training, (3) speech production, (4) language development, and (5) social skill development. Music, with its wider range and variety of frequencies and intensities, may often be more accessible to individuals who have hearing impairments than speech sound would be. Researchers, therapists, and educators have found that music activities involving experiences in singing, moving, listening, and playing instruments can all be perceived and enjoyed by people who have hearing impairments, especially when accommodations are made for their auditory limitations and the auditory input is supplemented by vibrotactile and/or visual input. When specially structured to reinforce rehabilitative or educational goals, these different types of music experiences can also have many potential therapeutic benefits. Working with speech pathologists, audiologists, and language specialists, music therapists bring an additional avenue for motivation and reinforcement of shared goal areas for clients who have hearing impairments, devising unique and enjoyable therapeutic intervention strategies based on the use of music as a tool to help teach and reinforce speech, language, listening, and social skills.

QUESTIONS FOR THOUGHT AND DISCUSSION

1. Briefly describe the different classifications and types of hearing loss. Discuss some impacts each might have on an individual's speech, language, and social skills. Also speculate on different adjustments or accommodations that might have to be made for different severities and types of hearing losses in the music setting, e.g., how might they impact choice of materials and experiences, instructional approaches, etc.?

2. Discuss some of the special characteristics and needs of individuals who have hearing impairments. What implications do these have for music therapy programming?

3. Why and how are music experiences useful in making contact with individuals who have hearing impairments? Are some types of experiences and activities more useful than other? Which ones? Why?

4. Describe some specific music therapy experiences that might be useful in (1) assessing auditory functioning, (2) assisting with auditory training, (3) improving speech production, (4) promoting language development, and (5) improving social skills. What unique benefits does music provide in each of these areas?

5. List several special considerations that may be important to remember when developing therapeutic intervention strategies for persons who have hearing impairments. Why are these important? What are their implications for the structure of music therapy intervention strategies?

6. For each of the situations listed below, (a) define the problem or areas of need for the client or group of clients, (b) describe one or more of the goals you might pursue in music therapy sessions with the client(s), (c) describe music activities you might use to help the client(s) meet those goals, (d) tell how the music activities you described relate to the goals and needs of the client(s), and (e) mention any special considerations you might want to take into account when working with the client(s).

Situation 1:

A group of six children, ages 7-8, has been referred to you for music therapy services. All of the children have moderate to severe hearing loss and wear hearing aids. Most can understand speech that is clear, loud, and distinct. These children make some speech sounds, but they have problems enunciating words clearly and have poor speech rhythm and inflection. Other problems include a limited ability to localize sounds and extreme frustration because of their lack of verbal skills with which to express their thoughts, wants, and feelings to the hearing people around them.

Situation 2:

You are working at a community center that offers special programs for individuals who are deaf or hard-of-hearing as well as programs for the general public. The manager of the center is looking for some experiences that will integrate these two groups, and is asking you for ideas.

SUGGESTIONS FOR FURTHER READING

Atterbury, B. W. (1990). *Mainstreaming exceptional learners in music.* Englewood Cliffs, NJ: Prentice-Hall.

Birkenshaw-Fleming, L. (1993). *Music for all: Teaching music to people with special needs.* Toronto: Gordon V. Thompson.

Bruscia, K. E. (Ed.) (1991). *Case studies in music therapy.* Phoenixville, PA: Barcelona Publishers.

Buechler, J. (1982). *Music therapy for handicapped children: Hearing impaired.* Washington, D.C.: National Association for Music Therapy.

Darrow, A. A. (1987). Exploring the arts of sign and song. *Music Educators Journal, 74*(1), 32-35.

Darrow, A. A. (1989). Music therapy in the treatment of the hearing impaired. *Music Therapy Perspectives, 6,* 61-70.

Darrow, A. A. (1993). The role of music in deaf culture: Implications for music educators. *Journal of Research in Music Education, 41*(2), 93-110.

Darrow, A. A., & Gfeller, K. E. (1988). Music therapy with hearing-impaired children. In C. E. Furman (Ed.), *Effectiveness of music therapy procedures: Documentation of research and clinical practice* (pp. 137-174). Washington, D. C.: National Association for Music Therapy.

Darrow, A. A., & Gfeller, K. E. (1996). Music therapy with children who are deaf and hard-of-hearing. In C. E. Furman (Ed.), *Effectiveness of music therapy procedures: Documentation of research and clinical practice* (2nd ed.) (pp. 230-266). Silver Spring, MD: National Association for Music Therapy. [Note: Pages 248-264 contain an annotated bibliography of research on music with individuals who are deaf or hard-of-hearing.]

Darrow, A. A., & Schunk, H. A. (1996). Music therapy for learners who are deaf/hard-of-hearing. In B. L. Wilson (Ed.), *Models of music therapy interventions in school settings: From institution to inclusion* (pp. 200-223). Silver Spring, MD: National Association for Music Therapy.

Edwards, E. M. (1975). Music and the hearing impaired. In R. M. Graham (Compiler), *Music for the exceptional child* (pp. 48-60). Reston, VA: Music Educators National Conference.

Gfeller, K. (1990). A cognitive-linguistic approach to language development for the preschool child with hearing impairment: Implications for music therapy practice. *Music Therapy Perspectives, 8,* 47-51.

Gfeller, K. (1992). Music therapy in the treatment of sensory disorders. In W. B. Davis, K. E. Gfeller, & M. H. Thaut, *An introduction to music therapy: Theory and practice* (pp. 209-233). Dubuque, IA: Wm. C. Brown.

Gfeller, K., & Bauman, A. A. (1988). Assessment procedures for music therapy with hearing impaired children: language development. *Journal of Music Therapy, 25*(4), 192-205.

Kapla, P. S. (1975). Music and the hearing handicapped child. In R. M. Graham (Compiler), *Music for the exceptional child* (pp. 61-71). Reston, VA: Music Educators National Conference.

Robbins, C., & Robbins, C. (1980). *Music for the hearing impaired and other special groups: A resource manual and curriculum guide.* St. Louis: Magnamusic-Baton.

Spicknall, H. W. (1968). Music for deaf and hard-of-hearing children in public schools. In E. T. Gaston (Ed.), *Music in therapy* (pp. 314-316). New York: Macmillan.

Standley, J. (1991). *Music techniques in therapy, counseling, and special education.* St. Louis: MMB Music.

Zinar, R. (1987). *Music activities for special children.* West Nyack, NY: Parker Publishing.

Chapter Ten

MUSIC THERAPY FOR INDIVIDUALS WHO HAVE VISUAL IMPAIRMENTS

DEFINITION

INDIVIDUALS WHO have severe visual impairments are generally classified as blind or as partially sighted. Usually, the term *blind* refers not only to those individuals who have no visual capability but also to legally blind persons (Codding, 1982). Individuals are considered to be *legally blind* when the visual acuity of their better eye is 20/200 or less after correction or when their peripheral vision is so restricted that its widest diameter subtends an angle of no greater than 20 degrees. *Partially sighted* persons have a visual acuity of between 20/200 and 20/70 in the better eye after correction (Atterbury, 1990; Birkenshaw-Fleming, 1993; Codding, 1982; Gfeller, 1992d; Lovejoy & Estridge, 1987; Nocera, 1979; Smith & Neisworth, 1975).

For educational purposes, children are sometimes classified as blind when they cannot read print but can learn to read braille, while they are classified as partially sighted if they can learn to read print under special conditions, as with special optic devices or with specially enlarged print (Smith & Neisworth, 1975). Individuals who are classified as blind because they do not have enough vision to read print may still have some *residual sight*; that is, they have may be able to perceive forms, motion, and light to some degree (Atterbury, 1990). There are varying degrees of blindness, depending on how much residual sight a person possesses (Birkenshaw-Fleming, 1993). Individuals who perceive forms well enough to move around are said to have *guiding vision*, while those who can see only within a range of two to four feet have *perception of form and motion*. Those who cannot distinguish forms or motion but can distinguish day and night have residual *light perception*, while those who have no light perception whatsoever are classified as *totally blind*.

Several other terms describing various vision problems and conditions may also be encountered when working with individuals who have visual impairments (Atterbury, 1990; Birkenshaw-Fleming, 1993; Codding, 1982). Persons with *myopia*, or severe near-sightedness, are unable to see objects clearly at a distance, while those who have *hyperopia*, or far-sightedness, can see distant objects clearly but have difficulty seeing close objects clearly. Individuals who have *peripheral vision* only can see only out of the sides of their eyes; they have little or no straight ahead vision. Those who have *tunnel vision*, on the other hand, have only a narrow field of vision (20 degrees or less) straight ahead. Severe *astigmatism* causes a distorted image due to light rays in the eye not converging on a focal point because of irregularities in the curvature of the cornea. In *amblyopia*, a person's eyes do not track together. A person who has *strabismus*, or crossed eyes, is unable to focus both eyes simultaneously on the same point. *Nystagmus* is a muscle disorder that causes rapid, involuntary, rhythmic oscillation of the eyeball. Individuals who have *albinism* have a lack of pigment that filters out light rays and can literally be "blinded" by the sun. When a person has *cataracts*, the lens of the eye loses its transparency, and vision becomes blurred and clouded. *Glaucoma* is an eye disease characterized by increased intraocular pressure that distorts the eye's ability to focus and may lead to blindness if untreated. *Retinitis pigmentosa* is a hereditary condition in which the retina (that part of the eye that contains that photoreceptive cells that receive the light images and send them to the brain by way of the optic nerve) gradually atrophies and degenerates. *Cortical blindness* is loss of sight due to an injury to the visual cortex; although the eye itself may be intact, the brain is unable to process or interpret visual stimuli.

CAUSES

Visual impairments may result when there are abnormalities or dysfunctions in any of the protective, refractive, directive, or receptive components of the visual system (Codding, 1982). *Protective structures* serve to guard and defend the eye from injury and include the orbit, orbital fat, eyelashes, eyelids and their lining, and tears. The *refractive components* serve to focus the light and visual stimuli; they include the cornea, lens, vitreous body (jelly-like material that fills the eyeball), and retina. *Directive structures* are those muscles that move the eyes up, down, or to the sides. *Receptive components* receive, transport, and interpret visual stimuli; they include the retina, optic nerve, and visual cortex (area of the brain where visual perception occurs).

Loss or impairment of vision may be caused by congenital defects, acquired eye disease, accidents and injuries, brain disorders, diseases affecting the whole body, or by unknown heredity factors (Birkenshaw-Fleming, 1993; Codding, 1982; Gfeller, 1992d; Lovejoy & Estridge, 1987; Miller & Keane, 1978). Common causes of blindness in newborns include congenital cataracts, congenital glaucoma, and disorders of the retina or optic nerve. Some former major causes of blindness during childhood, including damage to the eyes due to high concentrations of oxygen given to premature newborn (*retrolental fibroplasia* or *RLF*) and blindness from maternal rubella or gonorrhea during pregnancy, have become much less common. Later in life, loss of sight may be caused by accidents, cataracts, glaucoma, inflammation of the cornea, cancer of the retina (*retinoblatoma*), or diabetes. Problems or conditions leading to visual impairments may be stable or progressive in nature; some are treatable by medication or surgery.

Approximately eleven and one half million people in the United States have visual impairments, but less than one and one half million are disabled by their visual disorders (Codding, 1988). About four in every one thousand children are blind (Lovejoy & Estridge, 1987). Compared to other types of disability classifications or handicapping conditions, the incidence of legal blindness (especially by itself, with no other handicaps or disabilities) is relatively rare in children and young adults (Codding, 1988; Gfeller, 1992d). "Total blindness, of congenital origin, seems to be the exception rather than the rule" (Codding, 1988, p. 107). Among older adults, however, progressive decline in visual acuity is a more common problem. In the United States, over half of those persons who are classified as legally blind are age 65 or older (Miller & Keane, 1978).

When severe visual impairments are accompanied by other disabilities or handicapping conditions, individuals are said to have multiple disabilities (Codding, 1988). Information on these individuals is presented in Chapter Sixteen.

COMMON CHARACTERISTICS, PROBLEMS, AND NEEDS OF CLIENTS

As with any population, individuals who have visual impairments are a very heterogeneous group. The degree of visual impairment, the cause and time of onset of the impairment, and the expected course of the condition (whether it is stable or progressive), and the degree and type of support services available will all have varying effects on the individual's level of functioning, needs, and treatment program. In addition, individual clients all have unique combinations of abilities, needs, personality traits, strengths, and weaknesses that will impact their own particular responses and functional abilities; therefore, it is unwise to attempt to predict a particular person's skill levels or ceiling of abilities based on broad generalizations about a certain population. However, an awareness of some of those characteristics, problems, and needs which may be common to many clients who are blind or partially sighted will be beneficial both to the therapist who desires to work with this population and to the reader who is trying to understand how music therapy intervention strategies may benefit this population.

Since they have difficulty seeing where they are going, individuals who are blind or partially sighted often lack freedom and confidence in independent movement. This restriction in mobility is considered by many to be the most debilitating factor of severe visual impairment (Atterbury, 1990). Lack of mobility can also have detrimental effects on an individual's sense of independence and self-confidence. Individuals who have severe visual impairments need help in developing body awareness, spatial awareness, and locomotor skills, and independent interaction with the environment must continually be encouraged.

Because so much knowledge and information is acquired visually during the course of normal development, children who are blind or severely visually impaired from birth or early childhood may progress more slowly than their sighted peers in many areas, regardless of their overall level of intelligence (Codding, 1982; Lovejoy & Estridge, 1987). Early development of motor skills and language both rely on visual models of gross and fine muscle movements and lip and mouth positions. Later in life, much academic and practical skill information is acquired visually through pictures, demonstrations, and models.

Individuals who have severe visual impairments have to acquire concepts tactilely or auditorily rather than visually. They must often use their other senses to compensate for their impaired sight. Therefore, programs for these clients usually encourage high development of auditory skills. It is important to realize that other sense areas are not automatically strengthened when vision is impaired; skills in auditory and tactile perception must be developed through training and practice (Gfeller, 1992d).

Because of the lack of visual stimulation or because they have been overprotected by well-meaning relatives, individuals who have severe visual impairments sometimes become quite egocentric and have difficulty participating cooperatively in group activities (Codding, 1982; Gfeller, 1992d; Lovejoy & Estridge, 1987). Visual impairment may also be accompanied by emotional trauma and feelings of anxiety and insecurity, especially in those clients who have deteriorating vision or in those who have become blind after birth. Therefore, individuals who are blind or severely visually impaired may also need emotional support and benefit from experiences that promote psychological security and increase self-esteem (Codding, 1982; Gfeller, 1992d; Josepha, 1968; Lovejoy & Estridge, 1987). In addition, since society is for the most part geared for sighted people, persons with severe visual impairments may experience extreme frustration as they try to fit in with society, be accepted and understood by others, and seek meaningful relationships outside the protected environments of home and school (Codding, 1982). Consequently, they may need to find outlets for emotional expression and release of frustration and develop ways of interacting successfully and appropriately with sighted individuals.

SETTINGS FOR SERVICE DELIVERY

Individuals who have severe visual impairments may receive special programs to help meet their specific needs in a variety of settings, including public schools (in regular classrooms, with resource room support, or in self-contained classrooms), special residential or day schools for the blind and visually impaired, state schools, camp settings, psychiatric facilities or state hospitals, and adult rehabilitation facilities (Codding, 1982, 1988). In the United States,

approximately 85% of school-aged children who are classified as blind attend public schools; about half of these students have no other disability (McReynolds, 1988). The Individuals with Disabilities Act (IDEA) (Public Law 101-476), the 1990 revision of the 1975 Education for All Handicapped Children Act (Public Law 94-142) assures a free, appropriate public education to all children, ages 3-21, who have disabilities including those with visual impairments.

Incentives for early intervention programs to address the needs children birth through age 2 who have visual handicaps or disabilities are provided by Public Law 99-457 of 1986 (Adamek, 1996; Humpal, 1990). Special education services for children who have visual impairments are delivered according to the same general procedure outlined in Chapter Seven. After initial referral, assessment and identification of the disability, Individualized Educational Programs (IEPs) are written to guide instruction. The goals in IEPs are matched to the individual's specific strengths and weaknesses. IEPs also provide for appropriate support services in areas of need, placement in the least restrictive environment, and an annual evaluation of student progress in the program. The student is usually included with peers in a regular classroom for as much of the day as possible. When the IEP assessment finds that music therapy can provide a unique means of helping students achieve their educational objectives, music therapists may be called upon to provide traditional direct services, work with students in self-contained classes, work with students in inclusive classes, provide direct in-home services to students who are confined to their homes for medical reasons, provide consultation services to facilitate classroom instruction, inclusion, or music education, and/or provide staff development workshops (Wilson, 1996). Music therapy is usually classified as a related service in special education settings.

Music programs have been an important part of education and training programs at special schools for the blind since Lowell Mason initiated a music curriculum at Perkins School for the Blind in 1832 (Codding, 1988; Heller, 1987). Today, school-aged children who are classified as blind or severely visually impaired are much more likely to be served in public schools than in special schools for the blind (Zinar, 1987). Especially when visual impairment is their only disability, these students frequently are mainstreamed or included in regular classes in public school settings and receive music instruction from music educators (Atterbury, 1990; Codding, 1988; McReynolds, 1988;

Zinar, 1987). When music therapists work with individuals who have severe visual impairments in public school settings, they focus on using music to promote desirable physical, academic, and social changes, not on music instruction per se (Codding, 1988). At times, music therapists may consult with music educators to help them adapt instructional materials and procedures to the needs of students who are visually impaired. Some music therapists also contract their services to various agencies or see clients privately for individual therapy or specially adapted music instruction (Moog, 1987; Shoemark, 1991).

Since visual impairments affect adults more than children (Codding, 1988), music therapists may also work with individuals who have visual impairments in geriatric centers and adult rehabilitation facilities. Although blindness or visual impairment may not be the primary reason individuals are found in or referred to these settings, lack of sight will certainly impact their ability to function and interact with others and must be considered in planning and implementing rehabilitation programs. (For information on music therapy in rehabilitation and geriatric settings, see Chapters Eighteen and Nineteen.)

Individuals who have visual impairments, then, may receive services in any number of settings, depending on factors such as their age, degree of visual impairment, and the existence of other impairments or disabilities. Music therapists, too, may work with both children and adults who have visual impairments in many different settings, including public schools, state schools or hospitals, special schools for the blind, private schools or clinics, adult rehabilitation facilities, geriatric centers or nursing homes, music studios, private practice settings, or community programs. Music therapists may provide direct or consultant services and work with clients as individuals or in groups. In a recent survey of populations served by music therapists (AMTA, 1998), 330 of 1,620 music therapists responding said they worked with individuals who were visually impaired.

HOW MUSIC IS USED IN THERAPY

When people think of blindness and music, images of talented musicians like Ray Charles and Stevie Wonder may often come to mind. However, for persons with visual impairments as for the population in general, extraordinary musical talent is the exception rather than the rule (Codding, 1988;

Gfeller, 1992d). Nevertheless, the field of music, either in performance or in related activities like piano tuning, has long been considered by many to be a "natural" vocational choice for individuals who are blind (Zinar, 1987). In the United States, many schools for the blind, beginning with Perkins School for the Blind in 1832 and the New York School for the Blind in the mid-1800s, developed and maintained outstanding music programs that rivaled those of public schools, continuing to train excellent musicians well into the 1970s (Codding, 1988; Heller, 1987; Zinar, 1987). The therapeutic benefits of music for persons with severe visual impairments received some mention in these programs; however, most of the literature on these programs looked at the matter from the standpoint of music education rather than from the perspective of music therapy (Josepha, 1968; Codding, 1988). Music therapy, as a specific discipline, is a relatively recent addition to schools and training centers for individuals who are blind or severely visually impaired, first being introduced to any wide extent in schools for the blind in the mid-1970s (Codding, 1988). As the implementation of Public Law 94-142 in the mid-1970s led to the inclusion of more students with visual impairments in the public schools and to the provision of educational services for more severely disabled persons (Codding, 1988; Zinar, 1987), music therapy, with its emphasis not on music learning and music excellence for their own sake, but on the use of music to enhance learning and skill development in non-music areas and promote desirable changes in intellectual, social, motor, and emotional functioning, began to play a more prominent role in the education and training of individuals with severe visual impairments. Often, however, given the long history of music education for individuals who are blind or severely visually impaired and the prominence of some professional musicians who are blind, "music therapy, as a profession, is misunderstood by others who provide services to the visually disabled client" (Codding, 1988, p. 124).

Certainly the development of musical skills may be beneficial and rewarding to individuals who are blind or severely visually impaired, and music skills may be developed in the course of music therapy sessions, making the distinction between music therapy and music education vague or obscure at times (Josepha, 1968). However, music therapists always *primarily* focus on using music and its related learning and expressive experiences to help individuals gain skills or improve their functioning in non-musical areas, such as sensory, motor, cognitive, language, self-help, social, and emotional development (Codding, 1982, 1988; Gfeller, 1992d; Josepha, 1968; Kersten, 1981; Michel, 1976, 1985). Therapeutically directed music experiences can help (1) provide accessible, enjoyable sensory stimulation for individuals who have impaired vision, thus reducing self-stimulation, (2) develop motor skills and increase independent mobility, (3) develop auditory memory and discrimination, (4) develop and reinforce academic concepts, (5) enhance self-concept and assist in emotional development, (6) promote social interaction and increase communication with others, and (7) provide opportunities for relaxation, development of leisure skills, and aesthetic enrichment.

Music Therapy Experiences Provide Accessible, Enjoyable Sensory Stimulation and Help Reduce Self-Stimulation

Individuals who are blind or severely visually impaired, especially those who are very young or who are congenitally blind or who have additional disabilities, often engage in various types of self-stimulatory behavior, such as rocking, poking or rubbing the eyes, shaking the fingers in front of the face, moving the head side to side, head-rolling, head-bobbing, or head-banging (Codding, 1982, 1988; Gfeller, 1992d; Kersten, 1981; Lovejoy & Estridge, 1987). Some theorize that individuals with severe visual impairments who lack visual input and stimulation continue to engage in these mannerisms or ritualistic behaviors (sometimes termed *blindisms*) long beyond the period normal in infant development because these movements help relieve tension and frustration and/or provide satisfying sensations (Codding, 1982; Kersten, 1981). When individuals withdraw into self-stimulatory behaviors, however, it is difficult for them to attend to external cues and learn to interact successfully and appropriately with people and objects in their environment. Therefore, therapeutic and educational programs often try to reduce these self-stimulatory mannerisms.

Although music experiences may have visual

components, music is primarily an auditory phenomenon that is not dependent upon vision for its perception or performance. Therefore, music provides a source of sensory stimulation that is very accessible to individuals who are blind or visually impaired, as well as being something that is enjoyable to many and is viewed by society as a very appropriate and even desirable means of sensory stimulation and enrichment. Music activities, such as music listening or playing instruments, may be used as rewards for individuals who are working on reducing or extinguishing these ritualistic behaviors (Codding, 1982). Attractive music stimuli may also divert an individual's attention from self-stimulatory behavior and help focus attention on positive activities, such as grasping and playing instruments (Codding, 1982, 1988; Gfeller, 1992d; Kersten, 1981). In addition, the motor activity involved in playing instruments or moving to music may also help individuals discharge tension and frustration in a socially acceptable manner, reducing the need to relieve tension by stereotypic mannerisms (Kersten, 1981). Older persons with severe visual impairments may also learn to decrease tension and frustration and improve their control over stereotypic mannerisms by music-mediated relaxation exercises (Kersten, 1981) or other music experiences (e.g., instrumental improvisation, song writing) that focus on emotional expression, anxiety control, or the development of alternative behaviors or coping mechanisms.

Music Therapy Experiences Develop Motor Skills and Increase Independent Mobility and Interaction with the Environment

One of the greatest needs of persons with severe visual impairments is that of developing skills to move about their environment as independently as possible. This process involves (a) developing an *awareness of one's body parts* and their position in space, (b) developing *orientation* skills that allow one to use various sensory processes to develop spatial awareness and establish one's position in relation to other objects in the environment, and (c) developing *mobility* skills to move fluidly and confidently from one places to another in the environment (Codding,

1982; Gfeller, 1992d. These areas also greatly impact an individual's ability to explore and learn from the environment (Codding, 1982).

Many different types of therapeutically-directed music experiences can help clients who are blind or severely visually impaired develop body image, spatial awareness, orientation, mobility, and environmental exploration skills (Atterbury, 1990; Bachman, 1991; Birkenshaw-Fleming, 1993; Codding, 1982, 1988; Gfeller, 1992d; Jospeha, 1968; Kersten, 1981; Michel, 1976, 1985; Nocera, 1979; Salas & Gonzalez, 1991; Zinar, 1987). Songs that require clients to move or touch body parts can be used to help them develop an accurate body image, which is one of the prerequisites to moving about in space successfully. As the clients gain skills and confidence, spatial concepts and simple locomotor and non-locomotor movement patterns can be taught and practiced with action songs, musical games, and simple dances. Movement-to-music exercises and techniques from the Dalcroze eurhythmics approach, with their emphasis on large muscle movement, exploration of space, time, and energy, object awareness, tactile sensitivity, and consciousness of muscle movement, may also be very useful in developing confident and fluid movement in persons who have visual impairments (Atterbury, 1990; Bachman, 1991; Kersten, 1981). In fact, Dalcroze himself applied his approach to individuals who were blind and provided a number of specific exercises directed toward them (Bachman, 1991; Kersten, 1981). (For more information on the Dalcroze method and its applications to music therapy, see Chapter Twenty-two.)

Initially, music therapists might have the clients do movement activities on mats so that they have a defined, safe place in which to move. Later, environmental exploration can be encouraged by having clients reach out to find and play instruments and by having them walk across the room to find the instrument that is being played. Clients who are reluctant to move independently may be encouraged to explore the space around them if a guide rope is strung across the room at waist height or if they are paired with sighted partners. Scarves and streamers may also be used as aids to investigate the space around a client's body. Research has shown that rhythmic music facilitates travel-training and promotes a smooth walking gait, even in individuals who are congenitally blind (Unkefer, 1958, cited in Jospeha, 1968). Auditory cues and techniques such as pairing specific songs with specific rooms may also be used to facilitate mobility training and teach travel routes (Codding, 1988).

Successfully exploring and playing instruments in music therapy sessions may give clients the incentive and confidence to explore other aspects of their environment. For example, engaging in creative clinical musical improvisation with a music therapist using drum, cymbal, tambourine, piano, guitar, and voice helped a four-year-old who was blind develop the skills and confidence to reach out to and explore other aspects of the world (Salas & Gonzales, 1991). The ability, motivation, and confidence to explore and interact with one's environment is very important to an individual's overall development, for it is by exploring, manipulating, and interacting with objects and people in one's environment that one develops and refines many basic physical, cognitive, social, and emotional skills.

Music Therapy Experiences Help Develop Auditory Memory and Discrimination

When individuals are blind or severely visually impaired, their ability to receive information through their visual sense is absent, reduced, or distorted. Thus, other sensory modalities, especially the auditory sense, become vitally important for environmental awareness, learning, mobility, and interaction with others. Since music is largely an auditory phenomenon, it can play an important role in developing, training, and refining auditory skills. In addition, because many types of music experiences also often involve tactile and kinesthetic components, music may help individuals integrate their aural, kinesthetic, and tactile senses (Herlein, 1975).

Songs, chants, directed listening activities, movement-to-music games or exercises, and musical instruments can all be used as part of therapeutically directed music experiences designed to help individuals learn to become aware of and respond to sounds, localize and track sounds, discriminate between sounds or sound patterns, and recall and imitate sequences of sounds or words (Codding, 1982, 1988; Moog, 1987; Nocera, 1979). (See Chapter

Six for other examples of music activities useful in developing various auditory skills.) Memory skills developed as part of music auditory training programs may also help persons with visual impairments learn to recall longer and longer selections of vocal or instrumental music, enabling them to memorize parts needed to participate in instrumental or vocal performance ensembles.

Music Therapy Experiences Help Develop and Reinforce Academic Concepts

Most people acquire as much as 80% of the general information and knowledge they possess through their eyes (Birkenshaw-Fleming, 1993). Although persons who are blind or partially sighted have the same wide range of intellectual capabilities as their sighted peers, they must rely on senses and experiences other than visual ones for most of their learning. Songs and musical games dealing with various academic concepts, such as colors, numbers, days of the week, months of the year, shapes, and simple relationships, can help individuals who have severe visual impairments acquire much basic academic information and vocabulary in non-visual ways (Birkenshaw-Fleming, 1993; Codding, 1982, 1988; Nocera, 1979). (See Chapter Six for more examples of music activities for developing academic skills.) Music can also be used as a structure to help individuals recognize and discriminate among common environmental sounds (Codding, 1988; Michel, 1985) or to teach the sequence of steps needed to perform basic self-help, dressing, and grooming skills (Gfeller, 1992d; Michel, 1985). In addition, music activities can be formulated and structured to correspond to Piaget's stages of cognitive development (Codding, 1982; Rider, 1978, 1981), providing children who are blind or partially sighted with auditory and tactile experiences that will provide stimulation and learning experiences vital to successful academic development. Thus, auditory and tactile experiences can be used in place of visual experiences to help children with severe visual impairments master basic skills, facilitating their movement through the sensorimotor, pre-operational, concrete operations, and formal operations stages of cognitive development.

Music Therapy Experiences Enhance Self-Concept and Assist in Emotional Development

Visual impairments do not in and of themselves adversely affect emotional adjustment and self-concept; however, negative or overprotective reactions and attitudes of significant others to the disability and the person with visual impairments can lead to feelings of helplessness, dependence, lack of acceptance, and low self-esteem (Codding, 1982; Gfeller, 1992d). People with visual impairments may also experience many frustrations as they try to get along in a world geared for sighted people, and these frustrations may lead to feelings of anger or anxiety (Birkenshaw-Fleming, 1993; Kersten, 1981). Through their involvement in various types of music therapy experiences, individuals who are blind or visually impaired can learn how to express feelings and emotions appropriately, find constructive ways of coping with frustrations, and achieve successes and personal accomplishments that will help foster a healthy self-concept (Birkenshaw-Fleming, 1993; Codding, 1982, 1988; Gfeller, 1992d; Josepha, 1968; Kersten, 1981; Nocera, 1979; Salas & Gonzalez, 1991; Shoemark, 1991).

Many music activities, such as singing, writing songs, or playing musical instruments, can give individuals who are blind or partially sighted accessible, socially acceptable outlets for emotional expression. In addition, music, with its many timbres and wide range of dynamics, can provide a depth of expression that might otherwise be lacking for individuals with severe visual impairments, who are unable to perceive the nuances associated with gestures and facial expressions. Music therapists have also used musical exploration experiences incorporating improvisational music therapy techniques to help clients who were blind develop increased self-confidence and more positive affect (Salas & Gonzalez, 1991; Shoemark, 1991). Moreover, as they gain skills in singing or in playing a musical instrument ensemble, as they perform successfully with ensembles, or as they learn to move about freely and independently in dances, individuals who are visually impaired can gain a sense of belongingness and feelings of mastery and accomplishment that will help increase their self-confidence and build their self-esteem. "Music allows

for a degree of physiological and psychological equivalency with the sighted, a vital aspect of the self-image and esteem needs of nonsighted individuals" (Kersten, 1987, p. 132).

Adults who have declining vision or individuals who experience visual impairments later in life may also need assistance both in learning to accept the changes imposed by their visual disability and in developing skills to minimize the impact of the visual impairment on their daily life. Music therapy experiences that are structured to provide immediate success, personal gratification, and concrete evidence of personal accomplishment can help boost the confidence and self-concept of these clients and be important parts of their rehabilitation programs (Codding, 1988; Gfeller, 1992d; Josepha, 1968). In addition, music experiences involving song writing, lyric discussion, or instrumental improvisation techniques can be used to help individuals express and work through some of the emotions and psychological issues associated with their visual impairment and its effect on various aspects of their lives.

Music Therapy Experiences Promote Social Interaction and Increase Communication with Others

Music activities are often inherently social experiences. Whether they be one-to-one experiences involving interaction only between client and therapist or group activities involving interaction with others who have visual impairments or with sighted peers, music experiences can be structured by the music therapist to foster social interaction and interpersonal communication (Birkenshaw-Fleming, 1993; Codding, 1982, 1988; Gfeller, 1992d; Kersten, 1981, 1987; Moog, 1987; Nocera, 1979; Nordoff & Robbins, 1977; Salas & Gonzalez, 1991; Shoemark, 1991). For example, clinical improvisational techniques can be used in individual music therapy sessions to help clients learn to interact and participate with the therapist in music making. Shoemark (1991) found that interactional skills developed in individual music therapy sessions using piano improvisation also helped increase participation and cooperation in classroom activities.

Group music activities, such as dances, singing groups, or instrumental ensembles, can provide opportunities for clients who are visually impaired to interact and socialize with each other and/or with their sighted peers. As they participate in music groups, clients develop and practice social skills such as taking turns, listening to others, following directions, and cooperating with others. Group song writing or composition projects, lyric discussion activities, or group improvisation exercises may also be structured to provide opportunities to learn group problem solving skills. In addition, many music activities provide situations in which individuals who are visually impaired can communicate and interact as full participants, making physical contributions that are equal to those of their sighted peers. Kersten (1987) observed that "this feeling of belonging and equality is extremely important because their other opportunities for social and physical interaction are often limited" (p. 64).

Music Therapy Experiences Provide Opportunities for Relaxation, Development of Leisure Skills, and Aesthetic Enrichment

Like all people, individuals who are blind or severely visually impaired have needs for activities that are relaxing, that provide for constructive use of leisure time, and that provide for aesthetic enrichment and fulfillment. Music activities provide experiences that are easily accessible through senses other than vision and that are not subject to visual values (Moog, 1987; Zinar, 1987). Music therapists, with their specialized knowledge of the needs and learning styles of individuals with visual impairments and their knowledge of music activities and materials and ways these may be adapted, are well-equipped to structure music experiences in ways that will promote full, successful involvement and participation by individuals who are blind or partially sighted.

Persons who have limited vision must concentrate intently and attend vigilantly to auditory and tactile cues in their environment. This state of constant attention and alertness can lead to physical and mental tension and fatigue (Kersten, 1981, 1987). Relaxation or movement exercises to music can help relieve muscle tension, physical strain, and psychological tension, while also serving to reduce fatigue and revitalize mental processes (Birkenshaw-

Fleming, 1993; Kersten, 1981, 1987; Zinar, 1987). In addition, the acts of listening to music (live or recorded), moving or dancing to music, or actively participating in music-making, either by singing or playing instruments, all can provide both enjoyable leisure time activities and aesthetically rewarding experiences for individuals who have visual impairments. Although some adaptations to instructional methods may be necessary, individuals who are blind or partially sighted have few limitations when it comes to participation in most music activities (Atterbury, 1990; Birkenshaw-Fleming, 1993; Herlein, 1975; Kersten, 1981, 1987; Levinson & Bruscia, 1985; McReynolds, 1988; Moog, 1987; Zinar, 1987). Moreover, since persons with limited vision cannot relate to or contribute equally with sighted individuals in many other types of leisure pursuits (e.g., watching or participating in athletic contests, attending art exhibits, plays, or movies), music activities can provide welcome opportunities for individuals who have visual impairments to actively participate in leisure or recreational activities right alongside individuals who are not visually impaired (Birkenshaw-Fleming, 1993; Codding, 1982, 1988; Gfeller, 1992d; Kersten, 1981, 1987; Zinar, 1987).

While job training is not usually the focus of music therapy, some persons who are visually impaired do develop musical interests and skills that may eventually enable them to support themselves economically (e.g., by performing or tuning pianos). Some individuals who are blind or partially sighted have even become music therapists (Michel, 1985), using their music skills to help children and adults with many different kinds of disabilities improve their physical, psychological, social, or emotional functioning. While music therapists will certainly encourage interested and talented clients in these pursuits, they will also recognize that these music or music-related vocations are not right for every client who is visually impaired or even every client who is visually impaired and has musical talent. Certainly music can be a compensatory medium or device for persons who have visual impairments, but that is not the only benefit music can offer (Michel, 1976, 1985).

Therapists must always take care not to overemphasize the compensatory benefits of music for the visually handicapped, but to focus attention on the individual behind the music-making. (Michel, 1976, p. 34)

Finally, in a world that is devoid of visual stimulation and visual perceptions of beauty, the many timbres, dynamics, and styles of music can bring a richness of aesthetic experiences that might otherwise be lacking. Music is one aesthetic area that is completely accessible without sight (Moog, 1987).

Participation in music experiences can be very important to individuals who have visual impairments, for "music provides aesthetic experience in a world that can become barren and dreary" (Kersten, 1987, p. 132). "For people who are blind or partially sighted, music can be one of their most valuable experiences, bringing them joy and comfort" (Birkenshaw-Fleming, 1993, p. 57).

SPECIAL CONSIDERATIONS AND TIPS FOR SUCCESS

Because individuals with visual impairments have limited abilities to explore instruments visually or to observe them being played by others, they must be given plenty of time to touch and hold instruments and experiment with ways of playing and moving them. Since individuals who have severe visual impairments learn more successfully from multisensory experiences (Codding, 1982), verbal instruction should be reinforced by tactile or movement experiences whenever possible. When giving directions or instructions to groups that include persons who are blind or partially sighted, one must remember to verbally describe all visual demonstrations or to verbally repeat any information written on the board or displayed visually. In addition, one must learn to describe things in tactile as well as visual terms. Atterbury (1990), Birkenshaw-Fleming (1993), Codding, (1982), and Zinar (1987) provide many other practical suggestions for making different types of music experiences more accessible to persons with limited vision.

Different types of adaptations for printed material, including magnification, special lighting, enlarged print, or braille, may be useful with different individuals, depending on their degree of visual impairment (Atterbury, 1990; Birkenshaw-Fleming, 1993; Codding, 1982; Herlein, 1975; McReynolds, 1988; Smaligo, 1998; Zinar, 1987). A braille system of

music notation does exist; however, it is important for the sighted person to recognize that the braille system differs in concept from the print system of music notation and that it also involves a memory dimension (Herlein, 1975). Special electronic devices, such as the Varispeech machine, the Optacon, or the Kurzweil reader, may also be useful in making materials accessible to individuals who are blind or visually impaired (Levinson & Bruscia, 1985; Zinar, 1987). Printed materials should have large, black letters that contrast sharply with the background. Visual aids should also be large, simple, and uncluttered. When working with clients who read braille, it may be beneficial to label autoharp chord bars, resonator bells, and piano keys with braille letters. These clients may also be able to learn to read braille music notation.

Braille, large-print, and recorded music materials are available from the Music Division of the Library of Congress, Division for the Blind and Physically Handicapped, in Washington, D.C., as well as from other sources. For more extensive lists of resources and of organizations providing services and music materials to individuals who are blind or who have severe visual impairments, see Atterbury (1990), Codding (1982), Kersten (1981, 1987), Smaligo (1998), and Zinar (1987).

SUMMARY

Individuals who have severe visual impairments are usually classified as blind or partially sighted, depending upon the extent of their visual disability. Visual impairments occur when there are abnormalities or dysfunctions in any of the protective, refrac-

tive, directive, or receptive components of the visual system. Loss or impairment of vision may be caused by congenital defects, acquired eye disease, accidents and injuries, brain disorders, diseases affecting the whole body, or by unknown heredity factors.

Problems or conditions leading to visual impairments may be stable or progressive in nature; some are treatable by medication or surgery. Compared to other types of disability classifications or handicapping conditions, the incidence of legal blindness (especially by itself, with no other handicaps or disabilities) is relatively rare in children and young adults. Among older adults, however, progressive decline in visual acuity is a more common problem.

Music therapists serving individuals who have severe visual impairments use specially structured music experiences to help clients gain specific skills that will help them minimize the impact their visual impairment may have on their motor, social, intellectual, or emotional functioning. Therapeutically directed music experiences can help (1) provide accessible, enjoyable sensory stimulation for individuals who have impaired vision, thus reducing self-stimulation, (2) develop motor skills and increase independent mobility, (3) develop auditory memory and discrimination, (4) develop and reinforce academic concepts, (5) enhance self-concept and assist in emotional development, (6) promote social interaction and increase communication with others, and (7) provide opportunities for relaxation, development of leisure skills, and aesthetic enrichment. Certainly the development of musical skills may be beneficial and rewarding to individuals who are blind or severely visually impaired and some music skills may be developed in the course of music therapy sessions; however, music therapists primarily focus on using music and its related learning and expressive experiences to help individuals gain skills or improve their functioning in non-music areas, such as sensory, motor, cognitive, language, self-help, social, and emotional development.

QUESTIONS FOR THOUGHT AND DISCUSSION

1. How do varying degrees of visual impairment affect people's ability to interact with others and move about in their environment? What implications might this have for the structure and implementation of music experiences with this population?

2. Discuss some of the special characteristics and needs of individuals who have visual impairments. What implications do these have for music therapy programming?

3. Why are music experiences useful for therapeutic interventions with individuals who have visual impairments? Are some types of experiences and activities more useful or beneficial than others? Which ones? Why?

4. Describe some specific music therapy experiences that might be used with individuals who have impaired vision to (1) provide accessible, enjoyable sensory stimulation and reduce self-stimulation, (2) develop motor skills and increase independent mobility, (3) develop auditory memory and discrimination, (4) develop and reinforce academic concepts, (5) enhance self-concept and assist in emotional development, (6) promote social interaction and increase communication with others, and (7) provide opportunities for relaxation, development of leisure skills, and aesthetic enrichment. What unique benefits does music provide in each of these areas?

5. List several special considerations that may be important to remember when developing therapeutic intervention strategies for persons who have visual impairments. Why are these important? What are their implications for the structure of music therapy intervention strategies?

6. For each of the situations listed below, (a) define the problem or areas of need for the client or group of clients, (b) describe one or more of the goals you might pursue in music therapy sessions with the client(s), (c) describe music activities you might use to help the client(s) meet those goals, (d) tell how the music activities you described relate to the goals and needs of the client(s), and

(e) mention any special considerations you might want to take into account when working with the client(s).

Situation 1:

Sean is a five-year-old blind child who has been referred to you for music therapy. This is his first year in a school setting. Up to this point in his life, Sean's mother has done almost everything for him. She rarely lets him move around without holding her hand, except when he was in the safe confines of a large playpen. Sean is a very demanding and egocentric child who is used to having his every wish immediately fulfilled. He is an only child, and he has had almost no contact with other children his own age. His expressive and receptive language skills approximate those of a normal five-year-old child. Sean likes to manipulate objects and enjoys producing sounds on a piano or toy xylophone. He can walk, but he is reluctant to move around without holding someone's hand. Sean does not interact with his classmates; he either ignores them or pushes them away.

Situation 2:

Three young adult males who have become blind after injuries received in car and motorcycle accidents have been added to your music therapy group of developmentally disabled adults. Their short term memory skills have also been impaired. These men need to learn to adjust to their lack of vision and find ways to interact successfully, appropriately, and cooperatively with others in spite of their visual impairments. They also need to find constructive outlets to discharge anger and frustration and learn appropriate ways to express their feelings. These individuals are still working on mobility skills; at the present time they are a bit wary of moving about independently and lack confidence and freedom in independent movement. All three say they like music, especially rock music. They enjoy singing, and one used to play guitar before his accident.

SUGGESTIONS FOR FURTHER READING

Alvin, J. (1976). *Music for the handicapped child* (2nd ed.). London: Oxford University Press.

Atterbury, B. W. (1990). *Mainstreaming exceptional learners in music.* Englewood Cliffs, NJ: Prentice-Hall.

Birkenshaw-Fleming, L. (1993). *Music for all: Teaching music to people with special needs.* Toronto: Gordon V. Thompson.

Bruscia, K. E. (Ed.) (1991). *Case studies in music therapy.* Phoenixville, PA: Barcelona Publishers.

Codding, P. (1982). *Music therapy for handicapped children: Visually impaired.* Washington, D.C.: National Association for Music Therapy.

Codding, P. A. (1988). Music in the education/rehabilitation of visually disabled and multiply handicapped persons: A review of literature from 1946-1987. In C. E. Furman (Ed.), *Effectiveness of music therapy procedures: Documentation of research and clinical practice* (pp. 107-136). Washington, D. C.: National Association for Music Therapy.

Gfeller, K. (1992). Music therapy in the treatment of sensory disorders. In W. B. Davis, K. E. Gfeller, & M. H. Thaut, *An introduction to music therapy: Theory and practice* (pp. 209-233). Dubuque, IA: Wm. C. Brown.

Graham, R. M. (1975). Music and the blind or partially sighted. In R. M. Graham (Compiler), *Music for the exceptional child* (pp. 72-84). Reston, VA: Music Educators National Conference.

Herlein, D. G. (1975). Music reading for the sightless: Braille notation. *Music Educators Journal, 62*(1), 42-45.

Jospeha, Sr. M. (1968). Part III. Music therapy for physically disabled children and adults. In E. T. Gaston (Ed.). *Music in therapy* (pp. 97-171). New York: Macmillan.

Kersten, F. (1981). Music as therapy for the visually impaired. *Music Educators Journal, 67*(7), 63-65.

McReynolds, J. C. (1988). Helping visually impaired students succeed in band. *Music Educators Journal, 75*(1), 36-38.

Nocera, S. D. (1979). *Reaching the special learner through music.* Morristown, NJ: Silver Burdett.

Smaligo, M. A. (1998). Resources for helping blind music students. *Music Educators Journal, 85*(2), 23-26, 45.

Standley, J. (1991). *Music techniques in therapy, counseling, and special education.* St. Louis: MMB Music.

Zinar, R. (1987). *Music activities for special children.* West Nyack, NY: Parker Publishing.

Chapter Eleven

MUSIC THERAPY FOR INDIVIDUALS WHO HAVE ORTHOPEDIC IMPAIRMENTS

DEFINITION

ORTHOPEDICS is the branch of medical science that deals with disorders involving the skeleton, joints, muscles, and fascia (i.e., the membranes that cover and separate the muscles). Individuals who have orthopedic impairments have some neuromuscular or skeletal disorder or condition that temporarily or permanently interferes with the normal functioning of their bones, muscles, and/or joints. All orthopedic impairments interfere in some way with a person's physical abilities, having adverse affects on such things as mobility, muscular or joint strength, motor control and coordination, range of motion, muscle tone, muscle endurance, balance, posture, or locomotor patterns. Orthopedic impairments are often exclusively medical problems; they do not necessarily interfere with intellectual functioning. Other terms used to describe this general category of disability or impairment include *physically disabled, physically handicapped, physically impaired,* or *crippled* (Rudenberg, 1982; Staum, 1988; Thaut, 1992a).

Individuals who have orthopedic impairments may be described as *ambulatory, semi-ambulatory,* or *nonambulatory,* depending upon their ability to walk or move about independently or with varying types of assistance. Orthopedic impairments or handicaps may also be classified by degree, as *mild, moderate,* or *severe* (Atterbury, 1990; Rudenberg, 1982). Individuals who have mild impairments may require little special physical therapy or medical treatment, while those with more severe impairments may require extensive therapy and special educational or medical services.

CAUSES AND ASSOCIATED CONDITIONS

Orthopedic disabilities may be the result of either *congenital* (present at birth) or *adventitious* (acquired) neuromuscular or skeletal conditions or disorders, and may afflict the very young, the very old, and all age groups in between. The prognosis for any individual depends upon many factors, including the exact type of condition, disorder, or injury that caused the orthopedic impairment, the severity of the condition, the severity of any associated disabilities, and the availability of necessary medical, rehabilitative, and other support services. Some orthopedic impairments may be relatively uncomplicated and easily treatable (e.g., simple fracture), while others may be more complex and permanent (e.g., cerebral palsy) or even degenerative or terminal (e.g., Duchenne muscular dystrophy). Conditions frequently associated with physical disabilities or orthopedic impairments include cerebral palsy, spina bifida, muscular dystrophy, multiple sclerosis, poliomyelitis, arthrogryposis, malformations and joint dislocations, arthritis, spinal cord damage, severe head injury, stroke, severe burns, fractures, amputations, and brittle bone disorders (osteogenesis imperfecta and osteoporosis) (Atterbury, 1990; Rudenberg, 1982; Staum, 1988, 1996; Thaut, 1992a).

Cerebral Palsy

Cerebral palsy (CP) is a condition resulting from damage to the motor control centers of the brain. It is a nonprogressive disorder of the coordination of muscle action, not of individual joint and muscle function, that results in disorders of movement and posture. Eighty-five to ninety percent of all cases of cerebral palsy are congenital, resulting from faulty development of or damage to the brain in the womb or from brain injury during the birth process (Lovejoy & Estridge, 1987; Thaut, 1992a). Congenital causes of cerebral palsy include complications connected with prematurity, lack of oxygen to the fetal brain, maternal infections or heavy smoking or heavy alcohol or drug use, exposure to toxic substances, cerebral hemorrhage, severe newborn jaundice, or severe birth trauma. The 10% to 15% of the cases of cerebral palsy that are acquired in childhood, adolescence, or adulthood are most often caused by head injuries (e.g., skull fractures and brain lacerations), brain infections (e.g., meningitis and encephalitis), lead poisoning, cerebral anoxia, strokes, or brain tumors. Most children who have cerebral palsy live to be adults; life expectancy depends in part upon the severity of the condition and the severity of any associated disabilities (Lovejoy & Estridge, 1987).

Cerebral palsy may be classified according to *type of movement disorder* (spastic, athetoid, ataxic, tremor, rigidity, mixed, atonic), *body parts involved* (monoplegia – one arm or leg affected; hemiplegia – one side of the body [both arm and leg] affected; paraplegia – only the legs affected; diplegia – major involvement in the legs, minor involvement in the arms; triplegia – three limbs affected, usually one arm and both legs; quadriplegia – both arms and both legs affected), and *severity* or *degree of impairment* (mild, moderate, severe) (Atterbury, 1990; Lovejoy & Estridge, 1987; Rudenberg, 1982; Thaut, 1992a). Almost two-thirds of all individuals diagnosed with cerebral palsy have the spastic type, which is characterized by tight muscles (high muscle tone or *hypertonicity*), tense, stiff movements, and abnormal

movement patterns and postures resulting from the inability of the muscles to relax and the disturbance of normal muscle reflexes. About 15-20% of individuals who have cerebral palsy have the athetoid type, which is characterized by excessive, involuntary, purposeless movements and abnormal, irregular movement patterns. In ataxic type of cerebral palsy, which accounts for another 5%-8% of all cases, damage to the cerebellum results in a poor sense of equilibrium and poor balance control, unsteady and uncoordinated movements, an unsteady gait, and lack of muscle tone and power. The remaining types of cerebral palsy account for 10% or less of all cases. Individuals with the rigid type of cerebral palsy have a "lead-pipe" stiffness or inflexibility in their movements, caused by two opposite sets of muscles trying to work at the same time. Those with the tremor type have involuntary, vibrating movements of their limbs, especially when they attempt voluntary movements or are excited. In contrast to the irregular patterns of athetosis, these tremors are usually fairly rhythmic and regular. In mixed types, more than one type of cerebral palsy is present. Frequently, the mix includes both athetosis and spasticity, although ataxia or tremor may also be part of mixed conditions. Atonic cerebral palsy is found primarily in infants and is characterized by very low muscle tone (*hypotonia*). As affected individuals grow older, atonia may develop into athetosis.

Within each type of cerebral palsy, wide ranges of involvement and disability may occur. Those with mild involvement may have some awkward movements but usually can walk and talk and often have normal intelligence. Those with a moderate degree of impairment may walk unsteadily, have difficulty controlling and coordinating hand movements, and have some speech difficulties. Those who have severe involvement frequently are nonambulatory, have many speech and communication problems, and often have other associated disabilities.

Cerebral palsy does not necessarily result in deficits in intelligence; in fact, about one-third of all the individuals diagnosed with cerebral palsy have average or above average intelligence. Still, many individuals who have cerebral palsy have other impairments or disabilities (e.g., visual impairments, hearing impairments, perceptual problems, speech disorders, seizures, and learning disabilities), and over half have some degree of mental retardation (Atterbury, 1990; Lovejoy & Estridge, 1987; Rudenberg, 1982; Thaut, 1992a). (For more information on individuals who have multiple impairments or disabilities, see Chapter Sixteen.) There is no cure for cerebral palsy; however, interdisciplinary treatment, which may include things like medical services, physical therapy, speech therapy, special education, neurological services, orthopedic surgery, psychological services, social services, or vocational training, may help individuals develop skills to function as independently as possible.

Spina Bifida

Spina bifida is one of the more common congenital abnormalities of the nervous system, occurring in about 4 of every 1,000 live births (Lovejoy & Estridge, 1987). Spina bifida (literally, "cleft spine") results when one or more of the spinal rings in the vertebrae do not fuse properly during fetal development, leaving an opening in the spine through which some or all of the contents of the spinal canal may protrude (Atterbury, 1990; Lovejoy & Estridge, 1987; Rudenberg, 1982; Thaut, 1992a). In the mildest form, *spina bifida occulta*, skin covers the portion of the spine that had not fused properly; usually there is no pouching out of the spinal cord and the nerve tissues remain intact. In the more severe forms, there are sac-like protrusions that expose either the *meninges* (coverings of the spinal cord) or the spinal cord and its nerves. Spinal nerves do not develop past the opening in the spine. Therefore, depending on where the opening occurs, various nerve circuits, such as those needed for walking or for bowel and bladder control, may remain incomplete. Usually, the higher the location of the lesion or defect, the greater the functional impairment. Eighty-five to ninety percent of all children with spina bifida have some degree of *hydrocephalus*, in with the head is enlarged because the normal circulation of cerebrospinal fluid is blocked, and the fluid accumulates in the brain. Hydrocephalus is now commonly treated with a shunt operation in which a tube is inserted to drain the excess fluid from the brain to some other part of the body.

Although early surgery may be performed to close the spinal opening or to reinsert or protect the meninges and spinal cord, later treatment is usually required to correct or compensate for the accompanying neurological deficits. While the disorders or impairments associated with spina bifida usually cannot be eliminated, various types of surgery, therapy, and medical treatment can help to control them. Unless there are serious complications from hydrocephalus or severe infections, spina bifida usually does not affect an individual's level of intelligence. Also, while lower body paralysis may severely impact mobility, the lesions associated with spina bifida rarely impact the motor functioning of the arms or upper trunk.

Muscular Dystrophy

Muscular dystrophy (MD) is a degenerative muscle disease that is characterized by progressive muscle weakness. *Duchenne muscular dystrophy*, the most common and devastating type of muscular dystrophy, affects only young males and occurs in about one of every 3,500 live male births (Lovejoy & Estridge, 1987). The genetic defect that causes this condition usually results in an onset of symptoms between ages two and five, although symptoms may first occur as late as ages ten or eleven. Muscles in the lower body and spine are affected first, with a gradual progression to other muscles of the body. Initially, motor problems are minimal, with individuals having an abnormal swaying or waddling gait, difficulty climbing stairs, frequent falls, and a general lack of stamina. Children usually lose their ability to walk and become wheelchair-bound between the ages of ten and thirteen. As the disease progresses, muscles become thin, reflexes disappear, bone deformities and muscle contractures become more prevalent, and respiratory and heart muscles may also begin to deteriorate. Death usually occurs before age twenty, when muscle weakness becomes so severe that the individual succumbs to secondary complications such as heart failure or severe respiratory infections (Lovejoy & Estridge, 1987; Thaut, 1992a).

Other types of muscular dystrophy may also occur because of genetic defects (Lovejoy & Estridge, 1987). *Limb-girdle muscular dystrophy* mainly affects the muscles of the pelvic area. It can occur in both boys and girls, and it can range in severity from mild to extremely debilitating. Although death can result because of complications, death occurs less frequently than with Duchenne muscular dystrophy. Prognosis depends on the extent of muscle weakness and speed of muscle deterioration. *Facioscapulohumeral (FSH) muscular dystrophy* is a far more mild form of MD. It primarily involves the face, shoulders, and upper back, and can affect both males and females. Usually, symptoms do not appear until adolescence or adulthood and progression is very slow. Another less common and less severe form of MD is *Becker muscular dystrophy*. Although its symptoms may resemble those of mild forms of Duchenne muscular dystrophy, initial symptoms usually appear at a later age, and individuals may maintain the ability to walk well into adulthood. Heart involvement is less common than in Duchenne muscular dystrophy, and death usually does not occur until individuals are between the ages of 30 and 50.

Multiple Sclerosis

Multiple sclerosis (MS) is a chronic, progressive disease of the central nervous system that may involve the nerves affecting motor coordination and balance. MS most often strikes adults between the ages of 20 and 40; periods of improvement usually alternate with periods of worsening symptoms. Symptoms and effects of MS vary with the portion of the nervous system affected. Weakness, tremor of the limbs, impaired balance, and unsteady or stiff gaits are common motor problems associated with MS. In later stages, paralysis of various parts of the body may occur (Miller & Keane, 1978). MS is more prevalent in women than in men by a 3:2 ratio. About 250,000 Americans have MS; incidence is higher in the northern U.S. (30 cases or more per 100,000 people) than in the southern U.S. (5-29 cases per 100,000 people) (Clark et al., 1982).

Poliomyelitis

Poliomyelitis is a viral infection that attacks the central nervous system and injures or destroys nerve cells that control the muscles, causing temporary or permanent paralysis (Lovejoy & Estridge, 1987; Miller & Keane, 1978; Rudenberg, 1982; Thaut,

1992a). Also known as *polio* or *infantile paralysis*, this disease most often affects the leg muscles, although it may affect any muscles, including those involved in breathing and swallowing. About half of all patients with polio develop paralysis; with treatment and therapy, about half of these recover completely. Others require continued rehabilitation, which may include exercises for strengthening weak muscles or the use of braces, crutches, or wheelchairs to aid mobility. Although polio and post-polio rehabilitation programs were prevalent in the United States until the mid-1950s (Staum, 1988), vaccination programs have now made the disease quite rare in this country.

Arthrogryposis

Arthrogryposis is a congenital condition characterized by stiff joints and weak muscles. Depending on the extent and sites of involvement, these abnormalities in muscle and joint development result in various deformities such as turned-in shoulders, limited elbow flexion, pronated forearms, flexed wrists or fingers, dislocated hips, flexed or extended knees, curved spine (*scoliosis*), or turned in feet (Rudenberg, 1982; Thaut, 1992a). These deformities limit mobility and coordination to various extents, and muscle atrophy or joint enlargement and stiffness may increase as the child grows. Various types of orthopedic surgeries may help correct some deformities. Although deformities and conditions associated with arthrogryposis may severely impact coordination and mobility, speech and intelligence are usually unaffected.

Malformations and Dislocations

Malformations and dislocations may occur in different bone structures and joints for a variety of reasons throughout a person's life (Lovejoy & Estridge, 1987; Miller & Keane, 1978; Rudenberg, 1982; Thaut, 1992a). *Congenital malformations* exist when infants are born with some bone structure that deviates from the normal in any way. Examples include *clubfoot* (a common hereditary foot malformation, characterized by the heel being turned in under the ankle, the inner edge of the foot turned upward, and the sole and toes flexed downward), *clubhand* (hand and wrist deviated to one side as the result of a missing or shortened forearm bone), *webbed fingers, extra fingers, congenital flexed thumb* (thickened flexor tendon at the base of the thumb prohibits full extension), and some forms of *scoliosis* (abnormal spine curvatures to the left or right). *Congenital dislocations* usually occur when infants are born with bones displaced from joints because of some abnormality in bone development or joint construction that occurred during fetal development. One of the most common examples is *congenital dislocation of the hip.* Congenital malformations or dislocations may occur alone or in association with other conditions, syndromes, and deformities. Problems associated with congenital malformations and dislocations vary greatly according to the severity of the defect or to the severity of related conditions. Corrective treatment is available for most conditions, and may include various combinations of surgery, casting, bracing, splinting, and physical therapy.

Adventitious malformations or *deformities* of various bone structures and dislocations of various joints also have many causes. Deformities such as *scoliosis* (abnormal spinal curvature), *lordosis* (swayback), or *kyphosis* (humpback) may occur in connection with diseases (e.g., osteoporosis, rickets, muscular dystrophy, spina bifida, Marfan syndrome) that affect an individual's bones, muscles, or connective tissue. Contorted positions assumed in attempts to alleviate pain from tumors, injuries, spinal disk problems, or bone infections may also result in skeletal deformities. In addition, deformities may occur when bone fractures are not set properly or do not heal properly. *Adventitious dislocations* usually result from a blow or a fall, although some may occur in connection with extreme physical exertion. The most common sites for dislocation are *finger, thumb, shoulder, elbow, knee,* and *hip* joints. Problems associated with malformations and dislocations that occur later in life vary greatly and are often related to the severity of the defect or any associated diseases or conditions. Corrective treatment, which may include various combinations of surgery, casting, bracing, splinting, and physical therapy, is available for most orthopedic problems resulting from deformities or dislocations. In older persons with severe or chronic problems, the replacement of affected joints by artificial joints may be considered.

Arthritis

Arthritis is a relatively common disease that is characterized by inflammation or pain and stiffness in the joints. About 40 million people in the U.S. have some type of arthritic disease. Arthritis can occur in people of many different ages, from infants to elderly people. It can affect both the joints and the connective tissues throughout the body. Symptoms may come and go without warning; however, arthritis is a chronic condition that is always there even when symptoms are not present. Thus, arthritis usually requires long-term treatment and adjustments (Arthritis Foundation, 1987; Department of Health and Human Services, 1986; Lovejoy & Estridge, 1987; Miller & Keane, 1978; Rudenberg, 1982; Thaut, 1992a).

The most common form of chronic arthritis in children is *juvenile rheumatoid arthritis* (JRA) (Lovejoy & Estridge, 1987; Miller & Keane, 1978; Rudenberg, 1982; Thaut, 1992a). In the United States, about 200,000 children under age 16 suffer from this one of the three main forms of this disease: *systemic,* which involves the entire system, with symptoms like fever, rash, enlarged liver, spleen, and lymph nodes, muscle and skeletal aches and pains, and eventual inflammation of joints; *polyarticular,* which involves five or more joints severely, often affecting the small joints in the hands and feet along with ankles, knees, and hips; or *pauciarticular,* which involves less than five joints. JRA affects girls approximately two and one-half to five times more than boys; peak incidence occurs between two and five years of age and again from ages eight to eleven. Acute episodes of joint inflammation are very painful and may vary in length from a few days to several weeks. There is no cure for JRA; treatment focuses on easing pain and preserving or, if possible, improving joint function. Many individuals who suffer from JRA, however, do experience remission and freedom from active disease ten years after onset. Only about 10% have residual functional limitations.

In adults, the two main types of arthritis are *rheumatoid arthritis* and *osteoarthritis* (Arthritis Foundation, 1987; Department of Health and Human Services, 1986; Miller & Keane, 1978). *Rheumatoid arthritis*, the more serious, virulent, and disabling disease, usually starts between ages 20 and 45. Both men and women are affected, but about three times as many women as men develop severe symptoms that require medical attention. This chronic systemic disease causes inflammatory changes throughout the body's connective tissues, affecting many joints, especially the small joints in the hands. Eventually, especially in more severe cases, the inflammation and thickening of tissue around various joints may lead to deformities or destruction of bones. *Osteoarthritis*, a degenerative joint disease caused by the disintegration or wearing away of the cartilage that covers the ends of the bones, most often affects older people, with women being affected more often than men. Joints that receive the most use or stress from weight-bearing over the years, such as fingers, knees, big toes, hips, and lower spine, are most likely to be involved. Symptoms vary from mild to severe, depending on the amount of degeneration present. Pain and stiffness are felt when affected joints are used, and, in more severe cases, movement at the joint may be restricted.

Treatment for individuals suffering from arthritic diseases is concerned with relieving pain, reducing inflammation, maintaining or restoring motion of the joint, preventing crippling deformities, helping maximize independent functioning, and reducing emotional stress. Various combinations of medication, balanced regimens of rest and exercise, applications of heat and cold, prescribed physical therapy, and adaptive or assistive devices may be used to help treat or manage arthritis. For some individuals, surgical intervention involving joint repair or replacement may be recommended. Braces, casts, or splints may also be used to immobilize affected joints or to help prevent deformities by maintaining good joint position.

Spinal Cord Damage

Spinal cord injuries paralyze about 8,000 Americans each year (National Paralysis Foundation, n.d.), usually as the result of accidents or traumatic injuries (Rudenberg, 1982; Thaut, 1992a). When the spinal cord is damaged in neck or back fractures, the flow of electrical impulses from the brain is interrupted, and various degrees of paralysis and loss

of function result. The site of the injury determines the extent of the damage; the farther up on the spinal cord the injury occurs, the more extensive the loss of function. When the spinal cord is damaged in the thoracic area or below, *paraplegia*, the loss of use of the lower body movement and sensation, occurs. Damage to the cervical area of the spinal cord results in *quadriplegia*, the loss of body movement and sensation below the neck. When spinal cord nerve pathways are completely destroyed, they do not regenerate and cannot be repaired by current medical techniques; thus, paralysis from spinal cord injuries is usually permanent. However, recent research is offering new hope to persons who have been paralyzed by spinal cord injuries, challenging the belief that paralysis resulting from central nervous system damage is irreversible (National Paralysis Foundation, n.d.). For example, scientists have found that nerve tissue can be transplanted into the brain and grow and survive there and that nerve cells from an embryo can survive and function in the central nervous system of an adult host. In addition, new drugs are being discovered that minimize that process of paralysis and improve recovery following injury, and techniques like computer stimulation and biofeedback are being used to help restore functional control to previously useless muscles (National Paralysis Foundation, n.d.).

Paralysis often imposes many severe emotional, social, and occupational changes in a person's life. Therefore, treatment and rehabilitation of persons who have spinal cord injuries focuses on helping them adjust psychologically as well as helping them learn adaptive techniques to improve their daily functioning. (More information on the treatment and rehabilitation of individuals with spinal cord injuries is presented in Chapter Eighteen.)

Severe Head Injury

Severe head injuries (closed head injuries, head trauma, brain trauma) result from sudden mechanical force or blows to the head, such as may occur in accidents or falls, birth injuries, child abuse, or motor vehicle accidents (Rudenberg, 1982). These injuries can be life-threatening or result in residual dysfunctions in one or more sensory, motor, language, behavioral, or psychological areas, depending upon the extent and location of the brain injury. Motor problems that can occur as the result of severe head injuries include *hemiplegia* (loss of movement and/or sensation on one side of the body), difficulties with motor control, motor planning, balance, or coordination, restricted range of motion, and limited muscle strength and endurance (Lucia, 1987; Rudenberg, 1982). (More extensive information on various conditions resulting from head trauma and on the treatment and rehabilitation of individuals with closed head injuries is presented in Chapter Eighteen.)

Stroke

In a stroke, or *cerebrovascular accident (CVA)*, the blood supply to the brain is temporarily blocked, cutting off the brain's source of oxygen and causing damage to the brain cells (Prazich, 1985). As the brain cells are damaged or die, the functions they control (e.g., speech, muscle movement, emotions, understanding) are lost or impaired (Miller & Keane, 1978; Prazich, 1985; Zamula, 1986). Motor problems that occur include hemiplegia, muscle weakness, difficulties in balance, or difficulties in coordination and motor planning. About 400,000 Americans suffer strokes each year; about 160,000 die immediately or shortly after the stroke's onset. Of those who survive, about 10% return to work without significant impairment, about 40% will be slightly disabled, about another 40% will be seriously disabled and require some special services, and about 10% will require institutional care (Zamula, 1986). (Detailed information on causes and effects of strokes and the treatment and rehabilitation of individuals who suffer strokes is presented in Chapter Eighteen.)

Severe Burns

Deep second- and third-degree burns can cause temporary or permanent orthopedic handicaps because of contractures (i.e., permanent shortening and tightening of muscles), loss of body parts, or limitation of movement due to treatment procedures (Rudenberg, 1982; Thaut, 1992a). Burns may be caused by thermal, chemical, or electrical agents, or by radiation. Third-degree burns, the most severe

category of burns, involve all skin layers and may involve tendons, muscles, and even bones. Nerves are also damaged. These burns do not heal spontaneously; they require skin grafting and often leave severe scars. Individuals who have third-degree burns often require prolonged periods of hospitalization and rehabilitation. Treatment may include bathing in special solutions, debridement (removal) of dead skin tissue, dressing changes, blood tests, physical or occupational therapy, and surgical procedures, such as skin grafts.

Fractures

Fractures (broken bones) can impair movement either temporarily or permanently. Fractures are most often caused by trauma (e.g., in accidents, falls, severe blows to the affected part); they may also result from twisting caused by muscle spasms, indirect loss of leverage, or disease that causes decalcification of the bone (Miller & Keane, 1978). In simple or closed fractures, there are no open wounds. In compound or open fractures, the broken bone breaks through the soft tissues and skin, causing an open wound. Fractures are treated by aligning the broken ends of the bone and establishing bone continuity so healing can take place. Once the broken bone is set (and, in more severe breaks, internally stabilized by pins, nails, screws, or plates as necessary), the bone is immobilized by a cast or traction apparatus. Once the cast is removed, the patient will need to rebuild strength in the muscles that were not used while the bone was immobilized. After severe fractures or in cases where bones have not healed in proper alignment, range of motion or mobility may be permanently affected. Any muscle or nerve damage occurring along with a fracture may also impede a person's recovery of full function.

Amputations

Persons who have amputations are missing all or part of a limb or limbs (Lovejoy & Estridge, 1987; Miller & Keane, 1978; Rudenberg, 1982; Thaut, 1992a). *Congenital amputations* occur when limb buds of the fetus fail to develop, resulting in the baby being born without limbs or parts of limbs. *Elective* or *acquired amputations* occur when a limb is removed due to an accident or surgery to treat or arrest certain medical conditions, such as blood vessel disorders, infections, bone tumors, gangrene, and malignancies. Most acquired upper limb amputations are the result of severe trauma, while most leg amputations are due to some type of blood vessel disorder. *Traumatic amputations* are most often caused by accidents involving motor vehicles, farm machinery, or power tools, or by gunshot injuries.

Treatment and rehabilitation for individuals who have amputations includes exercises to strengthen surrounding muscles and prevent contractures and training in use of prosthetic devices (e.g., artificial limbs) for both functional and recreational activities. Since acquired amputations are usually very traumatic for a person, strong psychological support is also needed.

Brittle Bones

Abnormally brittle bones can be a problem for both children and adults, resulting in frequent fractures and possible deformities and restrictions in mobility. *Osteogenesis imperfecta* is a hereditary condition that affects both males and females and is marked by abnormally brittle bones that fracture easily (Miller & Keane, 1978; Thaut, 1992a). Limbs may become shortened or deformed by repetitive fractures and broken bones that heal in deformed positions. When the condition develops during intrauterine life (*osteogenesis imperfecta congenita*), the child is born with deformities. The condition may also develop after birth (*osteogenesis imperfecta tarda*), with fractures usually starting to occur when the child begins to walk. While physical activities for children with this condition may be severely restricted and repeated fractures and resultant deformities may limit mobility, they usually have normal intelligence and do well academically.

Osteoporosis, a disease in which bones become fragile and more likely to break, usually affects older people. More than 25 million Americans are at high risk for developing osteoporosis. Although women are five times more likely to suffer from osteoporosis, men also can develop the disease (National Osteoporosis Foundation, 1995). Principal causes of osteoporosis include lack of physical activity, lack of estrogens or androgens, and a chronic low intake of calcium. Osteoporosis may also occur in connection with endocrine disorders, bone marrow disorders, and nutritional disturbances (Miller & Keane, 1978). Complications of osteoporosis include increased risk of fracture (especially for spine, wrist, and hip bones), postural deformities, pain, and loss of mobility. Osteoporosis leads to 1.5 million fractures, including more than 300,000 hip fractures, each year (National Osteoporosis Foundation, 1995). Appropriate exercise (including stretching, strengthening, and walking), proper posture, and proper diet can help build and maintain strong bones and held avoid osteoporosis and its devastating effects. Special weight-bearing or resistive exercises to help preserve bone, strengthen back and hip muscles, and maintain flexibility are usually included as part of prevention and treatment programs for osteoporosis. Treatment may also include adjusting diet to insure adequate calcium and vitamin D intake and taking medications (e.g., estrogen replacement therapy for post-menopausal women; calcitonin or biophosphates that slow bone removal for men and women).

COMMON CHARACTERISTICS, PROBLEMS, AND NEEDS OF CLIENTS

As is evident from the preceding paragraphs, the population of individuals who have orthopedic impairments is quite a heterogeneous one, including persons with a wide variety of temporary or permanent conditions who range in age from infants to the elderly. Different types of conditions or diseases that cause orthopedic impairments also have wide ranges of impact, from very mild to very severe.

In addition, individuals who have orthopedic or physical disabilities often suffer from multiple handicaps (Thaut, 1992a). If an individual's orthopedic impairment is caused by some trauma or condition (congenital or acquired) that damaged a portion of the brain or nervous system, the damage rarely is confined to one isolated area and often impairs more than one area of functioning. Thus, although diseases and conditions that result in orthopedic impairments do not necessarily affect other areas of functioning, some individuals who have physical impairments also may have intellectual, sensory, or speech deficits. (For more information on the needs and treatment of individuals with multiple handicaps, see Chapter Sixteen.) Generally speaking, the more severe or extensive the individual's impairments or handi-capping conditions, the more adaptations or assistance the individual will need to carry out tasks of daily living. Of course, any individual client will have a unique combination of abilities, needs, personality traits, strengths, and weaknesses that will impact his or her treatment program and functioning level; therefore, it is unwise to attempt to predict a particular person's skill levels or ceiling of abilities based on broad generalizations. One must always remember that "each person is unique, and different adaptations must be made for each" (Birkenshaw-Fleming, 1993, p. 47). However, an awareness of some of those characteristics, problems, and needs which may be common to many clients who have some kind of condition that causes an orthopedic impairment will be beneficial both to the therapist who desires to work with this population and to the reader who is trying to understand how music therapy intervention strategies may benefit this population.

Whether their impairment is congenital or adventitious, whether it is permanent or temporary, clients who have orthopedic impairments need to make some personal and social adjustments because of their impairments. Some of their most immediate or obvious needs involve finding ways to carry out their normal activities of daily living in spite of limitations in mobility, range of motion, coordination, or muscular strength and endurance. Those with certain conditions (e.g., cerebral palsy) may need special positioning or handling techniques to help them make the most of their motor abilities (Rudenberg, 1982), while those with other conditions may need to learn to use prosthetic devices, wheelchairs, or other adaptive devices. Clients who are in constant pain from their orthopedic impairments also need something to relieve their pain to take their mind off of their pain. Most individuals who have orthopedic impairments must continually be encouraged to function as

independently as possible. Many will need to be encouraged to exercise regularly to improve or maintain muscle tone and joint function. Since immobility and muscle weakness are factors that increase susceptibility to respiratory infection, lung and breathing exercises may also be important to clients with orthopedic impairments.

Because many social activities, especially for children, often require physical mobility, those who have orthopedic impairments may miss out on opportunities to socialize with their peers (Thaut, 1992a). Therefore, they may need to seek out activities that can provide meaningful and enjoyable social experiences. Obvious physical deformities or lack of physical coordination may also lead to lack of social acceptance by peers, and individuals who have problems in these areas may need help in finding ways to deal with the reaction of others to their disability and to be accepted in spite of their impairments. Individuals who have been over-protected because of their physical frailties will need help in increasing their confidence in doing things independently to the extent of their abilities. Those who have a lower sense of self-worth because of their physical impairments will also need help increasing their self-confidence and self-esteem. Settings and activities that seek out and strengthen their talents and abilities while minimizing or compensating for their weaknesses will be most beneficial (Atterbury, 1990; Rudenberg, 1982; Thaut, 1992a).

Lack of mobility or decreased ability to move about independently can also adversely impact the social life of adults who have chronic conditions that cause orthopedic impairments. As moving about becomes more difficult, these persons may gradually stop going to activities they formerly enjoyed, have fewer opportunities to get out and interact with others, and gradually lose their social skills. This isolation can also decrease self-esteem. (For more information on the needs of elderly persons, see Chapter Nineteen.)

Persons who have orthopedic disabilities have the same needs for emotional development and emotional expression that all people do (Atterbury, 1990; Birkenshaw-Fleming, 1993; Rudenberg, 1982; Thaut, 1992a; Zinar, 1987); however, their physical disabilities may limit the options available to them for expressing emotions or releasing tension. For example, since clients who have a limited capacity for physical activity cannot use strenuous physical activity as an outlet for venting frustration, they must find other ways to express their frustration and release tension. Some may become verbally abusive, blaming others for their condition. Others may withdraw into fantasy or regress into less mature behavior patterns. Still others may overcompensate by trying to excel in some other area. All these individuals need experiences that will restore their self-esteem, improve their self-image, and give them more appropriate ways to express their emotions and relieve tension and anxiety. Depending on the nature of their disability or condition, individuals may also need to find ways of coping with feelings of loss, grief, depression, or loneliness. In particular, those who have lost motor functions in traumatic accidents or those who are suffering from degenerative, terminal conditions may have special needs for constant encouragement and emotional support from significant others as they find ways of coping with the realities of their condition. (For more information on the needs of those who are in rehabilitation settings or who are terminally ill, see Chapters Eighteen and Twenty.)

Along with the unique needs imposed by their particular condition or disability, individuals who have orthopedic impairments continue to have needs common to all people, including needs for independence, a feeling of accomplishment, opportunities to participate with others, opportunities to be involved in meaningful activities, enjoyable leisure and recreational experiences, outlets for emotional expression, sources of security and support, sources of comfort and love, intellectual stimulation, respect, and opportunities for aesthetic experience and fulfillment. Because of the limitations imposed by their conditions, they may need to find unique ways to meet these needs or have special adaptations made to enable them to participate with others or join in experiences as equal participants. Even those who are suffering from degenerative, terminal conditions need "opportunities to participate equally in expressive musical experiences and occasions to experience musical perception and experience" (Atterbury, 1990, p. 146). Physical impairments or deteriorations do not diminish a person's need for aesthetic experience. In fact, some of these individuals may have increased needs for aesthetic experience and expression as they seek ways to add meaning, fulfillment, and quality experiences to their lives.

SETTINGS FOR SERVICE DELIVERY

Individuals who have orthopedic impairments may receive special programs to help meet their specific needs in a variety of settings, dependent somewhat on their age, the nature and extent of their disability, and any other impairments they may have. Young children may receive services in their home or be seen in special early intervention programs, pediatric hospital units, burn centers, preschool programs, centers for the developmentally delayed, or clinics sponsored by agencies such as Easter Seals or United Cerebral Palsy (Humpal, 1990; Jacobowitz, 1992; Michel, 1985; Rudenberg, 1982; Rudenberg & Royka, 1989; Staum, 1988, 1996; Thaut, 1992a). Incentives for early intervention programs to address the needs children birth through age 2 who have handicaps or disabilities are provided by Public Law 99-457 of 1986 (Adamek, 1996; Humpal, 1990).

Since the Individuals with Disabilities Act (IDEA) (Public Law 101-476), the 1990 revision of the 1975 Education for All Handicapped Children Act (Public Law 94-142) assures a free, appropriate public education to all children, ages 3-21, who have disabilities, including those with orthopedic impairments, school-age children will most likely receive services through their local school district. They may also receive assistive technology devices and services through the provisions of IDEA or the Technology-Related Assistance for Individuals with Disabilities Act (Public Law 100-407) (Adamek, 1996; Johnson, 1996). Special education services for children who have orthopedic impairments are delivered according to the same general procedure outlined in Chapter Seven. After initial referral, assessment and identification of the disability, Individualized Educational Programs (IEPs) are written to guide instruction. The goals in IEPs are matched to the individual's specific strengths and weaknesses. IEPs also provide for appropriate support services in areas of need, placement in the least restrictive environment, and an annual evaluation of student progress in the program. Depending on the nature of their needs and abilities, children may be mainstreamed or included in regular classes for the entire day, be in regular classes part of the day and in a resource room part of the day, spend the entire day in a special classroom, or be placed in a special school for children with orthopedic disabilities (Rudenberg, 1982; Thaut, 1992a). When the IEP assessment finds that music therapy can provide a unique means of helping students achieve their educational objectives, music therapists may be called upon to provide traditional direct services, work with students in self-contained classes, work with students in inclusive classes, provide direct in-home services to students who are confined to their homes for medical reasons, provide consultation services to facilitate classroom instruction, inclusion, or music education, and/or provide staff development workshops (Wilson, 1996). Music therapy is usually classified as a related service in special education settings.

Adults who have orthopedic impairments also receive services in a wide variety of settings, including general hospitals, state hospitals, state schools, rehabilitation centers, extended care facilities, nursing homes, physical therapy clinics, neurological institutes, V.A. hospitals, burn centers, biofeedback clinics, pain clinics, or private homes (Michel, 1985; Staum, 1988, 1996). In addition, agencies like United Cerebral Palsy provide day treatment programs and services for adult clients in some communities (Michel, 1985).

Music therapists work with both children and adults who have various types of orthopedic impairments or physical disabilities. They may treat clients in any of the settings mentioned above as well as in music therapy clinics, music studios, community programs, or private practice. Music therapists may provide direct or consultant services and work with clients individually or in groups. Music therapists may also use their skills and training to help musicians overcome physical discomforts and problems related to music performance (Rider, 1987; Taylor, 1997; see also Chapter Seventeen). In a recent survey of populations served by music therapists (AMTA, 1998), 443 of 1,620 music therapists responding said they worked with individuals who were physically disabled.

HOW MUSIC IS USED IN THERAPY

Several different types of music experiences, such as singing, listening, playing instruments, moving to music, and creating music, can all be structured in specific ways to have therapeutic benefits for individuals who have various orthopedic impairments or disabilities (Birkenshaw-Fleming, 1993; Michel, 1985; Rudenberg, 1982; Staum, 1988, 1996; Thaut, 1992a; Zinar, 1987). The exact type of experience chosen will depend on the needs, capabilities, and interests of the client. While music therapy intervention strategies used with this population often primarily focus on increasing "efficient synergistically appropriate uses of muscles as they relate to movement" (Staum, 1988, p. 79), music therapy experiences may also have important social, emotional, and personal benefits for individuals who have orthopedic impairments. From early intervention (Humpal, 1990) to geriatric settings (Bright, 1972, 1981; Palmer, 1977), therapeutically directed music experiences can be a valuable asset to educational, developmental, and rehabilitative programs for individuals who have various types of orthopedic impairments.

The next sections of this chapter give an overview of ways music therapy interventions can complement a number of goal areas commonly found in rehabilitative, educational, or developmental programs for children and adults who have temporary or permanent orthopedic dysfunctions. Since orthopedic impairments primarily interfere with a person's physical abilities, attention will be directed primarily to ways music therapy interventions can positively influence physical and motor functioning. However, since orthopedic impairments also affect a person's entire life to varying degrees, mention will also be made of particular psychosocial benefits music therapy experiences may have for individuals with orthopedic impairments. The reader is also encouraged to consult other chapters in this text that present related information: Chapter Seventeen gives additional information on music therapy and pain management; Chapter Eighteen presents specific information on the use of music therapy in rehabilitation settings; and Chapter Nineteen deals with the special needs of geriatric clients.

Music Therapy Interventions Help Elicit Movement and Decrease Pain Perception

As anyone who has ever found themselves unconsciously tapping their foot or drumming their fingers or rhythmically nodding their head to a march or a dance tune with a strong, lively beat will attest, music has the capacity to stimulate movement. Musical instruments also arouse curiosity and interest, inviting and encouraging a person to reach out to make a sound. These inherent motivating aspects of music experiences can be structured by music therapists working with persons who have orthopedic impairments for a variety of purposes, "from stimulating exercise of large muscle groups to almost imperceptible movements in non-responsive patients" (Staum, 1988, p. 75).

Individuals who have orthopedic impairments or disabilities may be reluctant to move for a number of reasons, including the pain associated with their condition (e.g., arthritis, severe burns), the degree of neuromuscular involvement that renders movement extremely difficult (e.g., severe cerebral palsy, head injury, strokes), anxiety associated with fear of further injury or pain (e.g., brittle bone disorders), or, especially for those who have been overprotected, a lack of confidence in their abilities. Exercise and movement, however, are often vital aspects of the rehabilitation programs for these individuals, necessary to improve their level of functioning and help them reach their maximum level of independence. Therefore, music therapy interventions that help elicit and encourage movement and help decrease the perception of pain associated with movement can be most important in motivating individuals to actively participate in therapeutic movement programs and increase their functional independence (Bright, 1972, 1981; Jacobowitz, 1992; Michel, 1985, Palmer, 1977; Staum, 1988, 1996).

Rhythmic, stimulating music has frequently been used to motivate even the most reluctant individuals to participate in simple movement or exercise activities (Bright, 1972, 1981; Michel, 1985, Palmer, 1977; Staum, 1988, 1996; Thaut, 1992a). Since music is often associated with fun and pleasure, movement performed or requested in the context of music experiences "may not be thought of as exercises, and therefore may be attempted more readily, without the expectation of failure" (Ford, 1984, p. 11). Props like hoops or scarves used in conjunction with the movement-to-music experiences may further encourage movement. In addition, lyrics that request movements or action songs and music games may motivate some clients to participate. In her experience with pediatric burn patients, Christenbury (1979) found that "children seemed more willing to cooperate with commands to move when they were simultaneously singing action songs" (p. 141). The social aspects of dance or movement-to-music games and activities, along with the stimulating and motivating qualities of the music itself, may also encourage those who need help to allow themselves to be assisted to move, even if the movement is painful. In her work with geriatric clients, Palmer (1977) noted that "the sound of a polka or march was usually sufficient inducement to assure their cooperation even though it was painful" (p. 194).

Individuals are usually more likely to want to move or exercise to music that is meaningful or enjoyable to them. Thus, it is important to take into account an individual's preferences and cultural background when choosing music to accompany movement activities. Hearing preferred music may elicit movement even in seemingly nonresponsive clients. For example, contingent application of 15 seconds of preferred music (patient's preference determined from conversations with the patient's family) increased overt systematic responses in targeted behaviors (e.g., lateral head movement, mouth movement, eye focus, eye blinks, finger movement) for some comatose patients who were in a vegetative state (Boyle, 1987, 1989). Wolfe (1980) also found that contingent music, controlled by special head devices with mercury switches that played the music only when the subject's head was in an erect position, effectively improved head control in some subjects who had spastic cerebral palsy.

For some individuals, the pleasure obtained from making a sound on a musical instrument may provide the necessary motivation for movement. As they focus on the instrument and the sound being produced, clients may become less aware of pain associated with movement. For example, as Rudenberg and Royka (1989) found, the pleasure and comfort associated with the music experience of playing adapted instruments helped pediatric burn patients achieve "increased movement with lessened or decreased awareness of pain" (p. 41). If musical instruments are selected and adapted appropriately, they can be highly motivational tools in encouraging the development or rehabilitation of physical skills (Clark & Chadwick, 1979; Elliott, 1982; Ford, 1984; Humpal, 1990; Rudenberg, 1982; Staum, 1988, 1996; Thaut, 1992a). Once the client becomes motivated by an instrument and reaches out to play it, experiences can be shaped and guided by the therapist to complement movements and exercises being worked on in physical and occupational therapy programs. Instruments can also be set up in particular ways to encourage proper body positioning or increased range of motion. In addition, as electronic instruments and computer music technology continue to advance and as new devices for inputting and controlling electronic and computer music continue to become available, more musical devices and instruments are constantly added to the repertoire of the music therapist striving to encourage and motivate movement in individuals who have limited movement capabilities (Fegers et al., 1989; Howell, Flowers, & Wheaton, 1995; Krout, 1992a, 1995; Nagler & Lee, 1989; Swingler, 1994).

Certain types of music therapy interventions can also be beneficial for individuals who have much pain because of their orthopedic condition or the treatment procedures associated with it. For example, music therapy interventions such as music listening combined with deep breathing, progressive muscle relaxation, and age-appropriate imagery can help patients who have severe burns decrease anxiety and tension prior to and during surgery or painful procedures (e.g., daily debridement) or exercises (Barker, 1991, Christenberry, 1979; Robb et al. 1995; Rudenberg & Royka, 1989). Moreover, by providing a more relaxed, comforting, and soothing atmosphere, music can help divert the patient's attention, at least to some extent, from the pain. The use of music, relaxation, and imagery may also be useful in assisting in the management of postsurgical pain for various orthopedic surgeries, such as corrective surgery for scoliosis (Steinke, 1991). In addition, techniques like biofeedback and music (Godley, 1987; Rider, 1987) or vibroacoustic therapy, which combines music, vibration, and low frequency sound (Chesky & Michel, 1991; Skille, 1989), may be useful in managing or alleviating pain associated with arthritis or chronic muscle pain or fatigue. Other clients with chronic pain may benefit from techniques combining music and sound with mediation or imagery (Rider, 1987; Weissman, 1983). For example, Weissman (1983) found that when patients in hospitals or long term care facilities who constantly complained of pain were asked to state the location of the pain, moan or groan, and then create a pleasant or comforting vocal sound (e.g., "ah" or "mmm") and send it, on the breath, to the painful area, their pain and tension decreased.

Music Therapy Interventions Have Positive Influences on Muscle Tone

As was noted in Chapter Five, research has shown that music with different amounts of rhythmic activity and different degrees of percussive or sustained sounds (stimulative vs. sedative music) has different effects on several physiological responses, including muscle tension, motor activity, and relaxation responses (Edwards et al., 1991; Gfeller, 1992a; Hodges, 1980; Radocy & Boyle, 1988). Although individual preferences and experiences certainly affect the responses of a particular listener to a particular musical selection or style at any given time (Hanser, 1985), stimulating music (music that is fast or lively, with strongly enunciated rhythms and detached percussive sounds; e.g., marches, fast dances) usually tends to stimulate muscular action and physical activity, while sedative music (music that is slower, with more sustained sounds, flowing melodies; smoother, more quiet or monotonous rhythms; e.g., lullabies) tends to reduce physical activity, decrease tension, and promote relaxation (Gaston, 1968a). Music therapists may make use of these general principles, along with the information on music style preferences gained from their assessments of particular clients, to suggest musical stimuli that will positively influence a client's muscle tone and help that client engage in motor tasks more efficiently or effectively.

Individuals who have low muscle tone (hypotonia) need to increase their muscle tone to maintain proper posture and effectively perform tasks requiring motor activity. Music therapists have found that using various types of stimulating music (e.g., drum beats, recorded music, stimulating music improvised by the therapist) with these individuals often facilitates increased muscle tone and stimulates active movement, leading to greater physical alertness and enhancing responses to posture and motor control exercises (Sekeles, 1989). When movement is synchronized with musical and rhythmic stimuli, muscles usually become more active and work more efficiently (Thaut, 1992a). Therefore, techniques using rhythmic and musical stimuli to pace or time movements may be very useful in facilitating neuromuscular re-education for victims of strokes or traumatic brain injuries (Thaut, Schleiffers, & Davis, 1991). Exercising certain body parts by playing instruments or repeating dance movements can also help improve muscle tone in the body parts exercised (Rudenberg, 1982; Staum, 1988, 1996; Thaut, 1992a).

Individuals who have high muscle tone (hypertonia), muscle stiffness, or spasticity, on the other hand, need to find ways of relaxing their muscles. Relaxation exercises to soothing, sedative music prior to other activities may help some individuals calm and relax their muscles and then be more able to participate more effectively in activities requiring motor control (Rudenberg, 1982; Thaut, 1992a). Techniques combining sedative music with biofeedback-assisted relaxation training (Scartelli, 1982) or combining low frequency sound with music (Wigram, 1995) also helped decrease muscle tone and promote relaxation in some individuals who had spasticity. Continual advances in computer and electronic technology now provide the clinician with ways to control musical sound information (e.g., pitch, dynamics, timbre) by biological signals, offering new possibilities for music facilitated relaxation (Krout, 1995). In addition, techniques combining music and meditation or music and imagery have also been used effectively to reduce muscle tension in some clients (Rider, 1987;

Weissman, 1983).

When working with individuals who have cerebral palsy, it may be important to take into account the type of cerebral palsy when selecting music. For example, some research has shown that sedative and stimulative music may have quite the opposite effects on individuals who have spastic cerebral palsy as compared with those who have athetoid cerebral palsy: Generally, stimulative music seems to be more effective in promoting relaxation and controlled movement in clients with spastic cerebral palsy, while sedative music seems to be more effective for clients with athetoid cerebral palsy (Lathom, 1961; Schneider, 1954, 1957). Of course, individual responses will vary and these guidelines will not apply to every individual who has a given type of cerebral palsy. (For example, see Scartelli [1982] above.) Although general guidelines may provide useful starting points, the music therapist must always carefully observe, assess, and evaluate individual preferences for and responses to particular techniques, experiences, and selections of music and plan or revise music-based interventions accordingly.

When working with clients who have severe physical handicaps, such as those with severe cerebral palsy, music therapists must work closely with trained physical therapists and occupational therapists to learn specific positioning and handling techniques that will help normalize muscle tone (e.g., neuro-developmental treatment [NDT] techniques). Music therapists can then incorporate these techniques into music therapy treatment programs (F. Johnson, 1981; Rudenberg, 1982), as they position clients or instruments in ways that will maximize normal muscle tone and facilitate normal movement patterns. Using their knowledge of the physiological and psychological effects of music, music therapists may also work with physical therapists and occupational therapists to develop background music to accompany NDT exercises and help facilitate and structure normal, rhythmic muscle movement. For clients who are very tactile defensive or who have a high degree of spasticity or athetosis, listening to certain types of music prior to their work with the physical therapist may help them become calmer and more relaxed, facilitating an atmosphere and state of being more conducive to treatment.

Music Therapy Interventions Help Strengthen Muscles and Joints, Increase Endurance, and Promote Physical Fitness

Almost all individuals who have any type of orthopedic impairment must engage in some sort of motor development or rehabilitation program to help improve joint or muscle strength or function. Many types of music experiences can facilitate clients' involvement in and response to these programs. However, since music therapists usually do not have extensive training in kinesiology and functional motor assessment, they must consult with occupational and physical therapists or other motor rehabilitation specialists to see what particular types of exercises, movements, positions, or handling techniques are indicated (or contraindicated) for any individual client. Music therapists then use their expertise in music to plan music-based interventions that complement these efforts.

> Music-based motor rehabilitation demands interdisciplinary efforts. Whether the music therapist provides adjunctive functional training programs or serves as a consultant for music-based therapeutic facilitations, it is apparent that collaborative efforts are dictated. (Lucia, 1987, p. 37)

Many music therapy interventions that are used to help clients increase muscle or joint strength, improve range of motion, increase endurance, or promote physical fitness fall under the general category of "movement to music" (Thaut, 1992a, p. 174) and use specially selected music to accompany, guide, or structure movement activities. Depending on the situation, the music may be supplied by recordings or performed live by the therapist. The tempo and length of the music can be adjusted to correspond to the capabilities of the individual and to the desired speed and duration of the exercise. Demands can be increased gradually by playing the music for longer intervals as the individual gains strength (Michel, 1985).

Appropriate background music carefully selected by the music therapist can facilitate participation in and response to range of motion and muscle-strengthening exercises by (a) stimulating muscular activity, (b) facilitating desired changes in muscle tone, (c) motivating participation, (d) serving as a distraction from pain that may be associated with the movement, (e) setting a mood that matches and encourages the desired motor response, and (f) helping to rhythmically structure and synchronize movements (Gfeller, 1988; Lucia, 1987; Michel, 1985; Rudenberg, 1982; Staum, 1988, 1996; Thaut, 1992a; Thaut et al., 1991; Zinar, 1987). For example, range of motion and muscle-strengthening exercises can be a very necessary but very painful part of treatment and therapy for many individuals who have arthritis, cerebral palsy, spasticity, or contractures, as well as for those who may be recovering from burns, fractures, strokes, or traumatic brain injuries. Carefully selected music can facilitate clients' responses to these exercises by helping relax muscles prior to exercise and by providing a more pleasant atmosphere and/or a diversion from the pain that is often associated with the movement (Christenberry, 1979; Rudenberg & Royka, 1989). Vibroacoustic therapy techniques, which use music in combination with low frequency sound vibrations, have also been useful in increasing range of motion and decreasing high muscle tone in some clients (Wigram, 1995). Researchers have found that receiving vibroacoustic therapy treatment prior to range-of-motion exercises can significantly increase range of motion for some individuals with spastic cerebral palsy (Wigram, 1995). (See Chapter Twenty-two for more information on vibroacousitc therapy.)

Research has shown that carefully chosen music also can enhance general fitness programs by increasing motivation and by helping structure temporal and quantitative factors related to the required exercise movements (Gfeller, 1988; Thaut et al., 1991). Choosing music that incorporates client preferences as well as appropriate rhythmic and phrase structures further enhances participation by facilitating "active focus on an external event rather than on the discomforts that accompany strenuous exercise" (Gfeller, 1988, p. 40). Thus, the addition of music to exercise routines may help increase endurance and frequency of activity, as well as alleviate the boredom and tedium generally associated with repetition (Denenholz, 1959; Gfeller, 1988; Palmer, 1977; Staum, 1988, 1996; Wolfe, 1978). Individuals can also practice muscle or joint strengthening exercises in fun ways when specific, prescribed exercise movements are incorporated into dance routines or action songs. Some people who are reluctant to participate in structured exercise programs might be very willing or motivated to take part in dances. Judicious planning and coordination of efforts by music therapists and physical therapists can make enjoyable dance experiences double as goal-directed exercise programs.

Exercise-to-music programs and movement-to-music experiences, then, can be an important part of general physical fitness programs for many different types of clients, including frail older adults (Bright, 1972, 1981; Weissman, 1983), helping to improve breathing and circulation as well as assisting in maintaining muscle and joint function. Some clients may even process and respond to exercise routines better when music is added. For example, music can provide persons who are recovering from strokes or traumatic brain injuries with important cues that help increase their attention and focus on the task (especially important for language-affected persons with right hemiplegia) and provide a rhythmic structure for organizing and maintaining muscular effort and increasing endurance (Lucia, 1987; Thaut et al., 1991). For some clients, performing exercises to a rhythmic accompaniment may even improve stability of joints by facilitating an earlier onset and prolongation of muscle activation or by increasing co-contraction of antagonist muscle groups (Thaut et al., 1991).

Examples of specific movement-to-music and exercise-to-music programs for specific goals, types of movements, or body parts can be found in Bright (1981), Lucia (1987), Miller (1979), and Zinar (1987). Individuals who need to develop, strengthen, or reactivate large arm and shoulder muscles can also benefit from the arm movements associated with musical conducting (Tanner & O'Briant, 1980; Staum, 1988, 1996), while the use of hand signals associated with the Kodaly approach to music education can promote wrist rotation and finger flexion and extension (Zinar, 1987).

Other music therapy interventions make use of musical instruments to help clients increase muscle or joints strength, improve range of motion, increase endurance, or promote physical fitness. By carefully selecting instruments and matching them to the needs and interests of the individual, music therapists can help clients develop increased range of motion in certain joints or strengthen specific muscle groups

(Confrancesco, 1985; Denenholz, 1959; Farnan & Johnson, 1988b; Ford, 1984; Josepha, 1964, 1968; Miller, 1979; Rogers, 1968; Rudenberg, 1982; Rudenberg & Royka, 1989; Staum, 1988, 1996; Thaut, 1992a; Zinar, 1987). A careful analysis of basic physical abilities (e.g., muscle groups involved, range of motion and positioning requirements) needed to play many string, brass, woodwind, percussion, and keyboard instruments, such as that provided by Elliott (1982), will help therapists select instruments that will be most appropriate and beneficial for individuals with particular physical abilities and disabilities. Of course, an individual's preferences will also play a part in the selection, for individuals will be more motivated to play and practice instruments they like. Many traditional instruments can be adapted for successful use by clients who have orthopedic impairments (Clark & Chadwick, 1979; Josepha, 1964; Rudenberg, 1982; Zinar, 1987). Others may learn to make music with computers, developing skills which also increase their muscle and finger strength (Spitzer, 1989).

Musical instruments can be great motivational devices for encouraging movement and promoting sustained practice of a certain movement or sustained exercise of a certain muscle group. The pleasure and sense of accomplishment associated with making music on an instrument often distracts an individual from the pain that may be associated with the movement and encourages the individual to keep on moving to make the sound. For example, Rudenberg and Royka (1989) noted that pediatric burn patients had increased movement with less pain when they were playing adapted instruments. In addition to providing pleasant stimulation, the aural feedback provided by the instrument may help an individual gauge improvement and progress. Instrumental instruction is naturally linked to a series of gradual goals (Elliott, 1982), which can be easily matched to physical therapy goals for increased range of motion, strength, and endurance. Individuals also gain added strength and endurance as they practice their instruments outside the therapy session and maintain the program at home (Elliott, 1982).

By positioning instruments in certain ways, music therapists can encourage individuals to maintain proper posture. By gradually moving instruments farther away from individuals or by having individuals reach to xylophone bars or piano keys farther and farther from midline, music therapists can help encourage increase arm extension and upper extremity range of motion. Music therapists can also add interest to passive range of motion exercises as they assist clients in moving their arms or fingers to produce sounds on instruments. Producing a crash on a cymbal or a tap on a tambourine as one is assisted to stretch and extend one's arm may help give purpose and meaning to the exercise while adding an element of fun. Rhythmic background music may facilitate rhythmic structure of the movement and activation of appropriate muscle tone, as the sound produced by the instrument played with the assistance of the therapist provides feedback on the movement and adds pleasure to the exercise. Some music therapists have also used musical instruments to strengthen hand grasp strength in stroke victims (Confrancesco, 1985). Others use specific instruments in hospital rehabilitation and therapy programs to strengthen particular joints or muscle groups and increase general physical endurance (Elliott, 1982; Rogers, 1968). Josepha (1964) also found that, with special adaptations, piano and violin instruction could be used to help amputees strengthen muscle and improve coordination in the use of the prosthesis.

Music Therapy Interventions Help Regulate Physical Movement and Increase Motor Control and Coordination

Many individuals who have orthopedic disabilities have difficulties with the timing and coordination of their movements and need special programs to help them develop functional neuromuscular patterns, increase their control over their movements, and improve the coordination of their movements. Just like movement, music is a dynamic event, unfolding through time. By matching the qualities and rhythms of the music experience to the qualities and rhythm of the desired movement, music therapists can devise interventions that (a) help individuals perceive the rhythm and timing of normal movement patterns, (b) provide an enjoyable structure to facilitate the appropriate timing of movements, and (c) offer a rewarding and pleasurable means of practicing and working to improve movement control and coordination. Music therapists have used a variety of

experiences involving movement-to-music, playing instruments, or contingent music listening to help develop functional motor behaviors, increase neuromuscular coordination and motor control, and improve mobility and locomotion in clients who have some degree of coordination or motor control problems resulting from cerebral palsy, traumatic brain injuries, stroke, arthritis, muscular dystrophy, severe burns, fractures, aging, or other conditions causing skeletal, joint or muscular impairments (Bright, 1972, 1981; Denenholz, 1959; Farnan & Johnson, 1988a, 1988b; Ford, 1984; Josepha, 1964, 1968; Lucia, 1987; Michel, 1985; Miller, 1979; Palmer, 1977; Rogers, 1968; Rudenberg, 1982; Staum, 1988, 1996; Thaut, 1992a; Thaut et al., 1991; Zinar, 1987).

The rhythmic structure of music can be very beneficial in helping individuals time their movements or perceive the rhythmic flow and structure of desired movement patterns. As music is chosen to match the desired movement, the structure of music helps organize responses and make them purposeful:

> As the body responds to rhythm, reflexes and random movements can be changed to functional or purposeful movement. The signal, music, stimulates the person's nervous system, and can draw a motor response, movement. (Farnan & Johnson, 1988a, p. 11)

When rhythmic techniques are used to teach and accompany movement skills in neuromuscular reeducation programs, some individuals may experience quicker recovery of motor skills because of improved anticipation and timing of muscular effort (Thaut et al., 1991). Movement-to-music experiences can help individuals perceive normal, symmetrical movement patterns and then practice and reinforce these patterns (Birkenshaw-Fleming, 1993). By moving or being assisted to move to recorded music, by performing actions to songs, and by doing dancing or exercises that require movements in various directions, individuals can learn to become more aware of the position of their body in space and learn to control and coordinate their movements to perform specific actions. Coordination and control are approached gradually through successive steps of approximation, with difficulty, number, extent, and independence of movements gradually being increased as the individual's skills develop. Walking to music or a steady beat can also facilitate locomotion and gait training (Staum, 1988, 1996; Thaut, 1992a). In addition, the structure of music may help individuals who are recovering from strokes or traumatic brain injuries focus on tasks and sustain consistent muscular efforts by helping them organize their movements to a rhythmic beat (Lucia, 1987; Thaut et al., 1991). The cues provided by musical structure or song lyrics may also assist in motor planning, thus facilitating the development of functional motor patterns that an individual can use in daily routines (Lucia, 1987; Staum, 1988, 1996). For example, Gervin (1991) used song lyrics to train a patient recovering from a brain injury to dress independently. The external cues and pacing provided by the lyrics and music helped structure the activity and overcome difficulties in initiation, sequencing, and motor planning.

Many individuals who have severe neuromuscular impairments resulting from conditions like cerebral palsy, stroke, or traumatic brain injury need help developing or relearning functional movement patterns. For some of these individuals, musical instruments may provide the motivation to use their hands and arms and to develop functional hand skills (Farnan & Johnson, 1988b; Ford, 1984; Michel, 1985; Rogers, 1968; Rudenberg, 1982; Staum, 1988, 1996; Thaut, 1992a; Zinar, 1987). As individuals reach out to touch, grasp, hold, manipulate, and release instruments, they develop important functional hand skills that can then be used to perform other activities of daily living (Confrancesco, 1985; Farnan & Johnson, 1988b). As skills develop, music therapists can help encourage increased control and coordination by gradually asking individuals to play faster beats, more complex patterns, or more intricate rhythms. More complex instruments like xylophones, keyboards, guitars, and other band or orchestral instruments have also been used to help develop motor skills and increase motor control and coordination in individuals who have physical handicaps (Denenholz, 1959; Elliott, 1982; Howell et al., 1995; Rogers, 1968; Staum, 1988, 1996). When these instruments are specially adapted, they can also be used by individuals with upper limb amputations (Edelstein, 1987, 1989; Josepha, 1964) or others who have unique physical limitations (Birkenshaw-

Fleming, 1993; Clark & Chadwick, 1979; Rudenberg, 1982). In addition, electronic instruments and computers help individuals with severe physical impairments use instrumental instruction as a means of improving motor control and coordination (Howell et al., 1995).

While the feedback of improved sound production or the psychological satisfaction of creating a musical product may motivate individuals playing musical instruments to work longer and harder to a desired end (Staum, 1988, 1996), it is important to realize that an individual's degree of interest in an instrument will affect that individual's motivation and performance (Howell et al., 1995). Thus, for maximum benefit, musical instruments used to help develop movement patterns and increase motor control and coordination should be selected with regard to their interest to the individual as well as with regard to their ability to promote beneficial movement patterns (Elliott, 1982; Staum, 1988, 1996).

Clients who have severe orthopedic impairments may require special treatment techniques, such as neuro-developmental treatment (NDT) or sensory integration, to help them develop functional, controlled movement patterns. Music therapists can work with physical therapists and occupational therapists to learn these techniques and find ways to incorporate them into music therapy treatment programs (James, 1986; F. Johnson, 1981; Rudenberg, 1982). Music therapists who work with severely impaired clients must also be aware that the way clients are positioned can greatly affect their motor control (Farnan & Johnson, 1988b; Rudenberg, 1982). Rudenberg (1982, pp. 12-13) lists several guidelines for reducing the influence of abnormal reflexive activity and abnormal muscle tone in clients who have severe cerebral palsy. By careful positioning of both client and equipment, music therapists can use many instrumental and movement-to-music experiences to facilitate motor control and coordination in these clients. Clients may also increase tolerance for positioning equipment as they use it in the music therapy situation, where they are distracted from the pain or restrictions of the equipment by their interest in the music activity. In addition, operant conditioning procedures involving contingent music listening can help develop functional motor behaviors (Staum, 1988, 1996) or increase maintenance of desired positions and postures (Wolfe, 1980) in some clients.

Music Therapy Experiences Facilitate Communication and Emotional Expression

Persons who have orthopedic disabilities have the same needs for communication and emotional expression that all people do; however, their physical disabilities may limit the options available to them for expressing ideas and emotions. Some conditions that result in orthopedic impairments may also have speech or language disorders associated with them (e.g., severe cases of cerebral palsy, other conditions that affect muscles associated with speech or respiration, some strokes or traumatic brain injuries). Since both verbal and nonverbal communication and emotional expression are a natural part of many music experiences, such as singing, chanting, improvising, composing, song writing, and playing musical instruments, and since music experiences are usually perceived as enjoyable and nonthreatening and can be readily adapted to allow for participation by individuals of varying levels of abilities and disabilities, music therapy experiences can provide needed outlets for communication and emotional expression for many clients who have orthopedic impairments.

Music therapy interventions can stimulate communication by providing enjoyable, motivating activities that offer opportunities for self-expression and verbal or nonverbal communication, and favorite music activities can also effectively reward desired communication behavior (Thaut, 1992a). For those clients who have speech and language difficulties associated with their orthopedic impairment, music experiences can provide a non-threatening atmosphere to try out verbal communication skills as well as afford a potent avenue for nonverbal communication. For many of these individuals, music therapy interventions can also effectively complement many speech therapy goals. (See Chapter Twelve for more information.)

Since their physical impairments may limit their options for releasing tension and frustration, many individuals who have orthopedic impairments must find alternative ways to express strong emotions. Depending on the nature of their disability or

condition, some individuals may also need to cope with feelings of loss, grief, depression, or loneliness. Music, the language of the emotions (Whitwell, 1993), offers a natural, socially acceptable way of meeting clients' needs for emotional development and emotional expression. As they participate in music experiences by singing or by writing songs or by choosing songs to express the way they feel or by playing musical instruments or by moving or relaxing to music, individuals can express a wide range of emotions and find new ways to relax and relieve tensions. Specially structured music therapy experiences can also offer assistance in coping with frustrations or emotional problems that may be associated with an individual's disability. In addition, songs can offer comfort and emotional security to those individuals who have been scarred or disfigured by accidents or whose lifestyles have been drastically altered by the effects of strokes, spinal cord injuries, or traumatic brain injuries (Rudenberg & Royka, 1989). Song writing experiences can also be effective tools for helping patients release and discuss feelings related to their injuries (Christenberry, 1979). For those involved in rigorous physical rehabilitation programs, the opportunity to participate in fun and enjoyable creative music experiences can provide a much needed emotional outlet to help them release tension and cope with the strain and frustrations they are experiencing (Barker & Brunk, 1991). As family members become involved in music therapy experiences, music can give patients and families new ways of communicating with each other, provide ways of starting to deal with emotionally charged topics, give help and support in coping with multiple losses and adjusting to new life situations, and offer needed avenues of emotional release (Barker & Brunk, 1991; Rudenberg & Royka, 1989).

Since "access to musical experiences can be provided on many different levels of sensory, physical, and intellectual ability" (Thaut, 1992a, p. 177), music therapists can readily structure many different types of experiences in singing, song writing, music listening, playing musical instruments, improvising or composing music, or moving to music to fit an individual's unique abilities and needs for expression (Edelstein, 1987, 1989; Ford, 1984; Rudenberg, 1982; Thaut, 1992a). Recent advances in technology now allow even individuals who have severe physical limitations increased opportunities to create music independently through the use of computers and adaptive electronic equipment (Fegers et al., 1989; Howell et al., 1995; Krout, 1992a, 1995; Nagler & Lee, 1989; Swingler, 1994). As technology continues to advance, more and more individuals with physical limitations will have increased access to emotional expression through interaction with musical instruments and musical composition.

Music Therapy Experiences Increase Self-Esteem and Provide Opportunities for Personal Enrichment

Problems like lack of mobility, decreased independence, physical deformities, lack of motor coordination, or physical frailties can all adversely impact an individual's self-confidence and self-esteem. Along with the unique problems or needs imposed by their particular condition or disability, individuals who have orthopedic impairments continue to have needs common to all people, including needs for independence, success, a feeling of accomplishment, enjoyable leisure and recreational experiences, intellectual stimulation, and opportunities for aesthetic experience and fulfillment. Physical impairments or deteriorations do not diminish a person's need for aesthetic experience. In fact, some individuals with physical impairments may have increased needs for aesthetic experience and expression as they seek ways to add meaning, fulfillment, and quality to their lives. Through successful participation in music experiences, individuals can increase their feelings of confidence and self-esteem as well as develop viable avenues for personal expression and leisure time enjoyment that they can participate in throughout their lives (Birkenshaw-Fleming, 1993; Edelstein, 1987, 1989; Ford, 1984; Jacobowitz, 1992; Josepha, 1964, 1968; Michel, 1985; Rider, 1987; Rogers, 1968; Rudenberg, 1982).

Birkenshaw-Fleming (1993) observed that "developing a good self-image is very important for students with physical problems, especially as they grow older and become more aware of their disabilities" (p. 54). As these individuals participate successfully in carefully structured music

experiences, they can gain feelings of competence and increased confidence and self-esteem as they learn to independently control and interact with various aspects of music. Developing musical performance or compositional skills and talents can also be a boost to the self-esteem and self-confidence for many individuals. In addition, these skills can provide them with new avenues for personal enrichment, aesthetic expression, meaningful accomplishments, and participation in "normal" activities that are valued by society. With the use of adaptive devises (Birkenshaw-Fleming, 1993; Clark & Chadwick, 1979; Edelstein, 1987, 1989; Elliott, 1982; Josepha, 1964; Rudenberg, 1982; Zinar, 1987) or computer technology, adaptive switches and input devices, and electronic instruments (Fegers et al., 1989; Howell et al., 1995; Krout, 1992a, 1995; Nagler & Lee, 1989; Swingler, 1994), even individuals who have severe physical limitations can participate independently and successfully in musical performance and composition experiences. Persons who have had upper limb amputations or who are paralyzed on one side may also learn to play instruments by making use of adaptive devices (Edelstein, 1987, 1989; Elliott, 1982; Josepha, 1964) or may find much enjoyment and enrichment from the extensive amount of piano literature written for one hand (Edel, 1994). As music therapists adapt instruments and instructional approaches to the unique needs and capabilities of individuals with various orthopedic impairments, these individuals can develop many musical performance skills which will give them new avenues for personal enjoyment, use of leisure time, and aesthetic expression, and may also lead to increased opportunities for participation with others in vocal or instrumental ensembles or musical plays and operettas.

Other individuals may find additional aesthetic and personally enriching leisure opportunities through developing an active interest in and appreciation for listening to music (Birkenshaw-Fleming, 1993; Ford, 1984). Ford (1984) noted that, by developing music listening skills and interests as well as singing or playing skills, individuals who have physical impairments "will be able to enjoy music as an active force throughout life" (p. 13). Listening to music can be a source of comfort, enjoyment, learning, and personal enrichment no matter what the person's level of ability or disability (Birkenshaw-

Fleming, 1993). As music therapists structure music experiences to facilitate the acquisition of academic information, enhance the experience of and memory for certain concepts, and set moods conducive to learning (e.g., promote attention and reduce anxiety), music can also serve to enhance cognitive learning processes and promote the development of academic skills in individuals who have orthopedic impairments (Ford, 1984; Thaut, 1992a).

Music therapy interventions may also be useful in increasing self-esteem and positive attitudes in musicians who experience performance problems involving muscle pain and fatigue. For example, Rider (1987) found that music therapy interventions involving a combination of guided imagery and music, music improvisation, biofeedback, systematic desensitization, and cognitive restructuring effectively decreased a 34-year-old cellist's problems with shoulder pain and fatigue and with anxiety during solo performance, thereby increasing performance quality, self-esteem, and positive attitude toward performance. (See Chapter Seventeen for more information on Performing Arts Medicine.)

Music Therapy Experiences Provide Opportunities for Socialization and Increase Social Skills

Since many social activities, especially in childhood, are built around movement or require independent physical mobility (Thaut, 1992a), persons who have orthopedic impairments may have limited opportunities to participate in social experiences with their peers. Lack of mobility or decreased ability to move about independently can also adversely impact the social life of adults who have chronic conditions that cause orthopedic impairments. Specially structured music experiences can be very beneficial in developing, improving, or helping to maintain socialization skills in clients of all ages, from preschoolers (Hughes et al., 1990) to school-age children (Atterbury, 1990; Birkenshaw-Fleming, 1993; Ford, 1984; Humpal & Dimmick, 1995; Jacobowitz, 1992; Josepha, 1964, 1968; Michel, 1985; Nordoff & Robbins, 1971a; Rogers, 1968; Rudenberg, 1982; Rudenberg & Royka, 1989; Thaut, 1992a; Zinar, 1987) to adults (Barker &

Brunk, 1991) to geriatric clients (Bright, 1972, 1981; Glassman, 1983; Palmer, 1977; Weissman, 1983), as they give individuals who have orthopedic impairments opportunities to interact with their peers (both disabled and nondisabled) in meaningful and productive ways. Music experiences can also facilitate communication and healthy, enjoyable interaction between individuals with orthopedic disabilities and the members of their families (Barker & Brunk, 1991; Rudenberg & Royka, 1989).

Since music is accessible on many different physical, intellectual, and emotional levels, music experiences can be structured to include individuals of many different physical and intellectual abilities, giving them each a part to play in producing a meaningful product or achieving an enjoyable experience. For example, ambulatory and non-ambulatory clients can participate together in group singing or instrumental experiences or even in dance and movement-to-music experiences (especially if these incorporate adapted movements or wheelchair dancing for nonambulatory clients). Music play experiences and traditional music learning activities can be very useful in promoting interaction and socialization among children with and without disabilities (Atterbury, 1990; Birkenshaw-Fleming, 1993; Hughes et al., 1990; Humpal & Dimmick, 1995; Zinar, 1987). As they interact with others in music settings, children with physical disabilities receive important socialization experiences while they learn music skills. As individuals of all ages work with others to write group songs, produce instrumental improvisations, perform in instrumental or vocal ensembles, dance, or put on musical plays, they develop skills in interacting and working cooperatively with others (Barker & Brunk, 1991; Ford, 1984; Glassman, 1983; Jacobowitz, 1992; Josepha, 1964, 1968; Michel, 1985; Nordoff & Robbins, 1971a; Palmer, 1977; Rogers, 1968; Rudenberg, 1982; Rudenberg & Royka, 1989; Tanner & O'Briant, 1980; Thaut, 1992a; Weissman, 1983).

New electronic and computer technology make it possible for even those clients with severe physical limitations to work together with others in music performance groups. For example, the use of synthesizers with electronic control devices matched to an individual's physical abilities allows clients with physical handicaps to be integrated into ensembles with nonhandicapped individuals (Fegers et al., 1989). Individuals using switches connected to specific electronic or computer-controlled drum sounds can also learn to work together to produce the sound of a large drum set (Krout, 1995). During activities such as these, clients learn to focus on and attend to each other, thereby improving their social awareness and sense of group as they concentrate on the sounds being produced and work cooperatively to play the desired musical patterns.

Clients may also have the opportunity to take leadership roles as they conduct musical ensembles (Ford, 1984; Tanner & O'Briant, 1980) or direct musical plays. In addition, by leading or performing in ensembles or by participating in musical plays or talent shows, individuals have increased opportunities for social recognition by others as well as for interaction with others. For older adults, the enjoyment and satisfaction gained from music experiences like performing in vocal or instrumental ensembles, attending concerts or music appreciation programs, participating in musical plays or talent shows, or writing group songs, may provide the motivation necessary to keep them participating with others in group activities, helping them maintain their social skills and giving them ways to continue to interact with others in meaningful and satisfying ways (Bright, 1972, 1981; Glassman, 1983; Palmer, 1977; Tanner & O'Briant, 1980; Weissman, 1983; see also Chapter Nineteen).

SPECIAL CONSIDERATIONS AND TIPS FOR SUCCESS

When dealing with clients who have orthopedic impairments, music therapists must work closely with trained physical therapists and occupational therapists to learn exactly what exercises or types of movements the clients should be encouraged to do or exactly how the clients should be moved and positioned (Farnan & Johnson, 1988b; James, 1986; F. Johnson, 1981; Rudenberg, 1982; Thaut, 1992a; Zinar, 1987). The therapist will also need to consider the expected prognosis or developmental course of a client's condition to know what can reasonably be expected of the individual at various stages and in what particular ways the individuals and/or family members may need support as they deal with various stages of recovery or progressive deterioration (Atterbury, 1990; Barker & Brunk, 1991; Birkenshaw-Fleming, 1993; Christenberry, 1979; Rudenberg, 1982; Rudenberg & Royka, 1989).

Traditional musical instruments must often be adapted if they are to be used successfully by clients who have orthopedic impairments. For example, handles or mallets may have to be adapted to fit the client's grasping ability, or special stands may be needed to hold and position instruments. The music therapist should also be aware that, even when using simple rhythm instruments, certain instruments require more effort to produce sound than others. Participation may be facilitated by first having an individual play instruments which require less effort (e.g., wrist bells, hand drum), gradually moving to instruments that require more effort (e.g., rhythm sticks, drum with mallet) as the individual's skills develop. Farnan and Johnson (1988b, p. 45) provide a useful chart ranking the relative difficulty of common rhythm instruments.

When using musical instruments to mobilize, exercise, or strengthen certain muscles or limbs, it is also very important to observe the individual carefully to make sure the complex act of playing the instrument is not creating undue tension or strain elsewhere (Staum, 1988, 1996). While musical instruments can be very motivating and effective tools for developing increased muscle strength, range of motion, and motor control and coordination for many individuals, they may not offer the most direct means of rehabilitation for all individuals or all orthopedic disorders (Staum, 1988, 1996). The music therapist who works with individuals who have severe orthopedic handicaps should also strive to keep aware of technological developments that offer increased access to music playing and composition through the use of computers, adaptive switches and control devices, and electronic instruments.

Many resources are available to help music therapists find materials that are useful for persons who have various orthopedic impairments. For example, Edel (1994) has compiled a resource list of over 1,000 piano pieces for one hand alone that range in difficulty from basic to virtuoso. Special tape players and music materials are also available from the Library of Congress Division for the Blind and Physically Handicapped in Washington, D.C. Several excellent, practical ideas for adapting activities, instruments, and equipment to maximize independent participation by individuals who have physical disabilities and various orthopedic impairments can be found in Atterbury (1990), Birkenshaw-Fleming (1993), Clark & Chadwick (1979), Edelstein (1987, 1989), Elliott (1982), Farnan and Johnson (1988a, b), Humpal and Dimmick (1995), Rudenberg (1982), and Zinar (1987). The reader interested in more specific information about any particular disorder or condition is also encouraged to consult reference sources to find groups or organizations (e.g., United Cerebral Palsy, Muscular Dystrophy Association) specific to that condition.

SUMMARY

Individuals who have orthopedic impairments have some type of neuromuscular or skeletal disorder or condition that results in temporary or permanent physical dysfunction. Orthopedic impairments interfere in some way with a person's physical abilities, having adverse affects on such things as mobility, muscular or joint strength, motor control and coordination, range of motion, muscle tone, muscular endurance, balance, posture, or locomotor patterns. Other terms used to describe this general category of disability or impairment include *physically disabled, physically handicapped, physically impaired,* or *crippled.* Individuals who have orthopedic impairments may be described as *ambulatory, semi-ambulatory,* or *nonambulatory,* depending upon their ability to walk or move about independently or with varying types of assistance.

Orthopedic impairments have a variety of causes and may be associated with conditions that are congenital or acquired, acute or chronic, temporary or permanent, simple or complex, treatable or relatively unchanging or degenerative. Orthopedic disabilities may afflict the very young, the very old, and all age groups in between. The prognosis for any individual depends upon many factors, including the exact type of condition, disorder, or injury that caused the orthopedic impairment, the severity of the condition, the severity of any associated disabilities, and the availability of necessary medical, rehabilitative, and other support services. Conditions frequently associated with physical disabilities or orthopedic impairments include cerebral palsy, spina bifida, muscular dystrophy, multiple sclerosis, poliomyelitis, arthrogryposis, malformations and joint dislocations, arthritis, spinal cord damage, severe head injury, stroke, severe burns, fractures, amputations, and brittle bone disorders.

Different types of conditions or diseases that cause orthopedic impairments also have wide ranges of impact, from very mild to very severe. Orthopedic impairments are often exclusively medical problems; they do not necessarily interfere with intellectual or sensory functioning. However, in cases where the disease or condition that causes the orthopedic impairment also affects other areas of functioning, individuals may have multiple impairments, including intellectual, sensory, or speech deficits. Generally speaking, the more severe or extensive the individual's impairments or handicapping conditions, the more adaptations or assistance the individual will need to carry out tasks of daily living.

Since individuals who have orthopedic impairments lack normal muscle, joint, or bone function to some degree, they need to make various personal and social adjustments. Some of their most immediate or obvious needs involve finding ways to carry out their normal activities of daily living in spite of their limitations in mobility, range of motion, coordination, or muscular strength and endurance. Those with conditions such as cerebral palsy may need special positioning or handling techniques to help them make the most of their motor abilities, while those with other conditions may need to learn to use prostheses, wheelchairs, or various adaptive devices. Many individuals will need encouragement to exercise regularly to improve or maintain muscle and joint function. Others need assistance in developing muscle control and coordination. Some individuals may need assistance with pain management. In addition, lack of mobility, decreased independence, physical deformities, lack of motor coordination, or physical frailties can all adversely impact social life, self-confidence, and self-esteem. Persons who have orthopedic disabilities also have the same needs for emotional development and emotional expression that all people do; however, their physical disabilities may limit the options available to them for expressing emotions or releasing tension, and they must find unique ways to meet these needs.

From early intervention to geriatric settings, therapeutically directed music experiences can be a valuable asset to educational, developmental, and rehabilitative programs for individuals who have various types of orthopedic impairments. Many goals for these individuals focus on developing, improving, or maintaining some aspect of motor functioning abilities. Music therapy interventions can complement physical therapy programs and motor skill development goals by (1) helping to elicit movement while decreasing perception of pain, (2) positively affecting muscle tone in ways that will facilitate movement or relaxation, (3) providing activities that help strengthen muscles and joints, increase endurance, and promote physical fitness, and (4) providing activities that help regulate physical movement and increase motor control and coordination. Music therapy experiences may also have important social, emotional, and personal benefits for individuals who have orthopedic impairments. As they keep in mind the needs of the whole person,

music therapists may structure interventions to (5) facilitate communication and emotional expression, (6) increase self-esteem and provide opportunities for personal enrichment, and (7) provide opportunities for socialization and the development of social skills. This chapter provided several examples of music therapy experiences in each of these areas.

To maximize opportunities for independent participation by clients, music therapists must know how to adapt traditional instruments and mallets for individuals who have orthopedic impairments. Music therapists should also be aware of technological developments that offer individuals who have severe impairments increased access to music playing and composition through the use of computers, adaptive switches and control devices, and electronic instruments. In addition, music therapists should consult with occupational and physical therapists or other motor rehabilitation specialists to see what particular types of exercises, movements, positions, or handling techniques are indicated (or contraindicated) for any individual client. Therapists will also need to consider the expected prognosis or developmental course of a client's condition to know what can reasonably be expected of the individual at various stages and in what particular ways the client and/or family members may need support as they deal with various stages of recovery or progressive deterioration.

QUESTIONS FOR THOUGHT AND DISCUSSION

1. Discuss some of the special characteristics and needs of individuals who have various types of orthopedic impairments. What implications do these have for music therapy programming?

2. Are some types of music experiences and activities more useful than others in therapeutic programs for individuals who have orthopedic impairments? If so, which ones? Why?

3. Describe some specific music therapy experiences that might be used with individuals who have orthopedic impairments to (1) help to elicit

movement and decrease pain perception, (2) positively affect muscle tone to facilitate movement or relaxation, (3) help strengthen muscles and joints, increase endurance, and promote physical fitness, (4) help regulate physical movement and increase motor control and coordination, (5) facilitate communication and emotional expression, (6) increase self-esteem and provide opportunities for personal enrichment, and (7) provide opportunities for socialization and increase social skills. What unique benefits or qualities does music bring to each of these areas?

4. List several special considerations that may be important to remember when developing therapeutic intervention strategies for persons who have various orthopedic impairments. Why are these important? What are their implications for the structure of music therapy intervention strategies?

5. For each of the situations listed below, (a) define the problem or areas of need for the client or group of clients, (b) describe one or more of the goals you might pursue in music therapy sessions with the client(s), (c) describe music activities you might use to help the client(s) meet those goals, (d) tell how the music activities you described relate to the goals and needs of the client(s), and (e) mention any special considerations you might want to take into account when working with the client(s).

 Situation 1:

Wayne, a six-year-old boy with a diagnosis of athetoid cerebral palsy, has been referred to you for music therapy services. The physical therapist thinks that, given enough training, Wayne eventually will be able to use his upper extremities for functional movements. At this time, however, Wayne exhibits many jerks, writhing, uncontrolled movements. He cannot grasp or hold objects for more than two or three seconds. Wayne also has poor eye-hand coordination: Whenever he tries to reach out to touch or grab something, he usually misses on the first and second attempts. Wayne has fairly normal intelligence and often becomes frustrated by his inability to control his movements to get what he wants. The more frustrated he becomes, the more tense he gets, and the less he can control his movements. Consequently, Wayne needs to learn to relax so he can make the most efficient, controlled movements of which he is capable.

 Situation 2:

You are working as a music therapist on a hospital unit for patients recovering from orthopedic injuries. The physical therapists have asked you to help them devise programs that will decrease the patients' pain during range of motion exercises. They have also asked you to help devise activities that will motivate reluctant patients to participate in exercises designed to increase joint and muscle strength or to improve muscular control and coordination.

SUGGESTIONS FOR FURTHER READING

Alvin, J. (1976). *Music for the handicapped child* (2nd ed.). London: Oxford University Press.

Atterbury, B. W. (1990). *Mainstreaming exceptional learners in music.* Englewood Cliffs, NJ: Prentice-Hall.

Birkenshaw-Fleming, L. (1993). *Music for all: Teaching music to people with special needs.* Toronto: Gordon V. Thompson.

Bruscia, K. E. (Ed.) (1991). *Case studies in music therapy.* Phoenixville, PA: Barcelona Publishers.

Christenberry, E. B. (1979). The use of music therapy with burn patients. *Journal of Music Therapy, 16*(3), 138-148.

Clark, C., & Chadwick, D. (1979). *Clinically adapted instruments for the multiply handicapped.* Westford, MA: Modulations.

Edelstein, J. E. (1989). Musical options for upper limb amputees. In M. H. M. Lee (Ed.), *Rehabilitation, music and human well-being* (pp. 213-225)µ. St. Louis: MMB Music.

Elliott, B. (1982). *Guide to the selection of musical instruments with respect to physical ability and disability.* St. Louis: Magnamusic-Baton.

Farnan, L., & Johnson, F. (1988). *Everyone can move: Music and activities that promote movement and motor development.* New Berlin, WI: Jenson Publications.

Farnan, L., & Johnson, F. (1988). *Music is for everyone: A handbook for providing music to people with special needs.* New Berlin, WI: Jenson Publications.

Ford, S. C. (1984). Music therapy for cerebral palsied children. *Music Therapy Perspectives, 1*(3), 8-13.

Godley, C. A. S. (1987). The use of music in pain clinics. *Music Therapy Perspectives, 4,* 24-28.

Howell, R. D., Flowers, P. J., & Wheaton, J. E. (1995). The effects of keyboard iiexperiences on rhythmic responses on elementary school children with physical disabilities. *Journal of Music Therapy, 32*(2), 91-112.

James, M. R. (1986). Neurophysiological treatment of cerebral palsy: A case study. *Music Therapy Perspectives, 3,* 5-8.

Josepha, Sr. M. (1968). Part III. Music therapy for physically disabled children and adults. In E. T. Gaston (Ed.), *Music in therapy* (pp. 97-171). New York: Macmillan.

Miller, K. J. (1979). *Treatment with music: A manual for allied health professionals.* Kalamazoo, MI: Western Michigan University Printing Department.

Nagler, J. C., & Lee, M. H. M. (1989). Music therapy using computer music technology. In M. H. M. Lee (Ed.), *Rehabilitation, music and human well-being* (pp. 226-241). St. Louis: MMB Music.

Nocera, S. D. (1979). *Reaching the special learner through music.* Morristown, NJ: Silver Burdett.

Nordoff, P., & Robbins, C. (1971). *Music therapy in special education.* New York: John Day.

Nordoff, P., & Robbins, C. *Therapy in music for handicapped children.* London: Victor Gollancz Ltd.

Rudenberg, M. T. (1982). *Music therapy for handicapped children: Orthopedically handicapped.* Washington, D.C.: National Association for Music Therapy.

Rudenberg, M. T., & Royka, A. M. (1989). Promoting psychological adjustment in pediatric burn patients through music therapy and child life therapy. *Music Therapy Perspectives, 7,* 40-43.

Standley, J. (1991). *Music techniques in therapy, counseling, and special education.* St. Louis: MMB Music.

Staum, M. J. (1988). Music for physical rehabilitation: An analysis of literature from 1950-1986 and applications for rehabilitation settings. In C. E. Furman (Ed.), *Effectiveness of music therapy procedures: Documentation of research and clinical iipractice* (pp. 65-104). Washington, D. C.: National Association for Music Therapy.

Staum, M. J. (1996). Music for physical rehabilitation: An analysis of literature from 1950-1993 and applications for rehabilitation settings. In C. E. Furman (Ed.), *Effectiveness of music therapy procedures: Documentation of research and clinical practice* (2nd ed.))pp. 61-105). Silver Spring, MD: National Association for Music Therapy.

Thaut, M. H. (1992). Music therapy for the physically disabled child. In W. B. Davis, K. E. Gfeller, & M. H. Thaut, *An introduction to music therapy: Theory and practice* (pp. 164-179). Dubuque, IA: Wm. C. Brown.

Zinar, R. (1987). *Music activities for special children.* West Nyack, NY: Parker Publishing.

Chapter Twelve

MUSIC THERAPY FOR INDIVIDUALS WHO HAVE COMMUNICATION DISORDERS OR IMPAIRMENTS

DEFINITIONS

THE AMERICAN Speech and Hearing Association [ASHA] (1980) has defined communication disorders as the "inabilities of individuals to understand or appropriately use the speech and language systems of society" (p. 1). Communication disorders may range in severity from occasional misarticulations or sound repetitions to a complete inability to use speech and language for communication. There are two broad classifications of communication disorders: *speech disorders* and *language disorders*. According to ASHA (1980):

A language disorder is characterized by the inability to use the symbols of language through: (a) proper use of words and their meaning, (b) appropriate grammatical patterns, and (c) proper use of speech sounds.

A speech disorder is characterized by difficulty in (a) producing speech sounds (articulation),

(b) maintaining speech rhythm (fluent speech), and (c) controlling vocal production (voice) (p. 1).

Speech and language pathologists, more commonly referred to as speech therapists, are specialists in human communication, normal speech and language development, and communication disorders (ASHA, 1980; Michel & Jones, 1991). These professionals provide many clinical services, including assessing and treating speech and language disorders, helping individuals understand the types and severities of communication disorders, and assisting individuals who have communication disorders in finding ways to achieve more normal communication in social, school, and/or work settings (ASHA, 1980). The methods used vary depending on the nature and severity of the disorder, the individual's age, and the individual's awareness of the problem.

TYPES OF SPEECH AND LANGUAGE DISORDERS

Speech and language disorders may be grouped into several broad categories. Individuals who have communication disorders or impairments may have difficulties in one or more of these areas in varying degrees of severity. Speech or language problems may exist by themselves or be associated with other conditions, such as

hearing impairments or other sensory deficits, cerebral palsy, learning disabilities, traumatic brain injuries, mental retardation, autism, speech-motor deficits, severe environmental deprivation, or psychosocial problems (APA, 1994; Lovejoy & Estridge, 1987).

Articulation Disorders

Articulation disorders are the most numerous of all speech disorders, playing a part in 60-75 percent of all communication disorders (ASHA, 1980; Lovejoy & Estridge, 1987). Since these disorders involve phonological production, they are sometimes called *phonological disorders*. Individuals who have articulation disorders fail to produce speech sounds that are expected and appropriate to their age and dialect, and these difficulties often interfere with social communication or with academic or occupational achievement (APA, 1994; ASHA, 1980; Lovejoy & Estridge, 1987; Miller, 1982).

Individuals who have articulation disorders have difficulty producing speech sounds clearly. They may substitute one sound for another (e.g., "wight" for "light" or "wabbit" for "rabbit"), omit sounds (e.g., "at" for "hat" or "han" for "hand"), and/or distort sounds (e.g., "shlip" for "sip" or /s/ in "say" pronounced like /z/). A lisp (/s/ pronounced as /th/; e.g., "yeth" for "yes") is a common example of a slight distortion. Depending on their severity, articulation disorders may have minimal effects on speech intelligibility or cause speech to be completely unintelligible. Usually sound omissions are viewed as more severe than sound substitutions. Sound distortions are typically viewed as least severe. Phonological disorders may also involve errors in selecting or ordering sounds within words or syllables.

It is important to realize that some sound substitutions, omissions, or distortions are a normal part of language development or regional dialect. Thus, assessment of speech abilities must always take into account an individual's developmental age and cultural context (APA, 1994; ASHA, 1980; Lovejoy & Estridge, 1987; Michel & Jones, 1991).

Fluency Disorders

Individuals who have fluency disorders have disturbances or disruptions in the natural rhythm and time patterning of their speech that are inappropriate for their age or developmental level (APA, 1994; ASHA, 1980; Lovejoy & Estridge, 1987; Miller, 1982). Some dysfluencies frequently occur in young children in the normal course of language develop-

ment, and these are not considered to be disorders.

One of the most common and widely recognized fluency disorders is *stuttering*. Individuals who stutter frequently repeat or prolong sounds, syllables, words, or phrases when they speak (APA, 1994; ASHA, 1980; Lovejoy & Estridge, 1987; Miller, 1982). The extent of the disturbance may vary from one situation to another, often becoming more severe when there is particular pressure to communicate. Other types of speech dysfluencies include *interjections* (word or phrase inserted into an utterance that has no grammatical connection to it; e.g., "uh," "oh"), *broken words* (pauses or breaks within a word), *audible or silent blocking* (pauses in speech that may filled with interjections or left silent), and *circumlocutions* (substituting words to avoid problem words).

Voice Disorders

Individuals who have voice disorders have problems with vocal quality, vocal pitch, or vocal loudness or intensity. Individuals who have speech that is overly harsh, hoarse, breathy, or nasal have problems involving *vocal quality*. Those whose speech is higher (shriller) or lower than is standard for their age or sex and those whose speak in a monotone or have breaks in their voice have problems with *vocal pitch*. Individuals who have problems with *vocal loudness* or *intensity* speak too loudly or softly or may lose their voice (e.g., as in *aphonia* associated with chronic laryngitis). Unlike many other speech problems, some voice disorders may be only temporary (ASHA, 1980; Lovejoy & Estridge, 1987; Miller, 1982).

Delayed Language

Children who exhibit a marked slowness in developing language skills necessary to express and understand thoughts and ideas are said to have delayed language (ASHA, 1980; Miller, 1982). Children who have delayed language may have receptive language disorders (impaired ability to understand language), expressive language disorders (problems using speech/language to communicate meaning or problems using age-appropriate language and speech patterns), and/or auditory processing difficulties (problems distinguishing, focusing on, or remembering certain sounds) (APA, 1994; Lovejoy & Estridge, 1987).

Children who have *receptive language disorders* have difficulties comprehending the meaning of words or sentences. In milder cases, children may have difficulty understanding the subtleties of language (e.g., that the remark "You forgot your book" contains an implied message to go back and get the book) or difficulties understanding only certain types of words (e.g., spatial terms) or certain types of statements (e.g., more complex structures, like "if-then" sentences). In more severe cases, children have difficulty understanding even basic vocabulary and simple sentences. Since a child's ability to develop expressive language is dependent on acquiring receptive language skills, most receptive language disorders in children also include some expressive language disorder component (APA, 1994).

Children with *expressive developmental language delays* fail to develop speech skills expected for their age (APA, 1994; ASHA, 1980; Lovejoy & Estridge, 1987). They may have a limited amount of speech and a limited vocabulary, use simplified and limited varieties of grammatical structures, and use a limited variety of sentence types. They may have difficulty recalling words and difficulty learning new words. They may make frequent word-finding or vocabulary errors or may mix up the order of letters in words (e.g., "aminal" instead of "animal"). They may also use unusual word order in sentences or omit critical parts of sentences.

Children who have problems or deficits in some areas of auditory-processing have difficulty discriminating sounds, associating sounds and symbols, processing sounds, or storing, recalling, or sequencing sounds and ideas. Some may be easily distracted by irrelevant background noises, while others may have difficulty shifting their attention from one sound to another. Some may be unable to remember sounds even for a short time, and others may respond to a certain sound differently each time it is heard. Because of these symptoms, children with auditory processing problems may often appear to have attention deficit hyperactivity disorders or learning disorders (APA, 1994; Lovejoy & Estridge, 1987).

Aphasia

Aphasia is the loss or impairment of speech and language abilities because of damage or injury to certain cortical regions in the left hemisphere of the brain, often as the result of a stroke or head injury (Adamek & Shiraishi, 1996; Cohen, 1995; Miller 1982; Taylor, 1989). Depending on the location and extent of the damage, expressive language skills, receptive language skills, or both expressive and receptive language skills may be affected. For example, a lesion in Wernicke's area of the brain (*Wernicke's* or *receptive aphasia*) causes deficits in a person's ability to *understand* spoken or written language. In addition, individuals who have Wernicke's aphasia often are unable to find the proper words to communicate their intended messages, so they may produce fluent but non-sensical speech. In contrast, a lesion in Broca's area of the brain (*Broca's* or *expressive aphasia*) causes deficits in a person's ability to produce speech. Although they are able to understand speech reasonably well, individuals who have Broca's aphasia have difficulty expressing themselves in meaningful words, phrases or sentences. They may have problems retrieving words to name objects or express ideas, or they may have difficulties when they try to combine words into phrases or make sentences.

Two related communication disorders caused by brain damage or injury are apraxia and dysarthria (Adamek & Shiraishi, 1996; Cohen, 1992, 1995; Miller, 1982; Taylor, 1989). These may be found in conjunction with aphasia in some patients. In *apraxia*, the brain centers that control motor programming are damaged, and the motor memory needed for speech articulation is impaired. Individuals who have *verbal apraxia* may know what they want to say, but they cannot remember how to make their oral muscles produce the correct sounds. In *dysarthria*, the neuromotor mechanisms that regulate speech movements are damaged, resulting in incoor-dination of the muscles needed to produce speech and disturbances in respiration, vocal pitch, and phonation. "Dysarthric speech is characterized by limited verbal intelligibility, vocal intensity, and vocal range, as well as abnormal speech rates" (Cohen, 1995, p. 70).

Communication Disorders Associated with Other Conditions

Some conditions may affect the mechanisms associated with the production or development of speech, causing problems, impairments, or delays in speech and language. For example, malformations like *cleft palate* (a condition that occurs when the bones and tissues of the hard and soft palates fail to fuse) adversely impact vocal quality and phonation. The speech of individuals with cleft palates is characterized by hypernasality, nasal emissions (air escaping through the nasal passages during speech), and misarticulations (Lovejoy & Estridge, 1987; Miller, 1982).

Individuals who have *cerebral palsy* (see Chapter Eleven) may also experience speech and language difficulties. When cerebral palsy affects the motor control centers that govern the muscles for speech and/or breathing and breath control, individuals may have articulation, fluency, and/or voice disorders. If the impairments are extremely severe, the individual may be unable to develop oral speech.

Since hearing profoundly influences one's ability to develop or maintain speech and language skills, individuals who have *hearing impairments* may also have speech and language difficulties (Darrow & Gfeller, 1988; Gfeller, 1992d; Lovejoy & Estridge, 1987; Zinar, 1987). Problems may include delayed language development or various voice, fluency, and articulation disorders. Generally, the more severe the hearing impairment, the greater impact it will have on the development of language and other communication skills. (See Chapter Nine for more information.)

In addition, individuals who have conditions such as *mental retardation* (see Chapter Seven), *learning disabilities* (see Chapter Eight), *autism* (see Chapter Thirteen), *severe environmental deprivation,* or *psychosocial problems* (see Chapters Fourteen and Fifteen) may also have associated speech and language impairments. For more information on developing or remediating communication skills in these individuals, the reader is encouraged to consult the chapters discussing those conditions.

CAUSES

Communication disorders can be caused by many different physical, emotional, and environmental factors (APA, 1994; ASHA, 1980; Lovejoy & Estridge, 1987). Some speech and language impairments are the result of congenital or developmental factors or conditions (e.g., faulty development of brain and central nervous system centers related to language processing and speech production; hearing impairments; cleft palate; cerebral palsy); others are acquired later in life through injury to the brain or to any of the mechanisms or senses involved in speech and language. Problems with physical or mental development, psychological or emotional problems, and inadequate speech and language models in the home environment may also adversely impact speech and language development. In addition, voice disorders may be caused by excessive throat clearing, yelling, or screaming, and allergies or smoking can cause varying degrees of laryngitis.

Speech or language problems that have the same manifestation also may have entirely different causes in different individuals. For example, children may have an impairment or delay in expressive language that is not associated with any known injury to the brain (*developmental type*), or individuals may *acquire* an expressive language impairment after brain injury resulting from severe head trauma.

COMMON CHARACTERISTICS, PROBLEMS, AND NEEDS OF CLIENTS

As with any population, those individuals who have communication disorders or impairments are a very heterogeneous group. Factors such as the type and severity of the speech or language impairment, the cause and time of onset of the impairment, the existence of associated conditions or impairments, and the degree and type of support services available will all have varying effects on the individual's level of functioning, needs, and treatment program. In addition, each individual who has a speech or language impairment will have a unique combination of abilities, needs, personality traits, strengths, and weaknesses that will impact that individual's particular responses and functional abilities. Therefore, it is unwise to attempt to predict a particular person's skill levels or ceiling of abilities based on broad generalizations about a certain population. However, an awareness of some of those characteristics, problems, and needs which may be common to individuals who have various types of communication disorders will be beneficial both to the therapist who desires to work with this population and to the reader who is trying to understand how music therapy intervention strategies may benefit this population.

Individuals who have communication disorders or impairments have problems understanding language and/or problems using speech and language to express their thoughts and ideas. These speech and/or language difficulties may have varying degrees of severity, but they are serious enough that they interfere with the individual's social communication or with educational or occupational achievement (APA, 1994; Miller, 1982). When individuals have difficulty communicating with others, they often become isolated from friends, family, or society, in vocational, educational, social, and emotional areas (ASHA, 1980). Individuals who have communication disorders may also have emotional or self-confidence problems that arise from and/or contribute to their speech and language difficulties (APA, 1994; Wells & Helmus, 1968). In addition, they may feel angry, frustrated, or alienated because of the negative reactions of others to their poor speech or because of their inability to easily express their thoughts and ideas to others (Cohen, 1994). Consequently, these clients often need experiences that will enhance their self-esteem and self-confidence, provide outlets for emotional expression and release of anger and frustration, and present opportunities for interacting and communicating successfully with others.

Individuals who have speech impairments may have a number of problems, including poor coordination of breath and vocal mechanisms, poor articulation, lack of vocabulary, inability to remember speech sounds, inability to speak in complete sentences, poor grammar and syntax skills, inaccurate speech rhythms and inflections, and mixing up the order of words in a sentence or the order of syllables within a word (Nocera, 1979).

Clients with communication disorders will seldom exhibit all of these problems, but they will demonstrate a cluster of them consistently. Therapeutic goals for these clients may include areas such as increasing the ability to vocalize, improving breath and muscle control necessary for speech, increasing verbalization, developing accurate speech rhythms and inflections, and improving receptive and/or expressive language skills.

Individuals who have communication disorders that are the result of malfunction of or injury to the brain centers used in processing or producing speech and language (e.g., aphasia) may have difficulty with many different aspects of speech and language. For example, they may have a speaking voice that is pitched too high or too low, have a limited vocal range, or have difficulty controlling the intensity of their voice, have a speech rate that is uneven or abnormally fast or slow, or be difficult to understand (Cohen, 1992). Other individuals may be able to understand speech but not be able to produce it (APA, 1994; Cohen, 1995; Miller 1982; Taylor, 1989). Some individuals may also have problems with certain aspects of language, such as abstractions or spatial terms (APA, 1994; Bernstorf & Welsbacher, 1996), or they may have difficulty focusing on the main idea or take longer than normal to respond (Bernstorf & Welsbacher, 1996; Lovejoy & Estridge, 1987). Again, therapeutic interventions will be tailored to the individual's specific needs and problems, with the primary goal of giving the client some system of functional communication.

Augmentive Communication Systems

Some individuals have impairments or conditions, such as deformity of or damage to the vocal mechanism, certain types of brain damage, or profound hearing loss, that leave them unable to use oral speech for communication. These individuals need some alternative to oral speech, some augmentive means of communication, to help them communicate with those around them (Humpal & Dimmick, 1995; Miller, 1982). Several different types of augmentive or alternative communication systems are currently available, including (1) signing or manual communication systems, such as American Sign Language (ASL) (see Chapter Nine for more information), (2) Blissymbolics, a system of symbols designed by Charles Bliss to represent words and concepts (Blissymbolics Communication Foundation, 1978), and (3) electronic or manual communication boards, which use letters, words, or pictures to represent items and needs the clients encounter in their daily environment. Communication boards are usually designed by speech therapists, and are tailored to fit the individual's specific communication needs and physical and mental capabilities (Miller,

1982). The speech therapist helps the individual and those with whom the individual wishes to communicate learn how to use the system. Individual picture symbol cards (Coleman, McNairn & Shioleno, 1995; *Picture Communication Symbols Combination Book*, 1994) and various electronic devices and speech synthesizers (Humpal & Dimmick, 1995) may also be used to help nonverbal individuals communicate with those around them.

SETTINGS FOR SERVICE DELIVERY

Individuals who have communication disorders or impairments may receive special programs and services to help meet their specific needs in a variety of settings. Treatment settings may vary according to the type and severity of the impairment, the precipitating cause, and the time of onset (i.e., whether it is a congenital or developmental problem or whether it was acquired later in life). Speech and language pathologists are usually the primary professionals who help these clients develop or improve their communication skills. Speech and language pathologists provide services in many different types of facilities, including private clinics, public and private schools, colleges and universities, hospitals, rehabilitation centers, nursing homes, community clinics, state and local health departments, or state and federal government agencies (ASHA, 1980).

Many children who have speech and language disorders receive services through their local school district. The Individuals with Disabilities Act (IDEA) (Public Law 101-476), the 1990 revision of the 1975 Education for All Handicapped Children Act (Public Law 94-142) assures a free, appropriate public education to all children, ages 3-21, including those who have speech or language impairments. Both this law and the Technology-Related Assistance for Individuals with Disabilities Act (Public Law 100-407) also provide for assistive technology devices and services that may be needed by the individual (Adamek, 1996; Johnson, 1996). Incentives for early intervention programs to address the needs children birth through age 2 who have communication disorders are provided by Public Law 99-457 of 1986 (Adamek, 1996; Humpal, 1990).

Special education services for children who have speech or language impairments are delivered according to the same general procedure outlined in Chapter Seven. After initial referral, assessment and identification of the disability, Individualized Educational Programs (IEPs) are written to guide instruction. The goals in IEPs are matched to the individual's specific strengths and weaknesses. IEPs also provide for appropriate support services in areas of need, placement in the least restrictive environment, and an annual evaluation of student progress in the program. The student is usually included with peers in a regular classroom for as much of the day as possible. When the IEP assessment finds that music therapy can provide a unique means of helping students achieve their educational objectives, music therapists may be called upon to provide traditional direct services, work with students in self-contained classes, work with students in inclusive classes, provide direct in-home services to students who are confined to their homes for medical reasons, provide consultation services to facilitate classroom instruction, inclusion, or music education, and/or provide staff development workshops (Wilson, 1996). Music therapy is usually classified as a related service in special education settings.

Those individuals who acquire speech or language impairments later in life may also benefit from the services of speech and language pathologists to help them learn to adjust to their losses and/or to develop effect compensatory strategies to help maintain their abilities to communicate and socialize with their peers and families. This may be especially important for individuals who have lost some or all of their ability to communicate because of brain damage due to head injury or stroke.

Music therapists may work with both children and adults who have varying degrees and types of communication disorders or impairments. They deliver services to these clients in many different settings, including public schools, private schools or clinics, music studios, nursing homes, hospitals, rehabilitation centers, or community programs. Music therapists may provide direct or consultant services and work with clients as individuals or in groups. In a recent survey of populations served by music therapists in which respondents were permitted to list as many categories as appropriate (AMTA, 1998), 393 of 1,620 music therapists responding said they worked with individuals who had speech impairments, while 302 reported working with clients who were neurologically impaired and 290 reported working with stroke victims.

HOW MUSIC IS USED IN THERAPY

Speech and song have many similarities, sharing common features of fundamental frequency, variation and range of frequency or pitch, rate or rhythm, vocal intensity, correct breathing patterns and breath support, coordinated phonation, and accurate diction (Cohen, 1992, 1994; Coleman, McNairn & Shioleno, 1995; Michel & Jones, 1991; Staum, 1989). They are also both natural vehicles for human expression. In addition, involvement in music experiences increases many skills that are necessary for speech and language development, such as auditory attention and perception, auditory discrimination, auditory memory, a sense of body image and spatial relationships, motor planning and muscular coordination, vocabulary development, social interaction skills, and development of imagination and creativity (Zoller, 1991). Therefore, music experiences, especially those involving singing, would seem to be a natural way to help individuals improve speech and language skills. In fact, researchers have long noted the close connection between speech pathology and music therapy and continue to explore the relationships between the two fields (Cohen, 1994; Michel, 1985).

Music therapists who treat individuals with speech and language disorders must work closely with speech and language pathologists to determine the specific needs of each client (Michel, 1976, 1985; Michel & Jones, 1991). At times, music experiences may serve as an adjunct to traditional speech therapy approaches, as when songs are used to practice and drill specific words or sounds (Zoller, 1991). However, since "music provides an alternative neurological pathway for learning" (Coleman, McNairn & Shioleno, 1995, p. 3), music therapy approaches can also make many unique contributions to the treatment of persons who have communication disorders (Cohen, 1994; Michel, 1985; Miller, 1982). For example, music experiences can present material in an enjoyable, nonthreatening way, provide structure for the learning task and for the occurrence of appropriate responses, help cue or facilitate speech and language responses, and provide immediate positive reinforcement (Coleman, McNairn & Shioleno, 1995; Michel & Jones, 1991; Standley & Hughes, 1997; Staum, 1989). By providing multisensory learning and expressive experiences that involve the whole person, music promotes emotional engagement, increases motivation to participate in the task or treatment, and helps alleviate some of the boredom usually associated with repetitive drill (Coleman, McNairn & Shioleno, 1995; Miller, 1982; Staum, 1989; Zoller, 1991). In addition, "almost all reports in the literature suggest that both children and adults enjoy musically adapted speech learning experiences" (Staum, 1989, p. 64).

Music experiences can be structured to address several needs of clients who have various types of speech and/or language disorders. For example, therapeutic music experiences may focus on (1) increasing breath and muscle control, (2) stimulating vocalization, (3) developing receptive and/or expressive language skills, (4) improving articulation skills, (5) improving speech rate and fluency, and/or (6) correcting voice disorders. Music therapy approaches may also facilitate speech and language development or rehabilitation in individuals who

(7) have cleft palates, (8) have aphasia, or (9) use augmentive communication systems. Finally, music therapy interventions can help individuals who communication disorders (10) increase self-confidence, emotional expression, and social interaction. The next sections of this chapter provide examples of ways therapeutic music experiences can help clients gain skills in each of these areas.

Therapeutic Music Experiences to Increase Breath and Muscle Control

In order to produce speech sounds, an individual must have a certain amount of breath and muscle control. Music activities, such as playing simple wind instruments (e.g., kazoo, flutophone, Melodica), practicing breathing or blowing exercises to music (e.g., blowing bubbles to a song about bubbles), doing breathing and vocal exercises associated with singing instruction, and participating in singing and chanting, can help individuals develop the breath and muscle control needed for speech (Cohen, 1994; Miller, 1982; Nocera, 1979; Wells & Helmus, 1968; Zoller, 1991). Those who are bored by breathing exercises or simple instruments can develop their respiratory muscles and breath control by studying singing (Cohen, 1992, 1994) or learning to play more advanced wind instruments (Haas, Pineda & Axen, 1989). The aesthetic rewards inherent in making music can be important factors in motivating clients to develop and practice breath control and breath support skills. As they experience success in developing breath and muscle control in music contexts, client may also develop the confidence needed to transfer and apply these skills to speech production.

Therapeutic Music Experiences to Stimulate Vocalization

Before individuals can speak in words, they must learn how to use their vocal mechanisms to produce sounds. Vocalizations are preverbal behaviors that are part of speech development. Once an individual produces vocal sounds, these can possibly be shaped over time into words and communicative speech (Cunningham, 1986; Staum, 1989).

Music often acts as "a nonverbal catalyst to evoke vocal participation" (Staum, 1989, p. 64). For example, various types of specially selected background music can help elicit and increase vocalizations in children with cerebral palsy (Ditson, 1961), disadvantaged kindergarten children (Goolsby, Frary, & Rogers, 1974), children and adults with mental retardation (Cunningham, 1986; Pujol, 1994), and individuals who are speech-delayed or mute (Staum, 1989). Some research has found that soft music and flute melodies in major keys were particularly useful in significantly increasing vocalizations (Cunningham, 1986; Pujol, 1994). However, since all clients have individual preferences and unique responses, music therapists must always carefully observe each client's responses to various types of music and musical instruments to determine what particular background music (style, form, tempo, volume, etc.) or instruments will most effectively promote vocalizations for a particular individual or group of clients.

Sometimes, vocalizations can be encouraged and shaped as the therapist imitates the client's spontaneous sounds and then shapes or extends or structures them through vocal or instrumental improvisations (Loewy, 1995; Nordoff & Robbins, 1977). In other instances, contingent music may be used as a reinforcer to increase free verbalization (Talkington & Hall, 1970; Walker, 1972). Other participatory music experiences, such as humming, singing with sustained vowel sounds, singing or echoing consonant sounds or syllables, or vocally imitating instrument, animal, or familiar environmental sounds (e.g., sirens, horns, jets, wind) within the context of songs, may also encourage individuals to vocalize and stimulate the use of expressive speech (Loewy, 1995; Nocera, 1979).

Many of these musical vocal stimulation experiences can be structured to follow the normal sequence of language development (Loewy, 1995; Michel & Jones, 1991). For example, Loewy (1995) has suggested a series of music techniques to stimulate and activate vocalization at each stage of Van Riper's (1984) model of language acquisition. At the earliest stages, Loewy suggests tonal/vocal holding techniques to match and extend the child's cry and rhythmic drum beating to match and help organize the child's sounds. At the babbling/lalling stage, vocal mirroring techniques encourage vocal play and development. Later, vowels and phonemes are used in vocal improvisation and rhythmic consonant play, and specific action words are used and explored with instruments and in songs. Perhaps most importantly, while carefully sequenced music experiences help encourage vocalization within the context of an individual's particular stage or level of speech and language, they simultaneously help "integrate the cognitive, physical, and emotional aspects of growth" (Loewy, 1995, p. 71).

Therapeutic Music Experiences to Develop Receptive and Expressive Language Skills

Both receptive and expressive language skills can be developed, practiced, and reinforced through specially structured music experiences (Coleman, McNairn & Shioleno, 1995; Humpal, 1990; Michel & Jones, 1991; Miller, 1982; Nocera, 1979). Music may be especially useful in helping develop the listening, sound discrimination, and auditory sequencing and memory skills that are important in the development of *receptive language skills* (Michel & Jones, 1991; Miller, 1982; Nocera, 1979; Zinar, 1987; Zoller, 1991). Sounds of musical instruments and singing voices readily attract the attention of most clients, thus providing a useful starting point for auditory awareness training. At first, music therapists may work on basic auditory awareness and perception skills, asking clients to make gross discriminations (e.g., sound/no sound, fast/slow, loud/soft, high pitch/low pitch) in listening, movement-to-music, singing, and instrumental experiences. As the client's skills emerge and develop, these activities can be structured and adapted to lead clients to gradually make finer discriminations of sound qualities, pitches, dynamics, tempos, or rhythms. Music activities and experiences that gradually ask clients to remember more sounds, lyrics, and rhythms or more complex sequences of sounds, musical events, or directions can also help develop auditory memory and sequencing skills.

When individuals have good receptive language skills, they understand what words mean and are able to follow directions. Music therapists can readily structure a number of activities to help individuals develop and practice these skills. For example, songs, dances, and musical games can require individuals to

follow simple directions, identify or move specific body parts, or identify colors, pictures, objects, letters, numbers, etc. Clients can also demonstrate an understanding of language by pointing to pictures or word cards that go with song lyrics, performing actions or answering questions to demonstrate an understanding of song lyrics, or sequencing picture cards to tell the story of a song. Michel and Jones (1991, pp. 16-18), Miller (1982, pp. 43-45), Nocera (1979, pp. 24-54, 99-100), and Zinar (1987, pp. 175-176), give several detailed suggestions of music activities that may be useful in developing auditory perception and receptive language skills.

Different types of music experiences may also help motivate individuals to develop and practice various *expressive language skills*. For example, group singing can be a very effective tool for reinforcing communication, improving expressive language skills, and increasing self-initiated speech (Cohen, 1994). Individuals who have speech impairments or delayed language development may also become more confident in using expressive speech when they are asked to do this in the enjoyable, nonthreatening context of music experiences (Hoskins, 1988; Michel & Jones, 1991; Miller, 1982; Zinar, 1987).

> Children will frequently sing something they rarely or never say, and can often do so without demonstrating the same difficulties they have when they are speaking the same words. This can lead to increased self-confidence, and can encourage the child to use the words in everyday speech. (Miller, 1982, p. 31).

Sequentially structured songs and music games can gradually encourage the development of expressive language skills, first asking individuals to produce vowel or consonant sounds (e.g., sing with "ah" or "oo" or "buh"), then to sing one or two words or fill in the missing words to song lyrics, and then to sing phrases and whole songs (Michel & Jones, 1991; Miller, 1982). Hoskins (1988) also found that music activities like action songs, singing activities used to teach concepts like body parts, colors, and numbers, and antiphonal songs using picture word cards were particularly useful in encouraging spontaneous speech and improving expressive language skills in preschool children who had language delays. In addition, clients can also develop and practice expressive language skills as they participate in song writing experiences, supplying single words, phrases, or complete lyrics for original songs or parodies. Michel & Jones (1991, pp. 19-26), Nocera (1979, pp. 101-102), and Zinar (1987, pp. 175-176) provide several excellent examples of specific music activities that can be used to develop expressive language skills.

Music experiences may also be used to increase vocabulary, learn and understand rules of grammar and syntax, and develop, improve, or reinforce reading and writing skills. Music experiences, such as songs, chants, musical games, song writing activities, listening experiences, and movement or instrument playing experiences that incorporate the use of written symbols or directions, may all be structured to present information on these subjects, practice these skills, provide a structure for learning and remembering the information, or reinforce the learning (Coleman, McNairn & Shioleno, 1995; Michel & Jones, 1991; Miller, 1982; Standley & Hughes, 1997; Staum, 1989; Zoller, 1991). Moreover, the multisensory aspect of music experiences can facilitate the learning and retention of material. For example, Madsen (1991) found that first graders learned more new vocabulary when the words were presented with music paired with gesture over words paired with gesture alone. In addition, music experiences can accommodate a wide variety of learning styles.

Some music therapists have structured therapeutic music interventions to complement various approaches to language development. Gfeller (1987b) used song writing in a Language Experience Approach to increase reading and writing skills, and found that song writing increased motivation to participate and increased attention to the material by adding a novel teaching method. The lyrics and music also provided themes for discussion and a structure for teaching language skills. In another research project, music activities structured to complement a cognitive-linguistic approach to language development (a) increased multisensory and motor involvement in learning (instrumental and music-movement experiences), (b) encouraged dialogue and group interaction (question-and-answer, call-and-response, echo, or fill-in songs), (c) motivated and engaged client participation, and (d) provided opportunities to experience and practice

language skills in a different context (Gfeller, 1990). Another researcher found that, when books texts were set to music in a music-enhanced whole language approach, music became a structural prompt to pair the sung word to the written word, helping children "link oral to written language through rhyme, rhythm, and repetition of vocabulary and story structure" (Colwell, 1994, p. 240).

In early intervention settings, specially designed music activities can provide effective avenues for practicing language patterns, learning how to use books and printed materials, increasing language comprehension, and beginning to decode written language (Standley & Hughes, 1997). Research has found that music activities that intentionally target and focus on specific skills are most effective in teaching pre-reading and writing concepts (Standley & Hughes, 1997). Coleman, McNairn, and Shioleno (1995) provide several examples of songs and music activities that may be used to increase specific literacy skills.

Therapeutic Music Experiences to Improve Articulation Skills

Since individuals must be able to discriminate between correct and incorrect sounds to articulate words properly, musical experiences focusing on improving sound discrimination skills (e.g., same/different) may provide an important foundation for improving articulation skills (Michel & Jones, 1991; Nocera, 1979; Zinar, 1987; Zoller, 1991). Initial experiences may use instrumental sounds (e.g., identifying instruments by sound only; telling whether two sounds were played by the same or different instruments), with later experiences moving to finer distinctions of verbal sounds. For example, individuals may be asked to listen to two versions of a lyric to identify which uses the correct word sounds and which contains errors.

One of the most obvious types of beneficial musical experiences for individuals who have articulation disorders is the use of specially devised songs, chants, or musical games that help them practice certain speech sound or words (Cohen, 1994; Madsen, Michel, & Madsen, 1975; Marsh & Fitch, 1970; Michel & Jones, 1991; Michel & May, 1974; Miller, 1982; Nocera, 1979; Staum, 1989; Wells

& Helmus, 1968; Zinar, 1987; Zoller, 1991). The process may begin by setting specially targeted sounds or syllables to melodies or chants for the individual to sing. When specific sounds are mastered, the individual may then be asked to sing targeted words in songs that use these sounds (see Michel & Jones, 1991, pp. 19-21, and Zinar, 1987, pp. 182-187, for examples). Singing and music can motivate individuals to practice their articulation exercises by providing a more pleasurable way of communicating and by relieving some of the boredom often associated with the repeated drill necessary to improve articulation skills. As Staum (1989) noted, "the flexibility of music provides a perfect structure to alleviate the monotony that otherwise would prevail" (p. 63).

The rhythmic structure of music may provide additional benefits to persons with articulation disorders. Zoller (1991) suggested that individuals speak poems rhythmically while clapping, walking, or tapping the beat, for "rhythm often unconsciously helps correct misarticulations" (p. 275). The rhythmic and melodic cues provided by setting words to music may also help individuals remember sound sequences within words, another skill that is important to proper articulation (Staum, 1989).

Therapeutic Music Experiences to Improve Speech Rate or Fluency

The rhythmic and melodic structure of music can also be used to help individuals achieve a more normal *speech rate*. Individuals who speak too rapidly may learn to speak more slowly by singing question-and-answer songs that have slow or moderate tempi and one syllable per note. The structure involved in using sung questions (by the therapist) and sung responses (by the client) may help individuals relax and slow their rate of speech, enabling them to improve their ability to verbally communicate information and answer questions about themselves and their daily routine (Michel & Jones, 1991). Rhythmic games and exercises that involve walking, tapping, or playing instruments to the basic beat or melodic rhythm of songs may help individuals become more aware of tempo and speech rate (Miller, 1982). Speaking/chanting words or phrases rhythmically or

saying and clapping the rhythm of familiar words are other music- and rhythm-based techniques that may help individuals achieve a more appropriate speech rate (Miller, 1982). Cohen (1988) also found that superimposing a rhythm on verbal structure by tapping the beat while singing or by tapping the beat while practicing a tape of functional sentences helped decrease excessively fast speech rates in individuals who had brain damage. Persons with neurological impairments who received singing instruction (including breathing and vocal exercises and group singing) also showed some improvement in their speech rate (Cohen, 1992; Cohen & Masse, 1993). For persons with neurogenic communication disorders who had an abnormally slow speech rate, vocal instruction paired with Visi-Pitch™ feedback helped increase speech rate and vocal intensity (Cohen, 1995).

The rhythmic and melodic structure of music can also help decrease *fluency disorders*. Although Galloway (1974) reported that, contrary to popular belief, singing cannot cure stuttering, various studies have shown that white noise and rhythmic stimulation can significantly reduce stuttering (Altrows & Bryden, 1977; Brayton & Conture, 1978; Silverman, 1976; Yairi, 1976). Michel & Jones (1991) noted that researchers have hypothesized that some stuttering problems may be related to difficulties with speaking rate, controlling the breath stream, and synchronizing the breath stream with sound production at the vocal cord level, and that many techniques in singing instruction may help alleviate these difficulties. Therefore, they recommend that music therapists "apply techniques of good singing instruction, vocalizing, breathing, etc., with stutterers" (Michel & Jones, 1991, p. 23). Since stuttering problems often increase in stressful situations, persons who stutter may benefit from music relaxation techniques (Michel & Jones, 1991). Conceivably, there may be instances in which rhythmic or melodic structure could cue both relaxation and fluency for some individuals. Clearly, many questions about stuttering and its causes and treatments remain to be answered (Michel & Jones, 1991; Miller, 1982). The music therapist must work closely with qualified speech pathologists and carefully note the specific needs, strengths, preferences, and responses of each client.

Therapeutic Music Experiences to Correct Voice Disorders

Since singing and speaking both involve elements of vocal frequency (pitch), inflection (melodic contour and pitch change), sound quality, and intensity (volume), singing can be a valuable therapeutic tool to help correct various voice disorders (Cohen, 1992, 1994; Miller, 1982; Nocera, 1979; Staum, 1989; Zinar, 1987). Because breath control affects vocal resonance and voice timbre, individuals who have problems with v*ocal quality* (overly harsh, hoarse, breathy, or nasal speech) may benefit from breath control exercises to music or from learning proper breath support and control as part of vocalization exercises and singing instruction (Cohen, 1994; Miller, 1982). Humming or playing simple wind instruments like the kazoo or flutophone also help develop breath control and support and help individuals learn to direct their air stream for more open, less nasal sounds (Miller, 1982; Wells & Helmus, 1968; Zinar, 1987).

Various music experiences can also positively influence *vocal pitch* and *inflection.* For example, individuals whose speech is higher (shriller) or lower than is standard for their age or sex may benefit from music-movement and singing games that have them recognize and imitate high or low sounds and pitches. The use of hand signals that correspond to high, medium, and low pitches may help emphasize proper intonation and pitch level placement. Singing instruction and vocal training utilizing songs and vocal exercises have effectively improved the fundamental speaking frequency (vocal pitch) of children with hearing impairments (Cohen, 1994; Darrow & Starmer, 1986) and persons with neurological impairments (Cohen, 1992). In addition, specially adapted music education software used with a personal computer that increased singing range and accuracy in an individual with Down syndrome also caused his speech to become clearer and pitched in a higher, more appropriate frequency range (Spitzer, 1989).

Music can also be a valuable asset in teaching or practicing correct inflectional patterns for individuals who speak in a *monotone* or who have problems with proper vocal *inflection* (Miller, 1982; Nocera, 1979; Staum, 1989; Wells & Helmus, 1968; Zinar, 1987). When melodies and phrases of songs are carefully constructed so that the melodic and rhythmic treatment of the lyrics corresponds to the natural rhythms and inflections of speech, singing songs can help clients learn and practice correct rhythmic and inflectional patterns for words, phrases, and sentences (Nordoff & Robbins, 1971a). As individual clients learn to use more inflection through singing or chanting, the music can be gradually faded (Staum, 1989). Matching tones with a piano, moving or making diagrams to show the pitch contour of a phrase, and echo songs and chants are all experiences that can help increase awareness of vocal pitch and inflection. Miller (1982, pp. 47-48), Nocera (1979, pp. 102-103), and Zinar (1987, pp. 181-183) provide several examples of music- and rhythm-based experiences designed to improve vocal inflection.

When individuals speak too loudly or softly (disorders of *volume* or *intensity*), experiences in singing or playing the same song at different volume or intensity levels may help them become aware of differences in degrees of loudness and learn to control their own level of speaking, singing, or playing. Relating musical dynamic markings to speech situations, practicing getting gradually louder or softer (with voices or instruments), or using echo songs may also help individuals learn to use appropriate volume in singing and speaking (Zinar, 1987). Those who speak too softly may need to develop breath control and lung capacity. They may benefit from vocal and breathing exercises, singing sustained tones and gradually being encouraged to sing longer songs and phrases, vocally imitating the sounds of chimes or drums, playing the harmonica or kazoo, or learning to play a wind instrument (Wells & Helmus, 1968; Zinar, 1987). Cohen (1995) found that a treatment regimen including breathing exercises, speech tasks set to diatonic ascending and descending patterns that slightly exaggerate normal speech prosody, singing familiar songs, and Visi-Pitch™ feedback helped individuals with neurogenic communication disorders improve their vocal intensity. Subjects in this study noted that combination of singing and Visi-Pitch™ feedback enhanced their therapy and gave an incentive to practice at home. Again, it is evident music has a great ability to motivate individuals to participate in treatment and to practice repetitious drills (Staum, 1989).

Music Therapy for Individuals Who Have Cleft Palates

Individuals who have cleft palates often have problems with hypernasality and poor breath stream control. Several music experiences involving singing and playing simple wind instruments can help alleviate these problems (Michel, 1968; Michel & Jones, 1991; Wells & Helmus, 1968; Zinar, 1987). As mentioned above, humming and kazoo playing have been found to be most effective in reducing nasal sounds (Michel, 1968; Wells & Helmus, 1968; Zinar, 1987). Playing simple wind instruments like the harmonica, flutophone, melodica or pianica, whistle, or reed horn may also develop velopharangeal closure and help eliminate nasal emission of air (Michel, 1968; Michel & Jones, 1991; Wells & Helmus, 1968), while trumpet instruction can help older clients learn to direct their airstream properly (Wells & Helmus, 1968). In addition, group singing and vocalizing experiences can help develop proper breath stream control and provide a pleasurable way to practice correct speech sounds and improve tone quality (Michel, 1968; Michel & Jones, 1991).

Not only do music therapy interventions help individuals who have cleft palates increase ability to discriminate sound quality, improve breath stream control, and practice articulation exercises, but they also provide outlets for expressing feelings of frustration and aggression and help increase individuals' self-confidence as they make positive accomplishments in developing musical skills (Michel, 1968). Moreover, imbedding therapeutic treatment in music experiences often makes individuals more willing to participate in treatment. For example, Michel (1968) observed that even children who were uncooperative in speech therapy and usually disruptive in group settings responded positively to music therapy.

Music Therapy for Speech and Language Rehabilitation in Individuals with Aphasia

The benefits of singing for stimulating speech in individuals who have neurological impairments have been noted for many years. Cohen (1994) provides a summary of early anecdotal records (dating back to 1745) and research, all of which note how singing is often maintained in individuals with expressive aphasia who have little or no speech. While the ability of music therapy interventions to help a particular individual may depend on many factors, including the individual's premorbid experience with music and the exact site and extent of the brain damage (Cohen, 1994; Taylor, 1987b, 1989), music therapy techniques can be effective in treating speech dysfunctions for many individuals with traumatic brain injuries (Adamek & Shiraiski, 1996).

Early reports in the music therapy literature observed that individuals who were not able to speak as the result of a brain injury often were still able to sing songs that were learned before the injury. For some clients, these songs could provide a springboard for redeveloping some language ability (Goodglass, 1963; Palmer, 1953). Since those early years, many different music- and rhythm-based interventions have been developed to help restore speech and communication abilities in persons with aphasia.

Melodic Intonation Therapy

In the early 1970s, a technique called Melodic Intonation Therapy (MIT) was developed by a speech pathologist as a strategy to recover some functional speech in adults with aphasia who were not responding to more traditional speech therapy techniques (Albert, Sparks, & Helms, 1973; Sparks, Helms, & Albert, 1974; Sparks & Holland, 1976). In MIT, short phrases and sentences are intoned at a slow tempo to simple, unfamiliar melodic patterns that have a limited pitch range (designed to resemble the natural inflections of speech), with a precise rhythm that emphasizes the words' normal stress and inflection. The client is led through a sequence of specific steps and levels that gradually increase the length of phrases and sentences intoned, decrease dependence on the therapist, and minimize the client's reliance on the intonation. Techniques used in the MIT process include verbal cuing, hand tapping, control by hand signals, unison repetition, and eventual fading of the melodic patterns. (For a complete description of the method, see Sparks and Holland, 1976).

MIT techniques are based on the assumption that the right hemisphere of the brain is dominant for interpreting nonverbal processes such as music. The right hemisphere, then, also responds to the "musical" qualities of speech (rhythm, stress, inflection), especially when they are exaggerated. It is hypothesized that MIT is effective because the damaged left hemisphere of the brain, which is assumed to be dominant for speech, is stimulated and assisted by the melodic intonation that exaggerates the rhythm, stress, and melodic contour of the words and phrases, making use of speech functions contained in the undamaged right hemisphere (Kraus & Galloway, 1982). The best candidate for MIT is an adult with aphasia who has normal verbal comprehension but limited verbal output, who is emotionally stable, and who makes an active effort at self-correction.

Lucia (1987), a music therapist, has adapted MIT techniques for group use, focusing on word retrieval through songs and rhythmic chant. According to Lucia (1987), this approach is most useful for patients who have damage to the left frontal lobe (Broca's aphasia) or bilateral damage in which the right temporal lobe is still relatively intact. Kraus and Galloway (1982) have also successfully used MIT techniques to help develop speech in children who have apraxia and language delays.

Rhythm and Melody in Speech Therapy

This technique, developed by a music therapist (Rogers & Fleming, 1981), makes use of both musical and therapeutic principles, and employs "carrier melodies" to stimulate speech in persons with left hemisphere brain damage. The technique "capitalizes on residually intact melody and rhythm at some neurophysiologic level wherein correlates of speech/language share neural pathways with those elements of music salient to verbal communication, i.e., rhythm and melody" (Rogers & Fleming, 1981, p. 36). In contrast to MIT, this method uses familiar melodies "to take advantage of any 'automatic' ability present" (p. 34). After selecting a familiar melody with intervals and rhythms approximating those of conversational speech to be used as the carrier tune (e.g., "Yankee Doodle"), the therapist establishes the patient's ability to hum or sing the carrier melody. Next, phrases are added to the melodic pattern. Tongue exercises performed to the

music helped patients prepare to speak/sing the words. Later, vocabulary is increased, using a two-note pattern to introduce new words. Finally, the carrier melody and two-note patterns are reduced and eliminated, and more complex phrases are substituted, using melodies involving three pitches (e.g., C, D, E). Rogers and Fleming used the method in both group and individual sessions, and noted that "the simplicity of the program lends itself to family participation and carry-over to practice in the home during weekend passes and after discharge" (p. 35).

Other Techniques

Other music-based techniques can also enhance communication abilities in persons with aphasia and related disorders. Skille (1989) found that vibroacoustic therapy, a method in which musical sound waves are applied directly to the body, increased vocal sound production in persons with aphasia. Cohen (1992) used singing instruction and weekly Visi-Pitch™ feedback on vocal intensity, fundamental frequency, and percentage of pause time to help clients with both expressive aphasia and dysarthria increase their speech rate and vocal intensity, with some improvement in verbal intelligibility. Cohen and Masse (1993) found that singing and rhythmic instruction successfully increased verbal intelligibility in persons with neurogenic communication disorders. Cohen (1988) also worked with a patient who had right hemisphere brain damage and found that tapping the beat during singing or rhythmic speech helped decrease the patient's excessively fast speech rate.

Taylor (1987b, 1989) gives several recommendations for using music-based treatment interventions with clients who have communication disorders resulting from aphasia. His suggestions include:

1. Tailoring the music therapy intervention to the specific needs, strengths, abilities, and preferences of each client, to maximize music's ability to effectively treat the specific speech and language disorders of that individual;

2. Using slower than normal tempos to increase the time available to perceive and form syllables and

words; also using slowed conversational speech, emphasizing key words;

3. Using songs with few words, frequent repetitions, and fairly regular, repeated rhythm patterns for singing activities;

4. Singing songs more than once so clients have a chance to correct errors;

5. Pointing to the printed lyrics while singing, using large song cards or typed sheets with one song per page;

6. Using melodic settings of the words that enhance normal speech accents and inflections; and

7. Working separately on elements tempo, rhythm, pitch control, loudness, tone quality, articulation, breath control, so success in one area will generate motivation to work on other areas.

Taylor (1989) also suggests that song writing be used to help improve expressive language and believes "treatment objectives should include social, emotional and nonlanguage motor skills in addition to specific communication behaviors" (p. 177). (For more information on the use of music therapy in the rehabilitation of persons with traumatic brain injuries, see Chapter Eighteen.)

Therapeutic Music Experiences Using Augmentive Communication Systems

Individuals who use augmentive communication methods may readily participate in music experiences if the therapist is willing to learn the individual's system of communication and utilize it in giving instructions and allowing the individual to respond. For example, individuals who use communication boards may respond to questions or contribute to song writing exercises by using their boards. Herman (1985) worked with children who used Blissymbols and had them point to symbols to identify feelings represented by music, contribute to group "story songs," or tell what feelings they wanted to express. As mentioned in Chapter Nine, signing and manual communication systems can be used to

express song lyrics, and signs and singing can be used together for total communication experiences (Darrow, 1987a; Knapp, 1980). Music can also have a positive effect on learning signs. Buday (1995) found that, in simultaneous communication conditions, children with autism learned more signs when the signs were taught with music and speech than when they were taught with rhythm and speech.

Technology now makes it possible for individuals who are nonverbal to have an active "voice" in many music experiences (Humpal & Dimmick, 1995). For example, switches may activate tape players containing tape loops of repeated words or phrases in a song. Individuals who have augmentive communication devices that produce synthesized speech sounds may use these to supply words or phrases to songs or contribute to discussions or group compositions. Technology also allows individuals who have severe physical limitations increased opportunities to create music independently through the use of computers and adaptive electronic equipment (Fegers et al., 1989; Howell et al., 1995; Krout, 1992a, 1995; Nagler & Lee, 1989; Swingler, 1994).

Therapeutic Music Experiences Increase Self-Confidence, Emotional Expression, and Social Interaction

The opportunities for nonverbal communication inherent in group music activities can be very important to individuals who cannot use speech for communication. Through the acts of playing instruments or moving to music, individuals may express themselves and their feelings without the trauma, difficulty, or embarrassment of attempting to speak. The opportunity to express themselves through music, a socially acceptable, meaningful form of communication, "may serve to alleviate some of the frustration that often accompanies speech impairments and give the child [or adult] an opportunity for ventilation of feelings" (Miller, 1982, p.2). Those individuals who have acquired communication impairments as the result of brain injuries may also benefit from music therapy interventions, such as song writing, instrumental improvisation, or discussion of song lyrics, that help them process social and emotional issues related to their injury and losses (Adamek & Shiraishi, 1996;

Taylor, 1989). (See Chapter Eighteen for more information.)

Speech problems may cause individuals to have a lack of self-confidence (Wells & Helmus, 1968). As they participate in creative music experiences like song writing, instrumental improvisation, and creative movement to music that allow them to express their own feelings and personalities, individuals "visibly grow in power and self-possession" (Herman, 1985, p. 35). Individuals also increase their self-confidence and self-esteem as they participate successfully in music experiences, see their speech skills improve from practice in music situations, or acquire skills in singing or playing musical instruments (Haas, Pineda, & Axen, 1989; Michel, 1968).

Music therapy experiences are often conducted in group settings and provide opportunities for social interaction in the context of enjoyable activities. Group instruction provides many additional social and emotional benefits not present in individual instruction (Cohen, 1992; Rogers & Fleming, 1981). Participating in group singing or instrumental experiences can help increase cooperation, decrease shyness, and increase interaction with others (Michel, 1968). Group music experiences for individuals with aphasia also help increase social awareness, encourage successful interactions within a peer group, provide emotional support systems, give opportunities to see fellow patients at varying stages of progress, provide a safe environment to test new skills, and offer a forum for sharing issues, frustrations, concerns, and complaints (Cohen & Masse, 1993; Rogers & Fleming, 1981). Following their work in music therapy with persons who had aphasia, Cohen and Ford (1995) observed,

> The music therapy session provided them with a comfortable environment in which they were able to produce some words and apparently feel successful. Music therapy was valuable for them because it fostered participation and provided a means of expression, both verbal and nonverbal. (p. 54)

Researchers have also found that preschool children who have speech and language disorders can participate successfully in basic group music activities with their nondisabled peers (Cassidy, 1992). Thus, the practice of "mainstreaming" or including children who have communication disorders in "regular" music classes gives them opportunities to interact successfully with their peers and helps them practice various communication skills.

SPECIAL CONSIDERATIONS AND TIPS FOR SUCCESS

When music therapists work with clients who have speech and language disorders, it is essential that they consult and cooperate with speech therapists. Such cooperative efforts can have important beneficial results for the clients (Gfeller & Bauman, 1988; Michel, 1976, 1985; Michel & Jones, 1991; Michel & May, 1974). If a client uses an alternative means of communication, the music therapist should know how to understand and communicate through that system of communication.

The music therapist who uses music intervention to develop language skills should be familiar with the normal sequences of language development and with common language assessment tools (Michel & Jones, 1991). This will help the therapist determine the client's current level of functioning and help provide a sequence for skill development. Pairing concrete stimuli (e.g., pictures or gestures) with the aural/verbal stimuli of spoken words may help individuals respond correctly (Cassidy, 1992). Instructions and activities should use language that matches the functional language abilities of the client and should not attempt to teach too many items or give too many examples at one time (Michel & Jones, 1991).

Since many individuals with communication disorders may have emotional problems that arise from or underlie their speech and language problems, it is important to include consideration of their emotional needs in the total treatment plan (Michel, 1968; Michel & Jones, 1991; Miller, 1982; Taylor, 1989; Wells & Helmus, 1968). Since poor communication skills also negatively affect socialization, it may be important to help individuals develop and have opportunities to practice appropriate social interaction skills.

SUMMARY

When individuals cannot understand or appropriately use the speech and language systems of society, they have some type of *communication disorder*. There are two broad classifications of communication disorders: *speech disorders*, which include articulation, fluency, and voice problems, and *language disorders*, which are characterized by difficulties in using or understanding language (expressive and receptive language skills). Communication disorders or impairments can be caused by many different physical, emotional, and environmental factors. Some communication disorders result from *congenital* or *developmental* factors or conditions; others are *acquired* later in life through injury to the brain or the any of the mechanisms involved in understanding or producing speech and language.

Individuals who have communication disorders have problems understanding language and/or problems using speech and language to express their thoughts and ideas. These speech and/or language difficulties may have varying degrees of severity, but they are serious enough that they interfere with the individual's social communication or with educational or occupational achievement. Therapeutic interventions are tailored to the individual's specific needs and problems, with the primary goal of giving the client some system of functional communication. In addition, clients often need experiences that enhance self-esteem, provide outlets for expressing emotions and venting frustrations, and present opportunities to interact and communicate successfully with others. Individuals who are unable to use oral speech for communication often use augmentive or alternative means of communication, such as manual communication systems (sign language), Blissymbolics, or manual or electronic communication boards.

Speech and song are both natural vehicles for human expression and share many common features, such as fundamental frequency, variation and range of frequency or pitch, rate or rhythm, vocal intensity, correct breathing patterns and breath support, coordinated phonation, and accurate diction. Involvement in music experiences also increases many skills that are necessary for speech and language development, such as auditory attention and perception, auditory discrimination, auditory memory, a sense of body image and spatial relationships, motor planning and muscular coordination, vocabulary development, social interaction skills, and development of imagination and creativity. Music experiences facilitate the acquisition of speech and language skills in several ways: (1) by presenting material in an enjoyable, nonthreatening fashion, (2) by motivating clients to participate in treatment, (3) by providing structure for the learning task and for the occurrence of appropriate responses, (4) by cuing or facilitating speech and language responses, (5) by decreasing the boredom associated with repetitious drills, and (6) by providing immediate positive reinforcement.

Music experiences may be incorporated into traditional speech therapy approaches, as when songs are used to practice and drill specific words or sounds, or make unique contributions to the treatment of persons who have communication impairments by providing alternative neurological pathways and structures for learning (e.g., music therapy approaches for persons with aphasia or developmental language disorders). Therapeutic music experiences can be structured to help clients who have various types of speech and/or language disorders (1) increase breath and muscle control, (2) stimulate vocalization, (3) develop receptive and/or expressive language skills, (4) improve articulation skills, (5) improve speech rate and fluency, and/or (6) correct voice disorders. Music therapy approaches may also facilitate speech and language development or rehabilitation in individuals who (7) have cleft palates, (8) have aphasia, or (9) use augmentive communication systems. Finally, music therapy interventions can help individuals who communication disorders (10) increase self-confidence, emotional expression, and social interaction.

For interventions to be most effective, music therapists who treat individuals with speech and language disorders must work closely with qualified speech pathologists and carefully note the specific needs, strengths, preferences, and responses of each client.

QUESTIONS FOR THOUGHT AND DISCUSSION

1. Discuss some of the general characteristics and needs of individuals who have communication disorders. What implications do these have for music therapy programming?

2. Describe some general ways music experiences facilitate the acquisition of speech and language skills. Do some types of music experiences or modes of musical expression seem to facilitate the acquisition of speech and language skills more readily than others? If so, which ones? Why?

3. Describe at least three different types of augmentive communication systems. How might each of these be incorporated into music therapy experiences?

4. Describe some specific music therapy experiences that might be used to (1) increase breath and muscle control, (2) stimulate vocalization, (3) develop receptive and/or expressive language skills, (4) improve articulation skills, (5) improve speech rate and fluency, (6) correct voice disorders, (7) facilitate speech and language development in individuals who have cleft palates, (8) facilitate speech and language rehabilitation in individuals who have aphasia, (9) incorporate the use augmentive communication systems, and (10) increase client's self-confidence, emotional expression, and social interaction. What unique benefits does music provide in each of these areas?

5. List several special considerations that may be important to remember when developing therapeutic intervention strategies for persons who have communication disorders. Why are these important? What are their implications for the structure or implementation of music therapy intervention strategies?

6. For each of the situations listed below, (a) define the problem or areas of need for the client or group of clients, (b) describe one or more of the goals you might pursue in music therapy sessions with the client(s), (c) describe music activities you might use to help the client(s) meet those goals, (d) tell how the music activities you described relate to the goals and needs of the client(s), and (e) mention any special considerations you might want to take into account when working with the client(s).

Situation 1:

Because Mary seems to enjoy listening to records and playing the piano, she has been referred to music therapy in the hope that she can gain some needed nonmusical skills through music activities. Mary is ten years old, and she does not articulate consonant sounds clearly. Although her neurological evaluation showed that she should be able to develop the coordination needed for clear speech, Mary seems to have great difficulty coordinating the movements of her lips, tongue, and teeth. Mary rarely practices the exercises that the speech therapist gave her; she says they are boring and don't do any good.

Situation 2:

You are working as a music therapist in a long term care facility. Twelve of the residents have some degree of expressive aphasia. They are on the waiting list for speech therapy services. Many are depressed and frustrated by their lack of ability to communicate and socialize with others. Your administrator heard something about how music might help individuals with aphasia regain some speech, and she wants you to start a music group that might help these residents communicate and interact with others successfully.

SUGGESTIONS FOR FURTHER READING

Adamek, M. S., & Shiraishi, I. M. (1996). Music therapy with traumatic brain injured patients: Speech rehabilitation, intervention models, and assessment procedures. In C. E. Furman (Ed.), *Effectiveness of music*

therapy procedures: Documentation of research and clinical practice (2nd ed.) (pp. 267-278). Silver Spring, MD: National Association for Music Therapy.

Bernstorf, E. D., & Welsbacher, B. T. (1996). Helping

students in the inclusive classroom. *Music Educators Journal, 82*(5), 21-29.

Bruscia, K. E. (Ed.) (1991). *Case studies in music therapy.* Phoenixville, PA: Barcelona Publishers.

Cohen, N. S. (1992). The effect of singing instruction on the speech production of neurologically impaired persons. *Journal of Music Therapy, 29*(2), 87-102.

Cohen, N. S. (1994). Speech and song: Implications for therapy. *Music Therapy Perspectives, 12*(1), 8-14.

Coleman, K., McNairn, P., & Shioleno, C. (1995). *Quick tech magic: Music-based literacy activities.* Solana Beach, CA: Mayer-Johnson.

Galloway, H. G., Jr. (1975). Music and the speech handicapped. In R. M. Graham (Compiler), *Music for the exceptional child* (pp. 15-47). Reston, VA: Music Educators National Conference.

Loewy, J. (1995). The musical stages of speech: A developmental model of pre-verbal sound making. *Music Therapy, 13*(1), 47-73.

Michel, D. E. (1985). Speech and language disorders and disabilities. In D. E. Michel, *Music therapy: An introduction, including music in special education* (2nd ed.), (pp. 43-47). Springfield, IL: Charles C Thomas.

Michel, D. E., & Jones, J. L. (1991). *Music for developing speech and language skills in children: A guide for parents and therapists.* St. Louis: MMB Music.

Miller, S. G. (1982). *Music therapy for handicapped children: Speech impaired.* Washington, D.C.: National Association for Music Therapy.

Musselwhite, C., & Showalter, S. (1990). *Augmentive communication activity book.* Ashville, NC: The Irene Wortham Center.

Nocera, S. D. (1979) *Reaching the special learner through music.* Morristown, NJ: Silver Burdett.

Nordoff, P., & Robbins, C. (1971). *Music therapy in special education.* New York: John Day.

Nordoff, P., & Robbins, C. (1977). *Creative music therapy.* New York: John Day.

Robbins, C., & Robbins, C. (1980). *Music for the hearing impaired and other special groups: A resource manual and curriculum guide.* St. Louis: Magnamusic-Baton.

Rogers, A., & Fleming, P. L. (1981). Rhythm and melody in speech therapy for the neurologically impaired. *Music Therapy, 1,* 33-38.

Standley, J. (1991). *Music techniques in therapy, counseling, and special education.* St. Louis: MMB Music.

Standley, J. M., & Hughes, J. E. (1997). Evaluation of an early intervention music curriculum for enhancing prereading/writing skills. *Music Therapy Perspectives, 15*(2), 79-86.

Staum, M. J. (1989). Music as motivation for language learning. In R. R. Pratt & H. Moog (Eds.), *First research seminar of the ISME commission on music therapy and music in special education: Proceedings of 1986; Bad Honnef, W. Germany* (pp. 62-68). St. Louis: MMB Music.

Taylor, D. B. (1987). The theoretical basis for the use of music with aphasic patients. In R. R. Pratt (Ed.), *The fourth international symposium on music: Rehabilitation and human well-being* (pp. 165-169). New York: University Press of America.

Taylor, D. B. (1989). A neuroanatomical model for the use of music in the remediation of aphasic disorders. In M. H. M. Lee (Ed.), *Rehabilitation, music and human well-being* (pp. 168-178). St. Louis: MMB Music.

Wells, K. E., & Helmus, N. (1968). Music therapy for severe speech disorders. In E. T. Gaston (Ed.), *Music in Therapy* (pp. 159-162). New York: Macmillan.

Zinar, R. (1987). *Music activities for special children.* West Nyack, NY: Parker Publishing.

Zoller, M. (1991). Use of music activities in speech-language therapy. *Language, Speech, and Hearing Services in Schools, 22,* 272-276.

Chapter Thirteen

MUSIC THERAPY FOR INDIVIDUALS WHO HAVE AUTISM

DEFINITION

AUTISM IS A neurological disorder that affects brain function, causing a lifelong developmental disability. Autism is manifested by a variety of characteristic behaviors, including (1) disturbances and deficiencies in speech, language, and communication, (2) difficulties in relating to other people and failure to develop normal socialization, (3) abnormal responses to sensory stimuli, (4) resistance to any change in routines or in the environment, and (5) uneven rates of development (e.g., relatively normal motor skill development; delayed or uneven or out of sequence development of communication or cognitive skills). For a diagnosis of autism, these features must become evident during the first 2-1/2 to 3 years of life (Autism Society of America, 1995; Lovejoy & Estridge, 1987; Powers, 1989; Snell, 1996). Although some symptoms may become less severe over time, most continue to affect the individual, at least to some extent, throughout his or her life.

The American Psychiatric Association [APA] classifies autism as one of the pervasive developmental disorders. According to the APA (1994), "the essential features of Autistic Disorder are the presence of markedly abnormal or impaired development in social interaction and communication and a markedly restricted repertoire of activity and interests" (p. 66). Delayed or abnormal functioning in social interaction, language for social communication, or symbolic or imaginative play must be evident before 3 years of age. Asperger's disorder, another pervasive developmental disorder, has the impairments in social interaction and the repetitive and stereotypical patterns of behavior, interests, and activities that are characteristic of autism, but no delays in language development.

The syndrome of autism was first identified by Kanner (1943), who used the term *infantile autism* to describe the condition, since the symptoms became evident in infancy. Other terms or labels used to describe the syndrome or individuals with autistic traits include *autistic-like, childhood autism, early infantile autism, high functioning or low functioning autism, typical or atypical autism, severe or moderate or mild autism, Kanner's autism, learning disabled with autistic tendencies, pervasive developmental disorder, atypical pervasive developmental disorder, pervasive developmental disorder not otherwise specified* (APA, 1994; Powers, 1989; Snell, 1996).

CAUSES

When the syndrome was first identified, autism was thought to be caused by improper parenting, early emotional trauma, lack of parental affection, or faulty mother-child relations in early infancy. However, accumulated research since the 1960s has largely discounted that theory (Atterbury, 1990; Birkenshaw-Fleming, 1993; Del Olmo, 1998; Lovejoy & Estridge, 1987; Siegfried, 1997; Thaut, 1992d; Toigo, 1992). Lovejoy and Estridge (1987) unequivocally state:

One fact about the cause of autism has now become clear: the syndrome is not caused by improper parenting. It is certain that a child who is autistic is born with the disorder, that all different types of parents – regardless of their child-rearing practices – have autistic children, and that child-rearing practices have no bearing on the cause of the disorder. (p. 186)

Although the exact cause of autism is still unknown, there is now considerable evidence that autism is a neurological disorder caused by various types of brain damage or brain dysfunction (Atterbury, 1990; Del Olmo, 1998; Lovejoy & Estridge, 1987; Thaut, 1992d; Toigo, 1992). Diverse kinds of damage or abnormal development in brain centers handling sensory input may cause individuals with autism to react differently to sensory stimuli (light, sound, touch) and to have difficulty handling sensory input. These reactions interfere with learning and the ability to function normally in society. Furthermore, as individuals withdraw, "brain damage could be compounded as the brain is denied the stimulation necessary for normal development" (Toigo, 1992, p. 15). Current evidence shows no single brain structure or system that is defective in individuals with autism, but suggests that "molecular defects are spread throughout various parts of the brain in such a way that the ability to process complex information is diminished" (Siegfried, 1997, p. 7D).

Researchers continue to explore genetic, chemical, and biological causes of autism (Lovejoy & Estridge, 1987; Siegfried, 1997). Factors currently under investigation include (a) a combination of at least three genes that together generate the range of autistic symptoms, (b) defects in the nerve endings that receive chemical signals in the brain, (c) problems with the chemical messenger molecule, serotonin, or (d) problems in the fetal development of the brain (Siegfried, 1997). Although clues are increasing, researchers are still a long way from understanding exactly what causes autism.

COURSE OF DISORDER

By definition, autism has its onset prior to 3 years of age. It affects 2 to 5 children in every 10,000 births, and is four times more common in boys than in girls. Often, children who have autism show lack of interest in social interaction at or shortly after birth. Symptoms become more apparent after age 2, when deficits in communication and social skills and developmental delays and differences become easier to define. With properly structured individualized treatment programs, many individuals with autism can gain some communication, cognitive, and social skills and decrease some of their stereotypical behaviors. Generally, those individuals who are able to develop communicative speech and have higher overall intelligence have the best prognosis (APA, 1994; Lovejoy & Estridge, 1987; Powers, 1989). Researchers have found that "the degree of language development in the child with autism by age 5 is directly related to the child's degree of success later in life" (Snell, 1996, p. 159).

Autism is a lifelong disorder, so symptoms continue to be present into and through adulthood. Only a small number of individuals with autism are able to live independently as adults; about one-third can achieve some degree of partial independence given appropriate environmental supports (APA, 1994; Powers, 1989).

COMMON CHARACTERISTICS, PROBLEMS, AND NEEDS OF CLIENTS

Like any group of individuals, people who have autism vary widely in their abilities and behavior, so symptoms and behavioral manifestations of the syndrome will be somewhat different in each individual (APA, 1994; Lovejoy & Estridge, 1987; Powers, 1989; Snell, 1996). Factors such as the severity of the impairment, the existence of other disabilities, the age of the client, and the degree and type of support services available also affect an individual's level of functioning and prognosis. In addition, each individual's unique combination of abilities, personality traits, strengths, and weaknesses will impact that individual's particular responses and functional abilities. Therefore, it is unwise to attempt to predict a particular person's skill levels or ceiling of abilities based on broad generalizations about a certain population. However, an awareness of some of those characteristics, problems, and needs which may be common to individuals who have autism will be beneficial both to the therapist who desires to work with this population and to the reader who is trying to understand how music therapy intervention strategies may benefit this population.

Children who have autism often look physically normal and healthy; however, their abilities to communicate and interact with others are severely impaired. There are a wide variety and range of manifestations of autistic behaviors, but all individuals who have autism have at least some degree of difficulty in each of the following areas: (1) difficulties in social interaction and relating to other people, (2) severe language dysfunctions, (3) unusual, abnormal, and erratic reactions to routine sensory stimuli, (4) repetitive and restricted behaviors, activities, and interests and obsessive needs for sameness, order, and routine, and (5) disturbances in developmental rates or sequences (APA, 1994; Atterbury, 1990; Autism Society of America, 1995; Birkenshaw-Fleming, 1993; Lovejoy & Estridge, 1987; Nelson, Anderson, & Gonzales, 1984; Paul, 1982; Powers, 1989; Rutter & Schopler, 1978; Snell, 1996; Thaut, 1992d).

Difficulties in Social Interaction and Relating to Others

The word *autism* is derived from the Greek word meaning "self." Individuals with autism appear to be detached, aloof, and isolated from the world around them. They seem to live in a world of their own, unaware of people in their environment. They have difficulty understanding or expressing emotion and rarely form emotional attachments; they usually avoid eye contact and physical contact. They may appear to be apathetic and unresponsive and have few, if any, social affective gestures (e.g., smile,

frown, wave). Instead of seeking to share enjoyments, interests, and achievements with others or enjoying simple social play or games, they tend to treat people like objects and involve them in activities only as tools or mechanical aids.

Difficulties in relating to others frequently are one of the first signs of autism, already becoming noticeable in early infancy. As babies, individuals with autism often are indifferent or averse to being held (e.g., stiffen when picked up) and may not act cuddly or want to be cuddled. As toddlers, they rarely make meaningful eye contact or respond with social smiles and do not enjoy adult interaction games like "Peek-a-boo." As they grow, children with autism may become more aware of parents and other familiar adults, but they have little or no interest in establishing peer friendships, have difficulty mixing with other children, and lack the ability to play cooperatively with others. They may be oblivious to other children. They usually have no concept of the needs of others and may not notice another's distress. As they grow older, individuals with autism may have some interest in friendship but have difficulty establishing friendships because they do not understand the conventions of social interaction.

Severe Language Dysfunctions

The inability to use language for functional communication is one of the primary features of autism. *All* children with autism have severe difficulties understanding and communicating with language. "Extreme deficit in the ability to communicate in the broadest sense, specifically, the ability to use speech for purposive communication (even when the child has speech), is the common denominator of early childhood autism" (Boxill, 1985, p. 161). Both verbal and nonverbal communication skills and receptive language skills show marked and sustained impairments. The prognosis for individuals with autism is closely correlated to their ability to develop speech or a functional system of communication. If individuals can communicate with those around them, they have a better chance of being able to live and function successfully in the world.

Although they hear speech clearly, individuals with autism seem to have difficulty processing and understanding the meaning of speech sounds. To the individual with autism, human speech may just sound like senseless noise. Perhaps because of these processing difficulties, the development of spoken language is often delayed or absent. Approximately 40%-50% of individuals with autism never speak. Others often develop their own special language or repeat the words and sounds of others (*echolalia*). Echoing may occur immediately after a person speaks or be repeated at another time. For example, some individuals who have autism may remember whole passages from conversations or television programs and repeat them at various intervals over a long period of time.

Those individuals with autism who do develop some functional speech are often unable to initiate or sustain conversations. Their speech is often characterized by abnormal pitch, volume, intonation, rate, rhythm, or stress. In addition, it may be flat (lacking intonation or emotion) or have inappropriate changes in tone. They seldom use appropriate nonverbal communication features, such as gestures and facial expressions. Their speech also frequently contains grammatical errors, stereotyped or repetitive use of language, or jargon that is meaningful only to the individual or those who are familiar with the individual's communication style. Because of disturbances in language comprehension, individuals with autism may be unable to understand simple questions, directions, or jokes. Frequently, they have little or no ability to engage in imaginative play or simple imitation games.

Abnormal, Erratic Reactions to Routine Sensory Stimuli

Individuals with autism tend to have unusual reactions and responses to things they can see, hear, touch, smell, or taste. They are frequently over-responsive (*hypersensitive*) or under-responsive (*hyposensitive*) to various types of sensory input (e.g., light, sounds, touch, pain). In addition, these reactions may be very inconsistent, varying from day to day and within sensory categories (e.g., not hypersensitive to *all* lights, *all* loud sounds, etc.). Individuals with autism are sometimes described as falling on a "sensory processing continuum" (Grandin, 1995, p. 52), with those at the high-functioning end having mild sensory oversensitivity

problems and those at the lower-functioning end continually receiving severely distorted visual and auditory information.

Many individuals with autism are hypersensitive to sound (certain sounds or all sounds). However, responses are often erratic. For example, an individual "may overreact with startle reflex or tantrum to the sound of a dropped pencil but be oblivious to a loud siren" (Thaut, 1992d, p. 182). Or, an individual may be distressed by the sound of a distant lawn mower but seem not to notice a human voice in the same room. Individuals with autism may also have difficulty screening out sounds and may be enthralled by background noises (e.g., sound of heater; buzz of lights), becoming frenetically active or immobile and passive for long periods of time as they attend to these background sounds.

Individuals with autism also have erratic and unusual responses to other types of sensory stimuli. Some may not show pain when they are injured or may show no real fear of dangerous situations. Some may be fascinated with lights and color patterns or be preoccupied with certain surfaces or avoid certain textures. Individuals with autism may respond to motion in abnormal ways: some spin excessively with no dizziness, others fear certain movements, like the movement of elevators.

Children with autism also tend to use different senses than their peers do to explore the world (including people and objects) around them. Generally, children with autism use their senses of taste, smell, and touch more than their senses of vision and hearing to learn and explore (Lovejoy & Estridge, 1987; Powers, 1989). Thus, they tend to lick, mouth, and touch things (and people) in learning situations.

Repetitive and Restricted Behaviors, Activities, and Interests; Obsessive Need for Sameness, Order, and Routine

Individuals with autism frequently engage in bizarre, repetitive motor mannerisms, or *stereotypical behaviors*, involving the hands (e.g., hand or finger flapping, finger flicking, twisting or staring at their fingers or hands, hair-pulling, banging their head or ears) or the whole body (e.g., rocking, twisting, whirling, darting and lunging, or statue-like posturing). Some feel these are *self-stimulatory* behaviors individuals with autism use to create their own sensory input (Paul, 1982; Thaut, 1992d), while others suggest these repetitive motor mannerisms may be related to the individual's desire for sameness or their love of repetitive movement (Lovejoy & Estridge, 1987). Individuals with autism may also develop habitual abnormal movement patterns, like walking or running only on their tiptoes or holding their hands or bodies in odd postures.

Individuals with autism frequently develop fascinations, preoccupations, or fixations with certain objects (e.g., light switches, record players, vacuum cleaners, washing machines) or parts of objects (e.g., buttons, parts of the body). They may develop strong attachments to meaningless, inanimate objects, like a rubber band or a piece of string, and become very upset if that object is taken away. Repetitive movement also frequently fascinates these individuals, and they may become utterly absorbed in watching electric fans or toy tops, repeatedly opening and closing doors, or repeatedly spinning wheels or other objects. While both fixations and stereotypical behaviors can interfere with learning, communication, and socialization, fixations differ from stereotypical behaviors like hand flapping and twirling in that they are directed toward something *external*. If channeled correctly, fixations can motivate learning (Toigo, 1992). For example, if an individual is fixated on vacuum cleaners, one might use vacuum cleaners to teach counting concepts.

Individuals with autism usually have a very restricted range of interests. Frequently, they become preoccupied with one narrow interest, like amassing facts about dinosaurs or airplanes or statistics for a certain sport or team. Most individuals with autism also have an obsessive desire for order; everything must be in exactly the same place every time. They may set up toys, blocks, eating utensils, or other objects the same way over and over again. (Often, the system used to arrange or sort the objects is known only to the individual.) These individuals have a strong need and desire to maintain sameness in their lives and are very resistant to changes in their environment or routines. They may become extremely distressed over seemingly small changes, like a piece of furniture being moved or slight change in the route taken to school. Individuals with autism frequently develop many nonfunctional rituals and routines (e.g., continually touching certain objects in the same order) that they adhere to inflexibly.

Disturbances in Developmental Rates or Sequences

Individuals with autism characteristically have very uneven patterns of development, with disturbances or low abilities in some areas and normal or high abilities in others. Development in one area often lags far behind that in another. For example, a 7-year-old child may be able to dress and undress appropriately but may not be able to use a toilet. Even in the same general skill area, the rate of development may be uneven. For example, a child may sit up at an early age but not learn to walk for years (Lovejoy & Estridge, 1987).

Although the *functional abilities* of about 75% of people diagnosed with autism fall in the mentally retarded range (APA, 1994; Snell, 1996), most investigators agree that distribution of *IQ levels* for individuals with autism is similar to that of the general population (Thaut, 1992d): Some persons with autism are highly intelligent, others have average intelligence, and still others mild to serious mental retardation. Whatever their level of intelligence, individuals with autism usually have uneven cognitive abilities (APA, 1994). For example, an individual may have advanced math or reading skills but be unable to carry on a normal conversation. Many individuals with autism have certain isolated areas of ability, such as rote memory or special abilities in math, art, or music (subjects that do not depend on the use of language). Some cognitive deficits, like difficulties with abstract thinking, difficulties making sense of auditory and visual information, and problems organizing and sequencing information, are characteristic of autism. Many higher-functioning individuals with autism have a vocabulary that is higher than their level of language comprehension.

Characteristics of Adults with Autism

With appropriate treatment and therapy, many individuals with autism are able to gain some communication skills, develop basic functional skills, and decrease their stereotypical behaviors. Adults with autism usually do not acquire new behavior problems, nor do they lose progress they have made in controlling their behavior and meeting their own needs. Usually, they do not develop new medical problems (e.g., seizures) they did not have as children or adolescents. However, although some symptoms may become less severe, adults who have autism continue to have some degree of difficulty in all of the areas described in the preceding paragraphs (APA, 1994; Lovejoy & Estridge, 1987; Powers, 1989). About two-thirds of all individuals with autism remain severely handicapped throughout their adult years. The remaining third, usually those with higher intelligence and better language skill development, achieve some degree of partial independence.

Even higher-functioning adults with autism continue to have difficulties in social functioning and communication. They also maintain a very limited range of interests and activities, including some fixations. If properly directed, however, these interests and fixations might be developed into a career. For example, a person with autism who was fascinated with cattle chutes ended up with a career in animal science (Grandin, 1988, cited in Toigo, 1992). Artistically talented individuals might be able to work as graphic artists (Toigo, 1992), and musically talented individuals have become successful composers and pianists (Euper, 1968). Since adults with autism still have problems understanding how others

think and feel, however, even those who function well enough to have careers may still need persons who serve as "career mentors" and help them "deal with job-related social complexities" (Toigo, 1992, p. 17).

Whatever their level of functioning, adults with autism still have a great need for structure and routine. They frequently show an interest in rote activities, like memorizing sports statistics, bus schedules, or historic dates. They function best in a supportive environment that provides a balance between encouraging productivity and providing enough care and structure to help the individual feel secure and less anxious. Most retain a need for sameness and consistency in their environment, and some may continue to become upset or throw temper tantrums when changes occur.

As individuals with autism reach adulthood, treatment and therapy programs often begin to phase out academic training and place more emphasis on functional life skills and increasing independence. In addition, the focus shifts from *changing* behaviors to *channeling and redirecting* behaviors (e.g., flip through a magazine instead of flapping hands). Adults with autism continue to need structured training programs to help them improve and maintain communication skills, self-care skills, social skills, impulse control, ability to follow directions, and appropriate behaviors. No matter how high-functioning they are, most continue to need support services in some areas of their lives (Powers, 1989; Toigo, 1992).

RECOMMENDED TREATMENTS

Although there currently is no cure for autism, a number of different treatment techniques can benefit many individuals who have autism. These include *auditory training* (techniques that help individuals distinguish sounds more clearly) (Del Olmo, 1998), *behavior modification programs* (Adreon, 1994; Atterbury, 1990; Del Olmo, 1998; Grandin & Scarino, 1986; Thaut, 1992d), *exercise* (Grandin & Scarino, 1986), *facilitated communication* (training method where facilitator provides physical assistance to the client with a communication disorder, supporting their hand, wrist, or forearm to help

isolate index finger movement so the client can spell words using a keyboard or other letter display) (Adreon, 1994; Birkenshaw-Fleming, 1993), *music therapy* (Del Olmo, 1998; Grandin & Scarino, 1986), some forms of *play therapy* (using games and other forms of play to help individuals express emotions) (Del Olmo, 1998), *sensory integration therapy* (involves guidance series of activities that use gentle tactile stimulation, vestibular stimulation, and other sensory stimulation to help individuals learn to make successful, organized responses to sensory input) (Adreon, 1994; Del Olmo, 1998; Grandin & Scarino,

1986), *sound sensitivity training* (technique that tries to eliminate hypersensitivity to certain frequencies by playing music through earphones in which these sounds are filtered out or reduced in amplification and the other frequencies are played loudly) (Birkenshaw-Fleming, 1993), and *speech therapy* (Grandin & Scarino, 1986). Certain *medications,* including antidepressants and beta-blockers, have successfully reduced aggressive and self-injurious behaviors in some adolescents and adults who have autism (Toigo, 1992). Some individuals have also received beneficial results from special *diets* or extra doses of *vitamin B6* (Adreon, 1994; Toigo, 1992). Recently, *biomedical* research on how the brain can be taught to compensate for slow development or damage is beginning to generate new, effective treatment programs for individuals who have autism (Del Olmo, 1998). In addition, researchers are finding that some approaches designed to improve the mental skills of children who are slow learners (e.g., training exercises disguised as video games) also seem to help some children with autism (Siegfried, 1997).

Most current treatment programs for individuals with autism include some form of behavior therapy and utilize various behavior modification techniques. *Usually, programs that include a combination of approaches in a structured, individualized treatment plan are most*

successful (Grandin & Scarino, 1986; Lovejoy & Estridge, 1987; Snell, 1996; Thaut, 1992d). Good treatment programs promote the development of functional language and communication skills, social and interpersonal skills, independent living and self-help skills, cognitive skills, sensorimotor skills, and generalization of learned behaviors, as well as help individuals learn to control and diminish stereotypical and ritualistic behaviors (Lovejoy & Estridge, 1987; Snell, 1996; Thaut, 1992d). Since functional language and communication skills are crucial to interacting with others and are a prime indicator of success in later life for individuals with autism, language development is often the main focus of early intervention and educational programs (Snell, 1996; Thaut, 1992d).

With increasing frequency, parents of children with autism are looked upon as partners in the treatment of their child. They receive training in educational and behavior management techniques so they can help reinforce their child's program at home (Lovejoy & Estridge, 1987; Thaut, 1992d). Individuals with autism generally make the most progress when behavior expectations, management and interaction techniques, rewards, and consequences are consistent across all settings they encounter.

SETTINGS FOR SERVICE DELIVERY

Individuals who have autism receive special programs and services in a variety of settings, depending on their age, specific needs, level of functioning, and the types of services available in their community. These settings may include early intervention centers, home-based programs, public schools, public or private centers for persons who have various developmental disabilities, special clinic or treatment centers for individuals who have autism, special vocational training programs or sheltered workshops, and group homes.

Many children who have autism are served by special education programs from their local public school system. The Individuals with Disabilities Act (IDEA) (Public Law 101-476), the 1990 revision of the 1975 Education for All Handicapped Children Act (Public Law 94-142) assures a free, appropriate public

education to all children, ages 3-21, including those who have autism. Incentives for early intervention programs to address the needs children birth through age 2 who have handicaps or disabilities are provided by Public Law 99-457 of 1986 (Adamek, 1996; Humpal, 1990). Special education services for children who have autism are delivered according to the same general procedure outlined in Chapter Seven. After initial referral, assessment and identification of the disability, Individualized Educational Programs (IEPs) are written to guide instruction. IEPs set educational goals and establish programs that reflect the individual's specific strengths and weakness. IEPs also provide for appropriate support services in areas of need, placement in the least restrictive environment, and an annual evaluation of student progress in the program. The student is usually included with peers in a regular classroom for as much of the day as possible.

When the IEP assessment finds that music therapy can provide a unique means of helping students achieve their educational objectives, music therapists may be called upon to provide traditional direct services, work with students in self-contained classes, work with students in inclusive classes, provide direct in-home services to students who are confined to their homes for medical reasons, provide consultation services to facilitate classroom instruction, inclusion, or music education, and/or provide staff development workshops (Wilson, 1996). Music therapy is usually classified as a related service in special education settings. Snell (1996) provides a comprehensive overview of music therapy for students with autism in public school settings.

Music therapists may work with both children and adults who have autism. They deliver services to these clients in many different settings, including the client's home, early intervention centers, public schools, private schools or clinics, centers for the developmentally disabled, autistic treatment centers, music studios, community programs, or private practice situations. Music therapists may provide direct or consultant services and work with clients as individuals or in groups. In a recent survey of populations served by music therapists (AMTA, 1998), 376 of 1,620 music therapists responding said they worked with individuals who had autism.

HOW MUSIC IS USED IN THERAPY

The literature is filled with reports showing that almost all individuals who have autism respond positively to music, often showing unusual interests and abilities in music (DeMyer, 1974; Edgerton, 1994; Euper, 1968; Snell, 1996; Thaut, 1992d). After reviewing the literature on the musical behaviors of children with autism, Thaut (1992d) concluded that the evidence indicated that individuals who have autism (a) often perform much better in musical areas than they do in other areas of behavior, (b) often perform better in musical areas than many normal children do, and (c) usually respond to music more frequently and more appropriately than they respond to other auditory stimuli. Although little is known about the exact reasons for this responsiveness, people have speculated that music is attractive and pleasurable to individuals with autism because it bypasses language and is less specific than speech (Alvin & Warwick, 1991; Euper, 1968) or "perhaps because it is an absolutely predictable phenomenon in an unpredictable world" (Toigo, 1992, p. 17).

Left to their own devices, however, individuals with autism may use music as a device or stimulus to isolate themselves and further remove themselves from the real world (Benenzon, 1981; Hoffman, 1974). For example, some individuals will sit quietly listening for hours repeatedly listening to favorite pieces of music, totally unaware of things going on around them. If music is to be used to make contact with individuals with autism and help them gain skills in various areas, it is essential that the therapist be present to structure and guide the music experiences, leading the persons into constructive, reality-oriented activities that promote increased attention to and contact with the people and objects around them (Benenzon, 1981). Properly designed music experiences implemented by trained persons can be very effective both as vehicles for making initial contact with individuals who have autism and as structures or reinforcers for helping those individuals increase attention spans, awareness of people and objects, eye contact, purposeful use of objects, tolerance for sensory stimulation, concept of self, body awareness, acceptance of change, self-control, appropriate behavior patterns, verbal and nonverbal communication, self-expression, appropriate interactions with others, social skills, functional living skills, and basic cognitive concepts (Adreon, 1994; Alvin, 1978; Alvin & Warwick, 1991; Boxill, 1985; Hanser, 1987; Nelson, Anderson, & Gonzales, 1984; Nordoff & Robbins, 1968, 1971b, 1977; Paul, 1982; Snell, 1996; Thaut, 1984; 1992d; Toigo, 1992). As music therapists keep in mind the client's long-term goals, they structure increasingly more challenging musical activities and experiences to encourage the client to move forward to new levels of growth and development. In this way, progress continues and music therapy does not "degenerate into a form of musical coddling" (Nordoff & Robbins, 1971b, p. 108).

General Approaches and Techniques

Most of the literature and research recommends that highly structured approaches be used in the education and therapy of individuals with autism (Edgerton, 1994). However, both music therapy interventions employing highly structured, behavioral techniques (Adreon, 1994; Burleson, Center, & Reeves, 1989; Castellano & Wilson, 1970; Mahlberg, 1973; Staum & Flowers, 1984; Watson, 1979) and those employing freer, improvisational techniques (Alvin, 1978; Alvin & Warwick, 1991; Boxill, 1985; Edgerton, 1994; Nordoff & Robbins, 1968, 1971b, 1977; Saperston, 1973) have been used effectively with clients who have autism. Highly structured, *behaviorally-oriented* music therapy approaches use behavior analysis and systematic instruction coupled with reinforcement, often using preferred music activities as the reinforcer (Adreon, 1994). In this type of approach, "a firm directive strategy involves specific, frequent, clearly defined expectations of the child while being very careful not to let the child escape planned activities" (Nelson, Anderson, & Gonzales, 1984, p. 103). In *clinical improvisation*, however, the music therapist strives to meet the client at his or her level through music, and few demands are placed on the client, at least in the initial stages of therapy. Perhaps this seemingly less structured approach also works effectively with individuals who have autism because the improvised music itself serves to structure the experience.

Many music therapists use a *combination* of improvisational and more highly structured, behaviorally-oriented music intervention strategies in their work with individuals who have autism (Nelson, Anderson, & Gonzales, 1984; Saperston, 1982; Snell, 1996; Thaut, 1984; Toigo, 1992). The early stages of music therapy, which aim to establish contact with the client and promote feelings of safety and security, frequently employ less-directive interventions (e.g., clinical improvisation techniques) that allow for more open-ended responses on the part of the client. In later stages, music therapists frequently use more directive music interventions

that place more demands on the client's attention, interaction, and responses and seek to develop specific, targeted perceptual, language, cognitive, social, or motor skills. (For more information, see the section on "Stages of Development in Music Therapy Treatment" below.)

Several types of music techniques, including vocalization/singing/chanting, dances/action songs/ music-movement experiences, playing musical instruments (improvisation, structured performance, imitative games), musical games, Orff-Schulwerk activities, music-listening experiences, and background music, have been used successfully in the treatment of individuals with autism. Therapeutically-directed music experiences have been used to stimulate responses, reinforce responses, provide cues and structure for responses to occur, develop communication and interaction, focus attention, and mask distractions. More details on types of music activities and experiences that have been successful in helping individuals with autism reach particular goals are given later in this chapter.

Music Therapy Assessment

The unusual behaviors and many severe deficits in communication, social interaction, and sensory processing skills associated with autism often make it difficult for assessments relying on visual and verbal means of communication to assess the individual's potential. Since music therapy assessments do not depend on verbal and visual communication but rely on reactions to and interactions within music experiences, "a music therapy assessment may provide a glimpse of hidden potentials" (Snell, 1996, p. 170). In music therapy assessment sessions, the music therapist can adapt the music to support and encourage the individual, ensuring a positive experience that will keep the individual engaged in music making. As the music therapist observes the client's responses to different music experiences and interprets their relationships to nonmusical skill areas (e.g., communication, social, or cognitive abilities), important assessment information that complements the findings of other professionals is often gained (Snell, 1996).

Individual assessment may also help increase the

speed of clinical effectiveness. Careful assessment of a client's musical preferences enables the music therapist to use preferred musical activities and experiences in initial interventions so that the client responds favorably to the music environment more quickly, heightening the therapist's ability to begin using music experiences to develop skills in other areas (Adreon, 1994; Griggs-Drane & Wheeler, 1997). Since individuals with autism often have unusual responses to sensory stimuli (perhaps because of sensory processing abnormalities), music therapists must carefully observe and analyze each client's responses to different types of music stimuli, noting whether the stimuli elicit normal responses, little or no arousal, hyperreactive responses, or paradoxical reactions (e.g., client defensively withdraws and shows no response to excessive stimuli, or client overresponds because she or he is not receiving enough sensory input) (Nelson, Anderson, & Gonzales, 1984; Toigo, 1992). A client's behaviors may differ not only between musical and nonmusical environments, but also *within* the musical environment itself, depending on what particular musical styles, instruments, frequencies, modes of activity, etc., are being used and how these are perceived and processed by the client.

Griggs-Drane and Wheeler (1997) recommend the use of *functional assessment procedures* to help the music therapist define musical, environmental, and transitional variables that influence the client's behavior, so they can use the information to develop more effective music therapy intervention strategies and behavioral support plans. During the assessment session, a wide variety of musical styles, instruments, and experiences are used. In addition to the client's behavior before, during, and after the session, musical variables such as song name and style, instruments or voices used, key, live or recorded presentation, and selection duration are carefully noted and analyzed in relation to the client's responses. From this functional assessment, music therapists are able to determine which musical styles, keys, instruments, and modes of experiences are likely to be most reinforcing for that particular client and which are aversive or not tolerated. How the client responds will have definite implications for the type of stimuli that may be most effective in working with that particular client. Assessment information may

also help the therapist plan sessions alternating preferred and less-preferred activities, a structural technique that can be very effective in helping individuals with autism gain new skills (Adreon, 1994; Griggs-Drane & Wheeler, 1997). The pairing of a non-preferred activity with a preferred stimulus can also reinforce and facilitate performance of the non-preferred task (Griggs-Drane & Wheeler, 1997; Snell, 1996).

Music therapists who use clinical improvisation techniques as their primary mode of intervention also rely on careful observation, analysis, and assessment of the client's responses within the session to determine what music interventions will be most helpful in facilitating the client's positive growth and development (Alvin, 1978; Alvin & Warwick, 1991; Boxill, 1985; Nordoff & Robbins, 1968, 1971b, 1977). Nordoff and Robbins (1977) have developed two rating scales for evaluating individuals with autism and measuring changes in their behavior. One scale describes levels of participation and qualities of resistiveness in the client's relationship to the therapist in musical activity, beginning with the non-relating attitudes of the profoundly autistic state and progressing to awareness, acceptance, coactivity, and constructive participation in group work. The second scale rates the client's level of musical communicativeness as demonstrated by his/her instrumental, vocal, or body movement responses, again moving from noncommunicativeness to fragmentary responses to more sustained responses and free, confident participation and communication in musical experiences. In addition to their function as rating instruments, these scales "have proved to be important guides to therapists in imparting a sense of orientation and perspective in therapy, and in suggesting clinical approaches at various stages and in different situations" (Nordoff & Robbins, 1977,   p. 179). Boxill (1985, pp. 50-63) has also developed a music therapy assessment that can be used with individuals who have autism, as well as those who have other developmental disabilities.

Stages of Development in Music Therapy Treatment

Music therapy with individuals who have autism is often a very slow process; one must frequently work months or even years before seeing much progress (Alvin, 1978; Alvin & Warwick, 1991; Nordoff & Robbins, 1971b, 1977; Saperston, 1982; Thaut, 1984). Many authors speak of three general stages of development in music therapy treatment process with individuals who have autism (Alvin, 1978; Alvin & Warwick, 1991; Benenzon, 1982; Nordoff & Robbins, 1971b; Saperston, 1982; Snell, 1996; Thaut, 1984). Although they call these stages by different names, most authors agree on the general developmental progression and focus of therapy in each stage.

In the *first stage* of treatment, the music therapist tries to establish contact with the client, using music experiences to elicit and support the client's limited responses. Through this process, the client begins to feel safe and secure in the music environment, and the beginnings of musical communication are established. In the *second* or *intermediate stage*, specific forms of musical activity and responses are developed, and more demands are made on the client. The music therapist now becomes more involved in directing and shaping responses, as musical processes are used to develop and reinforce basic perceptual, language, social, cognitive, and motor skills. As the client develops skills and gains more awareness and confidence, there is more reciprocal communication and cooperation between client and therapist in the context of musical experiences. Activities at this stage also help prepare the client for group work as a "my turn-your turn" concept and imitation skills are developed. In the *third* or *complex stage*, the client is able to respond confidently and expressively in the music situation. The therapist aims to help the client integrate skills and use them to communicate with and relate constructively to the people and the world around him or her. The client may gradually be introduced to group music therapy settings to help increase his or her abilities to relate and respond appropriately to and to communicate and work cooperatively with other people. It is interesting to note how closely these general stages of music therapy treatment with individuals who have autism correspond to Sears's (1968) classifications of processes in music therapy: (1) experience within structure, (2) experience in self-organization, and (3) experience in relating to others.

Therapeutic Music Experiences to Make Contact and Initiate Communication

The first musical contact with the individual who has autism is often a nonverbal one. Music is a powerful means of nonverbal communication, which can be expressed and responded to through many modes of activity (e.g., listening, singing or vocalizing, moving, playing instruments). Music also has the ability to stimulate and touch many senses (auditory, visual, tactile, kinesthetic) and aspects of a person (physical, cognitive, emotional). Thus, as the client becomes aware of, attends to, and begins to respond to and/or interact with some aspect or aspects of the music experience, music can be a unique, nonthreatening way "of gently entering the client's world before demanding that he enter ours" (Toigo, 1992, p. 19).

Once the client feels secure in the musical environment, the therapist's presence can be gradually introduced within the context of music experiences (e.g., increasing physical closeness when singing or playing instruments; holding the hand while moving to music; guiding the client to a particular instrument; increased interresponsiveness such as echoing, imitation, responding to dynamic and tempo changes in music making) (Alvin, 1978; Alvin & Warwick, 1991; Hanser, 1987; Nordoff & Robbins, 1971b, 1977; Saperston, 1982; Thaut, 1984). Some individuals may also relate to the tactile qualities of sound stimuli. There is some evidence to suggest treating individuals who autism with particular combinations of low-frequency sound and music (vibroacoustic therapy) makes them subsequently more tolerant of contact and stimulation (Skille, 1989; Wigram, 1995).

Since individuals with autism usually relate better to objects than to people, musical instruments may be particularly useful in initiating contact with these clients (Alvin, 1978; Alvin & Warwick, 1991; Nordoff & Robbins, 1971b, 1977; Saperston, 1982; Thaut, 1984). As the music therapist presents various rhythm instruments and gives the client opportunities to listen to, observe, and explore them, the client may be attracted to a particular instrument's shape or sound, and, through this instrument, be prompted to participate actively in making music.

Instruments can serve as intermediary objects between client and therapist, providing a potential point for mutual contact, enjoyment without grasp of abstract concepts, and satisfaction of a need for self-expression. (Thaut, 1984, p. 10)

Contact and involvement are often facilitated by structuring experiences so they ensure a high rate of success while making few demands. For example, Orff xylophones might be set up with only those bars needed for a pentatonic scale, so that any note the client strikes will fit musically with the improvisation (Hollander & Juhrs, 1974).

Alvin (1978) has found that instruments that require physical pressure on a surface to play (e.g., drums, piano keys, mallet instruments, strings plucked or bowed) are most effective in establishing contact with individuals who have autism. Alvin theorized that the resistance of these instruments stimulates the individual's perceptual awareness and can give feelings of support. Shaking instruments (e.g., maracas) "do not convey the idea of meeting an object in space and time, connected with a certain rhythm or pulse" (Alvin, 1978, p. 15), and hence are usually not as useful for initial contacts with individuals who have autism. Care must also be taken to structure instrument exploration and improvisation experiences to minimize ritualistic, self-stimulatory behaviors and sensory overload (Thaut, 1984).

Several music therapists have had excellent results in establishing initial contacts with clients through clinical improvisation techniques in which the therapist improvises music that reflects the sounds, gestures, movements, and behaviors of the client (Alvin, 1978; Alvin & Warwick, 1991; Boxill, 1985; Hanser, 1987; Nelson, Anderson, & Gonzales, 1984; Nordoff & Robbins, 1968, 1971b, 1977; Paul, 1982; Snell, 1996; Thaut, 1984; 1992d; Toigo, 1992). As the process develops and the client's responses are reflected by and translated into musical structures, the music therapist, through the music, "helps the child move from a fragmented world into an integrated one, from *un*aware experiencing to *aware* experiencing" (Boxill, 1985, p. 161). Frequently, a particular song (composed or developed from improvisations) catches the attention of the client and is the catalyst for the first directed musical expression

or reciprocal musical communication initiated by the client (Boxill, 1985; Nordoff & Robbins, 1977; Snell, 1996). This "contact song" can then be used throughout the course of therapy to focus the client's attention and activity. It provides a familiar point of contact from which to expand skills and interaction and to which to return for stability and comfort.

Therapeutic Music Experiences to Develop Speech and Language

Since many individuals with autism begin to communicate nonverbally in music therapy sessions by using musical instruments, music therapists often find that instrumental activities are useful vehicles for helping clients develop receptive and expressive language skills. For example, once a client begins to respond musically with musical instruments, the therapist can gradually introduce techniques requiring more interaction (e.g., question-and-answer musical structures) or song lyrics that give directions or ask for specific responses from the client (Thaut, 1992d). As individuals with autism learn to play instruments rhythmically and participate in reciprocal play experiences, they experience and learn to follow the rhythmic give-and-take necessary for conversations (Toigo, 1992). In addition, approaches using Orff-Schulwerk instruments and techniques have effectively increased gestures, signed commands, and language development in individuals who have autism (Hollander & Juhrs, 1974). Clarkson (1991) found that the opportunity to choose instruments to use in instrumental activities increased use of sign language in a nonverbal adult with autism. Learning to playing wind instruments that develop oral motor and breath support skills can also help prepare clients to make and control speech sounds (Alvin, 1978; Thaut, 1992d).

In music therapy work with clients who have autism, improvisational music experiences that provide opportunities for nonverbal communication and self-expression frequently help pave the way to verbal expression. After clients have experienced musical give-and-take in instrumental activity, they may be stimulated to join the therapist in singing at least portions of the song that structures the improvisation (Nordoff & Robbins, 1971b; 1977). Edgerton (1994) found that improvisational music therapy techniques effectively increased the musical vocal behaviors of children with autism and discovered that, on the average, as children's musical vocal behaviors increased, nonmusical speech production also increased.

Music activities may also be used as a part behavioral strategies to encourage, reinforce, and structure verbal interactions. For example, an electively mute 14-year-old began to increase his verbal responses when opportunities to play a drum set were withheld if he did not respond verbally in a given amount of time (Castellano & Wilson, 1970). In a study by Watson (1979), verbalization among children with autism increased significantly when their spontaneous, unprompted speech was rewarded by tokens that could be redeemed for an afternoon music therapy session. The number of tokens needed to "buy" participation in the music therapy session varied from individual to individual, according to their baseline response level.

Songs and chanting techniques can also help students acquire and practice signed and spoken vocabulary and language patterns. For example, Buday (1995) found that children with autism learned signs more effectively when they were taught with music and speech than when they were taught with only rhythm and speech. In addition to the positive effect on speech and sign imitation, observations indicated that, when participating in the music condition, the children with autism had less hand flaying, fewer head movements, and less incoherent babbling. This would seem to indicate that music activities designed to improve expressive language skills in individuals with autism will be most successful when they employ a melodic component in addition to a rhythmic component.

Various music therapy techniques can also help reduce inappropriate or noncommunicative speech patterns for some individuals with autism. For example, improvised or composed songs designed to stimulate the client to sing answers to questions instead of echoing words can help decrease echolalia (Boxill, 1985; Nordoff & Robbins, 1971b, 1977). In addition, techniques where the therapist pauses while singing and waits for the client to fill in the appropriate word may stimulate appropriate use of language. Fischer (1991) also found that having a young man with autism and developmental delays write and then sing songs about his fears helped

reduce his inappropriate monologs reciting his fears.

Therapeutic Music Experiences to Encourage Social Interaction

Several studies have shown that music therapy interventions can help individuals who have autism increase eye contact, attention span, appropriate social behaviors, and awareness of people and objects in their environment, while decreasing instances of bizarre and self-abusive behaviors (Mahlberg, 1973; Saperston, 1973, 1982; Stevens and Clark, 1969). For example, as clients participate in dances and musical clapping games, they learn to increase their tolerance for physical closeness (Clarkson, 1991). Music therapists might also reinforce physical proximity by playing (or allowing the client to play) preferred musical recordings or instruments when the client came close to the therapist and withholding the music when the client withdrew or refused to come closer (Michel, 1985). Individual music lessons, structured so they are positive, success- producing experiences, can also reduce withdrawn and aggressive behaviors and increase positive social responses in children with autism (Jacobs, 1987).

Stereotypical and perseverative behaviors are a barrier to social interaction for many individuals with autism. Some music therapists have reported stereotypical behaviors may be decreased by joining in the behavior musically (e.g., reflecting it with improvisation) and then using musical structure to broaden the behavior into purposeful activity or active responses to the changes in the music (Nordoff & Robbins, 1977; Toigo, 1992). In addition, the technique of putting "stop" or ending commands into musical phrases at the end of songs (e.g., singing "and now we stop" or "we're done" on a V-I cadence) often helps individuals with autism stop compulsive or perseverative behaviors and increase self-control (Boxill, 1985).

When possible, music therapists usually work with clients who have autism in individual sessions at first in order to help the client develop and increase basic social responses. As the individual's skills develop, the music therapist can then gradually introduce the client to a group setting where these skills can be used and practiced. At first, the therapist may adapt songs and activities used in individual sessions for use in the group setting, thus maintaining a degree of familiarity and comfort in the music experience and helping to ease the transition for the client. As the client begins to accept the group situation, the therapist introduces small changes within the familiar experiences at levels the individual can handle, gradually building the client's repertoire of experiences and skills (Snell, 1996). As Snell (1996) observed, "acceptance of and participation in a group setting might be a significant accomplishment for the student who has a severe inability to accept change and a low tolerance for sensory input" (p. 176).

Many music experiences, such as group singing, partner or group dance and movement-to-music activities, action songs performed in circles, group instrument playing activities, playing or singing along with musical accompaniments, and Orff-Schulwerk ensembles employing combinations of movement, singing, body percussion, and instrument playing (Euper, 1968; Snell, 1996; Thaut, 1984, 1992d), can be structured to help individuals with autism increase their tolerance for and awareness of others, improve their ability to distinguish between themselves and other group members, develop appropriate social behaviors, and increase their ability to relate to and work cooperatively with others. As their social skills develop, some higher-functioning school-age individuals with autism may eventually be able to be included in some regular class settings (Atterbury, 1990; Snell, 1996). Pairing peer-tutors with the students who have autism can facilitate cooperation and learning experiences in inclusive classrooms (Almond, Rodgers, & Krug, 1979, cited in Atterbury, 1990).

Some music therapists have used music therapy sessions to increase positive interactions between autistic children and their parents (Alvin & Warwick, 1991), inviting the parent to participate in the music therapy session with the child. As both parent and child learned to communicate and interact through improvisational music sessions guided by the therapist, the child's tolerance for physical contact, social responsiveness, and emotional closeness gradually increased. Research has also shown that music can be an effective reinforcer for learning functional social behaviors. In a study by Staum and Flowers (1984), a 9-year-old girl who had a history of uncontrolled behavior in public settings and a strong

interest in music successfully acquired appropriate shopping behaviors (e.g., not touching merchandise and remaining with the accompanying adult on trips to the grocery store) when her appropriate behaviors were rewarded by music lessons. Staum and Flowers proposed that, in addition to being an effective reinforcer that could help develop other functional living skills, music might also give the client "a unique opportunity for self expression and personal satisfaction" (p. 17).

Therapeutic Music Experiences to Develop Identification and Appropriate Expression of Emotions

Many music therapists have found that active participation in music-making (e.g., singing, playing instruments, moving to music) can help individuals with autism experience and learn to express emotions accurately and appropriately (Alvin, 1978; Alvin & Warwick, 1991; Boxill, 1985; Nordoff & Robbins, 1971b, 1977). Individuals with autism can also learn to identify and express contrasting emotions by learning to associate different types of music with different feeling states, perhaps with the aid of activities that combine body language, movement, pictures of facial expressions, or verbal labeling with the music (Thaut, 1984, 1992d). Helping individuals who have autism learn to identify and express emotions can be a long process, however. In one case reported by Thaut (1984), it took two years of music therapy sessions for a ten-year-old boy to *begin* to respond to piano mood improvisations contrasting happy and sad by imitating the patterns on the piano and adding appropriate facial expressions and body postures.

Music can also help individuals with autism channel or control abnormal or excessive emotional responses. For example, rhythmic music, integrated with tactile or vestibular stimulation, and movement, can often have a calming effect on individuals with autism (Toigo, 1992). Individuals may also learn to control emotional outbursts by listening to particular songs or types of music that have calming effects for them (Snell, 1996). In other cases, active music-making experiences may be used to help channel and control emotional responses. For example, Clarkson (1991) reported that music therapy sessions utilizing structured and improvised instrumental and vocal activities and dancing to recorded music provided appropriate outlets for self-expression for a nonverbal, violent adult with autism, increasing his feelings of self-worth and decreasing his tantrums and violent outbursts. Fischer (1991) used an adapted song writing procedure ("song drawings") to help a young man with autism appropriately express his anxieties, which diminished his disruptive behaviors and reduced his monolog recitations of anxious thoughts. In later sessions, Fischer had the client write a song about things that made him a "fine young man." The act of constructing and rehearsing the song drawings helped reinforce concepts the client needed to learn and internalize, thereby helping him build a better sense of self. Skills and successes gained as they learn to play musical instruments can also help clients with autism internalize good feelings and build self-esteem (Jacobs, 1987).

Therapeutic Music Experiences to Increase Cognitive Skills

Music can facilitate the development of cognitive skills in individuals who have autism by (1) being a carrier of nonmusical information, (2) being part of the structure or background of the learning environment, or (3) serving as a reinforcement for learning (Thaut, 1992d). Since many individuals with autism are attracted to music, placing the nonmusical information in a musical setting or context "may motivate, facilitate attention and perception, and enhance memorization of the information" (Thaut, 1992d, p. 191). Song lyrics can convey basic information about body image, spatial concepts, self-help skills, number and color concepts, academic facts, etc. Other types of music experiences can also convey and reinforce nonmusical concepts (Thaut, 1984). For example, as individuals identify musical objects by pointing to them, playing them, recognizing their shape or sound, or recognizing the name of the object, they develop labeling skills. As individuals play different numbers of beats and use different numbers of instruments or different numbers of resonator bells or chime bars to play songs, they develop number concepts. Color concepts are

developed as individuals use instruments with different colors or color-coded tone bars or piano keys and as they follow colored graphic notation. Ordering instruments or sets of resonator bells by size helps develop form and size perception. Matching skills are developed as colors, shapes, and names of instruments are matched with graphic color-coded notation, pictures, like objects, word cards, or verbal responses. Individuals also develop auditory memory skills as they learn to imitate single tones and longer sequences of tones and as they learn to identify instruments by their sound. Performing body movements to songs or chants increases auditory-motor memory in addition to helping develop body awareness.

Structuring the learning environment by alternating periods of instruction with periods of music listening can have many beneficial effects for some individuals with autism. These benefits may include increased attention span and on-task behavior and decreased aggressive, ritualistic, and self-stimulatory behaviors (Hollander & Juhrs, 1974). Research also indicates that soft instrumental music with no strong rhythmic beat can increase the performance accuracy of individuals with autism on a color sorting task (Burleson, Center, & Reeves, 1989). The researchers suggested that music may mask extraneous auditory stimuli, increasing the individuals' ability to focus on the task. Several studies have also demonstrated that music can be a very effective reward or reinforcer that motivates individuals with autism to acquire nonmusical skills (Adreon, 1994; Burleson, Center, & Reeves, 1989; Castellano & Wilson, 1970; Mahlberg, 1973; Michel, 1985; Staum & Flowers, 1984; Watson, 1979). Both music listening and active music-making function as efficient reinforcers for many individuals who have autism (Thaut, 1992d).

When teaching cognitive and academic concepts in music therapy settings, it is important to remember that individuals with autism often have difficulty transferring learning and information from one context or setting to another. Therefore, music therapists must remember to specifically teach for transfer of learning and structure programs to promote generalization of skills from one setting to another (Nelson, Anderson, & Gonzales, 1984).

Therapeutic Music Experiences to Improve Sensorimotor Skills

Although some individuals with autism have relatively strong gross and fine motor skills, others have little functional hand use, delays in motor development, poor body awareness, poor laterality, and/or many nonfunctional stereotypical movements (Thaut, 1984). In addition, individuals who have autism frequently have some difficulties with motor coordination and motor planning (Nelson, Anderson, & Gonzales, 1984). Many also difficulty with sensorimotor integration (e.g., coordinating movements with auditory cues) (Thaut, 1992d; Toigo, 1992).

Nonfunctional stereotypical or perseverative movements can greatly impede the productive motor functioning of individuals who have autism. However, some music therapists have found that rhythmic activities that first match the tempo and rhythm of these movements and then change tempo or rhythm can be useful in interrupting stereotypical or perseverative movement patterns. Once these patterns are interrupted and broken, these rhythmic music activities can then be used to broaden the client's rhythmic movement responses into purposeful activity, as the client responds flexibly to or interactively with the music of the therapist (Nordoff & Robbins, 1977; Thaut, 1992d; Toigo, 1992). Changes in the rhythm or style of the therapist's improvisation can also help break patterns of compulsive beating (Hoffman, 1974; Nordoff & Robbins, 1971b, 1977; Toigo, 1992).

As individuals develop skills in playing musical instruments, motor control and coordination increases, along with skills in laterality patterns and right/left awareness (Thaut, 1984, 1992d). Action songs and music-to-movement experiences also help individuals with autism develop body awareness, motor control and coordination, and motor planning abilities (Alvin, 1978; Nelson, Anderson, & Gonzales, 1984; Stevens & Clark, 1969; Thaut, 1984; Toigo, 1992). For some clients, physical cuing may be necessary initially to help give the individual the feel of the movement or to help guide the individual into appropriate movement patterns (Snell, 1996; Thaut, 1984). In addition, music can enhance motor planning skills. For example, putting the steps of a process (e.g., shoe-tying) to song lyrics can help organize the steps of the experience for individuals with autism who relate well to music but may have difficulty with motor planning and visual-motor skills (Nordoff & Robbins, 1971b).

Many different music experiences can help individuals with autism integrate auditory, proprioceptive, tactile, vestibular, and kinesthetic stimulation (Thaut, 1984, 1992d; Toigo, 1992). For example, as individuals move to music (e.g., learning to move when music plays and stop when music stops or learning to match movements to musical accompaniments), movement is being coordinated to and integrated with auditory cues. Playing instruments combines the sensory input from the moving muscles and the feel of the instrument or mallet with auditory stimulation of the sound the movements produce. As individuals sing while moving or playing instruments, they also integrate auditory and movement-related stimuli. Using songs that are meaningful and reinforcing to clients as the basis for their instrumental activity may motivate clients to work hard to coordinate their beating to the song. In this way, familiar songs increase their capacity to integrate their beating with their singing, as in the case of Anna described by Nordoff and Robbins (1977, pp. 37-58, 207).

SPECIAL CONSIDERATIONS AND TIPS FOR SUCCESS

Since individuals with autism have a need for order and clear routines, expectations, and standards, it is important to provide structure, consistency, and predictability in music therapy treatment approaches. Structure can be provided by the music itself as well as by the session. Music therapy sessions with individuals who have autism are usually most successful when they use consistent opening and closing songs or rituals and follow a familiar, consistent pattern of songs and experiences within the body of the session. The technique of beginning and ending with preferred activities and then alternating more difficult tasks with easier, well-liked tasks during the session is often successful. Easiest, most favorite activities are often placed at the end of the session, to help end the session with positive experiences.

Since individuals with autism have difficulty adapting to change, it is important to prepare them for changes in activity. Musical phrases that signal the end of activities or specially devised "transition songs" may be useful in this regard (Boxill, 1985; Snell, 1996). Many individuals with autism also respond well to activity schedules, a sequence of pictures, words, and/or symbols that map out the sequence of tasks or schedules for the individual. These activity schedules provide stable consistent visual cues that "engage learners with autism, enhance learning, and reduce challenging behavior" (Griggs-Drane & Wheeler, 1997, p. 90).

It is important to remember that many individuals with autism are hypersensitive to some sounds. The therapist may need to adjust choices of music, instruments, and volume for the comfort level. When using a tape player for individual listening, showing how to adjust the volume and tone controls for comfort may help prevent behavior outbursts caused by overstimulation. Music therapists also need to be aware that some individuals with autism may not be processing auditory input normally, which may lead them to have abnormal responses to sound. Some clients may experience echoes of auditory stimuli, and others may not be able to tolerate multiple sounds and complex harmonies (Toigo, 1992). Careful observation and assessment are crucial to determine which sounds, instruments, keys, tempos, rhythms, musical styles, etc., are pleasant and reinforcing to the client and which are aversive. During the course of therapy, musical stimuli and experiences should be expanded gradually at a level the client will tolerate.

Gentle physical support or prompts (e.g., touch or support at shoulder, elbow, wrist) may be needed to encourage individuals with autism to initiate appropriate responses. These prompts should be faded as the client's skills emerge and develop. Adaptations of facilitated communication procedures may also have important implications for using musical instruments with individuals who have autism. As Birkenshaw-Fleming (1993) observed, "supporting/holding the hand or arm might be just the impetus necessary for some people to focus their minds on learning to play an instrument" (p. 94).

SUMMARY

Autism is a neurological disorder that affects brain function, causing a lifelong developmental disability. Autism is manifested by a variety of characteristic behaviors that become evident during the first 2-1/2 to 3 years of life. Although the exact cause of autism is still unknown, there is now considerable evidence that autism is a neurological disorder caused by various types of brain damage or brain dysfunction.

Children who have autism often look physically normal and healthy; however, their abilities to communicate and interact with others are severely impaired. There are a wide variety and range of manifestations of autistic behaviors, but all individuals who have autism have at least some degree of difficulty in each of the following areas: (1) difficulties in social interaction and relating to other people, (2) severe language dysfunctions, (3) unusual, abnormal, and erratic reactions to routine sensory stimuli, (4) restricted and stereotyped behaviors, activities, and interests coupled with obsessive needs for sameness, order, and routine, and (5) disturbances in developmental rates or sequences. Adults who have autism continue to have some degree of difficulties in all of theses areas. About two-thirds of all individuals with autism remain severely handicapped throughout their adult years.

Although there currently is no cure for autism, a number of different treatment techniques, including music therapy, have been shown to benefit many individuals who have autism. Most current treatment programs for individuals with autism include some form of behavior therapy and utilize various behavior modification techniques. Usually, programs that include a combination of approaches in a structured, individualized treatment plan are most successful.

The literature is filled with reports showing that almost all individuals who have autism respond positively to music, often showing unusual interests and abilities in music. Individuals who have autism usually respond to music more frequently and more appropriately than they respond to other auditory stimuli. Therefore, properly designed music experiences implemented by trained persons can be very effective both as vehicles for making initial contact with individuals who have autism and as structures or reinforcers for helping those individuals increase nonmusical skills (e.g., attention spans, awareness of people and objects, eye contact, purposeful use of objects, tolerance for sensory stimulation, concept of self, body awareness, acceptance of change, self-control, appropriate behavior patterns, verbal and nonverbal communication, self-expression, appropriate interactions with others, social skills, functional living skills, basic cognitive concepts).

Both music therapy interventions employing highly structured, behavioral techniques and those employing freer, improvisational techniques have been used effectively with clients who have autism. Many music therapists use a combination of improvisational and more structured music inter-

vention strategies in their work. The early stages of music therapy frequently employ less-directive intervention, allowing for more open-ended responses on the part of the client, while the later stages use more directive music activities that place specific demands on the client's attention, interaction, and responses. Careful observation and assessment are crucial to determine which sounds, instruments, keys, tempos, rhythms, musical styles, etc., are pleasant and reinforcing to the client and which are aversive.

In the last sections of the chapter, various music therapy intervention strategies that may be effective in helping individuals with autism develop nonmusical skills are described. These include therapeutic music experiences to (1) make contact and initiate communication, (2) develop speech and language, (3) encourage social interaction, (4) develop identification and appropriate expression of emotions, (5) increase cognitive skills, and (6) improve sensorimotor skills.

QUESTIONS FOR THOUGHT AND DISCUSSION

1. Discuss some of the special characteristics and needs of individuals with autism. What implications do these have for music therapy programming?

2. Why and how are music experiences useful in making contact with individuals who have autism? Are some types of experiences, activities, or instruments more useful than other? Which ones? Why?

3. Describe the three general stages of music therapy treatment with individuals who have autism and compare them to Sears's (1968) classifications of processes in music therapy (experience within structure, experience in self-organization, and experience in relating to others). What types of music experiences are most useful at each stage of treatment? Why?

4. Describe some specific music therapy experiences that might help individuals who have autism (a) develop speech and language, (b) improve social

interaction, (c) develop identification and appropriate expression of emotions, (d) increase cognitive skills, or (e) improve sensorimotor skills. What unique benefits does music provide in each of these areas?

5. List several special considerations that may be important to remember when developing therapeutic intervention strategies for persons who have autism. Why are these important? What are their implications for the structure of music therapy intervention strategies?

6. For each of the situations described below, (a) define the problem or areas of need for the client or group of clients, (b) describe one or more of the goals you might pursue in music therapy sessions with the client(s), (c) describe music activities you might use to help the client(s) meet those goals, (d) tell how the music activities you described relate to the goals and needs of the client(s), and (e) mention any special considerations you might want to take into account when working with the client(s).

Situation 1:

A five-year-old boy with autism has been referred to you for music therapy. He rarely gives eye contact or shows any social responsiveness to the people around him. He frequently rocks or flaps his hands. His parents reports he likes to listen to the classical music station on the radio. He has shown occasional interest in the tambourine and drum that are in his classroom. His teacher reports he likes to spin the jingles on the tambourine.

Situation 2:

You have been asked to provide music therapy sessions for a group of four boys, ages 7-9, all of who have been diagnosed as autistic. One knows a few basic signs; another is verbal but echolalic; the other two are nonverbal. The students rarely interact socially with one another. They are all used to using individualized activity schedules as a structural aid in their classroom. Their teacher reports they show an interest in tapes of children's activity songs, but rarely follow the directions. When she tries to use rhythm instruments, they bang on them indiscriminately or use them for self-stimulation. She has noticed that they occasionally stop and listen when she plays a few beats on the triangle or resonator bells. The teacher would like to see her students increase their awareness of each other while they continue to work on basic color, number, clothing identification, and body part concepts.

SUGGESTIONS FOR FURTHER READING

Alvin, J. (1978). *Music therapy for the autistic child.* London: Oxford University Press.

Alvin, J., & Warwick, A. (1991). *Music therapy for the autistic child* (2nd ed.). New York: Oxford University Press.

Birkenshaw-Fleming, L. (1993). *Music for all: Teaching music to people with special needs.* Toronto: Gordon V. Thompson.

Boxill, E. H. (1985). *Music therapy for the developmentally disabled.* Rockville, MD: Aspen Systems.

Bruscia, K. E. (Ed.) (1991). *Case studies in music therapy.* Phoenixville, PA: Barcelona Publishers.

Griggs-Drane, E. R., & Wheeler, J. J. (1997). The use of functional assessment procedures and individualized schedules in the treatment of autism: Recommendations for music therapists. *Music Therapy Perspectives, 15*(2), 87-93.

Nelson, D. L., Anderson, V. G., & Gonzales, A. D. (1984). Music activities as therapy for children with autism and other pervasive developmental disorders. *Journal of Music Therapy, 21*(3), 100-116.

Nocera, S. D. (1979). *Reaching the special learner through music.* Morristown, NJ: Silver Burdett.

Nordoff, P., & Robbins, C. (1971). *Therapy in music for handicapped children.* London: Victor Gollancz Ltd.

Nordoff, P., & Robbins, C. (1977). *Creative music therapy.* New York: John Day.

Nowicki, A. L., & Trevisan, L. A. (1978). *Beyond the sound: A technical and philosophical approach to music therapy* (Rev. Ed.). Porterville & Santa Barbara, CA: Nowicki/Trevisan.

Paul, D. W. (1982). *Music therapy for handicapped children: emotionally disturbed.* Washington, D.C.: National Association for Music Therapy.

Snell, A. M. (1996). Music therapy for learners with autism in a public school setting. In B. L. Wilson (Ed.), *Models of music therapy interventions in school settings: From institution to inclusion* (pp. 156-183). Silver Spring, MD: National Association for Music Therapy.

Thaut, M. H. (1984). A music therapy model for autistic children. *Music Therapy Perspectives, 1*(4), 7-13.

Thaut, M. H. (1992). Music therapy with autistic children. In W. B. Davis, K. E. Gfeller, & M. H. Thaut, *An introduction to music therapy: Theory and practice* (pp. 180-196). Dubuque, IA: Wm. C. Brown.

Toigo, D. A. (1992). Autism: Integrating a personal perspective with music therapy practice. *Music Therapy Perspectives, 10*(1), 13-20.

Chapter Fourteen

MUSIC THERAPY FOR CHILDREN AND ADOLESCENT WHO HAVE MENTAL OR BEHAVIORAL DISORDERS OR SEVERE EMOTIONAL DISTURBANCES

DEFINITIONS

THE FIELD OF CHILD and adolescent psychiatry deals with mental, behavioral, and emotional problems of childhood and adolescence. Children and adolescents who have mental disorders, behavioral disorders, or severe emotional disturbances *consistently* and *chronically* exhibit behaviors that are personally or socially deviant, maladaptive, or inappropriate. Since abnormal behavior is defined in terms of cultural norms, it is often difficult to determine precisely at what point behaviors are inappropriate or abnormal enough to be classified as disorders. One must consider many factors, including the frequency, duration, and intensity of the behavior and the circumstances in which it occurs (APA, 1994; Thaut & Gfeller, 1992). Many children or adolescents may exhibit some abnormal or inappropriate behaviors in isolated circumstances; however, those who are given diagnoses of mental or behavioral disorders or severe emotional disturbances exhibit "higher frequencies of inappropriate behaviors and less than average amounts of appropriate behaviors" (Paul, 1982, p. 2).

Many different terms, including behavior-disabled, childhood schizophrenic, conduct-disordered, emotionally handicapped, emotionally disturbed, hyperactive, socially maladjusted, juvenile offender, or delinquent, have been used to describe children and adolescents who have severe mental or behavioral disorders or serious emotional disturbances. Various degrees and types of persistent, repeated problem behaviors that significantly impair social or academic functioning are the common factor in all the conditions or disorders described by these labels (APA, 1994; Michel, 1985; Paul, 1982).

Mental Disorders

The American Psychiatric Association [APA] (1994) defines a *mental disorder* as

a clinically significant behavioral or psychological syndrome that occurs and that is associated with present distress (e.g., a painful symptom) or disability (i.e., impairment in one or more important areas of functioning) or with a significantly increased risk of suffering death, pain, disability, or an important loss of freedom. (p. xxi)

Common psychiatric or mental disorders of childhood and adolescence include *autism* (see Chapter Thirteen), *childhood schizophrenia* (psychotic state with delusions or hallucinations has onset after years of normal development), *learning disorders* (see Chapter Eight), *pervasive developmental disorders* (characterized by severe impairment in several areas of development such as social interaction and communication; often with stereotyped behaviors, interests, or activities), *attention-deficit/hyperactivity disorders (ADHD), conduct disorders* (repeated and persistent behavior patterns that violate basic right of others or age-appropriate rules and norms of society; may include aggression to people or animals, deliberate destruction of other's property, persistent deceitfulness or theft, or repeated serious violations of rules), *oppositional defiant disorders* (recurrent, persistent pattern of negative, defiant, hostile, or disobedient behaviors toward authority figures), *separation anxiety disorders, selective mutism, reactive attachment disorders* (developmentally inappropriate social relations that may be manifested in inhibited, hypervigilant, and ambivalent responses or in diffuse attachments and lack of selectivity in forming attachments), or *stereotypic movement disorders* (APA, 1994). Children and adolescents may also have *mood disorders* (e.g., depression), other *psychotic disorders* (e.g., delusional disorders or other severe disorders characterized by loss of contact with reality), *anxiety disorders* (e.g., phobias, panic disorders), or disorders related to *substance dependence* or *substance abuse* (APA, 1994; Cassity & Cassity, 1994b). In addition, some may receive clinical attention because of *relational problems* (significantly impaired functioning in parent-child or sibling relationships) or *problems related to physical abuse, sexual abuse, or child neglect* (APA, 1994).

Emotional Disturbances

In educational literature, children and adolescents who have mental, behavioral, and emotional problems are often classified as having severe "behavioral disorders" (BD) (see next section) or serious "emotional disturbances" (ED). "Generally, if a person acts in a manner that is detrimental to him- or herself and/or others, he or she may be considered in a state of emotional disturbance" (Newcomer, 1980, p. 6). According to Federal legislation related to the education of individuals with disabilities, children and adolescents are seriously emotionally disturbed when they demonstrate one or more of the following characteristics to a marked degree over a long period of time:

(A) An inability to learn which cannot be explained by intellectual, sensory, or health factors;

(B) An inability to build or maintain satis-

factory interpersonal relationships with peers and teachers;

(C) Inappropriate behaviors or feelings under normal circumstances;

(D) A general pervasive mood of unhappiness or depression;

(E) A tendency to develop physical symptoms or fears associated with personal or school problems.

(*Federal Register*, 1977, p. 42478)

This special education designation includes those who have diagnoses of childhood schizophrenia or autism (see Chapter Thirteen). It does *not* include those who are socially maladjusted, unless they are also seriously emotionally disturbed.

Behavioral Disorders

Children or adolescents who are capable of learning more socially acceptable and personally gratifying behaviors but who *repeatedly* respond to their environment in marked socially unacceptable and/or personally unacceptable ways are classified as having *behavioral disorders* (Kauffman, 1977). Those who repeatedly violate rules and laws exhibit *delinquent behavior* (e.g., repeated cheating in school, extreme hostility or disrespect to authority figures, frequent fighting or stealing, carrying weapons, substance use or abuse); when they violate governmental laws they are classified as *juvenile offenders* (Gardstrom, 1996; Michel, 1985; Paul, 1982).

In the past few decades, increased attention has also been focused on "at-risk" children and adolescents, those who, because of various circumstances (e.g., drug or alcohol abuse, poverty, unstable home structure, homelessness, AIDS infection, affected prenatally by crack or fetal alcohol syndrome, lead poisoning, repeated failure experiences in school), are at risk of not completing their education, of drug or alcohol addiction, of becoming teenage parents, of becoming involved in gangs and criminal activities, or of suicide (Taylor, Barry, & Walls, 1997). Again, because of the uniqueness of each situation, an exact definition of this category is difficult. At-risk tendencies are reflected in attitudes, choices, and acting-out behaviors, such as delinquency, problems with authority figures, suspension or expulsion from school, lack of involvement in school activities, high absentee or tardiness or truancy rates, history of failure in school, dropping out of school, unprotected sexual intercourse at an early age, pregnancy, and/or substance abuse (Taylor et al., 1997).

COMMON CHARACTERISTICS, PROBLEMS, AND NEEDS OF CLIENTS

As with any population, those children and adolescents who have mental or behavioral disorders or severe emotional disturbances are a very heterogeneous group. Factors such as the type and severity of the impairment, the cause and time of onset, the existence of associated conditions or impairments, and the degree and type of support services available will all have varying effects on the individual's level of functioning, needs, and treatment program. In addition, each individual will have unique combinations of abilities, needs, personality traits, strengths, and weaknesses that will impact that individual's particular responses and functional abilities. Therefore, it is unwise to attempt to predict a particular person's skill levels or ceiling of abilities based on broad generalizations about a certain population. However, an awareness of some of those characteristics, problems, and needs which may be common to children and adolescents who have mental or behavioral disorders or severe emotional disturbances will be beneficial both to the therapist who desires to work with this population and to the reader who is trying to understand how music therapy intervention strategies may benefit this population.

Children and adolescents who have mental or behavioral disorders or severe emotional disturbances frequently are troubled by a high degree of tension and anxiety. They may exhibit disruptive, withdrawn, or bizarre behaviors, causing trouble for themselves and the people around them. Those with more mild disturbances require constant structuring to keep them on task, while those with very severe disturbances may be unable to function within the boundaries of reality. Depending upon their level of learning skill and adaptive development, these clients may often need help developing basic academic, motor, communication, or social skills. Since most children and adolescents with mental or behavioral disorders or severe emotional disturbances have problems developing and maintaining satisfactory interpersonal relationships, social skill development is usually a primary area of need. Many of these clients also need help in the areas of improving their self-concept, learning positive coping strategies, developing self-control in dealing with fear and frustration, learning to predict consequences of behavior, and learning to interact cooperatively and appropriately with others (Nocera, 1979).

Several major categories or groupings may be delineated within the general population of children and adolescents who have mental or behavioral disorders or severe emotional disturbances. These may include schizophrenia or other psychotic disorders; anxiety disorders; mood disorders; eating disorders (anorexia, bulimia); autism; severe emotional disturbances; attention-deficit/hyperactivity disorders; disruptive behavior disorders/social maladjustment; substance abuse or dependence; juvenile offenders; those who have been abused; and those who are at-risk (APA, 1994; Paul, 1982; Taylor et al., 1997). In this text, individuals with autism are discussed in Chapter Thirteen, and schizophrenia and other psychotic disorders, anxiety disorders, mood disorders, and eating disorders (anorexia, bulimia) are described in Chapter Fifteen. Common characteristics and needs of youths in the remaining categories are described below.

Children and Adolescents Who Have Severe Emotional Disturbances

Children and adolescents who have severe emotional disturbances almost constantly function outside the boundaries of normal contact with reality (Paul, 1982). Other terms used to classify these clients include mentally ill, psychotic, or childhood schizophrenia. These clients have severe impairments that may include problems of identity, poor body image, perceptual problems, emotional lability, phobias, extreme anxiety, severe language disorders, bizarre or ritualistic behaviors, hallucinations, and severely delayed developmental stages. Relationships with other people and social interaction abilities are also usually grossly impaired. Some clients may seem oblivious to other people, not play with peers, or withdraw and refuse to make eye contact. Some may engage in behaviors that are injurious to themselves or others (e.g., biting themselves, head banging, or engaging in prolonged temper tantrums or violent outbursts). Lower functioning clients often lack basic self-help and personal hygiene skills (APA, 1994; Newcomer, 1980; Nowicki & Trevisan, 1978; Paul, 1982).

Children and adolescents who have been diagnosed as autistic are sometime included under the general category of severely emotionally disturbed. In this text, information on clients with autism is presented separately in Chapter Thirteen.

Children and Adolescents Who Have Been Abused

Children and adolescents who have been abused through physical violence, neglect, continual terrorism, continual rejection, and/or sexual exploitation may also display certain behaviors that cause them to be classified as behavior-disordered or emotionally disturbed (Paul, 1982). Some may be withdrawn and quiet, while others may be aggressive and destructive. Problems with assertiveness or anger management are common (Slotoroff, 1994). Many of these clients also have difficulty expressing feelings, low self-esteem, a poorly developed sense of self, poor internal controls, inadequate coping and defense mechanisms, much fear and anxiety, an extreme sensitivity to criticism, and an inability to trust people and establish effective relationships. Other characteristics that may be exhibited by children or adolescents who have been abused include short attention span, low frustration tolerance, fear of failure, emotional outbursts, poor impulse control, and delayed physical, academic, and/or social development (Clendenon-Wallen, 1991; Friedlander, 1994; Isenberg-Grzeda, 1995; Paul, 1982; Slotoroff, 1994).

Children and Adolescents Who Have Attention-Deficit/Hyperactivity Disorders

Children and adolescents who have attention deficit disorders [ADD] or attention-deficit/hyperactivity disorders [ADHD] have persistent difficulties paying attention and focusing on important tasks and/or difficulties delaying and controlling impulsive behaviors (APA, 1994; Bain, 1991; Children and Adults with Attention Deficit Disorders [CH.A.D.D], 1995). Individuals may have both attention deficit and hyperactivity problems, or they may have problems predominantly with inattention or predominantly with hyperactivity and impulsivity (APA, 1994). Children and adolescents with ADD or ADHD do not necessarily have emotional disturbances; however, without proper diagnosis and treatment, they may develop behavioral disorders, depression, or even substance abuse (CH.A.D.D, 1995).

ADHD involves a set of behavioral characteristics that impair a child's ability to function in his or her environment. Though biologically based, these characteristics are influenced by psychological and social factors. None of these behavioral characteristics taken alone would necessarily be considered abnormal. But taken in combination, or because of their intensity or pervasiveness, or because of the nature of the child's environment, they can create problems in the classroom, home, and other places. Moreover, they can initiate a spiral of problems. (Bain, 1991, p. 20)

Children with ADHD may seem to be constantly in motion, fidgeting, continuously changing activities, or talking incessantly. They frequently exhibit many of the following symptoms of inattention and/or of hyperactivity-impulsivity: short attention span; difficulty sustaining attention; easily distracted; failure to give close attention to details; inattention to verbal directions; difficulty following through on instructions (failure to finish tasks, chores, etc.); constantly shifting from one uncompleted task to another; difficulty organizing tasks and activities; frequent loss of materials necessary for tasks; fidgeting with hands or feet or squirming in seat; difficulty remaining seated as requested; difficulty waiting turns; blurting out answers before questions are completed; interrupting or intruding on others' activities or conversations; difficulty playing quietly; engaging in physically dangerous activities without considering the consequences. These characteristic behaviors of ADHD are *chronic and persistent,* showing repeated occurrences lasting at least six months, with onset before age seven (APA, 1994; Bain, 1991; CH.A.D.D., 1995; Paul, 1982; Wender & Wender, 1978).

Treatment of children and adolescents who have ADHD usually focuses on controlling or eliminating their problem behaviors at home, at school, and in the community. However, since their behaviors often cause these individuals to face criticism and rejection and experience failure, "possibly the greatest problems that ADHD children face are in the areas of their own self-esteem and their peer relationships" (Bain, 1991, p. 173). Many of these clients have low self-confidence, low appreciation for and acceptance of themselves, and do not feel loved and accepted by others. Therefore, they need experiences that will help them develop an internal sense of mastery, areas of competence, and ways of interacting appropriately and successfully with their peers.

Children and Adolescents Who Have Disruptive Behavior Disorders or Are Socially Maladjusted

There are two main types of disruptive behavior disorders: conduct disorders and oppositional defiant disorders (APA, 1994). Children and adolescents who have a *conduct disorder,* "one of the most frequently diagnosed conditions in outpatient and inpatient mental health facilities for children" (APA, 1994, p. 88), *chronically and persistently* engage in behaviors that violate the basic rights of others or that violate major age-appropriate rules and norms of society. They may repeatedly bully, threaten, or intimidate others; initiate physical fights; use weapons (e.g., brick, bat, knife, gun) that can seriously harm others; be physically cruel to animals or people; engage in crimes of theft like mugging, purse snatching, extortion, or armed robbery; or commit crimes of physical violence like rape, assault, or homicide. Individuals who have conduct disorders may also have a pattern of deliberately destroying

the property of others through fire setting, breaking or smashing, or other acts of vandalism. They may engage in theft or deceitful behaviors, such as breaking into others' houses or cars, conning others, shoplifting, or forgery. In addition, these clients often have a pattern, beginning before age 13, of staying out late at night without parental permission, running away from home and staying away overnight or for a more lengthy period, or being truant from school. They also are likely to have disturbed peer relationships. When onset is prior to age 10, "individuals are more likely to have persistent Conduct Disorder and to develop Antisocial Personality Disorder than are those with Adolescent-Onset Type" (APA, 1994, p. 86). Individuals who have conduct disorders usually have little concern for the feelings, well-being, or wishes of others. While they project a tough image, they may have low self-esteem. They frequently are easily irritated, have poor frustration tolerance, tend to blame others for their own mistakes, have outbursts of temper, and engage in reckless or high-risk acts. Conduct disorder is often associated with use of illegal substances, smoking, drinking, and an early onset of sexual activity. Individuals may also have ADHD, learning disabilities, anxiety or mood disorders, or substance-related disorders.

Children and adolescents who have an *oppositional defiant disorder* show "a recurrent pattern of nega-tivistic, defiant, disobedient, and hostile behavior toward authority figures that persists for at least 6 months" (APA, 1994, p. 91). These individuals frequently lose their temper, argue with adults, defy or fail to comply with requests of adult authorities, deliberately and persistently test limits, deliberately do things that annoy others, are verbally aggressive, or blame their mistakes or misbehaviors on others. They may be touchy and easily annoyed or be spiteful and vindictive. They are often stubborn, resist taking directions, and refuse to compromise or negotiate with adults. Oppositional symptoms usually become evident before age 8 and not later than early adolescence. Symptoms frequently occur first in the home setting; over time, they may spread to school and community settings. While individuals who have oppositional defiant disorder exhibit the disobedience and opposition to authority that are also observed in conduct disorder, they do not engage in serious aggression toward animals or people, deliberate destruction of property, or patterns of theft and deceit. However, oppositional defiant disorder may be a "developmental antecedent" to conduct disorder in a significant proportion of cases (APA, 1994, p. 92).

Sometimes adolescents who have persistent patterns of disruptive behaviors are classified as being *socially maladjusted.* These individuals consistently exhibit deviant or socially inappropriate behaviors because of "an inability to adapt to or cope with people and situations in the environment of daily living" (Paul, 1982, p. 58). Although their outward behavior may show defiance and aggression or an apathetic detachment, many of these individuals are actually insecure, fear failure, and have a poor self-concept. They frequently are not able to foresee consequences of behaviors and often have unstable and ineffective interpersonal relationships. Individuals who are *juvenile offenders* (see below) and children or adolescents who have problems with *substance abuse* or dependence (see below) are sometimes classified under the more general term *socially maladjusted* (Paul, 1982).

Children and Adolescents Who Are Juvenile Offenders

Individuals under age 18 who have been in trouble with the law may be described by various terms, including juvenile offenders, youthful offenders, or juvenile delinquents. They may have committed *status offenses* (e.g., truancy, curfew violations), acts that are illegal only when committed by juveniles, *misdemeanors* (e.g., trespassing, simple traffic violations), or more serious *felonies* (e.g., nonviolent crimes like car theft or violent crimes like armed robbery, rape, or murder). Before coming into contact with the juvenile justice system, these young people have typically displayed chronic patterns of antisocial behavior, such as cheating or missing assignments in school, being hostile and aggressive or being aloof and withdrawn, being disrespectful to or defying authority, destroying property, fighting, stealing, carrying weapons, or using illegal substances (Gardstrom, 1996; Michel, 1985).

Aggression is often the most problematic antisocial behavior manifested by children or adolescents who are juvenile delinquents. Many fear and

mistrust others and have difficulties establishing relationships, handling conflicts, and managing their own emotions. They are often aloof, guarded, indifferent, or superficial, and may be hostile and resistive, trying to project a "tough" image. Some may have symptoms of stress and anxiety. Factors such as alcohol or drug use and abuse, unplanned and problematic pregnancies, poor nutrition and poor personal hygiene, inadequate medical and dental care, a history of physical or sexual abuse, poor school performance or a history of repeated failure in school, poverty, or unstable and turbulent family situations may contribute to the problems of these clients. Many also have learning disabilities, mental disorders, or emotional impairments that interfere with learning. Most of these clients have needs in the areas of exploring and expressing feelings appropriately; increasing their self-esteem; learning to interact positively and successfully with others; acquiring skills for constructive use of leisure time; developing problem-solving, anger management, and coping skills; and improving functional academic and job-related skills.

Children and Adolescents Who Have Problems with Substance Abuse

Generally, substance abuse is more often a problem of adolescence than early childhood (Cassity & Cassity, 1994a, 1994b). Adolescents or older youth who have problems of substance or drug abuse, alcoholism, or substance or drug dependence or addiction use alcohol, illegal drugs, medications, toxins (e.g., lead, pesticides), or inhalants to such an extent that their health, safety, social or interpersonal relations, or performance at work, school, or home are impaired (APA, 1994; Paul, 1992). Individuals who develop patterns of substance abuse and dependence often use chemical substances or alcohol to help them escape or try to cope with their problems. Some may enjoy the "high" or feelings of euphoria they get when they are under the influence of their drug of choice. Others may begin substance use because of peer pressure, a desire to rebel, or a quest for adventure (Paul, 1982). Occasional or experimental use frequently develops into habitual substance abuse and substance dependence.

The problem of substance abuse becomes evident

when individuals repeatedly (a) demonstrate intoxication or other substance-related symptoms that leave them unable to fulfill their obligations at school, work, or home (e.g., repeated absences due to substance use; substance-related expulsions or suspensions from school; neglect of family or household); (b) use substances in physically hazardous situations (e.g., driving a car, operating machinery, swimming, rock climbing); (c) are arrested for substance-related problems (e.g., disorderly conduct, driving under the influence, assault and battery), or (d) have persistent inter-personal problems (e.g., arguments, physical fights) caused or exacerbated by the use or effects of the substance (APA, 1994). Many adolescents who have problems with substance abuse or substance dependence are depressed or insecure. They have a poor self-concept, low self-esteem, and ineffective or unstable relationships with others. Many also dread the future, have a fear or a history of failure, have difficulty developing or conceiving of long-range goals, and are often unable to perceive the consequences of behavior (Paul, 1982).

Children and Adolescents Who Are At-Risk

Since children and adolescents are at risk for many different reasons and each situation is unique, it is difficult, if not impossible, to describe the "typical" at-risk student. However, the literature does delineate several descriptive characteristics and high-risk behaviors that may indicate certain young people are likely to be at-risk (Taylor, et al., 1997).

Children and adolescents who are at-risk often are poverty-stricken, have a history of low grades and failure in school that contributes to decreased motivation and lack of self-esteem, have low level reading and academic skills, prefer gainful employment to school, have friends or relatives who have dropped out of school, have problems and stresses at home (e.g., dysfunctional family situation, emotional and/or physical abuse), feel alienated from the school environment, feel like outsiders because of numerous school transfers and family moves, or engage in self-destructive behaviors like substance abuse or early sexual intercourse. More obvious high-risk behaviors usually become evident during adolescence, when students may engage in delin-quent or acting-out behavior, defy or rebel against adult authority figures, be repeatedly truant or tardy, have frequent suspensions or expulsions from school, develop a pattern of substance abuse, engage in unprotected sexual intercourse (that may result in teen pregnancies), or drop out of school. Usually males are more likely to drop out of school and/or commit violent, aggressive acts, while females are at risk of becoming pregnant and have a greater tendency to attempt suicide.

Some children are at-risk because they are homeless (Staum & Brotons, 1995). They are deprived of emotional and social stability and frequently display delays in academic and behavioral skills. These children may need enrichment programs to help them develop interaction skills and group participation skills. Many also need experi-ences that will provide success, motivation, security, and improve their self-concept and feeling of self-worth.

TREATMENT APPROACHES

Several different treatment approaches, based on *biomedical models, psychotherapeutic models, behavioral models,* and *eclectic* or *multimodal models,* have been developed to treat children and adolescents who have mental or behavioral disorders or severe emotional disturbances (Atterbury, 1990; Brooks, 1989; Cassity & Cassity, 1994a; Thaut & Gfeller, 1992). The approach used will depend

somewhat on setting. For example, behavior modification techniques based on behaviorist princi-ples are most likely to be used in school settings (Atterbury, 1990). Outside the school setting, acute care facilities for adolescents often use psychotherapy as the primary treatment method, while chronic care facilities rely more on behavior modification (Brooks, 1989).

Biomedical Model

Those who approach treatment from a biomedical model maintain that biological factors (e.g., biochemical imbalances, genetic problems, physical abnormalities or illnesses) underlie emotional and behavioral disorders. They emphasize the impact of biological processes on human behavior. A specific diagnosis (e.g., schizophrenia, autism, psychosis, neurosis, conduct disorder) is given by a medical doctor (psychiatrist), who prescribes the course of treatment. Treatment often includes some type of medication or drug therapy. In cases where environmental stresses are believed to contribute to the individual's emotional, physical, or behavioral problems, a biomedical approach may also use changes in the environment or treatment interventions that change a person's responses to stresses (e.g., relaxation training, biofeedback) in conjunction with or in lieu of drug therapy.

Psychotherapeutic Models

In psychotherapeutic approaches, the psychiatrist, psychologist, or social worker looks beyond the overt or presenting behaviors to try to determine underlying causes of behavior. The presenting behaviors are not emphasized because they are viewed merely as symptoms of more severe disabilities or underlying conflicts. Psychotherapists help individuals find and examine the causes of their behaviors and learn better coping methods.

Those who work from a *psychoanalytic* or *psychodynamic* orientation (based on the theories of Freud and others) use various techniques to gain insight into an individual's unconscious conflicts, motivations, and symbols. Maladaptive behaviors are not dealt with directly, but decrease as individuals gain insight, work out underlying conflicts and anxieties, and build ego strength. Psychotherapists who work with young children may also use *play therapy* techniques, in which children reveal problems and anxieties on a fantasy level while playing with dolls, clay, or other toys, to help gain insights into the behaviors and responses of their clients (Kaplan & Sadock, 1991).

Some psychotherapists work from *humanistic* therapy models, such as Rollo May's existential therapy, Carl Rogers's person-centered therapy, or Perls's Gestalt therapy (Thaut & Gfeller, 1992). According to this model, emotional or behavioral disorders result when individuals fail to find meaning in their lives. These therapists try to develop a supportive relationship with the client, so clients can feel secure enough to confront basic questions about the meaning of life and achieve insights about their own life. Humanistic approaches emphasize the uniqueness, value, and worth of each individual, and believe all individuals have the capacity to control their own lives and make good decisions. Therapists often aim to help clients move to a state of "self-actualization" (Maslow, 1968), moving beyond the basics of existence to a life filled with meaning and a sense of well-being.

Those who follow *cognitive* treatment models maintain that disordered thinking about oneself and the world are at the root of emotional and behavioral disorders. Treatment focuses on (a) helping clients become aware of negative or irrational thought patterns or beliefs that create stress or cause feelings of inadequacy, (b) confronting these and identifying life experiences in which they operate, and (c) finding ways to reverse the negative or irrational thinking and thus alter behavior. Examples of cognitive approaches include Beck's cognitive therapy, Berne's transactional analysis (TA), Ellis' rational emotive therapy (RET), Glasser's reality therapy, Maultsby's rational behavior therapy, and Meichenbaum's cognitive behavior modification (Kaplan & Sadock, 1991; Thaut & Gfeller, 1992).

Behavioral Models

Behavioral models focus on the maladaptive or disruptive behaviors that affect the individual's ability to learn or to interact successfully and appropriately with others. These approaches are based on the work of Pavlov, Watson, Thorndike, and B. F. Skinner (Atterbury, 1990; Kaplan & Sadock, 1991). Therapists who work from a behavioral orientation believe that all behaviors are learned, and therefore can be unlearned. Focus is on observable behavior, not underlying processes. Overt behaviors are observed, measured, and quantified, to determine what behaviors need to be changed. Treatment plans use behavior modification techniques and principles of reinforcement and stimulus-response learning to decrease and extinguish inappropriate behaviors and responses and increase more adaptive, appropriate behaviors and responses. Brooks (1989) noted that, even when treatment facilities use psychotherapy as the primary treatment approach, "some form of behavior therapy is used for daily maintenance of the adolescent. Behavior therapy in such settings enhances the psychotherapeutic process because it provides a safe, concrete structure the adolescent needs" (p. 37). Since the behavioral model is the only treatment model that is education-based, it is the model most commonly used in school setting (Atterbury, 1990).

Eclectic or Multimodal Models

While particular therapists or clinics may favor a certain treatment model or approach, most therapists realize that no existing treatment model is effective for every client in every situation. Therapy teams often find that an eclectic approach, drawing from many models and combining the best features of several approaches, is most helpful in meet the unique needs of a particular client (Thaut & Gfeller, 1992). For example, experts have found that many clients with ADHD benefit most from multimodal approach (e.g., parent training in behavior management, appropriate educational program, individual and family counseling when needed, medication if required) that uses multiple types of interventions (medication, behavior therapy, family therapy, psychological and educational intervention) to help the client achieve therapeutic goals (Bain, 1991; CH.A.D.D., 1995).

Some therapists who work in psychiatric settings use Lazarus' (1976, 1989) Multimodal Therapy model to help classify a patient's problems and types of therapeutic interventions. This model is very eclectic; a variety of therapeutic approaches may be used to address the problems it identifies. "The Multimodal model involves comprehensive assessment and intervention across a person's BASIC-ID (or basic identity)" (Cassity & Cassity, 1994a, p. 134). Therapists who use this model carefully assess and describe clients' *Behavior* (habits, actions, gestures, reactions), *Affect* (emotions, moods, feelings), *Sensation* (how clients perceive what they see, hear, touch, taste, smell; includes negative sensations, such as tension, pain, dizziness, and client preferences or fixation), *Imagery* (recurring dreams, vivid memories, clients' self-image or body-image), *Cognitive* problems (ideas, values, beliefs, opinions, or attitudes that interfere with happiness or functioning), *Interpersonal* relations (ways clients socialize or interact with others; any problems with the way clients treat or are treated by others), and *Drug* use or health concerns (medication or drug use or abuse, any concerns about state of health or physical well-being). While, multimodal assessment attends to specific problems within each modality, it also focuses on the interaction between modalities, recognizing that a problem in one area or modality influences functioning in all other areas. Noting in what order clients exhibit BASIC-ID responses ("modality firing order") during a given response pattern can help a therapist determine what events trigger affective responses or emotional disturbances (Cassity & Cassity, 1994a, pp. 138-139).

SETTINGS FOR SERVICE DELIVERY

Children and adolescents who have mental or behavioral disorders or emotional disturbances may receive special programs and services to help meet their specific needs in a variety of settings, depending on the type and severity of their impairment. These may include outpatient and inpatient mental health facilities for children and adolescents, youth homes, private or public rehabilitation/educational facilities or clinics, private therapy, programs related to the juvenile justice system, or public schools. The

Individuals with Disabilities Act (IDEA) (Public Law 101-476), the 1990 revision of the 1975 Education for All Handicapped Children Act (Public Law 94-142) assures a free, appropriate public education to all children, ages 3-21, including those who have mental or behavioral disorders or severe emotional disturbances. Incentives for early intervention programs to address the needs children birth through age 2 who have handicaps or disabilities are provided by Public Law 99-457 of 1986 (Adamek, 1996; Humpal, 1990).

When children and adolescents receive services through their public school system, these special education services are delivered according to the same general procedure outlined in Chapter Seven. After initial referral, assessment and identification of the disability, Individualized Educational Programs (IEPs) are written to guide instruction. IEPs set educational goals and establish programs that reflect the individual's specific strengths and weakness. IEPs also provide for appropriate support services in areas of need, placement in the least restrictive environment, and an annual evaluation of student progress in the program. The student is usually included with peers in a regular classroom for as much of the day as possible. Sometimes school districts have special programs or campuses for adolescents who are at-risk of not completing their education due to teenage pregnancy, drug use, behavior problems, mild delinquency, or other factors (Gardstrom, 1996; Taylor et al., 1997). When the special education assessment finds that music therapy can provide a unique means of helping students achieve their educational objectives, music therapists may be called upon to provide traditional direct services, work with students in self-contained classes, work with students in inclusive classes, provide consultation services to facilitate classroom instruction, inclusion, or music education, and/or provide staff development workshops (Wilson, 1996). Music therapy is usually classified as a related service in special education settings.

Music therapists work with both children and adolescents who have mental or behavioral disorders or emotional disturbances. They deliver services to these clients in many different settings, including outpatient and inpatient mental health facilities for children or adolescents, special education programs in public or private schools, public or private clinics, substance abuse treatment programs, youth homes, juvenile corrections programs in long-term public or private rehabilitation/education settings, music studios, community programs, and private therapy settings. Music therapists may provide direct or consultant services and work with clients as individuals or in groups. Some music therapists are self-employed and work in private practice or contact their services to various agencies or treatment programs. In some instances, music therapy services may be funded by grants from the government, community, or private foundations (Gardstrom, 1996). According to a recent survey (AMTA, 1998), 21% of the music therapists responding served mental health populations, and 144 of 1654 respondents stated they specifically worked in child/adolescent treatment centers. Another 264 said they work in inpatient psychiatric settings, which may include some who serve children or adolescents. (The figures for self-employed/private practice and school settings did not specify populations served.)

HOW MUSIC IS USED IN THERAPY

Many aspects of music make it a useful therapeutic tool for children and adolescents who have various mental or behavioral disorders or severe emotional disturbances. As music therapists structure activities to focus on nonmusical behaviors and skills that can be learned and practiced through music experiences, music becomes something that children and adolescents with emotional or behavioral disorders can "identify with, relate to, and become an integral part of" (Levis & Lininger, 1994). For those who have severe emotional disturbances or psychoses, the rhythm, order, and structure of music can provide a link to reality (Sears, 1968) and provide stability that may be a significant factor in bringing meaning and order to other aspects of their lives (Salas, 1990). Since music is a potent means of nonverbal communication (Gaston, 1968a), it can be an effective tool for establishing contact with those who have difficulty expressing feelings and ideas verbally. As clients learn to express themselves and their feelings through music activities, such as playing musical instruments, singing, moving to music, or creating improvisations and songs, they also learn to relate more appropriately to others and begin to channel impulses into socially acceptable behaviors. Since music is a powerful affective medium that is integrally connected to emotions (see Chapter Five), it can be an effective medium for promoting desirable changes in moods and feelings (e.g., decrease depression, anxiety, anger; increase motivation, relaxation), thus developing more desirable affective behaviors that support therapeutic change and growth (Thaut, 1989a). In addition, music experiences can be structured to help clients learn to identify and appropriately express emotions, which can positively influence their ability to interact appropriately with others.

The gentle persuasion to group activity inherent in music (Gaston, 1968a) may motivate shy or withdrawn clients to begin to interact with others in the music setting. Instrumental ensembles and dances can be used to improve nonverbal communication and cooperation, while group singing, music discussion groups, and song writing activities can be used to facilitate verbal expression and interaction. As clients participate in rhythmic activities, instrumental ensembles, singing, and movement-to-music experiences, their imitation skills and amount of on-task behaviors also frequently improve. In addition, the experiences of successfully participating in music groups and learning musical skills also increase clients' self-esteem and contribute to an improved self-image.

Since music is usually an important part of adolescent culture, music therapy may be a particularly useful modality for enhancing treatment with adolescents (Brooks, 1989; Frisch, 1990). When music therapists approach adolescent clients by using the clients' preferred music, they are seen as "safe" adults with whom the adolescents may communicate through the common basis of music (Brooks, 1989; Wooten, 1992). Therapeutically structured music experiences provide positive, nonthreatening activities that offer a predictable, familiar context in which clients are able to relax and have a safe framework for taking risks and exploring difficult issues. These music experiences also offer nondirective and nonconfrontational control as the clients respond to the structure of the music and the music experience, not the adult authority. Especially in the initial stages of therapy, "the adolescent psychiatric inpatient may trust and relate to the music more quickly and more deeply than to another person" (Frisch, 1990). As well as being a way of establishing communication with adolescents, the preferred music of the adolescent can give the therapist insight into the patient's emotional issues (Wooten, 1992). For example,

Metzger (1986) found that adolescent psychiatric patients who had a history of violence, sexual abuse, or drug abuse often chose to listen to songs with themes related to their diagnosis and showed excitement over or fascination with songs about sex, violence, drugs, and Satanism.

General Music Therapy Intervention Strategies and Goals

When working with children and adolescents who have mental or behavioral disorders or severe emotional disturbances, music therapists structure different types of music experiences in many ways to help clients learn nonmusical behaviors that will help them relate more effectively and appropriately to the world around them. Whether the treatment model is primarily behavioral, psychodynamic, cognitive, humanistic, or eclectic, the music experience is an essential ingredient in the music therapy session. Whatever the treatment philosophy, music is both the primary tool used to establish contact with the clients and the primary means through which clients learn and develop desired nonmusical skills and behaviors.

Often, music therapy approaches with children and adolescents who have mental or behavioral disorders or severe emotional disturbances incorporate *active physical involvement* in making or responding to music, through playing or improvising on musical instruments, dancing or moving to music, singing or vocalizing, or composing songs or lyrics. Other more *passive approaches* are centered around music listening, using contingent music listening to modify behavior, teaching music-mediated relaxation and stress reduction techniques, using song lyrics as a basis for discussion, or using guided imagery and music. Some research suggests that music therapy experiences based on passive listening may be a better first approach for clients who are more fragile and who have strong needs for structure and security, while more active experiences (e.g., improvisation or rhythmic training on drums and other percussion instruments) may be better first experiences for clients who have aggressive, acting-out behaviors and/or severe attention deficit problems (Montello & Coons, 1998).

According to Friedlander (1994), music therapy

approaches in psychiatric settings for children may be grouped into two broad categories: music activity therapy and music psychotherapy. In *music activity therapy*, the emphasis is on structuring music activities to provide individuals with successful experiences within the music group while also increasing social, motor, and expressive skills or improving the client's internal organization. Therapeutic music experiences may include Orff-Schulwerk activities, instrumental ensembles, group singing, exercises to music, music as a reward for desired behaviors, song writing, lyric discussion, or music for stress reduction.

In *music psychotherapy*, the emphasis is on using the client's personal experience on music to explore personal issues, with the goal of acquiring and consolidating a sense of confidence and self-worth (see Chapter Fifteen). In *child music psychotherapy*, music therapists who have additional training in psychotherapy use music experiences such as improvisation, music listening, and creating new music to evoke or express imagery and emotion. However, the musical metaphors and images the children generate in these music processes are not interpreted by the therapist as they often are in adult music psychotherapy. Instead, change and learning come from the meaningful interpersonal interchanges experienced in the music activities that result in corrective emotional experiences (Friedlander, 1994). At first, the music therapist strives to "establish a safe musical container within which to accept the unique musical contributions of individual members" (Friedlander, 1994, pp. 95-96). In later stages of child music psychotherapy, clients explore their differences and learn to interact cooperatively and constructively with others in musical experiences and use music to express feelings, share with each other, and support one another.

Music therapists who serve adolescent patients in psychiatric settings treat adolescents with diagnoses of conduct disorders most frequently, followed by those with diagnoses of affective disorders, adjustment disorders, substance abuse, anxiety disorders, and psychotic disorders (Cassity & Cassity, 1994b). Music therapists who work with children in psychiatric settings also most frequently treat those with diagnoses of conduct disorders, followed by those with diagnoses of adjustment disorders, anxiety disorders, affective disorders, and psychotic disorders (Cassity & Cassity, 1994b). The majority of music

therapy interventions with adolescents address interpersonal, affective, or cognitive problems; with children, the majority address interpersonal, behavioral, cognitive, or physical problems (including problems with motor skills or receptive/expressive language) (Cassity & Cassity, 1994a, 1994b).

A careful assessment of clients' nonmusical and musical behaviors and preferences are a key part of developing effective music therapy treatment strategies. Important assessment areas include: music attitudes and preferences, how the client uses music, music skills and rhythmic abilities, interpersonal relationships, eye contact, attention span, posture, grooming, expressive abilities (verbal and nonverbal), concentration, retention, and problem-solving abilities (Cassity & Cassity, 1994b). Some music therapists find that Lazarus's (1976, 1989) Multimodal model (BASIC-ID) is also useful for categorizing information in music therapy assessments and treatment (Adelman, 1985; Cassity & Cassity, 1994a, 1994b; Cassity & Theobald, 1990).

Music therapists can use specially structured music experiences to help children and adolescents who have mental or behavioral disorders or severe emotional disturbances reach many different therapeutic goals, such as increasing behavior and impulse control, decreasing uncooperative and disruptive behaviors, increasing ability to follow directions, increasing ability to work cooperatively and constructively with others, decreasing withdrawn behavior, learning to develop relationships, increasing interaction with others, increasing appropriate social responses, learning to identify and appropriately express feelings and emotions, facilitating relaxation, decreasing tension and anxiety, increasing appropriate communication and self-expression, learning or practicing basic academic skills, increasing self-esteem, decreasing negative self-statements, and increasing problem-solving, decision-making, and coping skills (Cassity & Cassity, 1994a, 1994b; Zinar, 1987). Cassity and Cassity (1994a, pp. 47-80) and Zinar (1987, pp. 15-30) give several examples of general types of music interventions that may be used to help children and adolescents who have mental or behavioral disorders or severe emotional disturbances reach various goals.

Music Therapy Interventions for Children and Adolescents Who Have Severe Emotional Disturbances

Children and adolescents who have such severe disorders that they have lost contact with reality and have grossly impaired relationships and abilities to interact with other people still may be attracted to and reached through music. Creative or improvisational music therapy techniques, in which the therapist improvises music based on the child's movements, vocalizations, behaviors, or instrument beating to reach out to the child and establish contact through musical sounds, are frequently successful in establishing communication with severely impaired children (Nordoff & Robbins, 1971b, 1977). Once contact and communication have been established, the improvised music can help structure interactions, facilitate personality development, and lead to a working relationship between child and therapist and between child and peers. "The patient's musical personality, once affirmed and withstood, can change and grow within the musical relationship(s)" (Steele, 1987, p. 33).

By listening to the child's musical responses, reflecting these, setting them in a musical context (e.g., adding harmonies, form), and introducing variety, the music therapist structures the environment to let the music and the musical relationship move the child toward growth and positive change. For example, Steele (1987) described how a group of 6- to 9-year-old children who had emotional disturbances learned to share a basic beat in drum improvisations, which paved the way for them to accompany, imitate, and vary a melodic theme played by the therapist. As they became involved in more complex musical interactions, these children also learned to organize and control their responses and cooperate with and relate more constructively and appropriately to the other individuals in the music group. In another instance, as a 6-year-old girl who had a profound fear of novel experiences and unfamiliar objects learned to tolerate new musical instruments in passive listening experiences and in active music activities involving playing and improvising on instruments, she began to have a fear-free acceptance of other new objects, persons, and experiences (Hoelzley, 1991). In this case, the music therapist used improvisational music activities in combination with the behavioral techniques of reciprocal inhibition and counterconditioning as the client was gradually exposed to new instruments.

Music therapy techniques also have been incorporated successfully into various therapeutic educational approaches used to treat children with severe emotional disturbances. For example, specific music experiences have been matched to the various levels of the Developmental Therapy curriculum, resulting in an approach known as Developmental Music Therapy (DMT) (Graham, 1975; Wood et al., 1974). In DMT, music therapists structure the musical environment and plan therapeutic music intervention strategies to help the children sequentially develop needed behaviors, communication skills, and socialization skills. As clients progress, the focus moves from eliciting simple pleasure responses to music (Stage I) to developing individual skills for musical success (Stage II) to learning skills for increasingly more demanding types of group participation and involvement (Stages III-V). (See Chapter Twenty-two for more information on Developmental Music Therapy.)

Since music is a positive, reinforcing stimulus for many children, music therapy may also be an integral part of a behaviorally-oriented, levels system approach (Cleveland Music School Settlement Music Therapy Department, 1985; Presti, 1984). Music therapists who use this approach carefully plan, structure, and sequence music experiences to help clients learn more appropriate behaviors. Targeted behaviors are successively shaped using various types of specifically designed music activities to secure attention and cooperation, elicit desired behaviors, and/or reinforce the intervention process. Behavioral expectations, reinforcement, and consequences specified for each level, so clients are given the responsibility for their own behavior choices. By progressing through the levels as they learn to acquire, become proficient in, maintain, and generalize desired behaviors, clients are encouraged to "invest in the process, to learn the value of effort exerted and results achieved, and to strive toward goals that will improve social conduct and interaction" (Cleveland Music School Settlement Music Therapy Department, 1985, p. iii).

More recently, music therapy strategies have been incorporated into "Increase the Peace," a behavior management program to teach cooperation skills to elementary-age students, particularly those who have emotional disturbances (Levis & Lininger, 1994). This program combines a systematic program of behavioral expectations, positive reinforcements, and consequences with experiences centered around ten "focus words" (communication, encouragement, honesty, maturity, teamwork, composure, sportsmanship, consideration, compromise, and patience) designed to help students understand and experience cooperation. As the students participate in therapeutic music experiences based on listening, singing, music games, music ensembles, and music improvisation or composition, "music provides the rhythm, structure, and order to internalize the words, the meaning of the words, and the means by which to experience the words" (Levis & Lininger, 1994, p. 39). Levis and Lininger (1994, pp. 40-61) provide many specific activity plans that may be used in this approach.

Other music therapists and researchers have found that selected background music, used alone (Mitchell, 1966) or in conjunction with play therapy (Cooke, 1969) can decrease anxiety levels of children who have psychoses or severe emotional disturbances. Soothing, instrumental background music can also increase these clients' accuracy in performing sorting tasks (Burleson et al., 1989). In addition, music therapists have used singing, vocal dynamics groups, various instrumental activities, movement-to-music, music listening, music improvisation, music composition, and music with computers to help children who have severe emotional disturbances (1) achieve greater self- and group-awareness, (2) increase concentration and on-task behavior, (3) improve communication and self-expression, (4) identify and express emotions and feelings accurately and appropriately, and (5) increase cooperation with others (Cassity & Cassity, 1994a; Salas, 1990; Spitzer, 1989; Wasserman, 1972; Werbner, 1966).

Music therapists who work in *adolescent psychiatric settings* most often use structured music experiences to help their clients develop better interpersonal skills (e.g., increased self- and group-awareness, appropriate interactions with peers and adults, more cooperative behaviors, improved communication with adults), better affective processes (e.g., appropriate identification and expression of feelings, decreasing anxiety or stress reactions, increasing

impulse control, decreasing depression or suicidal feelings), and better cognitive processes (e.g., positive self-statements and increased self-esteem, sense of identity, organizational skills, decision-making and problem-solving skills, coping skills, insight into peer and family interactions) (Brooks, 1989; Cassity & Cassity, 1994a). Adolescents often do not communicate with adults; however, as they relate to the music used in therapy, they may also begin to see the music therapist as a "safe" adult, one whom they can trust and communicate with in and through the musical experience. Since music activities can be structured to be nonthreatening, offering nondirective and nonconfrontational control, adolescents often engage in music-mediated therapeutic processes with little resistance. Brooks (1989) called music therapy an excellent "sneak" therapy for adolescents, one in which they readily engage and through which they can work on any treatment goals. Haines (1989) noted that adolescents often respond more quickly in music, usually working together already in the first session.

Frisch (1990) observed that adolescents who have severe emotional disturbances frequently have difficulty using words to relate to other people; therefore, especially at the beginning of therapy, "the adolescent psychiatric inpatient may trust and relate to the music more quickly and more deeply than to another person" (p. 20). In addition, Frisch proposed that the musical symbols and structures adolescents choose to use can give the therapist an indication of where the client is in terms of identity formation, self-development, relatedness, and ego strength. She further suggested that the symbols and structural elements of the music used in music therapy provide adolescent patients with a safe medium for introspection that helps in developing ego strength and resolving identity crises.

Music experiences and techniques that can be useful in treating adolescents who have severe emotional or psychiatric disturbances include learning to play musical instruments, participating in music ensembles, rhythm training, improvisation, music listening and discussion, music-assisted relaxation, substitution song lyrics, song writing, guided imagery and music (GIM), group singing, musical story telling, and making music videos (Brooks, 1989; Edgerton, 1990; Edison, 1989; Ficken, 1976; Frisch, 1990; Haines, 1989; Henderson, 1983;

Montello & Coons, 1998). As adolescents take turns playing instruments and participate in structured instrumental ensembles, they develop impulse control and learn to take turns and cooperate with others (Frisch, 1990). Rhythmic training can help adolescents who have difficulty controlling behaviors and impulses channel and contain their "out of control" energy in a structured drumming format (Montello & Coons, 1998). As they learn to expand their expressive range and style, adolescents can experiment with and learn to control changes and transitions. Eventually, the ego strength and impulse control gained through success in music will carry over into other areas of life (Frisch, 1990).

Instrumental activities can also be used as part of a behavioral approach with older children and adolescents. In a study by Edison (1989), middle school students earned tokens for learning to perform rock or rap songs on keyboard, guitar, or percussion instruments. These tokens, as well as those used for good behavior in the classroom, could be used to purchase preferred roles in a music video. Students gained improved interpersonal skills through these experiences, with the results being more stable when students received specific instruction in generalizing those skills to the classroom.

Song writing is frequently a useful music therapy tool in both individual and group work with adolescents. For individuals, song writing can be a vehicle for self-expression and a means of developing self-esteem; for groups, it can be a tool for developing group cooperation and cohesion, increasing self-esteem, and providing an outlet for self-expression (Edgerton, 1990; Ficken, 1976; Haines, 1989). Usually, song writing experiences begin with a very structured approach, (e.g., filling in the blanks to complete a statement) so the client will be able to succeed easily and not be overwhelmed or threatened by the experience. Sometimes, the music therapist suggests a musical structure for the client's lyrics or uses precomposed tunes. At other times, the clients improvise to determine the melody. Edgerton (1990) suggested that it is valuable to have the clients determine the musical setting, because the clients are unable to "front" when they must work to make all the parts (rhythm, harmony, melody, etc.) fit together so the song will "sound good."

Music therapy techniques can also help adolescent clients learn to express and work through feelings. In

working with a 17-year-old girl with a diagnosis of adjustment reaction and borderline personality disorder who had been admitted to an inpatient psychiatric unit after a suicide attempt, Dvorkin (1991), working from a psychodynamic framework, mirrored the client's actions in music and then used improvised musical dialogues to help the client explore the meaning behind her actions. Other techniques included using composed songs as transitional objects to help bring primary issues, such as abandonment, to consciousness. Composed songs also helped the client comfort herself and contain and control her rage. As the client selected songs to respond to her own emotional needs, she used the musical structure as a tool to experience and work through feelings and find ways to cope. Henderson (1983) also found that group music therapy sessions using activities involving group discussion of moods and emotions expressed in songs, composing stories to recorded music, and drawing to music helped adolescent psychiatric patients increase their ability to correctly identify moods and emotions. In addition, after participating in these experiences, the group members showed an increased feeling of group cohesion and used more group pronouns (e.g., "our" instead of "my") to express feelings.

Music Therapy Interventions for Children and Adolescents Who Have Been Abused

Children and adolescents who have been abused frequently have a poor self-concept and low self-esteem, high degrees of fear and anxiety, and problems with assertiveness or anger management. Often, music therapists initially will use structured nonthreatening, "guaranteed success" music performance experiences (e.g., individual lessons on an instrument, improvisational musical dialogues between music therapist and client, group instrumental ensembles) to help encourage these clients to interact with others and develop social skills (Paul, 1982). Children and adolescents who have been abused may be more comfortable with music experiences that allow them to interact and express themselves nonverbally than they are with therapeutic experiences that require verbal responses; thus, instrumental music experiences can be important in establishing initial contact and communication with these clients. Many of these clients find experiences using musical instruments to be less threatening than vocal (e.g., singing, chanting) experiences, because musical instruments allow for some distancing of affect (Isenberg-Grzeda, 1995).

As music therapists use musical instruments in exploratory improvisational sessions and in structured dyadic or ensemble experiences, they begin to engage these clients in therapeutic group experiences that emphasize cohesiveness, identification, and universality. These experiences are also helpful in increasing positive relations with others, social coping skills, and problem-solving abilities (Friedlander, 1994). As clients succeed in playing musical instruments or participate successfully in music ensembles, their self-esteem also improves. In addition, they gain skills that can be used in many school settings or for enjoyable leisure time activities throughout their lives (Paul, 1982).

If clients are comfortable verbalizing in the music therapy setting, initial music therapy approaches may include small group sessions that use music listening and discussion to encourage social interaction and promote verbal expression (Paul, 1982). Some music therapists find that music therapy experiences based on passive listening are a better first approach for clients who are more fragile and who have strong needs for structure and security (Montello & Coons, 1998). Music therapists have also used song writing activities, improvisational musical dialogues, musical stories or fantasies, music dramas, painting or drawing to music, and guided imagery and music experiences to help children and adolescents who have been abused achieve therapeutic goals (Boyd, 1989; Dvorkin, 1991; Isenberg-Grzeda, 1995; Lindberg, 1995; Paul, 1982; Ritholz & Turry, 1994).

Both individual and group music therapy sessions can be effective treatment settings for children and adolescents who have been abused. In *individual music therapy sessions*, music experiences are used to help increase self-esteem, facilitate expression of feelings or emotions, facilitate communication and creative expression, assist in relaxation, and develop leisure skills (Boyd, 1989). Treatment frequently starts out in a less directive fashion, letting the client explore musical experiences and the use of music as an expressive tool. As therapy progresses, techniques may become more directive in order to offer the client a series of challenges that will facilitate and

encourage growth (Ritholz & Turry, 1994). Sometimes, musical fantasy and improvisational creative music therapy techniques can decrease a client's isolation and increase a client's ability to participate in a shared relationship with the therapist (Ritholz & Turry, 1994). In other instances, song writing experiences or improvised musical dialogues may be structured to help clients express and address their feelings (Dvorkin, 1991; Isenberg-Grzeda, 1995; Lindberg, 1995). According to Lindberg (1995), the act of creating songs gives adolescents who have been abused a means of expressing painful and hidden emotions, which then leads them to discover strengths and increases their assertiveness in expressing ideas and their confidence in decision-making. Precomposed songs (e.g., those written by popular recording artists) may also help bring issues to a client's conscious awareness or be used as a structure to help clients express feelings or comfort themselves (Dvorkin, 1991). In addition, Slotoroff (1994) found that structured and improvisational drumming techniques, used in a cognitive behavioral therapy framework to help clients increase awareness of their thoughts and feelings and practice ways of changing their behavior, were very effective in helping female adolescents who had been abused feel more empowered and become more assertive, with positive responses often being seen in only one or two sessions.

Group music therapy sessions with children or adolescents who have been abused frequently focus on facilitating social interaction and increasing social skills, facilitating the development of trust between group members, and facilitating opportunities for positive esteem and recognition by others (Boyd, 1989). Music techniques used in these group sessions include instrumental improvisation, instrumental ensembles (e.g., jazz or rock band with keyboard or synthesizer, bass, guitar, rhythm instruments, rhythm machine, etc., possibly using techniques like open chord guitar tuning or color-coded notes to facilitate success), Orff-Schulwerk experiences, music listening and lyric discussion/analysis, song writing, rap writing, playing rhythm instruments, creative movement to music, relaxation to music, guided imagery and music, and choosing songs to portray personality, feelings, or emotions (Boyd, 1989; Clendenon-Wallen, 1991; Paul, 1982). Initially, simple, safe, "instant success" activities, such as simple rhythm instrument, listening, or exercise/movement-to-music experiences, are used to help the clients feel safe in the music environment and develop trust of the therapist and each other (Friedlander, 1994; Paul, 1982). As the clients develop a feeling of trust and cohesion, more challenges are introduced, as the music therapist structures activities to explore and address issues and help the clients move toward positive growth and change. Often, music therapists will develop activities or sessions around a single issue, problem, or need that is common to most group members.

Music Therapy Interventions for Children and Adolescents Who Have Attention-Deficit/Hyperactivity Disorders

Music can be used in many different ways to improve the behavior and concentration of children and adolescents who have attention-deficit/hyperactivity disorders. For example, contingent music may be used within a behaviorally oriented approach to help eliminate disruptive behaviors and/or increase acceptable social behaviors. In a study by Wilson (1976), interrupting rock music selections played as background music during art class when specified disruptive behaviors occurred quickly eliminated those undesirable behaviors. In another study, recorded music used to reinforced appropriate social behaviors improved the walking habits and car-riding behaviors or a boy who was hyperactive (Reid et al., 1975).

Background music played before or during tasks may also decrease the activity level and increase the attentiveness of children who have ADHD. In a study by Scott (1970), arithmetic scores of boys who were hyperactive improved significantly when they worked on their math problems while rock music was playing in the background. Cripe (1986) also found that when subjects with ADD listened to rock music with a repetitive rhythm through headphones at a maximum volume of 58dB, their activity level decreased. However, just any background music will not necessarily decrease the activity level and increase the attentiveness of children with ADHD. Windwer (1981) found that when a tape of instrumental background music with a progressive

increase in tone frequency, tempo, and percussive elements was played during art class, the activity level of children with hyperactivity increased rather than decreased. Windwer suggested that, in this instance, a tape of music that progressively decreased in tempo, pitch, and intensity may have been more effective in decreasing activity and increasing attentiveness. Thus, optimal amounts of stimulation need to be determined by carefully observing behavioral responses if background music is to be an effective aid to decrease activity and increase attentiveness in children who are hyperactive.

Other researchers have suggested that it may be more beneficial to exposure children with attention and memory difficulties to music *prior* to cognitive processing tasks rather than using background music during the tasks. The results of a study by Morton and colleagues (1990) showed that listening to music prior to learning tasks increased classroom attention in students with ADD, suggesting a "music-induced enhanced ability to process information" (p. 205). These researchers theorized that, since music increases bilateral cerebral arousal levels, "ensuring right hemisphere arousal through music may facilitate concurrent left hemisphere arousal" (p. 204), leading to subsequent increased attention.

Other music therapy approaches work by directly involving children and adolescents with ADHD in experiential music activities. Children are frequently attracted to musical sounds and musical instruments. The pleasure they derive from making music and from being involved in music experiences can encourage children with ADHD to stay focused on tasks and modulate their behavior to produce desirable or pleasant musical products. For example, when Fles (1995) used gong improvisation with a group of children who were hyperactive, after a brief period of experimentation in playing as loudly as they wanted, the children, on their own, decreased the volume of their playing to a tolerable level of sound. After several sessions, they even began to produce very subtle effects. Caught up in the musical experience of playing the gong, "these usually restless children modulated their behavior because the softer sounds gave them personal satisfaction and aesthetic pleasure" (Fles, 1995, p. 89).

When children who have ADHD participate in experiential music activities like singing, playing instruments, and movement-to-music experiences, the music helps increase their tolerance for group activity by holding them together in sound (Hibben, 1991). Music can provide structure (e.g., stop when the music stops; play instrument for one verse and then pass it to the next person), boundaries in time (e.g., length of turns or task), repetition to reinforce learning of social routines or academic concepts, internal cues (e.g., song lyrics reminding child how to behave), rhythmic structure or pacing for movement or activity, and closure (Hibben, 1991; Jones, 1996). In addition, music provides pleasure and serves as a reward for group activity (Hibben, 1991).

Music therapists can also use rhythm and musical structure (e.g., repeated chorus that can be anticipated or focused on) to help clients increase and maintain their attention to task. Increased on-task behavior is usually achieved gradually, having the child participate in the musical task for increasingly longer periods of time (e.g., 1 minute, then 2 minutes, etc.) (Cassity & Cassity, 1994a). This gradual increase in length can be carried out subtly and unobtrusively, as verses or repetitions are added to a song or as the length of accompaniment music for movement activities is gradually increased or as the client is gradually given longer compositions to play.

Many children and adolescents with ADHD also have low frustration tolerance that causes them to quit, make excuses, yell, or become aggressive toward the objects or people involved as soon as tasks become difficult. When these clients are interested in learning to play musical instruments, music therapists design instructional approaches that assure the clients as much success as possible while simultaneously helping them increase their frustration tolerance and their ability to attend to and complete increasingly more difficult tasks (Jones, 1996; Paul, 1982). Often, the reward of making music will help keep the client working on the desired task, especially when successful completion of less preferred, more difficult tasks (e.g., note drills, repeating musical exercises until they are played correctly) is rewarded with preferred activities (e.g., composing own songs). For example, in individual music therapy sessions with a 9-year-old boy who was hyperactive, impulsive, depressed, and had aggressive, acting out behaviors, Herman (1991) used the autoharp to attract attention and initiate inter-

action. A key to increasing this client's frustration tolerance and willingness to experiment with music was the realization that musical mistakes just "floated away." Succeeding music therapy sessions them help the boy (1) gain expressive freedom (techniques included mirror, echo, and start-stop musical games and sand or water play to background music), (2) enjoy creative expression (painting and molding clay to music), and (3) learn structure (using a color-coded note system to play keyboard melodies and chords). Later, small group sessions (first with only one peer, then with two more) were used to help the boy work cooperatively with others in a group, using music games (e.g., conducting, reflection drumming, rhythm work, dancing) to increase frustration tolerance and develop appropriate interactions with peers. Herman (1991) reported that, following this course of music therapy (120 sessions), the boy could stay on task for 15 minutes, follow most directions, stay in a group and behave appropriately, had an increased frustration tolerance, an increased ability to wait his turn without frustration, improved social skills, clearer verbal communication, and decreased aggressive behaviors and temper tantrums.

Music Therapy Interventions for Children and Adolescents Who Have Disruptive Behavior Disorders

Interpersonal problems, such as uncooperative, disruptive, or socially inappropriate behaviors, are the most frequent types of problems treated by music therapists in psychiatric settings for both children and adolescents (Cassity & Cassity, 1994a). Since music experiences are rewarding to and viewed positively by most children and adolescents, including those who have behavioral disturbances or disorders, the desire to learn musical skills or participate in preferred musical experiences or listen to preferred music can be a powerful motivator to control behavior. In addition, music experiences that are structured to promote positive interactions and cooperative participation with others can help children and adolescents learn and practice more appropriate social behaviors in the context of enjoyable music activities (e.g., working cooperatively with others in an ensemble to produce a satisfying musical product; working cooperatively with others to plan and record a music video). As individuals learn more appropriate ways of interacting with others in music groups and as they develop increased self-confidence and self-esteem through successful participation in music experiences, they can transfer these more desirable behaviors to other areas of their lives.

Music therapy interventions that focus on helping clients with behavioral or conduct disorders develop more cooperative behaviors may take a number of different forms. Often, the therapist seeks to involve the client in an *instrumental group*, assigning responsibilities or musical roles so that group success depends on each client's cooperation (Cassity & Cassity, 1994a; Cleveland Music School Settlement Music Therapy Department, 1985; Presti, 1984). This approach may be structured to include behavior management techniques, where points are received for appropriate behavior in music, or be structured as a levels system (see description in "emotional disturbances" section above). Other music therapists use a variety of *music experiences* (e.g., listening, singing, music games, music ensembles, music improvisation or composition) *centered on themes* related to developing cooperative behaviors, combined with a systematic program of behavioral expectations, positive reinforcements, and consequences, to help clients understand and experience cooperation (Levis & Lininger, 1994).

In individual music therapy sessions, a music therapist might use *improvisational music techniques* to help children or adolescents develop more appropriate and cooperative behaviors (Nordoff & Robbins, 1977; Shoemark, 1991). For example, Shoemark (1991) used piano improvisation with a boy who was blind and had behavioral disturbances to help develop a relationship that encouraged positive interactions and cooperative participation. As the boy learned to interact spontaneously and cooperatively with the therapist in music making, his participation and cooperation in other areas of life also increased. In other instances, musical interaction and skill development in individual sessions may be structured from a more *behaviorist* point of view, using a system of rewards for appropriate behaviors and completion of tasks or structuring instruction on a levels system (Cleveland Music School Settlement Music Therapy Department, 1985; Kivland, 1986; Paul, 1982).

Computer and *electronic music resources* may also be used in individual or group sessions to help adolescents who have behavioral disorders increase on-task behavior, self-expression, problem-solving and decision-making skills, and improve relations with peers (Krout, 1992b; Krout & Mason, 1988). Since these instruments are versatile and attractive to most adolescents, they may help motivate clients to learn age-appropriate music skills which they can they use to participate successfully in school or community music programs and use throughout their lives for leisure time enjoyment. Music therapy sessions stress "music learning within socially acceptable boundaries" (Krout & Mason, 1988), so clients gain usable skills that will help them appropriately express feelings and work cooperatively with others.

In spite of their tough image, many children and adolescents who have disruptive behavior disorders actually have low self-esteem. As these clients experience success in music activities and learn new musical skills, their self-confidence and feelings of self-worth also increase. Increasing self-esteem can also be targeted as a specific music therapy goal. When this is the case, activities might be structured so that clients have opportunities to make positive statements about themselves or name specific things they did well in a music session. For example, Kivland (1986) used the format of individual piano lessons to help a 12-year-old girl with a conduct disorder learn to decrease negative self-statements and increase her ability to accept praise from others. Clear goals were presented for each lesson, so the girl knew what was expected for success. After 12 weeks of lessons, her negative self-statements decreased, she consistently was able to list three things she did well in each lesson, and she could accept praise from others. As her self-esteem and musical skills increased, her relations with her peers also improved as they saw her accomplishments in music.

Music therapy interventions can also help children and adolescents who have disruptive behavior disorders learn to channel aggressive impulses and express anger in more appropriate ways. Clients may select songs that express the anger they feel, and then be asked to identify appropriate ways to ventilate the anger (Cassity & Cassity, 1994a). Some clients may feel more comfortable playing out their angry feelings on musical instruments. As they learn to control their playing (e.g., vary dynamics and rhythms) and express their feelings in a musical framework, they may find ways of controlling their behavior. For example, structured and improvisational drumming techniques, used in a cognitive behavioral therapy framework, can help adolescents with conduct disorders increase awareness of their thoughts and feelings and practice ways of controlling their anger and impulsive behavior (Slotoroff, 1994). The discipline of learning to play a musical instrument through individual or group music lessons can also help clients learn self-control (Cassity & Cassity, 1994a) while simultaneously providing them with a socially appropriate outlet for emotional expression.

Some clients with behavioral disorders learn to control their anger and behavioral outbursts through *music-based relaxation training.* Saperston (1989) used music in the form of concept songs and chants as structural prompts to help a client who had behavioral disturbances and mental retardation learn to perform relaxation skills. Singing activities helped focus the client's attention on the relaxation task. Then, the music therapist directed the relaxation response, having the client lie still and perform breathing and muscle relaxation exercises with songs, chants, and rhythmic accompaniment to increase the client's awareness of relaxed feelings. Next, the songs and chants were faded and replaced with background music and verbal cues. Finally, music therapy sessions focused on developing transfer and generalization skills, helping the client recognize situations in which the procedure should be implemented and helping him practice and perform the relaxation procedure in different settings. Other music-mediated relaxation techniques, such as progressive muscle relaxation to music, guided imagery and music, and music and biofeedback, may also help children and adolescents with behavioral disorders learn to relax and help control their anger and disruptive, impulsive behaviors (Cassity & Cassity, 1994a). (For more information on music and relaxation/stress reduction, see Chapters Fifteen and Seventeen).

Music Therapy Interventions for Juvenile Offenders

Music therapy treatment goals for juvenile

offenders generally fall under one of four behavioral domains: emotional, social, physical, or cognitive/academic (Gardstrom, 1996). Since music addresses needs at a deeper, more expansive level, "the use of music and other creative arts therapies can affect aspects of treatment that are untouched by approaches relying on verbal communication alone" (Skaggs, 1997b, p. 74).

Music therapy interventions in the *emotional domain* help clients (a) identify, explore, and express feelings, values, opinions, and ideas, and (b) build self-esteem. Since music experiences are multimodal and multidimensional, "they allow increasing access to inner feelings and provide diverse modes for expressing them" (Skaggs, 1997b, p. 74). For example, music activities such as group singing of popular songs, dedicating songs to people, selecting songs to describe people, and choosing songs to express feelings have been shown to enhance the self-concept of clients who are juvenile delinquents while decreasing their feelings of rebellion and distrust (E. Johnson, 1981). Improvisational activities are also useful vehicles for helping youths in juvenile corrections programs share feelings and express both self-worth and self-doubt (Edelman, 1978). These nonverbal activities, which do not allow clients to hide behind words or tough talk, tend to promote honest and constructive responses.

In her work with male juveniles who were convicted sex offenders, Skaggs (1997b) found the techniques of guided imagery and music, improvising feelings and stories on Orff instruments, and favorite music days (clients bring in CDs; discuss, analyze how music affects or can be used to manage behavior) were useful in helping clients identify feelings, develop empathy with their victims, and learn ways of managing volatile feelings and of controlling behaviors. Other music therapists have used song lyrics to stimulate discussion about themes relevant to the client's current situation or rehabilitation process, or developed song writing experiences with varying degrees of structure to help clients express feelings or increase their self-awareness (Gardstrom, 1996).

Gaining skills in music performance or in successfully using technical musical production materials can also help youths who are incarcerated gain self-esteem while they develop technical and possible vocational skills. Technical advances, electronic instruments, and computer music have made music performance and production available to an increasing number of individuals. For example, Sheedy (1995) used the WaveRider, a system of hardware and software that takes readings from the body (e.g., muscle groups, heart rate, brain waves) and converts these to musical sound, with boys in a Wisconsin juvenile prison. The boys were eager to participate in the program and intrigued and motivated by the equipment. In addition to being useful in encouraging relaxation, initiating self-awareness, and encouraging experimentation, the process of using the WaveRider was very effective in facilitating introspective dialogue among the group members.

In the *social domain*, music therapy interventions help meet clients' needs for "peer interaction, appropriate competition, relaxation, and leisure" (Gardstrom, 1996). Various music experiences can be structured to decrease isolation, foster positive relationships and interactions, increase verbal interaction and self-disclosure, develop leadership skills, and give opportunities for healthy competition. Music experiences may provide the motivation for appropriate behaviors (e.g., facilitate appropriate group participation through group listening, singing, rhythm instrument, or movement-to-music experiences) or be used as a contingency for appropriate behavior (e.g., background music during free time stopped when any person failed to observe one of the established group behavior/interaction rules) (Michel, 1985).

Performance groups or improvisational experiences on musical instruments are frequently used to help clients who are juvenile offenders develop social skills such as following directions, listening to others, making positive contributions to a group, cooperating with others, and giving and receiving constructive feedback (Edelman, 1978; Gardstrom, 1996; Michel, 1985; Sheedy, 1995; Skaggs, 1997b). These techniques can easily be combined with group-oriented treatment models for the rehabilitation of youths who have delinquent behaviors, such as Positive Peer Culture (Gardstrom, 1987). When this structure is applied to music therapy treatment, peers meet in groups and assume responsibility for their own behavior and that of other group members. The music therapist serves as a facilitator, suggesting music experiences that are appropriately challenging

and using questioning techniques to help maintain group focus and increase insight. Challenging opportunities for growth and the chance to develop social and leisure skills may be provided through experiences like learning to play musical instruments (e.g., electric guitar, keyboard, percussion), learning to create music spontaneously (e.g., vocal or instrumental improvisation), or cooperating with group members to produce a musical product (e.g., group song writing). At first, group music experiences are relatively low-risk, involving whole group responses, minimal personal sharing, and minimal music skill requirements (e.g., learning a group rap chant). Later, group music experiences include higher-risk, more challenging activities, such as forming a band, where individuals learn responsibility to the group, learn to accept responsibility for helping each other, and are rewarded for working cooperatively with others by a more pleasing musical product.

In the *physical domain*, music therapy interventions that involve motor activity (e.g., dance, creative movement, or exercise to music; playing instruments; singing with sign language) can help provide clients with regular exercise and constructive physical activity that is vital to rehabilitation. In addition, these music therapy interventions involving motor activity can help clients improve general fitness and body image, develop or improve their gross and fine motor skills, and reduce physical stress (Gardstrom, 1996). Movement-to-music experiences, in particular, can be valuable tools for helping clients gain confidence in using their bodies to interact with others in socially acceptable ways and in helping them learn to appreciate personal boundaries and personal space. Song writing or music listening/ discussion activities can also be used to help generate open discussion about physical topics important to teens (e.g., sexuality, pregnancy, anatomy, feelings of anxiety over rapidly changing bodies) (Brooks, 1989; Gardstrom, 1996).

Music therapy interventions that focus on the *cognitive domain* may be structured to help clients increase their attending skills and their ability to follow directions, improve short- and long-term memory skills, and reinforce or teach specific academic concepts (Gardstrom, 1996). Music experiences may be used as a reinforcer for desired academic skills (e.g., being allowed to listen to favorite music or participate in music group only after successfully completing assignments) or as a vehicle for teaching specific academic concepts (e.g., practicing reading and writing skills through lyric analysis or song writing activities, song lyrics or rap chants that help clients learn and practice information like math facts or state capitals). The motivational elements and multisensory nature of music experience may have important benefits for youths who are used to experiencing failure in academic subjects or who have difficulty learning through more traditional means. For example, successfully expressing themselves nonverbally through instrumental or movement-to-music experiences may give some clients the confidence they need to try expressing themselves in written form. As they grow comfortable using words to express themselves in the context of music experiences (e.g., song writing), they may be more likely to try verbally expressing themselves in other contexts. In her work with juvenile sex offenders, Skaggs (1997b) observed that "story-telling on musical instruments flowed into story-telling through writing and art" (p. 78). In addition, creative music experiences (e.g., composition, song writing, group ensembles, producing music videos) help clients develop organizational, problem-solving, and decision-making skills that can be used in many areas of life.

Music Therapy Interventions for Children and Adolescents Who Have Problems with Substance Abuse

Clients who are seen by music therapists in treatment programs for substance abuse are usually of adolescent age or older (Cassity & Cassity, 1994a). The adolescents' preferred music is often used as a common ground to establish contact and communication with the patient, and the music therapists who use this music are perceived by the adolescents are "safe" adults with whom to relate (Brooks, 1989; Michel, 1985; Wooten, 1992). The adolescents' choices of music may also give the therapist insight into the patients' emotional and behavioral issues (Metzger, 1986; Wooten, 1992).

Once the music therapist has established communication with the patients, music can also be used as a "means for introducing and discussing alternative coping skills" (Wooten, 1992, p. 97). For

example, patients may be asked to listen to selected songs, discuss and analyze their lyrics, and process the themes and values suggested by the lyrics as a means of helping them become aware of the effects of chemical dependency and the consequences of various life style choices or as a means of generating discussion about feelings of helplessness, powerlessness, loss of relationships, and alternative responses to situations (Cassity & Cassity, 1994a; Gardstrom, 1987; James, 1988b). Such song lyric discussion used in the framework of a values clarification approach has been shown to positively influence participants' self-concept and sense of control over the environment, helping give them confidence in themselves and their ability to recover from chemical dependency (James, 1988b). Music therapists can also help patients see how certain music may be linked with their substance abuse behaviors and help them learn to break these links by avoiding music with negative influences (Metzger, 1986; Michel, 1985). In addition, music therapists can help clients learn to use music to positively influence their moods (an alternative "high") or to use music-based relaxation techniques as a chemical-free way to manage stress (Cassity & Cassity, 1994a; Michel, 1985).

Some music therapists have found that performance-oriented groups are more beneficial with adolescents than verbal/insight-oriented groups (Cassity & Cassity, 1994a). Group instrumental ensemble experiences or cooperative group projects like producing an accompaniment to poetry or making a music video can help clients learn to (a) work cooperatively with others, (b) explore different aspects of interpersonal communication, and (c) develop or improve decision-making and problem-solving skills (James & Freed, 1989). Other music therapists have used instrumental improvisation to role play different situations and increase clients' awareness of different options for solving problems (Gardstrom, 1987).

James and Freed (1989) have developed a sequential model for developing group cohesion and applied it to music therapy interventions in a residential treatment program for adolescents with chemical dependency. In the first stage, *Goal-Setting Activities*, assessments are conducted and clients are given an orientation to the format and rationale of the music therapy group, including a discussion of how progress in music therapy impacts the clients' treatment goals. In the next stage, *Individual/Parallel Play Activities*, music is used as a stimulus to encourage identifying with and relating to others in the group. Activities focus on what the group members have in common, and may include experiences in music-assisted relaxation, identifying moods and feelings expressed by music, and song lyric analysis. By moving slowly in the beginning stages of therapy, music therapists establish a healthy therapeutic atmosphere that will facilitate the groups' ability to accomplish tasks at the next levels. Stage three, *Cooperative Group Activities*, uses creative music performance experiences that require clients to interact more and work toward a group goal. Music activities at this stage include group compositions made up of individual contributions, improvisations led by the music therapist, performance groups with clients taking turns being conductors, music videos or musical puppet shows created by the clients, or group poetry writing accompanied by instruments. In stage four, *Self-Disclosure Activities*, music is used as a nonverbal language to support individual group members' expression of feelings and emotions as they communicate personal issues and receive insight and feedback from their peers in an accepting, nonjudgmental atmosphere. Musical experiences may including choosing songs to express feelings, moving to music that mirrors their feelings, peers picking songs or improvising on instruments or moving to music to show the moods they perceive other group members to have, or individuals improvising or creating tone poems to express their feelings. In the final stage, *Group Problem-Solving Activities*, music therapy experiences are used to support and stimulate verbal therapy. Activities from all of the preceding stages may be used, with their content focused more specifically on individual issues and skill-building to transfer new behaviors to real life situations.

Individual music therapy sessions may also be useful for adolescents who have substance abuse problems. For example, individual music therapy sessions using experiences in piano performance and relaxation and imagery to music helped a 16-year-old girl increase self-esteem, improve her relations with peers, decrease drug abuse, and learn to better organize and control her life (Lefebvre, 1991). As she learned she could control her life and positively influence her moods during music therapy sessions, the girl eventually came to the realization that: "It's up to me now as to how things are going to be from now on" (Lefebvre, 1991, p. 229).

Music Therapy Interventions for Children and Adolescents Who Are At-Risk

In recent years, both music therapists and music educators have begun to pay more attention to the role music can play in meeting the special learning needs of children and adolescents who are considered to be "at-risk." In music education as well as in music therapy programs, music helps these individuals gain skills in nonmusical areas. For example, participating in music ensembles or school music classes can help increase self-esteem, provide a sense of belonging, allow for expression of emotions in safe and positive ways, and develop many basic skills people need to succeed in the employment world (e.g., creative thinking, decision making, problem solving, the ability to see things in the mind's eye, self-management, teamwork, the ability to monitor and correct performance, the ability to work with diversity) (Taylor et al., 1997). As children and adolescents who are "at-risk" experience positive change, pleasure, creations of beauty, and aesthetic enrichment in music, they discover that there are positive things in the world and that artists can transform their world into a more beautiful, interesting, provocative place. Success in music or other arts experiences may help provide a sense of hope to those children and adolescents whose world seems full of hopelessness. Participating in creative music experiences also gives them opportunities to have an active part in creating beauty and demonstrating positive accomplishments. As they learn music skills, they discover that work and self-discipline (practice) *do* yield positive results (increase in skills, improvement in performance). For many, successful experiences in music may be a key factor in encouraging them to stay in school and succeed in other academic areas (Taylor et al., 1997).

Frequently, children and adolescents who are at-risk need help learning basic attending and social skills (e.g., staying with group, listening, following directions, taking turns, keeping hands to self, not talking out of turn, working cooperatively with others) necessary to succeed in the classroom. Music therapists often help clients develop these skills by combining a systematic program of behavioral expectations, positive reinforcements, and consequences with music experiences that teach and give the students a chance to experience and practice the desired behaviors (Cleveland Music School Settlement Music Therapy Department, 1985; Krout, 1986a, 1986b; Levis & Lininger, 1994; Staum & Brotons, 1995). For example, by using a simple token contingency in a "Good Listening Game," Krout (1986b) helped increase listening skills, on-task behavior, and correct responses to questions in 10- to 12-year-old students who were classified as underachievers and exhibited many disruptive behaviors. Students earned tokens, redeemable for group music listening time, when they correctly answered written questions about prerecorded musical compositions. Krout observed that these procedures really seemed to motivate students:

> Students appeared excited to be able to earn points, and comments such as, "We really earned our song today" were common during the token contingency portion of the study. (p. 15)

The "Increase the Peace" music therapy experiences described earlier in this chapter (see section on emotional disturbances) can also be used to teach cooperation skills to at-risk students (Levis & Lininger, 1994). In addition, music therapists sometimes work outside the school setting (e.g., in homeless shelters), using music activities as an enrichment/treatment program to help at-risk children develop interaction skills needed to function successfully in group learning situations (Staum & Brotons, 1995).

Children and adolescents who are at-risk have often experienced frequent failures with traditional learning methods in school. Music-based learning activities may give these students experiences that are more compatible with their learning styles and emotional needs, thus providing an effective, alternative method of learning for those at-risk students who have academic delays and who have difficulty learning through more traditional means (Taylor, et al., 1997). For example, music experiences can be structured to teach basic concepts (e.g., colors,

numbers, multiplication facts through song or rap lyrics or through music games). Music activities can also reinforce learning from other subjects and make the information more relevant to students' lives and interests (e.g., learning fractions by calculating subdivisions in rhythms and meters, exploring history through music of a particular period) (Taylor, et al., 1997). In addition, music lessons can serve as effective reinforcers to increase academic achievement and appropriate social behaviors in disadvantaged or at-risk students (Michel, 1971; Michel, 1985; Michel & Farrell, 1973).

Active participation in music activities can also help build self-esteem in those whose learning styles favor "hands-on" experiences. For example, self-esteem can be developed and enhanced as students learn simple skills (e.g., playing basic chords on guitar or ukulele to accompany simple songs) in music lessons (Michel, 1971; Michel & Farrell, 1973). Ensembles, such as school or community choirs or bands, can also be structured therapeutically to help participants develop self-confidence and leadership abilities. In addition, these ensembles provide opportunities for self-expression and group decision making and facilitate clients' adjustment to the school or community (Ragland & Apprey, 1974; Taylor, et al., 1997). The WaveRider program described earlier in this chapter (see section on juvenile offenders) has also been used in public schools with at-risk students to help them develop self-esteem, self-direction, and group cooperation skills while they receive technical and vocational training in the media arts (Sheedy, 1995).

Music Therapy Interventions in Family Therapy

Family relationships and interactions can greatly impact the behavior and well-being of any individual within the family group. In family therapy, family members are treated together, and "family relations and processes are explored as potential causes of mental disorder in one or more of the family members" (Kaplan & Sadock, 1991, p. 72). Miller (1994) has found that

> The experience of music can become a powerful asset to the therapy process because it provides

an opportunity to engage the family together in a profound experience, it enhances the impact of feelings experienced, and it facilitates the recollection of the events that occurred in the session. (p. 45)

Music and musical instruments are things that usually interest and are valued by both children and adults (Hibben, 1992). Since music offers a means of communication that is not dependent on words and since musical instruments usually evoke interest and curiosity, family members may participate more readily in music experiences than they do in verbal therapy (Miller, 1994). In addition, music experiences can readily include even young children in family work (Hibben, 1992). Experiences using musical instruments can facilitate nonverbal expression of emotions, creating involvement while allowing safe distancing. Songs and song writing may help families express feelings that are difficult to speak in words, bring families together, build bridges between generations, and facilitate the sharing of experiences and family stories (Bailey, 1984; Hibben, 1992).

Music also offers a neutral context to assess family relationships and may provide a metaphor for family functioning (Hibben, 1992; Miller, 1994). For example, observing family members as they improvise on melodic or rhythmic percussion instruments can give the therapist much information on family roles, communication patterns, balance of power, and symptoms of dysfunction. Adverse patterns of interaction and communication can also be addressed through music interventions that allow family members to recognize the dysfunctional patterns and practice more functional ways of interacting and communicating. Many music interventions, such as improvisation and musical role playing, echoing, soloing, playing duets, playing mood themes, conducting, and having adults guide children, can facilitate self-expression of individual family members, enhance family com-munication skills, and address issues of structural power imbalances within the family. Miller (1994) also found that, because of the extra visual, auditory, and kinesthetic cues and associations inherent in music experiences, the learning that takes place in music therapy sessions may be more readily accessible to and more likely to be retained by all family members. Therefore, multisensory music therapy interventions, used in combination with or in addition to standard "talking" therapy, can help the treatment process move faster.

Other family music therapy sessions may be designed not so much to look at family interactions as the source of pathology but to help other family members learn how to relate most appropriately and constructively to a child or adolescent who has an emotional disturbance or behavior disorder. Music can be an important factor in helping establish some positive contacts between family members. For example, some music therapists have used music therapy sessions to increase positive interactions between children who have autism and their parents (Alvin & Warwick, 1991), inviting the parent to participate in the music therapy session with the child. Family members can also learn how to use music experiences at home to help structure the environment or help the child or adolescent control his or her behavior (e.g., contingent music, music-mediated relaxation, songs to cue appropriate behaviors, removing detrimental music).

Finally, if individuals are to maintain new skills and behaviors they have learned in the clinical setting and generalize them to the home and community, the family must learn how to support these new behaviors. Therefore, sessions with family members may also be helpful toward the end of the treatment process to help clients learn to generalize their new skills and behaviors and apply them outside the therapy setting (James & Freed, 1989).

SPECIAL CONSIDERATIONS AND TIPS FOR SUCCESS

For children and adolescents who have mental or behavioral disorders or severe emotional distur-bances, "music represents a neutral, nonauthoritative force that allows them to relax and participate with-out fear" (Birkenshaw-Fleming, 1993, p. 101). Therefore, music therapy sessions with these clients are often most successful when directions and structure are provided through music or as part of a musical experience rather than verbally whenever possible. For example, instructions such as "sit down" or "now stop" might be sung to a simple melodic phrase (e.g., sol-do) or chord sequence (e.g., V7-I). In addition, songs and musical games can be used to structure length of turns (e.g., play/move/sing for certain number of beats/measures; use "now pass the ___ to ___" as part of lyrics), control movement from place to place, or focus attention on action while distributing or collecting instruments (Atterbury, 1990; Birkenshaw-Fleming, 1993; Nocera, 1979; Zinar, 1987). Therapists should strive to keep any verbal instructions short, simple, and concrete, reinforcing these instructions with visual aids or demonstrations whenever possible.

Children and adolescents who have mental or behavioral disorders or severe emotional disturbances usually function best in a secure, warm, structured, stimulating, success-oriented environment. Music therapists can help promote a safe, success-oriented environment by (a) starting with highly structured activities and gradually reducing structure as clients gain skills and confidence, (b) breaking large tasks down into smaller, more manageable steps, and (c) leading clients through activities with examples and clear instructions before asking them to improvise or make original contributions. Structuring sessions so that groups begin and end with routine, "ritual" activities also promotes security and predictability. In addition, alternating fun, easy, familiar activities with more difficult ones helps keep clients involved and interested in the process.

When working with these clients, it is important to emphasize the positive and build on the clients' strengths. Praise is important, but it must be genuine and should be given very specifically, telling the individual exactly what was good and how it can be made better. It is also important for teachers and therapists to provide good role models of desired social and interpersonal behaviors for these clients (Nocera, 1979; Paul, 1982): "Besides teaching academic skills, motor skills, social skills, etc., it is important that the children learn and see models of love, joy, peace, patience, kindness, goodness, faithfulness, gentleness, and self-control" (Paul, 1982, p. 71).

Many children and adolescents who have mental or behavioral disorders or severe emotional disturbances need firm, consistent discipline and behavior management approaches. Usually,

especially in group situations, these clients function best when there are clear, consistent expectations for behaviors. A few simple group rules for expected behaviors, along with consequences for infractions, should be clearly stated (Atterbury, 1990; Cleveland Music School Settlement Music Therapy Department, 1985; Levis & Lininger, 1994; Nocera, 1979; Presti, 1984; Zinar, 1987). These rules may be devised with the help of the group if the clients are functioning at a high enough level. It may also be helpful to post these rules so they are readily available for reference.

When working with children and adolescents who have mental or behavioral disorders or severe emotional disturbances, it is very important to set up or adapt the environment so as to minimize distractions. Therapists and teachers should consider the social and psychological implications of various group formations (Nocera, 1979, pp. 262-263) and use formations that maximize feelings of inclusion and cooperation and help focus attention on activity. Activities should also be structured carefully to minimize distractions and maximize on-task behavior. In planning, it is also important to pay special attention to *transitions* between activities, for these are often the points at which problem behaviors occur. In addition, if therapists and teachers know the warning signs of behavior outbursts for various individuals in the group, they can often do something to diffuse the situation before an outburst occurs (e.g., change activity, tempo, response mode, or dynamic level; position self closer to individual; point to chart of expected behaviors as reminder). Teachers and therapists must also carefully monitor their own reactions and take time to stop and think before they react or respond to inappropriate behaviors (Atterbury, 1990; Nocera, 1979).

The music that clients listen to in their leisure time can also positively or negatively influence their behavior and levels of tension and anxiety. Music therapists should make clients and staff aware of how music affects and influences behavior, so they realize that as simple an action as turning off or changing the music could help diffuse a potential crisis situation. After observing that incidents of sexual acting out and physical aggression on a psychiatric unit increased when adolescent patients listened to certain types of popular music, Metzger (1986) suggested that facilities establish an objective policy (by committee) on what types of music were suitable for leisure time use, which were suitable only if used under supervision in a therapy session, and which did not serve any clinically beneficial purpose. The later category included "music that tends to intensify or perpetuate the problems of patients, and is too shallow for use in discussions" (p. 22).

Lefebvre (1991) lists several additional important considerations for music therapy with adolescents who have mental or behavioral disorders. These include (1) taking time to *listen* to the adolescent, (2) thoroughly assessing clients, using both active and receptive techniques, to gain as complete an understanding as possible of the client's musical past (perhaps having the client do a "family music tree"), current music preferences and skills, and any musical goals, (3) letting the clients take an active part in setting treatment goals and evaluating progress, (4) using activities that are relevant to teenage needs and interests to motivate clients, (5) being flexible enough to change plans in response to the unpredictability of teenagers, (6) knowing when to empathize with clients and when to challenge them, being aware of how adept adolescents are at manipulation, and (7) giving the teenage client responsibility for his and her own life.

SUMMARY

The field of child and adolescent psychiatry deals with mental, behavioral, and emotional problems of childhood and adolescence. When children and adolescents consistently and chronically exhibit behaviors that are personally or socially deviant, maladaptive, or inappropriate, they may be classified as having some type of mental disorder, behavioral disorder, or severe emotional disturbance. This chapter discussed the characteristics and treatment of children and adolescents who have severe emotional disturbances, attention-deficit/hyperactivity disorders, disruptive behavior disorders, or substance abuse problems, as well as those children and adolescents who have been abused, who are socially maladjusted or are juvenile offenders, or who are "at-risk." All these conditions or disorders are characterized by various degrees and types of persistent, repeated problem behaviors that significantly impair social or academic functioning. Children and adolescents who have mental or behavioral disorders or severe emotional disturbances may be treated by approaches based on biomedical models, psychotherapeutic models, behavioral models, or eclectic/multimodal models. The approach used depends somewhat on the treatment setting.

Music therapists can use specially structured music experiences to help children and adolescents who have mental or behavioral disorders or severe emotional disturbances reach many different therapeutic goals, such as increasing behavior and impulse control, decreasing uncooperative and disruptive behaviors, increasing ability to follow directions, increasing ability to work cooperatively and constructively with others, decreasing withdrawn behavior, learning to develop relationships, increasing interaction with others, increasing appropriate social responses, learning to identify and appropriately express feelings and emotions, facilitating relaxation, decreasing tension and anxiety, increasing appropriate communication and self-expression, learning or practicing basic academic skills, increasing self-esteem, decreasing negative self-statements, and increasing problem-solving, decision-making, and coping skills. Often, music therapy approaches incorporate active physical involvement in making or responding to music, through playing or improvising on musical instruments, dancing or moving to music, singing or vocalizing, or composing songs or lyrics. Other more passive approaches are centered around music listening, using contingent music listening to modify behavior, teaching music-mediated relaxation and stress reduction techniques, using song lyrics as a basis for discussion, or using guided imagery and music. This chapter presented information on several specific music therapy interventions that may be useful in the treatment of children and adolescents who (a) have severe emotional disturbances, (b) have been abused, (c) have attention-deficit/hyperactivity disorders, (d) have disruptive behavior disorders, (e) are juvenile offenders, (f) have substance abuse problems, or (g) are "at-risk." Music therapy in family therapy was also discussed.

QUESTIONS FOR THOUGHT AND DISCUSSION

1. Discuss some of the special characteristics and needs of children and adolescents who (a) have severe emotional disturbances, (b) have been abused, (c) have attention-deficit/hyperactivity disorders, (d) have disruptive behavior disorders, (e) are juvenile offenders, (f) have substance abuse problems, or (g) are "at-risk." What implications do these have for music therapy programming?

2. Do some types of music experiences and activities more seem to be more useful than others in working with children and adolescents who have mental or behavioral disorders or severe emotional disturbances? If so, which ones? Why?

3. Which music therapy approaches described in this chapter reflect a psychodynamic orientation? humanistic orientation? cognitive orientation? behavioral orientation? eclectic or multimodal orientation? Do any reflect a biomedical orientation? How does the orientation affect the structure or implementation of music therapy strategies? How does it affect the interpretation of client responses?

4. Describe several music therapy experiences that might be useful in treating children and adolescents who (a) have severe emotional disturbances, (b) have been abused, (c) have attention-deficit/hyperactivity disorders, (d) have disruptive behavior disorders, (e) are juvenile offenders, (f) have substance abuse problems, or (g) are "at-risk." What unique benefits does music provide for each of these client groups?

5. What unique benefits can music provide in family therapy situations?

6. List several special considerations that may be important to remember when developing therapeutic intervention strategies for children and adolescents who have mental or behavioral disorders or severe emotional disturbances. Why are these important? What are their implications for the structure of music therapy intervention strategies?

7. For each of the situations described below, (a) define the problem or areas of need for the client or group of clients, (b) describe one or more of the goals you might pursue in music therapy sessions with the client(s), (c) describe music activities you might use to help the client(s) meet those goals, (d) tell how the music activities you described relate to the goals and needs of the client(s), and (e) mention any special considerations you might want to take into account when working with the client(s).

Situation 1:

You have been asked to conduct music therapy sessions with Carla, a fifteen-year-old girl who has been admitted to the adolescent unit of a county psychiatric hospital after an unsuccessful suicide attempt. Carla has a history of alcohol and drug abuse. She exhibits extreme fear and anxiety, is shy and withdrawn, and has low self-esteem and a poor self-image. She rarely interacts with others and often retreats into a world of fantasy. Carla sometimes laughs or cries for no apparent reason; she has difficulty expressing feelings accurately and appropriately.

Situation 2:

You have been asked to conduct music therapy sessions for a group of four boys, ages 7-9, who have been diagnosed with attention-deficit/hyperactivity disorder. They have short attention spans, difficulty completing tasks and following directions, and are easily distracted. All are fascinated by musical instruments, but they have difficulty using them appropriately for longer than 30-60 seconds at a time. Their teacher wonders if you can do anything to increase their attention span and help them learn more appropriate behaviors so they can be more successful in group learning situations.

SUGGESTIONS FOR FURTHER READING

Atterbury, B. W. (1990). *Mainstreaming exceptional learners in music.* Englewood Cliffs, NJ: Prentice-Hall.

Benenzon, R. O. (1982). *Music therapy in child psychosis.* Springfield, IL: Charles C Thomas.

Brooks, D. M. (1989). Music therapy enhances treatment with adolescents. *Music Therapy Perspectives, 6,* 37-39.

Bruscia, K. E. (Ed.) (1991). *Case studies in music therapy.* Phoenixville, PA: Barcelona Publishers.

Cassity, M. D., & Cassity, J. E. (1994). *Multimodal psychiatric music therapy for adults, adolescents, and children.* St. Louis, MO: MMB Music.

Cassity, M. D., & Cassity, J. E. (1994). Psychiatric music therapy assessment and treatment in clinical training facilities with adults, adolescents and children. *Journal of Music Therapy, 31*(1), 2-30.

Clendenon-Wallen, J. (1991). The use of music therapy to influence the self-confidence and self-esteem of adolescents who are sexually abused. *Music Therapy Perspectives, 9,* 73-81.

Cleveland Music School Settlement Music Therapy Department. (1985). *The music therapy levels system: A manual of principles and applications.* Cleveland, OH: The Cleveland Music School Settlement

Friedlander, L. H. (1994). Group music psychotherapy in an inpatient psychiatric setting for children: a developmental approach. *Music Therapy Perspectives, 12*(2), 92-97.

Frisch, A. (1990). Symbol and structure: Music therapy for the adolescent psychiatric inpatient. *Music Therapy, 9*(1), 16-34.

Gardstrom, S. C. (1987). Positive Peer Culture: A working definition for the music therapist. *Music Therapy Perspectives, 4,* 19-23.

Gardstrom, S. C. (1996). Music therapy for juvenile offenders in a residential setting. In B. L. Wilson (Ed.), *Models of music therapy interventions in school settings: From institution to inclusion* (pp. 127-141). Silver Spring, MD: National Association for Music Therapy.

Goodman, K.D. (1989), Music therapy assessment of emotionally disturbed children. *Arts in Psychotherapy, 16*(3), 179-192.

Graham, R. M. (1975). Music education of emotionally disturbed children. In R. M. Graham (Compiler), *Music for the exceptional child* (pp. 111-129). Reston, VA: Music Educators National Conference.

Isenberg-Grzeda, C. (1995). The sound image: Music therapy in the treatment of the abused child. In C. B. Kenny (Ed.), *Listening, playing, creating: Essays on the power of sound.* Albany, NY: State University of New York Press.

James, M. R., & Freed, B. S. (1989). A sequential model for developing group cohesion in music therapy. *Music Therapy Perspectives, 7,* 28-34.

Levis, L., & Lininger, L. (1994). *Increase the peace: A focused approach.* Austin & Buda, TX: Authors.

Metzger, L. K. (1986). The selection of music for therapeutic use with adolescents and young adults in a psychiatric facility. *Music Therapy Perspectives, 3,* 20-24.

Michel, D. E. (1968). Part IV. Music therapy for children and adolescents with behavior disorders. In E. T. Gaston (Ed.), *Music in therapy* (pp. 173-228). New York: Macmillan.

Nocera, S. D. (1979). *Reaching the special learner through music.* Morristown, NJ: Silver Burdett.

Nordoff, P., & Robbins, C. (1971). *Therapy in music for handicapped children.* London: Victor Gallancz Ltd.

Nordoff , P., & Robbins, C. (1977). *Creative music therapy.* New York: John Day.

Nowicki, A. L., & Trevisan, L. A. (1978). *Beyond the sound: A technical and philosophical approach to music therapy* (Rev. Ed.). Porterville & Santa Barbara, CA: Nowicki/Trevisan.

Paul, D. W. (1982). *Music therapy for handicapped children: emotionally disturbed.* Washington, DC.: National Association for Music Therapy.

Presti, G. M. (1984). A levels system approach to music therapy with severely behaviorally handicapped children in the public school system. *Journal of Music Therapy, 21*(3), 117-125.

Purvis, J., & Samet, S. (1976). *Music in developmental therapy: A curriculum guide.* Baltimore, MD: University Park Press.

Skaggs, R. (1997). Music-centered creative arts in a sex offender treatment program for male juveniles. *Music Therapy Perspectives, 15*(2), 73-78.

Slotoroff, C. (1994). Drumming technique for assertiveness and anger management in the short-term psychiatric setting for adult and adolescent survivors of trauma. *Music Therapy Perspectives, 12*(2), 111-116.

Standley, J. (1991). *Music techniques in therapy, counseling, and special education.* St. Louis: MMB Music.

Taylor, J. A., Barry, N. H., & Walls, K. C. (1997). *Music and students at risk: Creative solutions for a national dilemma.* Reston, VA: Music Educators National Conference.

Wilson, A. E. (1968). Music in the treatment and education of emotionally disturbed children. In E. T. Gaston (Ed.), *Music in therapy* (pp. 293-313). New York: Macmillan.

Zinar, R. (1987). *Music activities for special children.* West Nyack, NY: Parker Publishing.

Chapter Fifteen

MUSIC THERAPY FOR ADULTS WHO HAVE MENTAL OR BEHAVIORAL DISORDERS

DEFINITIONS

THE FIELD OF *adult psychiatry* deals with the prevention and treatment of mental, emotional, and behavioral disorders in adults. Although psychiatric illnesses and disorders may vary greatly in severity and exact type of symptoms manifested, all are "primarily characterized by behavioral or psychological impairment of function, measured in terms of deviation from some normative concept" (Kaplan & Sadock, 1991, p. 117). Just like the children and adolescents discussed in the previous chapter, adults who have mental or behavioral disorders consistently and chronically exhibit behaviors that are personally or socially deviant. However, adult disorders have usually developed over a longer period of time and tend to be more complex (Michel, 1985).

The American Psychiatric Association [APA] (1994) defines a *mental disorder* as

a clinically significant behavioral or psychological syndrome that occurs and that is associated with present distress (e.g., a painful symptom) or disability (i.e., impairment in one or more important areas of functioning) or with a significantly increased risk of suffering death, pain, disability, or an important loss of freedom. (p. xxi)

Although mental disorders may have a variety of manifestations and degrees of severity, they all are characterized by persistent, abnormal patterns of problem behaviors (Michel, 1976, 1985). Therefore, these clients are sometimes described as having *behavior disorders* or *behavioral disorders* (Gaston, 1968b;

Michel, 1976, 1985).

Mental or psychiatric illnesses and disorders traditionally have been classified into the two broad categories of neuroses and psychoses. A *neurosis* is a mental disorder primarily characterized by anxiety (Kaplan & Sadock, 1991). This anxiety may be experienced directly and be the main manifestation of the disorder, or it may be unconsciously controlled or modified to produce other distressing symptoms. A state of intense, persistent fear, dread, and discomfort is a prominent feature of many *Anxiety Disorders*, such as Panic Disorder, Agoraphobia, Phobias, Obsessive-Compulsive Disorder, Acute or Posttraumatic Stress Disorder, and Generalized Anxiety Disorders (APA, 1994). In the past, neuroses that involved a sudden impairment in function in response to emotional stress were termed *hysterical neurosis* (Kaplan & Sadock, 1991). Now, these are classified as *Conversion Disorders* (functional impairment in one of the special senses or voluntary nervous system) or *Dissociative Disorders* (disruption in the integrated functions of consciousness, memory, identity, or environmental perception; manifested as amnesia, fugue, identity disorder [multiple personality], depersonalization) (APA, 1994). Neurotic behavior is usually rigid, repetitive, and self-defeating. However, although their normal functioning is impaired to some degree, individuals who have neurotic behaviors maintain contact with reality and do not have any gross personality disorganization.

A *psychosis* is a more severe mental disorder that is primarily characterized by loss of contact with reality. Individuals who have psychoses have delusions, hallucinations, and an impaired ability to test reality (APA, 1994; Kaplan & Sadock, 1991). They may also have disorganized speech, disorganized or catatonic behaviors, and flat or inappropriate affective responses. Because of their severely impaired abilities to think, respond emotionally, communicate, interpret reality, and behave appropriately, these individuals usually have severe difficulties relating appropriately to others and are often unable to function independently in society. The American Psychiatric Association's listing of psychotic disorders includes Schizophrenia (paranoid, disorganized, catatonic, undifferentiated, or residual type), Schizoaffective Disorder, Delusional Disorder, and Brief Psychotic Disorder (APA, 1994). *Schizophrenia*, one of the more common psychotic disorders, is a severe mental disorder that lasts for at least six months, with at least one month of active symptoms that include at least two of the following: delusions, hallucinations, disorganized or incoherent speech, grossly disorganized or catatonic behavior, negative symptoms such as flattened affect, diminished thought processes, decreased initiative and motivation, or little interest in participating in work or social activities (APA, 1994). Schizophrenia does not refer to a split personality; rather, the term means "splitting of the mind," and refers to the disturbances or splits in thinking, feeling, and acting that are characteristic of schizophrenia (Thaut & Gfeller, 1992).

Other categories of mental disorders commonly encountered in adult psychiatric treatment include *Mood Disorders* (disturbances in mood, affect, or emotion that adversely influence the way an individual thinks, feels, and interacts with the environment; include Major Depressive Disorder, Bipolar Disorder, Dysthymic Disorder, Clyclothymic Disorder), *Personality Disorders* (enduring patterns of inner experience and behavior that deviate from cultural expectations, are pervasive and inflexible, and significantly disrupt social, emotional, or occupational functioning; include Paranoid, Schizoid, Schizotypal, Antisocial, Borderline, Histrionic, Narcissistic, Avoidant, Dependent, Obsessive-Compulsive, and Unspecified Personality Disorders), *Impulse-Control Disorders* (e.g., Intermittent Explosive Disorder, Kleptomania, Pyromania, Pathological Gambling), *Adjustment Disorders, Eating Disorders* (Anorexia Nervosa, characterized by a refusal to maintain a minimally normal body weight, and Bulimia Nervosa, characterized by repeated binge eating followed by self-induced vomiting, misuse of laxatives, excessive exercise, etc.), and *Substance-Related Disorders* (includes abuse of or addiction to or dependence on alcohol, drugs, or chemical substances) (APA, 1994; Thaut & Gfeller, 1992). For a more complete description of these and other mental illnesses, consult the *Diagnostic and Statistical Manual of Mental Disorders* (4th edition) [DSM-IV] (APA, 1994).

CAUSES

Whereas the psychiatric problems of children and adolescents are often related to factors of growth and development, those of adults "are more likely to be associated with stresses of every-day adaptation, either as an acute reaction to crises or a more chronic reaction resulting from distress over a longer period of time" (Michel, 1985, p. 49). No exact causes are known for most disorders; however, both biological (e.g., brain abnormalities, deficiencies in various neurotransmitters, genetics) and environmental

factors (e.g., traumatic experiences, family relationships) may contribute to many of the psychiatric problems of adults (APA, 1994; Goetinck, 1996b; Thaut & Gfeller, 1992). There is growing evidence that most mental disorders have some biological component (Siegfried & Goetinck, 1996; Taylor, 1997). "At root, 'mental' illnesses are all disorders of thought or emotion, stemming from physical problems – the biological equivalent of faulty wiring – in the brain" (Siegfried & Goetinck, 1996, p. 1F).

COMMON CHARACTERISTICS, PROBLEMS, AND NEEDS OF CLIENTS

As with any population, adults who have mental or behavioral disorders are a very heterogeneous

group. Factors such as the type and severity of the impairment, the cause and time of onset, the existence of associated conditions or impairments, and the degree and type of support services available will all have varying effects on the individual's level of functioning, needs, and treatment program. In addition, each individual will have a unique combination of abilities, needs, personality traits, strengths, and weaknesses that will impact his or her particular responses and functional abilities. Therefore, it is unwise to attempt to predict a particular person's skill levels or ceiling of abilities based on broad generalizations about a certain population. However, an awareness of some of those characteristics, problems, and needs which may be common to adults who have various types of mental or behavioral disorders will be beneficial both to the therapist who desires to work with this population and to the reader who is trying to understand how music therapy intervention strategies may benefit this population.

In the acute phases of their illness, adults who have mental or behavioral disorders often display behaviors of "intense confusion, agitation, excitability, fearfulness, or withdrawal" (Nowicki & Trevisan, 1978, p. 153). They have a need to learn and develop positive coping mechanisms to deal with the stresses and responsibilities of daily life. They may also have a need to find ways to control and channel aggressive or destructive impulses. In addition, many need help in developing or improving decision-making or problem-solving skills. Adults who have mental or behavioral disorders frequently lack the skills necessary to recognize and express feelings and emotions in an accurate and appropriate manner. Disturbances of affect, such as emotional lability, inappropriate outbursts of laughing or crying, or no affect, may also be present. Socialization is another common problem area for these clients. Usually, they have been unable to establish or maintain effective interpersonal relationships. Many clients also have a limited sense of trust in their own abilities and have low self-esteem. Of course, those clients who have severe psychotic disorders will need assistance in reestablishing contact with reality before they can begin to develop skills in communication, socialization, and expression of feelings. Some may also need to learn or relearn basic daily living skills (taking care of themselves and their house or apartment, budgeting, etc.).

Obviously, each particular mental disorder will have its own unique manifestations. For example, adults who have *schizophrenia* have symptoms such as delusions, hallucinations, impaired thinking, disorganized speech and behavior, emotional dysfunctions (e.g., affect that is blunted or reduced in intensity, flat affect, or inappropriate and unusual emotional reactions), social withdrawal, decreased ability to experience pleasure, and lack of motivation or perseverance (APA, 1994; Siegfried & Goetinck, 1996; Taylor, 1997; Thaut & Gfeller, 1992). Individuals who have schizophrenia also show markedly lower functioning in work, interpersonal relations, and/or self-care during the active phase of the disturbance (APA, 1994). Those who have *paranoid schizophrenia* are preoccupied with delusions, often with persecutory or grandiose themes, and/or have frequent auditory hallucinations, usually related to the delusions. Individuals may appear aloof, angry, argumentative, or anxious. Individuals who have the *disorganized type* of schizophrenia have disorganized speech and behavior and flat or inappropriate affect. Those who have *catatonic schizophrenia* have at least two of the following characteristics: motoric immobility (e.g., waxy flexibility or stupor), excessive motor activity that is purposeless and not influenced by outside stimuli, extreme negativism or mutism, peculiarities of movement (e.g., voluntarily assuming bizarre or inappropriate postures, stereotyped movements, prominent mannerisms or grimaces), or senseless imitation and repetition of another's words or phrases (*echolalia*) or movements (*echopraxia*) (APA, 1994).

Adults who have *major depressive disorders* feel sad or empty most of the time and show a markedly diminished interest in or ability to derive pleasure from activities. They may have insomnia or hypersomnia, a significant increase or decrease in appetite, and a significant weight loss or gain. Most usually feel tired or fatigued, seem unable to make decisions or get things done, have trouble concentrating, feel worthless, and have recurrent thoughts of death or suicide (APA, 1994; Siegfried & Goetinck, 1996; Taylor, 1997). These symptoms cause significant clinical distress or impairment in social or occupational functioning (APA, 1994). Those who have *manic episodes* have a persistent abnormally elevated or irritable mood, inflated self-confidence and feelings of grandiosity, decreased need for sleep, are extremely talkative and have racing thoughts, are easily distracted, have increased activity, and may be excessively involved in pleasurable activities that have a high potential for painful consequences (e.g., buying sprees, foolish investments, sexual indiscretions) (APA, 1994; Siegfried & Goetinck, 1996). Again, the severity of the mood disturbance causes marked impairment in occupational functioning in usual social relationships or activities (APA, 1994).

Adults who have *personality disorders* perceive or relate to their environment in unusual, inflexible, maladaptive ways that lead to disruptions in their social, occupational, or emotional life (APA, 1994; Thaut & Gfeller, 1992). They usually have difficulty forming or sustaining interpersonal relationships. They may perceive themselves and/or others in unusual ways and rarely recognize how their behaviors may contribute to their problems. Some may have problems with impulse control. Persons who have *paranoid, schizoid,* or *schizotypal* personality disorders have behaviors and beliefs that seem odd or eccentric, such as a pervasive distrust or suspiciousness of others (paranoid), detachment from and no desire for social relationships, emotional detachment and coldness, and flattened affect (schizoid), or acute discomfort with close relationships, odd beliefs and ideas, and peculiar or eccentric behaviors (schizotypal). Those who have *antisocial, borderline, histrionic,* and *narcissistic personality disorders* often have dramatic, emotional, or erratic behaviors. They may disregard or repeatedly violate the right of others and fail to conform to social laws and norms of behavior (antisocial), have a pattern of instability in self-image, affect, and interpersonal relationships, along with impulsivity and recklessness in areas such as spending, sex, and substance abuse that are potentially self-damaging (borderline), be excessively emotional or attention-seeking (histrionic), or have a pattern of grandiosity in fantasy or behavior, have a strong need for admiration, and have a lack of empathy (narcissistic). Individuals who have *avoidant, dependent,* or *obsessive-compulsive personality disorders* often seem to be anxious or fearful. They may be socially inhibited, have pervasive feelings of inadequacy, and be hypersensitive to negative evaluations (avoidant), have an excessive need to be taken care of and a pattern of submissive and clinging behaviors (dependent), or be preoccupied with orderliness,

perfectionism, and mental and interpersonal control, using repetitive, compulsive behavior to relieve anxiety (obsessive-compulsive). Adults who have *impulse-control disorders* are unable to resist impulses, drives, or temptations to perform acts that are harmful to themselves or others. Behaviors may include acting on aggressive impulses that result in serious assaults or destruction of property (*intermittent explosive disorder*), a pattern of stealing of objects not needed for personal use or for their monetary value that results in pleasure, relief, or gratification when the theft is committed (*kleptomania*), deliberately set fires for pleasure, gratification, or release of tension (*pyromania*), *pathological gambling,* or pulling out one's hair for pleasure, gratification, or release of tension (*trichotillomania*).

Adults who have *anxiety disorders* have persistent, excessive, uncontrollable fear or worry and avoidance behavior in response to certain stimuli (exogenous) or spontaneously without any obvious stressors (endogenous). They may have feelings of impending danger, overwhelming powerlessness, prolonged feelings of tension, and physical changes such as increased heart rate, disturbed breathing, sweating, trembling, etc. (APA, 1994; Kaplan & Sadock, 1991; Thaut & Gfeller, 1992). *Panic attacks,* sudden, discrete periods of intense fear or discomfort accompanied by at least four somatic or cognitive symptoms (e.g., palpitation, sweating, trembling or shaking, sensation of choking or smothering, chest pain, nausea, dizziness, feelings of unreality or being detached from oneself, fear of going crazy or dying, numbness, chills, or hot flashes), occur in the context of many anxiety disorders. Individuals who have *phobias* have irrational, excessive persistent fears of relatively harmless objects or situations, which often lead them to avoid the object or situation. Those who have *obsessive-compulsive disorders* have recurrent obsessions (persistent, unwanted thoughts, ideas, feeling, or impulses) or compulsions (repetitive or stereotyped behaviors or rituals) that are severe enough to be time consuming (take more than one hour a day), cause significant distress, or markedly interfere with the person's normal routine, occupational functioning, or social activities and relationships. In *posttraumatic stress disorder,* persons who have experienced some traumatic event (e.g., military combat, violent physical or sexual assault, witnessing severe accidents or natural disasters, being a prisoner of war or a prisoner in a concentration camp) continue to experience severe anxiety related to the event (e.g., recurrent memories or dreams of the event, intense distress to cues that symbolize or represent an aspect of the event) long after the event took place. Symptoms may include nightmares, efforts to avoid thought, conversations, activities, people, or places that arouse recollections or are associated with the trauma, guilt feelings or depression, restricted affect, difficulty falling or staying asleep, irritability, difficulty concentrating, hypervigilance, and exaggerated startle responses.

Individuals who have *eating disorders* often feel out of control in many or all areas of their lives (physical, emotional, mental, and behavioral). They try to substitute constant control over their eating behavior for the perceived lack of control over other aspects of their lives (Parente, 1989; Taylor, 1997). These individuals also have a disturbed perception of body shape and weight (APA, 1994). Those who have *anorexia nervosa* refuse to maintain a minimally normal body weight and are intensely afraid of gaining weight. This fear is not alleviated by weight loss. The condition may lead to self-starvation and become life-threatening. Those who have *bulimia nervosa* have recurrent episodes of binge-eating, during which they feel they cannot stop eating or control what or how much they eat. Following these binges, individuals use inappropriate compensatory behaviors (e.g., self-induced vomiting, misuse of laxatives or diuretics or enemas, fasting, excessive exercise) to prevent weight gain.

Adults who have *substance-related disorders* such as *alcoholism* or *chemical addictions* regularly use substances that affect the central nervous system, cause harmful changes in behavior, and result in health, social, and occupational impairments (APA, 1994; Thaut & Gfeller, 1992). When individuals are addicted to or dependent on a substance, they feel their psychological and spiritual well-being are dependent upon the experience gained from the particular substance (Skaggs, 1997a). People who are substance dependent have an increased tolerance for the substance, need continually greater amounts to achieve intoxication or the desired effect, have withdrawal symptoms when they abstain from the substance, and need the substance for daily functioning (APA, 1994; Thaut & Gfeller, 1992). They are unable to cut down or control substance use, spend much of their time trying to obtain and use the substance or recover from its effects, reduce or give up important social, occupational, or recreational activities because of the substance use, and continue substance use despite having persistent problems that they know are likely caused or exacerbated by the substance.

TREATMENT APPROACHES

Treatment for psychiatric disorders often involves a combination of approaches and interventions, including "a structured environment, a regime of medication, a variety of psychotherapeutic interventions, and a program of activity therapies" (Smeltekop & Houghton, 1990). For more acute phases of more severe disorders (e.g., schizophrenia, major depression), patients may require hospitalization, especially if they pose a danger to themselves or others. While medication may be very helpful in stabilizing individuals with severe psychosis, they are more likely to avoid relapses if they also receive training in basic life skills (Goetinck, 1996a).

It is important to remember that individuals with mental disorders are unique, and no one treatment or combination of treatments will be right for every person who has a particular disorder. The length of time available for treatment will also impact the choice of treatments. In short-term settings, treatment is intensive, very time-limited, and focuses on stabilizing patients, decreasing anxiety, helping them learn coping and problem-solving skills, and helping them recognize and change maladaptive behaviors (Murphy, 1992; Wolfe, 1996). More in-depth or insight-oriented interventions usually take longer periods of time.

Some therapists who work in adult psychiatric settings use Lazarus's (1976, 1989) *Multimodal Therapy model* to help classify a patient's problems and types of therapeutic interventions (Adelman, 1985; Cassity & Cassity, 1994a; Cassity & Theobold, 1990; Wilson, 1990a). Therapists who use this model carefully assess and describe clients' BASIC-ID: *Behavior* (habits, actions, gestures, reactions), *Affect* (emotions, moods, feelings), *Sensation* (clients' perceptions of what they see, hear, touch, taste, or smell; includes negative sensations, such as tension, pain, dizziness, and client preferences or fixation), *Imagery* (recurring dreams, vivid memories, clients' self-image or body-image), *Cognitive* problems (ideas, values, beliefs, opinions, or attitudes that interfere with the client's happiness or functioning), *Interpersonal* relations (ways clients socialize or interact with others; any problems with the way clients treat or are treated by others), and *Drug* use or health concerns (medication or drug use or abuse, any concerns about state of health or physical well-being). While Multimodal assessment attends to specific problems within each modality, it also focuses on the interaction between modalities, recognizing that a problem in one area or modality influences functioning in all other areas. The Multimodal Therapy model is very eclectic; a variety of therapeutic approaches may be used to address the problems it identifies.

As in child psychiatry, there are many different models for guiding the treatment of adults who have mental or behavioral disorders. Scovel (1990) identified six general psychotherapeutic treatment models currently in use in adult psychiatry: (1) the biomedical model, (2) the behavioral model, (3) the psychodynamic model, (4) the cognitive model, (5) the humanistic model, and (6) the holistic-wellness model.

In the *biomedical model,* mental disorders and the abnormal behavior that accompanies them are believed to be rooted in errant organic, physiological, or biochemical processes. Those who use this model search for germs or diseases, genetic history or abnormalities, or brain biochemistry, to see what might cause or influence the syndrome. Once a diagnosis is made, treatments that address the biological abnormalities (e.g., drugs or chemical therapies, relaxation training to decrease muscle tension and stress responses) are prescribed.

The *behavioral model* holds that abnormal or maladaptive behaviors are learned through conditioning, and, therefore, can be unlearned with appropriate therapy and training. The focus is not on underlying causes, but on the maladaptive behaviors exhibited by the client with a particular mental disorder. Classical or operant conditioning (pairing learning with positive or negative reinforcers) techniques are used to help the client develop desired

behaviors and diminish maladaptive responses. Behaviors are carefully observed, and specific undesirable behaviors are targeted for change. Often, contingencies are set up to help increase desired behaviors. A token economy system (clients receive tokens for desired behaviors, which may then be exchanged for privileges, rewards, etc.) or biofeedback techniques may be used in this model. Other techniques include modeling, systematic desensitization, self-management programs, and assertiveness training. The therapist assumes an active and directive role, structuring the environment and providing rewards and consequences to help the client achieve the desired changes. Change and progress is measured by a decrease in abnormal, maladaptive behaviors and an increase in new, more adaptive behaviors.

Persons who subscribe to a *psychodynamic model* believe that abnormalities and mental disorders are the results of hidden personality conflicts. Treatment helps patients uncover, identify, and work through these unconscious conflicts. As patients gain insight into the causes of their distress and work through conflicts, they make positive personality changes. Approaches in this model are based on the theories of Sigmund Freud, Alfred Adler, Carl Jung, Harry S. Sullivan, Erick Fromm, or Erik Erickson, and include techniques like free association, dream and imagery interpretation, and fostering transference.

Cognitive models assert that the emotional and behavioral problems of psychiatric disorders result from disordered thinking about self, others, and the world. Cognitive therapies include Ellis' rational emotive therapy (RET), Maultsby's rational behavior therapy, Beck's cognitive therapy, Meichenbaum's cognitive behavior modification, Glasser's reality therapy, and Berne's transactional analysis (TA). In cognitive approaches, therapy focuses on guiding the patient to discover unrealistic, irrational, or self-defeating thoughts, challenging these ideas, and assisting the client in developing healthier responses and thought patterns. Emotional and behavioral problems are eliminated as the thoughts that promote them are changed. As clients' ways of thinking and behaving become more logical, realistic, and mature, they develop the ability "to react more appropriately to life situations that demand a feeling response" (Scovel, 1990, p. 103). Techniques include examining thinking for "musts" and "shoulds," modifying "shoulds," changing language, homework to test new assumptions, open-ended questions, imagery, and role playing.

According to *humanistic models,* emotional and behavioral disorders occur when individuals fail to find or establish meaning in their lives. A key concept is humanistic theorist Abraham Maslow's (1968) idea of "self-actualization," a level of life rich in meaning and filled with a sense a well-being and completeness, the highest level of his hierarchy of human needs. Therapists who follow a humanistic approach give unconditional acceptance to the client and focus on the here-and-now of the therapeutic relationship. By relating to the client with genuine caring, acceptance, understanding, and respect, the therapist helps the client move beyond defenses and mental or emotional blocks to confront the basic questions of life, find meaning, and move to a higher level of functioning. Therapeutic techniques are experiential, oriented to building a trusting relationship, and designed to help the client make choices, build an internal frame of reference, and take personal responsibility to find purpose and meaning in life. Humanistic models of therapy include Fritz Perls's Gestalt therapy, Rollo May's existential therapy, and Carl Rogers's client-centered therapy.

Recently, the holistic movement, with its emphasis on considering all aspects of the person (physical/biological, mental/psychological, social, and spiritual) and treating the individual rather than the disease, has exerted an increasing influence on health care. The *holistic-wellness model* maintains that "the individual is an integrated whole with resources to promote personal health" (Scovel, 1990, p. 104), and that abnormalities occur when body, mind, and spirit are not in harmony or are not functioning in unity. The therapist's role is to educate, become involved with the clients, and share experiences with them, thus helping the clients gain information and promoting techniques that will help clients develop self-responsibility, better stress management, better health and fitness, and effective ways of counteracting environmental stressors. In a holistic approach, clients are encouraged to look within themselves to find healing. Techniques include imagery and visualization, meditation, acupuncture, bodywork, psychic healing, awareness training, applied kinesiology, and chiropractic therapy. Focus is on self-responsibility, self-care, self-examination, and self-healing to achieve a balanced state of wellness.

Although they differ in their emphases and ways of understanding mental disorders, all the models of treatment described above try to alleviate distress and affect growth and change. Whatever model is used, treatment follows the basic steps of (1) identifying the syndrome or disorder, (2) searching for a cause, (3) sorting out various possibilities and trying specific treatments, and (4) communicating the results in the language of the particular model (Scovel, 1990). Since no one approach will work for every client with a particular disorder, an eclectic approach that draws from more than one theory or treatment model (e.g., a combination of medication and behavioral or cognitive approaches) is often recommended (Goetinck, 1996a: Scovel, 1990; Smeltekop & Houghton, 1990; Wilson, 1990a). As will be seen later in this chapter and in Chapter Twenty-two, music therapists can work within the framework of any of these treatment models to devise goal-directed music interventions that help clients achieve positive growth and change.

SETTINGS FOR SERVICE DELIVERY

Adults who have mental or behavioral disorders may receive special programs and services to help meet their specific needs in a variety of settings. Years ago, many were confined to large state mental hospitals. Although the census of these hospitals has dropped dramatically in the last half of the twentieth century, long-term hospitalization is still a viable option in the continuum of mental health services (Wilson, 1990b). However, since the introduction of psychotropic medications in the mid-1950s and the passage of the Community Mental Health Center Act (Public Law 8-164) by the U.S. Congress in 1963, there has been an increasing move toward deinstitutionalization and community-based treatment for adults who have mental disorders. Short-term hospitalizations are becoming more and more the norm (Murphy, 1992; Wolfe, 1996). Now patients have a decentralized network of services to respond to their needs at various levels of illness and disability. The components of this network include (1) community-based services designed for those individuals who are able to live in the community while receiving treatment (e.g., outpatient clinics, community residences, after-care programs, half-way houses), (2) community hospital programs for those who are temporarily unable to function in the community or who may pose a danger to themselves or others (e.g., psychiatric units in general hospitals, community mental health center inpatient units), and (3) other sheltered settings for those who refuse traditional services but who cannot function independently. As society recognizes that a growing number of prisoners have severe mental problems, psychiatric services are also being given in correctional and forensic settings (Thaut, 1992b). In addition, there is a growing emphasis on discharge planning and finding ways to link patients or inmates with community support services once they are discharged from the hospital, treatment program, or prison. Many newly discharged clients need programs that will provide financial support, appropriate living arrangements, medical care, vocational rehabilitation, counseling, and leisure time activities to help them achieve a successful transition to community living (Wilson, 1990b).

Music therapy has a long history of use in psychiatric hospitals (Michel, 1985; Tyson, 1981), and the field of mental health is still one of the largest employers of music therapists (AMTA, 1998). Today, music therapists are established members of the interdisciplinary treatment team in many psychiatric hospitals (Choi, 1997). In a recent survey, most staff members at psychiatric hospitals that had music therapy departments and music therapy clinical training programs viewed the functional role of music therapists as highly favorable, but saw music therapy more as a supportive treatment than as a primary intervention (Choi, 1997). Music therapists who work with adult males in psychiatric hospitals most often treat those who have psychotic disorders, followed by those who have affective or mood disorders, substance abuse problems, personality disorders, anxiety disorders, and adjustment disorders. Music therapists

who work with adult female patients again most frequently treat those who have psychotic disorders, followed by those who have personality disorders, affective or mood disorders, substance abuse problems, adjustment disorders, and anxiety disorders (Cassity & Cassity, 1994b).

Music therapists also work with adults who have mental or behavioral disorders in many other settings, including community mental health centers, Veteran's Administration hospitals, drug/alcohol treatment programs, prisons or correctional programs, psychiatric units of general hospitals, public or private clinics, acute care inpatient or outpatient programs, music studios, community music schools, or in private practice (AMTA, 1998; Goldberg, 1989; Michel, 1985; Wilson, 1990b). Music therapists may provide direct or consultant services and work with clients as individuals or in groups. Music therapy can be part of both acute and chronic care programs and can be adapted to many different treatment models (Cassity & Cassity, 1994a; Scovel, 1990; Wilson, 1990a). Some music therapists who also have training in psychotherapy use music therapy as a primary intervention to facilitate exploration of personal issues (Goldberg, 1989).

In recent survey of music therapists' work settings (AMTA, 1998), 264 of 1,654 music therapists responding to a survey worked in inpatient psychiatric units, 116 worked in partial hospitalization programs, 92 worked in drug/alcohol treatment programs, 83 worked in community mental health centers, 31 worked in forensic facilities, and 20 worked in correctional facilities. When asked to list the populations they served, listing as many categories as appropriate, 559 of 1620 music therapists responding stated they worked with mental health populations; 467 reported treating clients who had behavioral disorders; 271 said they worked with clients who have substance abuse problems; 264, with clients who were abused or sexually abused; 142, with clients who had posttraumatic stress disorder; 114, with clients who had eating disorders; and 74, with forensic populations.

HOW MUSIC IS USED IN THERAPY

As has been noted earlier in this text, the beneficial effects of music on the mind, spirit, and emotions have been recognized since primitive and ancient

times (see Chapter Three). The field of mental and behavioral disorders has continued to be a prime venue for the therapeutic use of music in more modern times. In fact, Michel (1985) reported that "music in therapy with adults has had its most important development and widest acceptance in the realm of behavior disorders" (p. 71). Tyson (1981) also observed that "music therapy is a hospital-developed practice; it evolved particularly in psychiatric hospitals, which have borne the major responsibility for the care of the mentally ill in the United States for more than two hundred years" (p. 7).

As early as 1789, a case was being made for using music as a therapeutic agent in the treatment of depression (Heller, 1987). In the early 1880s, medical and psychiatric journals in the United States began to carry reports promoting music as a viable alternative treatment for various mental and physical disorders, and the physician/psychiatrist Benjamin Rush and his students, Edwin Atlee and Samuel Matthews, advocated for the therapeutic use of music in the treatment of psychiatric disorders, such as mania and depression (Davis, 1987; Heller, 1987). Much of the early music therapy treatment involved exposing patients to live or recorded music to help modify their moods and behaviors or help focus their attention on more healthy thoughts. In 1878, mentally ill patients at Blackwell's Island responded so favorably to an experimental music treatment employing live concerts and individual sessions that the New York City Charities Commissioner and the hospital's medical director supported additional experimentation on the use of music to alleviate suffering among the destitute mentally ill (Davis, 1987). Near the end of the nineteenth century, George Adler Blumer, a leading mental health reformer, advocated the use of music therapy to treat the mentally ill and also hired musicians to perform for the patients at Utica State Hospital in New York (Davis, 1987).

In the early to middle part of the twentieth century, several musicians in the New York area, especially Eva Vescilius, Margaret Anderton, Isa Maud Ilsen, and Harriet Ayer Seymour, promoted the use of music in healing by conducting experiments, providing music in hospitals, giving lectures and teaching courses on music therapy, and forming organizations dedicated to promoting the therapeutic use of music (see Chapter Four). As psychiatry became a more accepted form of medical treatment during World War I, music was used as both an adjunct to psychiatric treatment (e.g., helping attract

and increase attention, modify moods, stimulate intellectual functioning, relieve tensions, facilitate self-expression, stimulate resocialization) and as a general psychological stimulus in the hospital environment (e.g., during meals, calisthenics and exercises; to relax patients during hydrotherapy and electroshock therapy; as entertainment) (Tyson, 1981). The musician Willem Van de Wall, who worked in hospitals and prisons in New York and Pennsylvania, and the psychiatrist and composer Ira Altshuler, who worked at Wayne County General Hospital in Eloise, Michigan, developed significant music therapy programs in mental hospitals and prisons during this period (Boxberger, 1963; Clair & Heller, 1989; Collins, 1982; Davis & Gfeller, 1992; Graham, 1974; Van de Wall, 1936, 1946). Van de Wall observed that patients often exhibited more normal behaviors when they participated in music activities and noted that music provided structure and organization and was a powerful sensory stimulant that could awaken emotions, provide a means of appropriate emotional expression, and elicit memories. In addition, music gave patients a way to participate actively in their treatment, something that Van de Wall felt was beneficial to the recovery process (Clair & Heller, 1989).

In the 1920s–1940s, much of the use of music in mental hospitals and prisoners was educational, recreational, or entertaining in nature (Wilson, 1990b). Activities included record listening, group singing, patient bands and choruses, talent shows, and holiday and seasonal programs. Music programs were often conducted in group settings on the open ward, and aimed to modify patients' moods, moderate destructive physical activity, provide diversions, stimulate constructive use of energy, and promote cooperation and resocialization (Clair & Heller, 1989; Tyson, 1981). In the years during and immediately following World War II, music therapy became an accepted treatment in many Veteran's Administration and state psychiatric hospitals, as doctors discovered music could not only be a morale-booster but also facilitate the recovery process (Rorke, 1996; Tyson, 1981; Wilson, 1990b). Both active (e.g., singing or playing instruments alone or as part of a group) and passive (listening; listening and discussion) music experiences were prescribed as part of the Army's Reconditioning Program to facilitate exercise and assist with resocialization, education, and neuropsychiatric treatment (Rorke, 1996). On closed wards, live music was preferred to recorded music, for a "live" performer could adjust the music to the mood and responses of the patients. Other activities included singing, group or individual instruction for voice or instruments, rhythm bands, and special productions. On open wards, patient orchestras, record listening, exercises to music, and music quiz/variety shows were also used.

In state mental hospitals, group music activities provided some of the safest early group experiences for patients with serious mental illnesses, and music programs were conducted on the wards and in large groups to reach as many patients as possible (Tyson, 1981). One of the functions of the music therapist was to use music to stimulate and reinforce any positive responses, thus awakening or restoring the patient's interest in music which could then be used "as motivation for new learning and relationships, and reintegrating the patient into the social community" (Tyson, 1981, p. 11). Hospital music programs from the mid-1940s to mid-1950s included various patient instrumental and vocal groups (e.g., orchestra, band, instrumental "combos," chamber music groups, chorus, rhythm band); community sing-alongs on the wards; music-listening and music-appreciation groups; concerts by outside groups or patient groups; musical quiz, variety, and talent shows; musical, pageant, and holiday productions; individual music study including music or song writing; folk and square dance; religious choirs; training in instrument repair and maintenance or the construction of simple instruments (Tyson, 1981; Van de Wall, 1946).

As concepts in mental health care changed from custodial approaches to an emphasis on rehabilitation, musical activities in psychiatric hospitals moved from being regarded as mainly recreational or entertainment to being a part of therapeutic or educational methods that counteracted destructive processes and helped patients use some of their own physical and mental powers to improve their conditions (Tyson, 1981). The advent of tranquilizing drugs in the mid-1950s modified much of the acute, disturbed, psychotic behavior of individuals in mental institutions and made it possible to try to deal with the deeper psychological needs of these patients. Activity came to be seen as an important component of rehabilitation and recovery, and "hospitals began to mobilize all possible activities, music included,

into full schedules designed to encourage growth processes and resocialization" (Tyson, 1981, p. 12). In the 1960s, music therapists most commonly used music activities (a) to assist patients in establishing or reestablishing interpersonal relationships and (b) to increase or establish patients' self-esteem through self-actualization (Gaston, 1968b; Tyson, 1981).

In the 1970s and 1980s, music therapy practice continued to reflect changes in the field of mental health, as music therapists began to work in community mental health programs, private hospitals, and private practice, as well as in state and federal hospitals. During this time, music therapy program offerings also became more diverse, with less emphasis on performance-based activities (chorus, band) and more emphasis on activities with multidimensional approaches (creative movement and music, music listening and discussion, song writing, improvisation, guided imagery and music, etc.) that were based on assessments of the psychological, behavioral, and social needs of individual clients and had specific therapeutic goals and objectives (Braswell, Maranto, & Decuir, 1979a; Cassity & Cassity, 1994a; Lathom, 1982; McGinty, 1980; Tyson, 1981; Wilson, 1990b). With shorter hospital stays now becoming the norm, music therapists are working to develop treatment models that can achieve beneficial results in only a few sessions (Murphy, 1992; Wolfe, 1996). Acute care groups often focus on needs common to clients of varying diagnoses: (1) relaxation/anxiety management skills, (2) verbal interaction skills, and (3) leisure community skills (Wolfe, 1996).

Why Music Is Useful in the Treatment of Mental Disorders

Some of the strengths music brings to the treatment of adults who have mental or behavioral disorders are its flexibility, its almost universal appeal to people of all ages and levels of functioning, its ability to organize behavior and bring people together, and its usefulness as a vehicle for emotional expression (Gaston, 1968a; Goldberg, 1989; Sears, 1968; Thaut & Gfeller, 1992). As Goldberg (1989) observed:

A uniqueness of music in the psychiatric setting

is its flexibility. Music brings people together in a cohesive, supportive way; it provides external organization, narrows and focuses attention, and calms. Music reflects, evokes, and contains affect, stimulates imagery, and facilitates insight, support, and psychological safety. But most of all, its special quality lies in its unique ability to mirror the paradoxical, ambiguous, fleeting, dynamic nature of human emotions. (p. 42)

Since music is flexible and allows for participation at a wide variety of ability levels, music experiences used for therapeutic interventions can be readily adapted to the functioning level of the client. For example, simple experiential music activities, such as singing, playing musical instruments, selecting recorded music for listening activities, or moving to music, can help establish contact with clients who have severe psychotic disorders by providing safe, nonverbal relating experiences and a nonthreatening structure for reality orientation. Because of its inherent order and structure and its power to serve as a means of nonverbal communication and as a gentle persuasion to join in activity (Gaston, 1968a; Sears, 1968), music provides a "here-and-now" orientation that demands clients' attention and moment-by-moment commitment to the music experience. Since music is the language of emotions (Whitwell, 1993), music experiences also provide an important and unique way for clients to identify, experience, and express feelings in more appropriate ways. In addition, music may serve as a structure or reinforcer to control impulsive behaviors and practice more controlled, cooperative behaviors.

For higher functioning clients, experiences such as relaxation to music, guided imagery and music, instrumental improvisation, lyric discussion, and song writing, can reduce stress and anxiety, facilitate relaxation, increase self-esteem and feelings of well-being, improve verbal communication and social interaction skills, increase appropriate expression of feelings, and improve decision-making and problem-solving skills. In addition to helping clients improve their mental, social, and behavioral functioning, music therapy sessions can also provide clients with skills and abilities (e.g., singing with a group, playing instruments, appropriate behavior while listening to music, following a conductor) that can be used in

normal environments (Hadsell, 1974). Moreover, as goal-directed music experiences are used to foster the development of group cohesion, provide a unique mode for expressing feelings, and offer experiences in support, leadership, creativity, and play, music therapy services can play an important role in assisting adult psychiatric patients in their transition from the institution to the community (Langdon et al., 1989).

Since music is perceived as a nonthreatening, enjoyable stimulus by most people, participating in music therapy experiences may produce less fear and anxiety than other types of treatment. Heaney (1992) found that music therapy was viewed very favorably by most adult psychiatric inpatients, and suggested this may be related to the way music therapy interventions emphasize "increased socialization and group cohesion, provision of safe, expressive outlets for emotions, and the learning of new skills or the rekindling of previous interests which foster positive self-esteem" (p. 79). Music experiences also frequently stimulate the interest of apathetic clients and help motivate them to participate in goal-directed activities. As clients participate and cooperate in music therapy treatment, "the music therapist also actively promotes and attitude of cooperation with other aspects of treatment" (Smeltekop & Houghton, 1990, p. 122). In addition, music therapy interventions can complement treatment with psychotropic medications by addressing aspects or manifestations of the disease or syndrome (e.g., lack of insight, lack of judgment, impaired memory, poor affective expression, poor communication or socialization skills) that chemical interventions do not reach (Smeltekop & Houghton, 1990).

Recent advances in biomedical research techniques have also shown that music therapy interventions can directly influence biochemical and physiological functions that relate to the amelioration of psychiatric disorders (Taylor, 1997). However, it is important to realize that simple exposure to music alone does not necessarily promote positive changes in these functions. For the therapeutic use of music to be most successful, the music interventions must be carefully planned and directed by the therapist so they serve to promote positive growth and change. Used without planning and direction, music can at times intensify pathology, as when individuals with antisocial personality disorders use certain songs to validate their pathological thoughts and values. As Taylor (1997) explained:

> Music does not have the power to simply enter the brain and independently reverse a serious disorder by affecting neurological functions. It does, however, assist the therapist in eliciting certain mood changes and feeling states that allow the patient to exhibit and experience the effects of certain therapeutically beneficial responses. While the music alone does not rehabilitate the patient, it can affect reality contact through sensory stimulation and kinesthetic feedback. It is also used to structure interpersonal interaction and serve as a basis for participation in social groups or society at large. (p. 83)

General Music Therapy Intervention Strategies and Techniques

As with other client populations, music therapy interventions with adults who have mental or behavioral disorders can take a variety of forms, depending on the client's interests, preferences, abilities, and needs. Specific experiences used with particular clients are based on information gained in the music therapy and general assessments and are appropriate to the client's chronological and developmental age (Cassity & Cassity, 1994a, 1994b; Thaut & Gfeller, 1992; Wilson, 1990a; Wolfe, 1996). Music therapy interventions may employ *active* music-making techniques (e.g., singing, playing instruments, improvising or composing music, moving to music) or more *passive* techniques that are based on music listening (e.g., directed listening, listening and discussion, music for relaxation, guided imagery and music). While many music therapy interventions make use of familiar music that is preferred by the clients to help establish rapport with clients or use the lyrics of popular songs to help clients focus on a particular topic or bring up treatment issue for discussion, others effectively use less familiar, classical music to stimulate clients' imagery or expression of their unique inner feelings (Summer, 1994).

Music therapists may work with clients in individual or group sessions. Group music therapy is most often used in acute care settings. In addition to being more economical, group music therapy is more efficient at strengthening and building clients' interpersonal skills and is very effective in helping clients develop relevant, functional skills that can help them cope and function more effectively in their life in the community (Murphy, 1992; Wolfe, 1996). Music may also be used as general environmental stimulus to help control behavior. For example, when music from two local radio stations was played during patient free-time in the courtyard of a state mental hospital for patients who were hospitalized with behavioral problems, almost twice as many inappropriate behaviors (e.g., disruptive, exploitative, sexually assaultive, self-abusive, property destruction, selling contraband) occurred when the rock/rap station was playing than when the easy listening/country western station was used (Harris, Bradley, & Titus, 1992). The researchers noted that while it is a possibility that the easy listening music drove away persons more likely to act inappropriately and attracted those more prone not to act inappropriately, the change in music effectively controlled patients' behavior in a cost-free, instantaneous way where "frequent widespread attempts to control behavior in the mall area has been fruitless" (p. 15).

Levels of Intervention

According to Wheeler (1983, 1987), music therapy clinical practice with adult psychiatric clients falls into three general categories, (1) music therapy as activity therapy, (2) insight music therapy with reeducative goals, and (3) insight music therapy with reconstructive goals. Goldberg (1989) also distinguished two major types of music therapy practice used with adult psychiatric patients: music activity therapy (similar to Wheeler's level one) and music psychotherapy (similar to Wheeler's levels two and three). Music psychotherapy may use *focused* experiences, with themes determined by the therapist based on patient issues, or *open* experiences, where themes emerge from needs, images, feelings that arise from musical experience). Music therapists who use reconstructive insight music therapy or music psychotherapy techniques *must* have advanced clinical training in both psychotherapy and music psychotherapy procedures (Goldberg, 1989; Unkefer, 1990; Wheeler, 1983, 1987).

In *music activity therapy*, changing behavior, not understanding behavior, is emphasized, as music therapists actively involve clients in structured, success-oriented, goal-directed music experiences to help them experience and practice healthy behaviors. As they participate in these music activities, clients learn more adaptive and functional behaviors and develop behavioral and emotional control necessary to function in daily life. Goals include increasing internal/external organization, improving interpersonal interaction and relationships with peers, decreasing withdrawal and internal preoccupations, and increasing self-esteem. Techniques include Orff-Schulwerk activities, relaxation to music, exercises or movement to music, group singing, structured song writing, structured instrument playing, and other structured music experiences.

In *music psychotherapy* approaches, the focus is on the exploration of the client's personal issues. Techniques may include instrumental improvisation, music listening with discussion of lyrics or emotional reactions to music, or guided imagery and music. Music experiences are not limited merely to a short catalyst role at the beginning of the session, but are "used to expand, highlight, or contain emotional responses throughout the group session, depending on the needs of the group members" (Goldberg, 1989, p. 40). In contrast to child music psychotherapy, where the musical metaphors and images are not interpreted by the therapist (Friedlander, 1994), in music psychotherapy with adults, the metaphors and images generated with the client in music are usually verbally processed with the client (Goldberg, 1989). Thus, music therapists who use these techniques must have advanced clinical training in psychotherapeutic techniques (Goldberg, 1989; Unkefer, 1990; Wheeler, 1983, 1987).

Insight music therapy with reeducative goals uses music experiences to stimulate discussion of feelings, which lead to insights that help the clients reorganize their values or behavioral patterns, resulting in less anxiety and improved functioning. Music therapy interventions emphasize identification of feelings and attitudes, exploration of self-defeating attitudes and healthier ways of relating to others, creative problem-

solving, and using material presented in the musical experience or the feelings elicited by the musical experience to facilitate insight and behavioral change. In this level, music-based experiences and follow-up processing and discussion focus on relatively *conscious* material, such as the behavior patterns and feelings presented in the here-and-now interactions between the therapist and clients. As compared with music activity therapy, verbal processing plays a more prominent role in the therapeutic process.

In *insight music therapy with reconstructive goals*, the focus shifts to using therapeutic music experiences to help clients achieve insight into *unconscious conflicts* that negatively affect their behavioral patterns, thoughts, and feelings. The music therapist uses images and feelings elicited from music experiences that tap deeper levels of emotion and personality (e.g. Priestley's [1975] analytical improvisation techniques, Bonny's [1975] Guided Imagery and Music) to help the clients achieve insight into the causes of their current distresses or maladaptive behaviors and help them work through these conflicts and fears, which leads to positive personality changes. It is important to note that many states require licenses for private psychotherapeutic practices; therefore, trained music therapists who wish to use music psychotherapy techniques in private practice may need to complete additional graduate coursework and have a certain number of hours of supervised clinical work so they can meet the requirements for a counseling license in their particular state (Goldberg, 1989).

While each of these levels of music therapy may be useful in various situations, certain levels are generally more appropriate with specific types of clients (Goldberg, 1989, 1994; Wheeler, 1987; Unkefer, 1990). General, activity-oriented music therapy (level 1) is used with clients who have severe mental disorders (e.g., chronic schizophrenia, organic mental disorders) and more extreme personality disorganization, while insight music therapy with reeducative (level 2) or reconstructive goals (level 3) is more useful with those who have mental disorders with less severe personality disorganization (e.g., substance abuse, mood disorders, neuroses or anxiety disorders, personality disorders, situational disturbances). To benefit from insight music therapy with reconstructive goals, clients "have to be able and motivated to commit themselves to usually long-term therapy that challenges existent personality structures" (Unkefer, 1990, p. 147). It is highly recommended that music therapists who use insight-oriented techniques with reconstructive goals or music psychotherapy obtain advanced clinical training in psychotherapeutic and music psycho-therapy techniques (Goldberg, 1989; Wheeler, 1983, 1987; Unkefer, 1990).

Categories of Musical Experience

Using Wheeler's (1983) levels of practice along with ideas form Yalom's (1983) level of inpatient group psychotherapy, Unkefer (1990) classified programs and techniques used in music therapy treatment of adults with mental disorders into six general categories: (1) music performing, (2) music psychotherapy, (3) music and movement, (4) music combined with other expressive arts, (5) recreational music, and (6) music and relaxation. There are a number of techniques in each of these categories, any of which may be beneficial to adults who have various mental or behavioral disorders, depending on factors such as the exact nature of their presenting symptoms, their individual skills and preferences, the time and setting available for therapy, etc. Music therapists who work in psychiatric settings frequently employ many of these techniques in both the assessment and treatment of clients (Cassity & Cassity, 1994a).

Music performing techniques used by music therapists include group instrumental improvisation, instrumental or vocal performance ensembles (e.g., choir, jazz ensemble, Orff ensemble, hand bell choir, rock band, guitar ensemble, chamber music group), group singing, individual instrumental or vocal music lessons, and individual music improvisation/interaction. As these techniques are therapeutically directed, the therapist uses the context of music performance activities to increase skills such as appropriate socialization, cooperation, communication, expression of feelings, and frustration tolerance. In all of these performing activities, clients' self-esteem also increases as they master tasks and experience success in music performance.

According to Unkefer (1990), *music psychotherapy techniques* use music and music-based activities (a) to provide affective experiences that evoke thoughts, feelings, or associations or (b) as an objective focal point to elicit discussion or explore new behaviors or rediscover old skills. Techniques may include instrumental improvisation, GIM, lyric discussion, music listening with discussion of emotional reactions, song writing, and the like. Initially, group or individual approaches and activities may be *supportive*, as the music therapist structures music experiences to identify and clarify thoughts or feelings expressed by the client and facilitate/support appropriate interpersonal behavior. Later, group or individual approaches and activities may become more *interactive*, as the music therapist structures music experiences to express and reflect themes/issues relevant to the clients or group process or to clarify individual attitudes, feelings, motivations, or conflicts, thus facilitating the client's efforts to identify, express, and resolve conscious conflicts, to form new, healthier responses, and to practice the new behaviors. At the deepest level of music psychotherapy, *catalytic music group or individual therapy*, music experiences are used as a catalyst to tap unconscious levels of clients' emotional processes, which can then be processed and used to help the clients achieve insight and reorganize their existing personality structures to achieve healthier functioning. Music therapists who use these more in-depth experiences should have additional clinical training in psychotherapy and music psychotherapy techniques (Goldberg, 1989; Unkefer, 1990; Wheeler, 1983, 1987).

Music and movement experiences used in the treatment of adults who have mental or behavioral disorders include (a) movement awareness, (b) movement exploration, (c) movement interaction, (d) expressive movement, (e) dance, and (f) music and exercise. As these techniques are therapeutically directed, movement-to-music activities provide a context and structure to help clients increase body awareness and comfort in movement, physical fitness, social interaction skills, nonverbal expression of feelings, and self-confidence, while decreasing tension and anxiety. Live or recorded music can support and facilitate these experiences in several ways: (1) a *background accompaniment* to facilitate participation by matching the mood and tempo of the activity and providing sensory and psychological stimulation for the clients, (2) a *timing cue* to structure movements,

(3) a *catalytic stimulus* to provide a theme for expression or interaction through music, (4) a *representational accompaniment* to reflect or lead the character, tempo, flow, and mood of the movement, (5) a *content accompaniment* to help enhance the experience of internal aspects of the external movement characteristics, (6) a *designative accompaniment* to direct specific ways of moving (e.g., turn on trills, move up as music melody ascends), or (7) a *dance accompaniment* (Unkefer, 1990).

Music therapists who work with adult psychiatric clients may also *music combined with other expressive arts* in some of their treatment techniques. For example, music might be used to set a mood or provide a theme for clients to express themselves through fine arts such as drawing, sculpting, or drama. Music may also be used with prose or poetry, as clients develop musical accompaniments for existing works or as music experiences stimulate expressive writing experiences. These multisensory experiences often provide additional means of expression for non-verbal or withdrawn clients, helping them to express feelings without words or providing a structure to organize thinking and encourage expression through language (Unkefer, 1990). When the music therapist works with other creative arts therapists (e.g., art therapists, dance therapists, psychodramatists, poetry therapists), they may use a team approach to provide these multisensory experiences for the clients, with each therapist taking the lead in facilitating the experience in his/her area of expertise.

Frequently, music therapists use *recreational music activities* to help clients get comfortable with music-making so music can later be used as a tool for more in-depth group participation and therapeutic goals. These activities also provide initial steps toward resocialization and help clients develop constructive leisure time skills. Experiences may include (a) *music games* (e.g., music bingo, name that tune, concentration games, instruments play games), (b) *music appreciation awareness* (listening to and discussing or creating/performing a variety of types of music to encourage attention and on-task behavior and provide opportunities for asserting individual preferences and opinions in a non-threatening atmosphere), (c) *recreational music performance groups* (vocal and/or instrumental; emphasis on enjoyment and participating in process), and (d) *leisure-time skill development*. Leisure skills gained in music therapy can be an important part of a client's plan for post-discharge use of leisure-time and can play a vital role in assisting the client in his/her transition from an institution to the community (Langdon, et al., 1989; Unkefer, 1990; Wolfe, 1996).

Finally, since many adult psychiatric patients experience tension and anxiety, music and relaxation techniques can be an important part of music therapy programs for these clients (Unkefer, 1990; Wolfe, 1996). Music and relaxation training may be carried out in group or individual settings and utilize a number of techniques. These include (1) *music with progressive muscle relaxation training*, where appropriate music is paired with progressive muscle relaxation techniques and music becomes a conditioned stimulus for relaxation), (2) *music for surface relaxation*, in which clients learn to select music with characteristics that will help them relax and provide temporary relief from anxiety or stress), (3) *music imagery*, where clients listen to music in a relaxed state with therapist-suggested open-ended scenarios to promote imagery or aid concentration or relaxation (*not* intended to reach deep intrapsychic material that the specialized music psychotherapy technique Guided Imagery and Music does), and (4) *music-centered relaxation*, where music is used as a stimulus or focus to divert clients' attention from unpleasant thoughts and to block out feelings of anxiety, fear, or tension (Unkefer, 1990).

Music Therapy with the Multimodal Therapy Model

Some music therapists use Lazarus's (1976, 1989) Multimodal Therapy model to help assess clients and structure and integrate music therapy interventions in psychiatric settings. Music therapy activities can tie in with one or several areas of a client's BASIC-ID (behavior, affect, sensation, imagery, cognition, interpersonal relations, drugs) and be useful both for assessing a client's current level of functioning and for helping a client gain skills in needed areas (Adelman, 1985; Cassity & Cassity, 1994a, 1994b; Wilson, 1990a). Music therapy interventions may be structured to help clients increase concentration, attention span, and on-task behaviors; increase eye contact; increase ability to appropriately identify and express feelings and emotions; alter existing mood states (e.g., decrease depression or negative thought patterns); increase frustration tolerance, increase impulse control; decrease anxiety; facilitate muscle relaxation and release motor tension; increase self-esteem and improve self-concept (through success experiences, skill acquisition, positive sensory and social feedback); improve cognitive organization and memory skills; improve decision-making and problem-solving skills; increase ability to structure time and follow through on tasks; increase awareness of self and others; increase interaction and cooperation with others (through nonverbal as well as verbal means); increase group cohesion; and stimulate and/or structure perceptions and motor activity to increase alertness, increase coordination and confidence, and encourage social participation (Cassity & Cassity, 1994a; Thaut & Smeltekop, 1990).

Music Therapy Interventions for Adults Who Have Schizophrenic Disorders

Music therapists who work in psychiatric hospitals most frequently treat adult clients who have schizophrenia and other psychotic disorders (Cassity & Cassity, 1994b). Although schizophrenia is now recognized as a neurological disorder or brain disease whose symptoms often may be reduced with various psychotropic drugs (Goetinck, 1996a; Siegfried & Goetinck, 1996; Taylor, 1997), music therapy interventions can complement medication by treating and reducing symptoms (e.g., apathy, poor social skills, lack of involvement with others, blunted or inappropriate affect) that medications do not reach (Smeltekop & Houghton, 1990).

Many clients with schizophrenia or other psychotic disorders have severely disorganized personalities and initially benefit most from experiential music activities (e.g., singing, playing musical instruments, moving to music, selecting music for listening activities, music and relaxation) that provide a "here- and-now" orientation and demand moment by moment attention to the task (Nowicki & Trevisan, 1978; Unkefer, 1990; Wheeler, 1987; Wolfgram, 1978). Since verbal methods often do not reach individuals who have severe psychoses, movement-to-music or instrumental improvisation or performance activities that provide opportunities for nonverbal relating experiences can be very important in establishing contact with these clients and

helping them begin to become aware of and interact cooperatively with others. Recent research revealing that music reaches the emotional centers of the brain without the need for higher cortical analysis also suggests a biomedical explanation for the effectiveness of music as a vehicle for establishing contact with individuals who have schizophrenia or other psychoses:

> Through playing, singing, or otherwise participating in the production of music itself, the brain must act in direct relationship to the concurrent musical stimuli that enter the realm of neurological perception. . . . Sustained musical interaction, therefore, may be quite effective in helping the brain of the psychotic person regain its ability to receive, organize, and react appropriately to sensations perceived from the external environment. (Taylor, 1997, pp. 113-114)

Many music therapists have had success using improvisational music therapy techniques (see Chapter Twenty-two) to establish contact with and elicit communication and cooperative interactions from adults who have schizophrenia or other psychotic disorders (Aigen, 1990; Nolan, 1994; Nowicki & Trevisan, 1978; Pavlicevic et al., 1994). In one ten-week study, subjects with severe, chronic schizophrenia showed significant gains in their ability to interact more musically and for longer periods of time with the therapists and also showed significant improvement in their clinical state as measured by the Brief Psychiatric Rating Scale (Pavlicevic et al., 1994). Other therapists have used specially composed or selected songs to help develop and reinforce self-awareness, reality contact, and more socially adaptive behavior patterns in clients who have severe psychoses (Wolfgram, 1978, 1980).

Music Therapy Interventions for Adults Who Have Mood Disorders

Mood or affective disorders are the second most frequent disorders music therapists who work in psychiatric hospitals treat with adult male patients, and the third most frequent disorder treated in music therapy for adult female patients (Cassity & Cassity,

1994b). Many music therapists have found that the experiences of successfully participating with others in music activities or gaining skills in playing musical instruments help increase self-esteem in clients who are depressed or have low self-esteem (Cassity, 1976; Cassity & Cassity, 1994a; Morgan, 1975; Unkefer, 1990). Activities such as improvising on musical instruments, discussing music or song lyrics, and writing songs can also help clients learn to identify and express feelings accurately and appropriately (Behrens, 1988; Cassity & Cassity, 1994a; Cordobes, 1997; Dickens & Sharpe, 1970; Ficken, 1976; Langdon et al., 1989; Unkefer, 1990; Wolfgram, 1978, 1980). In addition, music psychotherapy approaches utilizing metaphoric music improvisation and Guided Imagery and Music (GIM) can help individuals with severe depression gain access to feelings, images, and insights (Warja, 1994).

For many clients, music seems to be a "safer" vehicle than words for experiencing and expressing feelings and emotions. For example, Cordobes (1997) found that, while both game-playing and song writing helped develop group cohesion in adults with depression, subjects used a greater number of emotional words and focused more on treatment issues during the song writing condition. Since it provides avenues for nonverbal as well as verbal expression, music allows comfortable modes of participation for clients who are reluctant to verbalize and provides authentic, physical experiences of affect for those who hide behind verbal intellectualizations (Langdon et al., 1989):

> Patients who do not want to verbalize and prefer to remain silent may be able to play a sound. Later, they may be able to express their feelings as a single word added to a song and eventually, elaborate verbally. For other patients who express themselves in complex intellectual concepts with little genuine affect, the music provides a place where they can express themselves on direct emotional and bodily levels. Through the physical work of playing and the exposure to the stimuli of melody, harmony, and rhythm, they can begin to experience real affect. (pp. 101-102)

Taylor (1969, 1997) developed a specific music therapy procedure, the Expressive Emphasis Technique, for clients who have severe *clinical depression accompanied by suicidal behaviors*. In the first phase, clients select musical materials for active participation and work with the therapist in a positive, nonthreatening atmosphere to concentrate on eliciting the full expressive potential of each musical phrase. Later in this phase, the therapist begins to ask clients for their ideas about various musical styles or elements. This training in musical expression helps clients learn to be more expressive of feelings in general, while the supportive atmosphere established by the therapist conveys the message that whatever feelings the clients have will be accepted and respected when they are expressed in appropriate ways. In the second phase, music performance, improvisation, or creative movement or drawing to musical stimuli, in combination with verbal processing, are used to help clients express their own personal emotions that are generated by the musical experience. In the third and most important phase, the therapist intentionally does things in the musical situation that create discomfort for the client (e.g., shortening session time by starting late or ending early, playing an accompaniment too slow or too fast, misplacing music), seeking to get the client to outwardly express negative or hostile emotions about these events rather than inverting these emotions. As the client learns to express hostile feelings outwardly toward appropriate objects and in acceptable ways, the client's requests must be fulfilled immediately so she or he learns this is an effective coping mechanism. When the client is able to express verbally the full range of hostile or negative emotions that previously had been directed inwardly, the therapist reestablishes the original positive atmosphere, further demonstrating the value of this coping technique.

Taylor (1997) reported that this Expressive Emphasis Technique was very successful in treating adults with severe clinical depression and suicidal behavior: suicidal episodes decreased in frequency throughout treatment, reaching zero at or near the beginning of phase three, and positive personality traits of extraversion, self-confidence, and motivation became evident during the music therapy session and began to generalize as the treatment progressed. According to Taylor's theory, this technique is so effective because the neuronal impulses stimulated by the release of negative emotions and by the realization of an effective means of self-expression "serve as monoamine agonists, resulting in reactivation of neuronal circuits that had been unable to produce these neurotransmitters in amounts sufficient to avert the suicidal depressive reaction" (p. 117).

Some research suggests that musical-rhythmic tasks may help distinguish mania from other mental disorders during the psychotic phase of the disorder. Cohen (1986) found that subjects with mania were superior to subjects with other psychotic disorders on tests of rhythmicity and tempo reproduction; subjects with mania also scored significantly higher on rhythmicity than on tempo, and the speed of item presentation did not affect their performance. Music therapy interventions may address various needs of patients with mania (Cassity & Cassity, 1994a; Unkefer, 1990). For example, activities such as singing, structured dances or movement-to-music, and instrumental improvisation may help channel energy or provide structured, appropriate outlets for energy release. Music programs that progressively move from more stimulating to more relaxing music or music and relaxation training can help individuals decrease physical restlessness, while involvement in goal-oriented performance or movement-to-music experiences or guided music listening experiences may help focus attention and increase concentration. Task-oriented music activities may also provide reality orientation, structure, and practice in impulse control, while music psychotherapy techniques can help clients learn to appropriately identify and express emotions.

Music Therapy Interventions for Adults Who Have Anxiety or Stress Disorders

Since music has the ability to affect both physiological and mood/emotional responses (see Chapter Five), it can be a powerful tool for reducing stress, tension, and anxiety. Jellison (1975) has shown that background music can reduce stress responses and help induce relaxation under stress. Music can also be combined with relaxation training (Alley, 1977) and biofeedback techniques (Epstein, Hersen, & Hemphill, 1974; Scartelli, 1984; Wagner, 1975) to reduce tension and stress responses and to facilitate relaxation responses. In addition, Lowe (1973) found

that excitatory responses to rock music could be used to countercondition fear of public speaking and fear of authority figures. It is important to note, however, that individual preference for the type of music being played often affects the listener's response to that music. Consequently, individual preferences should be considered in order to achieve maximum benefits in using music to facilitate reduction of tension and stress (Hanser, 1985; Logan & Roberts, 1984; Prueter & Mezzano, 1973; Stratton & Zalanowski, 1984; Taylor, 1973). Although precatagorized selections of stimulative and sedative music may be useful in some cases, they may have subtle elements which will evoke unpredicted responses in some individuals:

> For instance, slow, arrhythmic music which otherwise meets all criteria for sedative music may appear foreign or frightening to some listeners. Researchers must use care in generalizing beyond a single musical selection until more exhaustive efforts to quantify the effects of different music have been undertaken. (Hanser, 1985, p. 199)

Today, music-assisted relaxation training programs are an important part of many music therapy programs in acute care mental health settings (Wolfe, 1996). Techniques often involve pairing selected music with progressive muscle relaxation, self-suggestion, guided imagery, or biofeedback. Patients learn exercises through repetition with guidance from the therapist, and then are encouraged to include them in their daily lives for self-maintenance. Treatment interventions that combine selected music with vibroacoustic stimulation can also help clients decrease anxiety, increase feelings of calmness and relaxation, increase self-confidence in facing stressful situations, and decrease psychosomatic symptoms (Brodsky & Sloboda, 1997; Wigram, 1995). For some clients, using music plus vibrotactile stimulation within a cognitive-behavioral framework was just as effective as traditional psychotherapeutic counseling in reducing symptoms of anxiety (Brodsky & Sloboda, 1997). This equal effectiveness is important, for some clients who shy away from more traditional treatments may perceive music-based treatments as being less threatening, and therefore be more willing to participate in music-based interventions.

Many music therapists use some form of Guided Imagery and Music (GIM) procedures to help clients decrease anxiety, facilitate relaxation, and increase feelings of well-being (Blake & Bishop, 1994; Bonny 1978b; Peach 1984). Hammer (1996) found that state anxiety, or perceived situational stress, decreased significantly in subjects in a GIM group, and recommends this intervention for use with clients dealing with acute or chronic stress. In addition, Hammer's research indicated that GIM treatment programs "may have an overall effect on improving one's ability to react to stress, improving concentration and general contentment, and improving one's ability to relax in general" (p. 67). In their work with musicians who had severe performance anxiety, Brodsky and Sloboda (1997) found that music-based relaxation and imagery training used within a cognitive behavioral framework were equally as effective as traditional counseling and psychotherapy in reducing stress and performance anxiety. A specific form of music and imagery treatment, the Bonny method of Guided Imagery and Music, has also been used very effectively to treat individuals who have been abused or have witnessed or been a victim of some horrible or traumatic event that has resulted in a post-traumatic stress disorder (Blake & Bishop, 1994; Ventre, 1994b). Used with individuals or in groups, GIM techniques can help clients (a) decrease their hyperarousal and increase their concentration and physical/psychological relaxation, (b) gain access to memories, images, and the feelings associated with them, and (c) increase feelings of hope and empowerment by unlocking inner resources and directing energy to realistic solutions or resolutions, freeing the self from the effects of the past and healing/reconnecting with ordinary life and plans for a more fulfilling future. GIM techniques can be a very powerful form of music psychotherapy, and music therapists who use GIM techniques must have special, advanced clinical training (see Chapter Twenty-two for more information).

Music therapists who work with clients who have anxiety or stress disorders may also use intervention techniques that involve clients more actively in making or responding to music. For example, instrumental improvisation or performance techniques or movement-to-music activities can help reduce tension and anxiety by providing constructive outlets for physical energy and relief of muscular tension (Morgan, 1975; Unkefer, 1990; Wolfgram, 1978). Using music therapy as an adjunct to group therapy in a stress treatment program, Lienhard (1981) taught clients to listen to themselves by listening to music and their reactions to it. Instrumental improvisation activities were used to help make clients aware of the tome and volume of their communication. In addition, playing instruments served as vehicle for tension release in many clients. Lienhard also used music listening/discussion activities, using song lyrics as a catalyst for discussion to help clients (1) identify areas of stress, (2) identify and express feelings associated with stressful areas, (3) ventilate emotions, (4) share with the group and receive feedback, and (5) determine alternative positive coping mechanisms to deal more successfully with stressful situations. Other music therapists have used drumming techniques (e.g., improvisational drum groups, community drum circles, 1:1 sessions improvising and interacting with the therapist, storytelling with drum accompaniment) to help clients with post-traumatic stress disorder increase awareness of and express feelings, learn to modulate and control emotions, practice ways of changing or controlling behavior, increase feelings of control and empowerment, and, in group settings, help build feelings of group connectedness and group cohesion (Borczon, 1995; Burt, 1995; Slotoroff, 1994).

Music therapists may work within the framework of many different theoretical orientations as they structure music therapy interventions to help treat adults who have problems with stress or anxiety. For example, Tyson (1987) used an analytically-oriented approach based on a psychoanalytic interpretation of the symbolic content of the client's singing and playing and interactions with the therapist to treat a client with generalized anxiety disorder. Working with the client using singing and instrumental lessons, Tyson noted a close relation between the client's musical problems and his unconscious psychological conflicts. As the client analyzed the body movements he used in singing and playing, these became subjects for free association, searches for their psychodynamic meaning, and an experiential basis for creative problem solving and self-discovery.

Other music therapists work within cognitive or cognitive/behavioral orientations (Brodsky &

Sloboda, 1997; Bryant, 1987; Maultsby, 1977; Murphy, 1992), using song lyrics, music listening/discussion, music performance or music improvisation, or music/movement techniques as vehicles to help clients change their disordered ways of thinking and build healthier, more adaptive ways of thinking and relating to the world and others around them. A typical music therapy session structure in this orientation may include (1) an introduction by the therapist, focusing the clients on the task, (2) a music warm-up, with the therapist modeling response, (3) a music experience (e.g., improvisation, creating a group song), (4) therapist-facilitated verbal processing and discussion of the experience of the musical experience and how clients' responses/experiences/reactions relate to treatment issues, and (5) closure, led by the therapist (Murphy, 1992). Therapists have found that music activities often reach clients on an immediate, emotional level that is able to bypass verbal rationalizations and defenses. As Murphy (1992) observed, "While words can accomplish the same end results, for some patients it is the nonverbal experience that may best bring to conscious awareness recurrent, self-defeating patterns" (p. 105).

Still other music therapists take a biomedical approach, structuring music interventions to take advantage of the direct effect music has "on specific physiological processes whose functional variations are indicators of anxiety, tension or stress" (Taylor, 1997, p. 103). Many of the music-facilitated relaxation techniques mentioned earlier fall in this category.

Music Therapy Interventions for Adults Who Have Eating Disorders

Various types of music therapy interventions, from a variety of orientations, have been used to treat clients who have anorexia (Justice, 1994; Parente, 1989; Taylor, 1997) or bulimia (Justice, 1994; Nolan, 1989). The issue of being out of control is a prominent theme for many clients with eating disorders (Parente, 1989; Taylor, 1997), and "music therapy can provide support experiences in which the patient has control, new ways of expressing herself and coping with emotions, and connections with other people" (Justice, 1994, p. 105). Using a process musical theater structure where clients

developed, practiced, and performed music reviews using songs based on clients' fears and major issues, Parente (1989) helped clients with anorexia (a) identify, evaluate, and change faulty and self-destructive thought patterns, (b) discover new skills and behavior patterns, and (c) practice these new skills to transfer them to their daily lives. As part of the music therapy process, clients brought in "songs or musical selections expressing personal affirmations, current personal objectives, or troublesome thoughts and feelings" (p. 47), some of which were then selected for inclusion in the musical review. As they participated in the musical theater ensemble and rehearsed and performed songs and scenes for the show, clients practiced control of fear or phobias, learned to substitute positive attitudes and behaviors for destructive thoughts, emotions, or activities, learned to exercise personal power to improve their situation, supported one another and developed or strengthened meaningful friendships, and improved their self-esteem/self-confidence as they accepted, learned, and performed their roles and began to see themselves as capable, worthwhile individuals.

Justice (1994) also used music therapy interventions within a cognitive/behavioral framework to help clients with anorexia or bulimia increase self-awareness and self-esteem, increase awareness of irrational or destructive feelings and behaviors, decrease anxiety that may be experienced as they try to discontinue their eating disorder behaviors, and find new ways of taking control and coping with emotions. She presented three different levels of music therapy experiences that have been helpful in facilitating therapeutic processes with clients who have eating disorders: (1) music-reinforced relaxation, using music to complement, support, and ground muscle stretching, deep breathing, progressive muscle relaxation, and directed imagery techniques, (2) structured music therapy groups, using music and movement, handbells and choir chimes, group singing, or instruments improvisation, and (3) insight-oriented music/creative arts and imagery techniques, using group adaptations of the Bonny method of Guided Imagery and Music (GIM) or drawing or writing in response to stories or poems read to music. In *music-reinforced relaxation*, the music helps direct the clients away from obsessive thoughts connected with their eating disorders or control issues and nonverbally paces the experience.

Learning music-reinforced relaxation techniques give clients a method of self-regulation that helps them cope with stress and anxiety, increases their awareness of their physical and emotional reactions, and provides new options for dealing with anxiety without giving in to their old urges. In *structured music therapy groups*, clients have opportunities to experience success and connect with others and share experiences on a nonverbal level, which may be less threatening than trying to connect and share in verbal therapy groups. As clients participate successfully in music experiences, they begin to view themselves as an integral part of the group and begin to see their value as a person is based on qualities other than weight. These nonthreatening, structured experiences also help prepare the clients for more *insight-oriented music therapy techniques*, which use music experiences to help clients move past the defenses of or inability to use words, connect with deeper issues through symbol and metaphor, and help clients begin to identify and resolve the issues and feelings underlying their eating disorders.

Working from a more psychodynamic perspective, Nolan (1989) showed how music, in the form of structured and unstructured group improvisational techniques, could serve as a transitional object designed to interrupt the binge/purge cycle in the treatment of bulimia. Nolan hypothesized that

> musical expression, as a transitional object, may serve the purpose of redirecting unconscious feelings from the unsuccessful coping mechanism of bulimic behavior to conscious awareness and expression leading to mastery. (p. 51)

The experience of improvising and then discussing and processing roles and group process as they listened to a tape of the improvisation (a) helped reinforce reality contact for these clients, (b) assisted in identification of functional parts of their ego, (c) helped identify and intrude on distorted thoughts, and (d) provided a safe environment for testing new interpersonal behaviors. The act of playing musical instruments also provided clients with a wide range of expressive sounds over which they could have control, giving them a means of expression and a way to connect personally and subjectively with the music.

Focusing on the idea that being of out of control was one of the main issues of persons with anorexia, Taylor (1997) developed the music therapy procedure Control Reversal Therapy (CRT). CRT reverses the usual locus of control in therapy sessions, placing the control in the hands of the *client* and using experiential musical activities to generate feelings of internal control. Individual music therapy sessions are structured so that clients control the musical activity and participate on their own terms. Techniques include having the client (a) teach the therapist to sing/play specific songs or to play certain instruments, (b) use a rhythm instrument to signal or control the therapist's improvisations, (c) write song lyrics about a relevant topic and then choose the musical setting for these lyrics (therapist may offer suggestions, but clients must approve each note), (d) create music using interactive computer programs, or (e) use instruments to represent important people in her life. Reactions and feelings to these experiences are processed with the guidance of the therapist. Taylor has had great clinical success with CRT since 1988, with patients needing 12 sessions or less to make dramatic positive changes. Because of the biological processes that accompany feelings of internal control over external events (e.g., decreased blood levels of glucocorticoids, epinephrine and norepinephrine; increased activity in dopaminergic neurons of the brain stimulated by feelings of success), patients who are successfully treated by CRT techniques are able to release their cortical control over their eating and drinking behavior, allowing these processes to again be controlled normally by the endocrine glands and the hypothalamus. (For detailed information on the biological processes involved in CRT, see Taylor, 1997, pp. 79-83.) Taylor speculates that CRT techniques may also be effective with other clients for whom lack of control is an issue, such as victims of abuse or those who have some forms of post-traumatic stress disorder.

Music Therapy Interventions for Adults Who Have Problems with Substance Abuse or Addiction

Music touches all aspects of a person, physical, psychological, emotional, social, and spiritual (see

Chapter Five). Since "many researchers emphasize the need to treat the 'whole person' as opposed to 'their addiction'" (James, 1988a, p. 65), music therapy techniques can be a valuable treatment tool for adults who have problems with substance abuse or addiction. Music therapy interventions can readily be structured to complement many goals of addiction or alcoholism treatment programs, such as decreasing isolation, motivating clients to participate in treatment, increasing peer interaction and group involvement, facilitating group cohesion, increasing awareness of addictive behaviors and their consequences, clarifying values, accessing and expressing feelings and emotions, improving social skills, developing new coping skills, facilitating expression of issues and feelings related to recovery, decreasing tension and anxiety, facilitating relaxation and stress reduction, improving problems-solving skills, improving impulse control, developing a healthy self-image, finding constructive leisure time activities, and providing assistance in relapse prevention (Bednarz & Nikkel, 1992; Cassity & Cassity, 1994a; Freed, 1987; James, 1988a; Skaggs, 1997a; Treder-Wolff, 1990; Wheeler, 1985). In addition, music therapy interventions can enhance all stages of treatment, from engagement to recovery (Bednarz & Nikkel, 1992; Skaggs, 1997a; Treder-Wolff, 1990). Initially, techniques like discussing music interests or lyrics, improvising with rhythm instruments, or participating in music ensembles may help encourage rapport and facilitate interaction with and comfort in the group. Experiences that allow for nonverbal interaction and nonverbal expression, such as activities using rhythm instruments or sessions involving music and art (e.g., drawing to music), may be particularly useful in increasing clients' involvement (Wheeler, 1985). For many clients in this population, however, movement-to-music experiences may tend to decrease enjoyment and increase tension levels (Wheeler, 1985). Therefore, movement-to-music experiences are usually not a good choice for initial music therapy interventions.

As treatment progresses to more active intervention, "music is a channel of communication that penetrates the rigidity of defenses brought into early recovery, and is an objective conveyor of social attitudes and beliefs that can be used as a tool for exploration" (Treder-Wolff, 1990, p. 68). Techniques

used to help clients recognize addictive and maladaptive behaviors and share feelings associated with them include (a) lyric analysis and discussion of songs related to addiction or treatment issues, (b) choosing songs from a list of song titles to share something about one's feeling or life experiences, (c) group instrumental improvisations that can give insight into habits, feelings, or ways of interacting, (d) free or structured song writing procedures, and (e) Guided Imagery and Music (GIM). These same techniques can later be used to help clients explore issues on a deeper level, facilitating insight, assisting in the development and practice of new coping and problem solving skills, and facilitating the recovery process.

Music therapy interventions may also help clients become more aware of subtle social messages in advertising jingles for addictive products or of certain types of music/songs that are associated with or cue their substance abuse (Michel, 1985; Treder-Wolff, 1990). When clients become aware of these influences, music therapists can help them discover ways to counteract them. In addition, as clients recover and try to maintain an abstinent life style, they may continue use music-based relaxation techniques or music/leisure activities (listening, playing instruments, playing or singing in community or church musical groups) to deal with stress, structure leisure time, and find new ways of socializing with others (Bednarz & Nikkel, 1992; James, 1988a; Treder-Wolff, 1990).

Many music therapists have found that structured songwriting experiences are particularly useful in helping clients express feelings related to their individual situations, their addiction, and their recovery process (Freed, 1987; James, 1988a; Treder-Wolff, 1990). Music therapists also use GIM techniques to help clients deal with the chronic stress and anxiety that may be associated with recovery (Hammer, 1996; James, 1988a) or to help clients view life from different perspectives, access and build trust in their inner resources, identify and express emotions and feelings, resolve internal conflicts and heal old hurts, modify moods, develop internal control and support systems, discover optional modes of behavior, and find models for healthy responses (Skaggs, 1997a). In addition, techniques learned and insights gained in GIM sessions can assist clients in maintaining their recovery when treatment has ended. For example, "the music inside" can help clients get through the day by supplying all the things clients had formerly relied on their drugs to supply: support and strength during difficult times, the comfort of a familiar friend, a means of uplifting sagging spirits and facilitating clients' ability to move through emotional pain. Thus, music becomes "a readily accessible, economical and healthy choice" that both helps clients recover from addictions and assists them "in maintaining sobriety and continuing the healing and growth process" (Skaggs, 1997a, p. 46).

Music Therapy Interventions for Adults Who Have Antisocial Personality Disorders or Who Are in Correctional Facilities

Adults who have *antisocial personality disorders* may use certain songs to validate their pathological thoughts or values. Under the guidance of a music therapist, however, this same music can be used within the context of lyric analysis/discussion activities to help clients examine their role models, values, and goals (Taylor, 1997). Instrument playing activities that call for taking turns or for waiting to play one's part can help clients learn to control impulsive behaviors. These activities can also have a positive effect on brain processes that control behaviors:

> Waiting one's turn to play a handbell or tone chime, for example, forces the patient to make use of frontal lobe structures to overcome deficits in delayed response performance, thereby preventing impulsive behaviors from occurring. The frontal lobes also become occupied with evaluating the consequences of specific actions, a cognitive task not generally associated with the antisocial person. (Taylor, 1997, p. 84)

In addition, playing instruments can serve as a means of personal expression, a valuable leisure time skill, and a means of developing self-esteem. Group instrumental experiences can also be structured to provide opportunities for increasing problem-solving skills and practicing cooperative interactions with others.

Some research has shown that music therapy interventions may be an initial nonthreatening treatment approach with men who have physically abused women or children (Cassity & Theobold, 1990). Treatment approaches utilized music therapy experiences within the framework of cognitive/behavioral restructuring, anger management training, and relaxation training. Music therapy techniques included movement-to-music experiences to increase awareness of behavior, sing-alongs to elicit on-task behavior and cooperation as opposed to disruptive behavior, xylophone improvisation to facilitate appropriate nonverbal and verbal interaction, lyric writing to encourage expression of feelings, music listening/discussion and group music composition activities to promote cooperative interactions and facilitate discussion of treatment issues, and instrumental performance activities to improve impulse control and increase decision-making and organizational skills.

Music therapy techniques can assist in the rehabilitation of inmates, helping them gain new skills and behaviors that will enable them to function more appropriately and adaptively once they return to society (Elliot & McGahan, 1987; Hanser, 1987; Michel, 1985; Mitchell, 1978). For example, music skills learned in music therapy sessions can provide activities for constructive use of leisure time (Michel, 1985), either for personal enjoyment or for participating in community vocal or instrumental groups. In one instance, inmates who played together in a music combo in prison continued to play together after their release, even supplementing their income through this activity (Michel, 1976, 1985). After six years of research in providing music programs to prisoners, Elliot and McGahan (1987) were "convinced that music is one of the potentially most effective instruments for rehabilitation available to present-day society" (p. 170).

Prisoners who choose to be involved in music programs (e.g., instruction in music theory, instrumental music, or vocal music) can begin to rebuild their lives as they make positive decisions and take concrete actions to participate in music tasks which demand group cooperation and consideration of others (Elliot & McGahan, 1987). The mastery of even simple music tasks can help build feelings of confidence and group cohesiveness. In addition, inmates develop increased social and personal adjustment as they learn to conform to group expectations, experience group cohesiveness, and discover how each individual plays a unique role in cooperating with others to achieve a group goal. As their willingness to accept instruction and their skills increase, inmates also learn to put forth more effort in the face of challenges, leading to increased self-confidence, self-esteem, self-satisfaction, and pride in their physical self-image.

Hanser (1987) found that loosely structured music groups where participants were given the opportunity to choose the activities and goals they wished to work on in their music therapy hour helped increase self-esteem in inmates of a state correctional facility for women. In addition, these experiences provided the women with an opportunity to be themselves and to learn to trust others. Music and art therapy programs can also help prisoners express feelings and frustrations in socially acceptable ways, helping relieve anxieties and tensions which can lead to prison unrest. Moreover, these programs reinforce individuality and self-expression amid boring prison routines, thus making the prison environment more humanized and civilized (Mitchell, 1978).

Some music therapists work in the field of correctional psychiatry, treating inmates who have various psychiatric disturbances (Kaser, 1993; Nolan, 1983, 1994; Thaut, 1987, 1989b, 1992b). Involvement in structured therapeutic music interventions can have several benefits for prisoners who have psychiatric problems. These include (a) increasing reality contact; (b) engaging mood and emotional responses that promote active thinking and motivation toward goal achievement; (c) increasing self-esteem and learning respect for others; (d) providing a means to express, reflect upon, and deal with thoughts, feelings, and memories; (e) reducing tension and anxiety; (f) decreasing hostile and aggressive behaviors; (g) increasing constructive social interaction and improving group awareness and cohesiveness; (h) facilitating positive mood states and increasing coping abilities; (i) increasing physical and mental alertness; and (j) promoting ability to experience, identify, express, and perceive emotions accurately and appropriately (Thaut, 1987, 1992b). Music therapy techniques can be particularly effective in helping prisoner-patients feel more relaxed and in helping improve their mood and increasing positive thoughts about themselves and their lives (Thaut, 1989b).

Research and practice have shown that three types of music therapy techniques work very successfully with prisoners who have severe mental health problems (Thaut, 1987, 1989b, 1992b). *Music group therapy techniques* use guided music listening and supportive verbal interaction to help inmates learn to respect and cooperate others. In this process, prisoner-patients are also guided to set achievable personal goals (e.g., soothe and relax mind, recall good memories, increase inspiration or motivation to make progress or complete tasks, release or express inner feelings and thoughts, get mind off problems, relieve tension, clear confusion, think about loved ones) and then learn to select music experiences that will help them accomplish these goals. In the second category of techniques, *instrumental group improvisation*, the music therapist structures and guides simple improvisation tasks that have inmates play pitched and non-pitched percussion instruments, keyboards, or guitars. Through these experiences, prisoner-patients learn to express and communicate feelings, practice appropriate social interactions, experience success, release tension, and increase reality contact. Finally, music therapy programs in correctional psychiatry may use *music and relaxation techniques*, which teach inmates progressive muscle relaxation to sedative music of their choice. A few prisoner-patients may also benefit from insight-oriented Guided Imagery and Music (GIM) techniques used in combination with supportive group music therapy experiences. In some cases, GIM experiences can assist in temporarily lifting individuals' defenses so they can learn to recognize and deal with feelings that negatively impact their behavior and relations to others (Nolan, 1983).

Individual music therapy sessions may also benefit some prisoner-patients. For example, Nolan (1994) used music improvisation techniques to work with a 32-year-old prisoner who was fearful, isolated, did not speak, and possibly had hallucinations. After successfully using a xylophone set up with a pentatonic scale to engage in an improvisatory duet with the music therapist playing the guitar, and then hearing the tape of this duet, the prisoner-patient began to speak. Nolan hypothesized that as the prisoner-patient entered into the musical exchange, the musical experience elicited mental processes not effected by the psychosis and increased his level of functioning. In another instance, Kaser (1993) worked in a correctional setting with a prisoner-patient in the mid-stages of Alzheimer's disease, and found that, although the man was unable or unwilling to communicate his feelings verbally, he would communicate through songs he selected or sang. As he began to sing and express his feelings through songs he recalled, the prisoner-patient became more relaxed and less agitated. As his behavior improved in music therapy, he also behaved more appropriately on the cell block.

To work successfully in correctional settings, music therapists must understand rules, behavior codes, and social dynamics that are peculiar to the prison setting, always remembering that security takes priority over all other concerns and programs (Thaut, 1987, 1992b). Music therapists need to work cooperatively with security staff and be competent in handling security issues. The music therapist must also know something of the inmate's personality structure and criminal record to understand the behavior patterns and emotions that may be linked with his or her crime and expectations for the future. While therapy sessions in correctional settings must adapt to the limitations and restrictions of the prison system and usually do not have the degree of emotional sharing and openness that are present in other situations, therapeutic interventions that are brief, time-limited, focused on the here-and-now, and linked to clearly defined treatment goals (e.g., decreasing symptoms, increasing appropriate psychosocial functioning, adjusting to and coping with the reality of the present situation, preparing for reintegration with society for inmates who are about to be released) can be very useful in facilitating the inmate's therapeutic progress.

SPECIAL CONSIDERATIONS AND TIPS FOR SUCCESS

Music therapists who work with adults who have behavior disorders or mental illnesses have several responsibilities, which include the following (Wolfgram, 1978): (1) to create a warm, nonthreatening environment that bolsters self-esteem and motivation by emphasizing successful experiences; (2) to define limits and expectations for appropriate group behavior; (3) to direct and redirect the client's attention to the task at hand; (4) to be aware of individual responses and the significance of interaction; and (5) to perceive and address the clients as adults. Whatever the philosophical orientation of the music therapist, it is important that clear and specific goals and objectives for therapy be established. When this is done, appropriate affective or social behaviors that may at first seem very nebulous can become directly observable and specific, enabling both therapist and clients to determine whether progress is being made (Cooper, 1985; Hanser, 1984). For music therapy treatments to be most successful, music therapists must also structure their interventions to work within and support the particular orientation or treatment philosophy of the facility or program in which they are working (James, 1988a; Wilson, 1990a). A community-related approach to music therapy can facilitate the client's reintegration into society (Braswell, 1968; Rubin, 1973, 1975; Wilson, 1990b). For higher functioning clients, "it is essential that the therapist stress the importance of the program and even explain what is to be accomplished by it" (Nowicki & Trevisan, 1978, p. 155). Having these clients write or choose their own goals is one way of encouraging them to take responsibility for their own actions (Cooper, 1985; Nowicki & Trevisan, 1978). It is also important to remember that a therapist's concern for the client, reflected in actions as well as words, can affect the client's progress. "If the therapist is frequently late of inconsistent with the group, the clients tend to interpret it to mean that therapy is not important, and, further, that their mental health is no important" (Nowicki & Trevisan, 1978, p. 155).

SUMMARY

The field of adult psychiatry deals with preventing and treating mental, emotional, and behavioral disorders in adults. Although psychiatric illnesses and disorders may vary greatly in severity and exact type of symptoms manifested, they all are characterized by persistent, abnormal patterns of behavior. Mental or psychiatric illnesses and disorders traditionally have been classified into the two broad categories of neuroses and psychoses. A neurosis is a mental disorder primarily characterized by anxiety, while a psychosis is a more severe mental disorder that is primarily characterized by loss of contact with reality (e.g., schizophrenia). Other categories of mental disorders commonly encountered in adult psychiatric treatment include mood disorders, personality disorders, impulse-control disorders, adjustment disorders, eating disorders, and substance-related disorders. Behaviors characteristic of these various disorders are described briefly in the chapter.

Treatment for psychiatric disorders often involves a combination of approaches and interventions, including medication, some type of psychotherapeutic intervention, a structured environment, and a program of activity therapies. In short term settings, treatment is intensive, very time-limited, and focuses on stabilizing patients, decreasing anxiety, helping them learn coping skills and problem-solving skills, and helping them recognize and change maladaptive behaviors. More in-depth or insight-oriented interventions usually take longer periods of time.

As in child psychiatry, there are many different models for guiding the treatment of adults who have mental or behavioral disorders. These include: (1) the biomedical model, (2) the behavioral model, (3) the psychodynamic model, (4) the cognitive model, (5) the humanistic model, and (6) the holistic-wellness model. Music therapists can work within the framework of any of these treatment models to use goal-directed music interventions that help clients achieve positive growth and change. However, for music therapy treatments to be most successful, music therapists must work within the overall treatment philosophy of their particular facility. Music therapy has a long history of use in the treatment of mental illness, and the field of mental health is still one of the largest employers of music therapists. Some of the strengths music brings to the treatment of adults who have mental or behavioral disorders are its flexibility, its almost universal appeal to people of all ages and levels of functioning, its ability to organize behavior and bring people together, and its usefulness as a vehicle for emotional expression. As with other client populations, music therapy interventions with adults who have mental or behavioral disorders can take a variety of forms, depending on the client's interests, preferences, abilities, and needs. Specific experiences used with particular clients are based on information gained in the music therapy and general assessments and are appropriate to the client's chronological and developmental age.

Music therapy clinical practices with adult psychiatric clients may be grouped into three general categories: (1) music therapy as activity therapy, (2) insight music therapy with reeducative goals, and (3) insight music therapy with reconstructive goals (Wheeler, 1983, 1987). Music therapists who employ more in-depth music psychotherapy techniques must have advanced clinical training. Techniques used in music therapy programs generally fall into one of six general categories: (1) music performing, (2) music psychotherapy, (3) music and movement, (4) music combined with other expressive arts, (5) recreational music, and (6) music and relaxation (Unkefer, 1990). The last sections of this chapter described several specific music therapy interventions that may be useful in treating adults who have schizophrenic disorders, mood disorders, anxiety or stress disorders, eating disorders, problems with substance abuse or addiction, antisocial personality disorders, or who are in correctional facilities.

QUESTIONS FOR THOUGHT AND DISCUSSION

1. Discuss some of the special characteristics and needs of adults who have mental or behavioral disorders. What implications do these have for music therapy programming?

2. Why and how are music experiences useful in making contact with adults who have mental or

behavioral disorders? Are some types of experiences and activities more useful than others for certain types of clients? Which ones? Why?

3. Describe the six different models that may be used to guide the treatment of adults who have mental or behavioral disorders. Which music therapy

approaches described in this chapter reflect a biomedical orientation? behavioral orientation? psychodynamic orientation? humanistic orientation? cognitive orientation? Do any reflect a holistic-wellness orientation?

4. Describe Wheeler's three levels of music therapy practice with adult psychiatric clients. What is the difference between music activity therapy and music psychotherapy? Why do music therapists need advanced training to use in-depth music psychotherapy or insight music therapy with reconstructive goals?

5. Describe some specific music therapy experiences that might be used in treating adults who have (a) schizophrenic disorders, (b) mood disorders, (c) anxiety or stress disorders, (d) eating disorders, (e) problems with substance abuse or addiction, or (f) who are in correctional facilities. What unique benefits does music add to treatment in each of these areas?

6. List several special considerations that may be important to remember when developing therapeutic intervention strategies for adults who have mental or behavioral disorders. Why are these important? What are their implications for the structure of music therapy intervention strategies?

7. For each of the situations listed below, (a) define the problem or areas of need for the client or group of clients, (b) describe one or more of the goals you might pursue in music therapy sessions with the client(s), (c) describe music activities you might use to help the client(s) meet those goals, (d) tell how the music activities you described relate to the goals and needs of the client(s), and (e) mention any special considerations you might want to take into account when working with the client(s).

Situation 1:

You are working as a music therapist in a psychiatric hospital. One of your groups is comprised of five schizophrenic patients, ages 25-35. All have a history of previous hospitalizations, but none have been in the hospital for more than a week during their current admission. These patients are not yet stabilized on medication. They are confused and disoriented. Their problems include lack of reality orientation, inability to relate to others, disorganized and inappropriate verbalizations, and short attention spans.

Situation 2:

You are working at a university clinic. A 20-year old female with anorexia has contacted you about starting private music therapy sessions. She has heard that music therapy techniques can sometimes be useful in helping people overcome anorexia. So far, no other treatments she has tried have had lasting effects; she always goes back to her eating disorder behaviors. She says her life seems out of control. She enjoys music, and wonders whether music therapy could help her.

SUGGESTIONS FOR FURTHER READING

Bednarz, L. F., & Nikkel, B. (1992). The role of music therapy in the treatment of young adults diagnosed with mental illness and substance abuse. *Music Therapy Perspectives, 10*(1), 21-26.

Blake, R. L., & Bishop, S. R. (1994). The Bonny method of Guided Imagery and Music (GIM) in the treatment of post-traumatic stress disorder (PTSD) with adults in the psychiatric setting. *Music Therapy Perspectives, 12*(2), 125-129.

Braswell, C. E. (1968). Part IX. Development of music therapy in the community. In E. T. Gaston (Ed.). *Music in therapy* (pp. 345-406). New York: Macmillan.

Bruscia, K. E. (Ed.) (1991). *Case studies in music therapy.* Phoenixville, PA: Barcelona Publishers.

Cassity, M. D., & Cassity, J. E. (1994). *Multimodal psychiatric music therapy for adults, adolescents, and children.* St. Louis, MO: MMB Music.

Cassity, M. D., & Cassity, J. E. (1994). Psychiatric music therapy assessment and treatment in clinical training facilities with adults, adolescents and children. *Journal of Music Therapy, 31*(1), 2-30.

Goldberg, F. S. (1989). Music psychotherapy in acute

psychiatric inpatient and private practice settings. *Music Therapy Perspectives, 6*, 40-43.

Hanser, S. B. (1984). Music group psychotherapy: An evaluation model. *Music Therapy Perspectives, 1*(4), 14-16.

James, M. R. (1988). Music therapy and alcoholism: Part II – Treatment services. *Music Therapy Perspectives, 5*, 65-68.

Justice, R. W. (1994). Music therapy interventions for people with eating disorders in an inpatient setting. *Music Therapy Perspectives, 12*(2), 104-110.

Langdon, G. S., Pearson, J., Stastny, P., & Thorning, H. (1989). The integration of music therapy into a treatment approach in the transition of adult psychiatric patients from institution to community. *Music Therapy, 8*(1), 92-107.

Nolan, P. (1983). Insight therapy: GIM in a forensic psychiatric setting. *Music Therapy, 3*, 43-51.

Nolan, P. (1989). Music as a transitional object in the treatment of bulimia. *Music Therapy Perspectives, 6*, 49-51.

Nowicki, A. L., & Trevisan, L. A. (1978). *Beyond the sound: A technical and philosophical approach to music therapy* (Rev. Ed.). Porterville & Santa Barbara, CA; Nowicki/Trevisan.

Parente, A. B. (1989). Feeding the hungry soul: Music as therapeutic modality in the treatment of anorexia nervosa. *Music Therapy Perspectives, 6*, 44-48.

Plach, T. (1980). *The creative use of music in group therapy*. Springfield, IL: Charles C Thomas.

Rubin, B. J. (1975). Music therapy in a community mental health program. *Journal of Music Therapy, 12*(2), 59-66.

Schulberg, C. H. (1981). *The music therapy sourcebook: A collection of activities catagorized and analyzed*. New York: Human Sciences Press.

Skaggs, R. (1997). *Finishing strong: Treating chemical addictions with music and imagery*. St. Louis, MO: MMB Music.

Standley, J. (1991). *Music techniques in therapy, counseling, and special education*. St. Louis: MMB Music.

Taylor, D. B. (1997). *Biomedical foundations of music as therapy*. St. Louis: MMB Music.

Thaut, M. H. (1987). A new challenge for music therapy: The correctional setting. *Music Therapy Perspectives, 4*, 44-50.

Thaut, M. H. (1992). Music therapy in correctional psychiatry. In W. B. Davis, K. E. Gfeller, & M. H. Thaut, *An introduction to music therapy: Theory and practice* (pp. 273-284). Dubuque, IA: Wm. C. Brown.

Thaut, M. H., & Gfeller, K. E. (1992). Music therapy in the treatment of mental disorders. In W. B. Davis, K. E. Gfeller, & M. H. Thaut, *An introduction to music therapy: Theory and practice* (pp. 93-132). Dubuque, IA: Wm. C. Brown.

Treder-Wolff, J. (1990). Affecting attitudes: Music therapy in addictions treatment. *Music Therapy Perspectives, 8*, 67-71.

Tyson, F. (1981). *Psychiatric music therapy: Origins and development*. New York: Fred Weidner & Sons.

Unkefer, R. F. (1968). Part V. Music therapy for adults with behavior disorders. In E. T. Gaston (Ed.), *Music in therapy* (pp. 229-267). New York: Macmillan.

Unkefer, R. F. (Ed.). (1990). *Music therapy in the treatment of adults with mental disorders*. New York: Schirmer.

Wheeler, B. L. (1987). Levels of therapy: The classification of music therapy goals. *Music Therapy, 6*(2), 39-49.

Wolfe, D. E. (1996). Group music therapy in acute mental health care: Meeting the demands of effectiveness. In C. E. Furman (Ed.), *Effectiveness of music therapy procedures: Documentation of research and clinical practice* (2nd ed.) (pp. 106-143). Silver Spring, MD: National Association for Music Therapy.

Wolfgram, B. J. (1980). *Songs of life*. Sherman Oaks, CA: Alfred Publishing.

Chapter Sixteen

MUSIC THERAPY FOR INDIVIDUALS WHO HAVE SEVERE, MULTIPLE DISABILITIES

DEFINITION

INDIVIDUALS WHO are *multiply disabled* or *multiply handicapped* have two or more conditions that seriously interfere with functioning and learning (Nocera, 1979; Pfeifer, 1982, 1989). This term does not specify the *type* of disability, but only refers to the *number* of disabilities that impact a person's functioning. For example, one individual with multiple disabilities may be blind and have mental retardation, while another may have cerebral palsy, mental retardation, speech impairments, and visual impairments. Still another individual with multiple disabilities may have severe emotional disturbances, neuromuscular difficulties, and a seizure disorder, while a fourth may be nonambulatory, nonverbal, and have a chronic medical condition. Yet another individual with multiple disabilities may be hemiplegic and have expressive aphasia.

Individuals in programs for the multiply disabled frequently have disabilities that are very severe and pervasive. *Severe disabilities* impair an individual's ability to function to such an extent that the individual needs a high level of supports in many adaptive skill areas (AAMR, 1992; APA, 1994; Farnan, 1996). Other terms or labels frequently used to describe these individuals include *multi-handicapped, severely/profoundly handicapped (SPH), severely* or *multiply impaired,* and *severely disabled.*

CAUSES

Many individuals who have severe and multiple disabilities are born with these problems. Disabilities may arise from a variety of causes, such as genetic abnormalities, abnormal fetal development, prenatal trauma or injury, lack of oxygen at birth, or injuries during delivery. Other individuals acquire severe and multiple disabilities later in life as the result of diseases, accidents, brain or spinal cord injuries, or strokes. More information on the causes of a particular disability can be found in the chapter in this text that deals with clients having that specific disability.

COMMON CHARACTERISTICS, PROBLEMS, AND NEEDS OF CLIENTS

As with any population, those individuals who have severe multiple disabilities are a very heterogeneous group. Rarely do any two clients have the exact same combination of disabilities with the exact same degree of impairments. In addition, any individual client will have a unique combination of abilities, needs, personality traits, strengths, and weaknesses that will impact his or her treatment program and functioning level. Therefore, individual assessment is essential in determining the unique learning needs and capabilities of a particular client, and it is unwise to attempt to predict a particular person's skill levels or ceiling of abilities based on broad generalizations about a certain population. However, an awareness of some of those characteristics, problems, and needs which may be common to many clients who have severe multiple disabilities will be beneficial both to the therapist who desires to work with this population and to the reader who is trying to understand how music therapy intervention strategies may benefit this population.

Individuals with multiple disabilities often have severe numerous physical, mental, and/or social/emotional problems and delays which cause them to need a high degree of support services (AAMR, 1992; APA, 1994; Atterbury, 1990; Codding, 1988; Coleman, 1996; Farnan, 1996; Haring & Brown, 1976, cited in Pfeifer, 1982; Nocera, 1979). Many have low levels of environmental awareness and limited abilities to respond to the people and objects around them. Some individuals may engage in self-stimulatory and/or self-abusive behaviors. Individuals with severe multiple disabilities frequently lack basic skills in many areas and often have some degree of mental retardation. They may take a longer time to process and respond to information and directions, and their responses may be more subtle. Many have impaired motor control and coordination abilities; some have very limited mobility or are completely nonambulatory. Many of the most severely impaired individuals have few if any functional movements. Some cannot sit independently and need to be positioned in adaptive equipment.

Individuals who have multiple handicaps may have visual or hearing impairments or be very tactilely defensive. Many have some degree of speech or language impairment, and the more severely impaired are frequently nonverbal. They may be able to make some sounds, but, in most cases, speech never develops. Some may be able to communicate with simple sign language, assistive technology, or communication boards (see Chapter Twelve), but others are totally unable to communicate and must rely on others to anticipate their needs. Some individuals have complex medical needs and chronic medical conditions. They may have tracheotomies that enable them to breathe, be tube-fed, and/or experience seizures (which may or may not be able to be controlled by medication). Many lack basic self-skills (e.g., feeding, dressing, toileting) and are unable to protect themselves from common physical dangers. Most individuals who have severe multiple disabilities need constant care and supervision. Educational and therapeutic programs for these individuals often emphasize areas such as sensory stimulation, increasing functional motor, communication, and social skills, and learning basic self-help and survival skills.

It is important to remember that individuals with multiple disabilities do have *some* areas of strength and ability that can be nurtured and developed, even if these may seem to be hidden or masked by the severity of the individual's impairments. Whatever the degree or number of their impairments, all individuals also have basic human needs and longings to respond to and communicate with others, to love and to be loved. Although responses may be small (e.g., a change in breathing pattern, eyes widening slightly, a slight turn of a head, a small movement of a finger), *they are responses* that can be developed and expanded with patient work and guidance. More than one disability does not make an individual incapable of developing *some* level of functional skills and responses in *some* area of his or her life. Although a client with multiple disabilities might not make great gains in skill development, "the therapist is always about the business of helping the client to do his or her best, with hopes of always moving in the right direction" (Pfeifer, 1989, p. 60).

SETTINGS FOR SERVICE DELIVERY

Individuals who have severe multiple disabilities may receive special programs and services to help meet their specific needs in a variety of settings, depending on the nature and severity of their impairments, their age, and the types of programs and services in their community. Many infants and school-age children and adolescents receive services from special education programs administered their local public school system. The Individuals with Disabilities Act (IDEA) (Public Law 101-476), the 1990 revision of the 1975 Education for All Handicapped Children Act (Public Law 94-142) assures a free, appropriate public education to all children, ages 3-21, including those who have severe multiple disabilities. This law and the Technology-Related Assistance for Individuals with Disabilities Act (Public Law 100-407) also provide for assistive technology devices and services that may be needed by the individual (Adamek, 1996; Johnson, 1996). Incentives for early intervention programs to address the needs children birth through age 2 who have handicaps or disabilities are provided by Public Law 99-457 of 1986 (Adamek, 1996; Humpal, 1990).

Young children (ages 0-3) with multiple disabilities may receive services from early intervention programs in their homes, at day care centers, at special clinics, or at early intervention centers. From ages 3-21, individuals who have severe multiple disabilities often receive public school special education services "in segregated special schools, self-contained special education classrooms on age appropriate campuses, or in fully inclusive placements in their home school" (Coleman, 1996, p. 142). Special education services for children who have multiple disabilities are delivered according to the same general procedure outlined in Chapter Seven. After initial referral, assessment and identification of the disability, Individualized Educational Programs (IEPs) are written to guide instruction. IEPs set educational/habilitative goals that reflect the individual's specific strengths and weakness. IEPs also provide for appropriate support services in areas of need, placement in the least restrictive environment, and an annual evaluation of student progress in the program. When assessment finds that music therapy can provide a unique means of helping students achieve their educational objectives, music therapists may be called upon to provide traditional direct services, work with students in self-contained classes, work with students in inclusive classes, provide direct in-home services to students who are confined to their homes for medical reasons, provide consultation services to facilitate classroom instruc-

tion, inclusion, or music education, and/or provide staff development workshops (Wilson, 1996). Music therapy is usually classified as a related service in special education settings.

Some individuals with multiple handicaps receive services in other settings, including residential treatment settings, day programs in public or private centers for individuals with developmental disabilities, cerebral palsy, or physical handicaps, group homes, rehabilitation centers, and nursing homes. With the push for deinstitutionalization that began in the late 1970s, the population of residential centers has steadily declined as more community placement options have become available. As Farnan (1996) observed:

> Where in the past, a person with mild cerebral palsy, spina bifida, mild to moderate retardation, ambulation abilities, and no severe medical problems may have been admitted to a residential facility, only the person with the most profoundly medically fragile conditions (nonambulatory, profound retardation, failure to thrive, severe osteoporosis, and severe respiratory conditions including tracheotomies, etc.) will now be admitted. (pp. 114-115)

As individuals grow older, placement options often grow more limited, and appropriate settings for service delivery may be harder to find. However, as public awareness of the need increases, more community placement options may gradually become available. Those who acquire severe multiple disabilities later in life as the result of diseases, accidents, brain or spinal cord injuries, or strokes often receive services in rehabilitation or nursing home settings. More information on these settings is given in Chapters Eighteen and Nineteen.

Music therapists may work with both children and adults who have severe multiple disabilities. They deliver services to these clients in many different settings, including the client's home, public schools, private schools or clinics, centers for individuals with developmental disabilities, cerebral palsy, or physical handicaps, public and private residential facilities, group homes, private studios, nursing homes, rehabilitation centers, or community programs. Music therapists may provide direct or consultant services and work with clients as individuals or in groups. In a recent survey of populations served by music therapists, 401 of the 1620 music therapists responding said they worked with individuals who were multiply disabled (AMTA, 1998).

HOW MUSIC IS USED IN THERAPY

Every client has unique needs that can be addressed in music. The music "links" the therapeutic process. Music is not just entertainment; it is a means of discovering and meeting the basic needs of the child. (Pfeifer, 1989, p. 59)

Almost all individuals, even those who have severe multiple disabilities, respond positively to some form of music. Nordoff and Robbins (1977) speak of the concept of the "Music Child" – "that entity in every child which responds to musical experience, finds it meaningful and engaging, remembers music, and enjoys some form of musical expression" (p. 1). This entity often lies dormant in individuals who have severe multiple disabilities. As music therapists find that particular music, instruments, rhythm, or mode of response that attracts the individual's attention, the individual's inborn musicality begins to be awakened. Music therapists then structure music experiences to support, shape, and develop the individual's responses, thus facilitating increased awareness and perception and the development appropriate interactions and skills.

Music is a multisensory stimulus, something that heard, felt (vibrations), and seen (watching performer or instrument). Multisensory approaches are critical to work with individuals whose sensory systems are often severely impaired (Farnan, 1996). When music enters the environment, its pitch, rhythm, and/or the tactile sensation of its organized vibrations attract the individual's attention and provide that individual with a new and direct way of relating to the environment. Music can be both a stimulus for and a reinforcer of responses, motivating clients to reach out to their environment, rewarding these attempts with pleasure stimuli, and providing structures to learn and practice new skills.

Music experiences can help prepare clients for learning experiences by decreasing levels of tension, distractibility, and hypersensitivity and by positively influencing muscle tone (see Chapter Eleven).

Music also functions as a vehicle for emotional release and expression and as a means of verbal and nonverbal communication, providing opportunities for socialization and interaction with others. When music experiences are therapeutically structured, they can help individuals who have severe multiple disabilities increase environmental awareness, eye contact, attention span, awareness of self and others, functional social behaviors, functional motor skills, auditory and visual discrimination, receptive and expressive communication skills, cooperative and appropriate interactions with others, appropriate expression of emotions, basic self-help skills, or functional academic concepts (Boxill, 1985; Coleman, 1996; Cormier, 1982; Farnan, 1996; Farnan & Johnson, 1988b; Kay, 1981; Krout, 1987; Lathom, 1981a, 1981b; Lathom & Eagle, 1982; Nordoff & Robbins, 1971a, 1971b, 1977; Pfeifer, 1982).

General Approaches and Techniques

If music therapists are to work effectively with clients who have severe multiple disabilities, they must learn to (1) carefully *observe* the client, (2) *change* or *adapt* the environment, techniques, or activities, as necessary, based on the client's responses, and (3) *set realistic goals*, based on the information gathered in observing and responding to the client, that will help the client improve basic functional and adaptive skills in his or her areas of need (Pfeifer, 1982). One must also adjust expectations and realize that individuals who have severe multiple disabilities often take a very long time to develop responses or learn adaptive skills (Atterbury, 1990; Coleman, 1996). Responses may also be more subtle, and response time within activities may be longer (Farnan, 1996). As the individual continues to work on the same learning tasks over many months and years, the ability of the therapist to add slight variations to the music strategies and approaches can help maintain interest and attention, as well as promote generalization of that skill or concept. Repetition in various modes of expression also gives opportunities for different levels of participation and for introducing learning through various sensory pathways.

Music therapists who work with groups of individuals who have multiple disabilities face special challenges, for it is extremely unlikely that any two individuals will have exactly the same conditions, impairments, and needs (Atterbury, 1990; Farnan & Johnson, 1988b; Krout, 1987). However, with careful planning, music therapists can use the same activity to help different individuals work on different goals or objectives (Farnan & Johnson, 1988b; Krout, 1987). For example, the goal for one individual might be to hold his head up and look at the therapist during the "hello" song, while the goal for another individual on the same song might be to vocalize with the therapist and the goal for a third individual might be to wave "hello" at the appropriate place in the song. The key is to structure activities so each individual can participate at his or her own level of ability, while spontaneously changing and adapting the activity as necessary, based on the client's responses and/or immediate needs.

Another challenge in working with groups of individuals who have severe multiple disabilities is the "high degree of therapist involvement required to include the students in educational activities" (Krout, 1987, p. 3). Often, unless each client has their own assistant, the therapist must move from individual to individual, giving them prompts or physical assistance to participate in activities. Frequently, a group session with individuals who are severely multiply disabled may seem more like a series of individual sessions. However, the music does provide a stimulus and focal point all clients can perceive and attend to, even if the therapist is working directly with one client. Directing other group members to attend to the individual "performing" (or being assisted to perform) can help clients increase their awareness of others, sound localization, and attention span. Group members can also learn by watching others respond and be encouraged to participate themselves as they see their peers try to participate. For example, some individuals are more likely to vocalize if they are in a group and hear their peers vocalizing.

Several music therapists suggest that an effective way to plan group sessions for individuals who have severe multiple disabilities is to proceed from a general session outline (Coleman, 1996; Farnan & Johnson, 1988b; Krout, 1987). In this approach, the general progression of activities within each session is kept the same (e.g., greeting song, warm-up movement-to-music or action song, instrument play, targeted pre-academic or academic skill, singing, instrument play, movement-to-music, cool-down/session review, closing song), although the particular experience within each category may vary from session to session (e.g., use drum for instrument play one week, triangle the next). Of course, many different general session structures are possible, depending on the age of the clients, the needs and capabilities of the various individuals within the group, the time and space available, the equipment available, the particular music therapy objectives for the group members, etc. Coleman (1996), Farnan and Johnson (1988b), and Krout (1987) provide several examples of music therapy session outlines for various age and ability groups of clients with multiple disabilities.

Therapeutic Music Experiences to Increase General Awareness and Responsiveness

Many individuals who have severe multiple disabilities seem to have very little, if any, awareness of the people, objects, and events around them. Before these individuals can develop other adaptive skills, they must make some response, no matter how subtle (e.g., change in facial expression, pupils dilate or constrict, slight vocalization, increase or decrease in movement or respiration, slight movement or turning toward sound source), to the stimuli around them. "These responses indicate an awareness and basic processing of stimuli – a necessary life skill" (Farnan, 1996, p. 125). Music activities are often effective in eliciting awareness responses from these clients, even when other treatment intervention modalities have failed. Music provides a powerful sensory stimulus that is almost impossible to ignore (Lathom, 1981b) and can be adapted to allow for many different levels of response (Sears, 1968). As music is used creatively to reflect, mirror, and match the "here-and-now" of the client, and as it is used to identify and symbolize the relationship emerging between the client and therapist, an awakening of responsiveness often begins to occur. Boxill (1985) terms this "*a Continuum of Awareness*, the creative process of using music functionally as a tool of consciousness to awaken, heighten, and expand awareness of self, others, and the environment" (p. 71).

Several different types of music experiences can be useful in establishing contact with and eliciting initial responses from clients who have severe multiple disabilities. These include (1) music used in combination with intensive-play or play therapy techniques (Carter, 1982; Gonzales, 1981; Miorin & Covault, 1979; Monti, 1985), (2) music improvisations built around the client's vocal, movement, or instrumental responses (Boxill, 1985; Nordoff & Robbins, 1971b, 1977; Pfeifer, 1982), and (3) sensory stimulation experiences using the auditory and tactile input from musical instruments to attract attention and elicit responses, with gradual exposure to "hands-on" experiences with musical instruments (Cormier, 1982; Farnan, 1996; Schmidt, 1981). Positioning clients on a specially designed wooden sound floor may also help them feel the vibrations of live music and increase their responsiveness to the musical stimuli (Farnan, 1996).

Some music therapists are now having great success using electronic and high technology music resources to establish initial responses in individuals with multiple disabilities. For example, Swingler (1994) described Soundbeams, a technology that uses ultrasonic beams controlled by body movements to play electronic musical instruments at a distance without physical contact. Since the system may be set up so that tiny finger or head movements control the beams, it may be particularly useful in reaching those who have limited motions and limited abilities to respond to the world around them:

> For people, particularly children, with profound multiple disabilities . . . Soundbeam gives such a strong and rewarding experience of cause and effect and of control, that it can provide a foundation stone for learning and interaction. It is with these youngsters, who are so difficult to reach, that we have witnessed the most exciting and moving possibilities of the system. (Swingler, 1994, p. 5)

Computers, synthesizers, specially adapted switches and MIDI-input devices, and music composition software can also create new possibilities for participation and responses for individuals who have severely limited abilities, allowing them to independently control and initiate musical sounds (Krout, Burnham, & Moorman, 1993). As they learn to interact with others through these technological resources, clients develop increased eye contact, attention to task, and communication with others.

Therapeutic Music Experiences to Decrease Self-Stimulatory or Self-Abusive Behaviors

Some individuals who have severe multiple disabilities engage in various self-stimulatory or self-abusive behaviors. These can often be a barrier to appropriate interactions with the people and objects around them. Some music therapists have reported stereotypical or self-stimulatory behaviors may be decreased by joining in the behavior musically (e.g., reflecting it with improvisation) and then using musical structure to broaden the behavior into purposeful activity, as the client interrupts or modifies his or her behavior in response to the changes in the music (Nordoff & Robbins, 1977). Others have found that maladaptive and self-abuseive behaviors can be diminished or eliminated in individuals who have severe and profound mental retardation and multiple handicaps through a process known as "nurturance therapy" (Miorin & Covault, 1979). Consistency is a key to this technique; it works best used in the same location daily, with the same adult, at the same time. Three sections of music (slow, soothing section; a section of march tempo music; repeat of initial slow section), each approximately 7 minutes long, help structure the interactions between client and adult. During the session, the adult gives complete attention to the client, following the client's cues and body language to gauge the rate of introducing nonthreatening, positive interaction experiences (e.g., rhythmically stroking or patting the client's body; assisting client to rhythmically pat or stroke adult's body; stroking the client's hand to encourage close body contact, hand holding; rocking or swaying with the client in time to the music). It is theorized that the client's self-abusive and maladaptive behaviors are the result of the clients estrangement from others, and that the trusting interactions developed in the nurturance therapy process fulfill the client's basic need to develop a secure, sensitive relationship with another human being, thus causing the maladaptive behaviors to disappear or diminish. Case reports by Miorin and Covault (1979) show nurturance therapy is often effective in decreasing self-stimulatory or self-abusive behaviors in clients who have not responded to behavior modification techniques.

Since music is an attractive stimulus that catches the attention of even many individuals who have severe multiple disabilities, it can also be used effectively with behavior modification techniques, serving as a reinforcer or contingent stimulus to help clients increase eye contact, attention span, appropriate social behaviors, and awareness of people and objects in their environment, while decreasing instances of bizarre and self-abusive behaviors (Mahlberg, 1973; Saperston, 1973, 1982; Stevens and Clark, 1969). Music therapists can use active music making as well as passive music listening techniques to help individuals learn to channel and control responses. For example, Cormier (1982) reported that playing an electric piano with headset helped a nine-year-old boy who had developmental delays, vision and hearing impairments, and many autistic-like behaviors decrease his hyperactive behaviors and increase his attention span. Cormier (1982) observed: "The very act of playing at the piano provided spatial limitations so needed by J" (p. 12). In another example, Clarkson (1991) worked with a nonverbal, self-abusive, violent adult male with autism and found that, as music therapy sessions utilizing structured and improvised instrumental and vocal activities and dancing to recorded music provided appropriate outlets for self-expression, his tantrums, violent outbursts, and ritualistic behaviors markedly decreased, while his abilities to communicate and interact appropriately with others increased. Griggs-Drane and Wheeler (1997) also found that the aggressive, self-stimulatory behaviors of an adolescent female with multiple handicaps decreased during music therapy sessions. In addition, tapes with recorded music presented to the client after the session helped de-escalate the aggressive behaviors that frequently occurred when the music session was over.

Therapeutic Music Experiences to Increase Adaptive Social Responses and Promote Appropriate Social Interaction Skills

As individuals who have multiple disabilities learn to respond to and interact with adults and peers through specially structured music experiences, they can develop many basic social skills, like looking to the speaker, responding to their name, smiling to pleasurable stimuli, looking to others singing or playing instruments, and participating cooperatively in partner or group activities. In intensive play programs, a progression of prerecorded instrumental music (6 to 7 minutes of slow music, 7 to 9 minutes of fast music, 6 to 7 minutes of slow music) provides the environment and structure for movement activities involving close physical contact and stimulation that develop desired social skills like tolerating physical contact, indicating an awareness of others by smiling, vocalizing, or giving eye contact, moving cooperatively with another person, or engaging in simple imitation games. These techniques have been effective in building basic social behaviors in children with multiple disabilities and profound developmental delays who are normally unresponsive, unaware, and often fearful of physical contact and movement (Carter, 1982; Gonzales, 1981). Music may also be used with traditional play therapy approaches, using musical sounds, body percussion sounds (e.g., clapping, stamping), and exploration of musical instruments to facilitate interaction with others and the environment (Monti, 1985). The extensive range of sound possibilities available through music increase the likelihood that a sound can be found to attract the individual's attention and serve as a starting point to develop responsiveness to and interaction with others.

Music experiences can also facilitate social interactions between infants or young children with multiple disabilities and their parents or siblings. Witt and Steele (1984) described a case in which a 14-month-old girl with multiple disabilities learned to increase eye contact and positive interactions with her mother, appropriately play with rhythm instruments and sound-producing toys, and respond to her name through music therapy sessions involving both mother and child. Approaches used included singing early childhood action songs while assisting the child to participate, rhythmic experiences using a variety of instruments and sound-producing toys to attract attention and encourage interaction, and listening experiences to promote attention and eye contact. The mother would rehearse activities under the guidance of the music therapist and then continue to implement activities at home during the week, also involving other family members. The music activities gave family members a structure for interacting positively with the infant who had multiple disabilities and helped the infant develop basic social skills and responses. "The most important gain, however, was the improvement the family felt in their ability to relate to their handicapped member in a meaningful way" (Witt & Steele, 1984, p. 19).

After the individual develops basic social awareness responses in music activities, these responses can gradually be expanded through more complex and more demanding partner and group music experiences. In individual sessions, a music therapist might use improvisational music techniques to develop increased interactive responses between the client and the therapist (Boxill, 1985; Nordoff & Robbins, 1971b, 1977). For example, Shoemark (1991) used piano improvisation with a boy who was blind and had behavioral disturbances to help develop a relationship that encouraged positive interactions and cooperative participation. As the boy learned to interact spontaneously with the therapist in music making, his participation and cooperation also increased. More behaviorally oriented techniques that use music or music activities to reinforce desired social behaviors like eye contact and attention to task can also increase these responses in individual music therapy sessions (Witt & Steele, 1984). In group sessions, structured music activities involving singing, moving to music, or playing instruments with others can help individuals with multiple disabilities learn to participate and cooperate with others as they play/sing/move all together or as they wait their turn to play and learn to share with others (Coleman, 1996; Farnan, 1996; Farnan & Johnson, 1988a, 1988b; Kay, 1981; Krout, 1987; Lathom, 1981b; Lathom & Eagle, 1982; Nocera, 1979; Nordoff & Robbins, 1971a).

Music activities can be structured so individuals with wide varieties of abilities can participate simultaneously. Some may sing all the words of a song; others may vocalize on a single syllable (Krout, 1987). Some may play a complicated rhythmic or ostinato pattern; others may play one cymbal crash or a steady drum beat. With appropriate adaptations of traditional instruments (Clark & Chadwick, 1979; Coleman, 1996; Rudenberg, 1982), or with the use of electronic instruments and technological innovation, many individuals with multiple disabilities can eventually participate independently in instrumentally ensembles. New electronic and computer technology and special switches and control devices make it possible for even those clients with severe physical limitations to work together with others in music performance groups (Fegers et al., 1989). Technology also makes it possible for clients who cannot play traditional instruments to make the sounds of these instruments. For example, by using switches connected to specific electronic or computer-controlled drum sounds, clients can work together to produce the sound of a large drum set (Krout, 1995). Cooperative ensemble experiences like this help the clients focus on each other and improve their attention and sense of group as they concentrate on the sound being produced and work to play the desired sound patterns.

Music activities can also provide opportunities for individuals who have severe multiple disabilities to interact with their nondisabled peers. In some cases, individuals with disabilities may participate in ensembles with nondisabled peers (Fegers et al., 1989). In other instances, nondisabled students may function as "peer-helpers" in music classes for students who have multiple disabilities (Atterbury, 1990; Dykman, 1979). When each individual with multiple disabilities has a peer-helper, the peer-helper can help move the individual's feet or arms rhythmically, move the individual's wheelchair for wheelchair dances, and help hold instruments for the individual. As the students interact, they learn to cooperate in positive ways and develop new ways to socialize with persons who are in some ways different from them.

Therapeutic Music Experiences to Improve Motor Functioning

Many individuals who have severe multiple disabilities have limited functional motor skills. Those who are nonambulatory and immobile may need range-of-motion exercises to help them maintain or increase joint and muscle function. However, some individuals have such high muscle tone that these exercises become very difficult to perform. Music therapists can use their knowledge of the physiological effects of different types of music on muscle tone (see Chapter Eleven) to provide background music that will help reduce the client's muscle tone and facilitate responses to range of motion exercises (Schmidt, 1981). Action and body-part songs can also provide structure for movement exercises. As individuals are given assistance to participate in these movement-to-music experiences, they can be guided through normal movement patterns and increase their awareness of body position and body parts (Matteson, 1972).

In addition to facilitating appropriate muscle tone, musical stimuli may provide the incentive or motivation for clients to maintain proper posture or positioning. Wolfe (1980) used an operant conditioning procedure involving contingent music listening to help individuals with cerebral palsy increase their ability to maintain an upright head position. Krout (1987) found that the desire to participate in music activities could also help an individual who had multiple handicaps and poor head control learn to keep his head upright for longer periods of time. In addition, individuals who need to adjust to new positioning equipment may learn to tolerate it more readily in the music therapy situation, where they are distracted from the pain or the restrictions of the equipment by their interest in the music activity.

Musical stimuli, particularly the sounds of musical instruments, may also motivate clients to increase their purposeful active movements (Farnan & Johnson, 1988b; Schmidt, 1981; Witt & Steele, 1984). As the individual's attention is attracted by the sound, the individual will look to the sound, and then gradually reach toward it. At first, individuals may need assistance to reach out to touch and feel instruments (Farnan, 1996; Schmidt, 1981), but as their tolerance for tactile stimulation and their abilities to direct their movements increase, this guidance can gradually be faded.

Playing basic rhythm instruments can help individuals develop many functional hand skills, such as reaching, touching, grasping, holding, manipulating, and releasing (Farnan & Johnson, 1988b). However, some individuals who have multiple disabilities, especially those who are very tactilely defensive and who startle or seizure to the slightest touch, may need very gradual exposure to "hands-on" experiences with instruments over the course of many months. Still, with patience and carefully structured experiences (first listening, then being close enough to feel the vibrations, then being assisted to touch and play the instrument, and finally, perhaps, reaching out to play it themselves), most individuals are eventually able to tolerate touching and playing instruments. For example, as Schmidt (1981) reported, "a girl who used to seizure when the guitar was strummed within one foot of her body now, after 14 months, tolerates having her own hand used to strum the guitar for two to three minutes with no seizure activity" (p. 24).

Movement-to-music activities can also be very beneficial in helping individuals who have severe multiple disabilities increase their motor control and coordination and their sense of body image and awareness of self in space (Boswell & Vidret, 1993; Farnan & Johnson, 1988a, 1988b; Lathom, 1981b; Lathom & Eagle, 1982). Programs may include passive movements to music, active rhythmic movements to music, action songs and movement imitation songs or dances, songs or movement-to-music experiences that direct clients to move particular body parts or move their whole bodies in certain ways, creative movement responses to music, and relaxation exercises to music. (For more information on these types of experiences, see Chapter Eleven.)

Therapeutic Music Experiences to Facilitate Personal Expression

The opportunities for self-expression available in music experiences can be very important to those individuals whose severe multiple disabilities result in them having very limited means of personal expression. As individuals learn to make choices (e.g., choose an instrument to play, choose a note or word to fit in a song) and express preferences (e.g., for instruments, particular songs, types of music), they develop functional skills needed for a more independent life (Farnan, 1996). Even those who are nonverbal can find ways to express themselves in music. For example, individuals who use communication boards may respond to questions or contribute to song writing exercises by using their boards. Herman (1985) worked with children who used Blissymbols and had them point to symbols to identify feelings represented by music, contribute to group "story songs," or tell what feelings they wanted to express. As mentioned in Chapter Nine, signing and manual communication systems can be used to express song lyrics, and signs and singing can be used together for total communication experiences (Darrow, 1987a; Knapp, 1980). Technology now even makes it possible for individuals who are nonverbal to have an active "voice" in many music experiences (Humpal & Dimmick, 1995). For example, switches may activate tape players containing tape loops of repeated words or phrases in a song (Coleman, 1996; Humpal & Dimmick, 1995). Individuals who have augmentive communication devices that produce synthesized speech sounds may use these to supply words or phrases to songs or contribute to discussions or group compositions.

Music experiences also help stimulate emotional responses and develop appropriate means of emotional expression. At a basic level, emotional responses are developed as individuals indicate excitement, pleasure, or other emotions as the result of musical stimuli (Pfeifer, 1982). Emotional responsiveness is further demonstrated when individuals respond by synchronizing their instrument playing to match the tempo and dynamic changes of the therapist's improvisation (Nordoff & Robbins, 1971a, 1977; Pfeifer, 1982; Shoemark, 1991). This ability to participate freely in expressive musical activities can also positively influence general emotional state. For example, Shoemark (1991) noted that as a boy with multiple disabilities developed communicative responsiveness and spontaneous creativity in his piano improvisations with the music therapist, his positive affect and mood also increased. In addition, expressive music experiences (e.g., singing, playing the drum) can be a means of venting and releasing one's innermost feelings (Pfeifer, 1982), something that can be very important to clients who have limited means of personal expression.

As they sing or vocalize, move creatively to music, play instruments, create songs or improvisations, or choose songs that tell something about themselves or their feelings, individuals who have severe multiple disabilities gain new and appropriate avenues for self-expression. Participation can be encouraged at

each individual's level of ability (Krout, 1987). For example, verbal individuals may be encouraged to sing song lyrics, those who use sign may be encouraged to sign lyrics, and nonverbal individuals may be prompted to vocalize on "ah." With appropriate adaptations, many individuals can eventually learn to play some instruments independently (Birkenshaw-Fleming, 1993; Clark & Chadwick, 1979; Coleman, 1996; Edelstein, 1987, 1989; Elliott, 1982; Rudenberg, 1982; Zinar, 1987) and use them to express feelings and emotions. Recent advances in technology now allow even individuals who have severe physical limitations increased opportunities to create music independently through the use of computers and adaptive electronic equipment (Fegers et al., 1989; Howell et al., 1995; Krout, 1992, 1995; Krout, Burnham, & Moorman, 1993; Nagler & Lee, 1989; Swingler, 1994). With these technological tools,

A whole range of people, for whom the possibility of making any kind of musical performance would have been regarded as remote if not downright inconceivable, have discovered that the development of creative musical expression and performance is now entirely possible for them. (Swingler, 1994, p. 5)

Therapeutic Music Experiences to Develop Functional Academic and Life Skills

Once individuals who have severe multiple disabilities develop basic awareness of and attention to music experiences, music therapy activities can be structured to help these individuals gradually progress through higher levels of awareness and increase their basic academic and functional life skills (Coleman, 1996; Farnan, 1996; Kay, 1981; Krout, 1987; Pfeifer, 1982). Individuals may learn to follow directions and improve their imitation skills as they participate in action songs and musical games that require them to respond to verbal directions or imitate one-step and two-step sequences. Colors, numbers, shapes, and spatial concepts can be learned and practiced in structured music activities using songs, movement-to-music, or musical instruments. Music experiences can also be structured to improve skills in making choices, matching, and sorting. In addition, individuals who have multiple disabilities can often learn and practice the sequence of steps for specific life skills (e.g., spreading peanut butter on a cracker or brushing teeth) more easily when these steps are set to song lyrics (Griggs-Drane & Wheeler, 1997). Music can also establish an environment that makes it easier for individuals with multiple disabilities to acquire life skills. For example, when individuals with multiple disabilities received feeding training in a music-controlled environment, they remained calmer and more attentive (Ayres, 1987). In addition, the trainers said they felt more patient and tolerant when the background music was used.

SPECIAL CONSIDERATIONS AND TIPS FOR SUCCESS

Even though the clients discussed in this chapter often have severe and numerous physical, mental, and/or social/emotional problems and delays, they still deserve to be treated with dignity and respect. Therapists should talk to them as they would talk to any person of their age. Selections of music and music materials should also be as age-appropriate as possible. Even if the therapist does not think the client can understand, the therapist should still explain what she or he is doing and wants the client to do. Short, concrete statements should be used, with gestures and tone of voice helping to convey the message. Music therapists should describe what the clients are seeing, hearing, and feeling to help them label their experiences. It is also important to use many kinds of sensory experiences and multi-sensory stimulation.

Since individuals with multiple disabilities often take longer to process the information and make a response, therapists must be sure they wait long enough for the individual to respond. Music therapists who work with clients who have severe multiple disabilities often need to "fine tune" their observation skills, so that they become aware of very subtle responses, like a slight change in the client's breathing pattern or a widening of the eyes to a certain musical stimulus. Since these individuals often take many months or even years to learn and develop skills and responses, it is important to work on skills that will be functional for the individual in the long term. Therapists must be prepared to repeat the same information in many different ways to give clients opportunities to learn and practice skills. "Creative repetition is the key with this population" (Coleman, 1996, p. 155).

Because individuals with multiple disabilities often have very limited motor skills, instruments or materials frequently must be adapted so clients can participate as independently as possible (Clark & Chadwick, 1979; Coleman, 1996). When physically assisting instrument play or movement, the therapist should let individuals do as much independently as they can. For example, even though individuals may not be able to play tambourine independently, they may be able to move their hands or fingers to tap the tambourine when the therapist supports and guides their movement at the wrist or elbow and holds the tambourine in front of them. In some instances, computers, electronic instruments, and adaptive switches and control devices can enable even individuals with very severe multiple handicaps to control musical sounds and make music independently (Fegers et al., 1989; Krout, 1992, 1995; Krout, Burnham, & Moorman, 1993; Swingler, 1994).

Any of the special considerations mentioned for specific disabilities also apply when an individual has that condition in combination with some other impairment. In addition, many of the music therapy intervention strategies listed for individuals who have severe developmental disabilities (see Chapter Seven), those who have autism (see Chapter Thirteen), and those who have severe motor limitations (see Chapter Eleven) are also often useful and effective with individuals who have multiple disabilities. Since many individuals with multiple disabilities may have complex medical needs and conditions, "the music therapist practicing in this type of setting must have knowledge of infection control practices, emergency procedures, child development, education, and rehabilitation" (Farnan, 1996, p. 114).

In order to coordinate their treatment approach with that of other treatment team members, music therapists who work with individuals who have multiple disabilities must become familiar with the various theories and practices associated with abnormal/normal development, alternative communication, sensory integration, and neuro-developmental treatment and learn to incorporate those theories and techniques used by the other professionals in their facility into music therapy treatment programs (F. Johnson, 1981). Music therapists must also become aware of the methods of observation and assessment that are useful and

appropriate for work with multiply handicapped clients (F. Johnson, 1981). In addition, music therapists should also learn which methods of observation, assessment, and data collection are most useful and appropriate for individuals who have severe multiple disabilities and find ways of individualizing treatment within group settings (Coleman, 1996; Farnan, 1996; Farnan & Johnson, 1988b; F. Johnson, 1981; Krout, 1987; Pfeifer, 1982, 1989).

SUMMARY

Individuals who are *multiply disabled* or *multiply handicapped* have two or more conditions that seriously interfere with functioning and learning. This term does not specify the *type* of disability, but only refers to the *number* of disabilities that impact a person's functioning. Individuals who are multiply disabled frequently have severe and pervasive disabilities that impair functioning to such an extent that the individuals need high levels of support in many adaptive skill areas.

While individuals with severe multiple disabilities frequently lack basic skills in many areas, have low levels of environmental awareness, and have limited abilities to respond to the people and objects around them, it is important to remember that even these individuals are unique human beings who have some area of responsiveness, strength, or ability that can be nurtured, developed and, expanded with patient work and guidance. More than one disability does *not* make an individual incapable of developing *some* level of functional skills and responses in *some* area of his or her life. Although a client with multiple disabilities might not make great gains in skill development, "the therapist is always about the business of helping the client to do his or her best, with hopes of always moving in the right direction" (Pfeifer, 1989, p. 60).

Almost all individuals, even those who have severe multiple disabilities, respond positively to some form of music. As music therapists find that particular music, instruments, rhythm, or mode of response that attracts the individual's attention, the individual's inborn musicality begins to be awakened. As the individual's responses are

supported, shaped, and developed by the music therapist, awareness and perception is increased, and purposeful, appropriate interactions and skills develop. When music experiences are therapeutically structured, they can help individuals who have severe multiple disabilities increase environmental awareness, eye contact, and attention span, decrease self-stimulatory and self-abusive behaviors, increase awareness of self and others, facilitate adaptive social responses, increase cooperative and appropriate interactions with others, improve functional motor skills, facilitate functional communication and emotional expression, and help develop basic self-help skills and functional academic concepts.

If music therapists are to work effectively with clients who have multiple disabilities, they must learn to (1) carefully *observe* the client, (2) *change* or *adapt* the environment, techniques, or activities, as necessary, based on the client's responses, and (3) *set realistic goals*, based on the information gathered in observing and responding to the client, that will help the client improve basic functional and adaptive skills in his or her areas of need. Music therapists must also adjust their expectations and realize that individuals who have severe multiple disabilities often take a very long time to develop responses or learn adaptive skills. These individuals may also need a longer time to process information and respond within activities, and their responses may be very subtle (e.g., slight turning toward sound source, small change in facial expression, respiration rate increasing or decreasing slightly).

Because individuals with multiple disabilities often

have very limited motor skills and communication abilities, instruments, materials, and approaches frequently must be adapted so clients can participate as independently as possible. Computers, synthesizers, specially adapted switches and MIDI-input devices, and music composition software can also create new possibilities for participation and responses for individuals who have limited abilities, allowing them to independently control and initiate musical sounds.

QUESTIONS FOR THOUGHT AND DISCUSSION

1. Describe some of the general characteristics and needs of individuals who have severe multiple disabilities. What implications do these have for music therapy programming?

2. Why and how are music experiences useful in making contact with individuals who have severe multiple disabilities? Are some types of experiences and activities more useful than other? Which ones? Why?

3. Describe some specific music therapy experiences that might be used to help individuals who have severe multiple disabilities (a) increase general awareness and responsiveness, (b) decrease self-stimulatory or self-abusive behaviors, (c) increase adaptive social responses and promote appropriate social interaction skills, (d) improve motor functioning, (e) facilitate personal expression, and (f) develop functional academic and life skills. What unique benefits does music provide in each of these areas?

4. List several special considerations that may be important to remember when developing therapeutic intervention strategies for persons who have severe multiple disabilities. Why are these important? What are their implications for the structure of music therapy intervention strategies?

5. For each of the situations listed below, (a) define the problem or areas of need for the client or group of clients, (b) describe one or more of the goals you might pursue in music therapy sessions with the client(s), (c) describe music activities you might use to help the client(s) meet those goals, (d) tell how the music activities you described relate to the goals and needs of the client(s), and (e) mention any special considerations you might want to take into account when working with the client(s).

Situation 1:

Sue is a 19 year-old female who is non-ambulatory and has cerebral palsy, spastic quadriplegia, and severe mental retardation. She has flexion contractures at her elbows, hips, and knees, severe scoliosis, and very limited movement in her arms and legs. She sometimes can grasp and hold objects that are placed in her hands and occasionally uses her hands to slowly push objects placed on her wheelchair tray. However, these movements are too slow and limited to be of much functional use. Sue's most consistent and controlled movements are with her head, and the occupational therapist is teaching her to use a headstick and a switch controlled by head movements.

Sue is nonverbal, but she does answer yes-no questions with eye movements (eyes up-down = "yes"; eyes side to side = "no"). She has a receptive vocabulary approximating that of a 4-year-old child, and can identify most letters of the alphabet, numbers 1-10, and basic colors. She eye-points to communicate with her language board, which contains about 20 pictures and symbols for familiar people, food, objects, places, and feelings. Sue is a very social person, but has difficulty interacting with others because of her physical and speech limitations.

Sue enjoys music. She often smiles and turns toward the tape player or radio when music is playing. When Sue sees staff or ambulatory peers moving and dancing to music, she tries to move her arms and legs, too. Sue also tries to use what limited movement she has in her arms and hands to play musical instruments. With much concentrated effort, Sue can slowly draw her fingers across the strings of a guitar or autoharp held in front of her or ring bells suspended from a line or bar.

Situation 2:

You have been asked to provide music therapy services for a group of six children and adolescents who have multiple disabilities and who range in age from 7-16 years old. All are nonverbal and nonambulatory and have severe to profound mental retardation along with numerous medical and physical difficulties. Four have spastic quadriplegia and many muscle contractures; two have floppy muscle tone and some jerky athetoid movements. All have few if any functional movements; they are completely dependent on others to meet their needs. Three are tube-fed; two have tracheotomies. All have short attention spans, limited awareness of or interest in their environment, and limited abilities to respond to and interact with others. Staff members have noticed some slight changes in behavior, affect, and muscle tone when different types of music are played in the room, but these responses are currently inconsistent and unpredictable.

SUGGESTIONS FOR FURTHER READING

Alvin, J. (1976). *Music for the handicapped child* (2nd ed.). London: Oxford University Press.

Atterbury, B. W. (1990). *Mainstreaming exceptional learners in music.* Englewood Cliffs, NJ: Prentice-Hall.

Birkenshaw-Fleming, L. (1993). *Music for all: Teaching music to people with special needs.* Toronto: Gordon V. Thompson.

Boxill, E. H. (1985). *Music therapy for the developmentally disabled.* Rockville, MD: Aspen Systems.

Bruscia, K. E. (Ed.) (1991). *Case studies in music therapy.* Phoenixville, PA: Barcelona Publishers.

Clark, C., & Chadwick, D. (1979). *Clinically adapted instruments for the multiply handicapped.* Westford, MA: Modulations.

Coleman, K. A. (1996). Music therapy for learners with severe disabilities in a public schooliisetting. In B. L. Wilson (Ed.), *Models of music therapy interventions in iischool settings: From institution to inclusion* (pp. 142-155). Silver Spring, MD: National Association for Music Therapy.

Cormier, Sr. L. (1982). *Music therapy for handicapped children: Deaf-blind.* Washington, D.C.: National Association for Music Therapy.

Farnan, L. (1996). Music therapy for learners with severe disabilities in a residential setting. In B. L. Wilson (Ed.), *Models of music therapy interventions in school settings: From institution to inclusion* (pp. 113-126). Silver Spring, MD: National Association for Music Therapy.

Farnan, L., & Johnson, F. (1988). *Everyone can move: Music and activities that promote movement and motor development.* New Berlin, WI: Jenson Publications.

Farnan, L., & Johnson, F. (1988). *Music is for everyone: A handbook for providing music to people with special needs.* New Berlin, WI: Jenson Publications.

Krout, R. (1987). Music therapy with multi-handicapped students: Individualizing treatment within a group setting. *Journal of Music Therapy, 24*(1), 2-13.

Monti, R. (1985). Music therapy in a therapeutic nursery. *Music Therapy, 5*(1), 22-27.

Nagler, J. C., & Lee, M. H. M. (1989). Music therapy using computer music technology. In M. H. M. Lee (Ed.), *Rehabilitation, music and human well-being* (pp. 226-241). St. Louis: MMB Music.

Nocera, S. D. (1979). *Reaching the special learner through music.* Morristown, NJ: Silver Burdett.

Nordoff, P., & Robbins, C. (1971). *Music therapy in special education.* New York: John Day.

Nordoff, P., & Robbins, C. (1971). *Therapy in music for handicapped children.* London: Victor Gollancz Ltd.

Nordoff, P., & Robbins, C. (1977). *Creative music therapy.* New York: John Day.

Pfeifer, Sr. M. (1982). *Music therapy for handicapped children: Multi-handicapped.* Washington, D.C.: National Association for Music Therapy.

Pfeifer, Sr. M. (1989). A step in the right direction: Suggested strategies for implementing music therapy with the multihandicapped child. *Music Therapy Perspectives, 6,* 57-60.

Standley, J. (1991). *Music techniques in therapy, counseling, and special education.* St. Louis: MMB Music.

Zinar, R. (1987). *Music activities for special children.* West Nyack, NY: Parker Publishing.

Chapter Seventeen

MUSIC THERAPY IN MEDICAL TREATMENT SETTINGS

DEFINITION

MEDICAL TREATMENT involves the process of diagnosing and prescribing measures to cure or alleviate illness, disease, injury, or pain, and the science and art of preventing diseases and improving and preserving health. Individuals may seek or require medical treatment for a variety of acute or chronic conditions, injuries, diseases, or life events (e.g., labor and delivery) that impact their daily functioning. Medical treatment may be long term or short term and be given in a variety of settings, depending on the exact nature of the condition, injury, or disease and the particular needs and life situation of the individual patient. Some treatments may involve hospitalization, surgery, or specific medical procedures (e.g., injections, lumbar punctures, bone marrow aspirations, debridement, cardiac catheterization, dialysis, chemotherapy). Treatment may also include various types of medication or life style changes.

Conditions that cause acute or chronic health problems include heart disease, pulmonary (lung) disease, kidney disease, severe burns, broken bones, severe infections, cystic fibrosis, severe allergies, asthma, hemophilia, sickle cell anemia, leukemia, cancer, diabetes, or epilepsy. This chapter deals mainly with those conditions that are treated in general hospital, outpatient, office, or clinic settings. Conditions such as traumatic brain injuries, spinal cord injuries, or strokes that are treated in rehabilitation settings are discussed in Chapter Eighteen, while the treatment of individuals who are terminally ill is covered in Chapter Twenty. The treatment of individuals who have medical conditions that result in orthopedic impairments was discussed in Chapter Eleven. Wellness programs are described in Chapter Twenty-one.

COMMON CHARACTERISTICS, PROBLEMS, AND NEEDS OF CLIENTS

The population of individuals who are treated in medical settings is extremely diverse (Gfeller, 1992c; Maranto, 1991, 1996; Standley, 1986, 1996b). Clients or patients vary in age (newborns to elderly), diagnosis or condition, type or intensity of treatment needed, urgency of treatment (emergency to planned surgery or procedure; acute vs. chronic conditions; wellness programs vs. disease treatment), state of general health, and types of support available. Individuals also have different prognoses, different durations of treatment or hospitalization, and different responses to their illness or treatment. In addition, each disease or condition presents its own unique set of problems and challenges. In spite of this great diversity, some general physical and psychosocial needs that are common to many individuals undergoing medical treatment or experiencing acute or chronic illnesses can be identified (Gfeller, 1992c; Hurley, 1987; Purtilo, 1978; Schwankovsky & Guthrie, 1982).

Since many conditions or medical procedures are painful to some degree, one of the most common *physical needs* of many patients is finding a way to deal with, reduce, increase their tolerance for, or decrease their perception of pain (Gfeller, 1992c; Spintge, 1989). Patients who have conditions that are exacerbated by stress or who are experiencing extreme stress because they must learn to deal with chronic illnesses or with a change in life style may also need to learn effective relaxation and stress reduction techniques.

No matter what their particular medical condition, patients are often anxious about treatment procedures, anesthesia, impending hospitalizations (Spintge, 1989), or changes their illness or condition may bring to their lives. Therefore, a common *psychosocial need* is anxiety reduction. Severe illnesses or accidents may also cause an individual to experience several losses: loss of former self-image, loss of independence (at least for a time), and, if hospitalization is required, loss of home and privacy (Purtilo, 1978). Consequently, many patients need emotional and psychological support to help rebuild self-esteem and facilitate their adaptation to the

treatment procedures or the revised life style that may be mandated (temporarily or permanently) by their condition. Persons who are chronically ill, in addition to needing good medical care, also need comprehensive social and psychological services to help them deal with the daily complications and difficult circumstances that accompany many chronic conditions (Hurley, 1987). Other common psychosocial needs of individuals who need treatment for acute or chronic medical conditions include (1) learning to adapt to the illness and the limitations it imposes, (2) helping other members of the family adjust to the illness, (3) dealing with the stresses and confinements of hospitalization, (4) learning and using age-appropriate coping strategies and defense mechanisms, (5) decreasing fear and anxiety, (6) normalizing the environment as much as possible, (7) finding ways to continue school, work, and/or social contacts, (8) preventing or remediating developmental delays or regressive behavior patterns, (9) finding ways to return to normal physical activity and daily routines to the fullest possible extent, and (10) facing issues of one's own mortality (Schwankovsky & Guthrie, 1982).

SETTINGS FOR SERVICE DELIVERY

Individuals who have acute or chronic medical conditions may receive treatments and services to help meet their specific needs in a variety of settings, depending on factors such as their age and the exact nature and severity of their condition. These include hospitals, outpatient facilities, clinics, doctors' offices, or home health care programs. School-age children who have chronic health impairments may receive services from special education programs administered by their local school system. In these cases, health-related services necessary for the child to participate in his or her educational program are specified in the child's Individualized Educational Plan (IEP).

In medical settings, music therapists serve individuals of all ages who have a variety of acute or chronic medical conditions. Music therapists carry out their interventions in a variety of settings, including general hospitals, children's hospitals, clinics, outpatient facilities, hospice programs, wellness programs, home health agencies, childbirth

education programs, performing arts medicine programs, and special education settings (AMTA, 1998; Gfeller, 1992c; Maranto, 1991, 1996; Schwankovsky & Guthrie, 1982; Standley, 1996b). Music therapy interventions can complement and facilitate medical treatment in areas such as labor and delivery, neonatal care, pediatrics, coronary intensive care, pulmonology, surgery, anesthesia, pain control, radiology, oncology, burn units, specific medical procedures (e.g., laceration repair, lumbar punctures, kidney dialysis, bone marrow transplants, debridement, dressing changes, cardiac catheterization, bronchoscopy), or specific chronic medical conditions (e.g., asthma, cystic fibrosis, diabetes, epilepsy, heart disease, hemophilia, lead poisoning, leukemia, nephritis, sickle cell anemia) (Froehlich, 1996; Gfeller, 1992c; Maranto, 1991, 1996; Schwankovsky & Guthrie, 1982; Standley, 1986, 1996b). Music therapists may work as full-time, part-time, or contract employees or as consultants. They may provide direct services (e.g., prescribed individual or group interventions with patients) and/or indirect services (e.g., designing general music listening programs; staff development training; establishing/maintaining a tape/music library to meet patient needs; organizing or supervising volunteers who provide diversional, recreational, or entertainment music experiences for patients). In a recent survey of populations served by music therapists in which respondents were permitted to list as many categories as appropriate (AMTA, 1998),

152 of 1,620 respondents reported working with medical/surgical populations, 139 reported working with chronic pain patients, and 185 reported working with cancer patients. When asked to list their work setting, 70 of 1,654 music therapists responding designated children's hospital, 85 listed outpatient clinic, 49 designated general hospital, 39 listed wellness programs, 32 listed oncology, and 13 listed home health agency (AMTA, 1998).

HOW MUSIC IS USED IN THERAPY

As was noted earlier in this text, music has been associated with healing and treating diseases since ancient times (see Chapter 3). Since the late 1970s and early 1980s, as more research tools and methods that demonstrate the efficacy of music therapy as a viable tool for medical treatment have become available (Spintge, 1991), "the field of medicine and music have been experiencing a renaissance in the appreciation of music as an important component in the world of medicine" (Taylor, 1988, p. 86). Today, applications of music in medical settings are based on scientific knowledge about the physical, psychological, and socio-emotional effects of music that are substantiated by research (Gfeller, 1992c; Maranto, 1991, 1996; Spintge, 1989, 1991; Standley, 1986, 1996b; Taylor, 1988, 1997). Music therapists function as cooperative members of the medical team, assessing the needs of the patient, planning music therapy intervention strategies designed to meet these needs, and then applying specifically structured music experiences within the context of a therapeutic relationship to help the patient reach the prescribed medical/therapeutic goals that will enable him or her to regain as full a degree of health as possible (Gfeller, 1992c; Maranto, 1991, 1996).

Music therapy interventions can meet both physical and psychosocial needs of children or adults who require treatment for acute or chronic medical conditions. Studies have found that music therapy procedures are particularly useful in helping patients respond more favorably to medical treatment procedures and in facilitating their ability to deal with hospitalization (Barrickman, 1989; Chetta, 1981; Christenberry, 1979; Dunn, 1995; Froehlich, 1984,

1996; Gfeller, 1992c; Jacobowitz, 1992; Malone, 1996; Marley, 1984; McDonnell, 1984; Perez, 1989; Robb, 1996; Robb et al., 1995; Rudenberg & Royka, 1989; Schwankovsky & Guthrie, 1982; Standley, 1996b). Standley's (1996b) meta-analysis of research literature related to the use of music in medical treatment yielded the following generalizations: (1) women usually have greater responses to music than do men; (2) music has a slightly greater effect on children and adolescents than on adults, with infants showing the least response to music; (3) music has greater effects when some pain is present, but becomes less effective as pain increases; (4) effects of music vary with patient diagnosis, prognosis, and related levels of pain and anxiety; (5) live music presented by a trained music therapist has greater effects than recorded music; (6) studies using patients' preferred music demonstrated the greatest effects; and (7) results varied according to the specific dependent measures utilized.

Functions of Music Therapy in Medical Settings

Maranto (1991) defines *medical music therapy* as "the use of music therapy strategies in the treatment of illness and the maintenance of health" (p. 1). In medical settings, music therapy interventions may be used (1) *as* medicine, when music or music-based experiences affect the patient's health *directly* on a biomedical and/or psychosocial level (e.g., listening to music or doing music-mediated relaxation exercises to decrease pain perception; using music-based interventions to help the patient achieve life style changes needed to promote health), or (2) *in medicine*, when music or music-based experiences support or facilitate medical procedures (e.g., music listening or music and imagery to positively affect mood or decrease tension during procedures; various active and passive music-based techniques to reduce distress and anxiety related to illness, condition, or treatment) (Maranto, 1991). Sometimes, music therapy interventions function as primary treatments (e.g., music instead of pain medication). At other times, they are equal partners with medical treatments (e.g., using music and visualization/imagery in conjunction with respiratory therapy exercises to improve breathing). Music therapy interventions may also be used to augment, enhance, or support medical treatments (e.g., music-based experiences to motivate patients to participate in the treatment program).

Crowe (1985) identified five uses of music in the general hospital setting: (1) to decrease patients' overall anxiety level through guided relaxation techniques, (2) to assist in pain management, (3) to help patients actively cope with anxiety and stress and stimulate verbalization of fears and concerns, (4) to humanize an otherwise sterile environment and emphasize wellness rather than illness, and (5) to support the patients' religious/spiritual needs. At times, music therapy assessments can also provide information that may be helpful in giving a more complete picture of a patient's diagnosis, condition, problems, or needs. For example, patients may reveal fears, concerns, and anxieties in music and creative arts sessions that they do not mention in other settings (Froehlich, 1996). Music therapists who are trained and accredited in Guided Imagery and Music (GIM) procedures have also found that imagery associated with the pathway linking mind and body may be used as a projective diagnostic tool that complements standard medical and psychological procedures. For example, in situations where a patient is extremely ill or has had some trauma and is depressed or highly stressed, GIM techniques can elicit relevant physical imagery that elucidates psychological underlays, stress factors, or physical traumas or abuses that impact the patient's condition, or GIM imagery may point out areas that are of critical concern to the patient (Short, 1991). Of course, music therapists then share their findings with the other members of the medical team. When the treatment team is aware of

the patient's fears or concerns, they are better able to prioritize treatment approaches to meet the needs of the patient and enhance treatment effectiveness.

Cost-Effectiveness of Music Therapy Interventions

Music therapy can be a very cost-effective addition to medical treatment settings. Research shows that patients who participate in prescribed music therapy programs often have "shorter hospital stays and fewer side effects or complications, with little or no additional costs to the facility" (Standley, 1996b, p. 35). Many music therapy interventions are very effective in decreasing patient anxiety and increasing patient relaxation (Crowe, 1985; Froehlich, 1996; Maranto, 1996; Schwankovsky & Guthrie, 1982; Standley, 1986, 1996b; Taylor, 1997), and "physicians . . . have long recognized that a relaxed patient requires less medication, experiences less pain, and recovers more quickly than a patient whose level of anxiety creates a state of mental and physical turmoil" (Crowe, 1985, p. 46). Research has also demonstrated that structured application of the analgesic (pain relieving) and anxiolytic (tension and anxiety relieving) effects of music can reduce the use of or need for sedative or analgesic drugs, decrease amounts of anesthesia or postoperative medications needed, shorten recovery periods and hospitals stays, and decrease total medical costs (Halpern, 1989; Maranto, 1996; Spintge, 1989; Standley, 1986, 1996b; Taylor, 1997).

Effective, appropriate music therapy programs can be started with relatively minimal expenditures for basic equipment (Crowe, 1985). In contrast to other disciplines that rely heavily on nonreusable supplies, music therapy programs use materials that are reusable and have a long life span (Clark & Ficken, 1988; Crowe, 1985). Music therapy programs are also highly cost-effective because of their flexibility (Crowe, 1985). Music therapists can work effectively in many areas of medical treatment (e.g., surgery, orthopedics, general medical care, pediatrics, maternity, oncology/palliative care) and use their interventions to address and remediate many different patient problems. In addition, many music therapy services can be provided in groups, allowing for a greater number of patients to be served. As Crowe (1985) observed,

Because of the flexibility of music therapy and the predominance of group participation, the hospital receives maximum financial benefit from the decision to hire professional music therapists who provide services to an optimum number of patients meeting a broad spectrum of their needs. (p. 48)

General Music Therapy Goals and Treatment Techniques

Since many patients who seek medical treatment are dealing with some degree of pain, *pain abatement* is one of the more common and important uses of music in medical settings. Music therapy interventions can decrease awareness of pain, increase pain threshold or pain tolerance, reduce the need for or provide an alternative to pain medication or sedatives, decrease stress and its physiological results, and alter or eliminate the psychological perception of pain (Bonny, 1978b, 1983; Brown, Chen, & Dworkin, 1989; Chesky & Michel, 1991; Colwell, 1997; Crowe, 1985; Eagle & Harsh, 1988; Gardner, Licklider, & Weisz, 1960; Gfeller, 1992c; Gfeller, Logan, & Walker, 1990; Godley, 1987; Locsin, 1981; Maranto, 1996; Rider, 1985; Schwankovsky & Guthrie, 1982; Selm, 1991; Spintge, 1989; Standley, 1986, 1996b; Steinke, 1991; Taylor, 1997; Wolfe, 1978). Many music therapy interventions for pain management employ some type of structured music listening as a distraction from pain, a focus for attention, a stimulus for relaxation, or a masking agent (e.g., mask unpleasant sounds of dental drills, hospital equipment noises or sounds of other patients). Often, treatment is more effective when the patient is involved in selecting the music (Maranto, 1996; Spintge, 1989; Standley, 1996b), choosing from a selection of programs provided by the therapist (may include various styles of music, but all programs have certain structural elements known to facilitate relaxation or pain reduction) or his or her own preferred music. A notable exception to this is the special classical music programs used with Guided Imagery and Music (GIM) techniques, that have also proven effective in reducing pain (Bonny, 1978b, 1983). (See Chapter Twenty-two for more information on GIM.) In addition, some research has shown that "entrainment music" that contains a definite mood shift from unpleasant to pleasant or from tension to relaxation is significantly effective in reducing pain (Rider, 1985). For some patients, more stimulating music, such as drumming tapes or live drum music (Scartelli, 1991) or rock music (Gfeller, Logan, & Walker, 1990), may be the most effective in reducing pain.

Many factors, including the patient's age, medical condition, general health, music preferences, familiarity of music, and specific therapeutic goals, impact the selection of music for listening-based interventions (Gfeller, Logan, & Walker, 1990; Maranto, 1996); not all music will be equally effective for all patients. Music listening experiences may be presented together with the suggestion they will reduce pain (Lavine, Bucksbaum, & Poncy, 1976; Melzack, Weisz, & Sprague, 1963), with structured relaxation techniques (Clark et al., 1981; Godley, 1987; Standley, 1986, 1996b), in conjunction with biofeedback (Godley, 1987; Rider, 1985), or with imagery techniques (Bonny, 1978b; Godley, 1987; Rider, 1985). For some individuals, pain reduction may be facilitated when vibroacoustic stimulation is paired with the listening experience, through the use of a vibroacoustic recliner (Colwell, 1997) or table (Chesky & Michel, 1991). Other more active music-making techniques, such as singing and playing instruments, may also be used as distractions to help manage pain (Colwell, 1997).

In addition to its use as an audioanalgesiac, music may be used as a cognitive/affective structure to help patients control or manage pain (Brown, Chen, & Dworkin, 1989; Selm, 1991). Examples include experiences presenting positive or relaxing statements presented through song lyrics, using songs as a nonthreatening medium to explore and challenge distorted or irrational beliefs, and using music-mediated relaxation or GIM approaches to decrease tension and anxiety and increase feelings of overall well-being.

Music therapy interventions may be used in medical settings for many purposes besides pain relief. Other goal areas include (a) decreasing fear and anxiety about a condition or treatment procedure, (b) helping individuals cope with the trauma of hospitalization and/or illness, (c) facilitating relaxation, (d) promoting stress reduction, (e) increasing muscular function, (f) structuring movements or exercises, (g) increasing motivation to participate in treatment, (h) facilitating healing or recovery processes, (i) structuring and/or reinforcing healthy lifestyle changes, (j) increasing expression of feelings, (k) serving as an outlet for expressing frustration, (l) providing emotional support, (m) decreasing isolation, (n) facilitating communication between patients and families or patients and therapists, (o) reinforcing or serving as a vehicle for learning health principles or self-care routines, (p) structuring pleasurable interpersonal interactions, and (q) normalizing the medical environment (Chetta, 1981; Christenberry, 1979; Froehlich, 1996; Gfeller, 1992c; Herman, 1981; Maranto, 1996; Perez, 1989; Schwankovsky & Guthrie, 1982; Standley, 1986, 1996b; Taylor, 1997; Tims, 1981). Music therapists use a variety of techniques, both active and passive, directive and nondirective, within the context of the therapeutic relationship, to help individuals meet these goals. Techniques include music listening, GIM, Orff-Schulwerk activities, group or individual music improvisation, musical/rhythmic games, movement-to-music, singing, playing musical instruments, music lessons, music ensembles, lyric discussion, song writing, music-mediated relaxation, exercise to music, vibroacoustic therapy, music and biofeedback, contingent music, participating in musical plays, and producing music videos (Bonny, 1983; Froehlich, 1996; Herman, 1981; Levine-Gross & Swartz, 1982; Maranto, 1996; Perez, 1989; Schuster, 1985; Schwankovsky & Guthrie, 1982; Skille, 1989; Standley, 1986, 1996b; Tims, 1981). Some composers are also working to compose music that they believe will affect people directly on a cellular level to accelerate the healing process (Halpern, 1989).

Whatever music therapy techniques are used in medical settings, they must be structured to fit the medical model, using specific objectives that are relevant to medical diagnosis, prognosis, and treatment time line (Standley, 1986, 1996b). Like any drug or treatment, the music therapy interventions in medical settings should be specifically prescribed or ordered by the physician or treatment team for specific purposes (Spintge, 1989). Music therapists must also be able to describe music therapy treatment benefits in medical, not musical terms (Standley, 1986; Taylor, 1997). In addition, music therapists must work cooperatively with other medical personnel, communicating professional observations and striving to find ways to schedule and incorporate music therapy interventions so they enhance treatment and

do not jeopardize or interfere with crucial medical routines (Froehlich, 1996; Standley, 1986, 1996b). For music therapists to work successfully in a medical setting, "it is important that medical staff consider music therapy a priority due to its perception as a benefit rather that a disruption" (Standley, 1986, p. 102).

The next sections of this chapter present examples of specific music therapy interventions that have been found to be effective in various medical circumstances.

Music Therapy Interventions in Labor/Delivery

Since the 1980s, music has been used in connection with prepared childbirth methods as (1) an attention-focusing stimulus, (2) a distraction stimulus to divert attention from pain, (3) a stimulus for pleasure response, (4) a conditioned stimulus for relaxation, and (5) a structural aid to breathing (Clark, 1986; Clark, McCorkle, & Williams, 1981; Hanser, Larson, & O'Connell, 1983). Clark, McCorkle, and Williams (1981) reported that women who participated in a music therapy-assisted childbirth program "experienced significantly more positive perceptions of their childbirth experience than have their non-music therapy counterparts" (p. 98). With the music therapy-assisted approach, women perceived more support from significant others, spent more time practicing Lamaze techniques at home, and reported less anxiety and pain during childbirth. Hanser, Larson, and O'Connell (1983) also found that a specifically designed program of background music could make the labor experience more pleasant by decreasing the expectant mother's behavioral manifestations of tension and verbalizations associated with pain. In addition, Stein (1991) discovered that when patients who were undergoing Caesarean deliveries listened to structured tape programs of soft, melodious music in their preferred style of music (easy listening, classical, country/western, or jazz) via headphones, their anxiety decreased.

Music therapy interventions may also play an important role in the treatment of patients who have high-risk pregnancies. Winslow (1986) worked with women who were hospitalized during pregnancy due to high-risk complications, using group and individual music therapy sessions to help the women express their anxieties and find effective ways of coping with their feelings. These sessions helped increase these patients' quality of life while decreasing their anxiety and increasing their compliance with and responsiveness to medical treatment. Techniques used in individual session included music with progressive muscle relaxation and talking to the baby in utero. Group music therapy sessions were conducted weekly and used sing-alongs of children's songs and lullabies to help increase socialization and group discussion of concerns. Most of the women who participated in these music therapy sessions felt an increased degree of control over their lives, felt less anxious, had fewer somatic complaints, had a more positive attitude, and experienced increased physical relaxation.

In another study, progressive muscle relaxation training paired with music effectively decrease the state anxiety levels of adolescent girls in their third trimester of pregnancy (Liebman & MacLaren, 1991). After reviewing the literature related to music therapy in obstetrics, McKinney (1990) concluded that music therapy interventions using music listening, music-enhanced relaxation and/or imagery, GIM, and the singing of lullabies and children's songs "may have the potential to shorten labor and reduce obstetrical complications as well as to increase the patient's sense of well-being through the alleviation of anxiety and the reduction of conflicting feelings and issues" (p. 60).

In addition to facilitating the labor/delivery process and helping increase the mother's sense of well-being, music therapy interventions can play significant roles in integrating siblings into the birth process. For example, songs can act as a catalyst to help children express how they feel about becoming an older sibling. Music activities can also be used to initiate positive interactions between older siblings and the new baby. In one hospital setting, siblings were allowed to go to the nursery to sing "Happy Birthday" to the new baby as part of a "Welcome to Life" program (Linderman & Fridley, 1981).

Music Therapy Interventions in Neonatal Care

Although the results of Standley's (1996b) meta-analysis of research literature related to the use of music in medical treatment showed that, by age, infants showed the least response to music, perhaps because of their lower degree of neurological and musical development, research and clinical observation also demonstrate that many infants do have some positive responses to music and that selected music therapy interventions can play an important role in neonatal care. Various studies have shown that the rhythmic stimulation of the mother's heartbeat can effectively calm and quiet newborns (Murooka, 1975; Smith & Steinschneider, 1975). Murooka (1975) found that recordings of the sound of blood pulsating through maternal veins and arteries and recordings of these sounds combined with classical music effectively stopped the crying of newborns and served as a natural sleep-inducer. Sedative music also has a calming and stabilizing effect on premature infants (Lorch et al., 1994).

Appropriate music stimulation is usually pleasing to and well-tolerated by infants. For example, Cassidy and Standley (1995) found that music stimulation was not contraindicated even in the first week of life for very low birthweight infants, for whom sensory stimulation was usually restricted. In fact, short periods of listening to lullabies reduced their distress and had positive effects on oxygen saturation levels, heart rate, and respiration rate, helping premature infants thrive. Because music effectively reduces tension and stress-related responses in newborn and premature infants, "staff at a large hospital in central Wisconsin believe that the use of music may have life-saving significance in their attempts to give premature babies a better chance to survive" (Taylor, 1997, p. 108).

Results of a study by Chapman (1975) suggested that musical stimuli might help premature infants conserve energy, thereby enabling them to use more calories for weight gain. Caine (1991) also found that presenting taped lullabies and children's songs in 30-minute increments to infants in the newborn intensive care unit (NBICU) significantly reduced initial weight loss, increased caloric intake and average daily weight, and decreased both time in the NBICU and total hospital stay. Music may also be used to stimulate learning and development. For example, assisted participation in body part songs may stimulate tactile exploration (hand to mouth, face, head, nose, eyes) and movement that is necessary for development (Standley, 1991).

In addition to having positive effects on newborns, music interventions can help promote bonding and positive interactions between newborns and their parents. For example, since music is not contraindicated even for premature infants, it may be a tool for nurturing bonds between parents and their critically ill infants, who they may not be able to hold, feed, bathe, or touch (Cassidy & Standley, 1995). Songs can also structure positive interactions between parents and newborns, act as a catalyst for play, decrease stress and tension, give parents tools for stimulating or calming their infants, and facilitate daily care (Standley, 1991). To increase bonding and personalization, parents might add their own words to songs and lullabies. Owens (1979) speculated that music therapists could help produce happier babies and parents and possibly even prevent early child abuse by teaching parents how stimulation is important to infant development, showing them ways to use music to stimulate and soothe their infants and teaching them basic behavioral principles to promote desired behaviors and guard against the forming undesirable contingent behaviors.

Music Therapy Interventions for Children or Adolescents Who Have Acute or Chronic Medical Conditions

Music therapy interventions can help meet both the physical and psychosocial needs of children and adolescents who have acute or chronic medical conditions. For example, music therapy techniques may play a particularly significant role in helping children and adolescents (and their families) deal with the trauma of hospitalization and respond more favorably to medical treatment procedures (Barrickman, 1989; Chetta, 1981; Christenberry, 1979; Dunn, 1995; Froehlich, 1984, 1996; Jacobowitz, 1992; Malone, 1996; Marley, 1984; McDonnell, 1984; Newton & Redmond, 1995; Perez, 1989; Robb, 1996; Robb et al., 1995; Rudenberg & Royka, 1989; Schwankovsky & Guthrie, 1982; Standley, 1996b). In addition to facilitating pain management and tension/anxiety reduction, music therapy interventions can provide (a) opportunities for expressing and dealing with feelings related to hospitalization, injury, or one's medical condition, (b) diversionary experiences and opportunities for socialization, (c) normalization experiences that provide opportunities to continue age-appropriate motor, language, and social development, and (d) integrative experiences that help children with chronic conditions or traumatic injuries fit the changes that result from the injury or medical condition into their lives so they can made adjustments and live life to the fullest.

Many techniques used with children and their families involve active music making procedures, "because children are people of action" (Froehlich, 1996, p. 17). Music therapists may use singing, rhythm bands, Orff-Schulwerk experiences, movement-to-music, relaxation-to-music, music games, improvisation, song writing, music video production, and many other techniques in their work with hospitalized children. Music therapy interventions are frequently integrated with child life practices (Froehlich, 1996; Rudenberg & Royka, 1989), and "puppets, instruments, objects for manipulation, and toys can assist the therapist in establishing a relationship of trust," (Barrickman, 1989, p. 14), especially with young children who may be shy, confused, or fearful and reluctant or unable to communicate verbally. The results of a study by Chetta (1981) indicated that songs can be used to familiarize children with medical equipment and procedures and that songs and other music therapy activities can effectively reduce pre-operative anxiety in children. Marley (1984) also found that music therapy activities, such as relaxation to music, musical/rhythmic exploration and imitation games, movement to music, and simple songs, combined with direct interaction with the music therapist, could significantly reduce stress-related behaviors in hospitalized infants and toddlers. In a more recent study, Malone (1996) found that live singing of age-appropriate children's songs with guitar accompaniment was an effective, non-invasive means of pain management and stress reduction for even very young pediatric patients. In addition, music therapy sessions can be very beneficial to pediatric trauma patients, who often must be deprived of the most basic comfort of being held. Music activities can help reduce anxiety and increase feelings of security and safety by creating "a compensatory holding environment through the use of sound, rhythm, and association to familiar songs" (McDonnell, 1984).

Many music therapy experiences, such as those

using Orff-Schulwerk activities, instrumental improvisation, music-listening matching music to the child's mood or emotions, musical stories and games, fill-in-the blank song and chants, song writing, and musical dramatizations, can also stimulate children to talk about their fears and feelings associated with their hospitalization or medical condition (Barrickman, 1989; Dunn, 1995; Froehlich, 1984, 1996; Jacobowitz, 1992; Perez, 1989). Froehlich (1996) suggested that music therapists who work with hospitalized children follow a crisis intervention model to structure music therapy interventions that help children cope with the trauma of hospitalization and illness. In this model, therapists first use structured music experiences to help assess the individual patient and determine any particular needs or conflicts. Once these are determined, music therapists use music experiences to build a trusting relationship with the patient, facilitate the patient's expression of feelings, help the patient find alternative ways of coping and positive support systems, and offer the patient hope for the future. Froehlich (1996, pp. 25-36) also gives several examples of ways Orff-Schulwerk activities may be used with hospitalized children within the framework of this model.

Pediatric patients who have received traumatic injuries such as burns may receive many benefits from music therapy techniques. For example, when a combination of music listening, deep breathing, progressive muscle relaxation, and imagery were used prior to reconstructive surgery, the pediatric patients' anxiety significantly decreased as compared with standard pre-operative preparation (Robb et al., 1995). Music-assisted relaxation techniques also gave patients new coping strategies and provided ways for them to be involved actively in their own care. In addition, these music experiences used within a therapeutic relationship provided emotional support and comfort to both the patient and the family.

Music therapy experiences involving singing, movement-to-music (whole body or isolated body parts), and playing instruments can provide much-needed enjoyable, "normal" sensory stimulation for pediatric burn patients. In addition, these experiences may also be structured to complement and facilitate physical therapy and respiratory therapy goals (Christenberry, 1979; Rudenberg & Royka, 1989). As the child feels secure and experiences pleasure and success in the music therapy setting, various music

activities (e.g., singing, instrumental improvisation, fill-in or question-and-answer songs, lyric analysis and discussion, song writing) may be structured to help the child increase self-expression and build psychological strength needed to cope with painful and sometimes frightening treatments, deal with various losses, and successfully adapt to different stages of recovery (Christenberry, 1979; Froehlich, 1996; Rudenberg & Royka, 1989). Song writing experiences using fill-in-the-blank scripts, group song writing, instrumental and vocal improvisation, lyrical narration with instrumental accompaniments, and writing lyrics related to discharge may be particularly useful for helping adolescents increase self-expression, self-esteem, communication, psychological adjustment and coping skills, and socialization (Robb, 1996). Recent research shows that music therapy interventions that provide patients with active coping strategies and promote self-expression also have important physical benefits, such as increased immune function (Lane, 1991, 1994; Robb, 1996).

Usually, when a child is hospitalized or traumatically injured, not just the child but the whole family need help coping with feelings of anger, fear, and loneliness that may be associated with the health crisis. By including parents and other family members in music therapy sessions, the music therapist can reduce the stress and anxiety of both the child and the family, facilitate communication and expression of fears and feelings, and provide the child and the family members with meaningful ways of relating to each other in structures that safely contain emotions. In addition, by giving the child and family members active roles in facilitating the child's health and well-being and by providing them with something positive and constructive to do, family music therapy sessions can help both the child and the family deal with the events of the medical crisis and its aftermath (Dunn, 1995; Froehlich, 1996; McDonnell, 1984; Newton & Redmond, 1995). For example, a musical story may provide a young child with an avenue to express feelings of fear and anxiety directly in a way that does not overburden anxious and worried parents (Jacobowitz, 1992). In addition, active involvement in music experiences may provide important distraction from pain, worry, and waiting not only for the child but also for the parents (Barrickman, 1989).

Children and adolescents who have chronic medical conditions can also benefit from music therapy interventions. Herman (1981) found that music activities, such as playing instruments, singing, writing songs, moving to music, and putting on musical plays, helped provide children who had severe asthma with outlets for venting frustration and expressing emotions. Moreover, singing and playing wind instruments had the added medical benefit of helping the children develop and maintain their optimum level of respiratory status (Haas et al., 1989; Herman, 1981; Michel, 1985; Schwankovsky & Guthrie, 1982). As the children experienced success in music activities and acquired musical skills, their self-esteem also increased. In addition, group music activities provided opportunities for socialization and positive interactions with others.

Music therapy experiences can also be structured to meet the physical and psychosocial needs of children who have other chronic health impairments, such as cystic fibrosis, diabetes, epilepsy, heart disease, hemophilia, leukemia, nephritis, and sickle cell anemia. Schwankovsky and Guthrie (1982, pp. 27-63) provide several examples of how various music activities can provide these individuals with enjoyable ways to improve their physical status, provide sensory stimulation and appropriate levels of physical activity, improve coordination and sensorimotor skills, decrease anxiety and tension, increase socialization, self-esteem, and self-expression, facilitate positive interactions with peers, increase coping skills and psychosocial adjustment, provide developmental learning experiences and peer interaction, and improve self-concept.

Music Therapy Interventions for Adults Who Have Acute or Chronic Medical Conditions

With adults, music therapy interventions have been used successfully used in coronary intensive care units, prior to and/or during surgery, to facilitate post-operative recovery, in radiology, in oncology, for headache or chronic pain patients, with gynecological procedures, with burn patients, in podiatry, with dental patients, and with specific medical procedures, such as laceration repairs, lumbar punctures, or kidney dialysis (Maranto, 1996; Standley, 1986, 1996b). As was noted early, one of the most common uses of music therapy interventions in medical

settings is the use of music listening, music-assisted relaxation, or music and imagery to reduce pain perception and decrease tension or anxiety (Bonny, 1978b, 1983; Brown, Chen, & Dworkin, 1989; Chesky & Michel, 1991; Colwell, 1997; Crowe, 1985; Eagle & Harsh, 1988; Gardner, Licklider, & Weisz, 1960; Gfeller, 1992c; Gfeller, Logan, & Walker, 1990; Godley, 1987; Locsin, 1981; Maranto, 1996; Rider, 1985; Selm, 1991; Spintge, 1989; Standley, 1986, 1996b; Steinke, 1991; Taylor, 1997; Wolfe, 1978). Other music therapy interventions have adult patients take a more active role in music-making through individual or group improvisations, instrumental or vocal solos, song requests, lyric discussion, or song writing. These also help reduce anxiety, serve as outlets for emotional expression, and may even provide some patients with the motivation they need to continue living and participate cooperatively with medical treatments (Levine-Gross & Swartz, 1982; Tims, 1981). Those individuals who have medical conditions that force them to pursue less strenuous leisure activities than those to which they were accustomed may develop music skills or music-related interests that can provide them with new leisure-time interests they can also pursue outside the hospital setting.

Music Therapy in Surgery

Research has shown that music therapy interventions can have beneficial effects (1) as part of pre-operative procedures, (2) in the operating room during surgical procedures, and (3) postoperatively, during recovery (Standley, 1986, 1996b; Taylor, 1997). In her review of over 30 research studies that examined the influence of music on physiological and psychological parameters associated with surgery, Maranto (1996, pp. 46-52) found that most interventions involved music listening, often selected by the patient from programs of music offered by the therapist, and that music interventions usually positively influenced both physiological and psychological measures. Structured music interventions also helped decrease patients' fear, anxiety, and awareness of pain, reduced the amount of anesthesia or pain medication needed, and, in some cases, decreased recovery time (Maranto, 1996; Taylor, 1997).

Structured music listening experiences, used alone or combined with imagery or various relaxation techniques, can provide a very effective, noninvasive way of decreasing pre-surgical stress, fear, and anxiety. When patients listened to classical music selected for its relaxing or calming qualities over loud speakers in the pre-operative area, they reported substantial decreases in anxiety (Bonny & McCarron, 1984). Listening to individually selected music programs (from a choice of prerecorded music tapes of various styles constructed by the therapist for their anxiety-reducing qualities) using headphones can also effectively decrease pre-surgical anxiety (Miluk-kolasa et al., 1996). In addition, listening to preferred relaxing music (selected from taped music programs of various styles compiled by the music therapist) combined with vibrotactile stimulation from a Somatron™ mattress can effectively reduce pre-surgical anxiety (Walters, 1996). This procedure also decreased time in surgery and the amount of post-operative medication needed in women awaiting scheduled gynecological surgery (Walters, 1996).

Music used during surgery may have both physical and psychological benefits for patients. During surgery, the patient gives up many controls. Music therapy can help give some control back to the patient by providing the patient with individualized choices (e.g., music selection, setting or adjusting the volume, choosing the scene for imagery, determining self-suggestion statements, active techniques to be used for stress reduction or pain management). As these choices increase the patient's sense of control, they also tend to decrease the need for medication and facilitate both the patient's response to surgery and his or her recovery (Cowan, 1991; Mandel, 1988). In addition, music techniques can have specific benefits during particular surgical procedures. For example, patients undergoing punch biopsy in-office gynecological procedures showed significantly lower respiratory rates and overt pain scores when they used music listening combined with basic relaxation procedures, as compared with nonmusic controls (C. A. Davis, 1992). In addition, those using the music had fewer procedural complications and required less time to complete the medical procedures.

While listening to pre-selected music through headphones can have some beneficial effects, such as decreased anxiety and a reduced need for anesthesia (Bonny & McCarron, 1984), the presence of the music

therapist can be also very important in helping the patients achieve optimum benefits from music interventions. The music therapist can facilitate patient responses by focusing the patient's attention on the music and/or the music-assisted relaxation or imagery procedures, by providing comfort and reassurance, observing patient responses, and by changing music programs or techniques as necessary to meet the patient's changing needs (Cowan, 1991; Mandel, 1991). For example, Cowan (1991) found that therapist-assisted techniques like imagery, breathing exercises, stroking or direct pressure, or autogenic suggestions used in combination with music listening were very helpful in calming, relaxing, and comforting patients during surgery, thus increasing the quality of patient care. The presence of both the music and the music therapist are vital in giving the most effective, positive surgery experience for the patient (Cowan, 1991; Mandel, 1991).

> Although the exact nature of the intervention varies from patient to patient, the visual, physical, and auditory bond between the patient and therapist can provide a calming force at an extremely vulnerable point in the patient's life. The music alone may be helpful in relaxing or distracting the patient, but it is the presence of the therapist that is the driving force in comforting and providing the patient with controls. (Cowan, 1991, p. 44)

Music therapy interventions can also assist in post-operative recovery by helping increase alertness, by providing distraction from pain, by facilitating relaxation, by decreasing tension and anxiety, and by reducing the need for postoperative medication (Bonny & McCarron, 1984; Cowan, 1991; Taylor, 1997). Bonny and McCarron (1984) recommended that music listening programs used in recovery rooms have faster tempi and include more stimulative music to facilitate the patient's return to normal consciousness. However, since responses to music are very individualized, indiscriminate use of music in recovery rooms may hinder rather than help the patient's progress. Mandel (1991), a music therapist herself, related a personal surgical experience where the music tape played in the recovery room did not match her mood and actually increased her agitation rather than serving its intended purpose of decreasing tension and anxiety. She wished there had been an attending music therapist in the recovery room who could have observed her reaction and turned off the music or offered her another selection that would have been more relaxing for her individual needs and mood at that moment. Mandel observed that, despite her knowledge and training, in her postsurgical state in the recovery room, "I was unable to monitor the music myself effectively. The music and my lack of control became factors detrimental to my initial recovery" (p. 111). She suggested that, even in the recovery room, "it seems necessary to have a music therapist serve as coach, observe patient responses, and plan and implement changes as they are indicated" (p. 112). Cowan (1991) also recommended that the music therapist be with the patient in the recovery room, offering music therapy interventions as a means of increasing alertness, providing distraction from pain, or facilitating relaxation.

Music Therapy with Organ Transplant Procedures

Since music is pervasive in society, it is generally well-received by most patients. Music is also a very flexible therapeutic tool that can meet patients' needs at various physiological, psychological, and social response levels. For these reasons, music therapy interventions may be particularly useful in addressing the emotional and social factors associated with the anticipatory and recovery phases of organ transplantation processes.

Gibbons and McDougal (1987) have suggested several ways that music therapy interventions might be used in the care of kidney, liver, and bone marrow transplant recipients, donors, and their families. For example, in the *pre-transplant phrases*, music therapy procedures could be structured to present information and facilitate discussions that would help patients and family members realize the risks associated with the transplant procedures and help them form realistic expectations of post-transplant life quality. During the *waiting period*, active or passive music-mediated relaxation and stress reduction procedures could help reduce anxiety and tension. Music therapy interventions may also address agitation or depression that may be associated with fear of organ rejection, surgical risks, or prognosis. In addition, as in any

surgical procedure, music therapy techniques can help patients manage physical pain and provide sensory stimulation and pleasurable experiences in a sterile hospital environment. Through music and imagery experiences, patients may even "travel" out the hospital environment for a time. In the *post-transplant phase*, structured experiences involving improvisation, playing musical instruments with others, group singing or listening, song writing, or lyric discussion could be used to help recipients deal with feelings of indebtedness or guilt toward their donors, facilitate the establishment or reestablishment of social relationships, and support self-esteem and self-concept, which may be decreased when physical limitations force employment or life style changes.

Music Therapy in Coronary Care

Listening to special programs of taped music can increase the pain tolerance of patients in coronary intensive care units while helping to decrease their heart rates and lessen anxiety and depression (Bonny, 1983). Listening to self-selected tapes of anxiolytic music can also facilitate emotional relaxation and provide distraction from pain for cardiac patients in intensive care (Spintge, 1989). In addition, some research has found that patients who listened to anxiolytic music consistently demonstrated "a statistically significant reduction ($p < .01$) of stress response in the cardiovascular and endocrinological systems" (Spintge & Droh, 1987, p. 91).

In cardiac rehabilitation programs, music therapy interventions can be structured to deal with and reduce patient fears (e.g., of death or of job loss), to decrease pain and stress, and to motivate patients to cooperate with and participate in their treatment program (Taylor, 1997). MacNay (1995) found that adding preferred music to a cardiac rehabilitation exercise program decreased the patients' perceived feelings of exertion and estimations of time spent exercising and increased positive moods. These results seem to indicate that adding patients' preferred music to cardiac exercise programs may help motivate some patients to participate in exercises that are vital to their rehabilitation and may also increase endurance and performance levels. Mandel (1996) also found that music therapy techniques such as small group discussion of live and taped music or lyrics, music relaxation and imagery, song writing, identification of song lyrics or titles that described stressful situations or coping techniques, using songs to express personal feelings, and nonverbal expression of feelings on musical instruments, could facilitate stress management for individuals referred to music therapy by their cardiologist.

Music Therapy with Patients Who Have Severe Burns

Music therapy interventions may address both physiological and psychological needs of patients who have severe burns. On the *physical level*, music therapy interventions may provide sensory stimulation and reduce sensory deprivation that may be associated with the sterile hospital environment; help distract from or reduce the pain associated with the burns, dressing changes, debridement, or skin graft operations; motivate physical movement and exercise necessary for rehabilitation; facilitate relaxation and stress reduction, and encourage deep breathing to help restore respiratory function and prevent respiratory complications (Barker, 1991; Christenberry, 1979; Taylor, 1997). Techniques used to achieve these goals included music and progressive muscle relaxation (PMR), singing, humming, hand-clapping, guitar strumming, exercise- or movement-to-music, listening to sedative music, and music with imagery. Barker (1991) noted that the use of music interventions during painful treatment procedures such as daily debridement also have beneficial effects for the staff: "During music/PMR conditions, the burn technicians were more relaxed and jovial with the patients" (p. 137).

Adult patients who have been severely burned also undergo various stages of *psychological adjustment* as they recuperate. Music therapy interventions may benefit patients through all of these stages (Christenberry, 1979). In the first stage, physiological emergency, patients are dealing with many physiological stresses and may experience recurrent nightmares related to their accident or periods of delirium or disorientation and confusion. Experiential music activities (e.g., singing or listening to familiar songs) may provide a foundation for reestablishing order and reality contact. Other interventions, such as structured music-listening, music and imagery, or music-mediated relaxation techniques, may also help reduce stress, tension, anxiety, and pain perception accompanying this early experience of burn injuries (Taylor, 1997). During the second stage, psychological emergency, patients are physically stable but are becoming increasingly aware of the losses associated with their injuries and are "involved in a transition from denial to recognition" (Christenberry, 1979, p. 144). Music therapy activities employ techniques like song writing, lyric discussion, improvisation, and guaranteed-success experiences in singing, playing instruments, moving-to-music, or composing music, to help patients express feelings, fears, and frustrations and build or rebuild self-esteem. During the third stage, social emergency, patients may be confronted with changes in their life styles and may have to deal with differences in interpersonal relationships as they prepare for discharge and return to society. This is a time of great emotional adjustment, and patients may become shy, suspicious, withdrawn, discouraged, or depressed. Prior to discharge, music therapy sessions can help patients discuss problems they may face outside the hospital, continue to work on increasing self-esteem, structure and enhance communication between the patient and family members, and possibly provide patients with music skills they can use for their own enjoyment or to participate in community music groups (Christenberry, 1979; Taylor, 1997). "Ideally, music therapy should be continued on an out-patient basis to help in the readjustment to life outside the hospital" (Christenberry, 1979, p. 146).

Music Therapy with Hemodialysis

Many patients with kidney disease must repeatedly undergo an invasive blood-cleansing procedure known as *hemodialysis*. Music therapy interventions that reduce stress and anxiety may help keep a patient's emotions under control so that blood pressure will not be a problem during this procedure (Taylor, 1997). There is some evidence that listening to specially selected, preferred music reduces the anxiety of adult hemodialysis patients (Schuster, 1985). Biomedical data now explains how music is able to produce these effects (Taylor, 1997). Normally, an aversive stimulus, such as the invasive hemodialysis procedure, would produce reactions from the amygdala and hypothalamus that would produce blood pressure changes and release of stress-related hormones. However, music therapy interventions involve the amygdala and hypothalamus with reactions to musical stimuli, making them less able to respond or react to the aversive stimulus. As Taylor (1997) explains:

> With musically stimulated impulses occupying neural pathways throughout the brain, the orbitofrontal cortex is less able to focus on self-concerns in determining emotional responses. The positive responses are sustained and replicated as the individual's brain stores conditioned emotional responses resulting from the effects of music on the medial division of the medial geniculate nucleus in the thalamus. (p. 76)

Thus, the anxiety-reducing effects of music can have important benefits for adult patients undergoing hemodialysis.

Music Therapy in Pulmonology

Various types of music therapy interventions, including singing, breathing exercises to music, listening to tapes of sedative music, relaxing to music, and playing simple wind instruments to improve exhalation ability, have been shown to benefit individuals who have respiratory problems (Christenberry, 1979; Mandel, 1996; Maranto, 1996; Rider et al., 1991). For example, music may motivate some patients to perform necessary deep breathing exercises. In her work with burn patients whose respiratory function was impaired, Christenberry (1979) observed: "The personal satisfaction involved in singing may encourage the patient to willingly cooperate in deep breathing, and to complain less than he would if he perceived this as a medical procedure" (pp. 141- 142). Michel (1985) also found that singing and playing wind instruments helped individuals with asthma increase their ability to use abdominal breathing.

Other research has found that singing improved the clinical status of patients with pulmonary edema and that singing in vocal ensembles increased the patients' relaxation responses (Rider et al., 1991). In addition to exercising the lungs and requiring individuals to use about 90% of their vital capacity, singing stimulates the cough reflex and helps patients with chronic respiratory conditions clear secretions from their airways (Bolger & Judson, 1984). Staum (1996) suggested that singing's success as a treatment modality for patients who have respiratory problems "is possibly due to its sustained nature and to its ability to stop, start, and successively time respiration" (p. 75).

Toning (chanting sustained vocal sounds on individual pitches) also effectively increases deep breathing and reduces heart rate in many pulmonary patients (Rider et al., 1991). Other music-based techniques that benefit pulmonary patients include using music to accompany breathing exercises, using music-assisted relaxation techniques, and being involved in small group music therapy sessions that use techniques such as lyric discussion, matching songs to personal feelings, song writing, and instrumental improvisation to encourage expression of feelings and frustrations and to decrease anxiety (Mandel, 1996). Some respiratory patients have developed their lungs and intercostal and abdominal muscles and increased their endurance and breath control by learning to play wind instruments (Staum, 1988, 1996).

Music therapy techniques can also facilitate patients' responses to bronchoscopy procedures. For example, Metzler and Berman (1991) found that listening to tapes of classical and semiclassical sedative music decreased tension and anxiety in patients undergoing bronchoscopy procedures. During the music condition, bronchoscopy patients showed significantly less increase in heart rate, increased neck relaxation, and had warmer hands (a factor that is associated with increased relaxation).

Music Therapy to Affect Immune Response

Research has shown that stress decreases immune system activity, thus increasing a person's susceptibility to infection (Taylor, 1997). Immune system responses can be enhanced through many techniques, including imagery and music (Bartlett et al., 1993; Lane, 1991, 1994; Rider, 1985; Taylor, 1997; Tsao et al., 1991). Some research has shown that secretory IgA levels can be increased by conscious thought and the use of music, suggesting that "sedative music can be an effective method for enhancing the immune system" (Tsao et al., 1991, p. 113). Other research has found that when subjects listened to relaxing selections of music from their preferred genre (e.g., contemporary jazz, new age, classical), their cortisol levels decreased significantly, supporting the theory that music facilitates immune system recovery (Bartlett et al., 1993). Taylor (1997) suggested that a closer look at how music influences the biological structures that control the immune system shows how music may accomplish these effects. After a detailed explanation of the biomedical processes involved, he summarizes: "In short, music can calm neural activity in the brain, resulting in decreased glucocorticoid production and associated recovery of normal white blood cell activity" (p. 108).

Music Therapy in Oncology

Research and clinical evidence show that music therapy interventions, such as music listening, music-mediated relaxation, music and imagery, song writing, and lyric discussion, can have many benefits for patients who have cancer. These include (a) assisting in pain management, (b) increasing relaxation and decreasing tension and anxiety, (c) increasing positive mood, (d) decreasing feelings of fear and isolation, (e) enhancing ability to communicate and express feelings, and (f) decreasing the side effects of chemotherapy (Maranto, 1996; Taylor, 1997). Music therapy experiences, such as song selection or instrumental improvisation, can also be structured to enhance communication between patients and their families, helping them express and explore emotions and ideas that seem too threatening to verbalize or express in other ways (Bailey, 1984; Bright, 1986; Clair, 1996b; Edwards, 1976; Froelich, 1996; Gilbert, 1977; Hamilton & Bailey, 1981; Martin, 1989, 1991; Munro, 1984; Ridgway, 1983; Whittall, 1991). (See Chapter Twenty for more information.)

Some research in music therapy and oncology has focused on music therapy for patients undergoing bone marrow transplants. Gibbons and McDougal (1987) concluded that music therapy interventions could be structured to impact socio-emotional factors that affected the waiting and recovery processes of

patients and their family members. Boldt (1996) developed a specific music therapy protocol for bone marrow transplant patients to help increase their feelings of psychological well-being, physical comfort, and exercise endurance. Techniques included deep breathing exercises, progressive muscle relaxation to slow instrumental music, range of motion exercises to music, patient-selected songs sung with guitar accompaniment, and patient-selected music to accompany exercise routines. The use of music increased the patients' cooperation and participation in activities, self-reported relaxation and comfort, sense of well-being, and physical comfort. Boldt noted that patients who had previously used music as a coping device or intervention for pain relief or relaxation were more willing to participate in the music therapy exercise program.

Music Therapy for Chronic Pain Management

Individuals who have chronic pain often seek medical treatment to find ways to alleviate or better manage their pain. Recently, treatment of chronic pain patients has begun to focus not only on the physical processes of the person in pain, but also on his/her affective and cognitive processes, in an attempt to change the person's subjective experience of the pain, thus improving the person's ability to cope with or manage pain more effectively (Selm, 1991). In addition to having definite effects on biomedical processes that relate to pain and pain perception (Taylor, 1997), music therapy interventions can also positively impact cognitive and affective processes that affect pain perception. Techniques include using music as a cue for relaxation and tension/anxiety release (music-mediated relaxation, biofeedback and music, music and imagery, GIM) (Colwell, 1997; Godley, 1987; Selm, 1991), singing or playing musical instruments to distract attention from the pain (Colwell, 1997), assisting learning by presenting verbal material related to pain management in song lyrics or by discussing relevant songs (Selm, 1991), or using music experiences as a nonthreatening way to explore cognitive distortion and challenge irrational beliefs (Selm, 1991).

After learning music-based pain control procedures under the guidance of the music therapist, many patients can then use these music-based techniques as self-regulation procedures to facilitate relaxation and pain relief (Colwell, 1997; Godley, 1987; Selm, 1991). Godley (1987) found that approximately 70% of the chronic pain patients who received music therapy interventions experienced a decrease in their use of medication, with many substituting listening to their music tape for medication. The use of music also increased patients' positive attitudes, optimism about their health, and faithfulness in practice of relaxation and pain management techniques. Selm (1991) concluded: "Research suggests that music enhanced self-regulation training methods may be more effective than those without music for persons with chronic pain" (p. 94).

In her meta-analysis of music research in medical/dental treatment, Standley (1996b) found that, by population groups, headache patients showed the second greatest response to music interventions. Music-based relaxation training has effectively reduced pain in both tension and migraine headaches. In one study, relaxation training with music and imagery was superior to biofeedback training in relieving migraine headaches (Chance, 1987). One year after training, patients in the music group had only one-sixth as many headaches as before training, and the headaches they had were shorter and less severe. Using music-based relaxation techniques, some patients were even able to end a developing migraine headache before it became very painful.

Music-based interventions are also effective in relieving some of the chronic pain associated with arthritis. Vibroacoustic therapy, which combines music, vibration, and low frequency sound (Chesky & Michel, 1991; Skille, 1989), effectively decreases pain for some patients who have arthritis. Some research indicates that the combination of music and vibration is more effective in reducing pain than music alone or a placebo condition (Chesky & Michel, 1991). Other research has shown that listening to anxiolytic music reduces pain associated with movement or range of motion exercises for patients with arthritis (Spintge, 1989). Adding music to prescribed exercise routines or using musical instruments to motivate and structure movement can also distract individuals from the pain associated with movement. (See Chapter Eleven for more information).

Music Therapy and Performing Arts Medicine

In recent years, a new medical specialty, performing arts medicine, which is concerned with the treatment of health-related problems of performing artists, has begun to develop (Brotons, 1994a; Maranto, 1991; Habboushe & Maranto, 1991; Taylor, 1988, 1997). A significant portion of this specialty is devoted to treating the specific medical and psychological problems of musicians (Habboushe & Maranto, 1991). Performing arts medicine for musicians focuses on treating (a) those medical problems that result from playing/singing or practicing and directly affect musical performance and (b) those problems that are not directly caused by playing/singing or practicing but still directly affect musical performance. Musicians may seek treatment for problems such as nerve compression syndromes, tension and fatigue, muscle or tendon disorders, cardiac irregularities, problems with the respiratory apparatus or the vocal cords, overuse syndromes, vision problems, performance anxiety, the affects of aging, or brain damage that results in amusia (Habboushe & Maranto, 1991; Taylor, 1997). Since music therapists have a thorough knowledge of music and music performance as well as a knowledge of therapeutic and rehabilitation processes, they may have valuable insights into the problems of performing musicians and be able to structure effective treatment interventions to help improve the musician's medical and psychological functioning. By bringing this unique perspective to the treatment team, music therapists can provide a bridge between physician and musician, between music and medicine (Habboushe & Maranto, 1991; Rider, 1987).

Music therapy interventions can sometimes be very helpful in treating the problems of performing musicians. For example, Rider (1987) used a combination of music psychotherapy involving GIM and music improvisation techniques, biofeedback, systematic desensitization, and cognitive restructuring to relieve a cellist's problems with shoulder pain and fatigue, breathing, and anxiety when playing solos. Rider noted that, after music therapy treatment, the cellist's self-esteem, positive attitude toward performance, and performance quality also increased. Brodsky and Sloboda (1997) used music therapy techniques to treat performance anxiety in musicians and found that counseling supplemented with music relaxation and imagery techniques or with music plus vibrotactile stimulation from a Somatron* Acoustic Massage™ power recliner were just as effective as traditional cognitive-behavioral psychotherapeutic interventions in reducing performance anxiety. In addition, they found that musicians were more willing to participate in music therapy interventions than in traditional psychotherapy.

When working with musicians who have performance anxiety, it is important to remember that individual performers may need different strategies for relaxation, since all performers do not experience anxiety in the same ways or for the same reasons.

Performance anxiety may have various physiological (e.g., increased heart rate, shortness of breath, nausea, sweating, shaking), psychological/emotional (e.g., exaggerated apprehension, fear of failure, generalized panic), cognitive (e.g., loss of confidence, lack of concentration due to worrying, memory lapses), or behavioral (e.g., trembling knees or hands, stiff arms or neck, deadpan face), manifestations in different individuals. "By studying individual differences, performers with different anxiety modes can be matched to the most appropriate treatment interventions" (Brotons, 1994a, p. 78).

SPECIAL CONSIDERATIONS AND TIPS FOR SUCCESS

Since clients who have acute or chronic health impairments suffer from specific medical problems, it is imperative for music therapists to consult with medical personnel to find out exactly what medical precautions or restrictions apply to individual clients. It is also beneficial for music therapists to be aware of the client's prognosis and the expected effects the condition will have on the client. This type of knowledge will help music therapists anticipate the client's needs. It is also extremely important for music therapists to be aware of any special procedures that should be followed in the event of crisis or emergency situations, such as acute asthma attacks, diabetic insulin reactions, or epileptic seizures.

Like any drug or intervention, the use of music in medicine should be specifically prescribed (Spintge, 1989). As in any setting, it is important that music therapy interventions in medical settings be used for specific purposes, taking into account the individual preferences, needs, and responses of each patient and matching the music and the type of intervention (e.g., active or passive) to these (Maranto, 1996; Standley, 1996b). When music is used properly, "the data suggest that there may be no medical procedure where music cannot be used for the benefit of the patient" (Spintge & Droh, 1987, p. 100).

Music therapists who work in medical settings must learn to structure their treatments and reporting procedures to comply with the requirements and expectations of the medical model. "Music therapy patient objectives should be specific, and should be relevant to medical diagnosis, course of treatment, and discharge timeline; benefits should be described in medical, not musical terms" (Standley, 1996b, p. 36). Music therapists who work in medical settings should also pay particular attention to biomedical research that relates to music therapy. As music therapists learn to apply biomedical findings to their clinical practice and learn to describe the effects of music therapy interventions in terms and parameters familiar to other health professionals, they will elevate their professional status as they are "able to be understood on the same medically sound basis as other disciplines" (Taylor, 1997, p. 122).

Music therapists who work in hospital settings need to develop methods for quick, precise assessment charting, and documentation methods (Jacobowitz, 1992; Standley, 1996b). Because of factors such as uncertain scheduling due to other treatments, medical crises, and patients being transferred or discharged without notice, music therapists who work in hospital settings must also learn to maintain a balance between structure and flexibility (Jacobowitz, 1992). At times, the music therapist must work around tubes and medical equipment or adapt to different treatment settings. Strict infection control procedures must also be observed in many medical settings. The music therapist should always remember that "in a hospital, the medical condition of the patient has priority" (Perez, 1989, p. 248) and adapt music therapy interventions and approaches to the current condition, needs, and location of the patient.

SUMMARY

Medical treatment involves the process of diagnosing and prescribing measures to cure or alleviate illness, disease, injury, or pain, and the science and art of preventing diseases and improving and preserving health. This chapter primarily dealt with those conditions that are treated in general hospital, outpatient, office, or clinic settings.

Since the late 1970s and early 1980s, as research tools and methods that demonstrate the efficacy of music therapy as a viable tool for medical treatment have become available, "the field of medicine and music have been experiencing a renaissance in the appreciation of music as an important component in the world of medicine" (Taylor, 1988, p. 86). Today, music therapists serve individuals of all ages who have a variety of acute or chronic medical conditions. Music therapists carry out their interventions in a variety of settings, including general hospitals, children's hospitals, clinics, outpatient facilities, hospice programs, wellness programs, home health agencies, childbirth education programs, performing arts medicine programs, and special education settings. Music therapy interventions can complement and facilitate medical treatment in areas such as labor and delivery, neonatal care, pediatrics, coronary intensive care, pulmonology, surgery, anesthesia, pain control, radiology, oncology, burn units, specific medical procedures, or specific chronic medical conditions. Music therapists function as cooperative members of the medical team, assessing the needs of the patient, planning music therapy intervention strategies designed to meet these needs, and then applying specifically structured music experiences within the context of a therapeutic relationship to help the patient reach the prescribed medical/therapeutic goals that will enable him or her to regain as full a degree of health as possible.

One of the more common and important uses of music in medical settings is pain abatement. Music therapy interventions can decrease awareness of pain, increase pain threshold or pain tolerance, reduce the need for or provide an alternative to pain medication or sedatives, decrease stress and its physiological results, and alter or eliminate the psychological perception of pain. Music therapy interventions are also used to decrease a patient's fear and anxiety about a condition or treatment procedure, to help individuals cope with the trauma of hospitalization and/or illness, to facilitate relaxation or stress reduction, to increase muscular function, to structure movements or exercises, to increase a patient's motivation to participate in treatment, to facilitate healing or recovery processes, to structure and/or reinforce healthy life style changes, to increase expression of feelings, to serve as an outlet for expressing frustration, to provide emotional support, to decrease isolation, to facilitate communication between patients and families or patients and therapists, to reinforce or serve as a vehicle for learning health principles or self-care routines, to structure pleasurable interpersonal interactions, or to normalize the medical environment. This chapter surveyed several music therapy interventions used in labor/delivery, in neonatal care, in the care of hospitalized or health impaired children, in surgery, with organ transplant procedures, in coronary care, with patients who have severe burns, with hemodialysis, in pulmonology, to affect immune response, in oncology, for chronic pain management, and in performing arts medicine.

QUESTIONS FOR THOUGHT AND DISCUSSION

1. Discuss some of the special characteristics and needs of individuals who have various acute or chronic medical conditions. What implications do these have for music therapy programming?

2. Why and how are music experiences useful in making contact with individuals who have various types of acute or chronic medical conditions? Are some types of experiences and activities more useful than others for certain conditions or needs? Which ones? Why?

3. Describe some specific music therapy experiences that might be used (a) in labor/delivery, (b) in neonatal care, (c) in the care of hospitalized or health impaired children, (d) prior to, during, or

following surgery, (e) with organ transplant patients and their families, (f) in coronary care, (g) with patients who have severe burns, (h) with hemodialysis, (i) in pulmonology, (j) to affect immune response, (k) in oncology, (l) for chronic pain management, and (m) in performing arts medicine. How do music therapy interventions help facilitate medical treatment or provide unique ways to meet the medical and/or psychosocial needs of patients in each of these situations?

4. Discuss some special considerations that may be important to remember when developing therapeutic intervention strategies for persons who have acute or chronic medical conditions or when working as a music therapist in a medical setting. Why are these important? What are their implications for the structure of music therapy intervention strategies and the reporting/documentation of treatment outcomes?

5. For each of the situations described below, (a) define the problem or areas of need for the client or group of clients, (b) describe one or more of the goals you might pursue in music therapy sessions with the client(s), (c) describe music activities you might use to help the client(s) meet those goals, (d) tell how the music activities you described relate to the goals and needs of the client(s), and (e) mention any special considerations you might want to take into account when working with the client(s).

Situation 1:

A 4-year-old child entering the hospital for surgery is very anxious and frightened about the procedure. The child's fears and their concern about his condition are making his parents very anxious, too, but they are trying to hide this from the child because they don't want him to get more upset. The doctor has asked you to help in finding ways to calm and relax the child and parents and help them express and deal with their fears and concerns. She also would like you to help explain the procedure to the child in a way he can understand.

Situation 2:

A young mother-to-be in the sixth month of her pregnancy wants to have a medication-free childbirth experience and has heard that music might be helpful in relieving or distracting her from the pain. She is in good health, and her doctor supports her plan. She and her husband have contracted with you to develop a music therapy-assisted childbirth program for them.

SUGGESTIONS FOR FURTHER READING

Barrickman, J. (1989). A developmental music therapy approach for preschool hospitalized children. *Music Therapy Perspectives, 7,* 10-16.

Boldt, S. (1996). The effects of music therapy on motivation, psychological well-being, physical comfort, and exercise endurance of bone marrow transplant patients. *Journal of Music Therapy, 33*(3), 164-188.

Brown, C. J., Chen, A. C. N., & Dworkin, S. F. (1989). Music in the control of human pain. *Music Therapy, 8*(1), 47-60.

Bruscia, K. E. (Ed.) (1991). *Case studies in music therapy.* Phoenixville, PA: Barcelona Publishers.

Clark, M. E. (1986). Music therapy-assisted childbirth: A practical guide. *Music Therapy Perspectives, 5,* 23-27.

Cowan, D. S. (1991). Music therapy in the surgical arena. *Music Therapy Perspectives, 9,* 42-45.

Crowe, B. (1985). Music therapy and physical medicine –

expanding opportunities for employment. *Music Therapy Perspectives, 5*(1), 44-51.

Froehlich, M. A. R. (Ed.). (1996). *Music therapy with hospitalized children: A creative arts child life approach.* Cherry Hill, NJ: Jeffrey Books.

Gibbons, A. C., & McDougal, D. L. (1987). Music therapy in medical technology: Organ transplants. In R. R. Pratt (Ed.), *The fourth international symposium on music: Rehabilitation and human well-being* (pp. 61-72). NY: University Press of America.

Harvey, A. W. (Compiler). (1988). *Music and health: Sourcebook of readings.* Richmond, KY: Music for Health Services Foundation.

Jacobowitz, R. M. (1992). Music therapy in the short-term pediatric setting: Practical guideline for a limited time frame. *Music Therapy, 11*(1), 45-64.

Maranto, C. D. (Ed.) (1991). *Applications of music in medicine.*

Washington, D.C.: National Association for Music Therapy.

Maranto, C. D. (1996). Research in music and medicine: The state of the art. In M. A. R. Froehlich (Ed.), *Music therapy with hospitalized children: A creative arts child life approach* (pp. 39-66). Cherry Hill, NJ: Jeffrey Books.

McKinney, C. H. (1990). Music therapy in obstetrics: A review. *Music Therapy Perspectives, 8,* 57-60.

Rider, M. S. (1987). Music therapy: Therapy for debilitated musicians. *Music Therapy Perspectives, 4,* 40-42.

Robb, S. L. (1996). Techniques in song writing: Restoring emotional and physical well-being in adolescents who have been traumatically injured. *Music Therapy Perspectives, 14*(1), 30-37.

Rudenberg, M. T., & Royka, A. M. (1989). Promoting psychological adjustment in pediatric burn patients through music therapy and child life therapy. *Music Therapy Perspectives, 7,* 40-43.

Schwankovsky, L. M., & Guthrie, P. T. (1982). *Music therapy for handicapped children: Other health impaired.* Washington, D.C.: National Association for Music Therapy.

Selm, M. E. (1991). Chronic pain: Three issues in treatment and implications for music therapy. *Music Therapy Perspectives, 9,* 91-97.

Spintge, R. (1989). The anxiolytic effects of music. In M. H. M. Lee (Ed.), *Rehabilitation, music and human well-being* (pp. 82-100). St. Louis: MMB Music.

Standley, J. M. (1986). Music research in medical/ dental treatment: Meta-analysis and clinical applications. *Journal of Music Therapy, 23*(2), 56-122.

Standley, J. M. (1996). Music in medical/dental treatment: An update of a prior meta-analysis. In C. E. Furman (Ed.), *Effectiveness of music therapy procedures: Documentation of research and clinical practice* (2nd ed.) (pp. 1-60). Silver Spring, MD: National Association for Music Therapy.

Chapter Eighteen

MUSIC THERAPY IN PHYSICAL REHABILITATION PROGRAMS

DEFINITIONS

REHABILITATION IS the process of restoring an individual's ability to function as normally as possible in his or her daily life and work following a disabling injury or illness (Miller & Keane, 1978). *Physical rehabilitation programs* work on restoring functional abilities in the areas of cognition, communication, physical skills (e.g., motor learning and motor skills), activities of daily living, and psychosocial skills to individuals who have injuries or illnesses that have caused physical, cognitive, sensory, and/or perceptual deficits (Sandness, 1995). Interventions are directed toward helping patients achieve the maximum degree of independence possible in physical, psychological, and social/emotional functioning, so that they can return to the community to enjoy the best quality of life possible (Brunk, 1992). The three most common groups of individuals served by physical rehabilitation programs are survivors of traumatic brain injuries, strokes, and spinal cord injuries.

A *traumatic brain injury (TBI)* is a severe injury to the brain that causes widespread, diffuse brain damage. Other terms used to describe this condition include *closed head injury* (used when the brain is injured without the skull being penetrated) or *head trauma*. Traumatic brain injuries usually are caused by sudden mechanical force or blows to the head, such as may occur in accidents or falls, assault, gun shot wounds, or motor vehicle accidents (Brunk, 1992; Lucia, 1987; Rudenberg, 1982; Thaut, 1992c). Lack of oxygen to the brain (e.g., in near-drowning) or lack of blood supply to the brain (e.g., following cardiac arrest) may also cause TBIs. TBIs can be life-threatening or result in residual dysfunctions in one or more sensory, motor, language, behavioral, or psychological areas, depending upon the extent and location of the brain injury.

Most individuals who experience brain injuries are unconscious or in a comatose state for some period of time. A *coma* is "a state of unconsciousness from which the patient cannot be aroused, even by powerful stimuli" (Miller & Keane, 1978, p. 235). The longer patients are in a coma, the more likely they are to have widespread, severe brain damage (Thaut, 1992c). In the United States, TBIs are a major cause of death and disability for individuals under age 35. Ten to 15% of the approximately 700,000 Americans who suffer head injuries each year are permanently disabled to such an extent that they will never be able to return to their pre-injury life style (Thaut, 1992c).

In a *stroke*, or *cerebrovascular accident (CVA)*, the blood supply to the brain is temporarily blocked, cutting off the brain's source of oxygen and causing damage to the brain cells (Prazich, 1985). About two-thirds of all strokes are *ischemic strokes* or *infarctions*, resulting from blockages or clots that gradually form in arteries leading to the brain. When the obstruction is only temporary, a *transient ischemic attack (TIA)*, sometimes know as an incomplete, "mini," or "little" stroke, occurs. TIAs are brief, lasting only a few seconds to no more than 30 minutes, followed by a complete return to normal functioning. However, they usually are a warning sign that a complete stroke may occur sometime in the future. *Hemorrhagic strokes* occur when blood vessels in or around the brain leak or burst, as the result of artery walls being weakened by disease and breaking, or of a sudden increase in blood pressure that ruptures arteries, or of a cerebral aneurysm (thin tissue in a section of an artery wall that balloons out and eventually breaks).

As brain cells are damaged or die during a stroke, the functions they control (e.g., speech, muscle movement, emotions, understanding) are lost or impaired (Miller & Keane, 1978; Prazich, 1985; Zamula, 1986). Brain damage caused by strokes is usually more localized and specific than the diffuse brain damage that occurs in TBIs (Brunk, 1992; Thaut, 1992c). About 400,000 Americans suffer strokes each year; about 160,000 die immediately or shortly after the stroke's onset. Of those who survive, about 10% return to work without significant impairment, about 40% will be slightly disabled, about another 40% will be seriously disabled and require some special services, and about 10% will require institutional care (Zamula, 1986).

Spinal cord injuries paralyze about 8,000 Americans each year (National Paralysis Foundation, n.d.), usually as the result of accidents or traumatic injuries (Rudenberg, 1982; Thaut, 1992a). When the spinal cord is damaged in neck or back fractures, the flow of electrical impulses from the brain is interrupted, and various degrees of paralysis and loss of function result. The site of the injury determines the extent of the damage: The farther up on the spinal cord the injury occurs, the more extensive the loss of function. When the spinal cord is damaged in the thoracic area or below, *paraplegia*, the loss of use of the lower body movement and sensation, occurs. Damage to the cervical area of the spinal cord results in *quadriplegia*, the loss of body movement and sensation below the neck. When spinal cord nerve pathways are completely destroyed, they do not regenerate and cannot be repaired by current medical techniques; thus, paralysis from spinal cord injuries is usually permanent. However, recent research is offering new hope to persons who have been paralyzed by spinal cord injuries and challenging the belief that paralysis resulting from central nervous system damage is irreversible (National Paralysis Foundation, n.d.). For example, scientists have found that nerve tissue can be transplanted into the brain and grow and survive there and that nerve cells from an embryo can survive and function in the central nervous system of an adult host. In addition, new drugs are being discovered that minimize that process of paralysis and improve recovery following injury, and techniques like computer stimulation and biofeedback are being use to help restore functional control to previously useless muscles (National Paralysis Foundation, n.d.). Research is continuing on ways to apply these findings to the rehabilitation of individuals who have spinal cord injuries.

After injuries to the brain or nervous system, some patients may experience a gradual, spontaneous return of some cognitive, physical, or sensory functions that were lost immediately following the incident. The phenomenon is known as *spontaneous recovery*. Most spontaneous recovery occurs within three to six months of the injury; therefore, a prognosis is usually not given until after this period. Spontaneous recovery of some functions may continue for another 12-18 months; however, patients are usually best served by starting rehabilitation as soon as possible after their injury (Lucia, 1987).

COMMON CHARACTERISTICS, PROBLEMS, AND NEEDS OF CLIENTS

As with any population, those individuals who are served by rehabilitation programs are a very heterogeneous group. Factors such as the type and severity of the impairment, the cause and time of onset, the existence of associated conditions or impairments, and the degree and type of support services available will all have varying effects on the individual's level of functioning, needs, and treatment program. In addition, each individual will have a unique combinations of abilities, needs, personality traits, strengths, and weaknesses that will impact that his or her particular responses and functional abilities. Therefore, it is unwise to attempt to predict a particular person's skill levels or ceiling of abilities based on broad generalizations about a certain population. However, an awareness of some of those characteristics, problems, and needs which may be common to individuals who are served by rehabilitation programs will be beneficial both to the therapist who desires to work with this population and to the reader who is trying to understand how music therapy intervention strategies may benefit this population.

Government agencies, such as the Joint Commission on Accreditation of Healthcare Organizations [JCAHO] and the Commission on Accreditation of Rehabilitation Facilities [CARF], that set standards for physical rehabilitation programs emphasize providing therapeutic, educational, and training services that are consistent with the needs of the individual patient and that help the patient develop and maintain the highest possible level of independent functioning and community reintegration (Sandness, 1995). Thus, a measure of how well patients can function independently in various aspects of life activities is an important indicator of their treatment needs. Many physical rehabilitation programs use the *Functional Independence Measure (FIM)* from the Uniform Data System for Medical Rehabilitation to indicate the severity of a patient's disability (Sandness, 1995, p. 77). A patient's FIM score can change during the rehabilitation process as the patient makes progress in increasing his or her independent functioning in some area of life activities.

The FIM contains 18 items in six categories of life activities: self-care, sphincter control, mobility, locomotion, communication (receptive and expressive), and social cognition (includes social interaction, problem solving, memory). These items are rated on a seven-level scale that represents gradations of independent or dependent behavior and reflects the amount of help needed by the patient in each area. In levels 1 and 2, "complete dependence," the patient contributes less than 50% to less than 25% of the effort required for an activity. In levels 3-5, the patient is able to expend 50%-75% or more of the effort, but requires physical assistance or supervision from another person to complete the activity. Patients functioning at levels 6 or 7 do not require assistance or supervision from another person to perform the activity and are rated as "independent" in those areas.

The FIM is a useful tool for providing a general idea of the patient's overall level of functional independence and his or her progress toward independence during treatment. Other assessment tools specific to various population groups (e.g., coma patients) are also used in determining the needs of clients in physical rehabilitation programs. Some of these assessments are described briefly in the following sections, which deal more specifically with the characteristics and needs of individuals who have traumatic brain injuries, who are comatose, who have had strokes, or who have spinal cord injuries.

Individuals with Traumatic Brain Injuries

Individuals who survive traumatic brain injuries (TBIs) may have functional deficits in a number of areas, including speech and language, vision and/or hearing, motor function (e.g., paralysis, limited range of motion, limited muscle strength or endurance, difficulties with balance or motor planning), cognition (e.g., difficulties with concentration, memory, recalling sequences, reasoning, problem solving), and socio-emotional areas (e.g., labile affect, depression, poor motivation, poor self-image, difficulty initiating activities or carrying them through to completion, impulsivity or overactivity, rigidity, poor self-awareness, inappropriate social behaviors, lack of social judgment) (Brunk, 1992; Chance, 1986; Lucia, 1987; Thaut, 1992c). Persons who have had TBIs "are often irritable, quarrelsome, anxious, easily depressed, and excitable" (Chance, 1986, p. 64), and these qualities may affect their ability to interact effectively with others. TBI patients may also become confused and agitated by even slight variations in routine, or may laugh uncontrollably or become verbally abusive when they are under stress. Those who face chronic disability will, at some point in their recovery, experience feelings of grief over the losses they have sustained (Bright, 1986). Anger – at their helplessness, with the doctors, with society, etc. – is often a part of the grief over disability (Bright, 1986). It is important that professionals offer TBI patients considerable emotional support, along with assistance in gaining physical, cognitive, and social skills, to help these patients adapt successfully to the changes that have occurred in their lives. Since self-esteem is critical to the way individuals adapt to loss and change (Bright, 1986), it is also important to provide experiences that bolster or increase the patient's self-esteem.

Rehabilitation from traumatic brain injury is a long process, and individuals usually pass through several stages or phases of recovery (Brunk, 1992;

Claeys et al., 1989; Thaut, 1992c). In the *early* or acute *stages* of TBI, there is global suppression of cognitive functions and little or no response to stimuli. The patient may be in a coma. As the patients emerge from this phase, they often experience severe agitation and confusion and are disoriented to time and place. In the *middle* or *intermediate phases* of recovery, patients are generally oriented to time and place but still experience moderate confusion and may have disoriented, disorganized, or agitated responses to stimuli. With appropriate environmental structure, their performance and responses generally improve. At this stage, most TBI patients have marked to severe attention deficits, severe memory deficits, difficulties with problem solving and judgment, and social difficulties. During the *later phase* of recovery, patients may continue to have some cognitive impairments (e.g., mild to moderate memory, problem-solving, or organizational difficulties); however, their performance usually improves with direction and repetition and as they learn compensatory strategies for persistent deficits. With practice, social relationships and behaviors usually improve, and many patients regain a generally positive self-image. However, as they work on accepting their residual deficits and try to find ways to return to as many of their pre-injury responsibilities as possible during this stage, patients may also experience depression, anger, or anxiety. Behaviors and cognitive functioning levels of TBI patients are also often described by levels of the Rancho Los Amigos Scale (Brunk, 1992; Claeys et al., 1989), which is discussed in the next section of this chapter.

Individuals who have traumatic brain injuries frequently respond best to multi-modal, trans-disciplinary treatment processes that begin with the development of rapport between client and therapist (Claeys et al., 1989):

> TBI clients appear to respond to relationships far more than to techniques or processes. Thus, the more transdisciplinary training and clinical practice that occurs, the greater likelihood of the most therapeutic combination of relationship and technique occurring. (p. 71)

In working with individuals who have TBIs, it is important to incorporate positive expectations into all aspects of rehabilitation. Therapists should try to focus on abilities rather than disabilities and structure interventions to work with the patient's strengths. Rehabilitation programs often offer many services, including physical therapy, occupational therapy, speech therapy, psychotherapy, nutrition or dietary planning, creative arts therapies, therapeutic recreation, and group and family counselling (Brunk, 1992; Chance, 1986). Programs frequently focus on cognitive training or re-training, functional skills training (e.g., learning skills and routines for self-care, housekeeping, leisure, work or school, business and finance, consumer events, and personal/social activities) and environmental management (modifying the environment to minimize the effects of the individual's limitations) (Chance, 1986).

Individuals Who Are Comatose or Emerging from Comas

Individuals who have received brain injuries from head trauma or a stroke often are in a comatose state for at least a short time after their injury. The amount of time spent in coma impacts the patient's chances of recovery. Generally, "the longer a person is comatose the more likely the existence of severe and widespread brain damage" (Thaut, 1992c, p. 259).

Patients who are in deep coma states do not respond to their environment (Brunk, 1992; Boyle, 1989). They often appear to be in a sleep-like or vegetative state. Although they may seem to be awake at times, there is no external evidence of communication or complex behavior. Most movements are random and reflexive. Therapists who work with coma patients try to find some type of stimulation that will produce consistent alerting and orienting responses in the patients to help them gradually move out of the coma and begin to purposefully respond to and interact with their environment (Boyle, 1987, 1989; Claeys et al., 1989).

Several assessment scales have been developed to assess the severity of comatose states by rating various responses and behaviors of coma patients. Two of the most common are the Glasgow Coma Scale (Boyle, 1989; Sandness, 1995; Thaut, 1992c) and the Rancho Los Amigos Scale (Brunk, 1992; Claeys et al., 1989; Sandness, 1995; Thaut, 1992c). The *Glasgow Coma Scale* uses numerical scales to rate three areas of response: (a) *eye opening* (1=none; 2=to pain; 3=to speech; 4=spontaneous), (b) *motor response* to pain stimulus or command (1=no response; 2=extension; 3=abnormal flexion; 4=withdrawal; 5=localizes pain; shows purposeful movement; 6=obeys command), and (c) *verbal response* (1=none; 2=incomprehensible; 3=inappropriate; 4=confused; 5=fully oriented). Adding the three ratings gives an assessment of coma severity: a total of 13 or more is a mild coma, 9-12 is moderate, and 8 or below is severe (Thaut, 1992c).

The *Rancho Los Amigos Scale* uses eight levels to describe the cognitive functioning and behaviors typically demonstrated by patients as they emerge from coma (Claeys et al., 1989; Thaut, 1992c). In *Level I, no response*, the deepest state of coma, the patient seems to be in a deep sleep and is completely unresponsive to stimuli. In *Level II, generalized responsiveness*, the patient still appears to be asleep most of the time, but has limited, inconsistent, non-purposeful, nonspecific responses (e.g., physiological changes, body movements, vocalizations) to pain or sensory stimulation. Responses are often the same, regardless of the type of stimulation. Patients at *Level III* exhibit *localized* responses: They react specifically, although still inconsistently, with responses being differentiated according to the type of stimulus. These patients are beginning to be more aware of and responsive to some people. They may be alert for 3 or more minutes at a time, and may begin to follow simple commands, such as closing eyes or squeezing hand. At *Level IV, confused-behavioral*, patients become more active, with confused, bizarre, agitated, nonpurposeful, and sometimes aggressive behaviors. These agitated behaviors seem to be related to internal confusion. Patients do not seem to discriminate between people and objects and attend only very briefly to environmental events. If patients are able to talk, their speech is frequently incoherent or inappropriate to the environment. However, Level IV patients are beginning to take some independent actions and show some signs of processing information, even though they usually lack short- and long-term recall skills. As patients progress to *Level V, confused*, they are becoming more alert and are able to follow simple commands fairly consistently. However, responses to more complex tasks and new learning are often fragmented and confused. Patients are unable to sustain attention for any length of time

and have difficulty focusing on one task. With structure, patients can perform some previously learned tasks, but are usually unable to learn new information. Patients may be able to converse on a superficial social level for short periods, but verbalizations are still often inappropriate or confabulatory. Memory functions are still severely impaired. In *Level VI, confused-appropriate*, patients can follow simple commands consistently and show goal-directed behaviors, but they are dependent on cues and external structure for direction. They are usually able to preform previously known self-care activities with minimal assistance. Although many memory and processing deficits are still present, memory and attention span are increasing, as are awareness of self and others. Responses may be confused but are usually appropriate to the situation. Patients at this stage generally have more depth and detail for past memories than for recent memories. Patients who progress to *Level VII, automatic-appropriate*, behave appropriately and are oriented within hospital and home settings. They can perform daily routines automatically, and are able to learn some new information, although usually at a decreased rate. With structure, they can initiate some social or recreational activities, but they still have impaired judgment, planning, and problem-solving skills. At *Level VIII, purposeful and appropriate*, patients are alert, oriented, responsive to the environment, and are able to recall and integrate past and recent events. They can learn new activities and perform activities without supervision once they have been learned. These individuals can usually function independently at home and may be able to drive, although some impairments in abstract reasoning, judgment, and stress tolerance may persist.

Individuals Who Have Had Strokes or Cerebrovascular Accidents

Patients who have had strokes or CVAs may have a variety of physical, cognitive, or socio-emotional impairments, such as paralysis, memory problems, neglect of one side of the body, difficult with new learning, emotional lability, inappropriate affect, distorted sensory input, and difficulties regulating and checking their own speech and behavior ("social judgment") (Brunk, 1992; Fowler & Fordyce, 1974;

Prazich, 1985; Sandness, 1995; Thaut, 1992c; Zamula, 1986). Each individual will have different problems, depending on the particular part of the brain that was damaged. For example, a stroke that involves the right side of the brain generally causes weakness or paralysis on the left side of the body, while one that involves the left side of the brain causes weakness or paralysis on the right side of the body. Patients with right brain damage usually also have difficulties with spatial-perceptual tasks, tend to overestimate their abilities, may be impulsive or careless, and have memory deficits that impact performance of activities (Fowler & Fordyce, 1974). Those with left brain damage usually have a slow, cautious behavioral style and frequently have communication disorders, such as *aphasia* (impaired ability to understand or use language; may affect expressive or receptive language skills or both), *apraxia* (impaired speech ability due to loss of motor planning abilities involving the muscles used for articulation of words), or *dysarthria* (slow, slurred, monotonous speech, often with disruptions in flow and phrasing and imperfect articulation, due to motor control disturbances caused by central or peripheral nervous system damage affecting muscles related to speech production). Patients who have severe speech disorders may need to learn to use an augmentive communication system to communicate with others. (See Chapter Twelve for more information on communication disorders and augmentive communication systems.)

Patients who lose the ability to speak or who lose normal speech quality often also lose their self-confidence. Their difficulties in communicating and interacting with others may lead to frustration, withdrawal, and/or decreased self-esteem. Some patients may become depressed. Many individuals need time to grieve the losses caused by their stroke as well as emotional support to help them adjust to the changes in their abilities and roles (Bright, 1986; Clair, 1996b).

Although strokes may occur at any age, many stroke patients are elderly. Recent figures indicate that 75% of all strokes occur in people who are over age 65 and that the incidence of strokes is three times higher for individuals who are over age 75 than for those ages 65-74 (Clair, 1996b). Treatment for stroke patients generally involves three phases: acute, subacute, and chronic (Clair, 1996b). In the *acute* phase, treatment focuses on getting the individual medically stable and on identifying deficits and remaining abilities in cognitive processing, motor function, postural control, speech and language, sensory perception, and emotional responses. In the *subacute* phase, attention turns to preventing complications and further deterioration. During the *chronic* phase, treatment focuses on maintaining the patient's functioning at the highest possible level of independence and reintegration to their community. This phase presents many challenges to both stroke patients and their caregivers, as individuals may begin to experience depression because of their impairments. During the chronic phase, individuals must learn to adjust to their deficits and find ways to cope with changing roles and responsibilities. Some may need to learn to use adaptive equipment. Many will also have to face giving up at least some of their independence as they are forced to rely on others for various aspects of their care (Bright, 1986; Clair, 1996b).

Individuals with Spinal Cord Injuries

Spinal cord injuries usually result in some degree of paralysis (i.e., loss of motor function). The site of the injury determines the extent of the damage; the farther up on the spinal cord the injury occurs, the more extensive the loss of function. Paralysis imposes many severe emotional, social, and occupational changes in a person's life. For example, individuals who are quadriplegic may need to learn to cope with changes in relationships (e.g., with spouse, children, parents, friends) as well as with changes in body image and physical functioning abilities. They need much emotional support as they "adapt to being different, rather than remaining 'ill'" (Bright, 1986, p. 137).

Treatment plans for the rehabilitation of persons who have spinal cord injuries are based on interdisciplinary assessments that include a determination of motor impairments and functional limitations. "Functional assessment of the client includes all spheres of activity, such as home and family, recreation, employment, and independence in daily living skills" (Sandness, 1995, p. 78). Clients may help set treatment goals by indicating what activities are most important for them to learn in order to function more independently or be more comfortable. In addition to helping patients increase upper extremity function, increase endurance and respiratory function, and learn to use adaptive devices, treatment programs also help clients with spinal cord injuries deal with psychological adjustment issues (e.g., loss of privacy, loss of control, loss of independence, changed physical abilities, and changed self-image), vocational and independent living skills, and leisure education (Brunk, 1992).

SETTINGS FOR SERVICE DELIVERY

Individuals who need rehabilitation services because of traumatic brain injuries, strokes, or spinal cord injuries may receive special programs and services to help meet their specific needs in a variety of settings, including general hospitals, special rehabilitation hospitals, centers, or clinics, nursing homes, long-term care facilities, speech clinics (e.g., for aphasia rehabilitation), or in-home services. In addition, school-age individuals may receive services through special education programs of their local school districts. The Individuals with Disabilities Act (IDEA) (Public Law 101-476), the 1990 revision of the 1975 Education for All Handicapped Children Act (Public Law 94-142) assures a free, appropriate public education to all children, ages 3-21, including those who have orthopedic impairments (such as paralysis) or traumatic brain injuries. This law, as well as the Technology-Related Assistance for Individuals with Disabilities Act (Public Law 100-407), also provide for assistive technology devices and services that may be needed by the individual (Adamek, 1996; Johnson, 1996). Sometimes, rehabilitation may begin in one setting (e.g., hospital) and then, after the individual is medically stable, continue in another setting that is geared more specifically to rehabilitation.

Music therapists may work with individuals of varying ages who have traumatic brain injuries, strokes, or spinal cord injuries. Music therapists usually work as part of an interdisciplinary team that may include physicians, nurses, psychologists, social workers, dieticians, physical therapists, occupational therapists, speech therapists, educators, vocational rehabilitation specialists, therapeutic recreation specialists, other creative arts therapists, chaplains, and family counselors (Brunk, 1992; Thaut, 1992c). Music therapists can provide services to clients who have had traumatic brain injuries, strokes, or spinal cord injuries in many different settings, including hospitals, rehabilitation centers, Veteran's Administration facilities, public schools, private schools or clinics, music studios, nursing homes, clients' homes, or community programs. Music therapists may provide direct or consultant services and work with clients as individuals or in groups. They may be full- or part-time employees of facilities, contract their services to various agencies, or work in private practice.

In a recent survey of populations served by music therapists in which respondents were permitted to list as many categories as appropriate (AMTA, 1998), 205 of 1,620 respondents said they worked with clients who had sustained head injuries, 302 reported working with clients who were neurologically impaired, and 290 worked with clients who had had strokes. When asked to list their work settings, 119 music therapists specifically stated they were employed in physical rehabilitation settings (AMTA, 1998), as compared with 75 music therapists who listed physical rehabilitation as their work setting four years earlier (NAMT, 1994a). These figures seem to support Sandness' (1995) prediction that "the potential for increasing music therapy services in the area of physical rehabilitation is significant" (p. 76).

HOW MUSIC IS USED IN THERAPY

Unique Contributions to the Rehabilitation Process

As music therapists cooperate with other professionals in providing interventions that address the physical, cognitive, communication, and socioemotional needs of individuals in physical rehabilitation programs, they bring to the treatment program specialized sets of music-based activities and experiences that can address client needs in unique ways (Thaut, 1992c). Music provides an additional entryway to the brain, activating additional neurological pathways through which learning and skill development can occur (Hofmeister & Cole, 1986). For example, the rhythmic and temporal qualities of music can provide cues and structures that help patients structure and organize movement and sequence activities (Brunk, 1992, Clair, 1996b; Lucia, 1987; Staum, 1988, 1996; Taylor, 1997; Thaut et al., 1991). Music experiences also facilitate the establishment of a therapeutic relationship (Claeys et al., 1989), helping establish a common bond between therapist and client and reducing the barrier that tends to separate the helper and the helpee (Bright, 1986).

Since music is a normal activity that is valued by society, music therapy interventions can help humanize and normalize the treatment setting, providing a nonthreatening environment that increases motivation, decreases tension and stress, and helps individuals feel comfortable expressing their inner feelings (Confrancesco, 1985). Music experiences can also be adapted to allow for participation at different levels of ability and be individualized to include material that is meaningful to and motivating for a particular client. In her music therapy work with coma patients, Boyle (1987) observed:

> It [music] seemed suited to the limitations of the patients while simultaneously tapping their potential to be controlled by conditioned reinforcers from their own unique histories. . . . In addition, music is unobtrusive, easy to administer, unlikely to produce satiation, and unlikely to create resistance from caretakers, medical personnel, or members of patients' families. (p. 52)

Music therapy interventions can be structured as enjoyable leisure activities that help clients practice skills or as social experiences that family members can enjoy with the clients or help implement (Barker & Brunk, 1991). Because of the wide range of materials and methods of interaction available in music experiences, music therapy interventions can add interest and motivation to treatment programs, increasing patient participation and potential level of recovery (Thompson et al., 1990). In addition to targeting specific skill development areas, music therapy experiences can provide the setting for a holistic integration of physical, cognitive, and socioemotional skills (Brunk, 1992).

General Music Therapy Goals and Treatment Techniques

As with any population, music therapy treatment for individuals in physical rehabilitation programs begins with referral and assessment. Medical approval for music therapy treatment should always be given by the patient's physician, and specific recommendations may be provided by the physician or other treatment team members on precautions, adaptations, or goals that may apply to the music therapy setting (Brunk, 1992). When music therapists work in cooperation with other treatment team members, they can "develop a more comprehensive treatment program, ensuring maximal rehabilitation of the affected and residual functions, and providing quality of life at the highest level attainable" (Thompson et al., 1990, p. 29).

Much information concerning the patient's general level of functioning can be obtained from the assessments and reports of other disciplines; however, music therapists will also wish to obtain information on the individual's musical history, interests, and preferences and observe the patient's responses to various types of music materials and experiences (Sandness, 1995). Since music influences brain functions in unique ways (Taylor, 1997), patients may exhibit responses to music experiences that are not present with other types of stimulation. Music therapy assessments for coma patients may include observation of patients' responses to a sequenced presentation of musical stimuli (vibrating string with various pitches, recorded music, tuning forks, autoharp) (Claeys et al., 1989). Music therapy activities can also be used to assess the cognitive, motor, communication, social, and visual skills of stroke patients (Thompson et al., 1990).

Music therapy interventions can be structured to help individuals in physical rehabilitation programs improve their level of functioning in physical, cognitive, communication, and socio-emotional skills (Adamek & Shiraishi, 1996; Barker & Brunk, 1991; Brunk, 1992; Claeys et al., 1989; Hofmeister & Cole,

1986; Lucia, 1987; Sandness, 1995; Staum, 1988, 1996; Thaut, 1992c; Thompson et al., 1990). Potential applications of music therapy treatments are very broad. Boyle (1989) observed that "music can be an integral part of treatment programming ranging from contingent auditory stimulation to the development of new lifetime leisure skills for the traumatic brain-injured patient" (p. 144). Brunk (1992) noted that patients in a rehabilitation center could participate in music therapy at all levels of recovery, from coma stimulation (music for auditory stimulation and as a contingent stimulus) to active treatment (using goal-directed music experiences to work on speech, motor control and coordination, memory, or other concerns) to discharge (using music-based activities to facilitate discussion of discharge concerns or helping patients and their families find ways to continue using music activities to develop skills or to provide social integration after hospitalization). Music therapy interventions for patients in rehabilitation programs utilize a variety of structured music experiences (e.g., listening to music, playing instruments, singing or vocalizing, moving to music, improvising or composing music, and discussing music) to motivate or assist patients in working toward the greatest degree of independence possible in functional motor, communication, cognitive, self-care, and socio-emotional skills.

Music Therapy Interventions to Improve Physical Functioning

Music therapy interventions can help patients in rehabilitation programs improve physical functioning by providing (a) motivation for movement (especially if the movements are difficult for the patient), (b) purpose and direction for movement, (c) structure or timing cues for movement or physical exercises, (d) feedback for movement (e.g., tactile/kinesthetic feedback from the feel of strumming the strings of an autoharp as well as auditory feedback when a sound is produced), and (e) practice in motor coordination and motor planning (Brunk, 1992; Sandness, 1995; Thaut, 1992c). Restoring motor function following a stroke or traumatic brain injury is often a long, difficult, and frustrating task, involving such developmental steps as increasing the patient's ability to initiate move-

ment, increasing range of motion necessary to assume desired postures or to move far enough to accomplish desired tasks, and improving fluidity of movement or increasing motor control and coordination (Clair, 1996b). Research has shown that rhythmic auditory stimulation from music can facilitate this process as sound stimuli excite motor neurons and stimulate muscular responses and as rhythmic stimuli synchronize and organize motor activity (Clair, 1996b; Staum, 1988, 1996; Thaut, 1992c; Thaut et al., 1991; Taylor, 1997).

At a very basic level, music can reinforce and increase purposeful motor responses. Boyle (1987) found that 15 seconds of contingent music (using the patient's preferred music, as determined from conversations with the patient's family) effectively increased targeted behaviors such as lateral head movement, mouth movement, finger movement, eye focus, and eye blinks. Research has also shown that vibroacoustic therapy, "a process in which vibrations are applied directly to the body in the form of low frequency sinus tones in combination with selected music" (Skille, 1989, p. 62), can benefit stroke patients by decreasing muscle spasms, increasing responsiveness to range of motion exercises, and stimulating or facilitating independent movements. In addition, clinical studies in China have shown that music electro-acupuncture techniques, where music is electrically added to the acupuncture stimulation by attaching electrodes from the sound source to the acupuncture needle by metal clips as the subjects listen to the same music through headphones, can stimulate muscle function and increase muscle strength in patients with cerebral hemiplegia (Shi-jing et al., 1991).

Many music therapy programs in physical rehabilitation settings use movement to music (e.g., exercises to music, music with gait training) or the movements used in playing instruments to help motivate movement and to help increase motor control and coordination (Brunk, 1992; Hofmeister & Cole, 1986; Lucia, 1987; Sandness, 1995; Staum, 1988, 1996; Thaut, 1992c). Frequently, music and rhythmic stimulation are used as timing cues to organize and structure physical movements and exercise. According to Thaut (1992c), music is very useful as a timing cue for physical movement because of three factors. First, the rhythmic organization of music helps patients organize their movement in time. Secondly, music activates the auditory sense, the sense in which timing develops earliest and most efficiently. Thirdly, sound activates the motor neurons and puts the muscles in a state of readiness, and learning to move to rhythmically organized sounds (e.g., music) activates the muscles in synchrony with the auditory rhythm.

Recent neurophysiological research has shown that music not only stimulates movement but also serves as a "neurological entrainment mechanism" (Taylor, 1997, p. 121) for movement. For example, music and auditory stimuli can be very beneficial in facilitating gait training for individuals who have had strokes or who have Parkinson's disease (Clair, 1996b; Staum, 1988, 1996; Thaut, 1992a). In summarizing some of the research in this area, Clair (1996b) concluded:

> Although the work of Thaut and colleagues is complex and involves sophisticated measurement protocols, the outcomes are clear: Rhythmic auditory cues presented during gait training cause walking to become more symmetrical, more efficient, and better balanced. (p. 213)

Music may also be used in conjunction with behavioral techniques to improve physical functioning. For example, Kearney and Fussey (1991) found that contingent music administered by a headband with a special switch that allowed the music to be played only when the subjects held their head in the correct upright position significantly increased correct head position during ambulation in adult males who had brain injuries. The neurological entrainment power of music was incidentally shown in this study, as the researchers noted that the rhythmic auditory stimulation also decreased the patients' stride deviation and improved their gait rhythmicity.

From her analysis of the literature concerning music and physical rehabilitation, Staum (1996) observed that reinforcing the rhythmic stimulation of music with sounds of one's own production (as in singing, chanting, playing instruments) seemed to increase the inherent drive to synchronize movement with the rhythm of the music. In her work with patients who had traumatic brain injuries, Lucia (1987) found that singing familiar songs (selected to

match the time frame, tempo, and feel of the movement) during exercise routines developed by physical or occupational therapists motivated and facilitated patients' participation by helping them focus on the task and by providing diversion from the boredom of repeated exercises. The group practiced singing the songs before adding the movement. Lucia found that this technique was most beneficial to patients with right hemiplegia who had left frontal lobe damage or bilateral damage where the singing centers of the right brain hemisphere were still relatively intact.

Research has shown that auditory rhythm can enhance performance of upper extremity gross motor tasks, implying that the use of rhythmic techniques to teach and accompany movement in neuromuscular reeducation programs may lead to a quicker recovery of motor control and skill by improving the anticipation and timing of muscular efforts (Thaut et al., 1991). Organizing movements to a rhythmic accompaniment or practicing functional movements of upper extremities by playing musical instruments may help also patients who have had strokes or TBIs sustain consistent muscular efforts (Thaut et al., 1991). For example, Confrancesco (1985) used music instruments matched to the client's physical needs to increase hand grasp strength and functional arm and hand movements in stroke patients.

Using appropriate musical instruments to exercise specific physical movement gives patients immediate feedback and reinforcement (via the production of a tone or a beat) when the movement is performed correctly, adds enjoyment to the exercise and motivation to practice the movements, and helps patients remember the muscle movements that produce certain rhythmic and melodic patterns (Thaut, 1992c). Various instruments, from simple rhythm instruments to autoharps and guitars to recorders and keyboards to traditional band and orchestral instruments to electronic or computerized instruments, can be used in movement retraining. The key is to match the instrument to the physical needs, abilities, and interests of the patient (Elliott, 1982; Thaut, 1992c). For example, Erdonmez (1991) worked with a patient whose premorbid experience as a pianist motivated him to use the piano as an integral part of his rehabilitation following a left cerebral vascular accident. Sometimes, the music therapist will have to adapt instruments so patients can use them most effectively (Brunk, 1992; Clark & Chadwick, 1979; Elliott, 1982; Rudenberg, 1982). Other individuals, especially those who have severe physical limitations, may be able to use what limited movement they have to make music with electronic instruments, computers, and adaptive electronic equipment, such as special switches or input devices (Fegers et al., 1989; Howell et al., 1995; Krout, 1992a, 1995; Nagler & Lee, 1989; Swingler, 1994). For more information on music therapy interventions used in the rehabilitation of motor impairments, see Chapter Eleven.

Music therapy interventions can also help patients in rehabilitation deal with chronic pain that may be associated with their condition and improve their independence in activities of daily living (ADLs). Rider (1985) specifically explored music therapy techniques to reduce pain in patients with spinal cord injuries and found that "entrainment music," which began with much tension and dissonance to match the patients' pain and gradually shifted to more consonant, relaxed sounds, was most effective in reducing pain and muscular tension. Many of the other music-mediated pain reduction techniques discussed in Chapter Seventeen may be also be beneficial for these patients.

In the area of ADLs, cues provided by musical structure or song lyrics can assist in motor planning and facilitate the development of functional motor patterns that individuals can use in daily routines. For example, Gervin (1991) used song lyrics to train a patient recovering from a brain injury to dress independently. The external cues and pacing provided by the lyrics and music provide a structure for the activity that helped the patient overcome difficulties in initiation, sequencing, and motor planning and complete the task successfully.

Music Therapy Interventions to Improve Cognitive Functioning

Music therapy interventions can help patients in rehabilitation programs improve many areas of cognitive functioning, including alerting and orienting responses, awareness of self and others and the environment, reality orientation, attention span, memory, concentration and focus on tasks, ability to

follow commands, problem-solving skills, and ability to learn and retain new information (Brunk, 1992; Sandness, 1995; Thaut, 1992c). Many types of music experiences can be structured to stimulate and reinforce orienting or attention responses, focus attention and increase concentration, assist in increasing reality orientation and awareness of self and others, provide cues for memory and structure for learning or relearning information as well as motivation for individuals to participate in cognitive retraining programs, provide practice and reinforcement for following directions, and help individuals develop and practice problem-solving skills. Thus, therapeutic music interventions can facilitate cognitive response and skill development throughout the course of rehabilitation.

Music therapy is often included as part of a stimulation program for patients who are comatose (Boyle, 1987, 1989; Brunk, 1992; Claeys et al., 1989; Sandness, 1995; Thaut, 1992c). A primary treatment goal for coma patients is to increase their awareness of stimuli and their ability to exhibit consistent, appropriate responses to stimuli (Claeys et al., 1989). To make the musical stimuli as meaningful as possible for the patient, music therapists may interview the patient's family to find out what types of music were meaningful to the patient prior to the injury. Music therapists may then present these selections in short, distinct segments, "to provide a structure within which the client can process the musical experiences as being different form the random stimuli" (Claeys et al., 1989, p. 72). Other vibrational, rhythmic, harmonic (e.g., consonant and dissonant chords) and environmental sounds may also be used to elicit alertness or orienting responses or to signal times of the day or specific activities (Brunk, 1992; Claeys et al., 1989). It is important that musical stimuli be intentional and played for only short periods, so that they are perceived as unique events and not just part of the background noise. As the therapist presents stimuli, she or he can first match them to the tempo of the patient's breathing or to the rhythm of a patient's eye blinks or finger movements, and then later vary the tempo or rhythm of the music to see if the patient will show awareness of the change by matching his or her breathing or movement to the new tempo or rhythm (Brunk, 1992). In addition to evoking responses, music or sounds that are meaningful to the patient can be used contingently to help reinforce purposeful responses and increase the patient's ability to exhibit consistent, appropriate responses (Boyle, 1987, 1989).

As patients emerge from coma (levels II-III of the Rancho Los Amigos Scale), familiar music can be used to decrease agitation and anxiety (Thaut, 1992c). Improvised songs about the patient's movements or vocalizations can help increase the patient's awareness of his or her behavior, while songs incorporating information about place, date, time, and season can be used to increase reality orientation (Claeys et al., 1989). Even if there is no observable response, patients may still be hearing and, at least to some degree, processing the information. Therefore, all interactions should be encouraging and supportive, and persons conversing in the room should assume that the patient can hear and understand their conversations, even if she or he cannot respond (Claeys et al., 1989; Clair, 1996b). As patients progress to levels IV-VI of the Rancho Los Amigos Scale, music therapists use music experiences to support treatment goals related to areas such as following directions, short-term memory, reality orientation, attention and concentration, etc. For example, song lyrics can be used to present and structure information and help cue recall (Brunk, 1992; Claeys et al., 1989; Sandness, 1995; Thaut, 1992c). Learning (or relearning) how to play musical instruments can also help patients increase cognitive skills such as short-term memory, increased concentration, and perception of visual/spatial relationships (Erdonmez, 1991; Hofmeister & Cole, 1986; McMaster, 1991). As patients develop increased attention and concentration in music therapy sessions, their general concentration ability may improve, too. For example, McMaster (1991) found that, as a 40-year-old woman who was recovering from a stroke was able to attend to tasks in music therapy sessions for longer periods of time, she also began to attend to subjects that interested her outside of the session for up to one hour.

Music Therapy Interventions to Improve Communication Skills

Music therapy interventions can be often be very beneficial for patients who have speech and language impairments as the result of strokes or traumatic brain injuries (Adamek & Shiraiski, 1996; Brunk, 1992; Clair, 1996b; N. Cohen, 1988, 1992, 1994; Hofmeister & Cole, 1986; Lucia, 1987; Sandness, 1995; Taylor, 1987b, 1989; Thaut, 1992c). However, it is important to remember that a particular individual's response to various types of music therapy strategies will depend on many factors, including the individual's premorbid experience with music and the exact site and extent of the brain damage (Cohen, 1994; Taylor, 1987b, 1989). As has been noted in Chapter Twelve of this text, music therapy interventions can address both receptive and expressive language skills and may provide avenues for nonverbal as well as verbal communication.

The benefits of singing for stimulating speech in individuals who have neurological impairments have been noted for many years. Cohen (1994) provides a summary of early anecdotal records and research, all of which note how singing is often maintained in individuals with expressive aphasia who have little or no speech. In more recent times, special music therapy techniques, such as Melodic Intonation Therapy (Albert, Sparks, & Helms, 1973; Sparks, Helms, & Albert, 1974; Sparks & Holland, 1976), rhythm and melody in speech therapy (Rogers & Fleming, 1981), and the stimulation approach, where familiar song texts are used to trigger speech, (Lucia, 1987; Thaut, 1992c), have been developed to assist in aphasia rehabilitation. (See Chapter Twelve for a more detailed explanation of these techniques.) Many music therapy strategies used to facilitate or increase speech in persons who have had strokes or TBIs "capitalize on preserved right brain functions for singing, an automatic, non-propositional speech skill that generally precedes functional speech recovery" (Lucia, 1987, p. 36).

In addition to stimulating speech production, music therapy techniques may improve the speech rate, vocal intensity, and verbal intelligibility of clients who have neurogenic communication disorders (N. Cohen, 1988, 1992, 1994, 1995; Cohen & Masse, 1993). Chapter Twelve provides more detailed information on music therapy interventions used for these purposes, as well as examples of music therapy procedures used to improve receptive language skills. Chapter Twelve also discusses alternative or augmentive systems of communication (e.g., communication boards) and gives suggestions for incorporating these in music therapy experiences.

Music Therapy Interventions to Improve Social and Emotional Functioning

Since the social and emotional consequences of traumatic brain injuries, strokes, and spinal cord injuries are often as devastating as the physical and cognitive deficits, dealing with socio-emotional concerns is an important part of the rehabilitation process. Music therapy interventions can help meet the emotional and social needs of patients in rehabilitation programs by reducing anxiety, serving as a means of nonverbal expression and an outlet for releasing tension or expressing frustration, providing motivation to participate in treatment and interact with others, decreasing depression, facilitating emotional expression, providing opportunities for creativity and success experiences, helping patients find ways to cope with or adapt/adjust to their limitations, and providing group experiences that facilitate supportive, positive interactions with others (Brunk, 1992; Clair, 1996b; Sandness, 1995; Thaut, 1992c).

As part of the rehabilitation process, individuals who have experienced losses of physical functioning, independence, etc., due to a stroke, TBI, or spinal cord injury need opportunities to express their grief and/or anger over these losses (Bright, 1986; Clair, 1996b; McMaster, 1991). Since music is the language of feelings and emotions (Gaston, 1968a; Whitwell, 1993), it can facilitate this process, especially for those who have lost the ability to communicate verbally or who have limited insight and verbal processing capabilities. When individuals listen to, vocalize with, or play laments or other songs expressing grief and deep emotions, the songs may serve as a projection of their feelings and help them communicate emotions associated with their debilitation and express and work through their grief (Erdonmez, 1991; McMaster, 1991). The structured use of these songs within a therapeutic setting helps patients both express their grief deeply and helps them move out of their grief "into a lighter state" (McMaster, 1991, p. 555). Instrumental improvisations (McMaster, 1991) or improvised songs (Amir, 1990) can also help individuals express and work

through feelings. In addition, Guided Imagery and Music (GIM) techniques may help some patients who have brain damage work through feelings of depression, hopelessness, helplessness, and anger (Goldberg et al., 1988). Goldberg and her colleagues (1988) found that GIM techniques could be effective when more traditional psychotherapy techniques were not useful because of the patient's brain damage. However, they recommended that GIM be used only with "patients who are not psychotic, had good premorbid social, vocational, and psychological functioning, and evidence good current ego strength" (p. 45).

Music can also be helpful in providing comfort and emotional support throughout the long and often frustrating process of rehabilitation. Pre-composed, familiar songs that resonate with the patients' experience may provide tangible evidence that their grief and feelings are understood by others (Bright, 1986; Erdonmez, 1991; McMaster, 1991). For example, one patient who was recovering from stroke found comfort and help in expressing and dealing with his suffering from song cycles, such as Schubert's *Winterreise*, that he had known prior to his CVA (Erdonmez, 1991). In another case, the song "Climb Every Mountain," together with a sketch depicting a climb from a dark valley to a sunny mountain ridge, encouraged patients to keep on working toward their goals, even if the process seemed very slow:

> The image of slow but real progress from darkness into light, together with a familiar song which express much the same ideas and a sketch in the memory notebook, has provided comfort to a variety of people whose progress in therapy is slow, and the music has helped to keep the ideas in mind. (Bright, 1986, p. 144)

Song writing, both individual and group, can be another important element in the therapeutic process for clients in physical rehabilitation programs, providing opportunities for creativity as well as a means of facilitating emotional expression and working through issues associated with the rehabilitation process (Amir, 1990; Barker & Brunk, 1991; Brunk, 1992; Claeys et al., 1989; Robb, 1996). Amir (1990) used an "improvised song" technique to help a 20-year-old male, who had quadriplegia following a spinal cord injury from an automobile accident, express and work through his feelings of depression and despair over his lack of progress and his physical limitations. In this process, the therapist played an accompaniment as directed by the patient, who chose the instrument (e.g., guitar, keyboard), tempo, sounds, and general style of the music. As the patient listened to the music, he was asked to close his eyes and give words to his feelings.

> The music guides him to become attuned to his inner world and to feel his creative expressions. The therapist provides him with a musical framework in which he can free associate; the music serves as a constructive external support for expressing what might have otherwise gone unexpressed. (Amir, 1990, p. 70)

When involved in the creative process of improvised songs and poetic expression supported by music, this patient was able to see himself as a whole human being, in spite of his physical limitations. Through these songs, he not only mourned the loss of his previous way of life, but also discovered new symbols and strengths that gave meaning to his current life situation.

In addition to providing outlets for creativity and expression of feelings, group song writing can help provide mutual support for patients by developing relationships and a sense of community (Claeys et al., 1989). For example, Robb (1996) used fill-in-the-blank scripts and improvisational song writing (instrumental and vocal improvisation or lyric narration to an improvised instrumental accompaniment) with adolescents who had traumatic brain or spinal cord injuries. These song writing experiences led to increased communication and self-esteem, facilitated adjustment to the rehabilitation process, helped patients recover repressed material, and improved coping and socialization skills. Robb (1996) summarized:

> Most patients came away from the experience having discovered something about themselves, wanting to share their experiences with others, and feeling a sense of pride in what they have accomplished. (p. 36)

Sometimes, individual and group song writing

processes are combined, as when individual verses about feelings or goals alternate with a group chant or chorus (Barker & Brunk, 1991). Discharge songs may also help provide closure for the patients and help them integrate and synthesize their experiences (Robb, 1996).

Music experiences lend themselves well to group activity, providing opportunities for patients to interact with others in both verbal and nonverbal ways. For those patients who are unable to speak but are still able to sing, songs may provide a positive way of communicating and of socializing and interacting with others. Clair (1996b) described a case in which singing facilitated positive interactions between a stroke patient and her family. After the stroke, the patient was unable to speak and only responded to her families visits by crying. When the family members began to sing some well-known songs to her, the patient was able to join in singing, stopped crying, and began to laugh with delight that she could participate with her children in this way. Although the patient will face long hours of therapy to relearn skills,

> she was motivated to participate in rehabilitation because of the success she experienced in singing her much-loved music with her children. Her success also provided reassurance and joy to her children, who needed to feel that they were helping their mother rather than making her cry. (Clair, 1996b, p. 215)

Although not all patients will be able to respond by singing (the area and extent of brain damage may impact vocal responses), many will be comforted by well-known songs. It is also important to consult with the patient's physician to determine when sensory stimulation can safely begin (Clair, 1996b).

Group singing may also provide a way for patients to begin to socialize with each other and give them encouragement to work on regaining communication skills (Cohen, 1992; Lucia, 1987). As Cohen (1992) observed in her work with singing instruction for speech rehabilitation of patients who had experienced TBIs or CVAs, group singing provided patients with important social and emotional benefits that are not present in individual sessions.

Instrumental experiences can also be structured to provide emotional and social benefits for patients in physical rehabilitation programs (Barker & Brunk, 1991; Brunk, 1992; Claeys et al., 1989; Clair, 1996b). For example, instrumental improvisation can provide opportunities for patients to express feelings and frustrations within the safe container of the musical structure. Group instrumental experiences provide opportunities for nonverbal relating experiences, where group members need to be aware of and depend on each other to produce a pleasing musical product (Barker & Brunk, 1991). Participating in instrumental ensembles enables patients who are "isolated by illness or fear to become acquainted, to pool their strengths in mutually satisfying ways, and to develop skills and abilities that facilitate successful musical experiences" (Clair, 1996b, p. 218). With appropriate adaptations of instruments (Clark & Chadwick, 1979; Rudenberg, 1982) and the use of technology such as adapted switches, electronic instruments, and computers (Fegers et al., 1989; Krout, 1992a, 1995; Nagler & Lee, 1989), even patients who have severe physical limitations can independently create music and participate in music ensemble experiences.

Family participation can easily be incorporated into music therapy experiences, providing family members with a way to participate positively in the rehabilitation process and giving them opportunities to interact with their injured family member in experiences that are enjoyable and emotionally uplifting (Barker & Brunk, 1991; Bright, 1986; Brunk, 1992; Claeys et al., 1989; Clair, 1996b; Thaut, 1992c). Impairments from TBIs, CVAs, or spinal cord injuries impact families, too, as roles and life styles change. Since family support is critical to recovery rehabilitation, programs must find ways to incorporate families in positive experiences as both patient and family adjust to the social and emotional effects of the injury (Barker & Brunk, 1991). "Unlike other disciplines, music therapy offers a setting in which the family can function as a group, thereby often improving family relationships" (Claeys et al., 1989). Many types of music activities, from simple hand-holding and singing, to partner activities, to instrumental groups, to song writing, to combined art and music experiences, can be structured to provide a setting where patients and their family members or friends can focus on expression of feelings, meaningful social interaction, re-establishing or learning new ways of relating to each other, and healthy creativity (Barker & Brunk, 1991; Claeys et al., 1989). In addition, music and creative arts groups can help provide fun times in the midst of a serious, strenuous physical rehabilitation program, thus giving patients and families a necessary emotional outlet (Barker & Brunk, 1991).

Finally, music therapy can play an important role in patients' leisure education. Music therapists can help patients (a) learn how to use adapted devices to participate in music activities they enjoyed before their injury, (b) find ways to use music as enjoyable structure to practice functional skills and support rehabilitation goals, or (c) learn new music skills to substitute for old music skills (e.g., using computers or synthesizers to compose or play music instead of playing a guitar) (Brunk, 1992). Music therapy programs focusing on leisure skill development may include activities such as an introduction to adapted instruments and input devices (e.g., special switches), vocal or instrumental lessons, theory lessons or the development of composition skills, community outings, and the use of community resources.

Some patients may achieve a new interest in life and a purpose for living by learning to use previous musical skills or interests in new ways. For example, a young man who had played the bass guitar before a spinal cord injury from an automobile accident left him a quadriplegic was able to experience himself as a complete human being again through the creative process of improvising songs (Amir, 1990). In another instance, a physician who also had been a talented classical pianist before a stroke left his right hand and arm paralyzed learned to play many of the right-handed piano parts with his left hand as part of his rehabilitation process (Erdonmez, 1991). For this patient, "music became the focus of his life and gave him a purpose for his existence (Erdonmez, 1991, p. 569).

SPECIAL CONSIDERATIONS AND TIPS FOR SUCCESS

Music therapists who work with patients in physical rehabilitation programs need to find optimum ways to structure and manage the environment (adaptive aids, minimize distractions, cues for responses, etc.) to maximize patients' performance and minimize the impact of their disabilities (Brunk, 1992; Chance, 1986). When using musical instruments, "it is important to analyze the physical strengths and weaknesses of the patient and then match them with an instrument that requires positioning and motions appropriate to his or her physical ability" (Thaut, 1992c, p. 268). Electronic instruments, adapted instruments, special switches, and computers may help persons with physical limitations be involved in actively making music (see Chapter Eleven). Therapists may also want to consult references such as Edel (1994), that list resources for piano music of various difficulty levels that can be performed with one hand.

Tools like the Functional Independence Measure (FIM) can help provide a general idea of the patient's overall level of functional independence and his or her progress toward independence during treatment. Other assessment tools, such as the Glasgow Coma Scale and the Rancho Los Amigos Scale, are used to describe coma severity and describe cognitive functioning and behaviors typically exhibited by patients as they emerge from coma. Music therapists may make use of tools such as these to guide their planning. In addition, FIM scores may help demon-strate the effectiveness of some music therapy intervention strategies.

When working with patients who are comatose, it is important to remember that they may hear and understand conversations that are going on in the room, even though they may not be able to respond. Therefore, interactions should be positive, concrete, encouraging and supportive, and persons in the room should remember to talk *to* the patients rather than *about* them (Claeys et al., 1989; Clair, 1996b).

As research into the direct effects of music on the human nervous system continues to progress, music therapists should consider approaching "movement objectives with stroke and traumatic brain injury patients from the viewpoint of using music as a neurological entrainment mechanism rather than simply as a way to stimulate movement" (Taylor, 1997, p. 121). In addition, music therapists should also take into account the whole person when planning their treatment approaches, making use of the ability of music to provide emotional support and positive experiences for both the patient and his/her family during the long rehabilitation process.

For special considerations and tips for success in dealing with clients who have neurogenic communication impairments, see Chapter Twelve.

SUMMARY

Rehabilitation is concerned with helping patients achieve their maximum potential in physical, psychological, and social/emotional functioning, so that they can function as independently as possible and return to the community to enjoy the best quality of life they can. The three most common groups of individuals served by physical rehabilitation programs are survivors of traumatic brain injuries, strokes, or spinal cord injuries.

Music therapy interventions can provide unique ways to address the needs of individuals in physical rehabilitation programs. Since music influences brain functions in unique ways, patients may exhibit responses to music experiences that are not present with other types of stimulation. Music experiences activate additional neurological pathways through which learning and skill development can occur, facilitate the establishment of a therapeutic relation-ship, provide motivation and enjoyment, and facilitate emotional expression and social interaction. In addition, music activities can be structured and adapted to allow for participation at many different levels of ability.

Patients in physical rehabilitation settings can benefit from music therapy at all levels of recovery, from coma stimulation (music for auditory stimulation and as a contingent stimulus) to active treatment (using goal-directed music experiences to work on speech, motor control and coordination, memory, or other concerns) to discharge (using music-based activities to facilitate discussion of discharge concerns or helping patients and their families find ways to continue using music activities to develop skills or to provide social integration after hospitalization). Music therapy interventions for patients in rehabili-tation programs utilize a variety of structured music experiences involving listening to music, playing instruments, singing or vocalizing, moving to music, improvising or composing music, and discussing music to motivate or assist patients in working toward the greatest degree of independence possible in functional motor, communication, cognitive, self-care, and socio-emotional skills.

Family participation also can easily be incorporated into music therapy experiences, providing family members with a way to participate positively in the rehabilitation process and giving them opportunities to interact with their injured family member in experiences that are enjoyable and emotionally uplifting. In addition, music and creative arts groups can help provide fun times in the midst of a serious, strenuous physical rehabilitation program, thus giving patients and families a necessary emotional outlet.

QUESTIONS FOR THOUGHT AND DISCUSSION

1. Relate the levels of the Rancho Los Amigos Scale to the three stages of recovery from TBI. Describe the way patients function at each level or stage and discuss the implications of these behaviors for music therapy programming.

2. What are some unique contributions music makes to the rehabilitation? How/why can these be important for patients and their families?

3. Describe several music therapy interventions that might be used to help improve (a) physical functioning, (b) cognitive functioning, (c) communication skills, and (d) social or emotional skills in patients who have had strokes, traumatic brain injuries, or spinal cord injuries. What unique benefits does music provide in each of these areas?

4. List several special considerations that may be important to remember when developing therapeutic intervention strategies for persons who have had strokes, traumatic brain injuries, or spinal cord injuries. Why are these important? How might they impact the planning and implementation of music therapy programs?

5. For each of the situations listed below, (a) define the problem or areas of need for the client or group of clients, (b) describe one or more of the goals you might pursue in music therapy sessions with the client(s), (c) describe music activities you might use to help the client(s) meet those goals, (d) tell how the music activities you described relate to the goals and needs of the client(s), and (e) mention any special considerations you might want to take into account when working with the client(s).

Situation 1:

You have been asked to provide music therapy sessions for a small group of individuals between the ages of 25 and 40 who are recovering from closed head injuries or strokes. These individuals are currently residents of a rehabilitation center. Some have limited movement and weakness on one side of their body. All can say at least a few words, but have varying degrees of difficulties with communication. Several have difficulty with memory, concentration, and problem solving. Most need work on improving their ability to initiate tasks and carry them through to completion. All need to work on relearning appropriate social interaction and group cooperation skills. Individuals in the group are often irritable, quarrelsome, anxious, or easily depressed or excited. None of the group members were active musicians at the time of their injury, but a few had played in the band or sung in the choir in high school. All used to enjoy listening to the radio or recorded music. Music interests ranged from rock to easy listening to country to gospel.

Situation 2:

A 25-year-old female who sustained severe head and back injuries in a diving accident has been referred to you for music therapy. She is paralyzed from the waist down and has limited use of her upper extremities at this time. She sometimes experiences severe back pain. She also has difficulties with short-term memory and sequencing skills. She has just entered a rehabilitation center, but is angry and depressed and has little interest in trying to regain any functional skills. Since she can no longer lead the type of active life to which she is accustomed, she feels it would be better for her to be dead.

SUGGESTIONS FOR FURTHER READING

Adamek, M. S., & Shiraishi, I. M. (1996). Music therapy with traumatic brain injured patients: Speech rehabilitation, intervention models, and assessment procedures. In C. E. Furman (Ed.), *Effectiveness of music therapy procedures: Documentation of research and clinical practice* (2nd ed.) (pp. 267-278). Silver Spring, MD: National Association for Music Therapy.

Amir, D. (1990). A song is born: Discovering meaning in improvised songs through a phenomenological analysis of two music therapy sessions with a traumatic spinal-cord injured young adult. *Music Therapy, 9*(1), 62-81.

Barker, V. L., & Brunk, B. (1991). The role of a creative arts group in the treatment of clients with traumatic brain injury. *Music Therapy Perspectives, 9*, 23-31.

Boyle, M. E. (1989). Comatose and head injured patients: Applications for music in treatment. In M. H. M. Lee (Ed.), *Rehabilitation, music and human well-being* (pp. 137-148). St. Louis: MMB Music.

Bruscia, K. E. (Ed.) (1991). *Case studies in music therapy.* Phoenixville, PA: Barcelona Publishers.

Claeys, M. S., Miller, A. C., Dalloul-Rampersad, R., & Kollar, M. (1989). The role of music and music therapy in the rehabilitation of traumatically brain injured clients. *Music Therapy Perspectives, 6*, 71-77.

Clair, A. A. (1996). Music in physical rehabilitation. In A. A. Clair *Therapeutic uses of music with older adults* (pp. 195-227). Baltimore, MD: Health Professional Press.

Clark, C., & Chadwick, D. (1979). *Clinically adapted instruments for the multiply handicapped.* Westford, MA: Modulations.

Cohen, N. S. (1988). The use of superimposed rhythm to decrease the rate of speech in a brain-damaged adolescent. *Journal of Music Therapy, 25*(2), 85-93.

Cohen, N. S. (1992). The effect of singing instruction on the speech production of neurologically impaired persons. *Journal of Music Therapy, 29*(2), 87-102.

Cohen, N. S. (1995). The effect of vocal instruction and Visi-Pitch^{tm} feedback on the speech of persons with neurogenic communication disorders: Two case studies. *Music Therapy Perspectives, 13*(2), 70-75.

Cohen, N. S., & Ford, J. (1995). The effect of musical cues on the nonpurposive speech of persons with aphasia. *Journal of Music Therapy, 32*(1), 46-57.

Cohen, N. S., & Masse, R. (1993). The application of singing and rhythmic instruction as a therapeutic intervention for persons with neurogenic communication disorders. *Journal of Music Therapy, 30*(2), 81-99.

Confrancesco, E. M. (1985). The effect of music therapy on hand grasp strength and functional task performance in stroke patients. *Journal of Music Therapy, 22*(3), 129-145.

Elliott, B. (1982). *Guide to the selection of musical instruments with respect to physical ability and disability.* St. Louis: Magnamusic-Baton.

Lucia, C. M. (1987). Toward developing a model of music therapy intervention in the rehabilitation of head trauma patients. *Music Therapy Perspectives, 4*, 34-39.

Miller, K. J. (1979). *Treatment with music: A manual for allied health professionals.* Kalamazoo, MI: Western Michigan University Printing Department.

Nagler, J. C., & Lee, M. H. M. (1989). Music therapy using computer music technology. In M. H. M. Lee (Ed.), *Rehabilitation, music and human well-being* (pp. 226-241). St. Louis: MMB Music.

Rudenberg, M. T. (1982). *Music therapy for handicapped children: Orthopedically handicapped.* Washington, D.C.: National Association for Music Therapy.

Sandness, M. I. (1995). The role of music therapy in physical rehabilitation programs. *Music Therapy Perspectives, 13*(2), 76-81.

Standley, J. (1991). *Music techniques in therapy, counseling, and special education.* St. Louis: MMB Music.

Staum, M. J. (1996). Music for physical rehabilitation: An analysis of literature from 1950-1993 and applications for rehabilitation settings. In C. E. Furman (Ed.), *Effectiveness of music therapy procedures: Documentation of research and clinical practice* (2nd ed.) (pp. 61-105). Silver Spring, MD: National Association for Music Therapy.

Thaut, M. H. (1992). Music therapy in the rehabilitation of stroke and traumatic-brain-injured clients. In W. B. Davis, K. E. Gfeller, & M. H. Thaut, *An introduction to music therapy: Theory and practice* (pp. 251-272). Dubuque, IA: Wm. C. Brown.

Thompson, A. B., Arnold, J. C., and Murray, S. E. (1990). Music therapy assessment of the cerebrovascular accident patient. *Music Therapy Perspectives, 8*, 23-29.

Chapter Nineteen

MUSIC THERAPY WITH INDIVIDUALS WHO ARE ELDERLY

DEFINITION

ELDERLY IS A TERM used to describe individuals who have reached a certain arbitrary, chronological age that society defines as being "old." Some sources classify people as "older" or "elderly" when they reach 55 years of age; others reserve this classification for those who are ages 60 or 65 or older. Essentially, the only factor people in this population have in common is that they have lived past a certain chronological age (Prickett, 1996). Other terms used to describe these individuals include *older adults, aged, aging, senior, senior citizens,* or *geriatric.* The field of scientific study that deals with aging and the problems of the aged is called *gerontology. Geriatrics* is the branch of medicine that is concerned with the care of elderly persons and the treatment of problems associated with aging.

Due to many factors, such as improvements in life style, nutrition, and medical services, the aging of the "baby boom" generation (those born between 1946 and 1964), the general decrease in the birth rate, and the increase in life expectancy, the elderly population is one of the fastest growing segments of our society (Dychtwald, 1993). In 1900, about 4% of Americans were age 65 or older; by 1994, this percentage had tripled to 12.7% ("Aging Statistics," 1994; Richter, 1996). Two-thirds of all the people who have lived beyond age 65 are alive today. Many of these are in good health and are living active, independent lives (Hager, 1983; Horn & Meer, 1987; Jacobson, 1987; Richter, 1996). By

2030, more than 20% of the population is expected to be over age 65 (Horn & Meer, 1987; Richter, 1996).

People who are age 85 or older are sometimes called "old old" or the "oldest old" (Feil, 1982; Horn & Meer, 1987). From 1970 to 1987, this group increased by 165% to 2.5 million, and now represents more than 1% of the population (Horn & Meer, 1987). Many individuals over age 85 still lead healthy, active lives: more than half live in their own homes, and some still work for a living (Horn & Meer, 1987; Jacobson, 1987). 30% live by themselves, while more than a third live with a spouse or children. Many socialize in a variety of ways, attending religious services or professional, social, church-related, or recreational groups. Only about one-fourth are in hospitals or longterm care facilities (e.g., nursing homes).

Ageism is a term used to refer to the discriminatory treatment or prejudicial stereotyping of older people (Horn & Meer, 1987; Purtilo, 1978). Ageism is an attitude that old age means obsolescence, decline, deterioration, frailty, and uselessness, and that older people have nothing to do, no place to go, and nothing to become. Ageism assumes all people think, act, feel, and look pretty much the same. The reality, however, is that "there is no age group more varied in physical abilities; personal styles, tastes and desires; or financial capabilities than the older population" (Dychtwald, 1993, p. 5).

CHARACTERISTICS, PROBLEMS,
AND NEEDS OF CLIENTS

Individuals who are elderly are very diverse; in fact, "people grow less alike as they age" (Jacobson, 1987, p. A19). Although certain physiological, psychological, and socio-emotional changes are often associated with the aging process, these changes do not occur at the same rate or to the same degree in all individuals (Bright, 1986; Purtilo, 1978). Therefore, chronological age alone is a poor indicator of a person's physical, mental, or socio-emotional abilities. Many other factors, such as general physical and mental health, economic status, access to family or close friends, and involvement in meaningful activities, greatly impact an individual's level of functioning in all of these areas (Erikson et al., 1986; Prickett, 1996; Purtilo, 1978). Consequently, it is unwise to attempt to predict a particular person's skill levels or ceiling of abilities simply based on the fact that he or she has passed a certain chronological age. However, an awareness of some of those characteristics, problems, and needs which may be common to various groups of individuals who are elderly will be beneficial both to the therapist who desires to work with this population and to the reader who is trying to understand how music therapy intervention strategies may benefit these individuals.

For ease of discussion, this chapter will group elderly individuals into five general categories: (1) the well elderly, (2) those who are semi-independent, (3) those who are chronically ill or medically fragile and are being cared for in their own home or that of a caregiver, (4) those who are in nursing homes or long-term care facilities, and (5) those who have Alzheimer's disease (AD) or related dementias. Individuals who are terminally ill and receiving hospice care may be found in both categories 3 and 4, since some hospice programs are home-based and others are inpatient programs (Colligan, 1987; Palmer, 1989). Characteristics and needs of individuals who are terminally ill are discussed in detail in Chapter Twenty.

General Changes Associated
with the Aging Process

Primary aging is a gradual process that affects the efficiency of all body systems. This process is genetically determined and proceeds at different rates in different individuals. *Secondary aging* is the result of factors like disease, trauma, stress, abuse, and disuse. Many of these are life style factors that can be controlled to some extent by the individual. In fact, some research suggests that many of the problems of old age are primarily due not to aging, but to the improper care of the body over an individual's lifetime (Dychtwald, 1993). The overall rate at which an individual ages is determined by interaction of these primary and secondary factors (Horn & Meer, 1987).

People who are elderly have to contend with many biological, mental, and social changes (Purtilo, 1978; Smith, 1972). In some ways, the changes of old age are comparable to those experienced during adolescence. As Smith (1972) observed:

Just as adolescence is a process not only of growth but also of widespread change, so aging, from its start, is far from a process of mere decline. Instead it is in large measure a process of change in all aspects of the aging person's body, organs, senses, and mind, which in turn alters the aging person's conduct, emotions, self-control, personality and relations with others. (p. 3)

Common *biological* or *physiological changes* associated with aging include the following (Davis, 1992a; Lazarus, 1988; Purtilo, 1978; Smith, 1972):

- loss of skin elasticity
- a decrease in the body's ability to regulate temperature
- a decrease in skin oils
- more fragile blood vessels
- reduced function of superficial nerve endings (resulting in a decreased sensitivity to pain or pressures that can lead to injury)
- decreased lung elasticity and lung capacity
- decreased cardiac output and blood supply
- an increase in the time needed to recover from injury
- a generalized decrease in strength and stamina

- loss of brain tissue (a gradual process that occurs throughout life since neurons are not regenerated when they die)
- increased reaction or response time and decreased reflex strength due to changes in brain electro-chemical activity
- vision changes (*presbyopia*) such as decreased lens elasticity, decreased pupil size, and decreased speed of adjustment to light changes that may cause the need for more light or reading glasses and may make night driving difficult
- decrease in hearing acuity (*presbycusis*) due to increased rigidity of the bones in the middle ear and gradual loss of ability to hear high frequencies,
- loss of calcium in the bones decreased flexibility due to calcification of the ligaments
- a more compressed and less flexible spinal column
- decreased muscle strength and endurance
- increased time needed to recover between activities
- changes in gait (e.g., shorter steps, less steady with more lateral movement)
- deterioration of the teeth and gums
- reduced saliva output that may lead to difficulties chewing and swallowing
- decline in the size and number of taste buds
- deterioration in the sense of smell
- decreased strength and elasticity in the bladder and muscles controlling urination (may result in more frequent urination or some degree of incontinence)
- decrease in hormonal secretions in both males and females

It is important to remember that these changes occur at different rates in different individuals and that not all changes happen to the same extent in every individual.

Some *medical problems* or diseases also become increasingly common among individuals over age 65. These include *arteriosclerosis* (hardening of the arteries caused by thickening and loss of elasticity of the arterial walls, often because of fatty deposits, resulting in decrease or cessation of blood flow to various parts of the body, with concomitant decrease or loss of function), *heart disease, hypertension, stroke* (see Chapter Eighteen), *cancer, Parkinson's disease* (a condition affecting the basal ganglia of the brain; characterized by mask-like facial expression, tremor of resting muscles, slowing of voluntary movements, a hurried, shuffling gait, muscular weakness, and possible difficulties with speech flow; mental capacity remains intact), *hernia, enlargement of the prostrate* in men, *prolapse of the rectum or uterus, osteoporosis* (see Chapter Eleven), *arthritis* (see Chapter Eleven), *diabetes, glaucoma,* or *cataracts* (Davis, 1992a; Lazarus, 1988; Miller & Keane, 1978; Tomaino, 1992). However, although older people may have an increasing number of chronic, controlled health problems as they age, many individuals are not necessarily limited or bothered by them (Dychtwald, 1993).

Mental or psychological changes associated with aging may include changes in personality, intellectual functioning, and/or mental health (G. Cohen, 1988; Davis, 1992a; Lazarus, 1988; Purtilo, 1978; Smith, 1972). *Personality changes* that occur with aging include increased withdrawal, decreased ability to compensate or adapt to changes, decreased attention to world or community events, or increased preoccupation with self or trivial things. These changes in behavior patterns may often be the result of physical or social factors (e.g., diminished hearing or vision; decreased ability to get around independently; loss of friends and companions) or of a decreased self-concept. Changes in *intellectual functioning* include increased rigidity of thought patterns (possibly a means of coping with stress), decreased speed of perception and response time, decreased awareness of environmental cues due to diminished sensory perceptions, decreased immediate recall ability (especially if distracted), a need for longer rehearsal time to learn new material, a tendency to lose their train of though more easily, a decreased ability to spontaneously recall information, and increased memory difficulties or memory lapses. It is important to realize that aging, in and of itself, does *not* decrease a person's level of intelligence or ability to learn.

Most of the losses in mental capacity happen to the very old, not to people in their 60s, 70s, and early 80s, and are due not to age itself but to depression, drug interactions, lack of exercise, of one of many other reversible conditions. (Dychtwald, 1993, p. 5)

As older people continue to challenge themselves, they can learn new things, and their intelligence and understanding may actually increase with age. Also, many older people make up for loss of speed by their increased judgment, perspective, experience, insight, decision-making and problem-solving abilities. In addition, research has shown that the brain can continue to create new neural connections, that it can "rewire" itself to compensate for losses, and that diminished skills can be relearned with training.

Some *mental disorders* are also common among elderly people (G. Cohen, 1988; Davis, 1992a; Lazarus, 1988; Tomaino, 1992). The incidence of *depression* seems to increase with advancing age, with some estimating that 20% to 45% of individuals over age 65 have some degree of depression. Depression in elderly persons may have several forms and causes, ranging from clinical depression to drug-induced depression to depression in association with medical and neurological illnesses to depression in association with cognitive impairments such as Alzheimer's disease (G. Cohen, 1988). Depression in the elderly may also be masked by vague physical decline or multiple somatic complaints. Depression in elderly persons is treatable; however, it often goes undiagnosed (Bright, 1986; Lazarus, 1988). Persons age 65 and over continue to have the highest suicide rates in the United States (Aging Statistics, 1994; G. Cohen, 1988).

In addition to depression, elderly people may have other psychiatric disorders, such as *paranoid states* (for some, may be the result of isolation, illness, or sensory loss), *anxiety disorders* (often temporary, triggered by apprehension of traumatic events, decreased abilities, or illnesses), *substance abuse* (prescription or nonprescription medications, as well as alcohol or drugs; some may turn to these to try to alleviate loneliness or depression), *schizophrenia,* or *sleep disorders.* Organic mental disorders, such as *Alzheimer's disease, senile dementia, arteriosclerotic psychosis,* and *multi-infarction dementia,* are also increasingly prevalent with aging. These disorders affect brain processes and cause mental confusion and disorientation, personality changes, and physical problems. Some estimate that as many as 50% of all mental disorders in elderly people result from organic disorders.

In addition to physical and mental changes, most elderly individuals must also deal with a number of *social changes* (Bright, 1986; Purtilo, 1978). In the United States, aging is frequently accompanied by a loss of social status and a loss of opportunities for socialization. Many older people no longer seem to be needed by their children, their community, or their place of business. When they reach a certain chronological age, they are asked or forced to retire from their jobs. They may also be asked to step down from community boards to make way for younger people. These events may contribute to loss of income, loss of worth and respect, or loss of former self-image or identity. If older people are to maintain the image of themselves as useful members of society, they must have opportunities to engage in some kind of ongoing activity that makes them feel they are needed.

As their children or grandchildren move to other parts of the country and as their friends or spouses suffer debilitating illnesses or die, older people lose important social contacts and support systems. Their own physical deterioration may also lead to loss of mobility and opportunities for socialization. Elderly individuals who have severe physical and/or mental impairments may be forced to become more dependent on others. Increased dependency often leads to loss of self-esteem and, if alternate living arrangements are needed, to loss of home, possessions, and privacy. According to Purtilo (1978), one of the greatest conscious fears of elderly people is the fear of losing their independence.

Different people are affected by the changes associated with aging at different rates and in different ways. In addition, physical, mental, and social changes never have simple, isolated effects; changes in one area impact other areas. For example, decreased income may lead to poor nutrition which may cause changes in physical or mental health, or decreased sensory acuity may lead to decreased independence which may cause a diminished self-concept, withdrawal, and/or depression. Therefore, it is important to work with elderly persons from an interdisciplinary, holistic perspective, taking into account all areas of the person's life. And, while it is true that physical, mental, and social conditions all affect specific needs of individual elderly persons, it is important to remember that, on the whole, the essential needs of older people are the same of those of adults of any age: nourishing food, comfortable shelter, companionship, a sense of being useful and productive, intellectual stimulation, and spiritual refreshment (Otten & Shelley, 1977).

The Well Elderly

The well elderly constitute the largest segment of the population of older individuals. Most older Americans are healthy, have adequate economic resources, and lead active lives (Dychtwald, 1993; Hager, 1983; Horn & Meer, 1987; Palmer, 1989; Richter, 1996). They live independently in the community and consider being on their own proof of their mental and physical vigor. Only about 45% have some chronic problem, such as arthritis or hearing impairment, that causes come kind of limitation (Hager, 1983). The functional age of these healthy older Americans – "a combination of physical, psychological and social factors that affect their attitudes toward life and the roles they play in the world – is much younger than their chronological age" (Horn & Meer, 1987, p. 77).

The well elderly are a diverse group of individuals, whose members have very definite preferences. They are receiving increasing attention from businesses, especially the travel, housing, and health industries, since they represent a vast new market for goods and services. Since they represent a powerful voting block, the well elderly also receive a great deal of attention from politicians.

The well elderly are individuals who now have plenty of leisure time to pursue new interests. They have needs for experiences that provide opportunities for self-discovery and creativity (Whitwell, 1993). Many seek quality, enriching experiences and are self-directed, highly motivated learners. They gather at senior centers not to play cards but to get information on retirement investments, exercise, travel, and wellness (Richter, 1996). They may be active in clubs and associations, participate in park and recreation programs, care for grandchildren, travel, or take courses at universities that have special programs for older adults. Although the well elderly may have fewer physical needs than elderly persons who are institutionalized, they may have similar emotional needs: a need for meaningful activity, a need to fill their time constructively, a need to feel useful and worthwhile, a need for a support system, a need to find ways to cope with the stresses of

experiencing loss and grief with increasing frequencies, and a need to find ways to cope with social losses and physical changes associated with aging (Glassman, 1983).

Elderly Individuals Who Are Semi-Independent

Elderly individuals in this group live in their own home or that of a caregiver, but spend three or more days a week in an adult day care program for supportive or supervised care (Palmer, 1989). Others may live in assisted living centers, where meals, transportation, activities, and some personal care services are provided. These individuals have some mental or physical impairment that interferes with their ability to function independently. Many are physically frail and/or have memory impairments (Kay, 1996; Smith & Knudson, 1995). They need opportunities for socialization, programs that will increase and support their functional abilities, and opportunities to participate in meaningful activities that will give them a sense of accomplishment and self-esteem. Some may need assistance with activities of daily living, such as eating, bathing, or walking.

Adult day care centers have been in existence since the 1970s, but did not begin to grow in popularity until the mid-1980s and 1990s. The number of adult day care centers in the United States more than doubled between 1985 and 1994, growing from 1,200 to 3,000 (Kay, 1996). Some estimate that 10,000 adult day care centers will be needed by the year 2000. Adult day care centers help both elderly clients and their caregivers by providing (a) alternatives to premature or inappropriate institutionalization, (b) programs that maximize the functional abilities of their clients, and (c) respite to caregivers while giving psychosocial support to their clients (Palmer, 1989). Some adult day care centers work with specific groups of clients, such as individuals who have Alzheimer's disease. Most centers, however, serve clients who have a wide variety of abilities and disabilities. Adult day care centers usually operate five days a week and provide meals, recreational services and programs, transportation, and other therapeutic programs.

Other facilities and programs that provide alternatives to institutionalization for persons who need assistance in some areas of daily living are also being developed. For example, in the mid- to late-1990s, a number of assisted living residences have been opened in various areas of the country. These facilities may provide services such as meals, transportation, laundry and housekeeping, recreational programs, and medication supervision for persons who need some assistance in these areas.

Chronically Ill Elderly Individuals Receiving Home Care

Some elderly persons who have chronic or terminal illnesses are cared for in their own homes or the home of a caregiver. These caregivers often receive support from a community home health agency or a hospital or hospice program. Insurers and the federal government are finding that providing services to the chronically ill elderly in their homes through community-based agencies is a viable, less expensive alternative to traditional nursing home care (Palmer, 1989).

Chronically ill individuals have a variety of physical and medical needs which must be met by others; however, they (and their caregivers) also have important social, psychological, emotional, and spiritual needs. These include (a) meaningful contact and communication with others, (b) mental stimulation, (c) ways to express feelings and emotions related to their situation, and (d) spiritual refreshment and fulfillment. It is important to keep in mind the needs of the *whole person*, not just his or her obvious medical needs, for all aspects of a person affect each other and are important to quality of life.

Elderly Individuals Who Are in Nursing Homes or Long-Term Care Facilities

Although many people immediately think of nursing homes when they think of elderly people, most figures show that only 5%-10% of individuals over 65 live in nursing homes (Aging Statistics, 1994; Barna, 1993; Hager, 1983; Jacobson, 1987). According to the 1990 census, approximately 3.1 million of the 31.1 million people over age 65 lived in long-term care facilities (Aging Statistics, 1994). Of this group, many are in their 80s or older: Only

about 8% of all persons ages 65-85 live in nursing homes, while about 20% of those age 85 or older live in nursing homes (Aging Statistics, 1994; Barna, 1993). Over two-thirds of nursing home residents are women, most of whom are husbandless and in their late 70s or older. While some people enter nursing homes for short stays to recover from an acute medical condition and then return to the community or assisted living facilities, the vast majority are there on a long-term basis.

Most nursing home residents have multiple chronic illnesses, and over half have some kind of mental disorder or organic brain syndrome. However, it is important to remember that, as a whole, the population of elderly nursing home residents is a very diverse one. Nursing homes have residents who are very alert as well as residents who are very disoriented, residents who are middle-aged as well as residents who are very old, residents who have good family or community support systems as well as residents who are all alone. Some residents are sociable, and others prefer to keep to themselves. Physical abilities also vary greatly: Some residents have good sight, while others are very visually impaired or blind; some have good hearing, while others are very hard-of-hearing or deaf; some are ambulatory, while others are dependent on wheelchairs or bedridden; some can feed and dress themselves, while others are totally dependent in all areas of daily living. Thus, one must look at each individual carefully to determine his or her specific strengths and needs.

Factors leading to placement in a long-term care facility or nursing home include (1) some disturbance in thinking or feeling, (2) a physical illness that requires nursing care and supervision, (3) an individual becoming unmanageable at home because of potentially harmful behavior, (4) behavior that is harmful to oneself or others, and (5) environmental factors, such as having no other place to go when independent living becomes unfeasible or having no significant others (spouse, children, etc.) who can provide informal support. Most older people see moving to an institution as a prelude to death. Regardless of their situation, individuals often feel somewhat rejected. Therefore, a move to a nursing home is often accompanied by feelings of fear, guilt, and resistance.

When they move to a nursing home, individuals

lose much of their independence, their home, many of their personal possessions, privacy, familiar surroundings and routines, and at least some of their social contacts. These losses may negatively affect the person's self-image and self-esteem. In addition, people who live in long-term care facilities lose much of their freedom of choice: They must abide by the rules, schedules, and routines of the institution. They have little control over their circumstances and few opportunities to make decisions. These residents also are generally dependent on others for transportation and are often isolated from the general community.

Persons who live in nursing homes or other institutions for a long period of time may develop a pattern of behavior called *institutional neurosis*. This pattern of behavior is characterized by (1) an over-dependence on routines and other people, (2) a lack of initiative, (3) apathy, (4) lack of interest in the future, and (5) deterioration of personal habits, such as grooming. It is important to remember that those elderly people who live in nursing homes or long-term care facilities continue to have needs for (a) meaningful activities that make them feel useful and productive, (b) intellectual stimulation, (c) ways to communicate and express their feelings, (d) opportunities for socialization with others, and (e) opportunities for creative expression and spiritual affirmation. Nursing home residents will enjoy and benefit from many of the same activities and experiences other older adults enjoy, if these experiences are structured and adapted to take into account the special needs posed by individual physical and mental limitations.

Elderly Individuals Who Have Alzheimer's Disease or Related Disorders

When individuals have *dementia*, they have multiple cognitive deficits that are due to the direct physiological effects of a medical condition and that are severe enough to interfere with their normal daily activities and social relationships (APA, 1994; Carruth, 1997; McNeil, 1995). *Alzheimer's disease*, or *dementia of the Alzheimer's type*, is a progressive, age-related, degenerative brain disorder that is characterized by gradual onset and continuing, irreversible cognitive decline in areas such as memory, ability to

perform routine tasks, orientation in time and space, language and communication skills, abstract thinking, and the ability to do mathematical calculations. Other symptoms include personality and behavioral changes, impaired judgment, decline in grooming and self-maintenance, and decrease in social skills (APA, 1994; G. Cohen, 1988; Gwyther, 1985; McNeil, 1995; *Memory and Aging*, 1987). Alzheimer's disease is *not* a normal part of aging; it is a chronic, terminal brain disease marked by steady, progressive mental and physical deterioration that shortens one's expected life span.

Since the mid-1980s, research into Alzheimer's disease and programs for persons with Alzheimer's disease and related disorders have received increasing attention (Bright, 1988; Chavin, 1991; G. Cohen, 1988; Gwyther, 1985; McNeil, 1995). Alzheimer's disease is the leading cause of cognitive impairment in old age and the fourth leading cause of death in the United States. About 4 million Americans, including 50%-60% of all nursing home residents, have this progressive, degenerative brain disorder. Although early onset Alzheimer's disease (before age 65) occurs in some people, most cases of Alzheimer's disease occur in elderly persons, affecting approximately 6% of those over age 65 and 25%-35% of those over age 85. Studies show that the incidence of Alzheimer's disease increases dramatically with age: "After age 65, the percentage of affected people approximately doubles with every decade of life" (McNeil, 1995, p. 8).

At this writing, Alzheimer's disease is neither preventable nor curable. A definite diagnosis is still possible only on autopsy, when the characteristic structural changes in the brain can be detected. However, using diagnostic tools such as a detailed patient history, a comprehensive physical examination and laboratory tests to rule out other possible causes of dementia, brain scans and imaging, and neuropsychological testing, clinicians can now diagnose probable Alzheimer's disease with 85% to 90% accuracy (McNeil, 1995). Current research suggests that Alzheimer's disease may have many causes or a number of factors that combine over time to trigger the disease (Chavin, 1991; McNeil, 1995). Researchers are also testing drugs that may help control, delay, or possibly reverse the chemical changes that take place in the brains of individuals who have Alzheimer's disease.

Alzheimer's disease was first described by a German physician, Alois Alzheimer, in 1907. It is characterized by certain structural changes in the nerve cells of the brain: (a) *neurofibrally tangles* (pairs of filaments wrapped around each other in the cytoplasm of the neurons, (b) *neuritic plaques* (filamentous and granular deposits), and (c) *granulo-vascular degeneration* (fluid pockets and granular material in the neurons). Individuals with Alzheimer's disease also have much lower levels of some neurotransmitters as compared with people who are aging normally. In addition, the thinking center (*cortex*) of the brain shrinks or atrophies in individuals with Alzheimer's disease, and the spaces in the ventricles of the brain become enlarged. These changes take place throughout the frontal and temporal lobes of the cerebral cortex and result in progressive loss of memory, thinking, judgment, and, finally, general functioning abilities. The average course of the disease is seven years, although it may progress as quickly as 2-4 years or last as long as 15-20 years. The progression from onset of memory and cognitive disturbances to helplessness may take anywhere from a few months to several years (APA, 1994; Chavin, 1991; G. Cohen, 1988; Gwyther, 1985; McNeil, 1995).

In an attempt to measure the progression of Alzheimer's disease, researchers have devised various scales such as the Clinical Dementia Rating (CDR), which has five stages, and the Global Dementia Scale (GDS), which has seven stages (Chavin, 1991; Gwyther, 1985; McNeil, 1995). Most clinicians and family members, however, think of the progression of Alzheimer's disease in three stages: mild or early, moderate or middle, and severe or late (terminal) (Gwyther, 1985; McNeil, 1995).

In the *mild* or *early stage* of Alzheimer's disease, symptoms include confusion and memory loss, disorientation, getting lost in familiar surroundings, trouble handling money or paying bills, difficulties with routine tasks, loss of spontaneity or initiative, mood or personality changes, and poor judgment. This stage may last as long as 2-4 years, leading up to and including diagnosis. The *moderate* or *middle stage* may last from several months to 10 years after diagnosis. Symptoms include increasing memory loss and confusion; shorter attention span; difficulty with activities of daily living (e.g., feeding, bathing); increased anxiety, suspiciousness, or agitation; sleep

disturbances; late-afternoon or early-evening restlessness ("sun-downing"); wandering or pacing; difficulty recognizing family and friends; repetitive statements or movements; increased difficulty organizing thoughts or thinking logically; confabulation; and problems with reading, writing, and numbers. Individuals in this stage usually need full-time supervision. Individuals who are in the *severe* or *late (terminal) stage* of Alzheimer's disease lose their ability to speak, don't recognize family members or themselves in a mirror, lose weight even when given a good diet, lose bowel and bladder control, and sleep more. Individuals at this stage may try to put everything in their mouth or touch everything and may groan, scream, or make grunting sounds. They are totally dependent on their caregivers. This stage may last a few months to two or three years. It is important to remember that these stages merely provide a framework to help understand Alzheimer's disease and prepare for changes that will occur in patients over time. In reality, stages often overlap and the appearance and progression of symptoms varies greatly from individual to individual.

Even though there is no cure or definitive treatment for Alzheimer's disease at the present time, there are ways to *manage the symptoms* associated with the disease and improve the affected person's quality of life (Chavin, 1991; Gwyther, 1985; McNeil, 1995; Whitcomb, 1992). Research and experience have shown that, with the proper approach and facilitation, "the person with dementia can learn new skills, relearn old skills, and adjust to new situations" (Chavin, 1995, p. 4). Although routine is important, new experiences are also needed to provided intellectual stimulation. There is some evidence that keeping people with dementia intellectually stimulated can help keep them mentally alert and perhaps even slow the progression of the disease (Chavin, 1995). However, stimulation must be structured and adapted to the individual's level of functioning. For example, even small amounts of excitement may upset a confused person, but carefully structured activities within the limits of his/her abilities (e.g., a walk, a visit with an old friend) may add interest and meaning to life.

Individuals who have Alzheimer's disease still have a need for meaningful, purposeful activities that contribute to their self-esteem and quality of life. They also need opportunities to socialize and interact with others. Activities that draw on lifelong interests and are adapted to the individual's current level of functioning are generally most successful. To communicate effectively with individuals who have Alzheimer's disease, caregivers must remember to minimize outside distractions, secure the person's attention (a touch on the shoulder or holding hands may help sustain attention), use short sentences, be consistent, use distraction rather than confrontation, demonstrate when possible, physically guide and reassure the person during movement, reassure the person of sustained care, show respect for the person's adult feelings, and respond to what the person appears to be feeling, so she or he will sense the caregiver understands. Using body language that demonstrates respect and caring can also facilitate effective interactions with individuals who have dementia. As caregivers look for things the person still is able to do and focus on these, adapting activities and situations so the person can continue to be involved within the limits of his/her abilities, both caregiver and patient will benefit.

With each stage of dementia, there are issues, needs, and problems that affect caregivers as well as the person with dementia. Family members often experience a deep sense of loss as the disease progresses, for they are gradually losing the person they love. In addition, as their burden of responsibility and caring for the physical needs of the individual with Alzheimer's disease increases, that individual's ability to respond to them decreases. For all these reasons, caring for persons with Alzheimer's disease or related dementias can be very stressful. Therefore, goals of care for individuals with Alzheimer's disease also usually include providing support for the caregivers, be they family members or facility staff (Clair, 1996b; Gwyther, 1985; McNeil, 1995; Special Committee on Aging, 1992). This support may take various forms, including (1) emotional and social support (e.g., support groups, individual and family counseling, home visits from professionals), (2) services, such as respite care, that give family caregivers some temporary relief, and (3) knowledge and skills training that give caregivers information about Alzheimer's disease, including resources available to them, and help caregivers learn behavior management techniques, skills for coping with the symptoms of Alzheimer's disease, and practical ways to resolve day-to-day problems.

Although Alzheimer's disease is the most common form of dementia in elderly persons, accounting for 50-70% of all cases, there are also other conditions that may cause dementia in elderly persons (APA, 1994; Carruth, 1997; Chavin, 1991; G. Cohen, 1988; McNeil, 1995). For example, *multi-infarct dementia* is caused by a series of minor strokes that occur at different times and affect cognitive functioning. This disorder has an abrupt onset and a fluctuating rather than uniformly progressive course. Patterns of deficits are "patchy" and vary greatly from person to person, depending on which areas of the brain are affected. Approximately 20% of all cases of dementia in elderly individuals are the result of strokes or multi-infarct dementia, while another 18% are caused by a combination of multi-infarct dementia and Alzheimer's disease.

The remaining cases of dementia in elderly persons are caused by a variety of disorders, including *Pick's disease* (a degenerative brain disease that mainly affects the frontal and temporal lobes; most common in individuals between ages 50 and 60, although it can occur in older individuals; emotional blunting, loss of behavioral inhibitions, and prominent language abnormalities occur early in the disease; difficulties with memory and other features of dementia occur as the disease progresses), *Parkinson's disease* (a slowly progressive neurological condition, characterized by tremor, rigidity, postural instability, and a blank, staring facial expression; dementia eventually occurs in 20%-60% of cases, more often in older individuals or those with severe or advanced disease), *Huntington's disease* (hereditary progressive degenerative disease of brain tissue; affects cognition, emotion, and movement; usually begins in mid-life; characterized by involuntary spasmodic, jerky, twisting movements of neck, trunk, and extremities; more severe memory deficits, disorganized speech, and psychotic features are sometimes present as the disease progresses), *Creutzfeldt-Jakob disease* (central nervous system disease; manifests itself in dementia, twitching or spasmodic involuntary movements, and characteristic periodic sharp EEG readings; most often develops in adults between the ages of 40 and 69 and typically progresses very rapidly over several months), *HIV disease*, or *alcohol abuse*. All types of dementia have the characteristic features of memory loss, decline in language skills, personality changes, impaired judgment, disorientation, and eventual decrease in ability to perform activities of daily living and loss of motor function.

The severe deterioration and eventual incapacity that occur in persons with dementia differ dramatically from the symptoms of *Age-Associated Memory Impairment (AAMI)* or *benign senescent forgetfulness*, a decline in short-term memory that sometimes accompanies aging (G. Cohen, 1988; Gwyther, 1985; McNeil, 1995; *Memory and Aging*, 1987). AAMI is neither progressive nor disabling; it is characterized only by brief short-term memory lapses and does not progress to other cognitive

impairments as dementias do. AAMI is often most noticeable when an individual is under stress or pressure; once the person relaxes, she or he is often able to recall the forgotten material. Persons with "normal" memory loss or AAMI are usually able to continue to follow written or spoken directions, develop compensatory strategies to deal with their memory loss (e.g., notes and reminders), and continue to care for themselves. In contrast to the progressive losses of memory and cognitive functioning associated with dementias, the memory problems of AAMI do not interfere with the individual's ability to carry on daily activities.

PSYCHOSOCIAL THEORIES OF AGING

As the elderly population continues to grow, many people have become interested in finding out what helps individuals age successfully. Some have found that people age more successfully when they do not accept the myth that aging is a time of inevitable decline (Hager, 1983). However, individuals who are elderly *do* need to make adjustments in their ways of thinking, feeling, and coping to meet the demands of their changing internal and external circumstances (Muslin, 1992). If they face these problems and opportunities associated with aging thoughtfully and realistically, aging individuals can, as long as they have reasonably intact mental abilities, largely determine the course their aging will take (Smith, 1972). Individuals may also increase their positive outlook, coping abilities, and general life satisfaction in later life by continuing to be involved in cognitive activities (G. Cohen, 1988).

When individuals age successfully, they do not overreact to the external world and do not show symptoms of fragmentation or loss of self-worth. These individuals have not merely *adjusted* to aging, which may imply an acceptance of inadequacy, but have *adapted* successfully to aging, achieving a cohesive "elderly self" (Muslin, 1992). These individuals have made conscious adjustments and adaptations that enable them to be at peace with themselves and have a joyous, fulfilled life.

Whether they realize it or not, people who work with individuals who are elderly are influenced both directly or indirectly by their ideas on what

constitutes successful aging. The set of attitudes, perspectives, assumptions, and beliefs people have about aging "influence the way in which the elderly are approached and treated and the way that their hopes and aspirations are either thwarted or realized to the fullest" (Watts, 1980, p. 88). Often, people may draw some of their beliefs and attitudes from the various psychosocial theories that attempts to define successful aging. Two of the most common of these are the *disengagement theory* and the *activity theory* (G. Cohen, 1988; Schooler & Estes, 1979; Watts, 1980).

According to the *disengagement theory* of aging, which originated with the work of Cummings and Henry (1961), as people age, they gradually and voluntarily withdraw from various roles they have assumed in life and become increasingly introverted and interested in fulfilling personal needs while decreasing their involvement with others (G. Cohen, 1988; Davis, 1992a; Purtilo, 1978; Schooler & Estes, 1979; Watts, 1980). In this view, high satisfaction in old age is found by accepting the inevitability of reduced personal and social interactions and voluntarily disengaging from them. Elderly people are seen as withdrawing from social and psychological involvement in their environment at the same time society is withdrawing its support from them. This mutual dissociation results in decreased interactions between the individual and society. Some see this process as occurring both in response to a lower level of energy and as a preparation for death.

In recent years, the implication that disengagement is universal and unavoidable has been criticized by many gerontologists (Davis, 1992a). While some people will disengage with relative comfort as they age, others disengage with great discomfort and, in that process, show a great drop in life satisfaction (Schooler & Estes, 1979). Others have been relatively disengaged for most of their lives and continue to be satisfied with that state as they age. In some cases, however, disengagement may not be a normal part of aging but an indication of depression, one of the most unrecognized and undertreated illnesses in the elderly (Bright, 1986; Davis, 1992a). "It is now generally accepted that not all elderly people reduce their societal roles and that those who do may suffer from depression" (Davis, 1992a, p. 149).

The *activity theory* of aging originated with the work of Havighurst (1963). This theory focuses on engagement rather than disengagement. It contends that people age most successfully and maintain satisfaction, health, and self-esteem when they remain as active and involved as possible (G. Cohen, 1988; Davis, 1992a; Watts, 1980). According to this theory, middle-age roles and activities are still appropriate in the older years, although they may have to be modified to some degree. Thus, individuals have the most satisfaction in their older years when they are able to maintain the pursuit of activities that are congruent with the preferences and relationships they have developed throughout their lives. Because of this emphasis on continuing or maintaining activity, the activity theory of aging is sometimes called the *maintenance* or *continuity theory*. Research and surveys of the activity patterns of older adults (G. Cohen, 1988; Erikson, Erikson, & Kivnick, 1986) lend support to the activity theorists' contention that "the thirst for activity and involvement on the part of the aged is much greater than society may be willing to admit or allow" (Watts, 1980, p. 87).

Neither the disengagement theory nor the activity theory will be applicable to all elderly individuals. "Some elderly individuals will choose to withdraw and reduce the number and quality of their social contacts, whereas others will maintain and seek an active life style" (Davis, 1992a, pp. 149-150). Although the assumption that there is only one way to grow old may be appealing, the reality is that there are a tremendous variety of behaviors and experiences and levels of development among elderly individuals, just as there are among people of all age levels (Kastenbaum, 1979). As each person brings unique traits, strengths, and weaknesses to this stage of development, successful aging will be different for each individual. The personality patterns individuals have had throughout their lives, rather than some preconceived notions about aging, may be one of the best predictors of whether they will tend to disengage or to remain active as they age.

Some theorists choose to look at aging from a *developmental* perspective (Erikson, Erikson, & Kivnick, 1986; Kastenbaum, 1979; Schooler & Estes, 1979). For example, Erik Erikson (1963, 1968; Erikson, Erikson, & Kivnick, 1986), in his stages of psychosocial development, sees middle adulthood as a time of addressing the conflict of generativity vs. stagnation and old age as the stage of dealing with integrity vs. despair. Depending upon how they face and meet the challenges of each stage of psychosocial development, individuals can develop adaptive strengths or maladaptive/malignant tendencies. The adaptive strength of middle adulthood is caring, a taking of active responsibility for nurturing the next generation, while that of old age is wisdom. According to Erikson,

> *Wisdom* is detached concern with life itself, in the face of death itself. It maintains and learns to convey the integrity of experience, in spite of the decline of bodily and mental functions. (Erikson, Erikson, & Kivnick, 1986, pp. 37-38)

Developmental theories of aging recognize that old age, as any stage of life, has its own challenges, and that different individuals meet these challenges in different ways. Although movement to a new stage of psychological development may occur in later life, it is just one of several alternatives (Kastenbaum, 1979). Some elderly individuals will cling to the values, activities, and orientations of their middle adult years, feeling that to give these up would be a sign of regression. Others may experience decline due to multiple stresses, but regain a higher level of functioning and life satisfaction when these stresses are identified and alleviated or modified. Still others will enter a new phase of development, orienting their life around a somewhat different set of tasks and values that those that had been of primary importance to them in their middle adult years.

These individuals may develop a strategy of simplification or essentialization, voluntarily shedding some of their past activities and relationships as excess baggage. They have less energy, but it is under more efficient control. Without turning their backs on life, they begin to orient themselves toward death, although not in a morbid way (Kastenbaum, 1979).

Other theorists feel that the phenomenon of aging can best be understood in terms of an *aging subculture* (Davis, 1992a; Lewis, 1985; Rose & Peterson, 1965; Schooler & Estes, 1979). They look at the population of elderly people as a distinct subgroup of society, who are aware that they are old and that, because of their age, they are subject to certain deprivations and enforced loss of roles, which they resent and try to overcome. Different elderly people will respond to

their age-associated losses and role changes in different ways. Some, especially those who have been relatively disengaged for most of their lives, may experience no deprivation. Others resign themselves to their loss of roles and seek no alternative. A third group becomes re-engaged, either by creating new independent roles for themselves in the general society or by finding new roles for themselves among their peers in the aging subculture. Subculture theorists also believe elderly persons have a unique set of norms, feelings, and attitudes that are best understood by other elderly individuals and stress the importance of elderly persons communicating with other elderly people (Davis, 1992a; Lewis, 1985).

TREATMENT APPROACHES

A variety of treatment approaches and interventions have been developed to rehabilitate and/or improve the life quality of elderly individuals (Bright, 1972; Davis, 1992a; Feil, 1982; Hackley, 1973; Karras, 1985, 1987; Purtilo, 1978; Riegler, 1980; Smith, 1990). These include sensory stimulation (sensory training), reality orientation, remotivation, validation, reminiscence, and life review. Many of these interventions target those elderly persons who are impaired or institutionalized. However, some approaches, like reminiscence or life review, can be used with most segments of the elderly population. Smith (1990) also noted that gerontological studies are increasingly finding that behavioral interventions provide effective ways to deal with many problems of the elderly.

Many rehabilitation programs for elderly individuals who are institutionalized use different approaches and techniques depending upon the individual's level of functioning. These programs often have three components: sensory stimulation (sensory training), reality orientation, and remotivation (Davis, 1992a). *Sensory stimulation* or *sensory training approaches* are usually recommended for the most severely impaired individuals. These programs aim to restore or improve the individual's contact with his/her environment by providing short, simple, concrete, highly structured activities that stimulate as many senses as possible. As individuals respond to

this sensory input, they begin to interact with their surroundings, often nonverbally at first. Passive activities that require few independent physical or verbal responses from the client are frequently used in the initial stages of the program. For example, the therapist may rub the client's arm with various textures, describing the feel of each, or present samples of various smells, describing what each is. Goals include improved awareness of and responsiveness to the environment, improved body awareness, increased attention span, improved motor function, and increased communication and interaction with others.

Reality orientation (RO), the next level up in a staged program, is used with people who are confused and disoriented but who are still able to participate in a group. This technique, pioneered by the psychiatrist James C. Folsom in the Veterans Administration Hospital in Topeka, Kansas, in 1959, uses consistent reminders of everyday facts as tools to decrease confusion, apathy, and isolation and to increase independence and improve awareness of self, others, and the environment (Hackley, 1973). Consistency and repetition within a calm, structured environment are the keys to success. RO programs have two components: (1) daily classes that review basic facts, help orient the clients to person, place, and time, and encourage socialization and maximum independence, and (2) constant, consistent reality-based communication in the course of everyday conversation and activities by all people interacting with the clients that reminds clients of who they are and who is talking to them (person), where they are (place), time (day, year, time of day, time in sequence of activities [e.g., just before lunch], season, etc.), why they are there, and what is expected of them. RO boards that list information such as the place, day of the week, date, next meal, next holiday, and weather, are integral parts of both aspects of the RO program. Other materials, such as clocks, calendars, pictures, color-coded hallways and doors, names plates, charts or pictures outlining the steps of a routine, and pictures of friends and family members, are also used as cues to promote reality orientation. Research has shown that consistent RO programs can arrest and, in many cases, reverse confusion and disorientation (Hackley, 1973).

Remotivation is the final step of the three-tiered rehabilitation program. It tries to stimulate cognitive abilities, verbal interaction, and improved social skills among individuals who may be moderately confused or apathetic but who are aware of their immediate surroundings, have some verbal abilities, and have enough of an attention span to participate in a 30- to 60-minute group. Remotivation programs use structured, small-group discussions to promote communication with and among the group members, trying to get them reinterested in simple, objective features of everyday life that are unrelated to any emotional difficulties they may have. The group leader uses pictures, slides, objects, recordings, or other concrete examples of the chosen topics to focus attention on the topic, and then encourages interaction and discussion through structured, objective questions. Goals include initiating a renewed interest in one's surroundings, increasing interaction with others, encouraging reality-based discussions, improving socialization, and increasing one's desire to take an active role in the society in which she or he lives.

Other treatment approaches are used with various groups of elderly individuals. For example, the technique of *validation*, also known as *validation/ fantasy therapy* or *the Feil method*, was developed in the mid-1960s by Naomi Feil in her work with individuals ages 80-100 plus (the "old-old") who were severely disoriented. Feil (1982) discovered that these individuals often withdrew or became hostile when she attempted to orient them to their present reality using traditional RO techniques, but did respond positively to experiences that used music, movement, feeling exploration, and reminiscence. She theorized that reality orientation, although useful with younger people who were disoriented and who might return to the community, did not relate to the lives of these old-old individuals who were disoriented or to the conflicts they were trying to resolve (e.g., justifying their lives in preparation for death). Many of these individuals had used denial as a coping mechanism throughout their lives. Because of permanent damage to their senses, mobility, memory, etc., that resulted from the normal processes of aging and a loss of familiar roles, they chose to retreat from their painful present reality and live on a subliminal level of awareness. These disoriented old-old people coped and survived by recreating or living in the past, when they were useful and rewarded, instead of acknowledging the unbearable present.

A person using validation techniques respects the unique differences in individuals and uses empathy to tune into the feelings of the disoriented old-old. By picking up on the clients' cues and helping them put their feelings into words, the therapist acknowledges the legitimate feelings behind the clients' disoriented statements, thus validating the clients and restoring their dignity. Goals of validation include restoring self-worth, reducing stress, justifying life, resolving unfinished conflicts from the past, and increasing positive feelings. Universal feelings (e.g., missing ones' parent, spouse, home, or job; fear of being alone; boredom, uselessness; anger at uselessness or rejection; need to belong and be loved) are explored through words, symbols, music, and movement in a nurturing environment, with the therapist acknowledging through words and actions that the person's feelings are true and valid. The technique of discovering and validating the feelings behind confused words or actions can also be very useful in relating to and calming individuals who have Alzheimer's disease or related dementias (Clair, 1996b; Feil, 1993; Whitcomb, 1992).

Reminiscence techniques can be beneficial for almost all groups of elderly people (Bright, 1972, 1981, 1986; Butler, 1963; Davis, 1992a; Merriam & Cross, 1981; Purtilo, 1978; Wylie, 1990). Many elderly people naturally recall past events and think or talk about them. In fact, at least a periodic retreat into the past is a normal phenomenon for individuals who are elderly (Feil, 1982; Purtilo, 1978). Reminiscence may be a natural and important part of the lives of elderly individuals for two reasons: (1) it serves as their way of *daydreaming* and (2) it provides a means of *life review* (Butler, 1963; Purtilo, 1978).

Daydreams are vehicles that carry people's hopes and help them see what they might become. As people become older and less oriented to the future, their thinking often becomes more focused more on what they were rather than on what they will become. Thus, their reminiscing about the past, about times of pleasure and self-worth, becomes their way of expressing hope in daydreams. As they reminisce, individuals also have an opportunity to put their life in order and perspective, to form a clear image of their legacy, and to determine the significance of who they are now. As they relate their reminiscing to the present, reminiscence may also assist in reconciliation and resolution of conflicts individuals may have (Bright, 1972, 1986; Butler, 1963).

The haphazard flow of memories that sometimes occurs in reminiscence may lead others to think the elderly person is confused and disoriented when he or she may, in fact, be merely engaged in the process of life review, in which memories from the past are so vivid they seem to be actually happening in the present (Feil, 1982; Purtilo, 1978). For example, a 94-year-old woman described her feelings and thoughts this way:

> To me, there is no past, present, or future; the 1960's or the 1900's are equally current for me. . . . Actually I am well aware of most situations but with things flashing through my mind the way they do, I'm likely to speak of my school days in the same breath as I talk about traffic outside my window. I know it's confusing to others but I can't help it. (Purtilo, 1978, p. 219)

Reminiscence is now recognized as a healthy process that can provide satisfaction, increase socialization and interpersonal interactions, facilitate adaptation to change or stress, aid in the resolution of grief over various losses, help validate and give meaning to one's life, strengthen self-esteem, and provide access to personal strengths and resources that were used in the past (Bright, 1972, 1981, 1986;

Butler, 1963; Davis, 1992a; Merriam & Cross, 1981; Purtilo, 1978; Wylie, 1990). The process of reminiscence can be effective in both individual or group situations and can be done in an informal (e.g., casual conversations) or formal matter (e.g., structured groups or individual sessions with therapeutic goals). Various materials, such as photographs, scrapbooks, antique objects, clothing, movies, magazines, posters, and music, are often used to stimulate reminiscence and focus discussion in structured groups. Many elderly people find pleasure in sharing their recollections with others, especially with those who lived through the same events and times.

Since reminiscence is so important to the life and mental health of elderly people, many facilities that serve the elderly offer *structured reminiscence groups* as part of their programs. Reminiscence can positively influence many aspects of an elderly person's life. A study conducted in the mid-1980s showed that nursing home residents who met in weekly small groups with a discussion leader where they told stories about themselves and their families were happier with their lives and rated themselves as healthier after only three months of meetings (Meer, 1985). Forty percent of the participants also showed an improved short-term memory, leading the researchers to conclude that talking about past events and their relationship to the present stimulated the participants cognitively as well as emotionally. Reminiscence techniques may also stimulate memories of the past for some individuals with Alzheimer's disease, providing connections that give them back some awareness of a positive sense of self (Clair, 1996b).

Recent research has also shown that *behavioral approaches* can be very effective, efficient tools for enhancing self-control and self-management in individuals who are elderly (Smith, 1990). Many behavioral techniques, such as positive reinforcement, systematic desensitization, assertiveness training, relaxation training, cognitive-behavioral approaches, and procedures based on social learning principles, can be used successfully with elderly individuals. These techniques can help deal with many behavioral problems commonly seen among elderly persons, including

(a) wandering and disorientation, (b) dependence in aging, (c) age-related changes in social activities, (d) sleep disturbances, (e) urinary incontinence, and (f) family management of the elderly. (Smith, 1990, p. 37)

Smith (1990) provides many references and summaries of studies documenting the successful use of behavioral interventions with elderly individuals. These techniques seem to show much promise for alleviating specific behavioral problems in at least some elderly individuals, especially those who are institutionalized. However, for behavioral interventions to be most effective, it is also important for therapists to determine both the most effective cues and reinforcement schedules for elderly clients and the variables which are most likely to increase, maintain, and generalize positive treatment effects.

SETTINGS FOR SERVICE DELIVERY

Individuals who are elderly receive special programs and services in a variety of settings, depending on their individual needs and levels of functioning. These include community senior centers, church groups, adult or senior learning programs at community colleges, adult day care settings, retirement communities, assisted living centers, private homes (home health care), private or public clinics or medical centers, nursing homes or long-term care facilities, general hospitals, rehabilitation facilities, psychiatric facilities, or hospice programs. Music therapists may work on a full-time or part-time basis in any of these settings, or they may provide contractual services to a number of different groups or agencies. In addition, music therapists may provide services to elderly clients through music stores or music studios or in private practice settings. Depending on the situation and the needs of the clients and the agencies, music therapists may provide direct and/or consultant services and work with clients as individuals and/or in groups.

In a recent survey of populations served by music therapists in which respondents were permitted to list as many categories as appropriate (AMTA, 1998), 646 of 1,620 respondents said they worked with elderly persons. 595 respondents specifically reported working with persons who had Alzheimer's disease or related dementias, while 290 reported they worked with individuals who had had strokes and 204 said they worked with individuals who had Parkinson's disease. When asked to list their work settings (again listing as many as appropriate), 417 of 1,654 music therapists responding said they worked in nursing homes, 162 in adult day care settings, 155 in geriatric psychiatric units, 125 in non-nursing geriatric facilities, 84 in assisted living centers, 42 in adult education settings, and 13 with home health agencies. The population of elderly individuals continues to be a growing area of employment for music therapists, both in the traditional areas of long-term care (nursing homes) and in the newer areas of home health, adult day care, community centers, assisted living centers, special programs for individuals with Alzheimer's disease and related dementias, programs for the well elderly, and the like (Clair, 1996b; Palmer, 1989; Prickett, 1996; Special Committee on Aging, 1992).

HOW MUSIC IS USED IN THERAPY

Music and Elderly Persons – Myths and Facts

People often have many false assumptions about elderly persons and their musical capacities and preferences (Davis, 1992a; Gibbons, 1988). Common misconceptions include the following:

1. Most elderly people are frail, malfunctioning individuals who lack any capacity for musical development.

2. The vocal ranges of most elderly people are so deteriorated that they cannot adequately sing most melodies.

3. Because auditory abilities decline with age, many

elderly people are unable to aurally discriminate-differences between familiar and unfamiliar melodies.

4. Most elderly people have no desire to learn or relearn musical skills.

5. Most elderly people prefer passive music activities requiring minimal skills and minimal involvement.

6. Most elderly people prefer religious music to all other types of music.

7. Elderly people who do not prefer religious music prefer music of the late 1800s or early 1900s to all other time periods.

8. Elderly people prefer quiet, sedative music at all times.

9. Elderly persons cannot and do not strive for quality musical products.

Research and clinical examples, however, give quite a different picture of the musical interests and capabilities of individuals who are elderly (Bowles, 1991; Clair, 1996b; Gibbons, 1985, 1988; Jonas, 1991; Moore, Staum, & Brotons, 1992; Prickett, 1988, 1996; Smith, 1989). In reality, musical ability does not decrease significantly as people age (Gibbons, 1982, 1985; Prickett, 1988, 1996). For example, Gibbons (1982) found that the composite Music Aptitude Profile score of subjects in three age groups (ages 65-70; 71--75; 76-93) did not differ significantly. Research and practical experience also show that the arts continue to be integral to development throughout life (Erikson, Erikson, & Kivnick, 1986; Gibbons, 1982; Weisberg & Wilder, 1985). However, although *ability* for music and other arts experiences does not diminish with age, *opportunities* society gives to participate in certain arts experiences or to learn or relearn skills often do decrease as people age (Gibbons, 1985).

For most elderly people, the physical changes associated with normal aging seem to have little effect on musical enjoyment or aptitude. Research shows that most elderly people are able to aurally discriminate melodies and rhythms (Gibbons, 1982,

1983b, 1988). In addition, research shows that the functional vocal range of most elderly people is between 13 semitones (A below middle C to G above middle C) (Greenwald & Salzberg, 1979) and 19 semitones (F below middle C to C above middle C) (Moore, Staum, & Brotons, 1992), which is large enough to provide satisfying singing experiences of most melodies, especially if the melodies are transposed to lower keys so that most of the notes lie within the individuals' most comfortable singing range. Those who assume that music played for older individuals should automatically be played at a louder than normal levels to compensate for decreased hearing acuity may also be in error. Smith (1989) found that, in music listening situations, older adults generally preferred *lower* loudness levels than younger adults. In addition, older adults did *not* compensate for decreased hearing capabilities by increasing the loudness level of the music.

Gibbons (1977) found that many elderly people enjoy and sometimes even prefer lively, upbeat music to slow, sedative music. Thus, although elderly people do enjoy some sedative music, it is not their exclusive choice. Another study found that, in the context of sing-alongs, many elderly clients preferred songs of moderate or slower tempos to those of faster tempos (Moore, Staum, & Brotons, 1992). This may indicate that different types and tempos of music may be appropriate for elderly people in different situations (e.g., listening or dancing/moving vs. singing). What music will be most useful and most preferred by particular clients in a given situation will depend on factors such as the task associated with the music, activity goals, individual preferences, etc.

Elderly people enjoy a wide variety of music and musical experiences and are able to discriminate and express definite preferences. Although factors such as community size and location, living situation, state of health, educational level, and previous life experience may influence their initial expressed preferences (Gilbert & Beal, 1982; Jonas, 1991), their interests may broaden as they are exposed to and educated about music of various styles (Gibbons, 1977). While religious music may be important to many (but certainly not *all*) elderly people , it is not the only type of music most enjoy (Gibbons, 1977, 1988; Gilbert & Beal, 1982; Moore, Staum, & Brotons, 1992).

Researchers have also found that, while older

people do enjoy music of many styles and periods, most show a significant preference for songs that were popular in their young adult years (approximately ages 18 to 30) (Gibbons, 1977; Jonas, 1991; Prickett, 1988, 1996). Thus, the popular music preferences of a 65-year-old person will be quite different from those of an 85-year-old. Other studies have found that many elderly people prefer patriotic, old popular, and religious songs over folk songs (Moore, Staum, & Brotons, 1992) and country music, traditional jazz, or art music over current popular music (Jonas, 1991).

Elderly people frequently show a strong desire to gain musical skills and to improve their skills in singing, playing, and general musical knowledge (Bowles, 1991; Gibbons, 1977, 1985; Myers, 1991, 1992). Elderly people also show a strong commitment to quality musical performances and products and are able to develop musically when given appropriate opportunities (Boswell, 1992; Darrough, 1992; Ernst & Emmons, 1992; Gibbons, 1977, 1985; Myers, 1991, 1992). Some research has shown that elderly persons are most likely to develop new musical skills when they are able to observe other elderly persons succeeding at musical activities and when they receive support and encouragement from their peers (Gibbons, 1985).

Even elderly individuals who have Alzheimer's disease retain some musical capabilities and enjoy participating in musical experiences (Bright, 1988; Brotons, Koger, & Pickett-Cooper, 1997; Chavin, 1991; Clair, 1996b; Cordrey, 1994; Gfeller & Hanson, 1995; Prickett, 1996). In some individuals with severe dementia, musical behaviors are maintained while all other cognitive functions decline (York, 1994). Many individuals with middle- to late-stage dementia retain rhythmic abilities even when singing ability is lost and overall cognitive functioning is severely compromised (Clair & Bernstein, 1990; Clair, Bernstein, & Johnson, 1995; Lipe, 1995).

Why Music Is Useful with Elderly Individuals

Since music has been an enjoyable part of the lives of most people, it can be a very effective tool for establishing communication with older adults, motivating them to participate in treatment programs, and helping them improve or maintain their level of physical, mental, social, and/or emotional functioning (Bright, 1972, 1981; Clair, 1996b; Gibbons, 1988; Karras, 1987; Palmer, 1977, 1989; Prickett, 1988, 1996; Smith & Lipe, 1991; Tanner & O'Briant, 1980).

Regardless of one's language, culture, or abilities, music

"speaks" to all of us. It motivates, enriches, touches, relaxes, energizes. From "Rock-a-bye-Baby" to "Blest Be the Tie That Binds," our lives are filled with music. (Karras, 1987, p. 1)

Music is an experience that is structured in time. As such, it can help structure many situations, interactions, and activities. The rhythms and melodies of music capture an individual's attention and evoke physical, intellectual, and emotional responses on many different levels. Memories and life experiences are often associated with music and the emotions tied to certain pieces of music; thus, music can stimulate reminiscence and be an ideal tool for life review (Bright, 1981, 1986). Music communicates at a feeling level, touching and serving as an expressive medium even for those who are unable to communicate with words. Music is also a very flexible modality that, through improvisation, can be changed to fit the tempos and responses of the moment. Since music experiences can be adapted to many levels of functioning and degrees of participation, most elderly people, from the healthiest, most independent to the most severely impaired, can participate successfully in some type of music experience (Clair, 1996b; Palmer, 1989; Special Committee on Aging, 1992).

The Older Americans Act Amendments of 1992, Public Law 102-375, recognizes that musical or rhythmic interventions specifically selected and structured by a music therapist can help restore, maintain, or improve the social or emotional functioning, mental processing, or physical health and functioning of older individuals. This law added music therapy to a list of supportive and preventative services that are provided for older individuals. Provisions were also made for research and demonstration projects and education, training, and information dissemination projects regarding the use of music therapy with elderly individuals (*Congressional Record*, September 22, 1992, No. 130-Part II, H. 8969-H. 9007).

General Music Therapy Treatment Goals with Older Adults

Music experiences can be used therapeutically with older adults in many ways. Various types of music experiences involving activities such as listening, playing musical instruments, singing, moving to music, creating music, or discussing music, can be structured by music therapists (a) to evoke and stimulate desired physical responses, from relaxation to structured movements or various degrees and types of physical activity; (b) to influence mood and affect and facilitate transitions to more desirable emotional states and reactions; (c) to facilitate verbal and/or nonverbal communication; (d) to improve social skills and facilitate social integration; (e) to serve as an outlet for and a vehicle of emotional expression; (f) to provide intellectual stimulation and improve mental functioning; (g) to stimulate meaningful associations; or (h) to provide purposeful, enjoyable activities that add meaning and quality to life and help improve and maintain self-esteem (Bright, 1972, 1981, 1988; Clair, 1996b; Douglass, 1985; Karras, 1987; Palmer, 1977; Special Committee on Aging, 1992).

As with any population, music therapists design treatment goals and interventions for older adults based on an individual assessment of client needs, abilities, and preferences. A national survey of music therapists working with older adults found that the most frequent goal areas for music therapy treatment were, in rank order: (1) socialization skills, (2) sensory stimulation, (3) cognitive skills, (4) expression of feelings, (5) physical functioning, (6) relaxation/anxiety reduction, (7) creative expression, (8) problem behaviors, and (9) spiritual affirmation (i.e., using the client's spiritual resources to help maintain overall well-being) (Smith & Lipe, 1991, p. 209). The next sections of this chapter provide more specific examples of music therapy goals and interventions with various subgroups of the population of elderly individuals.

Music Therapy Approaches with the Well Elderly

Therapeutically structured music experiences can have many benefits for elderly people who remain in the community and are relatively healthy and independent. For example, music experiences can provide (1) opportunities to find new roles, (2) meaningful and challenging activities, (3) mental and physical stimulation, (4) appropriate and enjoyable social experiences, and (5) new ways to contribute to society (Clair, 1996b; Palmer, 1985, 1989; Special Committee on Aging, 1992). Research on the leisure activities of older adults found that they show an overwhelming preference for music (Birkenshaw-Fleming, 1993). Other research has shown that involvement in music groups can enhance life satisfaction and that involvement in meaningful activities correlates strongly with both longevity and life satisfaction (Palmer, 1989). Many older adults are finding that music can be a great motivator for exercise and that involvement with music (e.g., learning music skills, participating in ensembles and community music activities) can help them maintain physical, mental, and emotional well-being (Clair, 1996b). Both music therapists and music merchants are also beginning to recognize the major contributions learning and participating in music can make to wellness and disease prevention in older adults (Bruhn et al., 1996; Farbman, 1994).

Since music has been an enjoyable part of the past experience of most elderly people, it can become a natural bridge to new and meaningful activity later in life (Palmer, 1985). Music therapists can design music experiences in which even people who have little or no previous musical experience can participate with success. Research has also shown that elderly persons continue to have ability to develop musically and retain the capacity to learn new musical skills, even at advanced ages (Clair, 1996b; Gibbons, 1977, 1982, 1985; Special Committee on Aging, 1992).

Some older people may find that they finally have the time to learn an instrument they have wanted to play all their lives; others may now have that time to participate in community or church choirs and ensembles (Birkenshaw-Fleming, 1993; Clair, 1996b; Erikson et al., 1986; Palmer, 1985). Developing music skills and then using them in social situations (e.g., ensembles, sing-alongs) also facilitates positive interactions with others and provides a sense of belonging and being needed. As individuals develop new skills and make meaningful contributions to a music group, their self-esteem increases and they have increased opportunities to receive positive recognition from others. Intergenerational music programs can also facilitate interactions and understanding between younger people (e.g., children, teens, college students) and older adults (Bowers, 1998; Darrow et al., 1994; Frego, 1995; Wilder, 1985).

Older adults who develop or redevelop music skills have expanded opportunities for self-expression. In addition, music skills can give them enjoyable activities to fill the time they spend alone (Clair, 1996b). Moreover, music offers opportunities for varying degrees of intellectual stimulation and challenges as older adults develop performance skills, learn more about music styles and music theory, or compose and create song lyrics and/or instrumental parts. Older people who prefer to be consumers (passive participants) rather than performers or composers can also receive intellection, emotional, and social benefits from music as they attend school and community concerts, contribute to fund-raising efforts of arts organizations, or participate in music appreciation or music discussion groups (Clair, 1996b; Palmer, 1985, 1989).

Older adults can enjoy and participate successfully in many different types of music experiences, including singing, listening, learning about or discussing music, playing instruments, moving or exercising to music, and creating music. As Clair (1996b) noted, "At some level of participation, music is available and accessible to most individuals who have an interest in it" (p. 58). Music experiences that have been used to help older adult improve or maintain their level of physical, mental, social or emotional functioning include

- vocal ensembles or choirs (Clair, 1996b; Darrough, 1992; Glassman, 1983; Palmer, 1985)
- sing-alongs (Glassman, 1983)
- individual vocal or instrumental lessons to develop or relearn musical skills (Bowles, 1991; Clair, 1996b; Gibbons, 1977; Glassman, 1983; Gold, 1982; Hoerning, 1982)
- bell choirs (Palmer, 1985)
- bands, orchestras, or small instrumental ensembles (Clair, 1996b; Ernst & Emmons, 1992; Gibbons, 1985)
- intergenerational music programs, choirs, or instrumental ensembles (Bowers, 1998; Clair, 1996b; Darrow et al., 1994; Frego, 1995; Wilder, 1985)
- rhythm bands (Glassman, 1983)
- talent shows (Glassman, 1983)
- spontaneous, creative group experiences to produce sound collages and vocal and instrumental improvisations and compositions (Carle, 1982)
- groups that attend and discuss concerts (Clair, 1996b; Palmer, 1985)
- music appreciation groups (Bowles, 1991; Clair, 1996b; Palmer, 1985)
- reminiscence through music (Palmer, 1989)
- musical journeys through time or life review through discussion of music associated with various periods of life (Bright, 1981; Kellman, 1986)
- music as an accompaniment to and motivation for exercise (Clair, 1996b)
- music-based or music mediated relaxation, stress management, and pain control (Clair, 1996b)
- song lyric analysis to facilitate discussion of issues associated with aging (Smith, 1991), and
- studying music in a societal context (Coates, 1984).

The well elderly are vital, capable, alert adults who value and demand quality experiences and expect to achieve and learn (Erikson et al., 1986; Myers, 1991, 1992). Many have a high interest in music performance skills and perceptive listening/music appreciation activities (Bowles, 1991). For music programs to be successful with this population, therapists must accurately define and assess the capabilities and interests of the participants and gear programs to the participants' strengths (Coates, 1984; Davidson, 1980; Gibbons, 1985). Participants must not only know the benefits involvement with music can have for their physical, mental, and emotional health, but also have opportunities to participate in programs and activities that have meaning for them and their life situation. To engage the healthy elderly and facilitate their use of music as a tool for continued growth and development, therapists must plan quality, challenging experiences using materials that are age-appropriate, interesting, and personally relevant to the participants (Boswell, 1992; Coates, 1984; Davidson, 1980; Gibbons, 1985; Myers, 1981, 1982). As Smith (1991) observed:

> The challenge for the future is to devise techniques and treatment strategies that not only accomplish specific treatment objectives but are sought out by the growing number of higher functioning older adults. (pp. 11-12)

Music Therapy Approaches with Elderly Individuals Who Are Semi-Independent

The rapid growth of adult day care centers and assisted living residences offers a tremendous new potential area for music therapy services. Music therapy treatment techniques have been used effectively with frail elderly individuals in nursing homes and long term care facilities for many years (Gibbons, 1988; Karras, 1987; Prickett, 1988, 1996), and most, if not all, of these interventions can also be used successfully with elderly individuals who have physical or mental impairments that cause them to need some degree of supervised care in adult day care or assisted living situations (Palmer, 1985, 1989; Smith & Knudson, 1995; Special Committee on Aging, 1995).

Since music experiences are flexible, adaptable, and accessible at many different levels of ability and participation, they can be important aspects of programming in day treatment centers that serve clients with a wide range of abilities and disabilities. Experiences such as listening to music, playing instruments, singing or humming, creating or improvising music with voices or instruments, relaxing or stretching and exercising to music, creating movements to music, or discussing song lyrics, can be structured by music therapists to maximize elderly clients' opportunities to socialize appropriately, develop a sense of belonging as they draw together for a common cause and function successfully within a group, discover or rediscover talents, enhance self-esteem through new accomplishments and positive recognition by others, express feelings and emotions (nonverbally as well as verbally), and improve their physical and mental functioning (Smith & Knudson, 1995). As the elderly clients participate successfully in music therapy experiences, they can enjoy and be

appreciated for their *current* accomplishments, rather that being appreciated only for their life work in the distant past. "For many disabled older persons, music therapy can be a key to the best possible quality of life" (Smith & Knudson, 1995, p. 24).

Smith and Knudson (1995) provide an excellent description of a model music therapy program for frail elderly and disabled adults in adult day care settings. Interventions included (a) instrumental and vocal improvisation (used to encourage expression of feelings, provide opportunities for verbal and non-verbal communication); (b) music-assisted reminiscence (to facilitate communication, interaction, life review); (c) music-meditated relaxation (to reduce physical and mental tension; to improve coping techniques and stress management); (d) music and rhythmic movement (to improve physical coordination and physical functioning; to encourage social interaction, creative expression, and cognitive awareness: (e) song writing (to express feelings, encourage creativity); (f) developing or redeveloping music skills by learning to play musical instruments such as hand chimes, Orff and percussion instruments, autoharp, piano or organ, band and orchestral instruments (to improve physical and mental functioning, decrease depression, provide meaningful activities); and (g) solo or group musical performances in talent shows, bell choirs, singing groups, instrumental groups, choral readings, etc. (to enhance self-esteem, provide opportunities for praise by others, increase interaction with others and feelings of belongingness, and improve physical and mental functioning). Some interventions, such as vocal or instrumental performing groups and rhythm/movement groups, were carried out in large group situations (15-30 members), while others, such as music-based discussion or reminiscence groups, smaller performing groups (e.g., bell choir, drum circle), improvisation groups, creative arts groups, relaxation/guided imagery groups, or groups with clients who had a certain diagnosis (e.g., dementia-specific groups) were more effective in medium (8-15 members) or small groups (4-8 members). While participants were sometimes grouped according to similar needs and levels of functioning, other groups integrated clients who had a variety of diagnoses, abilities, levels of physical and mental functioning, and ages. Individual music therapy sessions were also used to help clients learn or relearn/maintain music skills, facilitate expression of feelings and concerns, decrease agitation, or work on other individual needs in a more intensive situation.

The music therapy program also included some music experiences, such as sing-alongs, client talent shows, patriotic or seasonal programs, and melodramas, that involved whole group participation by 30 or more clients. These whole group activities emphasized general participant enjoyment and enhanced self-esteem. Smith and Knudson (1985) frequently included performance activities as part of the music therapy process, noting the great benefits these experiences had for both the performers/clients (e.g., increased self-esteem, sense of accomplishment, improved mental and physical functioning as they mastered new skills) and the audience.

> Whether the performance is done by one very frail individual, only in the presence of the music therapist and a family member, or by the large Bell Choir before a national conference audience of 400, laughter, tears, hugs, and standing ovations all attest to the fact that these elderly/disabled performers carry a message more powerful than words. (Smith & Knudson, 1995, p. 77)

Music therapists who work at adult day care or assisted living centers may be full-time employees, part-time or contract employees, or consultants (Palmer, 1989; Smith & Knudson, 1995; Smith & Lipe, 1991). It is important to remember that for music experiences to be music *therapy*, rather than just generalized music *activity*, they must be based on individual *assessment* of clients' needs, strengths, and weaknesses and have specific, measurable individual *goals* within a treatment plan designed to help clients use the music experiences to gain skills or improve their functioning in *nonmusical* areas. In addition to conducting specific music therapy sessions for certain clients or groups in adult day care or assisted living settings, music therapists might also supervise goal-directed music programming that is designed by the music therapist but implemented by other staff or volunteers. Some of these programs might include daily exercise to music, music listening or music and reminiscence groups, music and reality orientation groups, singing groups, ensembles using simple percussion or recreational instruments, or individual

tapes for clients with special needs (Palmer, 1989; Smith & Knudson, 1995). To help ensure the quality and appropriateness of this programming in meeting client needs, music therapists would meet regularly with those carrying out the programs to evaluate the program and make any necessary changes, either in the group structure as a whole or in particular approaches with individual clients.

Music Therapy Approaches with Chronically Ill Elderly Individuals Who Are Cared for at Home

As more and more chronically ill individuals are cared for in their home or that of a caregiver with assistance from community or home health agencies, music therapists are developing innovative ways to help meet the social, psychological, emotional, physical and spiritual needs of these individuals and their caregivers (Palmer, 1989; Special Committee on Aging, 1992). For example, music therapists may (a) contract with home health or community agencies to give an added dimension to their services, (b) work through outreach programs of hospitals or rehabilitation facilities or community agencies, (c) work for or contract with agencies that provide in-home hospice programs, or (d) contract privately with individuals or their families. In addition to providing direct services in the home, music therapists may assess the elderly client to determine his/her capabilities, needs, and interests and then train family members or other volunteers or caregivers to implement goal-directed music programming under the music therapist's supervision. When family members implement or participate in music therapy experiences, they can interact with the elderly individual in meaningful ways within the context of enjoyable activities that are within the physical, social, and psychological capabilities of the elderly individual. Some innovative programs have also used teleconferencing to connect homebound senior citizens, allowing them to participate in many different types of programs, including sing-alongs and discussion groups, by using their telephones (Kadaba, 1995). Being able to interact with others through teleconferencing gave these homebound elderly adults who were mentally alert but physically impaired something to look forward to and increased their mental stimulation and feelings of connectedness while decreasing depression.

Specific benefits of music therapy services to homebound chronically ill elderly individuals include (1) decreasing stress, anxiety, and depression, (2) providing alternatives for pain relief and relaxation, (3) decreasing isolation and facilitating communication and interaction with others, (4) integrating family members, (5) providing additional avenues for communication and emotional expression, (6) facilitating reminiscence and life review, (7) helping individuals and family members deal with the emotional impact of the individual's illness or condition, and (8) facilitating the grieving process (Bright, 1986; Clair, 1996b; Hanser, 1990; Special Committee on Aging, 1992). Music therapy interventions often utilize approaches that are low-cost and easily accessible. For example, Hanser (1990) found that an 8-week music listening program facilitated by a music therapist helped homebound older adults who were clinically depressed increase their ability to cope with stress and decrease symptoms of depression, anxiety, and physical complaints. Music listening selections specially selected by the music therapist after assessing the client could also be used to facilitate reminiscence and life review and help bring closure to life (Bright, 1981, 1986; Palmer, 1989). In addition, music listening and discussion, improvisation, song writing, and other techniques could be used to help clients and family members communicate with each other and share information, emotions, and feelings (Special Committee on Aging, 1992). Many of the techniques for music-facilitated relaxation, stress reduction, and pain management or for music therapy and physical rehabilitation described elsewhere in this text (see especially Chapters Seventeen and Eighteen) may also be useful for homebound elderly clients who have needs in these areas (Clair, 1996b). Specific information on music therapy goals and approaches with individuals who are terminally ill will be presented in Chapter Twenty.

In addition to the interventions described above, many of the music therapy treatment techniques described in other sections of this chapter can also be adapted for use with elderly individuals in their private homes. Of course, the exact types of music therapy interventions and approaches used with any particular individual will depend on that individual's specific needs, interests, preferences, and abilities, as determined by the music therapist's assessment.

Music Therapy Approaches with Elderly Individuals Who Are in Nursing Homes or Long-Term Care Facilities

Music therapy treatment techniques have been used effectively with frail elderly individuals in nursing homes and long term care facilities for many years, adding quality and meaning to the lives of the residents while assisting them to increase or maintain their level of physical, mental, social, and/or emotional functioning (Bright, 1972, 1981; Davis, 1992a; Gibbons, 1988; Karras, 1987; Palmer, 1977, 1985, 1989; Prickett, 1988, 1996). Music therapy interventions can be an integral part of a comprehensive treatment and rehabilitation programs for elderly residents of long-term care facilities, both by providing a unique way of engaging residents and helping them improve or maintain physical, mental, and social/emotional skills (Bright, 1972, 1981; Clair, 1996b; Karras, 1987; Palmer, 1977, 1985, 1989; Prickett, 1988, 1996; Special Committee on Aging, 1992; Weissman, 1983), and by complementing and enhancing other rehabilitative approaches commonly used with geriatric residents, such as sensory stimulation/sensory training, reality orientation, remotivation, resocialization, validation, reminiscence, life review, and behavioral approaches (Bumanis & Yoder, 1987; Davis, 1992a; Karras, 1985, 1987; Riegler, 1980; Smith, 1990; Wylie, 1990).

Weissman (1983) divided music therapy treatment goals and objectives with elderly clients who are institutionalized into six areas: (1) *sensory* (includes sensory awareness and discrimination, identifying, locating, and recalling objects in the environment), (2) *perceptual-motor* (includes identifying body parts, maintaining balance, walking unassisted), (3) *cognitive* (includes comprehension, judgment, memory, reasoning, problem-solving), (4) *physical fitness* (includes breathing, circulation, ability to care for oneself), (5) *self-image* (includes maintaining self-identity, having realistic expectations, grieving appropriately for losses, expressing a perspective on one's life), and (6) *social* (includes giving and receiving concern and support, engaging in meaningful activity, sharing life experience).

Comprehensive music therapy programs in nursing homes and long-term care facilities use a wide variety of music experiences (listening, moving, singing, playing, creating, discussing) to help clients reach goals in these areas (Bright, 1972, 1981; Davis, 1992a; Gibbons, 1988; Hylton, 1983; Karras, 1987; Palmer, 1977, 1985). Music activities commonly found in nursing homes include solo or small group singing, large group sing-alongs, resident choirs, music listening or appreciation groups, listening to performances of outside musical groups, recorded music or radios in rooms or lounges, musical games, music-assisted relaxation, music-mediated reminiscence programs, solo instrument playing, rhythm bands, bell choirs, resident bands or other instrumental ensembles, instrumental improvisation, dances, exercise to music, creative movement to music, song writing, and music discussion groups (Hylton, 1983; Karras, 1987; Palmer, 1977). Since music experiences impact individuals physically, mentally, and socio-emotionally, therapeutically directed music experiences can do much to help meet the total spectrum of needs of elderly individuals in extended care facilities (Palmer, 1977, 1985, 1989).

Many elderly individuals who reside in extended care facilities need help improving or maintaining their *physical functioning* abilities. Needs in this area may include increasing or maintaining range of motion, identifying body parts, maintaining balance, improving locomotion, increasing tolerance for physical activity, improving breathing and circulation, increasing self-care abilities, rebuilding muscle strength and function after illness or stroke, decreasing muscle tension, decreasing pain perception, or improving sensory abilities (Bright, 1972, 1981; Clair, 1996b; Karras, 1987; Palmer, 1977, 1985, 1989; Weissman, 1983). Therapeutically structured music experiences can provide individuals with enjoyable activities that also help them improve their functioning in these areas. For example, music used to accompany exercise routines may help take the clients' minds off the pain that is often associated with physical exercise and provide the motivation and incentive to join in exercise and movement activities (Bright, 1972, 1981; Clair, 1996b; Palmer, 1977, 1985). Lively, rhythmic music that is meaningful to the residents (e.g., something from their ethnic heritage) may motivate even those with

arthritic fingers to open their hands and straighten their fingers to clap along (Palmer, 1977, 1985; Tanner & O'Briant, 1980). Even though some residents, at least initially, may require physical assistance from the therapist to participate actively in movement-to-music experiences, Palmer (1977) noted that "the sound of a polka or march was usually sufficient inducement to assure their cooperation even though it was painful" (p. 194).

Movement-to-music experiences can both stimulate independent movement and help residents improve motor control and coordination. Activities such as marching, dancing, walking rhythmically to music, or moving creatively to music can give ambulatory residents increased confidence, grace, and security in independent movement. For nonambulatory residents, activities like kicking and stamping to music can provide flexion and extension in the lower extremities, improve circulation, and increase muscle strength and tolerance for activity. Scarves, hoops, ribbons, and other props can provide additional visual and tactile stimulation along with additional motivation to participate in creative movement-to-music experiences. Such props can help encourage movement in both ambulatory and nonambulatory residents. In addition, many dances and music-movement exercises can be adapted for participation by nonambulatory as well as ambulatory residents (Bright, 1972, 1981; Douglass, 1985; Karras, 1987; Palmer, 1977, 1985). Music and rhythmic stimuli can also help organize movement and facilitate gait training in residents who are recovering from strokes or who have Parkinson's disease (Clair, 1996b; Staum, 1988, 1996; Thaut, 1992a; see also Chapter Eighteen).

Musical instruments can also be used to encourage physical movement, increase range of motion, improve motor control and coordination, and increase muscle strength (Confrancesco, 1985; Karras, 1987; Palmer, 1977; see also Chapters Eleven & Eighteen). Some residents may enjoy playing rhythm instruments or recreational instruments, while others may prefer the piano, more traditional band or orchestral instruments, or bell choirs. As the length of time residents play instruments is gradually increased, residents develop increased physical endurance as well as improved motor skills (Palmer, 1977). As music therapists carefully match the characteristics of instruments to the physical movement needs of individual residents, musical instruments can also be used to reinforce or help achieve physical therapy goals (Elliott, 1982). For example, Confrancesco (1985) used rhythm instruments, piano playing, and autoharp playing to help increase hand grasp strength and functional hand and arm movements in individuals who were recovering from strokes. The hand and arm strength and control developed through playing musical instruments can then be used to perform some self care activities (e.g., holding brush or comb to brush/comb hair; holding adaptive spoon and feeding self).

The act of musical conducting can also have important physical benefits. Residents may serve as client-conductors for vocal or instrumental ensembles, or they may conduct to recorded music. As they move their arms to conduct, individuals reactivate and revitalized large arm and shoulder muscles, release tension, and improve physical coordination and endurance. In addition, clients who act as conductors for the group reap the psychological and socio-emotional benefits of increased self-confidence and improved leadership abilities (Tanner & O'Briant, 1980).

Therapeutic music experiences can also improve the physical functioning of geriatric residents by helping to decrease pain, reduce tension, and facilitate relaxation (Clair, 1996b; Karras, 1987; Weissman, 1983). Most of the techniques for music-mediated relaxation and pain reduction already described in Chapters Seventeen and Eighteen can be used effectively with geriatric residents. With some adaptations, even Guided Imagery and Music (GIM) approaches may be beneficial (Summer, 1981). Vocal improvisational/meditative exercises, where residents state the location of their pain, moan and groan to acknowledge and pain, and then create a pleasant, comforting vocal sound to send to the painful area to reduce tension, may also be useful in helping nursing home residents alleviate pain (Weissman, 1983).

In addition to having numerous physical needs, many elderly individuals who reside in extended care facilities need help improving or maintaining their *mental functioning*. Therapeutic music activities can play important roles in stimulating cognitive functioning, in helping to maintain good mental health, and in improving or rehabilitating cognitive

awareness for geriatric residents. For example, mental functioning can be stimulated by learning new skills in vocal or instrumental lessons (Gibbons, 1985; Gold, 1982: Hoerning, 1982). Learning new songs (lyrics and melody), either from song sheets or through a "lining out" procedure (therapist sings line; clients repeat), also helps individuals redevelop or maintain memory skills (Palmer, 1977, 1985). Procedures such as having residents supply missing phrases in songs or naming songs or tunes played by the therapist continue to develop residents' recall and memory skills. In addition, critical thinking skills, increased attention span, comprehension, judgment, memory, reasoning, problem solving, and spontaneous verbal interaction can be improved as residents discuss song lyrics or events associated with songs, participate in music appreciation classes, or write their own songs or parodies (Karras, 1987; Palmer, 1977, 1985; Scalenghe, 1984; Weissman, 1983).

Music therapy interventions can also be structured to promote and encourage active decision-making in geriatric clients who, as nursing home residents, often have few opportunities to make choices or decisions. Opportunities for decision-making may be as simple as choosing a songsheet folder or ribbon of a certain color or selecting a particular rhythm instrument to play from a choice of two or more (Palmer, 1977). Increased independence in decision-making is often approached through carefully structured successive steps of approximation. For example, Kemper (1982) gradually developed geriatric residents' ability to independently select songs for the group to sing in a sing-along by first having group members pull slips of paper listing a song titles from a bag and then, as group members gained confidence, having them select titles from a multiple choice listing of song titles.

Music experiences can also play an important role in promoting good mental health among nursing home residents. Shaw (1988) found that ragtime music was very useful in eliciting attention and stimulating responsiveness in depressed, apathetic nursing home residents. In addition to increasing attention and responsiveness, the ragtime music was also comforting to the residents, for it was performed on an instrument that was familiar and enjoyable to them (the piano) and had lyric melodies as well as stimulating rhythms. As residents participate in enjoyable music experiences, they are engaging in a form of adult play. According to Tanner and O'Briant (1980), "'play' appears to a necessary part of maintaining good mental health in adulthood" (p. 30). Some who subscribe to Gardner's (1983) theory of multiple intelligences have observed that, in certain aging individuals, some intelligences (e.g., verbal/linguistic, logical/mathematical) may fade while others (e.g., musical/rhythmic, bodily/kinesthetic) may become more prominent (Kay, 1998). Since music can address and integrate all of these intelligences, it can engage people at many levels and help them develop and exercise whatever aspect of intelligence is strongest for them (Kay, 1998).

Therapeutic music experiences can be particularly beneficial for residents who have problems with memory loss and mental confusion. For residents who are very disoriented and nonresponsive, music therapy interventions can be effective components of *sensory stimulation* or *sensory training* programs (Davis, 1992a; Olson, 1984; Weissman, 1983; Wolfe, 1983). Since music is a multisensory stimulus and something that has been an enjoyable part of the past life experience of many residents, music often stimulates attention responses or physical movement in even the most severely regressed individuals. By studying the resident's social history and speaking with family members, the music therapist can find clues as to what types of music or instruments are most likely meaningful to a particular resident and elicit a response. For example, Palmer (1985) used the song "Take Me out to the Ball Game" to increase attention and responsiveness in a nonverbal, withdrawn resident who had always loved baseball. At first, this resident merely opened her eyes and looked toward the therapist when she heard the singing. With individual attention and gentle encouragement, the resident gradually joined the music group, eventually singing along, joining in conversation, and even playing instruments and participating in movement activities to the best of her ability. In another situation, Olson (1984) found that listening to player piano music increased physical activity, rhythmic participation, and feelings of well-being in geriatric patients who were severely regressed.

Music therapy activities used in sensory training or sensory stimulation programs are usually short, predictable, and highly structured experiences designed to elicit responses, improve awareness and responsiveness to simple directions and people and objects in the environment, and increase body awareness, motor function, and attention to activities (Davis, 1992a; Weissman, 1983). Passive activities (e.g., therapist physically assisting the individual in moving to music or in playing musical instruments) may be used initially to help develop awareness and responsiveness. Activities are often paired with short phrases, sometimes in the form of improvised song lyrics, describing the action or giving concise directions (e.g., "move your arm up; move your arm down"). Physical guidance is gradually faded as the individual's independent responses increase.

At the next level of cognitive rehabilitation, music therapy interventions can both encourage participation in *reality orientation programs* and increase elderly individuals' ability to learn and recall important information about person, place, and time (Bright, 1972; Bumanis & Yoder, 1987; Davis, 1992a; Riegler, 1980). For example, Riegler (1980) found that geriatric patients who participated in a music-based reality orientation program showed marked improvement in reality orientation and behavior functioning, while those who participated in a reality orientation program without music showed no improvement over the same period of time. The music-based reality orientation program included activities such as "listening to and discussing music written about a particular place or time" and "singing and playing rhythm instruments to accompany songs and jingles dealing with names, numbers, day, date, and year" (p. 30). Music/dance-based reality orientation programs, using hello songs incorporating group member's names, multisensory creative movement-to-music and dance activities, hand dancing and mirroring exercises, songs with added gestures, seasonal songs, songs that incorporate names or weather or place, and rhythm instrument activities, can also be effective with geriatric nursing home residents (Bumanis & Yoder, 1987). Other research has shown that singing can improve face-name recognition in nursing home residents with memory loss (Carruth, 1997).

In the third step or level of cognitive rehabilitation, music can both provide motivation for elderly residents of long-term care facilities to participate in *remotivation* programs and be used to set moods or introduce topics and stimulate discussion for remotivation sessions (Bright, 1972; Davis, 1992a; Gibbons, 1988). For example, an opening welcome song may be used to encourage residents to join in the group and help set a climate of acceptance. Songs about particular topics (e.g., springtime, laughing, World War II) can then be used to focus attention and act as a starting point for sharing memories and opinions. Related songs, pictures, props, instrumental, or songwriting activities might then be used to help develop the topic and expand the discussion. Music may also be very helpful in refocusing the group at the end of the session. For example, one or more of the songs used might be sung with the group to help summarize the discussion. A concluding song (perhaps composed by the therapist to fit the specific activities and dynamics of the group) can help establish closure and be used to express appreciation to the group members for their contributions to the session.

Music therapy interventions can also be an important component of *validation* approaches with disoriented "old-old" nursing home residents (Bumanis & Yoder, 1987; Feil, 1982). Songs, listening experiences, instrument play, and movement-to-music experiences can be structured to validate and explore universal feelings the confused residents may be experiencing. Experiences that acknowledge and validate their feelings make these individuals feel they are understood and give them a reason to participate actively and begin to interact more positively with others. In addition, music is an ideal stimulus for *reminiscence and life review* (Bright 1972, 1981, 1986; Davis, 1992a; Feil, 1982; Karras, 1985, 1987; Wylie, 1990). Music can be used in reminiscence groups in several ways (Karras, 1987): (1) as a background when residents are gathering, to set the mood for the discussion to come (e.g., dance music from the 1940s if discussing that period); (2) as a topic for discussion (e.g., favorite movie musicals, singing stars of the 1930s); (3) songs about particular topics (e.g., songs mentioning items of clothing for a discussion of fashions; songs mentioning places for a discussion of travel or vacations; songs about animals for a discussion of pets or farm animals); (4) focussing on words of song lyrics that lead to discussion of other topics or memories of certain times or activities (e.g., writing on slates in "School Days"; "My Merry Oldsmobile" as lead-in to discussion of early cars); (5) to start and end groups (focus and summarize

discussion); (6) occasional use of more recent songs as a basis of talking about the past (e.g., "Those Were the Days"; "Sunrise, Sunset" from *Fiddler on the Roof*); (7) as a bridge to discussions of more serious topics (e.g., life and death, the Great Depression, war times); (8) identifying singers and theme songs; (9) songs of historical significance (e.g., World War I: "Over There"); or (10) the use of old sheet music to stimulate discussion. Songs of residents' teen and adult years are usually most useful for eliciting memories of adulthood activities (e.g., dances, when they first heard songs) (Karras, 1987; Wylie, 1990). Activities such as taking musical journeys through time or discussing songs associated with a certain period in an individual's life can also facilitate the life review process (Bright, 1981, 1986; Kellman, 1986).

Like any group of people, geriatric residents of long-term care facilities have *social* and *emotional needs* that impact their overall level of functioning. Because many residents have lost not only their home, their role in society, and some significant others in their lives but also some of their mental or physical functioning abilities, they often have a poor self-image and may try to withdraw into a world of their own (Palmer, 1985; Purtilo, 1978). Since music has been an enjoyable part of the past experience of most residents and can be structured for successful participation at many different levels, music therapy interventions can be an excellent tool for increasing self-esteem in geriatric nursing home residents and for drawing them back into contact with others. Interpersonal contact may first be established in individual interactions with the music therapist and then gradually expanded to include small and large group experiences. For example, Redinbaugh (1988) described a slow, 15-month process in which music therapy interventions (shaping attention responses to songs that interested the resident, clapping and foot-tapping, instrument play, ball and parachute activities, sing-alongs, and opportunities to choose instruments, props or songs) increased nonverbal and verbal communication and social interaction for a depressed, 91-year-old nursing home resident. As her communication and interaction skills redeveloped in music activities, the resident eventually increased her participation in other social activity groups as well, which gave her an increased system of social support.

Music experiences provide many opportunities for both verbal and nonverbal interaction, through sharing the experience of listening to a particular piece of music, singing or playing instruments together, moving or dancing to music, creating or composing songs, or discussing music. As residents participate successfully in these activities, learn new skills, and have the opportunity to make choices and decisions, their dignity is enhanced and their self-esteem is increased (Kemper, 1982, Palmer, 1977). Vanderark and colleagues (1983) found that nursing home residents who participated in structured 45-minute music sessions twice a week showed significantly improved life satisfaction and self-concept, along with some increases in socialization and self-confidence. Music activities in these sessions included singing familiar songs, learning simple chordal accompaniments on autoharp or tone bells, playing rhythm instruments, and performing motions to songs. Residents who perform as soloists or as members of musical ensembles also have increased opportunities for positive recognition by others, another means of enhancing self-esteem (Glassman, 1983; Gold, 1982; Hoerning, 1982; Palmer, 1977).

Music therapy interventions may also be useful in helping residents develop realistic expectations, grieve appropriately for losses, and place their lives in perspective (Bright, 1986; Weissman, 1983). The simple activity of a therapist singing a song about loss and inviting residents to hum along if they have lost something can help residents begin to express grief nonverbally (Weissman, 1983). More complex activities like song writing can help residents who are mentally alert but physically disabled learn to accept their new limitations. Palmer (1977) found that writing ballads initiated communication and facilitated more positive perspectives among a group of hostile, withdrawn residents by providing a structure that allowed them "to air complaints and interact with each other while working on a meaningful project" (p. 196). Adaptations of Guided Imagery and Music (GIM) techniques can also help nursing home residents who have physical disabilities address and deal with many past, current, and future issues, including disability, grieving, sexuality, and the aging process (Short, 1992). In addition, using GIM techniques in a group setting increased residents' participation and encouraged sharing and support among residents. Summer (1981) also found that GIM could increase self-esteem, help residents recall strengths and assets from their past

and find ways to use these in their current setting, break the cycle of rumination over certain thoughts and memories by bringing different thoughts to conscious awareness, and give residents new experiences (e.g., an imaginary GIM trip to Hawaii) without leaving the nursing home. The group support developed during discussions of GIM experiences "can help to increase self-awareness and self-acceptance, an internal change that fosters interpersonal relationships at the nursing home" (Summer, 1981, p. 41).

Music therapy interventions can be important *behavior management* tools for nursing home residents, helping both to increase active participation in appropriate, meaningful social activities and to eliminate undesirable behaviors (Clair, 1990, 1996b; Smith, 1990). The music therapist can use music to provide structure to control the behavior of elderly nursing home residents by intentionally modifying tempo, pitch, loudness, timbre, harmony, rhythmic activity, or accompaniment to elicit the desired responses. "Active participation in carefully designed and structured musical activities can ease the need for other types of behavior management, at least for a time" (Clair, 1990, p. 74).

Music therapy interventions can help manage or alleviate many behavioral problems of elderly nursing home residents, including depression, insomnia, agitation, eating problems, problems during activities of daily living (ADLs) (e.g., bathing, dressing, toileting), and catastrophic reactions (Clair, 1996b; Thomas et al., 1997). Music-based relaxation or guided imagery techniques may be helpful in alleviating depression or insomnia. Since music provides structure and predictability through rhythm, form, and familiarity, participation in music activities such as singing, dancing/moving, or playing rhythm instruments can decrease agitation and promote appropriate social interactions in disoriented as well as alert nursing home residents (Clair, 1990, 1996b). Eating problems can be reduced through the use of background music that establishes a positive mood, focuses attention, and masks distracting sounds. According to Clair (1996b), "upbeat music with moderate, danceable tempos and familiar, singable melodies is most appropriate" (p. 106).

Hearing familiar songs sung by caregivers during ADLs may also help establish a secure environment and decrease confused residents' agitation during these activities. Clair (1990) has observed that many caregivers have found that singing to elderly residents during ADLs helps the residents gradually become more physically relaxed. For these residents, "singing may provide access to feelings of comfort that are associated with time when they were nurtured . . . and with feelings of belonging" (p. 107). Familiar, preferred music may also help diffuse emotional stress and decrease catastrophic reactions. In addition, contingent music can be used with nursing home residents to reinforce desired behaviors and eliminate negative behaviors, such as chronic screaming (Smith, 1990). Since research has shown behavioral interventions can effectively ameliorate many of the more common problems of elderly nursing home residents, Smith (1990) suggested that music therapists strongly consider an "increased use of behavioral techniques within music therapy treatment programs for the elderly" (p. 39).

Music Therapy Approaches with Elderly Individuals Who Have Alzheimer's Disease or Related Disorders

Music therapy interventions can be important components of treatment during the early, middle, and late stages of dementia (Bright, 1988; Brotons et al., 1997; Chavin, 1991; Clair, 1996b; Gfeller & Hanson, 1995; Hanson et al., 1996; Prickett, 1996; Special Committee on Aging, 1992). A recent analysis of the literature by Brotons and colleagues (1997) indicated that "in general, music/music therapy is an effective intervention to maintain and improve active involvement, social, emotional and cognitive skills, and to decrease behavior problems of individuals with dementia" (pp. 204-205).

Most individuals with dementia respond positively to music, for its rhythm, form, and familiarity provide them with a sense of security and structure. Some research suggests that individuals with Alzheimer's disease use alternative cognitive, memory, and neural mechanisms to process and respond to auditory stimuli, allowing some individuals with severe dementia to maintain musical behaviors after other cognitive functions have declined (York, 1994). In many cases, music that holds significance and meaning for individuals with dementia can help them

regain access to memories they have lost and restore, at least for a time, some of their 'lost' personality (Brotons et al., 1997; Sacks & Tomaino, 1991). In addition, music tasks can be very useful in assessing cognitive functioning in older adults with dementia (Lipe, 1995; York, 1994). Thus, music has great potential for providing individuals with dementia with important tools for relating positively to themselves, their caregivers, and others around them.

However, not all music or type of music experience will be suitable for all individuals who have dementia. If they are to be effective, music and music interventions must (1) have meaning for the individual (relate in some way to his/her preferences or life experiences), (2) be suited to the individual's current needs and functional abilities in the verbal, cognitive, and physical skills it requires, and (3) be implemented by a sensitive music therapist who can adapt the activity to the responses and needs of the individuals at a particular moment (Bright, 1988; Brotons et al., 1997; Chavin, 1991; Clair, 1996b; Cordrey, 1994; Gfeller & Hanson, 1995; Sacks & Tomaino, 1991).

> The effectiveness of music therapy depends on a careful selection of music materials, the type of activity, the difficulty of the task, and the appropriate implementation of the activity by a sensitive therapist. One music therapy activity does not fit all situations and all needs. . . . Furthermore, undifferentiated uses of music, such as simply setting up a radio or record player, do not qualify as a truly therapeutic use of music, and in fact they have the potential to contribute to agitation or confusion. (Gfeller & Hanson, 1995, p. 123)

Experiences in singing, moving (folk or ballroom dances, scarf dances, exercises or creative movement to music), and playing instruments (rhythm activities, bell choirs, accompaniment instruments such as the autoharp) can all be structured at high or low levels of demand to meet the needs of individuals at various stages of dementia. Some individuals can also participate successfully in structured composition/ improvisation experiences or musical games (e.g., musical bingo, Name that Tune) (Brotons, 1994b; Chavin, 1991). Generally, individuals are able to continue to participate more purposefully through their stages of decline in movement and rhythm activities than in singing activities (Brotons, 1994b; Clair, 1996b; Gfeller & Hanson, 1995; Hanson et al., 1996). As the dementia progresses, music therapy interventions that have lower demands (simpler, nonverbal, requiring less precise responses) and do not require as many active responses continue to offer successful, purposeful experiences for individuals who have Alzheimer's disease or related disorders (Gfeller & Hanson, 1995; Hanson et al., 1996). Books by Chavin (1991), Cordrey (1994), and Gfeller and Hanson (1995) specifically describe several music therapy activities and session plans suitable for individuals at various stages of Alzheimer's disease.

Music Therapy Interventions for Early Stage Dementia

Music therapy interventions can give persons with early stage dementia many opportunities for successful experiences, meaningful and purposeful activities to structure time, and feelings of accomplishment, thus adding to life quality, facilitating positive moods, and helping to relieve some symptoms of fear, anxiety, and depression (Clair, 1996b). Participation in goal-directed music activities can also significantly increase overall cognitive functioning, as indicated by scores on the mini mental status questionnaire (Smith, 1986), while singing can help some individuals retain memory functions (Prickett & Moore, 1991). Individuals with early stage dementia are most likely to participate in music experiences that (a) utilize skills that have been practiced over many years (e.g., singing for people who have always enjoyed singing; prompting a person to play a favorite song on an instrument he/she has played most of his/her life; doing familiar dances or creative movement using actions from well-known activities like sweeping the floor), (b) use songs, dances, movements, instruments, or activities that have personal significance and meaning for the individual, and (c) draw on cognitive, physical, or verbal skills that are still accessible to the individual at an appropriate level of challenge and demand (Brotons et al., 1997; Chavin, 1991; Clair, 1996b; Gfeller & Hanson, 1995; Hanson et al., 1996).

Many different types of structured music inter-

ventions can be used therapeutically with individuals in the early stages of dementia, either individually or in groups. For example, group sing-alongs or adapted choir experiences can facilitate successful interactions with others, help maintain socialization, increase awareness of self and others, increase self esteem through successful participation and positive recognition by others, help individuals release tension and frustration, and provide opportunities for choice (e.g., choosing song) and creative expression (Bright, 1988; Brotons et al., 1997; Chavin, 1991; Clair, 1996b), while one-to-one singing experiences can distract individuals from depression and facilitate positive mood changes, promote communication and emotional closeness between family members or caregivers and the individual, and serve as an auditory cue to help individuals retain language and memory functions (Brotons et al., 1997; Clair, 1996b; Prickett & Moore, 1991). Music-based reminiscence groups (Chavin, 1991; Smith & Knudson, 1995), music groups using songs and activities centered around a certain theme (Bright, 1988; Cordrey, 1994), and music games (e.g., finishing a lyric line, Name that Tune, music trivia) (Bright, 1988; Chavin, 1991) promote verbal interaction and socialization, decrease loneliness and isolation, provide opportunities to discuss/express feelings and voice opinions, provide opportunities for choice and decision-making, stimulate cognitive and memory functions, maintain attending skills, and enhance self-esteem and self-concept through successful participation with others and recollections of past accomplishments, significant life events, and significant others. Props and prompts from the group leader (e.g., multiple choice or yes-no questions rather than open-ended questions) can greatly facilitate individuals' responsiveness to reminiscence and song-related discussion activities (Chavin, 1991).

Structured song writing experiences (e.g., lyric substitution; lyrics on a theme given by therapist) can also help increase communication, socialization, cognitive function, creative expression, and self-esteem (Chavin, 1991; Silber & Hes, 1995). Since it utilizes the "feelingful" parts of the brain that may still be intact when other cognitive functions have declined, song writing can help individuals with early stage dementia temporarily overcome memory and language deficits and give emotionally withdrawn individuals a way to express repressed feelings that they are unable to express in speech (Silber & Hes, 1995). Individual "lessons" on previously learned instruments can help individuals retain music skills, enhance self-expression and feelings of self-worth, decrease agitation and depression, facilitate positive affect, and stimulate cognitive and physical functioning (Clair, 1996b; Smith & Knudson, 1995), while group instrumental ensembles, such as bell choirs (Chavin, 1995; Smith & Knudson, 1995) or rhythm groups (Bright, 1988; Gfeller & Hanson, 1995; Smith & Knudson, 1995) can promote active participation and interaction with others, decrease withdrawal and isolation, increase cognitive awareness and help maintain cognitive functioning, improve/maintain motor functioning and eye-hand coordination, provide opportunities for creative self-expression, provide ways to nonverbally express feelings, and increase self-esteem and feelings of belonging.

Many individuals in the early stages of dementia also enjoy participating in dances (especially ballroom dancing or square dancing, if these are in their past experience) or music-movement experiences (e.g., exercise to music, actions to songs, scarf dancing, creative movement to music, massage to music) (Bright, 1988; Brotons et al., 1997; Clair, 1996b; Gfeller & Hanson, 1995; Hanson et al., 1996; Shively & Henkin, 1986; Smith & Knudson, 1995). Therapeutically structured music and movement sessions using familiar, enjoyable music can provide a nonthreatening environment that increases feelings of comfort and security while decreasing anxiety and agitation (Shively & Henkin, 1986). Music/movement experiences also increase socialization and interaction with others, promote creativity and nonverbal expression of feelings, help increase or maintain physical functioning, and increase awareness of self and others. Bright (1988), Chavin (1991), Cordrey (1994), Gfeller and Hanson (1995), and Smith and Knudson (1995) provide many examples of plans for specific interventions using singing, song writing, reminiscence, instrumental, and music/movement experiences.

Music Therapy Interventions for Middle Stage Dementia

Although the mental and physical abilities of individuals in the middle stage of dementia are steadily declining, these individuals still have needs for appropriately challenging activities that can help them maintain their highest level of functioning for as long as possible (Chavin, 1995; Gfeller & Hanson, 1995; Hanson et al., 1996). Given appropriate structure and adaptations, they can still participate successfully in ensembles like bell choirs (Chavin, 1995; Smith & Knudson, 1995) or fairly demanding dances and music/movement experiences (Clair, 1996b; Gfeller & Hanson, 1995; Hanson et al., 1996). These experiences provide interaction with others and help reduce isolation and maintain physical and cognitive functioning. Some individuals may also still be able to sing familiar songs, especially ones that were learned early in life. In addition to providing socialization, enjoyment, and emotional expression, singing may positively influence other behaviors. For example, Millard and Smith (1989) found that, during sing-alongs, individuals in the middle stage of Alzheimer's disease vocalized and verbalized more than during discussion sessions, increased sitting or walking with others both during and after the sessions, showed more awareness of and concern for others, and showed pleasure by smiling more often. During sing-alongs, clients also showed more attention to task and less wandering than they did in the discussion activity.

Those clients who are not able to sing may still derive benefits and pleasure from singing experiences, as they interact by vocalizing with the melodies and as they show attention or affective reactions to the songs (Clair, 1996b; Lipe, 1991). In addition, songs can help individuals communicate feelings and emotions they are no longer able to express verbally. Kaser (1993) tells of an elderly man in the middle stage of Alzheimer's disease who selected songs to express feelings he was experiencing and eventually began to verbalize and interact more through this process. The songs enabled this man to form a supportive, meaningful relationship and gave him a unique way to "converse" and discuss his feelings. In addition, these positive experiences in music therapy sessions led to less agitation, more relaxation, and decreased hostile and inappropriate behaviors outside the sessions as well.

Familiar music can also give meaning and order to the environment at a time when so many experiences are becoming confused and meaningless, thus adding pleasure and quality of life and helping restore some sense of mental and emotional well-being (Clair, 1996b). Music that has been part of the individuals' past life experience "carries with it a full range of well-integrated associations, emotions, and memories," enabling it to provide the individuals with pleasant, satisfying experiences that "are immediate and do not require cognitive processing for success" (Clair, 1996b, p. 74). Recorded selections of familiar music can be very useful in establishing rapport with clients, in facilitating positive mood shifts, and in evoking initial responses. Some clients may show excitement at hearing familiar selections and may spontaneously begin to hum or sing along (Lipe, 1991). After trust and a common bond are established through listening to tapes of the clients' preferred music, therapists can add more active goals and activities, such as singing on cue, playing instruments with songs, manipulating objects associated with songs, following directions to start and stop, increasing attention span and amount of on-task behavior, or participating in music activities away from the client's room (Prange, 1990). Eventually, clients may begin to fill in titles or even talk about the songs and memories associated with them (Lipe, 1991).

Structured rhythmic activities are also very successful for engaging these clients in purposeful, enjoyable activities that encourage interaction with others. Even individuals who are severely regressed can still participate successfully with others in rhythmic activities, such as playing drums (Clair, 1996b; Clair & Bernstein, 1990; Clair et al., 1995). Rhythm activities can be done one-to-one (Pollack & Namazi, 1992) or in small groups of four to six (Clair et al., 1995; Gfeller & Hanson, 1995). Research has found that vibrotactile stimulation, such as that obtained from larger drums that emit strong vibrations, promotes longer, more active participation in severely regressed persons in the middle or later stages of Alzheimer's disease (Clair, 1996b; Clair & Bernstein, 1990). Often, some participation will occur spontaneously. However, it takes the structure and guidance of the music therapist to help the clients sustain participation and develop awareness of others in the group (Clair et al., 1995). Modeling by the therapist (Clair, 1996b) or by higher performing peers (Christie, 1995) can also positively influence the participation level of group members.

Over time, group members can significantly improve their ability to successfully strike the drum and to imitate simple rhythm patterns (Clair et al., 1995). Nonverbal interaction in music activities can also help offset the void in interaction caused by the loss of expressive language skills and foster social interaction of severely regressed individuals with Alzheimer's disease both during and after the music therapy sessions (Pollack & Namazi, 1992). As successful as rhythm activities are for many individuals with Alzheimer's disease, however, it is important to realize that not all clients will respond positively to rhythmic activities. Some may react with pain or increased agitation to the loud noise, while others may simply not be interested in playing (Clair, 1996b). For these individuals, singing or movement activities may offer better avenues of expression and interaction.

Research and clinical experience have shown that a structured, predictable session format is most successful as a treatment protocol for group music therapy with individuals in the middle stages of dementia (Clair, 1991; Gfeller & Hanson, 1995; Smith & Knudson, 1995). Groups are usually small (4-6 members), about 30 minutes in length, and begin and end with a greeting song that stays the same from week to week. The body of the session (treatment portion) usually includes two to four activities involving familiar songs, rhythmic activities, and/or music/movement activities. These activities focus on encouraging active involvement and increasing social interaction, awareness of self and others, self-expression, attention span, communication (verbal and non-verbal), and self-esteem.

Clair's (1991) protocol included (1) a greeting song, using each group member's name, (2) singing of familiar songs (e.g., those from group member's young adult years, patriotic songs) led by the music therapist with guitar accompaniment, (3) individual rhythm instrument play, in which clients select an instrument from a choice of two and imitate the music therapist's two- and three-beat patterns, (4) rhythm ensemble work, unaccompanied and with singing/acoustic guitar, and (5) a good-bye song, using each group member's name. Smith and Knudson (1995) also recommended a 5-part session structure: (1) greeting song using clients' names; (2) warm-up songs; (3) rhythm instrument playing (clients choose instrument; play with songs);

(4) singing familiar songs/individual performances; (5) closure with good-bye song using clients' names and thanking them for their contributions to group. Gfeller and Hanson (1995) utilized a three-part session structure: (1) an opening, introductory activity to greet group members and signal the beginning of the session; (2) a 20-minute treatment portion, using two activities, with each activity representing one of the three categories of singing, movement, or rhythm at an appropriate complexity level to the group; (3) a short closing activity to thank the group members and say good-bye.

Clients' participation is usually enhanced when activities use music materials and instruments that correspond to the group members' preferences and draw on lifelong music skills or interests (Gfeller & Hanson, 1995; Smith & Knudson, 1995). The therapist's ability to guide and lead participation and to adjust the demands of the task to the responses and functional abilities of the participants helps optimize on-task behavior while reducing agitation and disruptive behaviors (Clair, 1996b; Clair et al., 1995; Gfeller & Hanson, 1995). In addition, some research has shown that including a peer with a high level of performance/participation in music therapy groups helps motivate and increase the active participation of lower functioning persons with middle stage Alzheimer's type dementia (Christie, 1995).

Music therapy interventions can also help manage many of the behavior problems that may occur in middle stage dementia. Research has shown that music therapy can effectively facilitate sleep and reduce agitation and disruptive behaviors in many individuals with middle stage dementia, particularly if their preferences are taken into account (Brotons et al., 1997). Both live and taped music, as well as participation in singing, playing instruments, music games, music/movement experiences, or composition/improvisation activities can be used to decrease agitation (Brotons et al., 1997). Some studies have found that individualized taped music programs, tailored to the patients' preferences, can help soothe patients prior to and during bathing, reducing agitation and aggressive behaviors (Thomas et al., 1997). In developing taped music programs to decrease agitation, it is very important to identify the precise music that has traditionally satisfied or comforted the individual, so the taped program will have meaning and relevance for the individual.

For many individuals with middle stage dementia, participation in music activities also decreases wandering and promotes attention to and positive interactions with others (Brotons & Pickett-Cooper, 1996; Fitzgerald-Cloutier, 1993; Groene, 1993; Millard & Smith, 1989). Fitzgerald-Cloutier (1993) found that unaccompanied singing was particularly effective in maintaining the attention of a wandering, agitated 81-year-old female resident with middle stage Alzheimer's dementia, keeping her seated in one place for as long as twenty minutes. Brotons and Pickett-Cooper (1996) found that music therapy sessions using singing, instrument playing, dance/movement, musical games, and simple composition/improvisation activities (e.g., playing name or feelings on instruments) decreased the agitation and wandering of individuals with Alzheimer's disease both during and for at least twenty minutes following the session. Ninety-eight percent of these subjects stayed for the entire session and 88% stayed for the entire post-session observation period.

Since music therapy experiences like singing, dancing, or playing rhythm instruments can be easily be done while standing or moving, they can be adapted for use in a "Walker's Club" and used to provide constructive, meaningful activities for individuals who need to pace (Chavin, 1991). Generally, music that is not too loud and movements that are not too fast help hold attention and prevent overstimulation.

Music Therapy Interventions for Late Stage Dementia

Although persons with late-stage dementia have lost all verbal articulation and physical ambulation abilities, are incontinent of bowel and bladder, and may sleep for long periods of time and be unresponsive to most stimuli, they still need programs and activities that contribute to their dignity and quality of life. Music-listening is one experience that is still accessible to most of these individuals, but taped music programs and radios must be used with care if they are to be most beneficial.

Although this music can provide needed stimulation, it can be harmful if it does not match the musical taste of the individuals who must listen to it or if it plays incessantly. . . . Music preferred by staff, especially if the resident responds to it with cries, tensed muscles, and pained facial affect, must never be used in the resident's room unless it can be established that the resident also likes it. (Clair, 1996b, p. 82)

When working with individuals in the late stage of dementia, music therapists must be alert for small changes in facial expression or tension, short increases in eye contact or a slight turning toward the sound, or a slightly more alert posture, as well as more obvious observable responses such as a change in vocal activity or movement of arms/fingers or legs/feet. Movement responses may be very small, such as slight foot or finger movement. Goals for these individuals include sensory stimulation, increased awareness of self and others, increased interaction with others, increased opportunities for creative self-expression and nonverbal communication, increased participation in positive, meaningful experiences, and increased self-esteem through successful participation in structured, nonthreatening, enjoyable activities (Chavin, 1991; Clair, 1996b). Most interventions with these individuals will take place in one-to-one interactions, in the individual's room or at his or her bedside. Persons may also be gathered in groups around a table or in a circle, but interactions will still be on an individual basis, with the therapist going from person to person and repeating the same activity with each (Chavin, 1991).

Some research has shown that persons with late stage dementia have the most frequent alertness and attention responses during live, unaccompanied singing (Clair, 1996a). Singing provides a point of contact with another human being on an emotional and sensory level, making no cognitive demands (Clair, 1996b). At some level of awareness, individuals may also perceive that they are receiving attention that is out of the ordinary when a person takes the time to sing with them (Clair, 1996a). Many individuals' alerting and attention responses to singing increase over time; persons who are relatively nonresponsive in initial sessions may begin to show some responsiveness in the fourth or fifth session (Clair, 1996a). Different music will evoke

alerting responses in different individuals. Some will respond best to familiar songs of youth, while others may respond more to lullabies. An additional level of contact can be provided by adding touch (e.g., holding hands; rocking or swaying; sitting in close proximity; stroking the shoulder, arm, or face; massaging with creams or oils) to the singing (Clair, 1996b).

During the final stages of dementia, music therapy interventions often take on a palliative form, helping to provide physical and psychological comfort (Lipe, 1991). In addition to the comfort derived from being sung to, persons may also benefit from individualized recorded music programs that provide them with a sense of security and familiarity. Whitcomb (1992) gives the example of an 86-year-old French priest with late stage dementia whose agitation and screaming were replaced with relaxation and peace when a tape of Gregorian chants was played at his bedside. This familiar music touched him on some level of awareness and helped bring him back to a place of serenity and comfort.

To be most effective, recorded music must not be played continuously but at specific times or for specific purposes. Clair (1996b) recommended managing the music on a schedule determined by individual responses to music and individual sleep patterns. For some people, this may be 15 to 20 minutes of music an hour, while for others it may be an hour of music followed by an hour of quiet. Recorded music programs may be appropriately used any time the person is awake, during the day or night.

Caregivers and Music Therapy

Shared music experiences can be an important means of increasing communication (verbal and nonverbal), facilitating meaningful interactions, enhancing emotional closeness, triggering positive memories, and deepening relationships between caregivers and care recipients, especially when the recipients are in the middle and late stages of dementia where they have lost the physical, cognitive, verbal, and social abilities to independently interact meaningfully with others (Clair, 1996b; Clair et al., 1993; Clair & Ebberts, 1997; Lipe, 1991; Prickett & Moore, 1991; Special

Committee on Aging, 1992; Whitcomb, 1992). Even in the early stages of dementia, music therapy interventions can help caregivers and care recipients nonverbally express the feelings associated with knowing the care recipient has a progressive, incurable disease (e.g., anger, grief). As music-making taps some of the still intact skills and abilities of the care recipient, music experiences can also provide opportunities for pleasant, meaningful interactions between caregiver and care recipient. This positive interactive experience can evoke feelings of success and satisfaction for both caregiver and care recipient. In addition, they help caregivers focus on their loved one's strengths and residual abilities, rather than on all the disease is taking away (Clair, 1996b).

Many different types of music experiences can be used to enhance the interactions of caregivers and care recipients. Those who have played instruments together may continue to interact in this way (Clair, 1996b), while others may prefer to sing favorite songs (Clair, 1996b; Prickett & Moore, 1991) or listen to music together (Clair, 1996b; Lipe, 1991). Favorite songs can also evoke reminiscences that caregiver and care recipient can share (Chavin, 1991; Clair, 1996b; Palmer, 1989). Many of these experiences can continue to give satisfaction to both caregiver and care recipient into the middle and late stages of dementia. For example, dancing together or sitting next to each other while singing or while one plays the piano or guitar and both hum or sing can provide caregivers and care recipients with moments of emotional closeness and intimacy (Clair, 1996b; Clair et al., 1993; Special Committee on Aging, 1992). As the structure of these musical experiences provides the focus and encouragement for care recipients to reach out to their caregivers with loving, physical gestures, they also allow the caregivers to receive something back from the care recipients and contribute to fulfilling the caregivers' needs for emotional closeness with their loved ones.

Other benefits of music therapy interventions for caregivers dealing with care recipients in the middle and late stages include (1) providing a means of decreasing agitation or boredom of care recipients and (2) providing a structure for positive, meaningful interactions between caregivers and care recipients. Caregivers may sing care recipients' favorite songs or use tapes of their favorites songs to help focus care recipients' attention on positive experiences and decrease their agitation, boredom, or restlessness (Clair, 1996b; Lipe, 1991). Songs and singing may also be vehicles for providing satisfying interpersonal interactions between caregivers and care recipients when fluent speech no longer can (Prickett & Moore, 1991). Even care recipients in late stage dementia will frequently respond to their loved ones' singing by making eye contact, having a more relaxed or more alert facial expression, or by vocalizing at certain points of the song (Clair, 1996b). In addition, hearing caregivers sing familiar, comforting songs or hearing tapes of familiar, comforting music may help decrease care recipients' agitation and combativeness during assisted personal care activities (e.g., bathing, changing soiled clothing), thus making the caregiver's job easier and less stressful (Clair, 1996b; Thomas et al., 1997; Whitcomb, 1992).

Music therapy interventions can also help give structure and meaning to visits between family members and their loved ones in the middle and late stages of dementia, making the experience less frustrating and more pleasant for both parties (Clair, 1996b; Clair & Ebberts, 1997; Lipe, 1991). Using music that is familiar and well-liked by both family members and their loved ones with dementia, be it live singing by the family member, tapes of preferred songs or dance music that can be listened to, sung with, or moved to, or tapes of performances by children or grandchildren, can help alleviate much of the anxiety and frustration family members often feel at visits. As the music structures and enhances the time they have together, "caregivers can let go of the responsibility they feel to maintain their loved ones' comfort by allowing the music to take over" (Clair, 1996b, p. 271). A recent model music therapy program used structured 10-minute singing, dancing, and drum playing experiences to enhance interactions between family members and their loved ones who had late stage dementia and were in residential care (Clair & Ebberts, 1997). These experiences elicited active responses from both caregivers (family members) and care recipients, giving purpose and direction to their interactions. Family members participating in the study showed a statistically significant increase in satisfaction with the visits using music therapy, as compared with previous visits without music therapy.

Music therapy interventions may also be used

with caregivers alone, to help alleviate stress (Clair, 1996b; McCarthy, 1992; Palmer, 1989) or to facilitate the process of dealing with their own emotions of grief, anger, and disappointment as they gradually lose their loved one to dementia (Bright, 1988; Clair, 1996b). For example, music-mediated relaxation techniques can be used to help release tension, manage stress, and gain temporary respite from worry and fear (Clair, 1996b; Palmer, 1989). These techniques can be useful to individual caregivers in the home or to staff members in residential facilities. McCarthy (1992) designed a music therapy program to decrease the stress and reduce burnout among staff members in a nursing home unit for patients with Alzheimer's disease. Techniques taught to staff members included deep breathing and progressive muscle relaxation to music, simple yoga and gentle stretching to music, imagery with music, and massage therapy with music.

Other caregivers may be helped by repeating positive, self-affirming statements rhythmically to appropriate accompaniment music (Clair, 1996b). In addition, songs, groaning vocalizations, and instrumental improvisations can provide a safe container for caregivers to express their grief, anger, fear, pain, or other emotions (Bright, 1988; Clair, 1996b). Structured song writing experiences (e.g., filling in the blanks about things they miss about the person, things the disease is taking from them, things they hate about the care process but still love about the care recipient, etc.) may also help some caregivers safely express strong emotions.

SPECIAL CONSIDERATIONS AND TIPS FOR SUCCESS

Careful individual assessment of client needs, interests, previous experiences, strengths, and preferences and ongoing assessment and evaluation of treatment interventions and client responses are key ingredients to effective music therapy programming with any population of elderly individuals. Generally, activities will be most successful when they (a) use materials that are interesting and personally relevant to the participants or that incorporate their previous life experience, (b) provide appropriate levels of challenge, (c) take into account the physical and mental capabilities of the participants and make any necessary adaptations for these, (d) are age-appropriate (geared to characteristics, needs, interests of older adults), (e) use high-quality equipment and materials, (f) focus on using the strengths of participants, (g) are designed for sequential skill-building, using preferred methods and materials, (h) emphasize the personal meaning each individual gains from the experience, and (i) promote success and enhance the self-concept and self-esteem of the participants (Chavin, 1991; Clair, 1996b; Coates, 1984; Cordrey, 1994; Davidson, 1980; Douglass, 1985; Gfeller & Hanson, 1995; Gibbons, 1977, 1985, 1988; Karras, 1987; Myers, 1991, 1992; Smith & Knudson, 1995; Weissman, 1983). While enthusiastic, confident leadership enhances participation and success (Davidson, 1980), group leaders must remember they are not performing for the clients but structuring the music to elicit certain responses and help the clients reach specific goals.

It is also important to realize that music may have negative and well as positive effects (Chavin, 1991; Clair, 1996b; Karras, 1987). What is comforting and relaxing or enjoyable to one person may be distressing and even painful to another; music or instruments that are preferred by one may be hated by another; experiences that are just right for one may be overstimulating for another. Therefore, music therapists must always observe individual reactions carefully and be ready to change or adapt materials and experiences to meet individual needs.

Purtilo (1978) observed that a therapist's success in working with geriatric clients will be enhanced if the therapist recognizes that most older people fear dependence and if the therapist is aware of differences in sensory or motor acuity that may affect the responses of elderly clients. Because of motor and sensory limitations, many geriatric clients may have difficulty performing music with small intervals or complex rhythm patterns; however, they can have successful musical experiences if the therapist chooses music that has marked changes in pitch and duration and employs simple rhythm patterns (Gibbons, 1983a). Large-print song sheets may be needed to compensate for deteriorating vision. Adequate lighting and good acoustics will also enhance the music experience for geriatric clients (Nowicki & Trevisan, 1978). In addition, because the functional vocal range of most geriatric clients is rather limited, many songs will have to be transposed if they are to be used most easily and successfully with geriatric clients (Greenwald & Salzberg, 1979; Moore, Staum, & Brotons, 1992). In addition, providing musical cues or prompts for songs (rather than just announcing titles) may increase lyric recall and facilitate the participation for many elderly clients (Bartlett & Snelus, 1980; York, 1994). Acknowledging clients by name and thanking them for their contributions to the group, along with some physical contact (e.g., handshakes, hugs), are also important aspects of establishing therapeutic relationships with geriatric clients, for those actions help rebuild a sense of dignity and self-esteem in the clients (Palmer, 1977).

It is also important to remember that geriatric clients, like any group of people, have a wide range of musical interests (Gibbons, 1985). Elderly people are not interested exclusively in religious music or popular music from the turn of the century. The type of popular music people prefer tends to vary with their age. Usually, older people tend to prefer music that was popular during their early adult years (Gibbons, 1977). There are also indications that older people prefer stimulative music to sedative music and place a high premium on quality musical experiences (Gibbons, 1977, 1985). Finally, it is important to remember that musical aptitude does not necessarily deteriorate just because an individual has reached the age of sixty-five. Both older people in the community and many institutionalized geriatric clients maintain the capacity to develop musically as they age (Gibbons, 1983b, 1985; Kellmann, 1986).

[*Note:* For more information on special considerations with elderly clients who have specific disabilities or conditions (e.g., hearing or visual impairments, orthopedic problems, aphasia, recovering from a stroke), please see the chapters relating to those conditions.]

SUMMARY

Elderly is a term used to describe individuals who have reached a certain arbitrary, chronological age that society defines as being "old." The field of scientific study that deals with aging and the problems of the aged is called *gerontology*. *Geriatrics* is the branch of medicine that is concerned with the care of elderly persons and the treatment of problems associated with aging. After describing some common physiological, mental, and social changes associated with aging, this chapter described general characteristics of five subgroups of elderly individuals: (1) the well elderly, (2) elderly individuals who are semi-independent, (3) chronically ill elderly individuals receiving home care, (4) elderly individuals who are in nursing homes or long-term care facilities, and (5) elderly individuals who have Alzheimer's disease or related disorders.

Two common psychosocial theories of aging are the *disengagement theory of aging*, which holds that successful aging consists of gradually and voluntarily withdrawing from society, and the *activity theory of aging*, which contends that people age most successfully and maintain satisfaction, health, and self-esteem when they remain as active and involved as possible. Others have proposed *developmental theories of aging* that look at old age as a distinct stage of life with its own tasks and challenges. Still others look at the population of elderly people as a distinct subgroup of society (*aging subculture*), who have a unique set of norms, feelings, and attitudes.

A variety of treatment approaches and interventions have been developed to rehabilitate and/or improve the life quality of elderly individuals. This chapter described sensory stimulation/sensory training, reality orientation, remotivation, validation, reminiscence, life review, and behavioral interventions. Many of these interventions target elderly persons who are impaired or institutionalized. However, some approaches, like reminiscence or life review, can be used with most segments of the elderly population.

Elderly people enjoy a wide variety of music and musical experiences and retain the capacity to develop musically as they age. Since music has been an enjoyable part of the lives of most people, it can be a very effective tool for establishing communication with older adults, motivating them to participate in treatment programs, and helping them improve or maintain their level of physical, mental, social, and/or emotional functioning. After describing general music therapy treatment goals for older adults, this chapter discussed specific music therapy approaches for five subgroups of elderly individuals: (1) the well elderly, (2) elderly individuals who are semi-independent, (3) chronically ill elderly individuals receiving home care, (4) elderly individuals who are in nursing homes or long-term care facilities, and (5) elderly individuals who have Alzheimer's disease or related disorders. In addition, music therapy interventions that could be used by and with caregivers were discussed.

QUESTIONS FOR THOUGHT AND DISCUSSION

1. Discuss some of the special characteristics and needs of (1) the well elderly, (2) those elderly individuals who are semi-independent, (3) those who are chronically ill or medically fragile and are being cared for in their own home or that of a caregiver, (4) those who are in nursing homes or long-term care facilities, and (5) those who have Alzheimer's disease or related disorders. What implications do these have for music therapy programming?

2. Briefly describe the disengagement, activity, developmental, and aging subculture theories of aging. What are some implications of each for programming for elderly individuals? Which do you feel are most applicable to music therapy interventions with the elderly? Why?

3. Describe some of the major treatment approaches (e.g., sensory stimulation/sensory training, reality orientation, remotivation, validation, reminiscence, life review, behavioral approaches) used with individuals who are elderly. For which groups of clients might each be most useful? How might music experiences be incorporated into each of these approaches?

4. Discuss some of the myths and realities about elderly persons and music. What are the implications of these for music therapy programming?

5. Why are music experiences useful for individuals who are elderly? Are some types of experiences and activities more useful than others for particular types of clients? Which ones? Why?

6. Describe some specific music therapy experiences that might be used to help (1) the well elderly, (2) those elderly individuals who are semi-independent, (3) those who are chronically ill or medically fragile and are being cared for in their own home or that of a caregiver, (4) those who are in nursing homes or long-term care facilities, (5) those in the early, middle, and late stages of dementia, and (6) caregivers. What unique benefits does music provide for each of these groups?

7. List several special considerations that may be important to remember when developing therapeutic intervention strategies for persons are elderly. Why are these important? What are their implications for the structure of music therapy intervention strategies?

8. For each of the situations listed below, (a) define the problem or areas of need for the client or group of clients, (b) describe one or more of the goals you might pursue in music therapy sessions with the client(s), (c) describe music activities you might use to help the client(s) meet those goals, (d) tell how the music activities you described relate to the goals and needs of the client(s), and (e) mention any special considerations you might want to take into account when working with the client(s).

Situation 1:

Mr. H. is 65 years old. He recently retired and is looking for constructive ways to fill his time. He just started attending a senior center with his wife. One day he mentions that although he and his wife have always enjoyed music (in fact, they still go to concerts and love to sing and listen to records), he never learned to play an instrument because he never had enough time. Now that he has the time, he wonders if he might be too old to learn. Mr. and Mrs. H. have a piano at home that their children or grandchildren play when they come to visit. Mr. H. also enjoys country music and has thought about learning to play the guitar.

Situation 2:

Mrs. C. is a 75 year old widow who has been in a nursing home for about three months. She is slightly confused and uses a walker to help her get around. She rarely goes out of her room, because she is afraid she will get lost. She has few visitors. She often seems to be very nervous and has occasionally been observed to be crying silently, but she will not say what is wrong. She rarely initiates conversation with staff or other residents. She hardly even talks to her roommate, because she doesn't want to bother anyone. Mrs. C. keeps herself busy by reading her Bible, napping, listening to tapes of religious music, or watching TV. Her social history says that her husband played the violin and that she used to play the piano and sing in the church choir.

Situation 3:

You have been contracted to provide music therapy sessions for a small group of residents on the newly formed Alzheimer's care unit of a local nursing home. There are three women and two men in the group. All are ambulatory. Their dementia has progressed to the point where they now have trouble recognizing close friends and family members. Most still speak, but they frequently have problems finding the words they need to express their thoughts and feelings. These residents often engage in repetitive motions like pacing and tapping; a few also repeat certain phrases like "help me" or "Where's my mother?". Their restlessness and agitation tends to increase in the late afternoon and early evening. The activity director has scheduled your music therapy group for a late afternoon time in the hope that you can decrease their agitation and get them engaged in some purposeful activities.

SUGGESTIONS FOR FURTHER READING

Boxberger, R., & Cotter, V. W. (1968). Part VI. *Music therapy for geriatric patients.* In E. T. Gaston (Ed.), Music in therapy (pp. 269-290). New York: Macmillan.

Bright, R. (1972). *Music in geriatric care.* New York: St. Martin's Press.

Bright, R. (1981). *Practical planning in music therapy for the aged.* Lynbrook, NY: Music-graphics.

Bright, R. (1986). *Grieving: A handbook for those who care.* St. Louis: MMB Music.

Bright, R. (1988). *Music therapy and the dementias: Improving the quality of life.* St. Louis, MO: MMB Music.

Brotons, M., Koger, S., & Pickett-Cooper, P. (1997). Music and dementias: A review of literature. *Journal of Music Therapy, 34*(4), 204-245.

Bruscia, K. E. (Ed.) (1991). *Case studies in music therapy.* Phoenixville, PA: Barcelona Publishers.

Caplow-Linder, E., Harpza, L., & Samberg, S. (1979). *Therapeutic dance/movement: Expressive activities for older adults.* New York: Human Sciences Press.

Chavin, M. (1991). *The lost chord: Reaching the person with dementia through the power of music.* Mt. Airy, MD: ElderSong Publications.

Clair, A. A. (1996). *Therapeutic uses of music with older adults.* Baltimore, MD: Health Professions Press.

Cordrey, C. (1994). *Hidden treasures: Music and memory activities for people with Alzheimer's.* Mt. Airy, MD: ElderSong.

Davis, W. B. (1992). Music therapy and elderly populations. In W. B. Davis, K. E. Gfeller, & M. H. Thaut, *An introduction to music therapy: Theory and practice* (pp. 133-163). Dubuque, IA: Wm. C. Brown.

Erikson, E. H., Erikson, J. M., & Kivnick, H. Q. (1986). *Vital involvement in old age.* New York: W. W. Norton & Co.

Feil, N. (1982). *Validation – the Feil method: How to help the disoriented old-old.* Cleveland, OH: Edward Feil Productions.

Feil, N. (1993). *The validation breakthrough: Simple techniques for communicating with people with "Alzheimer's-type dementia."* Baltimore, MD: Health Professions Press.

Gfeller, K., & Hanson, N. (Eds.). (1995). *Music therapy programming for individuals with Alzheimer's disease and related disorders.* St. Louis: MMB Music.

Gibbons, A. C. (1988). A review of literature for music development/education and music therapy with the elderly. *Music Therapy Perspectives, 5,* 33-40.

Hanson, N., Gfeller, K., Woodworth, G., Swanson, E., & Garand, L. (1996). A comparison of the effectiveness of differing types and difficulty of music activities in programming for older adults with Alzheimer's disease and related disorders. *Journal of Music Therapy, 33*(2), 93-123.

Karras, B. (1985). *Down memory lane: Topics and ideas for reminiscence groups.* Wheaton, MD: Circle Press.

Karras, B. (Ed.). (1987). *"You bring out the music in me": Music in nursing homes.* Binghamton, NY: Haworth Press.

Kellman, R. H. (1986). Developing music programs for older adults. *Music Educators Journal, 72*(5), 30-33.

Palmer, M. D. (1977). Music therapy in a comprehensive program of treatment and rehabilitation for the geriatric resident. *Journal of Music Therapy, 14*(4), 190-197.

Palmer, M. (1989). Music therapy in gerontology: A review and a projection. *Music Therapy Perspectives, 6,* 52-56.

Prickett, C. A. (1988). Music therapy for the aged. In C. E. Furman (Ed.), *Effectiveness of music therapy procedures: Documentation of research and clinical practice* (pp. 285-299). Washington, D.C.: National Association for Music Therapy.

Prickett, C. A. (1996). Music therapy as a part of older people's lives. In C. E. Furman (Ed.), *Effectiveness of music therapy procedures: Documentation of research and clinical practice* (2nd ed.) (pp. 144-166). Silver Spring, MD: National Association for Music Therapy.

Schulberg, C. H. (1981). *The music therapy sourcebook: A collection of activities categorized and analyzed.* New York: Human Sciences Press.

Short, A. E. (1992). Music and imagery with physically disabled elderly residents: A GIM adaptation. *Music Therapy, 11*(1), 65-98.

Smith, D. S., & Lipe, A. W. (1991). Music therapy practices in gerontology. *Journal of Music Therapy, 28*(4), 193-210.

Standley, J. (1991). *Music techniques in therapy, counseling, and special education.* St. Louis: MMB Music.

Summer, L. (1981). Guided imagery and music with the elderly. *Music Therapy, 1*(1), 39-42.

Weisberg, N., & Wilder, R. (1985). *Creative arts with older adults.* New York: Human Sciences Press.

Weissman, J. A. (1983). Planning music activities to meet needs and treatment goals of aged individuals in long-term care facilities. *Music Therapy, 3*(1), 63-70.

Chapter Twenty

MUSIC THERAPY FOR INDIVIDUALS WHO ARE TERMINALLY ILL

DEFINITION

INDIVIDUALS ARE said to be *terminally ill* when they have been diagnosed with some fatal, incurable disease or condition. Many terminally ill patients have incurable diseases, such as certain types of cancer (especially cancer that has metastasized, or spread to other parts or organs of the body) or AIDS. Others are in the advanced stages of degenerative neurological diseases, such as amyotrophic lateral sclerosis (ALS, or Lou Gehrig's disease), Alzheimer's disease, Huntington's disease, multiple sclerosis, muscular dystrophy, or Parkinson's disease. As Purtilo (1978) observed, one of the main difficulties with this term is its generality: Both individuals who may live for years before dying from a malignant or degenerative condition and those who will almost certainly die within a few days or weeks are labeled "terminally ill."

When people are terminally ill, they usually receive palliative care rather than active, aggressive medical treatment. *Palliative care* serves to alleviate the distressful symptoms of the disease or condition (e.g., reduces pain as much as possible) but does not strive for a cure. Palliative care focuses on providing individualized, supportive care that improves life quality and preserves dignity. This term is often used interchangeably with the term "hospice care" (Munro, 1984). *Hospice programs* coordinate supportive and palliative services from a variety of professionals and disciplines to help meet the total needs (physical, psychological, social, emotional, and spiritual) of terminally ill individuals and their families. Some hospice programs are home-based,

some are inpatient programs, and others provide continued support for the patient both at home and during periods of hospitalization (Colligan, 1987; "Life's Work," 1987; Palmer, 1989; Visiting Nurses Association of Dallas, 1981). Hospice programs aim to keep the integrity and personal choices of the patient and the family intact by providing individualized, supportive, interdisciplinary care that encourages each patient to live as fully as possible and then allows them to die in peace and with dignity, surrounded by their loved ones. In hospice program, health care workers "view death not as a medical failure, but as a part of life" ("Life's Work," 1987, p. 55).

The modern hospice movement began in England in 1967 when Dame Cicely Saunders founded St. Christopher's Hospice near London ("Life's Work," 1987; Martin, 1989). The first modern hospice programs in Canada and the United States were established in the mid-1970s, and the National Hospice Organization was founded in 1978. Since that time, the hospice movement and interest in dignified, holistic care for the dying have experienced tremendous growth. Speaking at a symposium in 1989, Patrice O'Connor, Coordinator of the Palliative Care Program at St. Luke's/Roosevelt Hospital Center in New York City observed:

The growth and the development of Hospice in the United States from three programs in 1975 to over 1800 programs in 1988 shows the interest and concern of people in taking control of this aspect of their lives in a highly technical health-care system. (Martin, 1989, p. 79)

In 1998, the United States had over 25,000 hospice programs. About half of these were associated with hospitals or home health agencies ("Hospice Web," 1999).

COMMON CHARACTERISTICS, PROBLEMS, AND NEEDS OF CLIENTS

As with any population, those individuals who are terminally ill are a very heterogeneous group. Factors such as the type and severity of the illness or condition, the expected time left before death, the existence of associated conditions or impairments, the reactions of family and friends, and the degree and type of support services available will all have varying effects on the individual's level of functioning, needs, and treatment program. In addition, each individual who is terminally ill will have a unique combinations of abilities, needs, personality traits, strengths, and weaknesses that will impact his or her particular responses and functional abilities. Therefore, it is unwise to attempt to predict a particular person's skill levels or ceiling of abilities based on broad generalizations about a certain population. However, an awareness of some of those characteristics, problems, and needs which may be common to many individuals who are terminally ill will be beneficial both to the therapist who desires to work with this population and to the reader who is trying to understand how music therapy intervention strategies may benefit this population.

According to Kübler-Ross (1969), most terminally ill people go through five stages in their confrontation with death: (1) denial and isolation, (2) anger, (3) bargaining, (4) depression, and (5) acceptance. Since individual patients move through these stages in different ways and some patients may revisit any or all of them (often at different levels) many times before their death, it may be more accurate to think of these stages as a range of responses likely to be exhibited by terminally ill individuals, rather than as a progression of discrete phases through which they will pass (Purtilo, 1978; West, 1994).

Others view the progression from life to death as consisting of four phases, each of which presents new tasks, challenges, and emotions (West, 1994). The length of each phases can vary greatly from patient to patient. In phase 1, *Early Phase*, the patient is adjusting to the reality of a terminal diagnosis,

deciding to shift from aggressive to palliative treatment, and learning to adapt to various role and body image changes. During phase 2, *Stabilization*, the acute crisis of being diagnosed as terminally ill has subsided and there may be few significant changes in health or life style. The patient's focus moves between tasks of living and tasks of dying, as she or he processes any "unfinished business," attends to such things as will preparation, funeral plans, and care for family members after his or her death, engages in life review or values clarification, and finds ways to keep on living fully while she or he is still alive. This lingering stage, between diagnosis and disease progression/imminent death, may be one of the hardest stages for many family members (Bright, 1986; Purtilo, 1978). The third phase, *Disease Progression*, may occur only once or several times before death. Some patients cycle between disease progression and stabilization many times before approaching imminent death. Disease progression is a crisis phase, during which the patient experiences many physical, psychological, and spiritual challenges as she or he adjusts to more losses, decreased functioning, and diminished energy. During this phase, patients may also be placed in hospitals or care facilities, resulting in additional losses and changes in quality of life. In phase 4, *End-Stage and Death*, the patient's death is imminent. During this phase, the patient is becoming detached and disengaged, adjusting to changes in sensory awareness, and physically, psychologically, and spiritually shifting from living to dying. Patients in this phase often become increasingly isolated and unresponsive. Others may get confused or anxious. Some patients may have a decrease in affective expression and a decreased tolerance for light, sound, or other stimuli.

Throughout the course of their terminal illness, individuals will have many physical, psychological, social, and spiritual needs (Bright, 1986; Colligan, 1987; "Hospice Web," 1999; "Life's Work," 1987;

Martin, 1989; Munro & Mount, 1978; Munro, 1984; Purtilo, 1978; Visiting Nurses Association of Dallas, 1981). *Physical needs* may include relief of acute or chronic pain and physical distress, muscle relaxation, appropriate medication and medical care procedures to manage medical conditions and symptoms, nutritional counseling, or assistance with activities of daily living (bathing, toileting, grooming, eating, etc.). Individuals with terminal illnesses may also need programs or strategies that help facilitate their participation in physical activities for the greatest extent possible. *Psychological needs* may include help in increasing or maintaining a healthy self-concept and high self-esteem, decreasing depression or anxiety, finding ways to keep on living to the fullest until death, facilitating expression of a broad range of conscious and unconscious feelings, having time and space to grieve or express anger, discussing and finding ways to deal with or work through present concerns, continuing to be involved in decision-making about one's own life or care to the fullest possible extent, reviewing part or all of one's past life, finding outlets for fantasy and creativity, and finding ways to tap and give expression to those parts of the individual that are still vital and healthy.

Many individuals who are terminally ill also need support and guidance in dealing with some of the fears that are often associated with the dying process. These include fear of isolation or of being alone, fear of increasing pain, fear of increased dependence on others (loss of independence and control), fear of indignity or rejection because of one's condition, fear of mounting medical costs, fear of the unknown (what comes after death), and fear mingled with grief and sadness over the impending loss of relationships (Bright, 1986; Maranto, 1988; Purtilo, 1978). When children are terminally ill, their chronological and development age will affect both their conception of death and their ways of expressing fears and feelings associated with dying (Froehlich, 1996; Schwankovsky & Guthrie, 1982). For many, having access to nonverbal means of expression may be important to eliciting and working through questions and emotions. When an individual who is terminally ill has a condition that has some societal stigma attached to it (e.g., AIDS), fears of rejection or

isolation and feelings of shock, guilt, panic, and worry over what others will think may be compounded, giving rise to additional needs for psychological counseling and support (Maranto, 1988).

The physical changes and psychological concerns associated with terminal illnesses may also impact an individual's ability to relate to and communicate with others. *Social needs* of individuals who are terminally ill include physical touch, companionship, private times with family and friends, ways to stay involved with others in meaningful activities, links to the individual's life before the terminal diagnosis, entertainment or diversion from dealing with the painful reality of terminal illness, and ways to facilitate conversations between themselves and their family members, including discussion of difficult, emotional, or intimate issues. For some individuals, religion or exploration of spiritual issues become increasingly important as they face death. *Spiritual needs* may include pastoral counseling, grief counseling, finding ways to express and discuss spiritual feelings and questions, finding comfort and reassurance in religious or spiritual beliefs and/or rituals, obtaining support for one's beliefs, confronting questions about the meaning of life and what comes after death, and facilitating the transition from life to death ("Hospice Web," 1999; Munro & Mount, 1978; West, 1994).

Health care for individuals who are terminally ill emphasizes (1) managing pain and related symptoms to decrease suffering and maximize comfort; (2) helping individuals maintain independent physical function and encouraging them to live life as fully as possible; (3) providing patients and family members with information on the patient's illness and care (including what to expect as the illness progresses), along with the reassurance that everything possible is being done; and (4) attending to the emotional and spiritual needs of patients and family members, supporting them rather than abandoning them (Purtilo, 1978; Visiting Nurses Association of Dallas, 1981). The overall goal of treatment is to enhance and maintain the individual's quality of life until the moment of death, thus facilitating the adaptation of the individual's family (Purtilo, 1978; Schwankovsky & Guthrie, 1982).

COMMON NEEDS OF FAMILY MEMBERS

Most hospice or palliative care programs are concerned not only with the needs or the individual patient but also with the needs of the patient's family members (Bright, 1981, 1986; "Hospice Web," 1999; "Life's Work," 1987; Martin, 1989; Purtilo, 1978; Schwankovsky & Guthrie, 1982; Visiting Nurses Association of Dallas, 1981; West, 1994). Since family members, too, are unique individuals, each responds to their loved one's illness in different ways; therefore, it is unwise to attempt to predict a particular person's needs or responses based on broad generalizations. However, an awareness of some of those needs which may be common to the family members of individuals who are terminally ill will be beneficial both to the therapist who desires to work with this population and to the reader who is trying to understand how music therapy intervention strategies may benefit this population.

The terminal illness of one family member, be it spouse, parent, or child, impacts all other family members, for their roles in the family will change, at least to some extent, as they care for the ill family member and try to go on living with and interacting with that family member while making preparations to go on with life without them after their death. Family members, too, need much support in all areas of their lives. They may need to be reminded to take time for their own physical or nutritional needs. Some need help in finding workable stress management, relaxation, tension release, or anxiety reduction techniques. Family members, especially primary caregivers, need to have breaks or diversions from dealing with the pain and realities of their loved one's terminal illness. In many cases, respite care arrangements or helpful friends or neighbors can provide needed relief and time off. Some families may also need practical assistance in dealing with financial or legal matters in arranging for in-home care, or in making funeral arrangements.

Family members need time to be with their loved one, to share fun and diversional activities as well as quiet companionship, life review, and discussion of emotional and difficult topics. They need acceptance and permission both to look back over the past and to enjoy what time they have left together. They need to find ways to draw out and celebrate those parts of the patient that are still intact and healthy, so they can have enjoyable, meaningful interactions together. Family members also need time by themselves, both to solve practical and emotional difficulties and to continue their lives. They need to be informed (in words they can understand) about the patient's condition, treatment, and what to expect as the illness progresses. In addition, they need freedom to express all kinds of emotions, along with psychological and spiritual support, as they deal with fears and questions both throughout the patient's illness and after the patient's death.

Family members continue to need support and follow-up care during the bereavement period (Bright, 1981, 1986; "Hospice Web," 1999; Munro, 1984; Visiting Nurses Association of Dallas, 1981). During this time of grieving, family members are (a) learning to accept the reality of the loss, (b) experiencing the pain of the loss, (c) adapting to life without the loved one, and (d) withdrawing emotional energy from the former relationship with the loved one (Worden, 1982). Feelings may include shock, bewilderment, intense emptiness, sadness, despair, depression, restless anxiety, or fatigue and lethargy. Over time, most will experience a kind of "recovery," when they can finally think of their deceased loved one without overwhelming sadness. As their grief and sorrow give way to treasured memories, family members will begin to invest energy in other thoughts and activities and carve out new or revised identities and social roles for themselves. A good social, emotional, and spiritual support network can do much to help bereaved individuals maintain good physical and psychological health as they work through their grief over the death of their loved one.

SETTINGS FOR SERVICE DELIVERY

Individuals who are terminally ill may receive special programs and services to help meet their specific needs in a variety of settings, including nursing homes, hospitals, clinics, private homes, and inpatient or home-based hospice programs. Music therapists may provide direct or consultive services to individuals or agencies. While much work with terminally ill clients is done on an individual basis, music therapy services can also be provided to groups of patients or to patients and family members. In a recent survey of populations served by music therapists in which respondents were permitted to list as many categories as appropriate (AMTA, 1998), 254 of 1,620 respondents said they worked with terminally ill clients, while 185 reported working with individuals who had cancer and 119 reported working with individuals who had AIDS. Fifty music therapists said they worked in hospice facilities or bereavement services.

HOW MUSIC IS USED IN THERAPY

Music, with its ability to affect all aspects of a person's being, enhance emotional expression, and facilitate interactions between and among people (see Chapter Five), can be a very powerful and beneficial tool in helping patients and their families deal with the physical, psychological, social, and spiritual effects and challenges of the various phases of terminal illnesses. In addition to accomplishing clinical goals (e.g., pain or anxiety reduction, strengthening self-concept, facilitating emotional expression), "music can be a source of deep, meaningful interaction – between patients and families, patients and patients, and patients and [music therapist]" (Martin, 1991, p. 630). Songs and music experiences also have the power to reawaken vitality and "build intimate relationships between human beings and life" (Bailey, 1984, p. 16). Since hearing is the last sense to leave the body, music can even provide comfort and support in the final stages of death (Froehlich, 1996). Of course, each individual patient's reaction to a particular intervention or selection of music will be unique; therefore, music therapists constantly assess and evaluate patient responses and adjust music experiences accordingly (Bright, 1986; Froehlich, 1996; Martin, 1989; Munro, 1984; Munro & Mount, 1978; Schwankovsky & Guthrie, 1982; West, 1994). A particular patient's type of pain, phase of dying, cognitive style, functional defenses, spiritual and cultural background, and readiness to connect with or express feelings will also influence the type of music therapy interventions selected. In hospice work, music therapists are generally concerned less with facilitating change and more with supporting the patient, enabling the patient and family to make choices and have experiences that will "enhance the quality of life in the face of death" (West, 1994, p. 120).

Many music therapy techniques, such as music listening, Guided Imagery and Music (GIM), music-mediated relaxation, music and massage, discussion of music or music experiences, song choice, lyric interpretation and discussion, song writing, lyric substitution, singing or instrumental performance, music improvisation, use of music vibrations (from instruments, tuning forks, or mattresses/chairs that provide a kinesthetic experience of music vibrations), selecting/writing songs or taping musical performance as a lasting gift or legacy to friends/family members, and music-facilitated life review, have been used effectively to help meet the physical, psychological, social, and spiritual needs of both children and adults who have terminal illnesses, as well as those of their friends and families (Bright, 1986; Froehlich, 1996; Martin, 1989; Munro, 1984; Munro & Mount, 1978; Schwankovsky & Guthrie, 1982; West, 1994). Under the skillful direction of a sensitive music therapist, these techniques can enhance the quality of life of patients in palliative or hospice care in several ways. Benefits of music therapy interventions for individuals with terminal illnesses include decreasing pain, facilitating relaxation, diminishing stress and anxiety, providing enjoyment and recreation, providing an increased sense of control over one's life, decreasing depression, facilitating emotional expression and providing a safe container to hold and organize all kinds of feelings, providing psychological and/or spiritual support, increasing interaction and communication with family members, identifying and eliciting strengths and coping resources, stimulating reminiscence and life review, reinforcing identity and strengthening self-concept, providing outlets for creativity and self-expression, renewing interest in life, increasing self-esteem, and easing the transition from life to death (Bailey, 1984; Bright, 1986; Clair, 1996b; Colligan, 1987; Froehlich, 1996; Maranto, 1988; Martin, 1989, 1991; Munro, 1984; Munro & Mount, 1978; O'Callaghan, 1996; Schwankovsky & Guthrie, 1982; Standley, 1996b; West, 1994). Age-appropriate music therapy experiences and interventions can also help children who have terminal illnesses appreciate and connect to life and the healthy, vital creative parts of themselves, meet developmental milestones, and participate in regular childhood activities (Froehlich, 1996). In addition, music therapy interventions can provide stress relief and emotional or spiritual support to family members, enhance or facilitate their interactions with the patient, assist them in understanding and accepting their loved one's illness, and support them during the period of bereavement (Bailey, 1984; Bright, 1986; Edwards, 1976; Froehlich, 1996; Maranto, 1988; Martin, 1989, 1991; O'Callaghan, 1996; Schwankovsky & Guthrie, 1982; West, 1994). The next sections of this chapter provide more specific examples of music therapy interventions that can be used effectively to help meet various needs of terminally ill patients and their families.

Therapeutic Music Experiences to Help Meet Physical Needs

One of the important uses of music therapy in palliative care is pain relief (Bright, 1981, 1986; Maranto, 1996; Martin, 1989; Munro, 1984; Munro & Mount, 1978; Schwankovsky & Guthrie, 1982; Spintge, 1989; Taylor, 1997). For many individuals who are terminally ill, "the most immediate need is often managing pain or other symptoms of illness" (Skaggs, 1997c, p. 41). According to Achterberg (1985), as sound travels through the reticular activating system of the brain stem, it can activate the entire brain and hold the individual's entire cognitive awareness, thus closing out or diminishing the perception of other sensory stimuli, such as pain or nausea. Although music therapy interventions cannot change the cause of the pain, they can "help patients alter their perception of and responses to the pain" (Froehlich, 1996, p. 229). Froehlich (1996) developed a music therapy model for pain management with

individuals who are terminally ill that uses live or taped music in five different ways: (1) for pain distraction, (2) for relaxation, (3) for mood alteration, (4) for attention-focusing or concentration in a relaxed state, and (5) for dissociation, especially near the end stages of the illness (requires advanced clinical training).

Some patients find that listening to recordings of favorite, preferred music can decrease pain perception and help them to relax and become more comfortable (Bright, 1981, 1986; Curtis, 1986; Munro, 1984). Often, songs that have slower tempos and calmer rhythms are most effective in facilitating relaxation and decreasing pain. Individual patients, however, may also be comforted by music of other styles or tempos that holds particular meaning for them. For example, Bright (1986) tells of a man who received pleasure, peace, and comfort from a tape of Bach's organ "Toccata and Fugue in D Minor." Recorded music choices effective for pain reduction and relaxation are unique to each individual (Curtis, 1986); what works for one may be totally ineffective for another. When tape-recorded music is used as a specifically prescribed treatment to facilitate relaxation and pain relief, patients are often given individual tape players and headphones "so that the music can be played at any time of the day or night as the patient feels the need" (Bright, 1981, p. 38). Since background *noise* usually increases discomfort and tension (Curtis, 1986), background *music* that masks unpleasant environment sounds may also help decrease pain and discomfort.

Many patients find that relaxation and pain relief are facilitated when they do relaxation exercises to music (Froehlich, 1996; Martin, 1989; Munro, 1984; Munro & Mount, 1978) or are massaged in time to music (Clair, 1996b). Others achieve optimum relaxation, comfort, and pain relief through imagery coupled with music (Rider, 1985; West, 1994) or through the specific techniques of the Bonny method of Guided Imagery and Music (GIM) (Bonny, 1978b; Colligan, 1987; Froehlich, 1996; Munro, 1984; Skaggs, 1997c; Wylie & Blom, 1986). GIM techniques facilitate deep relaxation and may help individuals "journey" to places of peace and comfort. Imagery, emerging from the individual with the guidance of the therapist and the music, can also help patients exercise control over their pain (Skaggs, 1997c). Many patients are then able to learn to apply these techniques on their own to help them manage their pain at times when the therapist is not present (Colligan, 1987; Skaggs, 1997c; Wylie & Blom, 1986). Follow-up discussion of GIM experiences also help individuals achieve insights into their feelings and needs (Colligan, 1987). Music therapists who use GIM techniques need specific advanced clinical training. (See Chapter Twenty-two for more information on GIM.)

Live music, too, can be very effective in reducing pain and providing comfort for individuals who are terminally ill (Bailey, 1983; Froehlich, 1996; Martin, 1991; Taylor, 1997). In fact, Bailey (1983) found that listening to live performances of music decreased tension and anxiety and increased vigor in hospitalized cancer patients significantly more than did listening to tape recordings of the same music. As therapists perform live music with individual patients, they can also readily adapt tempos to the patient's breathing, using gradual changes in mood and tempo and gradual lengthening of musical phrases to help calm and soothe rapid breathing, thus facilitating peace and relaxation (Forinash & Gonzalez, 1989; Martin, 1991).

Other individuals are distracted from their pain and have increased feelings of comfort and decreased feelings of anxiety when they *actively participate* in live music experiences by singing or playing instruments (Froehlich, 1996; Levine-Gross & Swartz, 1982; Martin, 1989; Schwankovsky & Guthrie, 1982; Taylor, 1997; Tims, 1981). For example, one woman with chronic pain from terminal pancreatic and liver cancer experienced her first pain-free, full night of sleep in many months after singing Christmas songs for about ninety minutes (Taylor, 1997, p. 61). (For more information on music therapy and pain relief, see Chapter Seventeen.)

In addition to being an important tool for pain management, music therapy interventions can help alleviate some of the unpleasant side effects of chemotherapy. Studies have shown that listening to preferred music during chemotherapy can help decrease nausea, delay the onset of nausea, reduce the length of vomiting, and/or reduce anxiety (Maranto, 1996; Standley, 1992; Taylor, 1997). Standley (1992) found that music of many different styles could achieve these effects for various patients; the effectiveness depended not so much on the musical selection itself, but on the associations an individual had with the music.

Music experiences can also be structured therapeutically to motivate and facilitate individuals' participation in physical activities to the fullest extent possible (Bright, 1981; Froehlich, 1996; Munro & Mount, 1978; Schwankovsky & Guthrie, 1982). Since music can lessen pain perception and gently persuade client to be part of the group (Gaston, 1968a), putting exercise routines to music may provide the motivation needed for clients to participate in physical exercises (Bright, 1977; Munro & Mount, 1978). In some cases, instruments may provide the motivation for physical activity and a renewed interest in life. For example, reviving an 86-year-old terminally ill man's interest in playing the violin increased his interest in doing things for himself and in taking part in some physical activities (Beggs, 1991). In another instance, guitar lessons helped increase a terminally ill 15-year-old boy's level of physical activity and participation (Standley, 1996b). Music therapy activities can also be structured to help terminally ill children reach developmental goals and milestones (Froehlich, 1996).

Therapeutic Music Experiences to Help Meet Psychological Needs

Since music gives expression to a wide range of emotions while providing structure, grounding, and presence, it can help support both children and adults with terminal illnesses in times of joy, anger, doubt, and sorrow, through all the challenges of the various phases of terminal illness (Bailey, 1984; Bright, 1986; Edwards, 1976; Fagen, 1982; Froehlich, 1996; Gilbert, 1977; Hamilton & Bailey, 1981; Martin, 1989; Munro, 1984; Munro & Mount, 1978; Schwankovsky & Guthrie, 1982; West, 1994). In the face of the many role and body image changes that accompany terminal illnesses, music experiences can be structured to help reinforce identity and self-concept, increase self-esteem, and restore or maintain feelings of usefulness. For example, song lyrics can help reinforce identity and self-concept and provide a springboard for discussion of present concerns (Bailey, 1984; Edwards, 1976; Fagen, 1982; Munro, 1984; Munro & Mount, 1978; Schwankovsky & Guthrie, 1982). Renewing interest in previously played instruments or learning to play new instruments can also help increase self-esteem, interest in life, and feelings of being worthwhile and useful (Beggs, 1991; Bright, 1986; Bunt & Marston-Wyld, 1995; Standley, 1996b). Bright (1986) tells of a patient who played the harmonica to entertain fellow patients and staff during his many hospital admissions for inoperable cancer. Through this contribution, the patient gained much self-esteem and feelings of usefulness that "helped to defuse much of the anger which he had experienced when his diagnosis first became clear" (Bright, 1986, p. 130). Performing songs on instruments can also help decrease depression, motivate cooperation, and increase interest in life for both terminally ill adolescents (Standley, 1996b) and adults (Beggs, 1991). Other terminally ill individuals increase their self-esteem through the pride they get from creating lyrics or musical settings (O'Callaghan, 1997).

Other music therapy experiences bolster patients' self-concept and self-esteem by giving them opportunities to make decisions and positively affect outcomes. The simple act of selecting songs to sing or play, instruments to use, music to listen to, or music-mediated options to control their pain can provide patients with welcome opportunities for choice and control in a situation that is so often beyond their control (Bailey, 1984; Bright, 1986; Dunn, 1995; Fagen, 1982; Froehlich, 1996; Gilbert, 1977; Hamilton & Bailey, 1981; Martin, 1989, 1991; Munro, 1984; Munro & Mount, 1978; Schwankovsky & Guthrie, 1982; Standley, 1996b; West, 1994). GIM techniques also can be used to provide terminally ill patients with opportunities to control some aspect of their lives (e.g., images, thoughts, feelings) and to be creative (Colligan, 1987; Skaggs, 1997c; Wylie & Blom, 1986). Other patients find creative outlets in song writing, lyric substitution, or composing musical settings for poems or pictures (Fagen, 1982; Froehlich, 1996; Hamilton & Bailey, 1981; Martin, 1989; O'Callaghan, 1996, 1997; Schwankovsky & Guthrie, 1982). Through these creative acts, they also control the elements of their creation (e.g., words, musical sounds) and form them into things of beauty.

Adults as well as children need fun, recreational activities, even when they are terminally ill. One of the challenges of being diagnosed with a terminal illness is finding ways to enjoy life and keep on living fully until the time of death. Having opportunities for appropriately structured diversional and creative

music experiences can help in this regard. By adapting singing, listening, instrumental performance, improvisation, or dance/movement-to-music experiences to fit the functioning levels of individual patients, music therapists can devise unique music experiences that give terminally ill patients and their families much-needed opportunities for enjoyment and diversion, creativity, and connection with health and life (Bright, 1986; Bunt & Marston-Wyld, 1995; Clair, 1996b; Edwards, 1976; Froehlich, 1996; Martin, 1989, 1991; Munro, 1984; Munro & Mount, 1978; Schwankovsky & Guthrie, 1982). In addition, passive or active participation in enjoyable music experiences can give both terminally ill children and adults a new focus for interest and stimulation that helps relieve boredom, renews interest their in life, and increases positive interactions with other people. Other patients (and family members) may enjoy being transported in their minds and imaginations to more pleasant times and places through songs or imagery associated with music (Bright, 1981, 1986; Colligan, 1987; Dunn, 1995; Fagen, 1982; Froehlich, 1996; Hamilton & Bailey, 1981; Martin, 1989; Schwankovsky & Guthrie, 1982; Skaggs, 1997c; Wylie & Blom, 1986).

Since most individuals have enjoyed music throughout their lives, music can be an important tool for stimulating reminiscence and life review with terminally ill clients. Hearing songs and music from different time periods of an individual's life can facilitate recall of events, experiences, and feelings associated with these times (Bright, 1981, 1986; Clair, 1996b; Martin, 1989; Munro, 1984; Munro & Mount, 1978; West, 1994). Songs can be suggested by the therapist, requested by patients, or chosen by patients from a list provided by the therapist. The act of taping a life review with music and reminiscence may help individuals recall strengths and increase feelings of self-worth, thus helping to reawaken their interest in life (Beggs, 1991; Bright, 1986). For individuals who play instruments, the act of performing songs they learned in years past may facilitate reminiscence and life review (Beggs, 1991). Other palliative care patients may enjoy writing songs that express themes significant to their life experiences (O'Callaghan, 1996, 1997). GIM techniques can also help stimulate reminiscence and life review in clients who have terminal illnesses (Bruscia, 1991b; Colligan, 1987; Skaggs, 1997c; Wylie & Blom, 1986). In addition, video or audio tapes of musical life review sessions can be a significant gift to family members that will give them pleasant memories even after the patient has died (Beggs, 1991; Bright, 1986; Clair, 1996b). Collections of songs chosen by or written by the patient can also provide family members with lasting gifts of love or musical legacies from the patient (Froehlich, 1996; Standley, 1996b; Whittall, 1991).

Because music has the ability to access and express feelings directly and immediately, music therapy experiences can have a very unique and important role to play when individual clients or their families have feelings to communicate but no words to name or express them (Bunt & Marston-Wyld, 1995). As Kübler-Ross (1974) stated: "Music is a much-neglected form of language and can be used with these patients in a very effective way" (p. 43). Various music experiences can be structured therapeutically to provide terminally ill clients and their family members with many ways to express a wide range of emotions, both verbally and nonverbally. Often, action-based, nonverbal experiences, such as instrumental improvisation, help individuals play out and express feelings they are unable to verbalize (Froehlich, 1996; Hamilton & Bailey, 1981; Martin, 1989; Schwankovsky & Guthrie, 1982). Learning to access and express these feelings nonverbally helps many individuals gain the insight, awareness, security, and confidence to then articulate these feelings verbally as they feel the need (Bunt & Marston-Wyld, 1995). Other individuals are more comfortable choosing song lyrics to give symbolic, structured expression to feelings they have difficulty verbalizing (Bailey, 1984; Bright, 1986; Martin, 1989, 1991; Whittall, 1991).

> Often patients express, through the lyrics of the songs, that which they are either unable or unwilling to state verbally and directly. . . . Songs provide an element of safety . . . it is the therapist, who, when singing the lyrics chosen by the patient, gives voice to the thought or feelings. Songs seem to provide the support and distance necessary to broach frightening or otherwise difficult topics. (Martin, 1989, p. iv)

Song selection may be followed by verbal discussion, if the patient seems to be ready for verbal exploration of the topics and feelings brought up in the songs.

Some patients will be ready to talk, while others will just want to let the song lyrics do the talking for them, at least for a time. The therapist must be sensitive to cues from the patient as to whether or not to encourage additional verbal exploration of the material described by the song lyrics (Martin, 1989, 1991; West, 1994).

Familiar songs can also provide emotional comfort and support and help decrease anxiety (Clair, 1996b; West, 1994) or help stimulate verbalization about fears and feelings associated with hospitalization or terminal illness (Brodsky, 1989; Fagen, 1982; Froehlich, 1996; Hamilton & Bailey, 1981; Martin, 1989; Munro, 1984; Schwankovsky & Guthrie, 1982). In some cases, repeated listening to selected songs can help patients work through the pain associated with leaving loved ones (Whittall, 1991). Other music therapy approaches used in facilitating expressions of fears and emotions include drawing or painting to music, creating collages to background music, orchestrating poems or pictures or stories, lyric substitution, and song writing (Fagen, 1982; Froehlich, 1996; Hamilton & Bailey, 1981; Martin, 1989; Munro, 1984; Munro & Mount, 1978; O'Callaghan, 1996, 1997; Schwankovsky & Guthrie, 1982). Structured song writing experiences "offer creative non-intrusive opportunities for patients to connect with and process feelings at their own pace" (O'Callaghan, 1997, p. 32), while giving both verbal and musical validation to the individual's emotional expression. Music therapists who have advanced clinical training may use GIM techniques to help patients confront the emotional challenges of living with a terminal illness, discover lessons they can learn from the experiences, find resources and creative strengths within themselves, and discover incentives to continue living life to the fullest until death (Bruscia, 1991b; Skaggs, 1997c).

Finally, music therapy experiences can provide support and release in last moments of life, easing the transition to death (Clair, 1996b; Forinash & Gonzalez, 1989; Skaggs, 1997c; West, 1994). Some patients may benefit from using GIM procedures to mentally rehearse their death (Skaggs, 1997c). For many, familiar music can help provide an environment of love, support, and comfort during the last hours of life (Clair, 1996b; West, 1994). Music therapists may use a variety of techniques, including the singing and playing of precomposed songs (e.g., familiar songs that are meaningful to the patient, hymns), improvised songs, and vocal and guitar improvisation, to help relax patients who are near death and support them as they let go of life. Live performance allows the therapist to match rhythms and tempos to the patient's breathing, providing additional nonverbal support and connection.

Forinash and Gonzalez (1989) described one experience of using music to connect with and support a patient just prior to and through death. This patient, who could no longer communicate verbally and whose death was imminent, was referred to music therapy because "the staff sensed she might need support to let go of life" (p. 40). The music therapists began with simple guitar progression, gradually adding improvised "oo" and "ah" vocal sounds. During this time, the patient's breathing was deep and jerky. As they moved to structured songs with soothing melodies and lyrics focusing on love being a shelter and leaving troubles behind, the patient's breathing became softer and gentler. This continued during a transition to improvised lyrics and vocal sounds over guitar chord progressions matched to the patient's breathing. The session ended with a soft, gentle instrumental guitar improvisation, during which the patient died. Through nonverbal (changes in chord progressions, tempos, styles) and verbal (words of lyrics and improvised songs, images associated with them) means, music had supported and facilitated this patient's transition from life to death.

Therapeutic Music Experiences to Help Meet Social Needs

Songs and shared musical experiences can be very helpful in decreasing feelings of isolation and loneliness that often occur in clients who have terminal illnesses (Bright, 1986; Clair, 1996b; Edwards, 1976; Froehlich, 1996; Martin, 1989, 1991; Munro, 1984; Munro & Mount, 1978; Schwankovsky & Guthrie, 1982). As they passively or actively participate in music experiences with one or more other individuals (e.g., therapist, other patients, friends, family members), patients can interact and communicate verbally or nonverbally with others in a nonthreatening, supportive, and pleasurable atmosphere. The acts of singing or sharing familiar songs (Bailey, 1984; Hamilton & Bailey, 1981), writing

songs together (Cordobes, 1997; Froehlich, 1996; O'Callaghan, 1996, 1997), playing or improvising on instruments together (Brodsky, 1989; Bunt & Marston-Wyld, 1995; Froehlich, 1996; Martin, 1989; Schwankovsky & Guthrie, 1982), choosing songs and/or discussing song lyrics or memories associated with songs (Bailey, 1984; Bright, 1981, 1986; Clair, 1996b; Froehlich, 1996; Martin, 1989, 1991), and/or dancing/moving to music (Bright, 1981; Clair, 1986; Froehlich, 1996; Martin, 1989; Schwankovsky & Guthrie, 1982) can help establish a bond of trust between group members, increase group cohesion, and facilitate communication (verbal and nonverbal). Shared music experiences can also help bridge cultural differences (Munro, 1984; Munro & Mount, 1978), facilitate sharing of memories (Beggs, 1991; Bright, 1981, 1986; Clair, 1996b; Martin, 1989; West, 1994) and provide a socially appropriate context for touching and tactile stimulation (Clair, 1996b). In addition, group music projects like song writing or improvisations allow patients to support each other, work with others on meaningful projects, and transcend their illness, at least for a time, through creative aesthetic expression (Bunt & Marston-Wyld, 1995; Cordobes, 1997; O'Callaghan, 1996, 1997). With appropriate precautions and adaptations, shared music therapy experiences, including instrument playing, singing, song selection, song writing, lyric substitution, relaxation, imagery, and improvisation, can even be used with patients in isolation rooms (Brodsky, 1989; Froehlich, 1996). For example, Brodsky (1989) described how small portable electronic instruments (e.g., keyboard, Omnichord) could be played inside a plastic bag, thus adhering to the sanitary requirements of isolation while still allowing the patient to have a "hand-on" musical experience. This "hand-on" participation in music-making helped decrease the patient's feelings of isolation and facilitated the development of positive coping mechanisms. In addition, the act of making music provided an appropriate vehicle for emotional expression, that helped increase motivation, socialization, and ego strength.

Therapeutic Music Experiences to Help Meet Spiritual Needs

Spiritual support is an important part of hospice

care. Given that "music and religion are integrally related" (Gaston, 1968a, p. 22) and "hospice patients frequently make associations between music and spirituality" (West, 1994, p. 119), music experiences can be an important source of spiritual support for many terminally ill clients. Religious music of the patient's particular heritage and culture or inspirational music and lyrics may provide a source of comfort and reassurance for some patients (Bailey, 1984; Bright, 1981, 1986; Clair, 1996b; Gilbert, 1977; Kübler-Ross, 1974; Martin, 1989; Munro, 1984; Munro & Mount, 1978; West, 1994). Some music therapists have found that music from religious rituals can trigger awareness responses (e.g., opening eyes, turning head, speaking, smiling, becoming more relaxed) even in patients who no longer seem to be aware of or responsive to their surroundings (Clair, 1996b). Relaxing music combined with scripture readings can also provide comfort to patients with religious faith and help reinforce the idea of a spiritual self that will continue after death (Colligan, 1987). In other cases, using spiritual readings with GIM techniques may help patients come to terms with their spiritual identity (Colligan, 1987). Music therapists who work with terminally ill clients must be prepared to provide music from a variety of religions and cultures so they can use music to help meet the spiritual needs of clients from all cultural and religious backgrounds (Bright, 1986; West, 1994).

Some clients who are terminally ill may have a need for spiritual and existential exploration, expressing doubts, anger, fears, and questioning the meaning of life. Music can also provide a safe structure or container for exploring and expressing these types of feelings and questions (Bailey, 1984; Bright, 1986; Edwards, 1976; Maranto, 1988; Martin, 1989, 1991; Munro, 1984; Munro & Mount, 1978; West, 1994). Some patients may approach these feelings and questions from the lyrics of pre-composed songs (Bailey, 1984; Edwards, 1976; Martin, 1991) while other may explore them through instrumental improvisation or by writing original songs (O'Callaghan, 1996). GIM techniques may also help some patients explore the meaning of their lives, address spiritual questions, and/or prepare for death (Bruscia, 1991b; Colligan, 1987; Skaggs, 1997c).

Music Therapy with Family Members

Martin (1989) lists five ways music therapy interventions may be used with families of terminally ill patients between the time of the diagnosis of terminal illness and the time of death. *First,* music activities like singing, playing instruments, or creating music can give family members "something to do" (p. 24) with or for the patients. Beggs (1991) tells of a terminally ill patient who played the violin while his family members sang and the music therapist played the piano. This activity was very pleasurable and emotionally fulfilling for both the patient and his family members. Clair (1996b) and Martin (1991) also noted that music activities can play important roles in helping structure family members' visits with palliative care patients, thus making the visits more positive experiences for both family members and patients. Songs chosen by family members can have the added benefit of giving them meaningful emotional and cognitive connections to past pleasurable experiences with the patient or to sources of spiritual support and comfort. When music experiences help fill and enhance the time family members have with their loved ones, family members "can let go of the responsibility they feel to maintain their loved ones' comfort by allowing the music to take over" (Clair, 1996b, p. 271). Other music-based activities that family members might use to interact with their loved one include massaging or moving rhythmically with the patient to familiar music, listening to familiar music or tapes of family members playing instruments, or using songs to stimulate reminiscence and life review. Family members can also help inform the music therapist of the patient's preferences and background in music. Song choice can be another very beneficial activity for patients and family members (Bailey, 1984; Martin, 1989, 1991), helping them to broach difficult or emotional topics and enhancing their communication. For example, Bailey (1984) found that music therapy sessions in which family members and cancer patients chose songs about hope, pleasure, the world, reminiscence, needs and desires, feelings, loss and death, and peace, helped patients and family members (a) establish trust and a working relationship, (b) express feelings, needs, and desires, and (c) process issues, thoughts, and feelings. Many other music therapists have also found that songs or instrumental improvisations can be very important tools for helping patients and families express and explore emotions and ideas that seem too threatening to verbalize or express in other ways (Bailey, 1984; Bright, 1986; Clair, 1996b; Edwards, 1976; Froehlich, 1996; Gilbert, 1977; Hamilton & Bailey, 1981; Martin, 1989, 1991; Munro, 1984; Ridgway, 1983; Whittall, 1991). In other cases, combined music therapy and social work approaches can help children and adults learn more about the illness and one another's needs while creating a relaxed environment in which they can explore and express deep thoughts and emotions, share intimate feelings, and increase their coping skills (Slivka & Magill, 1986).

Secondly, music therapists can make video or audio tapes of sessions that include the patient and the family members and give the tapes to the family (Martin, 1989). These recordings can be very meaningful to family members after the patient's death, providing positive memories and giving a concrete representation of the patient's spirit (Beggs, 1991; Bright, 1986; Clair, 1996b; Martin, 1989; Whittall, 1991). *Thirdly*, music therapists can help family members use music in rituals (Martin, 1989). For example, songs and music might be used as a way of saying good-bye to family members (Froehlich, 1996; Whittall, 1991) or to support religious rituals and beliefs (Bright, 1986; Clair, 1996b; Colligan, 1987; West, 1994). Hearing or singing along with favorite or religious songs can also help family members share emotional closeness and connect with their loved one in a special way in the final moments of his or her life. These songs may evoke movement or speech responses in patients who have been unresponsive for days or weeks, which "indicate a level of conscious that families yearn to experience while they wait at the bedside of loved ones who are no longer responsive to their touch or voices" (Clair, 1996b, p. 189). *Fourthly*, Martin (1989) suggests that music can offer a way for families to connect and interact with patients who are neuropsychologically impaired. (See Chapters Eighteen and Nineteen for examples of music therapy techniques.) *Finally*, music therapists can help family members and patients plan music to be used at the patient's funeral (Martin, 1989).

In addition to facilitating family members' interactions with their loved ones, music therapy interventions can be important *self-care tools* for the family members themselves, especially for the primary caregivers. For example, music-mediated relaxation exercises can help family members deal with and manage the stress associated with caring for and being with the dying patient (Clair, 1996b). After the patient's death, music therapy interventions can also help family members through the grief process, facilitating their acceptance of the reality of the loss and their expression of the emotions of grief as well as serving a source of support and comfort (Bright, 1986; Munro, 1984; Ridgway, 1983; West, 1994). Audio or video tapes of the patient's work or collections of songs written or chosen by the patient can be important tools in providing grieving family members with positive, soothing memories of their loved one (Beggs, 1991; Bright, 1986; Clair, 1996b; Martin, 1989; Whittall, 1991). These articles might serve as transitional objects during the bereavement process, for they give those who are grieving something comforting that is a real presence of the person from whom they are now separated by death (Whittall, 1991).

Songs can be a very important tool for facilitating the expression of unresolved grief and reducing associated physical and emotional distress during times of bereavement. In fact, songs seem to be a cross-cultural means of supporting and facilitating the grieving process (Wexler, 1989). Other music therapy techniques used in bereavement follow-up include providing family members with copies of tapes they had used with the patient for relaxation or reminiscence, assisting with music for funerals or memorial services, song writing to express feelings associated with grieving or missing the loved one, listening to songs and music that affirm the positive and triumphant aspects of life and death or that affirm spiritual beliefs, lyric analysis and discussion to help survivors identify feelings and actualize their loss, music-based support groups to facilitate stress management or release of emotions, songs and music to facilitate reminiscence about the loved one, music-mediated relaxation techniques to decrease stress and/or facilitate normal sleep patterns, and attending music programs or joining music performance groups (e.g., church or community choirs) as a way of maintaining social contacts and/or developing new interests (Martin, 1989; Munro, 1984; Ridgway, 1983). Techniques such as nonverbal instrumental improvisations, music play, music/movement techniques, improvised songs or stories, and music-mediated relaxation exercises can be particularly helpful in bereavement follow-up or grief counseling sessions with children (Froehlich, 1996). In addition, music combined with grief counseling techniques and guided imagery may be used to help survivors revisit the relationship and work through issues left unresolved at the time of the patient's death (Bright,

1986). Music associated with the relationship may elicit unresolved and conflicting feelings and bring them to conscious awareness where they can be dealt with under the guidance of a trained therapist. Music therapists who use music in in-depth grief counseling should have advanced training in psychotherapeutic techniques.

SPECIAL CONSIDERATIONS AND TIPS FOR SUCCESS

Working with terminally ill clients is stressful and painful. Flexibility is essential to deal with the constantly changing condition of the patient (Fagen, 1982). Those who work with terminally ill people also need "initial and ongoing support in order to adjust to the daily confrontation with death" (Schwankovsky & Guthrie, 1982, p. 19). Because of the constant exposure to pain, suffering, sadness, and grief, therapists may at times experience emotional overload. When this happens, "it is important to seek staff support or, if necessary, to request a short respite period" (Munro, 1984, p. 83). It is also essential that those who work with terminally ill clients come to terms with their own fears of death (Bright, 1986; Kübler-Ross, 1969; Martin, 1989; Munro, 1984; Schwankovsky & Guthrie, 1982; West, 1994).

> To work with the dying patients requires a certain maturity which only comes from experience. We have to take a good hard look at our own attitudes toward death and dying before we can sit quietly and without anxiety next to a terminally ill patient. (Kübler-Ross, 1969, p. 269)

Music therapists must also realize that although music therapy may diminish the impact of the crises associated with death and dying and thus facilitate the client's continuing adjustment to dealing with terminal illness and impending death, music therapy will not necessarily resolve all these crises (Munro, 1984). Thus, while music therapists must take risks in order to motivate and challenge terminally ill clients, they must also "be wary of delving into patient and family issues which cannot be resolved" (Munro, 1984, p. 79). It may be beneficial for music therapists to remember that creative life need not be dismissed

as secondary in times of severe illness, but that it can share equal importance with other physical and intellectual needs (Bright, 1986; Fagen, 1982; Froehlich, 1996; Martin, 1989; Munro, 1984; O'Callaghan, 1996, 1997; Schwankovsky & Guthrie, 1982; Skaggs, 1997c; Wylie & Blom, 1986). Music therapy can help build up the client's sense of personhood by speaking to these creative needs and dealing with that creative part of the client's life that still may be a symbol of health and vitality. As Munro (1984) wrote: "Music reflects the depth of experience of humanity and is accessible to the uniqueness in each person. The challenge for the music therapist in terminal care lies in searching for ways to link the uniqueness of music with the uniqueness of the dying patient" (p. 33).

Music therapists who work with terminally ill patients focus on supporting and encouraging the patients, offering them choices that will give them some degree of control over their situation and providing experiences that will help them to live to the fullest until death (Bright, 1986; Bruscia, 1991; Froehlich, 1996; Martin, 1989, 1991; Munro, 1994; Schwankovsky & Guthrie, 1982; West, 1994; Whittall, 1991). Music therapists must continually assess the patient to determine which particular tasks of living or dying are most important to him or her at that particular point in time (West, 1994). "It is important to give the person space, and to take cues form him or her as to the content and depth of music therapy sessions" (Whittall, 1991, p. 610). Music therapists must also be sensitive to the individual's perceptions, defenses, receptiveness to music therapy, cultural background, and religious or spiritual beliefs so they can provide appropriate support through music (Bright, 1986; Munro, 1984; Schwankovsky & Guthrie, 1982; West, 1994).

Moreover, music therapists will be able to plan more effective support and intervention strategies if they have technical knowledge about the patient's illness and treatment procedures (including isolation or infection control procedures if applicable), as well as what the illness means to the patient and the family (in physical, psychological, social, spiritual, and financial terms) (Bright, 1986; Maranto, 1988; Martin, 1989; West, 1994). In addition, since the family, not just the patient, is the unit of care in hospice settings, music therapists may be concerned with providing support and comfort to family members as well, helping them accept and adjust to the patient's deteriorating condition, facilitating communication and interaction with their loved one, and assisting them during the period of bereavement as necessary (Bailey, 1984; Bright, 1986; Martin, 1991; Munro, 1984; West, 1994).

SUMMARY

Individuals who are terminally ill have been diagnosed with some fatal, incurable disease or condition. When people are terminally ill, they usually receive palliative care rather than active, aggressive medical treatment. Palliative care serves to alleviate the distressful symptoms of the disease or condition (e.g., reduces pain as much as possible) but does not strive for a cure. Hospice programs coordinate supportive and palliative services from a variety of professionals and disciplines to help meet the total needs (physical, psychological, social, emotional, and spiritual) of terminally ill individuals and their families. Health care for individuals who are terminally ill emphasizes (1) managing pain and related symptoms to decrease suffering and maximize comfort; (2) helping individuals maintain independent physical function and encouraging them to live life as fully as possible; (3) providing patients and family members with information on the patient's illness and care (including what to expect as the illness progresses), along with the reassurance that everything possible is being done; and (4) attending to the emotional and spiritual needs of patients and family members, supporting them rather than abandoning them. The overall goal of treatment is to enhance and maintain the individual's quality of life until the moment of death, thus facilitating the adaptation of the individual's family. Individuals who are terminally ill may receive special programs and services to help meet their specific needs in a variety of settings, including nursing homes, hospitals, clinics, private homes, and inpatient or home-based hospice programs.

Music, with its ability to affect all aspects of a person's being, enhance emotional expression, and facilitate interactions between and among people, can be a very powerful and beneficial tool in helping patients and their families deal with the physical, psychological, social, and spiritual effects and challenges of the various phases of terminal illnesses. Many music therapy techniques, such as music listening, Guided Imagery and Music (GIM) music-mediated relaxation, music and massage, discussion of music or music experiences, song choice, lyric interpretation and discussion, song writing, lyric substitution, singing or instrumental performance, music improvisation, use of music vibrations (from instruments, tuning forks, or mattresses/chairs that provide a kinesthetic experience of music vibrations), selecting/writing songs or taping musical performance as a lasting gift or legacy to friends/family members, and music-facilitated life review, have been used effectively with both children and adults who have terminal illnesses. Benefits of music therapy interventions for individuals with terminal illnesses include

- decreasing pain,
- facilitating relaxation,
- diminishing and providing a means of managing stress and anxiety,
- providing enjoyment and recreation,
- providing an increased sense of control over one's life,
- decreasing depression,
- facilitating emotional expression and providing a safe container to hold and organize all kinds of feelings,
- providing psychological and/or spiritual support,
- increasing interaction and communication with

family members,
- identifying and eliciting strengths and coping resources,
- stimulating reminiscence and life review,
- reinforcing identity and strengthening self-concept,
- providing outlets for creativity and self-expression,
- renewing interest in life,
- increasing self-esteem, and
- easing the transition from life to death.

In addition, music therapy interventions can provide stress relief and emotional or spiritual support to family members, enhance or facilitate their interactions with the patient, assist them in understanding and accepting their loved one's illness, and support them during the period of bereavement. This chapter provided several specific examples of various music therapy experiences that might be used to help meet (a) physical needs, (b) psychological needs, (c) social needs, or (d) spiritual needs of individuals who have terminal illnesses. Several types of music therapy experiences that could be useful for family members of terminally ill patients, both before and after the patient's death, were also presented.

QUESTIONS FOR THOUGHT AND DISCUSSION

1. What is meant by palliative care? Briefly describe the main features of hospice programs. What are the implications for music therapy programming in these settings?

2. Discuss some of the special characteristics and needs of individuals who are terminally ill. What are the primary emphases of health care for children or adults who are terminally ill? What implications do these characteristics/needs and emphases have for music therapy programming?

3. Discuss some of the special characteristics and needs of the family members of individuals who are terminally ill. What implications do these have for music therapy programming?

4. Why and how are music experiences useful in making contact with individuals who have terminal illnesses? Are some types of experiences and activities more useful than other? Which ones? Why?

5. Describe some specific music therapy experiences that might be used to help meet (a) physical needs, (b) psychological needs, (c) social needs, or (d) spiritual needs of individuals who have terminal illnesses. What unique benefits does music provide in each of these areas?

6. Describe some ways music therapy experiences might be used with family members of terminally ill patients, before and after the patient's death. What unique benefits does music provide in each of these areas?

7. List several special considerations that may be important to remember when working with persons who have terminal illnesses. Why are these important? What are their implications for the structure of music therapy intervention strategies?

8. For each of the situations listed below, (a) define the problem or areas of need for the client or group of clients, (b) describe one or more of the goals you might pursue in music therapy sessions with the client(s), (c) describe music activities you might use to help the client(s) meet those goals, (d) tell how the music activities you described relate to the goals and needs of the client(s), and (e) mention any special considerations you might want to take into account when working with the client(s).

Situation 1:
   Mrs. Keith is a 73-year-old woman with terminal cancer. Her cancer is inoperable, and radiation and chemotherapy treatments have been ineffective. She is in great pain, very weak, and bedridden. She often asks why God just doesn't let her die, as she's lived a long life and is now in so much pain. Mrs. Keith has few visitors. When her family comes, they stay only a few minutes, stand

nervously at the foot of her bed, and try to cheer her up with small talk. One time, just after the family had left, a nurse came in and found Mrs. Keith sobbing softly to herself. When the nurse asked what was wrong, Mrs. Keith just put her lips tightly together and turned toward the wall. Her social history shows that Mrs. Keith has enjoyed music throughout her life, so her doctor prescribed music therapy sessions to try to help Mrs. Keith communicate with her family, facilitate her emotional expression, and provide her with support and comfort.

Situation 2:

Mr. Jones is 46 years old and has terminal cancer. He has been discharged from the hospital and is now receiving home hospice care services. Mr. Jones is married and has three children, ages 15, 12, and 7. He feels sad and guilty about no longer being able to take care of his wife and children and about leaving them without a husband and father. He is searching for ways to stay involved in their lives as much as he can while preparing them for life without him. He would like to leave them some sort of legacy and/or happy memory of their times with him. Mr. Jones is also in a lot of physical pain. He does not like the way the pain medication makes him feel groggy and drowsy, so he is interested in finding alternate means of pain management.

Situation 3:

You have been asked to provide music therapy services for a group of terminally ill patients who are not imminently dying but who must be hospitalized for short periods to receive various treatments. They have needs for diversional or enjoyable activities so they do not have to focus constantly on their illness during their hospital stay. They also need programs that will help decrease their anxiety about treatment procedures. In addition, many of these individuals are looking for creative, meaningful activities to make their life still seem worthwhile and help them put the time they have left to good use.

Situation 4:

A social worker from a local hospice program has just started a support groups for family members of terminally ill patients. The group will meet twice a month to discuss issues related to living with and caring for a terminally ill family member. The social worker has heard that music can facilitate discussion of emotionally-laden, difficult issues, and has asked you to help lead this group.

SUGGESTIONS FOR FURTHER READING

Bailey, L. M. (1984). The use of songs in music therapy with cancer patients and their families. *Music Therapy, 4*(1), 5-17.

Bright, R. (1986). *Grieving: A handbook for those who care*. St. Louis: MMB Music.

Bruscia, K. E. (Ed.) (1991). *Case studies in music therapy*. Phoenixville, PA: Barcelona Publishers.

Bunt, L., & Marston-Wyld, J. (1995). Where words fail music takes over: A collaborative study by a music therapist and a counselor in the context of cancer care. *Music Therapy Perspectives, 13*(1), 46-50.

Colligan, K. G. (1987). Music therapy and hospice care. In B. Karras (Ed.), *"You bring out the music in me": Music in nursing homes* (pp. 103-122). Binghamton, NY: Haworth Press.

Cordobes, T. K. (1997). Group song writing as a method for developing group cohesion for HIV-seropositive adult patients with depression. *Journal of Music Therapy, 34*(1), 46-67.

Curtis, S. L. (1986). The effect of music on pain relief and relaxation of the terminally ill. *Journal of Music Therapy, 23*(1), 10-24.

Fagen, T. S. (1982). Music therapy in the treatment of anxiety and fear in terminal pediatric patients. *Music Therapy, 2*(1), 13-23.

Forinash, M., & Gonzalez, D. (1989). A phenomenological perspective of music therapy. *Music Therapy, 8*(1), 35-36.

Froehlich, M. A. R. (Ed.). (1996). Section V: Terminal illness. In M. A. R. Froehlich (Ed.), *Music therapy with hospitalized children: A creative arts child life approach* (pp. 207-242). Cherry Hill, NJ: Jeffrey Books.

Gilbert, J. P. (1977). Music therapy perspectives on death and dying. *Journal of Music Therapy, 14*(4), 165-171.

Maranto, C. D. (1988). AIDS: Information and issues for music therapists. *Music Therapy Perspectives, 5*, 78-81.

Martin, J. A. (Ed.)-(1989). *The next step forward: Music*

therapy with the terminally ill. Bronx, NY: Calvary Hospital.

Munro, S. (1984). *Music therapy in palliative/hospice care.* St. Louis: Magnamusic-Baton.

O'Callaghan, C. C. (1996). Lyrical themes in songs written by palliative care patients. *Journal of Music Therapy, 33*(2), 74-92.

O'Callaghan, C. C. (1997). Therapeutic opportunities associated with the music when using song writing in palliative care. *Music Therapy Perspectives, 15*(1), 32-38.

Schwankovsky, L. M., & Guthrie, P. T. (1982). *Music therapy for handicapped children: Other health impaired.* Washington, D.C.: National Association for Music Therapy.

Skaggs, R. (1997). The Bonny method of guided imagery

and music in the treatment of terminal illness: A private practice setting. *Music Therapy Perspectives, 15*(1), 39-44.

Slivka, H. H., & Magill, L. (1986). The conjoint use of social work and music therapy in working with children of cancer patients. *Music Therapy, 6A*(1), 30-40.

Standley, J. (1991). *Music techniques in therapy, counseling, and special education.* St. Louis: MMB Music.

Standley, J. M. (1992). Clinical applications of music and chemotherapy: The effects on nausea and emesis. *Music Therapy Perspectives, 10*(1), 27-35.

West, T. M. (1994). Psychological issues in hospice music therapy. *Music Therapy Perspectives, 12*(2), 117-124.

Wylie, M. E., & Blom, R. C. (1986). Guided imagery and music with hospice patients. *Music Therapy Perspectives, 3,* 25-28.

Chapter Twenty-one

MUSIC THERAPY TO PROMOTE HEALTH AND WELL-BEING IN THE GENERAL POPULATION

DEFINITION

IN A NARROW sense, *health* is often defined as the absence of disease, infirmity, or abnormality. However, in recent decades, the concept of health has expanded so that mere absence of disease alone does not necessarily constitute health. In the broad sense, then, health may be defined as a state of optimal functioning and complete mental, physical, and social well-being (Purtilo, 1978; World Health Organization, 1964). Others view health not as an all-or-nothing state of wellness or illness, but as something that exists on a continuum, from optimum health to suboptimal health to overt illness or disability to approaching death to death (Itoh & Lee, 1989). Most people move back and forth along this continuum throughout their lives, although they are always striving to maintain optimum health. In general, the task of medical professionals, then, is to help individuals maintain good health and to cure those who become ill in as short a time as possible (Itoh & Lee, 1989).

The increased emphasis on health and wellness in recent years has led members of the medical community to focus more on *preventative medicine*, which strives to help individuals maintain optimum health. From the preventative point of view, "good medical care acts on a person's health rather than reacting to a person's health problems" (Itoh & Lee,

1989, p. 27). *Follow-up care* provided to an individual after acute medical treatment may also be considered part of wellness or preventative services, for this follow-up care aims to help an individual achieve and maintain the highest possible degree of health and independent functioning (Purtilo, 1978).

In recent decades, increased awareness of and interest in holistic medicine and alternative healing practices have also helped focus the public's attention not just on curing disease but on striving for and maintaining optimum wellness by "adopting a life style that focuses on health" (Scovel, 1990, p. 105). The *holistic* (or wholistic) view proposes an integrated approach to health and wellness, in which body, mind, and spirit are seen as integrated parts of the whole system. Holistic medicine treats the whole person (body, mind, and spirit), not just the symptoms or disease (Scovel, 1990; Trevisan, 1978). It encourages individuals to take responsibility for their own health and stresses self-care, self-help, prevention, and striving for optimum wellness and balance in all areas of life (Adelman, 1985; Scovel, 1990; Trevisan, 1978). Holistic practices focus on the individual and encourage furthering of one's potential, self-awareness, and growth through finding answers within one's self (Bonny, 1986; Scovel, 1990; Summer & Summer, 1996).

COMMON CHARACTERISTICS, PROBLEMS, AND NEEDS OF CLIENTS

Those people in the general population who are basically healthy may need to find life styles that will

help them maintain optimum health and independent functioning. General needs often include maintaining healthy diet and exercise regimens, having adequate social, emotional, and spiritual support systems, developing coping strategies and creative problem-solving techniques to weather difficult times that may occur, finding ways to manage stress and relieve frustration, and having outlets for creative or emotional expression. According to Maslow (1968), when more basic needs (e.g., food and shelter, safety, love and belongingness, self-esteem) are met, individuals strive for self-actualization and the full realization of all their potentialities. Some individuals in the general population, therefore, may be interested in finding tools for personal growth and increased self-awareness and personal fulfillment. Many individuals also desire experiences that add meaning, joy, or beauty to their lives.

Specific characteristics and needs of older individuals who are healthy, have adequate economic resources, and lead active lives were discussed in detail in Chapter Nineteen. Some of these characteristics and needs may be applicable to people in other age groups as well.

SETTINGS FOR SERVICE DELIVERY

Health and wellness programs and services for the general public are found in variety of settings, including hospital-sponsored programs, community health fairs, park and recreation programs, workshops and seminars, fitness centers, wellness centers, stress reduction clinics, schools or community colleges, corporate wellness programs, and churches or community centers. Individual service providers may also work in private practice, contracting their services to individuals or groups. Music therapists could possibly work in any of these settings, providing direct or consultant services and working with clients as individuals or in groups (Peters, 1989). In addition, music therapists may provide services through music stores or music studios or in private practice settings. In a recent survey of work settings of music therapists (AMTA, 1998), only 39 of 1,654 respondents specifically said they worked in wellness programs or wellness centers. Thus, while some music therapists are beginning to work in this area of practice, it is one that still may have great potential for growth.

HOW MUSIC IS USED IN THERAPY

The arts can be a part of health maintenance and prevention. They can offset the meaningless that induces senility, and prevent a youngster's involvement with drugs and crime. . . . Perhaps someday doctors will prescribe some involvement in the arts just as they now tell pre-coronary patients to change their diet, relax, or ease their work schedules. (Spencer, 1978, p. 9)

One of the pioneers of music therapy, Willem van de Wall, was advocating the use of music for wellness as early as the 1930s. Van de Wall believed that music could not only provide aesthetic satisfaction for adults in the general population but also enhance "muscle relaxation, emotional expression, and relief from routine, which could lead to increased efficiency when responsibilities were resumed" (Clair & Heller, 1989, p. 173). In recent years, music therapists have given increasing attention to ways they can expand their services beyond the institutional setting and clients with disabilities to also promote health and wellness in the general population (Broucek, 1987; Clair, 1996b; Clark & Ficken, 1988; Peters, 1989). Chapter Nineteen has already described several ways music therapists are helping maintain and promote health in well elderly people by therapeutically structuring music experiences to provide opportunities for finding new roles, meaningful and challenging activities, mental and physical stimulation, appropriate and enjoyable social experiences, and new ways to contribute to society.

As Chapter Three noted, the use of music as

preventative medicine and as a strengthener of health and character made a resurgence in the United States in the latter part of the twentieth century. The holistic health movement, with its focus on interdependence of body, mind, and spirit for maintaining health and well-being, has generated interest in ancient healing practices using music and in contemporary ways to use music to facilitate healing, relaxation, centering, stress reduction, emotional release, consciousness expansion, and the highest possible state of well-being (Bonny, 1986; Bonny & Savary, 1973, 1990; Campbell, 1988, 1991a, 1991b; Crowe, 1991; Feder & Feder, 1981; Goldman, 1988; Halpern, 1978, 1989; Hamel, 1976/1979; Harvey, 1987, 1991; Kenny, 1982; Trevisan, 1978). The therapeutic use of music is finding its way into the board rooms and wellness programs of businesses, hospitals, and major corporations as employers recognize the need to reduce stress, alleviate staff burnout, and promote wellness, and seek innovative and effective ways to encourage team work and enhance creativity (Clark & Ficken, 1988; Mandel, 1996; McCarthy, 1992; Weitz, 1993). The medical community is also beginning to recognize the important role music and the arts can play in preventive care and health maintenance (Guzzetta, 1991; Itoh & Lee, 1989; Spencer, 1978). For example, medical doctors Itoh and Lee (1989) observed:

> If food is a nutrient for the body, music is for the mind. . . . As music is closely related to human well-being, it does have therapeutic value. In the total concept of health care, music therapy should be recognized as another modality for Prevention and Health Promotion. (p. 28)

Music educators, too, are beginning to recognize the lifelong health benefits of music and are finding ways to help people enjoy music throughout their lives (Boswell, 1992; Bowles, 1991; Clair, 1996b; Coates, 1984; Darrough, 1992; Davidson, 1980; Ernst & Emmons, 1992; Gibbons, 1985, 1988; Kellman, 1986; Logan, 1996; Myers, 1992).

Previous chapters have shown how music experiences are highly adaptable to various populations, kinds of involvement, situations, and needs. With its ability to structure order out of chaos and be a transcendent event (Crowe, 1991; Spencer, 1978),

music can "match an individual's level of functioning whatever it may be and help the person move toward the wholeness of healing" (Crowe, 1991, p. 119). Music is also a natural vehicle for addressing the whole person (body, mind, and spirit). Since "people can enjoy participating in music at every stage of life" (Logan, 1996, p. 42), music can be an important tool for promoting wellness and productively channeling creativity in the general population with individuals of all ages.

> Even though music may not be the natural vehicle for everyone's creativity, it can be an experimental ground in which to try out creative processes and apply them through a powerful medium. (Kenny, 1982, pp. 79-80)

Music experiences can help individuals in the general population maintain health and well-being in many ways. Sometimes, individuals will be able to use music in therapeutic or beneficial ways for themselves, as when they listen to certain types of music to relax or lift their spirits or when they listen to music while they are jogging or when they play musical instruments to release tension. However, this is not truly music therapy, since it does not have the interaction between therapist, client, and music (Priestley, 1985; see also Chapter One). At other times, music experiences will be more beneficial if they are structured by and performed under the direction or supervision of a trained music therapist, who bases interventions on an assessment of the unique needs of the particular individual or individuals and adapts programs to their specific responses.

People who wish to use music to increase their total health must realize that sound and music can have both positive and negative effects (Harvey, 1987). In addition, certain experiences, like Guided Imagery and Music (GIM), can sometimes bring up painful issues that are best dealt with under the guidance of a trained therapist (Bonny, 1989, 1994). The next sections of this chapter provide some examples of music experiences that can facilitate relaxation and reduce stress, decrease isolation and facilitate cooperative interactions, improve coping and problem-solving abilities, promote healthy habits and behaviors, humanize the environment, and expand consciousness and increase personal awareness. All these experiences can play a role in helping people in the general population reach a state of optimal functioning and complete mental, physical, and social well-being.

Music Experiences for Relaxation and Stress Reduction

"Historically, the most widely accepted application of music as a therapeutic agent is its use as a calming agent to combat anxiety, tension, and stress" (Taylor, 1997, p. 102). As previous chapters (especially Fourteen, Fifteen, Sixteen, Seventeen, Eighteen, Nineteen, Twenty) have already discussed, music can be an important tool in facilitating relaxation and stress reduction, both for individuals with various disabilities and for their caregivers. Many of these same music-mediated relaxation and stress reduction techniques will also work very well for most people in the general population.

Listening to specially chosen music (e.g., music that is familiar and has pleasant, calming, or uplifting associations) may by itself help improve emotional states and allay anxiety in some situations (Giles et al., 1991). In fact, biomedical research has shown that "music has a direct effect on physiological processes whose functional variations are indicators of anxiety, tension, or stress" (Taylor, 1997, p. 103). However, not all music categorized as relaxing will have the same effect on all listeners (Guzzetta, 1991; Hadsell, 1989; Hanser, 1985; Logan & Roberts, 1984; Stratton & Zalanowski, 1984; Taylor, 1973, 1997), and "depending on the individual's psychophysiology, mind state, and mood, music can produce different feelings at different times" (Guzzetta, 1991, p. 161). Music therapists, therefore, can play an important role in helping individuals learn how to select the most effective music for relaxation and stress management at various times in their lives. Since research indicates that music specifically composed or marketed for relaxation is no more effective in reducing tension than music personally selected by the individual (Thaut & Davis, 1993) and that music preferred by the individual generally best facilitates his or her relaxation (Hadsell, 1989; Hanser, 1985; Taylor, 1973), music therapists can often help individuals find appropriate selections from their preferred type of music. In addition, music therapists can help individuals experience a variety of types and styles of music that may help them relax effectively. Music therapists may also help individuals learn more about ways music can affect moods and attitudes (Giles et al., 1991; Harvey, 1991) and facilitate their exploration of additional techniques, such as imagery, biofeedback, or progressive muscle relaxation, that can be combined with music listening to facilitate relaxation and decrease tension (Scartelli, 1989).

Music listening can be combined with many specific group or individual and relaxation training techniques. These include: (1) *music with progressive muscle relaxation training* (appropriate relaxing music is paired with progressive muscle relaxation techniques; music becomes a conditioned stimulus for relaxation), (2) *music for surface relaxation* (individuals learn to select music with characteristics that will help them relax and provide temporary relief from anxiety or stress), (3) *music imagery* (listening to music in a relaxed state with therapist-suggested open-ended scenarios to promote imagery or aid concentration or relaxation), and (4) *music-centered relaxation* (music is used as a stimulus or focus to divert individuals' attention from unpleasant thoughts and to block out feelings of anxiety, fear, or tension) (Unkefer, 1990). In these approaches, individuals usually learn relaxation exercises through repetition with guidance from the therapist, and then are encouraged to include the exercises in their daily lives for self-maintenance.

Music can also facilitate relaxation responses to biofeedback relaxation techniques (Scartelli, 1989; Scartelli & Borling, 1986; Wagner, 1975). For example, Scartelli and Borling (1986) found that, when sedative music was used with biofeedback, both subject reports and microvolt readings showed that the music "maintained and in many cases fostered an enhanced state of relaxation" (p. 163). Subjects in this study reported that music helped keep their minds from wandering, facilitated relaxation, and was a positive part of the procedure.

Music therapists who have appropriate special training (see Chapter Twenty-two) may use the Bonny Method of Guided Imagery and Music (GIM) to help individuals decrease anxiety, facilitate relaxation, and increase feelings of well-being (Bonny 1978b, 1986, 1989; Bonny & Savary, 1990; Gregoire et al., 1989; Hammer, 1996). Hammer (1996) found that state anxiety, or perceived situational stress, decreased significantly in subjects in a GIM group, indicating GIM could be an effective intervention for persons dealing with acute or chronic stress. In addition, Hammer's research indicated that GIM programs "may have an overall effect on improving one's ability to react to stress, improving concentration and general contentment, and improving one's ability to relax in general" (p. 67). Thus, GIM may help a person gain and maintain a state of optimal health.

Active participation in singing or playing instruments, dancing or creative movement, or writing songs can also provide important forms of emotional release, helping reduce stress and discharge tension. For example, Priestley (1985) suggested that individuals use improvisational drumming as a means of releasing physical tension. Creative improvisation and composition activities based on the Orff-Schulwerk approach (see Chapter Twenty-two) can also help relieve stress and tension (Gregoire et al., 1989). In addition, the pleasant social interaction involved in music experiences like playing or singing in ensembles and the cathartic effect of releasing repressed emotions through singing or playing instruments may help people "de-stress" (Clynes, 1991, p. 135). Lyric discussion, song writing, and instrumental improvisation exercises could also be used to help individuals identify stressors and stress reactions, explore emotions, and develop positive coping and stress management techniques.

Music Experiences to Decrease Isolation and Facilitate Cooperative Interactions

Since the dawn of time, one of the primary functions of music has been as communal activity. People have always gathered together to make music as a group experience, sharing the joyous spirit and life energy inherent in the creation of music. (Goldman, 1988, p. 31.)

Group music experiences are still prevalent in society today. They can decrease isolation by giving people a reason to get together: to listen to music, to go to concerts, to practice or perform, to dance, to learn and discuss (e.g., music appreciation or theory classes). Throughout life, music experiences can offer many opportunities for positive interactions with others and for volunteer opportunities (e.g., mentoring younger students, involvement in church or community choirs and instrumental ensembles, helping with paperwork or publicity for school or community groups), things which research shows are vital components of good health (Logan, 1996). Especially as they actively make music together, people find they "are not singular, isolated units, but rather an interrelated web of unified beings whose purpose is to work together as one" (Goldman, 1988, p. 32). Thus, interesting and meaningful non-threatening group music experiences can turn indifference and isolation into interest and involvement. One study demonstrated how gifted students, who were isolated, vulnerable, and interacted poorly with others, learned to work together cooperatively, share ideas and feelings, and improve their self-concept through music therapy experiences using GIM and Orff-Schulwerk techniques (Gregoire et al., 1989). Another study showed that group singing increased trust and cooperation among group members significantly more than music listening, games, or film viewing (Anshel & Kipper, 1988).

In ancient cultures, music and dance were part of communal ceremonies and rituals that helped the group maintain the health, well-being, and identity of their community (Kenny, 1982). Some people today are also taking an interest in finding ways to use music for the health and good of society in general. For example, the organization Music Therapists for Peace was founded in 1988. The members of this worldwide movement sponsor various projects and activities, with the aim of "making more conscious use of the possibilities of music to promote healing and unite people" (Moreno, 1992, p. 87). Perhaps, "if the nations of our world were willing to play a new kind of music together that allows for the beauty of each unique player to remain while creating a unified and harmonious piece that has room for all," (Hesser, 1995, p. 49), they could also learn to live and work together in peace.

Music Experiences to Improve Coping Strategies and Problem-Solving Skills

In the mid-1930s, Willem van de Wall, one of music therapy's early pioneers in the United States, "spoke of music as a means for adults to be physically, mentally, and culturally developed despite the ever-increasing burdens of life" (Clair & Heller, 1989, p. 173). Throughout history, people have used songs and music to help lift their spirits and cope with difficult life situations (Kenny, 1982; Peters, 1989). Even today, involvement in various kinds of music experiences (singing, playing, listening, moving, creating), can help people experience beauty, joy, personal satisfaction, and meaning that lifts them, at least for a time, above and beyond their not-so-pleasant life situations (Taylor et al., 1997; Whitwell, 1993). Studies have shown that children and adolescents who are "at risk" often respond more positively to music experiences than to verbal interventions or traditional teaching methods (Staum, 1993; Taylor et al., 1997; see also Chapter Fourteen). For all people, participation in structured singing, instrumental, listening, movement-to-music, or improvisation/composition experiences can stimulate creativity, help sustain a sense of wonder and curiosity (something people often lose after childhood), lead people to see problems in new ways and find innovative solutions, and give people courage to improvise, experiment, explore alternatives, and try different things (Kenny, 1982; Taylor et al., 1997; Whitwell, 1993). Even major corporations are now using music experiences such as drum circles to help increase creative problem solving, break pre-existing molds and barriers, and facilitate innovative thinking (Weitz, 1993).

Music therapists have also found that music therapy experiences can be effective crisis intervention and prevention techniques. For example, having individuals improvise music that expresses feelings or conflicts about an anticipated or recently experienced traumatic event may help them maintain or regain an accurate reality perspective, while shared group music experiences (e.g., active listening and discussion, singing, group improvisations) can provide needed support from others (Luetje, 1989). In addition, structured experiences involving lyric analysis, song writing, improvisation, and music-assisted guided imagery may (a) assist with cognitive and emotional processing of the crisis event, (b) lead individuals to discover alternative solutions or responses, (c) help individuals find new ways of coping, (d) increase identification and awareness of inner strengths, and (3) facilitate the internalization of affirmative messages (Luetje, 1989).

Governments, too, are recognizing the power of music to help people cope with difficult situations. For example, during the 1991 Persian Gulf War, the Israeli Broadcasting Authority intentionally used music to help its citizens cope with the crisis, playing songs stressing strength and national unity, using parodies of popular tunes to give specific instructions for safety and defense preparations, and broadcasting soothing, nostalgic music during attacks to help reduce fear and anxiety (Brodsky, 1991). During the war, only Hebrew songs were broadcast, and special children's music was played in the evening to help the children cope with the stress and trauma of the situation. In these ways, "through mass communication, the power of music was used to assist the entire population in developing more adaptive coping methods, which included instilling feelings of national unity and establishing support systems" (Brodsky, 1991, p. 99).

Music Experiences to Promote Healthy Habits and Behaviors

As they strive for improved health and well-being, many people know the things they should do, but have difficulty making these things a regular part of their lives. Exercise, for example, is often perceived as being boring and tedious. Adding music to the exercise, however, may make it more enjoyable and provide the needed motivation to participate in and sustain exercise (Beckett, 1990; Brody, 1988; Gfeller, 1988). According to NASA, music can promote compliance with exercise routines, decrease the tedium of repeated movements, and help individuals attain the desired level of intensity (Brody, 1988). Gfeller (1988) found that music helped young adults increase their motivation, pacing, strength, and endurance during aerobic activities. Beckett (1990) reported that individuals who listened to music walked farther and with less effort than when they exercised without music. Other research has found that people who listen to music during exercise perceive the exercise as being less stressful (Brody, 1988). Moreover, music with phrases and tempos that correspond to those of the physical movement can facilitate muscle coordination and rhythmic movement (see Chapter Eleven). In fact, many cultures historically have used marching songs and work songs to decrease fatigue, increase rhythmicity and fluidity of movement, and help lessen injury (Itoh & Lee, 1989). The music best facilitates exercise when it (a) matches the individual preferences of the person who will be doing the exercise, (b) provides appropriate rhythmic and structural support for the movement, and (c) evokes pleasant associations (Gfeller, 1988).

Many music activities, such as singing, playing instruments, conducting, dancing/creative movement-to-music, are also in and of themselves enjoyable forms of physical activity that can provide exercise for the circulatory and respiratory systems and various muscle groups. These activities, as well as music therapy interventions involving listening and discussion or improvisation and discussion, can also be used to help individuals identify healthy life style patterns and coping techniques and increase compliance with exercise routines (Beckett, 1990; Mandel, 1996). In addition, some research indicates that involvement in music listening, music and imagery, and music therapy interventions that provide patients with active coping strategies and promote self-expression can enhance immune system responses (Bartlett et al., 1993; Lane, 1991, 1994; Rider, 1985; Robb, 1996; Taylor, 1997; Tsao et al., 1991; see also Chapter Seventeen). Halpern (1989) even speculated that as the emphasis in health care shifts to individuals taking a more conscious and active role in their own healing and growth, health specialists may begin "prescribing a proven therapeutic listening program for home or institutional follow-up" (p. 80).

Carefully chosen background music may also assist people trying to control their eating habits. Some research has shown that relaxing music can help decrease the number of bites per minute, causing people to eat more slowly and consume less food, while fast music made them chew faster and eat more ("Eating," 1991). Even though they ate less food, individuals who dined to slower music reported feeling fuller and more satisfied than they did when dining to no music or fast music.

Finally, structured music therapy interventions can precipitate the development of more healthy behavior patterns in individuals who are "at risk" for various reasons, by increasing their self-esteem and motivation, providing a form of emotional support

and emotional or creative expression, and decreasing depression and isolation (Shiraishi, 1997; Spencer, 1978; Taylor et al., 1997; Whitwell, 1993). For example, Shiraishi (1997) developed a home-based music therapy program for multirisk mothers who were experiencing high levels of distress, low self-esteem, and depression. Clients consulted with a music therapist to choose and be instructed in the use of one or more taped music programs, which they then implemented at home. The music therapist contacted clients weekly by phone or visit to discuss progress and determine whether any changes or additions would be made. General formats of available music programs included (1) familiar, upbeat music for gentle exercise to decrease muscle tension, (2) pleasant, calming familiar vocal or instrumental music to be used with gentle facial massage to decrease face and neck tension, (3) slow instrumental music for progressive muscle relaxation and full body relaxation, (4) preferred calming music for deeper relaxation after programs 1, 2, or, 3, to facilitate sleep, and (5) energetic, rhythmic music for more vigorous exercise. The majority of the participants enjoyed the music protocol and found the techniques helpful in decreasing stress, decreasing depression and increasing self-esteem. "Participants reported a sense of pride that they were able to do something positive and enjoyable for themselves" (Shiraishi, 1997, p. 21). In addition, some of these multirisk mothers found that "the music was able to help them interact more positively with their children, a skill that all the mothers acknowledged was important" (p. 21).

Music Experiences to Humanize the Environment

In a world that is becoming increasingly computerized and mechanized, human beings still need and long for experiences that speak to the imaginative, creative, feelingful side of their life (Leonhard, 1982; Whitwell, 1993). Music has been recognized by societies and cultures throughout history as an important vehicle for giving expression to feelings and imagination and for connecting human beings to each other (Gaston, 1968a; Kenny, 1982; Merriam, 1964; Radocy & Boyle, 1988). Music both evokes aesthetic responses and provides a vehicle for creative expression of beauty, meaning, and order (Gaston, 1968a; Radocy & Boyle, 1988). Therefore, music programs that stimulate imagination, creativity, feelingful thought, and thoughtful feeling, can do much to restore humanness and "counter the sterility, the depersonalization, the retreat into isolation that pervade contemporary society" (Leonhard, 1982, p. 24).

Chapter Five has already shown how music is an essential part of human behavior and discussed some ways that music provides unique forms of emotional expression, aesthetic and creative experiences, and enjoyment and personal gratification. In addition, Chapters Seventeen to Twenty have described some ways music can help "humanize" sterile medical environments by providing experiences that speak to the psychoemotional needs of patients and by masking stress-producing sounds of medical machinery. These chapters also discussed ways music experiences could provide necessary diversion from the more stressful or painful aspects of treatment or therapy, help patients relate to aspects of their lives that were outside of the treatment setting, and provide expression for those parts of the patient that were still intact and healthy.

In the general population, too, appropriate background music can help mask stressful and annoying environmental noises, help aid concentration and improve work capacity, and positively influence moods and behaviors (Clearwater, 1985; Prueter & Mezzano, 1973; Radocy & Boyle, 1988). Scientists have also recognized the powerful physical, mental, and emotional effects music can have and have used music as a stimulus to provide sensory variety and set the proper moods for various work and rest activities aboard space stations (Clearwater, 1985). In addition, people are becoming more aware of the facts that high noise levels can increase stress and damage hearing (Brody, 1982; Jaret, 1991; Ponte, 1989) and are learning to structure their "sonic environment" in ways that promote rather than detract from health (Harvey, 1987; Ponte, 1989). As people utilize aesthetic and creative processes through active participation in music experiences, they also develop a better capacity to cope with and find meaning in life (Aigen, 1995a; Edelman, 1978; *The Healing Role of the Arts*, 1978; May, 1975; Spencer, 1978; Taylor et al., 1997). Thus, music experiences can play a vital role in helping individuals connect with the feelingful side

of their being and in helping them realize their full human potential (Leonhard, 1982; Whitwell, 1993).

Music Experiences to Expand Consciousness and Increase Personal Awareness

With the holistic health movement's emphasis on taking responsibility for one's own health, striving for optimum wellness and balance in all areas of life, and furthering of one's potential, self-awareness, and growth through finding answers within one's self (Adelman, 1985; Bonny, 1986; Scovel, 1990; Summer & Summer, 1996; Trevisan, 1978), many people are looking for ways to increase their personal awareness and add more meaning and fulfillment to their lives. Because it acts on *both* the mind and the body and affects *all* aspects of a person – physical, mental, emotional, and spiritual – *simultaneously*, music can be an ideal stimulus for facilitating truly holistic methods of healing (Clynes, 1991; Goldman, 1988). Music experiences have the capacity to be both curative and preventative, both enjoyable and rehabilitative, both artistic and therapeutic (Aigen, 1995a; Edelman, 1978; Kenny, 1982; Spencer, 1978). Therefore, music therapy experiences aimed at tapping and productively channeling an individual's emotional energy for growth, nondestructive self-expression, personal satisfaction, and increased self-awareness can do much to increase the total health and life quality of the average person. As Broucek (1987) observed:

> For average people, the satisfaction, affirmation, identification, and exploration offered in music therapy may mean the difference between sickness and full health. . . . Music therapy becomes an affirmation of the risky but rewarding growth choice toward health, iirather than a sanction for the stagnation of safety. (pp. 54-55)

Many music therapy techniques and approaches can be used with individuals or groups to help enhance cognitive functioning, expand consciousness, increase creativity and self-expression, improve life satisfaction, facilitate self-awareness, and promote personal growth and optimum health. Recently, some research has indicated that listening to certain types of music (particularly classical music and especially that composed by Mozart), can facilitate learning and increase brain functioning, while other research has demonstrated connections between piano lessons and increased abstract reasoning abilities (Chism, 1999; Knox, 1994; "Music Education Linked," 1994). Listening to and performing music also seems to improve an individual's spatial-temporal reasoning abilities (Knox, 1994; "Music Education Linked," 1994). Studies in these areas are still in the beginning stages, however, and "it's risky to draw broad conclusions from limited studies" (Chism, 1999, p. 5C).

Some individuals may find that improvisation or composition exercises help stimulate creative problem solving, encourage creative exploration of different possibilities and provide a safe structure for experimenting and taking risks, and lead to increased boldness in personal exploration (Broucek, 1987; Kenny, 1982; Priestley, 1985). Others may find that song lyric discussion and personal or group song writing can stimulate increased personal awareness and help them see other points of view or other possible solutions. Many music therapists also utilize various music and imagery techniques to help individuals expand consciousness, explore alternatives, facilitate access to and expression of emotions, enhance self-awareness, and increase life satisfaction (Bonny 1978b, 1986, 1989, 1994; Bonny & Savary, 1973, 1990; Campbell, 1991a; Crowe, 1991; Ventre, 1994a). One of most widely-used methods is the Bonny Method of Guided Imagery and Music (GIM) (Bonny 1978b, 1986, 1989, 1994; Bonny & Savary, 1990). According to its founder, Helen Bonny, GIM is

> a process that focuses on the conscious use of imagery which arises in response to a formalized program of relaxation and music to effect self-understanding and personal growth processes in the person. Used one-to-one with a trained guide, GIM may be a powerful uncovering process in exploring levels of consciousness not usually available to normal awareness. (Bonny, 1989, p. 7)

GIM helps individuals in their "quest for individuation, for creative life living, for healing and health" (Ventre, 1994a, p. 35) and "may be used as an ongoing process by anyone who is a seeker after that truth which lies within each of us" (Bonny & Savary, 1990, p. 9). Research into the GIM process has demonstrated that GIM is usually most effective as tool for personal transformation, growth, and self-discovery when it is carried out in dyads (i.e., one-to-one sessions with therapist and client), with a planned series of sessions (usually five) under a competent, specially trained GIM therapist/guide (Bonny, 1989, 1994; Bonny & Savary, 1990).

GIM sessions have four basic phases: prelude, induction, music program, and postlude (Bonny, 1994; Summer, 1988). During the *prelude*, the GIM process is explained and goals are set for the session. This is followed by the *induction*, in which the therapist leads the client through a relaxation and focus procedure to facilitate deep relaxation and new levels of consciousness. During the *music program*, the therapist plays a GIM tape program suited to the client's needs and goals. As the music plays, the therapist guides or interacts with the client as the client relates images that are elicited by the music. GIM taped music programs are 20 to 40 minutes in length and consist of specially selected pieces of classical music designed to facilitate the moods and visualization themes reported by the client. Research has found that, for in-depth GIM work, "personal music preferences were not usually applicable or healing when used in therapeutic settings" (Bonny, 1986, p. 8). Sessions conclude with a *postlude*, an integration and processing phase during which the therapist guides the client in returning to a normal state of consciousness, discusses images or experiences from the music program with the client, and helps the client process these and relate them to personal goals or session goals. Since the GIM process transcends word and thought, helps individuals tap into and gain strength from their creative forces, breaks through denial, facilities new insight and understanding, and leads to a new level of acceptance and integration of all facets of an individual (Ventre, 1994a), it can be a potent tool in the quest for increased self-awareness, wholeness, and optimum health and well-being. (See Chapter Twenty-two for more information on GIM and GIM training.)

POTENTIAL HARMFUL EFFECTS OF SOUND OR MUSIC

"Not all uses of music are therapeutic" (Priestley, 1985, p. 257); therefore, individuals must be aware of both the positive and negative effects of sound and music if they are to use music most effectively as a source of individual and group health (Harvey, 1987). As Chapters Fourteen and Fifteen noted, some song lyrics or types of music may reinforce unhealthy thought or behavior patterns in certain individuals. Some types of music or music experiences also have the potential to overstimulate the nervous system, even causing musiogenic seizures in some individuals (Priestley, 1985). In addition, the same piece of music or the same type of instrument or experience will not have the same effect on every person. What is helpful or relaxing or uplifting to one person may have no effect or the opposite effect on another person. Therefore, it is important to monitor individual reactions and adjust music and experiences accordingly. Certain music therapy techniques may also be contraindicated for some individuals. For example, individuals who have poor ego strength, are incapable of symbolic thinking, have difficulty distinguishing between symbolic thinking and reality, or are unable to relate their experiences to the therapist, are poor candidates for GIM (Bonny, 1986; Summer, 1988).

Since prolonged exposure to loud music or sounds from powerful speakers at concerts, personal stereo headphones, customized car stereos, and television sets can lead to noise-induced hearing damage (Brody, 1982; Jaret, 1991; Lovejoy & Estridge, 1987; Ponte, 1989), therapists and clients should always carefully monitor the volume or decibel level of music used in music experiences. In addition to damaging hearing acuity, noisy environments can increase stress levels, irritability, and fatigue, and possibly contribute to increased blood pressure, cardiovascular injury, ulcers, accidents, and reduced work efficiency (Jaret, 1991). High environmental noise levels may also disrupt sensory and motor skill development in infants and toddlers (Jaret, 1991). Thus, by alerting people to the dangers associated with prolonged exposure to loud sounds or noisy environments, music therapists might do much to improve the general health and well-being of the population at large as well as helping to prevent noise-induced hearing losses.

MUSIC THERAPY VERSUS NEW AGE MUSIC HEALING AND SOUND HEALING TECHNIQUES

During the last two to three decades of the twentieth century, the new age movement has brought with it an increased interest in both the healing practices of non-Western cultures and the possible direct healing effects of certain types of music or sounds (Campbell, 1991a, 1991b; Crowe & Scovel, 1996; Halpern, 1978; Hamel, 1976/1979). Usually, these techniques focus on the direct impact of physical, acoustical vibrations on body structures and functions and on neural activity (Bruscia, 1989a; Crowe & Scovel, 1996; Summer & Summer, 1996). Crowe and Scovel (1996) enumerated six categories of sound healing techniques: (1) *self-generated sound for healing*, which usually involves some form of toning (producing long, pitched vowel sounds that are directed inward to release stress or resonate with certain body parts or energy fields); (2) *projecting sound into the body*, which uses special machines or tuning forks to apply healing vibrations of appropriate frequencies directly to the body; (3) *sounding the body*, which includes techniques that involve "reading the state of the body or energy fields of another person and projecting the missing sound or vibration back to the person to re-establish the natural state of balance" (p. 24); (4) *listening technologies*, such as the Tomatis method, that seek to improve hearing, listening acuity and focus, and sound perception in order to increase communication skills, learning ability, and social adjustment; (5) *compositions and specific sounds combinations for healing*, which include songs, chants, and compositions written specifically for healing purposes, therapeutic voice work (singing freely for emotional release and personal empowerment), community drum circles, the use of external sounds and rhythmic input to entrain and synchronize brain waves, and the use of instruments believed to have healing properties (e.g., Peruvian healing whistles, Oriental singing bowls, and meditation gongs); and (6) *sound environments or vibratory equipment*, such as the Somatron™ beds or chairs, that provide both auditory input and vibrotactile stimulation to the entire body.

While some of the music composed by new age music healers may be useful for such activities as relaxation and stress reduction, either in therapy or for personal use, the therapist or individual using the music must always be careful to monitor individual reactions to see if the music really is having the intended effects. The healing sounds tapes and techniques marketed and espoused by music healers often claim to heal or cure certain ailments for *all* people, not taking into account the possibility of unique individual reactions and responses. Many of these techniques falsely assume that music with certain tones and qualities will affect *all* people (or all those who have a certain condition) in the *same* way and that *all* individuals listening to the tape will do so in an *identical* state of mind (Summer, 1995). Instead of individual solutions for personal growth and health, these quick, "one-sound-or-vibration-is-right-for-all" cures tend to produce simplistic behavioral solutions, in spite of their use of holistic terminology (Summer & Summer, 1996). Rather than supporting the holistic goals of individualization, self-awareness, and growth, they seem to point to a predefined universally correct model of health, behavior, and thought (Summer & Summer, 1996). Individuals should be aware that much of the support for many of these techniques and procedures is based on testimonials or mis-applications of research findings. In addition, many of these approaches are "fatally flawed by the over-simplification of complex psychological, physio-logical, acoustical and musical phenomena" (Summer & Summer, 1996, p. 9). So, while some of these techniques may be beneficial to *some* people in *some* situations, it is unwise to place total faith in universal healing claims. In order to be most effective, music used for healing purposes, like medicine, must be *individually prescribed and applied*, taking into account the unique physical,

psychological, emotional, and spiritual make-up of the individual. In addition, the personal relationship and interaction between therapist and client can add much to the healing potential of music and sound.

> Any serious application of the power of sound must take into account the human element of compassion. The compassionate music healer is one who looks each client in the eye, hears his/her individual music, and develops a client-centered, holistic music healing process. (Summer, 1995, p. 64)

Readers who are interested in a more extensive critique of new age music healing claims and techniques are encouraged to consult Summer and Summer (1996).

In the last few decades of the twentieth century, there has also been an increasing interest in and growing market for self-help audio tapes containing subliminal messages (Walls et al., 1992). However, most of the evidence for their efficacy is based on testimonials and reports from the companies that manufacture the tapes (Staum & Brotons, 1992; Walls et al. 1992). Experimental studies conducted by Staum and Brotons (1992) showed

> no significant effects of subliminal stimulation on detection and awareness, on overt behavior, or on subconscious written or pictorial imagery. Furthermore, commercially purchased tapes did not show significance in perceived personal improvement when compared to placebo tapes. (p. 177)

This last finding may indicate that it is the power of suggestion, rather than any subliminal messages, that produces many of the positive effects of subliminal self-help tapes. In addition, the poor musical quality of many commercial tapes may even make them contraindicated for relaxation purposes (Staum & Brotons, 1992). Readers who desire more information on this subject may wish to read the extensive review of auditory subliminal suggestion literature by Staum and Brotons (1992).

SPECIAL CONSIDERATIONS AND TIPS FOR SUCCESS

Individuals who wish to use music for health and well-being must remember that each individual responds in unique ways to particular sounds, instruments, compositions, or musical instruments. In addition, the responses of one individual to a certain musical stimulus may vary from time to time, depending on his/her emotional, physical, and mental state. Therefore, it is always important to monitor individual reactions and adjust music materials or techniques accordingly. In addition, "anyone who use music for healing, either for their own benefit of for others, should be aware that unsuspected effects may occur" (Campbell, 1991a, p. 251). Therefore, it is often beneficial to work with or consult a trained therapist who can deal effectively with any problems that may arise. This is especially true with techniques that involve altered states of consciousness (e.g., GIM) and that work on self-discovery and increased personal awareness. The skills of trained music therapists can also be helpful in initially selecting and then monitoring the most effective music or musical techniques for individual self-help programs, such as music to motivate and accompany exercise.

It may be helpful to think of the use of music to promote health and well-being in the general population as a continuum, with self-prescribed activities at one end (e.g., listening to music to relax or get in a happier mood) and individualized treatment programs implemented by a music therapist on the other. This continuum might then be compared to the range of general medicine services available, from self-prescribed over-the-counter medications and home remedies to individualized prescribed medications or treatment implemented by a physician. Just as consumers or clients self-medicate for common colds or take vitamins to promote health, so they can "self-musicate" as they find certain types of music or musical activities that effectively relieve their stress, increase their mental alertness, help them exercise,

elevate their mood, etc. And, just as physicians sometimes use nonprescription medications in treatment for specific purposes in dosages matched to the individual patient, so music therapists may sometimes use commercially available tapes and materials (e.g., pre-packaged relaxation tapes or exercise tapes) in treatment interventions matched to the needs and interests of individual clients or instruct clients on ways to use these materials for health maintenance. However, just as consumers/clients seek the help of trained physicians for more severe problems, for guidance in using over-the-counter medications and remedies, or for help when the nonprescription medications or home remedies are not effective, so they must also learn to seek the help of trained music therapists when commercially available music materials or self-prescribed music programs or activities are no longer having the desired effects. As they seek to move into the mainstream of wellness services, music therapists must take the lead in educating the consumers about the entire spectrum of music and wellness treatments and help individuals identify which may be most beneficial for their personal use at particular times or for particular purposes. Music therapists must also help the general public develop guidelines for when they can safely "self-musicate," when they might need to consult with a professional music therapist, and when they might need the direct services of a professional music therapist to help them reach their desired goals for improving their total health and quality of life. Finally, music therapists must be able to back up their claims for the preventative, health maintenance, and health enhancement effects of music with solid scientific research. Then music therapy will be able to find a place as an important part of wellness/ preventative medicine services as well as rehabilitative services, as a vital service for the general population as well as for individuals with disabilities.

SUMMARY

Health is more than the mere absence of disease; it is a state of optimal functioning and complete mental, physical, and social well-being. In recent decades, a growing emphasis on health and wellness

has led to an increased focus on preventative medicine. In addition, a heightened interest in holistic medicine and alternative healing practices has helped to focus the public's attention not just on curing disease but on striving for and maintaining optimum wellness by adopting life styles that focus on health. Holistic medicine treats the whole person (body, mind, and spirit), not just the symptoms or disease, and encourages individuals to take responsibility for their own health and to strive for optimum wellness and balance in all areas of life.

In recent years, music therapists have given increasing attention to ways they can expand their services beyond the institutional setting and clients with disabilities to also promote health and wellness in the general population. This chapter provided some examples of music experiences that can facilitate relaxation and reduce stress, decrease isolation and facilitate cooperative interactions, improve coping and problem-solving abilities, promote healthy habits and behaviors, humanize the environment, and expand consciousness and increase personal awareness. It also addressed potential harmful effects of sound and music. Finally, some new age music healing and sound healing techniques were briefly discussed. While some of these techniques may have potential for therapeutic use and, in fact, be beneficial to some people in some situations, readers were cautioned against placing total faith in any universal healing claims. In order to be most effective, music used for healing purposes, like medicine, must be specifically and individually prescribed, taking into account the unique physical, psychological, emotional, and spiritual make-up of the client. In addition, the personal relationship and interaction between therapist and client can add much to the healing potential of music and sound.

QUESTIONS FOR THOUGHT AND DISCUSSION

1. What implications do the expanded concept of health, the increased focus on wellness and preventative medicine, and the growing interest in holistic medicine have for the expansion of music therapy services?

2. Discuss some of the characteristics and needs of individuals in the general population who are interested in obtaining, maintaining, or regaining optimal health and well-being. What implications do these have for music therapy programming?

3. Why and how are music experiences useful in promoting health and well-being in general population? Are some types of experiences and activities more useful than other? Which ones? Why?

4. Describe some specific music therapy experiences that might be used to help individuals (a) facilitate relaxation and reduce stress, (b) decrease isolation and facilitate cooperative interactions, (c) improve coping and problem-solving abilities, (d) promote healthy habits and behaviors, (e) humanize the environment, and (f) expand consciousness and increase personal awareness. What unique benefits does music provide in each of these areas?

5. Discuss some potential harmful side effects of sound or music. What implications might these have for music therapy services?

6. Describe some new age music healing and sound healing techniques. How do these differ from music therapy? Are there any ways some might be included as part of music therapy intervention strategies? If so, how?

7. List several special considerations that may be important to remember when using music to promote health and well-being in the general population. Why are these important? What are their implications for the structure of music therapy intervention strategies?

8. For each of the situations listed below, (a) define the problem or areas of need for the client or group of clients, (b) describe one or more of the goals you might pursue in music therapy sessions with the client(s), (c) describe music activities you might use to help the client(s) meet those goals, (d) tell how the music activities you described relate to the goals and needs of the client(s), and (e) mention any special considerations you might want to take into account when working with the client(s).

Situation 1:

A local hospital is starting community outreach wellness program. The hospital staff is looking for ways to make these programs as enjoyable and appealing as possible, and they want your ideas on ways music therapy interventions could be a part of this effort. Initially, community outreach programs are focusing on stress reduction, coping skills, and developing good exercise habits.

Situation 2:

Ms. F. is a 49-year-old successful business woman. She is divorced and has two grown children. Even though she is successful, her life seems void and empty at times. She is seeking experiences that will expand her self-awareness and add more meaning, fulfillment, balance, and wholeness to her life. In addition, she is interested in activities that will help her maintain optimal physical, mental, and emotional health as she grows older.

SUGGESTIONS FOR FURTHER READING

Bonny, H. L. (1986). Music and healing. *Music Therapy, 6A*(1), 3-12.

Bonny, H. L. (1989). Sound as symbol: Guided imagery and music in clinical practice. *Music Therapy Perspectives, 6*, 7-10.

Bonny, H. L. (1994). Twenty-one years later: A GIM update. *Music Therapy Perspectives, 12*(2), 70-74.

Bonny, H. L., & Savary, L. M. (1990). *Music and your mind: Listening with a new consciousness* (Rev. ed.). Barrytown, NY: Station Hill Press.

Broucek, M. (1987). Beyond healing to "whole-ing": A voice for the deinstitutionalization of music therapy. *Music Therapy, 6*(2), 50-58.

Campbell, D. G. (1988). The cutting edge: Personal transformation with music. *Music Therapy, 7*(1), 38-50.

Campbell, D. G. (Ed.) (1991). *Music: Physician for times to come.* Wheaton, IL: Quest Books.

Crowe, B., & Scovel, M. (1996). An overview of sound healing practices: Implications for the profession of music therapy. *Music Therapy Perspectives, 14*(1), 21-29.

Harvey, A. W. (Compiler). (1988). *Music and health: Sourcebook of readings.* Richmond, KY: Music for Health Services Foundation.

Itoh, M., & Lee, M. H. M. (1989). Epidemology of disability and music. In M. H. M. Lee (Ed.), *Rehabilitation, music, and human well-being* (pp. 13-31). St. Louis: MMB Music.

Kenny, C. B. (1982). *The mythic artery: The magic of music therapy.* Atascadero, CA: Ridgeview Publishing.

Kenny, C. B. (Ed.). (1995). *Listening, playing, creating: Essays on the power of sound.* Albany, NY: State University of New York Press.

Leonhard, C. (1982). Humanizing music in a mechanized society. *Music Educators Journal, 68*(9), 23-24.

Logan, K. (1996). Music is key to lifelong wellness. *Teaching Music, 3*(4), 42-43.

Scartelli, J. P. (1989). *Music and self-management methods.* St. Louis: MMB Music.

Schulberg, C. H. (1981). *The music therapy sourcebook: A collection of activities categorized and analyzed.* New York: Human Sciences Press.

Standley, J. (1991). *Music techniques in therapy, counseling, and special education.* St. Louis: MMB Music.

Staum, M. J., & Brotons, M. (1992). The influence of auditory subliminals on behavior: A series of investigations. *Journal of Music Therapy, 29*(3),130-185.

Summer, L., & Summer, J. (1996). *Music: The new age elixir.* Amherst, NY: Prometheus Books.

Chapter Twenty-two

OVERVIEW OF SELECTED "SCHOOLS" OF MUSIC THERAPY

FROM THE MANY clinical examples of music therapy practice presented in Chapters Seven to Twenty-one, it becomes evident that the use of music in therapy involves many different procedures, approaches, and techniques. As the profession of music therapy has developed during the last half of the twentieth century, certain "schools" of music therapy practice have evolved. Some of these are based on particular music techniques, such as improvisation, music and imagery, or vibroacoustic techniques. Others draw from music education approaches, adapting Orff, Kodály, Dalcroze, or Suzuki methods to clinical use. Still others are centered around specific educational, psychotherapeutic, or medical models and theories. However, although they may emphasize different types of music experiences or use different language, terminology, and frameworks to process, explain, and evaluate client responses, all these approaches to music therapy have one basic principle in common: they seek to "enhance the quality of life of individuals with various types of or potential clinical problems through the use of music and the therapeutic relationship" (Maranto, 1993a, p. 706).

This chapter attempts to overview some of the more common schools of music therapy practice that currently exist in the United States. Certainly, this listing is by no means exhaustive, and other groupings or classifications are indeed possible (for example, see Bruscia, 1989a, 1991a; Maranto, 1993b; Taylor, 1997; Unkefer, 1990). In addition, as the profession of music therapy continues to develop and as new medical, psychotherapeutic, and educational treatment theories continue to emerge, new schools of or approaches to music therapy treatment will likely continue to evolve. It is hoped that the overview presented in this chapter, however, will give the reader a basic understanding of at least some of the more common approaches to music therapy treatment that are used in the United States at this time.

NORDOFF-ROBBINS CREATIVE MUSIC THERAPY

In their work with handicapped children, Nordoff and Robbins developed an approach to music therapy centered around the technique of piano improvisation. Nordoff and Robbins (1968, 1971a, 1971b, 1977) found that improvisational music therapy techniques were very effective in eliciting responses from profoundly handicapped, seemingly unresponsive children.

The music therapist's primary aim in this technique of clinical improvisation developed by Nordoff and Robbins is to develop contact with the client within the context of the musical experience. Initially, the music therapist works supportively, creating a musical-emotional environment that accepts and enhances the client's responses (Nordoff & Robbins, 1977). For example, the music therapist might base an improvisation on some rhythm found in the client's movement or drum-beating or try to relate the tonal content of the improvisation to a tonal pattern found in the client's cries or vocalizations. Once contact and rapport have been established, musical interaction between the music therapist and client becomes the focus of the sessions. Throughout the course of therapy, the music therapist works progressively with the client, building on the responses elicited and skills developed in previous sessions.

Creative music therapy uses improvisation (usually piano and/or vocal) to musically reflect the client, to evoke movement, vocal, or instrumental responses from the client, to develop the client's musical skills and expressive freedom, and to develop communication and interresponsiveness between therapist and client (Bruscia, 1987, 1989c; Nordoff & Robbins, 1971a, 1971b; 1977; Robbins & Robbins, 1980). Improvisations used in creative music therapy make free use of dissonances and employ many different meters, modes, scales, structures, and styles. Through these improvisations, the therapist creates music situations and sequences that engage the client in active music-making to enhance cognitive, motor, behavioral, and affective growth and development (Aigen, 1995b; Bruscia, 1987; Nordoff & Robbins, 1977). Verbal instructions and interventions are kept to a minimum; musical expression is "both the stimulus and response medium for therapeutic growth" (Bruscia, 1987, p. 67). Nordoff and Robbins (1977) have also developed evaluation scales to show how a client's responses to musical improvisation reflect various degrees of participation, resistiveness, and communicativeness.

Nordoff-Robbins creative music therapy focuses on working with those parts of the client that are essentially human and non-exceptional. There is a great emphasis on the power of music to awaken emotional responses and to act as an ego-organizing or self-actualizing force.

In the Nordoff-Robbins approach, it is believed that music bypasses areas of pathology or dysfunction to access and individual's healthy core. . . . Cognitive and affective processes not otherwise detected are activated in and through music. (Aigen, 1995b, p. 24)

Creative music therapy is perhaps one of the most well-known systems of improvisational music therapy. It is useful in both individual and group sessions with clients who have a wide range of disabilities and functioning levels, including those with autism or emotional disturbances, developmental disabilities, physical or neurological impairments, hearing or visual impairments, or severe multiple disabilities (Aigen, 1995b; Nordoff & Robbins, 1968, 1971a, 1971b, 1977; Pfeifer, 1982; Robbins & Robbins, 1980; Salas & Gonzalez, 1991; Shoemark, 1991). Although it was developed for children, the approach has also been used effectively with adolescent and adult populations (Bruscia, 1987, 1991a; Clarkson, 1991; Pavlicevic et al., 1994; Ritholz & Turry, 1994). Clients need not have any preexistent musical or verbal skills to benefit from creative music therapy; however, music therapists who use the approach need to be highly competent, skilled, expressive and sensitive musicians who have a broad range of skills, particularly in piano and vocal improvisation, as well as a high degree of clinical awareness (Bruscia, 1987; Forinash, 1992). Training programs in the Nordoff-Robbins creative music therapy approach are located in England, Germany, the United States, and Australia.

OTHER MODELS OF IMPROVISATIONAL MUSIC THERAPY

Many other models of music therapy also rely on musical improvisation as their primary tool for assessment, treatment, and/or evaluation. For example, in her work with children who had autism and various other handicaps, Alvin (1978; Alvin & Warwick, 1991) developed an approach that gives the client complete freedom to improvise on a variety of musical instruments and find his or her own way to order sounds. As sessions progress, the therapist guides the client in developing appropriate relationships with objects, self, and others through improvisations that form a dynamic part of the therapist-client interaction and relationship. In Alvin's method, improvisation is used in conjunction with other active and receptive music experiences, and music therapy is seen as "a developmental process which must be planned and implemented in sequential stages of intellectual, physical, and social-emotional growth" (Bruscia, 1987, p. 108). Bruscia (1987, 1989c) calls this model *Free Improvisation Therapy*. This approach has been used successfully in individual, family, and group therapy sessions, with children who have autism or other developmental or psychiatric disabilities. It has also been used to a limited extent with adults.

Another improvisational model, *Analytical Music Therapy*, was developed by Priestley (1975, 1985). This model is based on the theories of Jung and Freud and uses words and symbolic improvisations to explore the client's inner life and facilitate growth. In this approach, after issues for emotional investigation are identified, improvisation is often based on programmatic titles. Clients choose from a wide variety of instruments, and their improvisations are usually accompanied by the therapist. Client and therapist roles in improvisation are defined according to the issue at hand. Verbal discussion and processing are used throughout the session. To use this model effectively, therapists must be trained and experienced in both analytical psychotherapy and analytical music therapy. The Priestley model has been used with normal adults, adults who have psychiatric or neurotic problems, couples, prisoners, therapy students, and, occasionally, with children (Bruscia, 1987, 1991a; Priestley, 1975, 1985).

Boxill (1985, 1989) developed a method of clinical improvisation she called the *Continuum of Awareness*. This approach, specifically designed for use with individuals who have developmental disabilities, uses improvisation along with specially structured and adapted experiences in singing/chanting, instrument playing, and moving to music, to build relationships with clients and increase their levels of awareness and adaptive functioning. The three primary strategies used to awaken and expand awareness and develop relationships are (1) *reflection* (mirroring, imitating, or synchronizing with client's actions, movements, or sounds, while simultaneously structuring the musical improvisation to reflect and support underlying moods and feelings), (2) *identification* (providing instantaneous feedback to the client in improvised songs and chants of who the client is, who the therapist is, what is taking place, what client and therapist are doing together, and what client is doing independently, heightening awareness of

experiences), and (3) *our contact song* (developed through strategies 1 and 2; the first vehicle, either compose or improvised, through which client initiates musical communication toward therapist; provides a base that may be adapted in various ways to affirm or reaffirm client-therapist relationship). This procedure has been used effectively in both individual and group settings with all age groups of clients who have developmental disabilities.

Another model of improvisational music therapy, the *Experimental Improvisation Therapy*, was developed by Bruscia as adaptation of Riordan's method of using improvisation dance or movement to help individuals with disabilities "develop creativity, self-expression, and interpersonal skills" (Bruscia, 1987, p. 211). This model may use group improvisations in dance, music, or both. The therapist provides themes or "givens" to direct the group's attention to a limited area of music and/or dance. The group then experiments with the possibilities within that area. Improvisation and discussion alternate throughout the session, helping the group to refine and connect themes. This approach has been used successfully with adults and children with disabilities, normal adults, and therapy students. The model emphasizes "the development of personal self-expression, interpersonal freedom and responsibility, and creativity, all within a group situation" (Bruscia, 1987, p. 211).

Bruscia (1987, 1989c) has identified and provided a comprehensive description of several other improvisational models of music therapy, including *Orff Improvisation Models, Paraverbal Therapy, Metaphoric Improvisation, Adult Improvisational Therapy, Integrative Improvisation Therapy, Developmental Therapeutic Process, Music Psychodrama,* and *Vocal Improvisation Therapy*. While different improvisational models have slightly emphases or utilize slightly different aspects of musical or improvisation experience, have different theoretical orientations, and may be directed toward different client populations, all these models use musical stimulation or verbal direction to engage the client in some sort of musical improvisation, through various expressive modes (e.g., playing instruments, singing/chanting, moving/dancing, drama/mime), that will evoke increased nonverbal communication and self-expression. By reviewing the improvisation, either musically or verbally, through active or receptive techniques, the therapist helps the client identify skills that have emerged, clarify or concretize ideas that have been elicited, or connect new insights and behaviors to their lives (Bruscia, 1989c).

Through his extensive study of and clinical practice with improvisational models of music therapy, Bruscia (1987) also developed the *Improvisation Assessment Profiles* (IAPs), which "provide a model of client assessment based upon clinical observations, musical analysis, and psychological interpretation of the client's improvisation" (p. 403). The IAPs focus on both the client's experience of the improvisation process and the resultant musical product in an attempt to discover general tendencies the client exhibits and how the client responds under various conditions (e.g., solo, dyad, group; move-ment, different instruments, vocal). Each musical element or improvisational component (rhythm, melody, harmony, texture, phrasing, volume, timbre, body-motor, program/lyrics, interpersonal) is rated on six profiles: integration, variability, tension, congruence, salience (which elements are given more control or prominence), and autonomy (deals with role relationships in dyadic or group improvisations). The IAPs can be used effectively with normal or disabled children or adults who have a develop-mental age of at least 18 months. Tasks can be adapted for clients with severe motor or hearing impairments. IAPs are used mainly to gather information about the client, which can then be interpreted according to any relevant psychological theory (Bruscia, 1987, 1989c).

THE BONNY METHOD OF GUIDED IMAGERY AND MUSIC

The technique that eventually became known as the Bonny Method of Guided Imagery and Music (GIM) was first developed by Helen Bonny in the early 1970s. GIM grew out of work with music in LSD therapy (controlled, clinical use of lysergic acid diethylamide, a potent psychotogenic drug to increase self-awareness and expand consciousness) and the subsequent search for alternate ways to achieve altered states of consciousness that would enhance self-awareness, induce deep relaxation, and facilitate personal transformation or peak experi-ences without mind-altering chemicals (Bonny 1975, 1978b, 1986, 1989, 1994; Bonny & Savary, 1973, 1990; Summer, 1988). Because "the multidimension-al qualities of musical sound allow it to touch many levels of consciousness both simultaneously or in sequence" (Bonny, 1975, p. 130), it was found that listening to music in a state of deep relaxation could give a person access to altered states of conscious-ness and increased awareness without the use of drugs. Since the 1970s, research into the GIM process has steadily refined methods of practice and procedures. GIM is now recognized as a powerful form of music psychotherapy that can reach deep intrapsychic material and help individuals go beyond ordinary levels of consciousness to reach emotional material normally hidden from conscious awareness as well as higher states of expanded awareness (Bonny, 1994; Goldberg, 1989; Jarvis, 1988; Unkefer, 1990). As such, it should only be used by specially trained practitioners.

According to its founder, Helen Bonny (1989), GIM is

> a process that focuses on the conscious use of imagery which arises in response to a formalized program of relaxation and music to effect self-understanding and personal growth processes in the person. Used one-to-one with a trained guide, GIM may be a powerful uncovering process in exploring levels of consciousness not usually available to normal awareness. (p. 7)

GIM sessions have four basic phases: prelude, induction, music program, and postlude (Bonny, 1978a, 1989, 1994; Summer, 1988). During the *prelude*, the GIM process is explained and goals are set for the session. In the *induction*, the therapist leads the client through a relaxation and focus procedure to facilitate deep relaxation and new levels of consciousness. During the *music program*, the therapist plays a GIM tape program suited to the client's needs and goals. GIM taped music programs are 20 to 40 minutes in length and consist of specially selected pieces of classical music designed to facilitate the moods and visualization themes reported by the client. As the music plays, the therapist verbally guides or interacts with the client as the client relates images that are elicited by the music. The exchange and interaction may prompt the therapist to change music tapes "to facilitate the fast movement which is taking place in inner dynamics" (Bonny, 1989, p. 8). Sessions conclude with the *postlude*, an integration and processing phase during which the therapist guides the client in returning to a normal state of consciousness, discusses images or experiences from the music program with the client, and helps the client process these and relate them to personal goals or session goals. This integration and processing is essential to the GIM process, for "the validity of GIM as a therapeutic technique rests on its capacity for giving insights for the solution of problems in the real world" (Summer, 1988, p. 41).

GIM is based on a humanistic, transpersonal orientation and uses client-centered interpretation of the images generated by the music that, "with the guide, serves as therapist and healer" (Bonny, 1994, p. 70). Music is central to the GIM process, for the music evokes changes that occur in perception and helps create and elicit movement through and into various state of consciousness (Bonny, 1989, 1994). As noted above, GIM uses classical music (i.e., art music of the Western culture) almost exclusively. While popular music usually has fixed meanings and specific agendas or referents and directs attention to itself, classical music has no fixed meanings and is perceived anew by each listener with each hearing (Summer, 1988; Whitwell, 1993). Classical music can be experienced on many levels and in many ways, is able to provide depth of experience and variety of musical color and form or melodic and harmonic complexity, can stimulate imagery that is not bound to specific words or situations, and may elicit archetypal images (Bonny, 1994; Summer, 1988; Ventre, 1994a). Thus, classical music is particularly well-suited to the deep, intra-psychic work associated with GIM. Music designed only to create a state of relaxation (e.g., new age or minimalist music with much repetition, lack of dissonance, and a very simple structure) is not useful for GIM (Summer, 1988), since the goal of GIM is not relaxation but active exploration of the psyche. Thus, GIM requires music that includes contrasts, tensions, dissonances, variations, and complex structures to facilitate this movement.

Music programs for GIM sessions are chosen not by the clients but by the therapist, who is specially trained in selecting and preparing music listening programs to evoke imagery and facilitate psychic exploration (Bonny, 1978b, 1989). In contrast to many other music therapy approaches, research into the GIM process has found that music choices based on the client's preferences are not usually helpful for in-depth GIM work (Bonny, 1986). While the therapist may wish to note these preferences for diagnostic purposes or to use with other music therapy techniques,

> the use of client preferred music in GIM creates problems similar to those found with the use of popular music, that is, specific and rigid associations that draw the client out of an altered state and into an alert state of consciousness associated with his listening habits. (Summer, 1988, p. 6)

GIM is usually most powerful and effective when it is carried out in dyads (i.e., one-to-one sessions with therapist and client), with a planned series of sessions (usually five), under a competent, specially trained GIM therapist/guide (Bonny, 1978a; 1989, 1994). Therefore, intensive GIM work is usually carried out in individual sessions, in private practice or other clinical settings, often as a primary psychotherapeutic approach (Bonny, 1994; Goldberg, 1989; Jarvis, 1988). GIM techniques have also been adapted for group use (Blake & Bishop, 1994; Peach, 1984; Short, 1992; Skaggs, 1997a, 1997b; Summer, 1981, 1988). Generally, group GIM is less intense and may therefore be more useful in hospital or acute inpatient settings (Bonny, 1994). The music listening portion in group sessions is usually shorter, often consisting of a single selection, and may, especially in sessions designed to be less intrusive, use appropriate instrumental popular music as well as classical music. In group GIM sessions, the guiding takes place not during the music listening section but during the postlude, as the guide asks for a report of each member's imagery and then facilitates a discussion of that imagery with the client and other group members, aiming to apply the GIM experience to individual and group goals (Bonny, 1994; Summer, 1988).

GIM can be beneficial for many different client populations, including normal clients who desire to increase personal awareness and personal growth (Bonny & Savary, 1990; Goldberg, 1989; Ventre,

1994a), those with relationship problems (Bonny, 1989), individuals with depression or other affective disorders (Bonny, 1989; Goldberg, 1989; Summer, 1988), those with anxiety, phobias, obsessive-compulsive disorders, borderline personality disorders, or sexual identity or dysfunction problems (Bonny, 1978a, 1989), short-term psychiatric inpatients who are dealing with specific situations or traumatic events (Blake & Bishop, 1994; Goldberg, 1989; Short, 1991; Ventre, 1994b), prison populations (Nolan, 1983; Skaggs, 1997b), alcoholics and substance abusers who are in treatment and abstinent (Skaggs, 1997a; Summer, 1988), individuals with physical disabilities (Short, 1992) or traumatic brain damage (Goldberg et al., 1988), elderly individuals (Summer, 1981), individuals who have AIDS (Bruscia, 1991b; Jarvis, 1988), individuals who are terminally ill (Skaggs, 1997c; Wylie & Blom, 1986), adult children of alcoholics (Jarvis, 1988), children and adolescents with emotional disturbances (Summer, 1988), and normal children who wish to increase creativity and problem-solving abilities (Summer, 1988). Short (1991) has also found that GIM can be useful in helping to diagnose physical illness or trauma.

Generally, in order to benefit from GIM therapy, individuals must be able to think symbolically, be able to differentiate symbolic thinking from reality, and be able and willing to report their experiences to the therapist (Bonny, 1989, 1994; Summer, 1988). GIM is usually contraindicated for patients with active psychoses, as the GIM experience, with its lack of reality referents, may be assimilated into and reinforce psychotic thinking and fantasies (Bonny, 1994; Summer, 1988). GIM is also contraindicated for those who are actively abusing drugs or alcohol (Summer, 1988). In addition, patients who have insufficient ego strength or certain types of neurological impairments (e.g., those that make communication difficult or impossible) are less likely to

benefit from GIM (Bonny, 1989). However, some individuals with affective disorders who do not have the necessary ego strength to benefit from *individual* GIM sessions can be treated effectively in *group* GIM sessions (Summer, 1988).

Therapists who use GIM techniques must have additional special training including "tutelage with a trained GIM practitioner" (Summer, 1988, p. v). The various texts and monographs describing GIM practice provide material for theoretical study and information on additional applications, but simply reading about GIM does not qualify one to be a GIM practitioner. GIM training is at the postgraduate level and encompasses both didactic and experiential in-depth learning experiences in the processes of music and psychotherapy over a period of at least three years. The intermediate and advanced levels of training include personal and supervised GIM sessions with a trained GIM facilitator as well as readings and both instruction in and practice of advanced clinical applications for both individual and group GIM work. GIM training programs are endorsed and regulated by the Association for Music and Imagery (AMI), and those who satisfactorily complete the total GIM training regime become Fellows of the Association for Music and Imagery (FAMI) (Bonny, 1994). GIM training programs and institutes are offered at various locations in the United States and in England, New Zealand, Australia, Denmark, Sweden, Switzerland, and Germany.

Individuals who have completed at least one level of approved GIM training are eligible for membership in the AMI. The AMI serves to create a professional network, resource, and authority on GIM, to provide conferences for sharing, nurturing, and continuing education, and to stimulate research and publication on GIM theory and practice. AMI has published its own journal since 1992 (Maranto, 1993b).

OTHER MUSIC AND IMAGERY TECHNIQUES

The use of music and imagery in music therapy practice is not limited to the Bonny Method of GIM. For example, Summer (1988, pp. 37-38) described three "GIM-like music listening exercises" that can be used by those who have not had formal training in

GIM to focus on specific goals with groups of clients. In these exercises, after a brief relaxation exercise and short focusing statement by the therapist, clients draw, write stories, or make up movements in reaction to classical music. After the music, the therapist facilitates group discussion of the clients' work or experience, possibly comparing an individual's work to real life feelings or situations. Music and imagery techniques can also be used to take clients on imaginary vacations or help them experience places outside their current situation (Summer, 1981).

Other techniques combine music and imagery for the purposes of relaxation and/or pain reduction (Campbell, 1991a; Rider, 1985; Summer, 1988; Unkefer, 1990). In these techniques, imagery seeks only to facilitate the relaxation process. After being taken through some sort of progressive muscle relaxation exercise, with or without music, clients are asked to concentrate on peaceful and relaxing images suggested by the therapist while listening to music that helps to support and sustain a relaxed feeling. Such music and imagery techniques have been effective in a number of different situations, including labor and delivery (Clark et al., 1981; McKinney,

1990), stress reduction programs (Hanser, 1985), pain management programs for persons who had chronic pain from spinal cord injuries (Rider, 1985), preoperative situations (Robb et al., 1995), acute care mental health settings (Wolfe, 1996), pain clinics (Godley, 1987), and palliative/hospice care (Munro, 1984). In addition, some research has shown that music and imagery can enhance immune system responses (Bartlett et al., 1993; Lane, 1991, 1994; Rider, 1985; Taylor, 1997; Tsao et al., 1991).

When music is used with imagery for relaxation purposes, music that is preferred by the client may be most effective (Clark et al., 1981; Hanser, 1985; Munro, 1984). However, environmental sounds (Munro, 1984), new age music (Campbell, 1991a; Summer, 1988), entrainment music (Rider, 1985), or sedative classical music (Summer, 1988) may also induce relaxed states when combined with imagery.

VIBROACOUSTIC TECHNIQUES

Vibroacoustic techniques use special equipment to provide both auditory input and vibrotactile stimulation to the entire body, applying both the auditory and tactile aspects of music for clinical purposes. According to Skille (1989), who originated vibroacoustic treatment techniques in Norway in 1968,

> VibroAcoustic therapy is the therapeutic use of VibroAcoustic (VA) equipment and software that emit low frequency sound signals [range of 30 Hz to 120 Hz] mixed with special audio cassettes. It is a process in which vibrations are applied directly to the body in the form of low frequency sinus tones in combination with selected music. (p. 62)

Skille requires potential users to go through instruction courses in the proper use of the equipment before purchasing it. When the VA equipment is used for therapy, music and low tone frequencies are selected and calibrated to the individual needs of each patient. Thus, the music therapist plays an important role in matching the music and vibrational components to the unique needs and responses of the client, in monitoring responses and adapting

treatment accordingly, and in supporting the client before, during, and after the treatment (Wigram, 1995). VibroAcoustic Therapy has been used in Norway, Denmark, Finland, England, Germany, and Estonia. In the United States, Chesky and Michel (1991) have clinically applied vibroacoustic techniques through their specially designed piece of equipment, the Music Vibration Table (MVT)™, which "consists of a base table, a sound system, a vibrating membrane (tabletop), and a computerized vibration feedback system that measures and controls the transmission of vibrations as they affect a subject's body" (p. 34). Studies and clinical work using VibroAcoustic Therapy and the MVT™ have shown that the combination of music and low frequency sound vibrations can have a number beneficial effects, such as pain reduction, alleviation of bronchospasm in asthmatic conditions, increased contact allowed by children with autism, reduced muscle tone and increased range of motion in individuals with spastic conditions, reduction of heart rate and blood pressure, and decreased anxiety (Chesky & Michel, 1991; Skille, 1989; Wigram, 1995).

Some controversy exists over whether vibroacoustic techniques are actually a form of music therapy (Skille, 1989). However, when these techniques are used for specific clinical goals by a trained therapist who establishes a relationship with the client, assesses the client, selects the music and vibration with the specific needs, reactions, and preferences of the client in mind, monitors and supports the client before, during, and after the music/vibration treatment, and adapts treatment to the client's responses and progress toward clinical goals, then vibroacoustic techniques can certainly be classified as music therapy. As Wigram (1995) pointed out, both the therapist's skill in applying these techniques and his or her ability to form a therapeutic relationship with the client during the treatment process play an integral role in gaining optimum benefits from vibroacoustic treatment techniques:

> It is important to realize in this modality of therapy, that despite the passive nature of the treatment, the relationship between the client and the therapist, and the relationship between the client and the music, share equal importance. . . . As in any other form of therapy, the individual needs of the client should be carefully considered by the therapist, and so the relationship that develops is just as significant and important as between the therapist and the client in a more active and interactive form of music therapy. (pp. 18, 19)

Since clients can also move into altered states of consciousness as they listen to music in states of deep relaxation during vibroacoustic treatment techniques, therapists must be aware that some clients may need support in dealing with or working through images or feelings that have resulted from this experience, while others may need time to recover from or come out of their deep state of relaxation/altered state of consciousness (Crowe & Scovel, 1996; Wigram, 1995).

CLINICAL ORFF-SCHULWERK

Clinical Orff-Schulwerk, or Orff music therapy, has developed from and is closely related to Orff-Schulwerk, the approach to music education developed in Germany by Carl Orff (Barclay, 1987; Bitcon, 1976; Froehlich, 1996; Orff, 1980; Schulberg, 1981). Orff-Schulwerk is a multisensory approach that integrates music, movement, speech and drama, and guides participants through several phases of musical development, including exploration, imitation, improvisation, and creation. Rhythm is the starting point and basis for most music making. The rhythms and sounds of the words of songs and chants provide rhythmic and melodic fragments for accompaniment figures, introductions, and codas. Creativity and exploration (through speech, sound, rhythm, song, movement, and instruments) are important components of Orff-Schulwerk, and materials for songs and chants ideally come from the participants themselves and their immediate world and experience (Froehlich, 1996; Landis & Carder, 1972).

Orff-Schulwerk uses a special instrumentarium that "is easily accessible to children's abilities and offers a variety of timbres and textures" (Froehlich,

1996, p. 25). Instruments used in Orff-Schulwerk include xylophones, metallophones, and glockenspiels of different sizes, tunable drums, cymbals, and recorders. Orff-Schulwerk experiences also use many "body percussion" sounds, such as snapping, clapping, *patschen* (tapping the upper legs), and stomping. Beginning Orff-Schulwerk activities use many simple musical elements or forms, such as pentatonic scales, ostinato patterns (repeating rhythmic, harmonic, melodic, or speech patterns), repetition and exploration/development of simple motives, rondos, canons, chants, call-response, folk songs, children's songs, and musical games. Advanced activities gradually incorporate more complex scales and modes, harmonies, textures, meters, instruments, musical forms, musical dramas, and dance forms. Although Orff-Schulwerk was originally developed for elementary school-age children, it has been widely adapted to other populations and age levels. When experiences are matched to the interests and capabilities of the group, Orff-Schulwerk can be an enjoyable learning process for all age groups, preschoolers through senior citizens (Bitcon, 1976; Shamrock, 1986).

In Orff music therapy, or clinical Orff-Schulwerk, the music therapist uses the Orff-Schulwerk materials (instrumentarium, speech, movement, supplementary props), processes, and forms to stimulate participation and create situations that allow the clients to express themselves musically, experience themselves as a person through music, make music with others, and use the music experiences to develop needed motor, social, behavioral, communication, cognitive, or emotional skills or deal with current issues (Froehlich, 1996; Hollander & Juhrs, 1974; Orff, 1980; Ponath & Bitcon, 1972; Tonchick, 1981). According to Gertrud Orff (1980), the Orff-Schulwerk instrumentarium can have three important therapeutic applications: (1) allowing for acoustic-active participation, (2) acting as a link between therapist and client, serving both as a distancer and a binding force, and (3) giving the client a means of communication and social practice. Furthermore, as the Orff-Schulwerk materials are applied therapeutically, they make possible a "threefold non-verbal communication" (Orff, 1980, p. 13): from client to material, from client to therapist via the material, and from client to client.

Many components of Orff-Schulwerk offer numerous possibilities for clinical applications (Bitcon, 1976; Froehlich, 1996; Orff, 1980; Ponath & Bitcon, 1972; Tonchick, 1981). For example, the emphasis on rhythm and the integration of speech, body, and musical rhythms can facilitate motor skill development. The emphasis on body movement and on playing instruments also helps develop motor skills in addition to facilitating development of concepts such as body image, directionality, laterality, and spatial orientation. Chanting and singing, important parts of many Orff Schulwerk activities, can stimulate vocalization and help develop speech and language skills. The contents of chants and songs can also help clients learn information, develop coping skills, or explore and verbalize feelings (Bitcon, 1976; Froehlich, 1996; Ponath & Bitcon, 1972). Clients who are nonverbal still can participate freely in many aspects of chants and rondos through movement, body percussion, or use of instruments. McRae (1982) gives several suggestions for adapting traditional Orff-Schulwerk activities to the needs of special populations.

The musical forms used in Orff-Schulwerk activities, too, can have important uses in therapy. For example, the rondo form (alternation of group chant and individual responses) can structure routines, such as turn-taking and group versus individual participation, while allowing individuals to give creative contributions within a nonthreatening atmosphere and receive immediate reinforcement from the group (Bitcon, 1976; Froehlich, 1996; Ponath & Bitcon, 1972). Small, repetitious forms also work well with clients who have limited attention spans; in addition, they can easily be expanded or lengthened as the clients' attention spans increase (Tonchick, 1981). Improvisation (using instruments, movement, speech, rhythm, etc.) and creativity, which are so much a part of Orff-Schulwerk, can also be important tools for therapy (Bruscia, 1987, 1989c; Froehlich, 1996; Orff, 1980). Since Orff-Schulwerk activities are usually group experiences, they can also help clients develop important socialization and group cooperation skills.

Orff-Schulwerk techniques have been used clinically with a wide variety of populations, such as individuals who have mental retardation (Bitcon, 1976; Dervan, 1982; McRae, 1982; Orff, 1980; Ponath & Bitcon, 1976), autism (Hollander & Juhrs, 1974), behavioral disturbances (Orff, 1980), learning disabilities (Rink, 1989), hearing impairments (Bitcon, 1976; Darrow, 1985; Darrow & Gfeller, 1991; McRae, 1982; Orff, 1980), visual impairments (Bitcon, 1976; McRae, 1982; Orff, 1980), speech impairments (McRae, 1982; Orff, 1980), or orthopedic impairments (McRae, 1982; Orff, 1980), hospitalized children (Froehlich, 1996), and elderly persons (Bitcon, 1976). In addition, since the Orff-Schulwerk instrumentarium is so readily accessible to clients with little musical experience or training, music therapists often use Orff instruments in other improvisational activities and techniques (e.g., Goldberg, 1989). Of course, Orff-Schulwerk activities and experiences will not by themselves facilitate therapeutic changes in clients; they are only a framework for therapeutic work and direction. The therapist must always keep individual goals in mind and consciously direct, structure, and adapt the experiences based on individual client responses to help the clients reach their therapeutic goals (Orff, 1980; Ponath & Bitcon, 1972).

CLINICAL APPLICATIONS OF KODÁLY CONCEPTS

Kodály believed that everyone in his native Hungary, not just the musically gifted, "should receive training in the reading and writing of music just as he received training in the reading and writing of his native language' (Landis & Carder, 1972, p. 41). To this end, Kodály devised a carefully planned, sequential music curriculum that used native Hungarian folk songs to teach basic musical concepts to young children. The Kodály approach emphasizes relative solmization, rote-learning, and "inner hearing" (i.e., mental rehearsal). Techniques include "signs, games, clapping, reading musical notes, rhythmic notation, and, most centrally, singing" (Hurwitz et al., 1975, p. 45). Intellectual concepts are introduced only after performance skills have been thoroughly acquired.

The *Education through Music (ETM)* approach of Mary Helen Richards, first developed in the late 1950s and early 1960s, adapts Kodály methods to American children and American folk songs (Bennett, 1987). In developing ETM, Richards met with Kodály and incorporated his suggestions. ETM utilizes characteristic rhythms and melodic patterns of American folk songs (which are somewhat different than those of Hungarian folk songs) to reach children *through* music, using active involvement in making music (especially singing) to focus and organize responses and gradually develop more refined levels of musical knowledge. Grounded in Kodály methodology, ETM also focuses on developing music skills experientially through singing, listening, and music games before introducing notation. ETM begins with general skill development: Level one focuses on developing the psychological and emotional comfort within in group, while level two gives priority to developing social and communication skills through cooperative group music activities involving "singing, playing, problem solving and studying" (Bennett, 1987, p. 41). Level three refines skills in listening to and producing music through experiences that focus on ear training. Procedures for increasing awareness of sounds and patterns include "chinning" (substituting syllables like 'loo' for song words), movement, inner hearing, and "antiphoning" (procedure for singing familiar song where followers immediately continue singing song when leader stops, dropping out again when

leader starts sings; differs from echo singing in that the whole song is kept intact). Music literacy begins in level four, as students study musical concepts through singing, writing, and reading. Techniques include the use of singing games and folk songs, the moveable *do* system and Curwen hand signals, rhythm syllables, sight-singing exercises, folk dances, and a gradual progression from sound to symbol. All levels of ETM materials have a strong music/language connection, using English language folk songs as a basis for presenting, organizing, and sequencing information in a way that emphasizes musicality as rhythmic and tonal patterns are learned and studied within the context of songs. Teachers are trained to elicit student responses, incorporate these into lessons, and use the information gained from observation and assessment of student responses to shape subsequent teaching strategies and lesson plans (Bennett, 1987).

Some music therapists and music educators who work with students who have disabilities have found that Kodály methods, techniques, and approaches can be very useful for working with individuals who have various disabilities, such as mental retardation (Lathom, 1974), hearing impairments (Darrow & Cohen, 1991; Darrow & Gfeller, 1991), learning disabilities (Hurwitz et al., 1975; Lathom, 1974), or emotional disturbances (Lathom, 1974). Froehlich (1996) and Schulberg (1981) also observed that several aspects of Kodály philosophy, such as the belief that every individual should be able to participate in and enjoy music, the careful attention given to the structure of and presentation of music and musical learning, the use of music indigenous to the culture as a basis for learning, and the emphasis on experiential involvement rather than note-reading, are used in many music therapy approaches.

Lathom (1974) noted several ways Kodály methods could be useful in music therapy contexts. In the Kodály approach, carefully selected and sequenced materials provide for thorough learning and repetition along each step of the way, giving the clients security in the learning situation and providing them with the skills to progress successfully. Learning is first accomplished through imitation, not by following complex verbal instructions. Musical performance skills are learned thoroughly by rote before being connected with symbols or intellectual concepts. Thus, difficulty with symbols or concepts does not prevent a client from developing and deriving pleasure from musical performance skills. The visual aids provided by the solmization hand signals which are a trademark of the Kodály approach provide an additional form of sensory input that may facilitate the learning process. In addition, these hand signals can provide important visual and kinesthetic pitch references for individuals with hearing impairments (Darrow & Cohen, 1991; Darrow & Gfeller, 1991) or provide wrist rotation and finger flexion/extension exercises for those with motor difficulties in these areas (Zinar, 1987). Arm signal variations have been developed for those who are unable to use hand signals (Bennett, 1987), so individuals with fine motor difficulties may also benefit for the additional sensory input of this method.

Other researchers have found that many components of the Kodály method, such as its emphasis on sensorimotor involvement to develop rhythmic skills, its strong connection between music and language, its structured, sequential approach to singing, and its emphasis on building listening skills and auditory memory, can help individuals with learning disabilities improve rhythmic, attention,

spatial, and sequencing skills that are important for reading and academic achievement (Hurwitz et al., 1975). Moreover, since the Kodály approach tries to promote close and secure relationships by emphasizing eye contact and individual attention and by incorporating various degrees of physical closeness or touching in musical games, it can also be helpful in developing social skills. However, those who work with individuals who have emotional disturbances must be careful to see that degree of contact required is within the tolerance limits of the individual (Lathom, 1974).

In looking over the goals and philosophy of Mary Helen Richards' ETM approach described briefly above, one can also see where the techniques of this approach could be very congruent with and adaptable to therapy contexts. In fact, the overview of ETM provided by Bennett (1987) noted that some ETM materials have even been developed for individuals who were hearing impaired or who had other disabilities or special needs. Since ETM materials are based on the indigenous patterns of North American folk songs, rather than those of Hungarian folk songs, they can provide important resources for North American music therapists who wish to use Kodály-based approaches to develop language skills with their clients.

CLINICAL APPLICATIONS OF DALCROZE EURHYTHMICS

While the singing voice in predominant in the Kodály approach, the Dalcroze method focuses on natural movement responses to rhythm as the vehicle for learning and internalizing music skills (Bachman, 1991; Froehlich, 1996; Landis & Carder, 1972; Mead, 1986; Schulberg, 1981). Dalcroze used the term *eurhythmics* to describe his system of rhythmic movement exercises that used body motion to help individuals develop an internal feel for musical rhythm, flow, and phrasing by linking experiential movement with cognitive processing. Both mind and body are mobilized in eurhythmics experiences as individuals act, react, and adapt to the rhythmic/musical environment (Bachman, 1991). Eurhythmics, however, is only one component of the Dalcroze method, which also includes ear training and solfege singing to develop inner hearing as well as improvisation through movement, speech, song,

and instruments to encourage spontaneity, creativity, and freedom in music-making that would move students beyond mere mechanical reproduction of notes. As students work on developing both inner hearing and their kinesthetic or muscle sense, rhythmic body movement links with cognitive awareness (Froehlich, 1996) and individuals experience with their "whole being the elements of time, space, and energy as they happen in music" (Mead, 1986, p. 46). As they help individuals learn to mobilize their mind and body in response to music, Dalcroze programs can enhance any person's ability "to act, react, and adapt to the surrounding world in order to cope with it to best advantage" (Bachman, 1991, p. 21). In addition, since they require no preexistent musical talent on the part of the participant and can be adapted for and enhance the functioning of individuals of many different age and ability levels,

Dalcroze techniques can be very useful for music therapy as well as music education programs.

Since the early twentieth century, some Dalcroze teachers have been using eurhythmics programs therapeutically to help individuals who were blind or deaf or who had mental or physical impairments or serious maladjustment problems (Bachman, 1991). Dalcroze himself taught music to blind students in Barcelona (Bachman, 1991; Landis & Carder, 1972). He devised special eurhythmics exercises to help blind people develop spatial awareness and spatial concepts, tactile sensibility, muscular sense and consciousness, and increased auditory skills. Dalcroze felt that the interaction between teacher and class through music helped compensate for the loss of the usual nonverbal cues of teacher approval (e.g., smiles). Kersten (1981) also found that Dalcroze rhythmic movement exercises were very useful in helping individuals who were visually impaired gain confidence in exploring space.

Since the movement to music activities of eurhythmics programs can reach the level of unconscious emotional response, eurhythmics exercises can serve as tools for educating and expressing feelings, something that may be an important aspect of therapy for individuals who have emotional disturbances, behavior disorders, developmental disabilities, or mental illnesses. As music therapists accompany an individual's movement with improvised music, thus placing the movement in a musical context, they can also nurture the individual's physical self-expression, facilitate purposeful interactions with music and others, and

guide individuals in exploring feelings and ideas as they move to different types of music (Hibben, 1984).

Clinically, eurhythmics programs have been used to benefit individuals who have behavioral and learning disabilities (Hibben, 1984), serious maladjustment problems (Bachman, 1991), visual impairments (Bachman, 1991; Kersten, 1981), hearing impairments (Bachman, 1991; Brick, 1973; Darrow, 1985; Swaiko, 1974), mental retardation (Bachman, 1991; Hibben, 1984), physical disabilities (Bachman, 1991), mental illness (Benenzon, 1981; Schneider, 1961), or autism (Bachman, 1991), or who are elderly (Heidenreich, n.d.). Eurhythmics programs may be particularly helpful in improving speech rhythms and auditory perception and awareness in individuals who have hearing impairments (Brick, 1973; Darrow, 1985; Swaiko, 1974), increasing freedom of movement and spatial awareness in individuals who have visual impairments (Kersten, 1981), improving motor planning and coordination in individuals who have mental retardation (Hibben, 1984), strengthening body image/awareness, improving awareness of physical and emotional boundaries, increasing motor control and coordination in individuals who have behavior and learning disabilities (Hibben, 1984), increasing rhythmic awareness and awareness of self and others in individuals who have mental illnesses (Benenzon, 1981), and improving physical, mental, and spiritual health in elderly individuals (Heidenreich, n.d.). Schneider (1961) also found that eurhythmics programs improved reaction time in patients who had schizophrenia.

CLINICAL APPLICATIONS OF THE SUZUKI METHOD

The Suzuki method is based on the mother tongue concept, the idea that, just as children learn their native language by being immersed in its sounds from birth, so they also can develop exceptional musical abilities if they are immersed in rich musical environments (Froehlich, 1996; Kendall, 1986; Suzuki, 1969). Suzuki believed all people are born with musical ability that can be developed if given a proper environment and sufficient repetition of stimuli. His talent education approach begins with a listening program at birth and introduces the playing of musical instruments (e.g., violin, cello, piano, flute,

harp) at age 2-1/2 or 3. Early learning is based on imitation, using exercises and games as well as instrument playing, with constant repetition leading to mastery and intimate knowledge of material. Parents, teachers, and children are cooperative partners in the learning process, with parents being actively involved in home teaching and practice. Note reading is postponed until the child is technically well-established on the instrument. The Suzuki talent education approach promotes joyful music making and self-development while minimizing competition (Kendall, 1986). The Suzuki method also embodies an approach to living that emphasizes success, self-esteem, and total well-being. Focus is on the child, not the musical product, and learning takes place in a positive, affirming, safe environment (Froehlich, 1996).

Some music therapists, noting similarities between Suzuki's philosophy of and approach to music education and music therapy principles and practices, are beginning to explore clinical applications of the Suzuki method (Froehlich, 1996; Metzler, 1982). Suzuki (1969) himself related how his method of violin instruction, with patient and persistent application, could help students who were physically disabled improve muscle strength and motor control (pp. 27-29) and make violin playing accessible to students who were blind (pp. 58-60). Suzuki's belief that all individuals had potential to develop musical abilities led him to encourage teachers to apply his talent education method to children of all ability levels. The Suzuki method has been used effectively with individuals who have developmental disabilities, visual impairments, learning disabilities, cerebral palsy, or chronic illnesses, as well as with elderly individuals (Froehlich, 1996; Suzuki, 1969).

Metzler (1982) suggested that music therapists might use aspects of Suzuki's talent education approach in working with individuals who were gifted as well as those who were physically disabled. Froehlich (1996) noted that Suzuki methods, used at a slower place with more repetitions and smaller tasks, provide an excellent approach for teaching instruments to those who are visually impaired or to those who are unable to read because of intellectual limitations. In addition, Suzuki classes can give students who are visually impaired an excellent foundation that will prepare them to learn Braille music. Since individuals of all ability levels can learn effectively with the Suzuki approach, it can be an ideal method for mainstreaming situations. The cooperative group experiences that are typical of the Suzuki method can also become tools to foster positive social interactions.

> Suzuki's life approach to developing a music making ability in any individual, regardless of age or ability, gives evidence that he would not conceive of music therapy and music education of the exceptional as separate fields, but rather view them as extensions of one another. (Froehlich, 1996, p. 334)

DEVELOPMENTAL MUSIC THERAPY

Developmental Music Therapy (DMT) is particular system of music therapy techniques that is based on the Developmental Therapy model. Developmental Therapy, which originated at the rutland Center for emotionally disturbed children in Athens, Georgia, is "a psychoeducational approach to therapeutic intervention with young children who have serious emotional and behavioral disorders" (Wood et al., 1974, p. 2). DMT draws its theoretical orientation from child development, child psychology, special education, and learning theory, and uses the changes and sequences of normal child development to sequence goals and facilitate therapeutic development (Sandness, 1991). The process is geared primarily to children ages two through eight, but it has been used successfully with children as old as fourteen.

Music therapists who work with children who have emotional disturbances or behavior disorders in childhood education settings face the additional challenge of translating traditional music therapy activities and practices into an approach that incorporates sequential patterns of growth and development. The DMT system was developed to help meet this challenge. Since music skills develop sequentially just as skills in other areas do, music therapists using the DMT approach must also "consider the musical capabilities at various ages, in order to design therapeutic experiences appropriate to each child's level of functioning" (Wood et al., 1974, p. 6).

The DMT program provides a series of sequential music therapy experiences that are designed to complement the Developmental Therapy curriculum. There are five stages in DMT: (1) responding to the musical environment with pleasure; (2) responding to the musical environment with success; (3) learning music skills for successful group participation; (4) investing in group music processes; and (5) applying individual and group music skills in new situations. In each stage, various types of music activities are used to pursue goals in four basic curricular areas: behavior, communication, socialization, and academics. In stage one, children learn to respond to the sound environment with pleasure and to trust the music therapist and themselves. In stage two, children learn specific musical skills while learning to participate successfully in routines, use words to affect others in constructive ways, interact appropriately with others, and perform activities incorporating concepts of same/different, labels, colors, and numbers. In stage three, children learn to apply their individual music, behavior, communication, academic, and motor skills in group situations. Activities used during this stage require cooperation and sharing between group members to produce a group product. In stage four, the focus of music therapy shifts to group commitment as children learn to value the group and function in a less clinically oriented environment. In stage five, children learn to generalize their skills to non-clinical settings. During this stage, the music therapist may function as a consultant to help children become involved in music situations common to their everyday environment (Wood et al., 1974). As children progress through the DMT stages, they become increasingly well-adjusted. The role of the music therapist, the amount and type of intervention required, and the type of musical environment and musical experiences needed by the children vary with each DMT stage (Graham, 1975; Purvis & Samet, 1976; Wood et al., 1974).

BEHAVIORAL MUSIC THERAPY

Behavioral models focus on observable behaviors, not underlying processes. These approaches are based on the theories and work of Pavlov, Watson, Thorndike, Skinner, and Wolpe (Atterbury, 1990; Kaplan & Sadock, 1991; Scovel, 1990). Therapists who work from a behavioral orientation carefully observe a client's behaviors and target specific undesirable behaviors for change. They then strive to create an environment that rewards positive, desirable behaviors and does not reward negative, undesirable behaviors. Treatment uses operant or classical conditioning techniques, employing various types of reinforcers to increase more appropriate or adaptive behaviors and responses. Therapists may also set up contingencies to help increase desired behaviors. Other techniques include token economies, modeling methods, systematic desensitization, self-management programs, and assertion training. In behavioral approaches, the therapist assumes an active and directive role, structuring the environment and providing rewards and consequences to help the client achieve the desired changes (Scovel, 1990).

Music is a powerful contingency and motivator for appropriate behaviors that can be used effectively in both group and individual settings, and applications of behavioral principles and techniques to music therapy treatment approaches have been investigated extensively and widely documented (Hanser, 1987, 1995; Madsen, 1981; Standley, 1996a). A survey conducted in the mid-1980s found that behaviorism was used by music therapists more than any other single treatment strategy or approach (Taylor, 1987a). Research has shown that many different types of music experiences (e.g., music listening, instrumental lessons, preferred creative experiences or group music activities) can serve as a means of positive reinforcement to help increase or maintain desired behaviors (Hanser, 1987; Madsen, 1981). In her meta-analysis of 98 studies employing music as a contingency for therapeutic or educational objectives, Standley (1996a) found that contingent music was a more effective reinforcer than either contingent nonmusic stimuli or continuous music. While the contingent presentation of music can effectively increase behaviors, the contingent withdrawal or interruption of music (e.g., stopping or interrupting music listening, removing instruments, or taking away participation in music group when undesirable behaviors occur) can effectively decrease behaviors.

Behavioral music therapy techniques have been used successfully with many different age groups and client populations in a variety of clinical settings (Hanser, 1987; Michel, 1985). For example, several studies mentioned in previous chapters show the effectiveness of behavioral music therapy approaches with individuals who have mental retardation (Bellamy & Sontag, 1973; Dileo, 1975; Dorow, 1976; Edison, 1989; Garwood, 1988; Johnson & Phillips, 1971; Madsen, 1981; Metzler, 1974; Saperston et al., 1980; Underhill & Harris, 1974; Walker, 1972), are electively mute (Castellano & Wilson, 1970), have autism (Mahlberg, 1973; Staum & Flowers, 1984; Watson, 1979), are disadvantaged or at-risk (Michel, 1971), are hyperactive (Reid et al., 1975; Scott, 1970),

have behavior problems or behavioral disorders (Presti, 1984; Steele, 1968; Wilson, 1976), are receiving acute care mental health services (Wolfe, 1996), have cerebral palsy (Wolfe, 1980), are comatose (Boyle, 1987, 1989), or have Alzheimer's disease or related dementias (Fitzgerald-Cloutier, 1993). Many music-based relaxation training approaches or self-management techniques also make use of behavioral techniques (Scartelli, 1989; Scovel, 1990).

PSYCHODYNAMIC MUSIC THERAPY

According to psychodynamic theory, a person's behavior results from the interaction of various components of the personality, including motivations, past and present events, and segments of the personality (e.g., id, ego, superego). Much of therapy centers on bringing unconscious material into consciousness so that it may be dealt with and worked through. Therapists use various techniques, such as free association, dream and imagery interpretation, and transference, to help clients gain access to and insight into unconscious conflicts, feelings, motivations, and symbols in order to facilitate positive personality changes. Approaches in this model are based on the theories of Freud, Adler, Jung, Fromm, and Erickson (Scovel, 1990).

Psychodynamic music therapy approaches can be used with effectively with clients of all ages who are seeking relief from various mental, emotional, or behavioral disorders. Individuals who have autism (Alvin, 1978; Alvin & Warwick, 1991; Bruscia, 1991a; mood disorders (Bruscia, 1991a; Priestley, 1985; Warja, 1994), eating disorders (Nolan, 1989), personality disorders (Bruscia, 1991a; Dvorkin, 1991), anxiety disorders (Priestley, 1985; Tyson, 1966, 1981, 1987), or schizophrenia (Bruscia, 1991a; Priestley, 1985) have all benefitted from psychodynamically oriented music therapy approaches. Music can be a very effective tool of psychodynamic therapy because of its ability to bypass verbal censorship and reach emotions and the deeper parts of an individual's psyche (Wheeler, 1981). In addition, it is a powerful nonverbal form of expression and communication that can be used to access and explore unconscious materials at a nonverbal, feeling level,

before clients are ready or able to verbalize them (Ruud, 1980; Wheeler, 1981). Music activities can also give clients an outlet for expressing anger or other urges or feelings in nondestructive ways, providing a form of sublimation (Ruud, 1980). Finally, as clients successfully participate in music experiences, they can gain a sense of mastery, control, and confidence that will build ego strength and increase feelings of self-worth (Ruud, 1980; Wheeler, 1981).

Some of the models based on music techniques discussed earlier in this chapter are forms of psychodynamic music therapy. For example, Juliette Alvin's (1978; Alvin & Warwick, 1991) *Free Improvisation Therapy* has psychoanalytical orientation, based on the work of Sigmund Freud (Bruscia, 1987). Another improvisational model, Priestley's (1975, 1985) *Analytical Music Therapy*, is based on the theories of Jung and Freud. Priestley noted that different types of instrumental improvisation activities could be used psychodynamically to help clients access emotions, achieve insight, and facilitate behavior change. Warja (1994) also used metaphoric improvisation techniques to help individuals with depression gain access to feelings, images, and insights. Additional examples of improvisation in psychodynamic music therapy are provided by Bruscia (1991a), Dvorkin (1991), and Nolan (1989). Other music techniques that can be applied within a psychodynamic framework include movement and relaxation (Priestley, 1985; Tyson, 1987), music listening/discussion activities designed to elicit emotional or cognitive reactions and insights into feelings and behaviors (Wheeler, 1983), individual music lessons (Tyson, 1966, 1981, 1987), and the use of songs or improvisations as transitional objects (Bruscia, 1991a; Dvorkin, 1991; Nolan, 1989). Some music therapists have also applied psychodynamic or psychoanalytic interpretations to their use of GIM techniques (Bruscia, 1991b; Warja, 1994).

Since music therapists who work from psycho-dynamic orientation often strive to help clients elicit and work through unconscious material, it is vital that they have advanced training in psychodynamic clinical techniques and have a thorough understanding of individual psychopathology (Priestley, 1975, 1985; Unkefer, 1990; Wheeler, 1983).

COGNITIVE MUSIC THERAPY

In cognitive therapy approaches, treatment focuses on helping clients become aware of negative or irrational thought patterns or beliefs that create stress or cause feelings of inadequacy, confronting these and identifying life experiences in which they operate, and finding ways to reverse the negative or irrational thinking and thus alter behavior. Examples of cognitive approaches include Beck's cognitive therapy, Berne's transactional analysis (TA), Ellis's rational emotive therapy (RET), Glasser's reality therapy, Maultsby's rational behavior therapy (RBT), and Meichenbaum's cognitive behavior modification (Kaplan & Sadock, 1991; Scovel, 1990; Thaut & Gfeller, 1992). Music therapy interventions have been combined with several these approaches, including transactional analysis (Arnold, 1975; Schulberg, 1981; Shreffler, 1976; Williams, 1979), rational behavior therapy (Maultsby, 1977), and rational emotive therapy (Bryant, 1987). Some music therapists also structure music experiences within a cognitive behavioral framework as part of their treatment interventions (Brodsky & Sloboda, 1997; Cassity & Theobold, 1990; Justice, 1994; Murphy, 1992; Parente, 1989; Slotoroff, 1994).

Music Therapy and Transactional Analysis

Transactional analysis is an approach to therapy that was developed by Eric Berne. According to Berne's theory, all humans have three go states: Parent, Child, and Adult. Each of these ego states have specific behaviors and thought patterns.

In clinical work, music activities have most often been used within a transactional analysis framework to achieve therapeutic progress with adult psychiatric clients. For example, Arnold (1975) used structured music activities to help activate the Child state in clients whose thoughts and behaviors were inhibited by parental injunctions. In these music therapy sessions, tapes of specific songs were used "to shape behavior through the six ways of structuring time as described by Berne – withdrawal, through rituals, pastimes, activities, games, and into intimacy" (Arnold, 1975, p. 116). Communication at a nonverbal level with music as the unifying factor played an important part in these sessions.

Music therapy activities can also be used to help touch the Adult and Parent ego states. For example, Shreffler (1976) used song writing to activate the Adult state of clients to help with problem-solving. Songs related to nurturing or critical parenting have also been used to help clients activate the nurturing Parent within themselves (Williams, 1979).

Music Therapy and Rational Emotive Therapy

Rational emotive therapy (RET) conceives of behavioral events as occurring in three steps: (a) an activating event or situation to which the person responds, (b) the person's beliefs about or perceptions and interpretations of the situation, and (c) the emotional and behavioral consequences. RET aims to help clients detect irrational beliefs (step b) that result in unhealthy emotional and behavioral consequences (step c). Intervention is based on debating and refuting irrational beliefs, especially by examining "musts" and "shoulds" that are often evidence of unrealistic or irrational thinking and self-imposed demands. After identifying and disputing these irrational beliefs or self-defeating ideas, clients learn to replace them with new, healthier ways of thinking and reacting. The therapist acts as a guide, helping clients detect irrational beliefs and facilitating their efforts to express and resolve conflicts and adopt healthier thought patterns (Bryant, 1987; Scovel, 1990).

According to Bryant (1987), clients perceive and approach music therapy experiences in the same way they approach all life experiences.

> Values, attitudes, and beliefs, both rational and irrational, are brought to bear in all experiences, and are therefore subsequently projected upon the client's approach to the music therapy setting. (p. 31)

Consequently, by superimposing cognitive frameworks on music-related behaviors, music therapists can use music therapy experiences to help clients examine the behavioral or emotional consequences of irrational or unrealistic beliefs, define and challenge these beliefs, develop new attitudes, and relate these to other life situations, thus ameliorating emotional disorders. Music therapy techniques that can be used in this process include using discussion of song lyrics to explore beliefs and emotional reactions and exploring beliefs about and emotional/ behavioral reactions to music performance situations (Bryant, 1987; Scovel, 1990; Thaut & Gfeller, 1992). Once irrational beliefs are identified, challenged, and replaced with healthier attitudes and thought patterns in the context of music experiences, the therapist can help clients see how these attitudes may also relate to their approach to other life situations (Bryant, 1987).

Music Therapy and Rational Behavior Therapy

Maultsby's (1977, 1984) rational behavior therapy (RBT) is derived from Ellis's rational emotive therapy and based on a logical synthesis of several learning theories that apply only to human beings. RBT is a comprehensive method that deals with cognitive, emotional, and physical behaviors and aims to help people solve problems in these areas by teaching them practical, rational techniques for emotional self-help. According to RBT theory, people's thoughts and perceptions create, maintain, or eliminate their emotions. Therefore, if they wish to change emotive feelings without drugs, people must change their

thought or perceptions. RBT also recognizes that emotive feelings are only a small fraction of total emotion, which includes perceptions and thoughts that give logical support to the feelings.

RBT helps individuals assess how emotionally health or unhealthy their behaviors are by providing five rules or criteria for healthy or rational behaviors (Maultsby, 1977, 1984). According to RBT, rational or healthy cognitive, emotive, and physical behaviors (1) are based on obvious fact or objective reality, not subjective opinions, (2) help individuals protect themselves, (3) help individuals achieve their short- and long-term goals in the best or most efficient way possible, (4) help individuals avoid significant undesirable conflict with others, and (5) help individuals feel the emotions they want to feel.

Since music can both stimulate and be a powerful reinforcer of new learning, therapeutically structured music experiences can be a valuable tool for rational behavior therapy (Maultsby, 1977). For example, song lyrics (often specially composed or adapted by the therapist to express rational ideas) can help individuals learn and practice new thought patterns. Positive emotive reactions can be reinforced through repetition of the lyrics, and, eventually, the lyrics can become cues for rational, logical emotive, cognitive, and physical behaviors. With the aid of the therapist, clients might also use song writing or lyric discussion activities to identify motivations of behaviors or discuss solutions to personal problems. In addition, singing or listening to recordings of song lyrics that restate insights or ideas gained in RBT sessions could provide clients with "an excellent emotional self-defense against unhealthy, negative emotions between therapy sessions" (Maultsby, 1984, p. 105). Music therapists might also structure song writing, listening/discussion, or instrumental improvisation activities could to guide clients through RBT techniques like the rational self-analysis or to facilitate practice of rational emotive imagery to help establish new, healthy patterns or habits of thought, perception, and behavior.

Music Therapy and Cognitive Behavioral Approaches

In recent years, more music therapists have been using music therapy techniques within a cognitive behavioral framework as they strive to develop approaches and interventions that help clients achieve lasting, positive results within only a few sessions (Murphy, 1992). Some of these approaches are based on Yalom's (1983) model of group psychotherapy. Music therapy interventions following cognitive behavioral models such as this have two important facets: (1) the musical experience that provides the activating event in which the clients are involved and to which they respond and (2) the verbal discussion (processing and feedback) of the clients' experience in and responses to the musical event.

A typical music therapy session structure in this orientation may include (a) an introduction by the therapist, focusing the clients on the task, (b) a music warm-up, with the therapist modeling response, (c) a music experience (e.g., improvisation, creating a group song), (d) therapist-facilitated verbal processing and discussion of the experience of the musical experience and how clients' responses/ experiences/reactions relate to their own specific emotional or behavioral issues, and (e) closure, led by the therapist (Murphy, 1992). Music activities are often very effective in quickly illuminating the clients' maladaptive thought processes and/or modes of interaction, for they reach clients on an immediate, emotional level that is able to bypass verbal rationalizations and defenses. "While words can accomplish the same end results, for some patients it is the nonverbal experience that may best bring to conscious awareness recurrent, self-defeating patterns" (Murphy, 1992, p. 105).

Music therapists can use a variety of techniques and music-based interventions, such as song lyrics, music listening/discussion, music performance, music improvisation, or music/movement techniques, within a cognitive behavioral framework to help clients change disordered ways of thinking and build healthier, more adaptive ways of thinking and relating to the world and others around them. For example, Slotoroff (1994) found that structured and improvisational drumming techniques and cognitive behavioral processing approaches could help adolescents with

conduct disorders increase awareness of their thoughts and feelings and practice ways of controlling their anger and impulsive behavior. These same techniques also were very effective in helping female adolescents who had been abused increase awareness of their thoughts and feelings and practice ways of changing their behavior, so that they felt more empowered and become more assertive. These changes occurred very quickly in music therapy treatment, with positive responses often being seen in only one or two sessions. In another study, Brodsky and Sloboda (1997) found that, for some clients who have extreme stress and anxiety over certain situations, using music plus vibrotactile stimulation or music-based relaxation and imagery training within a cognitive behavioral framework can be just as effective as traditional psychotherapeutic counseling in reducing symptoms of anxiety.

Music therapy interventions used within a cognitive/behavioral framework are also effective in helping clients who have eating disorders (a) increase self-awareness and self-esteem, (b) increase awareness of irrational or destructive feelings and behaviors, (c) decrease anxiety that may be experienced as they try to discontinue their eating disorder behaviors, and (d) find new ways of taking control and coping with emotions. Music therapy interventions that have been helpful in this regard include (1) music-reinforced relaxation, using music to complement, support, and ground muscle stretching, deep breathing, progressive muscle relaxation, and directed imagery techniques, (2) structured music therapy groups, using music and movement, handbells and choir chimes, group singing, or instruments improvisation, (3) insight-oriented music/creative arts and imagery techniques, using group adaptations of the Bonny method of Guided Imagery and Music (GIM) or drawing or writing in response to stories or poems read to music, and (4) musical theater productions utilizing songs expressing personal affirmation or relating to treatment issues (Justice, 1994; Parente, 1989).

HUMANISTIC MUSIC THERAPY

Humanistic therapy models include Rollo May's existential therapy, Carl Rogers's person-centered

therapy, and Fritz Perls's Gestalt therapy (Scovel, 1990; Thaut & Gfeller, 1992). Humanistic approaches emphasize the uniqueness, value, and worth of each individual, and believe all individuals have the capacity to control their own lives and make good decisions. Therapists who follow a humanistic approach give unconditional acceptance to the client and focus on the here-and-now of the therapeutic relationship. They try to develop a supportive relationship with the client, so he/she can feel secure enough to confront basic questions about the meaning of life and achieve insights about his/her own life, moving beyond the basics of existence to a state of "self-actualization" (Maslow, 1968), a life filled with meaning and a sense of well-being and completeness.

Music therapists who work within a humanistic framework use various types of music experiences (e.g., music listening or discussion, music improvisation, GIM) as a vehicle for building and developing a supportive relationship with clients and a means through which clients can achieve insight and increase their life quality and sense of meaning and fulfillment (Thaut & Gfeller, 1992). Music therapy techniques described earlier in this chapter that have

humanistic orientation include the improvisational models of Nordoff-Robbins (*Creative Music Therapy*) and Boxill (*Continuum of Awareness*) and the Bonny Method of Guided Imagery and Music. In addition to various clinical improvisation and GIM techniques, music therapists who work from within a humanistic framework may also use interventions employing techniques and experiences such as song selection, fantasy and lyric improvisation, music listening, song writing, and music-facilitated life review (Bruscia, 1991a). Humanistic music therapy approaches can be used successfully with almost every client population, including both those who have various disabilities and those in the general population who are seeking greater meaning or quality in their lives (Blake & Bishop, 1994; Bonny, 1978a, 1989; Bonny & Savary, 1990; Boxill, 1985, 1989; Bruscia, 1991a; Goldberg, 1989; Jarvis, 1988; Nolan, 1983; Nordoff & Robbins, 1968, 1971a, 1971b, 1977; Pfeifer, 1982; Robbins & Robbins, 1980; Short, 1991, 1992; Skaggs, 1997a, 1997b, 1997c; Summer, 1981, 1988; Ventre 1994a, 1994b; Wylie & Blom, 1986).

BIOMEDICAL MUSIC THERAPY

Those who approach treatment from a biomedical model maintain focus on the biological factors (e.g., biochemical imbalances, genetic problems, physical abnormalities or illnesses) that underlie emotional, physical, cognitive, or behavioral disorders. Once a diagnosis is made, treatments that address the biological abnormalities or problems are prescribed (Scovel, 1990; Thaut & Gfeller, 1992). These may include medications, special procedures (e.g., surgeries), changes in diet or life style, or changes in environment. In those disorders where stress is a factor, treatments may also focus on changing behavioral responses to stressors, including such things as structured relaxation training.

As medical research technology has developed to the point where the actual effects of music on physical processes can be observed and measured precisely, biomedical explanations for the effectiveness of music therapy procedures have increased. Drawing on decades of research related to the physiological effects of music and music therapy procedures, Taylor (1997) recently proposed a

biomedical theory of music therapy that focuses on establishing a medical basis for music therapy treatment procedures, independent of other psychological theories or intervention strategies. The key to Taylor's approach is the idea that, since research in neuroscience now indicates that the brain generates all human behavior, investigations into the influence of music and participation in music experiences on brain functioning will provide a objective framework for explaining the effectiveness of *all* types of music therapy applications and procedures.

According to Taylor (1997), biomedical music therapy is "the enhancement of human capabilities through the planned use of musical influences on human brain functioning" (p. 121). This definition is based on his Biomedical Theory of Music Therapy, which, in summary, states that

Music influences human behavior by affecting the brain and subsequently other bodily structures in ways that are observable, identifiable, measurable, and predictable, thereby providing the necessary foundation for its use in treatment procedures. (p. 52)

In the biomedical music therapy, then, the brain and investigations of the direct effects of music on the brain and the human nervous system are essential components for defining music therapy and for guiding music therapy practice. The four hypotheses included in Taylor's Biomedical Theory of Music Therapy deal with the specific brain and nervous system structures involved in music's effect on (1) pain perception, (2) emotional behavior, (3) motor activity (includes both physical functioning and interpersonal communication skills), and (4) the physiological processes that indicate anxiety, stress, and tension. These hypotheses cover all areas of human functioning commonly addressed by music therapy interventions, making interventions based on biomedical music therapy approaches applicable to almost any client population.

In citing clinical examples to support his theory, Taylor (1997) provides biomedical explanations for the positive influence of music and music-based experiences on (a) pain management in surgery, childbirth, cancer treatment, coronary treatment, burn treatment, and pain rehabilitation, (b) emo-

tional control in physical medicine situations (organ transplants, oncology, pediatrics, hemodialysis) and the biomedical determinants of eating disorders and behavior disorders, (c) the recovery of physical and communication skills, and (d) anxiety and stress management for infants and children, individuals undergoing dental procedures, patients with psychotic disorders, and individuals who are suicidal. Biomedical music therapy procedures include all the types of music experiences commonly used in other approaches: singing, playing instruments, listening to music, discussing music, moving or relaxing to music, and creating or improvising music. The difference lies not in the techniques themselves but in the music therapist looking to explain the effectiveness of these techniques primarily with regard to their direct effects on the human nervous system. Taylor (1997) believes that the biomedical theory of music therapy, grounded as it is in extensive and expanding amounts of empirical, scientifically verifiable data, can both elevate the status of the music therapy profession in medical and health care circles and "provide a unifying conceptual framework for many of the various theoretical positions and clinical modalities existing within music therapy" (p. 121).

THE PROS AND CONS OF FOLLOWING ONE APPROACH OR ORIENTATION

According to Wheeler (1983), integrating music therapy techniques into a specific psychotherapeutic theory or system can have two important benefits for music therapists: (1) providing explanations for what happens in music therapy and serving as a basis for making predictions about client responses, evaluating treatment, and finding ways to improve results, and (2) increasing the credibility and professional stature of music therapists, particularly in psychiatric settings. Taylor (1997) also suggested that explaining the effects of music therapy treatment procedures in biomedical terms could elevate music therapy to levels of professional respect and credibility equivalent to those accorded other medical professions and disciplines that have treatment techniques and approaches firmly grounded in verifiable, scientific data. Others have noted the

importance of integrating music therapy interventions into specific treatment models and approaches used by other professionals in special education settings in order to minimize confusion on the part of the client and to assure that all interventions complement and reinforce one another (F. Johnson, 1981; Wood et al., 1974).

As important as it is to coordinate therapeutic efforts with other professionals, music therapists must also remember to heed the warning of Gaston (1968b), who cautioned against ceasing to observe and report behavior because of adopting a specific theory or treatment model "so emotionally that the adoption has all the earmarks of a religious conversion" (p. 230). No one theory or treatment model can possibly have all the answers for all clients in all situations. While particular therapists or clinics may favor a certain treatment model or approach, therapy teams often find that an eclectic approach, drawing from many models and combining the best features of several approaches, is most helpful in meeting the unique needs of a particular client (Thaut & Gfeller, 1992). After a thorough study of the relationship of music therapy to various treatment theories, Ruud (1980) observed that adopting one model to the exclusion of all others would decrease human beings' potential views of themselves and concluded that music therapy "ought to be an open field where different models of understanding are given the possibilities to collaborate with each other" (p. 71).

In addition to subscribing exclusively to a particular theory or treatment model, music therapists may also face the temptation of adopting one particular musical technique (e.g., piano improvisation) to the exclusion of all other musical techniques and approaches. As this text has repeatedly noted, music therapy interventions are usually most effective when they incorporate, at least initially, instruments, music, and modes of musical experience and expression that are preferred by the client. While some specific musical techniques, instruments, or types of experiences will be helpful in working with most individuals of given client populations on certain goals, there will always be those individuals for whom those techniques are not particularly effective or for whom they are even contraindicated. Music therapists must *always* carefully assess *individual* client preferences, needs, strengths, and weaknesses and continually observe and evaluate *individual* client responses and behaviors to structure music therapy intervention strategies most effectively. In addition, over the course of their careers, music therapists are very likely to work with individuals of many different age groups who have a wide variety of needs and disabilities (Lathom, 1982). Therefore, music therapists would do well to be informed about and relatively proficient in a variety of musical techniques and approaches that can be used effectively with a wide range of client populations.

Recognizing that no one existing treatment model or musical technique will be effective for every client in every situation, most music therapists in the United States have adopted an eclectic approach to treatment (Maranto, 1993b; Taylor,

1987a). In writing about an eclectic approach to music education, Landis and Carder (1972) observed:

> The individual teacher has always carried an important responsibility for awareness of current trends in educational thought, for making judgments of the value of those trends, and for putting into practice those procedures he believes best suited to his students. (p. 4)

This statement might be paraphrased to apply to music therapists, who are responsible for being aware of current trends in music, music therapy, psychotherapy, special education, and medicine, for judging the value of these trends, and for putting into practice those procedures they believe are best-suited to their clients. Integrating music therapy techniques into the psychotherapeutic or educational model used by other professionals on the treatment team will certainly benefit the client, in that all will be working toward a common goal in a common way. However, fanatically adopting one theory, model, approach, or technique to the exclusion of all others serves neither clients nor therapist, for no single theory, model, approach, or technique can be most beneficial for all clients in all situations.

Music therapists would also do well to remember that their skills and abilities to assess individual client needs, relate to clients in and through music experiences, and structure music experiences to facilitate clients' movement toward positive growth and change, as well as the personal attributes and qualities they bring to their work (e.g., musical creativity, insight, empathy, confidence) are in many ways *more* important to the success of their music therapy interventions than is their adoption of any particular technique, approach, or theoretical perspective. As Aigen (1993) observed:

> There is no evidence that the adoption of any one theoretical perspective leads to more efficacious therapy than any other perspective. This is not to say that music therapists do not subscribe to and use elements of a particular theoretical approach, but rather to emphasize that the *person* who makes the interventions is more important than the actual technique or method. (p. 23)

SUMMARY

As the profession of music therapy has developed during the last half of the twentieth century, certain "schools" of music therapy practice have evolved. Some are centered around particular music techniques, such as improvisation, music and imagery, or vibroacoustic techniques. Others draw from music education approaches, adapting Orff, Kodály, Dalcroze, or Suzuki methods to clinical use. Still others are based on specific educational, psychotherapeutic, or medical models and theories. However, although they may emphasize different types of music experiences or use different language, terminology, and frameworks to process, explain, and evaluate client responses, all these approaches to music therapy seek to use music and the therapeutic relationship that develops within the context of music experiences to help individuals ameliorate various physical, mental, emotional, or social difficulties and achieve positive growth, change, and enhanced quality of life.

This chapter attempted to give the reader a basic understanding of some of the more common approaches to music therapy treatment that are used in the United States at this time. Several models of music therapy practice were discussed: Nordoff-Robbins Creative Music Therapy and other methods of improvisational music therapy; the Bonny Method of Guided Imagery and Music [GIM] and other music and imagery techniques; Vibroacoustic Music Therapy; clinical applications of Orff-Schulwerk methods, Kodály concepts, Dalcroze eurhythmics, and Suzuki methodology; Developmental Music Therapy; behavioral music therapy; psychodynamic music therapy; cognitive music therapy; humanistic music therapy; and biomedical music therapy. While specific approaches may have distinct advantages in certain settings or with certain types of clients, music therapists are cautioned against fanatically adopting one theory, model, approach, or technique to the exclusion of all others. No one method or set of techniques can possibly have all the answers for every situation.

QUESTIONS FOR THOUGHT AND DISCUSSION

1. List and briefly describe some "schools" or models of music therapy practice centered around *particular music techniques*. What special skills or types of training does the music therapist need to use these models of practice? Are there any particular groups of clients who are most likely to benefit from these approaches? Which ones? Why?

2. List and briefly describe some "schools" or models of music therapy practice centered around particular *music education approaches*. What special skills or types of training does the music therapist need to use these models of practice? Are there any particular groups of clients who are most likely to benefit from these approaches? Which ones? Why?

3. List and briefly describe some "schools" or models of music therapy practice based on specific *educational, psychotherapeutic, or medical models and*

theories. What special skills or types of training does the music therapist need to use these models of practice? Are there any particular groups of clients who are most likely to benefit from these approaches? Which ones? Why?

4. What one basic principle unites all these schools of practice? Why is this important?

5. What are some advantages and disadvantages of adopting a particular theory or approach to treatment? Of what must music therapists who work primarily from one technical approach or theoretical orientation always be aware? Why?

6. Is it important for music therapists to be aware of and perhaps even skilled in a number of different treatment techniques and approaches? Why or why not?

SUGGESTIONS FOR FURTHER READING

Arnold, M. (1975). Music therapy in a transactional analysis setting. *Journal of Music Therapy, 12*(3), 104-120.

Bachman, M. L. (1991). *Dalcroze today: An education through and into music.* New York: Oxford University Press.

Bitcon, C. H. (1976). *Alike and different: The clinical and educational use of Orff-Schulwerk.* Santa Ana, CA: Rosha Press.

Bonny, H. L. (1978). *Facilitating guided imagery and music sessions.* Baltimore, MD: ICM Publishing.

Bonny, H. L. (1978). *Guided imagery and music therapy: Past, present, and future implications.* Baltimore, MD: ICM Publishing.

Bonny, H. L. (1978). *The role of tape music programs in the guided imagery and music process: Theory and product.* Baltimore, MD: ICM Publishing.

Bonny, H. L. (1989). Sound as symbol: Guided imagery and music in clinical practice. *Music Therapy Perspectives, 6,* 7-10.

Bonny, H. L. (1994). Twenty-one years later: A GIM update. *Music Therapy Perspectives, 12*(2), 70-74.

Bonny, H. L., & Savary, L. M. (1990). *Music and your mind: Listening with a new consciousness* (Rev. ed.). Barrytown, NY: Station Hill Press.

Bruscia, K. E. (1987). *Improvisational models of music therapy.* Springfield, IL: Charles C Thomas.

Bruscia, K. E. (1989). The practical side of improvisational music therapy. *Music Therapy Perspectives, 6,* 11-15.

Chesky, K. S., & Michel, D. E. (1991). The Music Vibration Table (MVT™): Developing a technology and conceptual model for pain relief. *Music Therapy Perspectives, 9,* 32-38.

Froehlich, M. A. R. (1996). Orff-Schulwerk music therapy in crisis intervention with hospitalized children. In M. A. R. Froehlich (Ed.), *Music therapy with hospitalized children: A creative arts child life approach* (pp. 25-36). Cherry Hill, NJ: Jeffrey Books.

Froehlich, M. A. R. (1996). Introduction to current music education methods applicable to music therapy. In M. A. R. Froehlich (Ed.), *Music therapy with hospitalized children: A creative arts child life approach* (pp. 330-340). Cherry Hill, NJ: Jeffrey Books.

Hibben, J. (1984). Movement as musical expression in a music therapy setting. *Music Therapy, 4*(1), 91-97.

Landis, B., & Carder, P. (1972). *The eclectic curriculum in American music education: Contributions of Dalcroze, Kodály, and Orff.* Reston, VA: Music Educators National Conference.

Lathom, W. (1974). Application of Kodály concepts in music theory. *Journal of Music Therapy, 11*(1), 13-20.

Madsen, C. K. (1981). *Music therapy: A behavioral guide for the mentally retarded.* Lawrence, KS: National Association for Music Therapy.

McRae, S. W. (1982), The Orff connection . . . reaching the special child. *Music Educators Journal, 68*(8), 32-34.

Metzler, R. K. (1982). Suzuki and therapy: Nurtured by love. *Voice of the Lakes* (Newsletter of the Great Lakes Regional Chapter, National Association for Music Therapy), *26*(2), 14-19.

Nordoff, P., & Robbins, C. (1971). *Therapy in music for handicapped children.* London: Victor Gollancz Ltd.

Nordoff, P., & Robbins, C. (1977). *Creative music therapy.* New York: John Day.

Orff, G. (1980). *The Orff music therapy.* London: Schott & Co., Ltd.

Ponath, L. H., & Bitcon, C. H. (1972). A behavioral analysis of Orff-Schulwerk. *Journal of Music Therapy, 9*(2), 56-63.

Priestley, M. (1985). *Music therapy in action* (2nd ed.). St. Louis: MMB Music.

Purvis, J., & Samet, S. (1976). *Music in developmental therapy: A curriculum guide.* Baltimore, MD: University Park Press.

Ruud, E. (1980). *Music therapy and its relationship to current treatment theories* (Rev. Eng. ed.). St. Louis: Magnamusic-Baton.

Schulberg, C. H. (1981). *The music therapy sourcebook: A collection of activities categorized and analyzed.* New York: Human Sciences Press.

Scovel, M. A. (1990). Music therapy within the context of psychotherapeutic models. In R. F. Unkefer (Ed.), *Music therapy in the treatment of adults with mental disorders* (pp. 96-108). New York: Schirmer.

Skille, O. (1989). *VibroAcoustic therapy. Music Therapy, 8*(1), 61-66.

Standley, J. M. (1996). A meta-analysis on the effects of music as reinforcement for education/therapy objectives. *Journal of Research in Music Education, 44*(2), 105-133.

Summer, L. (1988). *Guided imagery and music in the institutional setting.* St. Louis: MMB Music.

Taylor, D. B. (1997). *Biomedical foundations of music as therapy.* St. Louis: MMB Music.

Wheeler, B. (1981). The relationship between music therapy and theories of psychotherapy. *Music Therapy, 1*(1), 9-16.

Wigram, T. (1995). The psychological and physiological effects of low frequency sound and music. *Music Therapy Perspectives, 13*(1), 16-23.

Wood, M. M., Graham, R. M., Swan, W. W., Purvis, J., Gigliotti, C., & Samet, S. (1974). *Developmental music therapy.* Lawrence, KS: National Association for Music Therapy.

Chapter Twenty-three

CLINICIANS AND RESEARCH

THE IMPORTANCE OF RESEARCH

SINCE THE EARLIEST days of the modern music therapy profession, leaders in the profession have viewed research as an essential element in establishing the therapeutic use of music as a viable treatment approach. The father of modern music therapy, E. Thayer Gaston (1968b), strongly emphasized that research, along with theory and practice, is vital to the continuing existence and viability of the discipline of music therapy:

> Without practice and research, theory is impotent and unproven; without theory and research, practice is blind; and without theory and practice, research is inapplicable. To fail to have some understanding of research is to remove one leg of the tripod supporting music therapy. (p. 408)

Although research and clinical practice may at times seem to have little in common, research can be very important to practicing music therapy clinicians in several ways. Research can help clinicians (1) understand normal or usual reactions to musical stimuli that will guide them in initial selections of music to accomplish certain effects; (2) determine and select music therapy methods and intervention strategies that are most likely to be most effective and efficient in accomplishing certain goals with particular client populations; (3) refine and create theories and conceptual models to guide practice; (4) confirm and substantiate methods of practice; or (5) reflect on and improve methods of practice (Gfeller & Davis, 1992; Kenny, 1998; Shuler, 1990; Siegel et al., 1986). Thus,

an understanding of research techniques and methods is important to music therapy clinicians as well as music therapy researchers, for clinicians must be able to effectively judge the quality of the research on which they base their practice and theories (Colwell, 1990; Prickett, 1989). As Duerksen (1968) noted: "The advancement of knowledge and practice in music therapy depends on the quality of the research performed and used by its practitioners" (p. 409).

Already during the 1920s, 1930s, and 1940s, music therapy pioneers like Willem van de Wall were stressing the need for "scientific research that could establish the validity and practical efficiency of music in institutions" (Clair & Heller, 1989, p. 171). When a professional organization, the National Association for Music Therapy, was established in 1950, the Research Committee became its first standing committee (Boxberger, 1963; Smith, 1998). Since that time, professional music therapy organizations have continued to emphasize the importance of research to the growth and acceptance of the music therapy profession. In fact, NAMT, AAMT, and AMTA have all listed encouraging, developing, or promoting research in music therapy as part of their goal or purpose statements (AAMT, 1993; AMTA, 1998; NAMT, 1980).

A survey by Nicholas and Gilbert (1980) found that music therapists do hold a generally positive attitude toward research: Over 95 percent of the respondents agreed with the need for research classes for music therapy students at both the graduate and undergraduate levels, and over 96 percent cited the need for more research in the field of music therapy.

Moreover, "81.3 percent felt that increasing accountability regulations and budget restrictions would force music therapists to become more aware of research results in the next five years" (p. 209). In the late 1980s and 1990s, there has indeed been an increasing emphasis on documenting (and researching) the cost effectiveness as well as the treatment effectiveness of music therapy procedures (Clark & Ficken, 1988; Furman, 1988, 1996). Recently established music therapy research grants and funds also demonstrate that research continues to be perceived as a key component of the future development of music therapy (Smith, 1998).

TYPES OF RESEARCH

Research, or systematic inquiry, in music therapy and related disciplines (e.g., music education, special education, education, psychology) can take many forms. These various forms of research can also be grouped or classified in several ways, such as by purpose, degree of formality, topic, method, or general orientation/perspective (Gay, 1981; Madsen & Madsen, 1978; Isaac & Michael, 1971; Merrion, 1990; Wheeler, 1995). Each of these divisions or classifications "serves a different purpose and may contribute in a different way to our understanding" (Wheeler, 1995, p.8).

When research is classified *by purpose*, it is often grouped into the two broad divisions of *basic* or *applied* research (Merrion, 1990; Wheeler, 1995). *Basic research*, also known as *pure research* or *fundamental research*, is done to increase fundamental knowledge about phenomena or to provide explanations for observed events. It is not concerned with practical applications. However, the knowledge gained from basic research (e.g., information regarding auditory processing or basic acoustics or how the brain responds to music) may lead to changes in practice or refinements of theories. Therefore, basic research frequently "provides the building blocks for applied research" (Merrion, 1990, p. 23). *Applied research* focuses on practical problems, devising ways to test hypotheses or models of practice to solve concerns in real life situations. Gay (1981) also includes evaluation research, research and development, action research in his classification of research by purpose. *Evaluation research* systematically collects and analyzes data to guide individuals in selecting alternatives and making decisions. *Research and development* is concerned with developing and testing products that will be most effective for specific purposes. *Action research* applies the scientific method to devise solutions for a specific problem in a specific setting. Its goal is a local solution, not a contribution to science or general knowledge.

Research sometimes is classified by *degree of formality*, as formal educational or therapeutic research, action research, or casual research (Isaac & Michael, 1971; Rutkowski, 1996). *Casual* or *"common sense" research* is frequently used by teachers and therapists as an approach to identifying problems and finding solutions that will improve teaching/ therapy methods and increase student/client learning or adaptive functioning. Observation is casual and methods do not involve rigorous procedures or require any special training. The focus is on making changing in current procedures that seem likely to improve the situation. Individuals who conduct *formal research* need extensive training in research methods, statistics, and measurement procedures. Formal research tries to find knowledge or solutions that will be generalizable to broad populations. It is also used to develop and test theories of practice. *Action research* is not as rigorous as formal research, but does provide a framework for problem solving that is more orderly and directed than casual inquiry. Individuals who conduct action research need some training in measurement techniques, research methods, and possibly statistics. Rigorous designs and complex statistics are usually unnecessary in action research; the research simply tries to show some numbers that demonstrate change. The goal of action research is obtaining knowledge or developing new skills and approaches that can be applied directly to solve problems in a classroom or therapy situations. Action research takes a flexible, adaptive approach to problem solving, "sacrificing control in favor of responsiveness and on-the-spot experimentation and innovation" (Isaac & Michael, 1971, p. 27). Subjects are students, clients, or staff with whom the researcher works. Since the sample is restricted and unrepresentative of the general population, findings are useful within the practical dimensions of the specific situation, but usually not generalizable to broader populations.

In discussing the boundaries of music therapy research, Bruscia (1995a) classified research in still another way, *by topic*, as discipline, profession, or foundational research. *Discipline research* is concerned with how music therapists interact with clients and use music to help clients improve their health or level of functioning. It may include *assessment studies* that show how clients use or respond to various musical materials, musical experiences, or types/styles of music under a variety of conditions and then relate this data to their treatment needs, as well as *treatment studies* that focus on specific methods of intervention used in music therapy and *evaluation studies* that measure the outcomes or effects of music therapy treatment. *Profession research* focuses on music therapists and socioeconomic, educational, or political concerns that affect the profession. Topics may include *employment practices, characteristics or opinions of music therapists, professional education and training, professional standards, legislative and public relations* issues that impact the profession and its relationship to other disciplines, the *history of music therapy* (organizational, cultural, or individual), and *meta-analyses or compilations of research and clinical literature. Foundational research*, though not itself directly about music therapy, provides knowledge, evidence, or support for concepts that are related to music therapy and may impact music therapy practice. Examples include studies on *music psychology, music physiology, sociology or anthropology of music, acoustics, psychoacoustics, music education, general needs and characteristics of client populations, other therapeutic methods, theories, or approaches*, or *characteristics of and issues in other health professions*.

One of the most common ways to classify research is *by method*. Traditionally, research methods have been grouped into four main types: philosophical, historical, descriptive, and experimental (Gfeller & Davis, 1992; Madsen & Madsen, 1978; Merrion, 1990; Wheeler, 1995). *Philosophical research* asks why and is concerned with analyzing and synthesizing ideas to discern truths or principles that are founda-

tional to music therapy or certain music therapy methods. It involves speculation based on logical thinking, analysis, and criticism and uses argument as its primary mode of inquiry and presentation (Aigen, 1995d; Gfeller & Davis, 1992; Madsen & Madsen, 1978; Wheeler, 1995). Philosophical methods clarify terms, expose and evaluate underlying assumptions, and relate ideas as systematic theories. Philosophical research is useful for (a) developing theories and value systems for practice, training, and research, (b) evaluating current theories and paradigms, (c) increasing the integration of the field of music therapy, (d) comparing concepts and theories from different disciplines, (e) drawing implications of music therapy practice to related areas, (f) suggesting conceptual solutions to alleviate practical problems in music therapy, and (g) discussing relating the scientific and artistic aspects of music and music therapy (Aigen, 1995d).

Historical research describes what was, systematically studying the evidence of the past to gain knowledge about the past and understand it in relation to the present (Gay, 1981; Gfeller & Davis, 1992; Madsen & Madsen, 1978; Solomon, 1995; Solomon & Heller, 1982; Wheeler, 1995). Historical researchers may study people, places (e.g., geographic regions, institutions, organizations), or events and ideas, using evidence from pictorial records, official records, personal correspondence, interviews, published books or articles, artifacts, or handwritten materials. Researchers must take care to analyze any historical evidence for credibility and accuracy. Historical research can help educate and inform music therapists about past practices, problems, and trends, increase their collective sense of purpose and identity, and help them use and draw on the accumulated wisdom of the past (Solomon, 1995; Solomon & Heller, 1982).

Descriptive research is concerned with what is and uses systematic methods to observe people, places, settings, or things, gather information about a current situation, and identify themes and patterns or examine the relationship between certain observed phenomena (Aigen, 1995c; Gay, 1981; Gfeller & Davis, 1992; Lathom-Radocy & Radocy, 1995; Madsen & Madsen, 1978; Merrion, 1990; Wheeler, 1995). Although descriptive research often uses numbers to help quantify observations or describe probabilities or correlations (Lathom-Radocy & Radocy, 1995; Merrion, 1990; Wheeler, 1995), it may also focus on identifying themes and constructs suggested and supported by detailed descriptions of human experiences (Aigen, 1995c; Wheeler, 1995). While descriptive research may be concerned with the relationships among variables, it does not manipulate the variables in question, but simply describes their current relationship. Types of descriptive studies include *surveys, ex post facto research* (includes *correlational* and *causal-comparative* studies), *case studies, developmental studies* (includes *longitudinal studies, activity analyses* [i.e., tasks and procedures needed to do a certain job], *trend studies,* and *cross-sectional studies*), *ethnographic studies,* and *interpretational research* (Aigen, 1995c; Lathom-Radocy & Radocy, 1995; Merrion, 1990; Wheeler, 1995).

Experimental research carefully selects groups and systematically manipulates a certain variable or variables to determine what will be given certain factors, parameters, and conditions (Gay, 1981; Gfeller & Davis, 1992; Hanser & Wheeler, 1995; Madsen & Madsen, 1978; Wheeler, 1995). Experimental research is the *only* research method that can precisely establish cause-and-effect relationships. It does this "by isolating the experimental variable and manipulating certain other factors under highly controlled conditions to ascertain how and why a particular event occurs" (Madsen & Madsen, 1978, p. 17). Procedures in experimental research are characterized by exactness and rigor. Variables are isolated by precise definition and/or design structure, and extreme care is taken to insure validity and reliability in measurement. Data are usually subjected to statistical analysis. Experimental research may use one-sample, two-sample, or multiple-sample designs. A single subject design known as *applied behavior analysis,* which systematically examines "the functional relationship between music therapy or other treatments and the particular behavior(s) of interest" (Hanser, 1995, p. 151), can be very useful in examining or testing the effectiveness of music therapy treatment procedures.

In recent years, research has frequently been classified not so much by method as *by the general orientation or perspective of the researcher* and has been divided into the two major categories of quantitative or qualitative research (Rutkowski, 1996; Wheeler, 1995). These methods differ significantly in philosophy, research focus or interest, and methodology (Bruscia, 1995b). *Quantitative research* strives to

quantify events or observations, focusing on things that can be measured or counted and using numbers to describe data and report outcomes (Aigen, 1995e; Bruscia, 1995b; Prickett, 1995; Rutkowski, 1996; Wheeler, 1995). It is an objective, cut-and-dried approach to investigation, based on the empirical method. Quantitative researchers hold a positivistic view of the word. They believe that absolute truth exists and can be revealed through research. They focus on objectivity and the discovery of time- and context-free generalizations that can be transferred from one setting to another in a value-free manner. Quantitative research looks at specific variables and uses operational definitions and deductive reasoning in a directed search for truth. This type of study always proceeds from a basic research question that serves to focus the investigation (Bruscia, 1995d). Through carefully methodology and rigorous research design, the researcher tries to maintain the position of an impartial observer.

Until recently, most music therapy research utilized quantitative methods, such as quantitative descriptive research (Lathom-Radocy & Radocy, 1995; Prickett, 1995), experimental research (Hanser & Wheeler, 1995; Prickett, 1995), or applied behavior analysis (Hanser, 1995; Prickett, 1995). Quantitative methods have the advantages of yielding reliable results and measurements that are easily understood by professionals in other disciplines and of using research designs, methodology, and analysis procedures that can be replicated by others (Prickett, 1995; Taylor, 1997). Some music therapists believe that quantitative research methods must be used "in order to establish music therapy firmly within the community of medical and scientifically based disciplines" (Taylor, 1997, p. 123). However, some research questions, such as preliminary investigations to identify basic variables, holistic comparisons of therapeutic processes, or complex issues that deal with deeply held values or depend on fluctuating emotional responses, do not lend themselves well to quantitative methods and may be better approached in other ways (Prickett, 1995).

Qualitative research takes a more subjective, humanistic, holistic view and relies on detailed verbal descriptions rather than measurements or numbers (Aigen, 1993, 1995e, 1998; Brusica, 1995b; Forinash, 1995; Forinash & Lee, 1998; Kenny, 1998; Rutkowski, 1996; Ruud, 1998; Wheeler, 1995).

Instead of trying to reduce experience to isolated, quantifiable variables, qualitative researchers strive to describe and interpret the entire process or experience using sounds, music, words, and pictures. Qualitative research takes place in natural settings. It has a broad focus and uses inductive reasoning and analysis to draw hypotheses and conclusions from the events and descriptions that emerge from the research process. Qualitative researchers believe that there are multiple levels of knowing (affective, intellectual, sensory, intuitional) and multiple truths and realities dependent on individual perspectives and perceptions. They believe that all research is value bound and that findings are context-specific. Therefore, they seek not to uncover universal truths but to discover the meanings, patterns, and essences of specific acts.

Qualitative studies may focus on (a) holistic description, identifying all facets of an experience, (b) definition of essence, identifying aspects of an experience that define it, (c) analysis, looking at how an experience is organized, (d) theory building, striving to find how things work, (e) interpretation, trying to identify the meaning of an experience, (f) re-creation, reproducing behaviors, phenomena, or interactions to try to understand them from the participant's point of view and verify meaning with the participants, (g) critique, determining value according to a particular system of beliefs or standards, or (h) self-exploration, analyzing and interpreting the researcher's own personal understanding and experience (Bruscia, 1995e). In qualitative methods, interactions between the researcher and participant(s) are essential to the process, the researcher takes on the role of participant-observer, and the researcher and participant(s) often work together in gathering data and interpreting phenomena. Instead of trying to eliminate their own values and beliefs, qualitative researchers delineate them and use them as tools in the research process.

Instead of choosing a method or design beforehand, qualitative researchers allow the method to evolve during the course of the investigation. Qualitative methods also have standards which, though very different from those of qualitative methods, still assure research value and integrity (Bruscia, 1998). Qualitative research methods include (1) *grounded theory*, which focuses on generating and

testing theory; (2) *naturalistic inquiry*, which studies events and interactions in natural contexts or settings and uses the researcher's whole self as a tool for data collection and analysis; (3) *phenomenology*, which studies participants' holistic experience of a given phenomenon or situation, and (4) *hermeneutics*, an interpretive-descriptive approach that studies, describes, and interprets human actions and practices (Aigen, 1995c, 1995e, 1998; Forinash, 1995). These methods have been used increasingly in music therapy research since the late 1980s as music therapists have looked for methods that could provide insights into the *entire* music therapy experience, including its subjective, creative, and aesthetic aspects (Aigen, 1993, 1995e, 1998; Bruscia, 1995b; Forinash, 1995; Kenny, 1998; Taylor, 1997; Wheeler, 1995). Forinash and Lee (1998) provide a comprehensive bibliography of books and articles dealing with qualitative music therapy research approaches.

From the preceding paragraphs, it is evident that there are many different types, philosophies, and methods of research. However, it is important to realize that no research method or philosophy is inherently better than or superior to any other, and all methods or approaches have their own strengths and weaknesses in given situations (Bruscia, 1995b; Gfeller & Davis, 1992; Ruud, 1998). The question, therefore, becomes not so much which approach or method is better, but which is best suited to (a) the nature of the particular phenomenon to be studied, (b) the nature of the research question or problem, (c) the research setting, (d) the type of researcher-subject relationship needed to achieve the objective, and (e) the purpose of the study and the type of information needed by the researcher and his or her audience (Bruscia, 1995b; Isaac & Michael, 1971). For example, music therapists who are interested in focusing on *behaviors* changed by music therapy interventions or on evaluating *outcomes* of music therapy treatment will be more likely to look to *quantitative* approaches, while those who wish to focus more on the *process* of therapy, including unconscious issues and subjective *experiences* that occur *during* therapeutic treatment may find *qualitative* methods are more suited to their needs (Wheeler, 1995). In order to develop as complete a picture of their discipline as possible, music therapists need to develop a "comprehensive research culture"

(Kenny, 1998, p. 215) that values and utilizes all forms and methods of research and has "the intellectual flexibility to envision more than one path to knowledge" (Prickett, 1995, p. 99). As Bruscia (1995b) concluded after surveying, comparing, and contrasting quantitative and qualitative research paradigms:

Music therapy is too broad and complex to be defined, contained, or limited by one approach to research. . . . Both quantitative and qualitative research are needed to enhance our mission. (p. 71)

THE RESEARCH ATTITUDE

The research attitude is a certain way of thinking, a way of systematically investigating and studying phenomena to learn more about the world. According to Madsen and Madsen (1978), the research attitude has three primary components; "(1) an objective state of mind, (2) a structured mode of action, and (3) evaluation for future action' (p. 5). A research attitude enables individuals "to analyze, critique, make transfers, and choose alternative in light of all possible evidence" (Madsen, 1986, p. 51).

When individuals approach problems with an objective state of mind, they gather information or data without any preconceived notions as to what this information means. This attitude is important both to quantitative researchers, who try to eliminate personal biases and values and look at situations as objectively as possible, and to qualitative researchers, who focus on letting meaning and research design evolve from the data itself. For example, phenomenological researchers strive to describe indigenous phenomena as completely as possible and then question, analyze, and critique their descriptions. The information gained from this process then guides further inquiry (Forinash, 1995). All researchers, then, start objectively by gathering information and analyzing or critiquing this information to determine

patterns and themes, make implications, and/or choose alternatives. This type of thinking is not limited to researchers; it is also used regularly in decision-making processes in everyday life.

The next characteristic of the research attitude is a structured plan for action, which may be a predetermined design or methodology (quantitative approaches) or may be a more flexible, fluid process that evolves as the information gathered in one step of the research process, along with the interactions between researcher and participants, impact the process and procedures in the next step (qualitative approaches). This structured mode of action and thoughtful observation and inquiry allow individuals both to organize their activities and investigations in a way that is consistent with their thoughts, ideas, values, and interests and to test the worth or value of their ideas and actions. Finally, a research attitude prompts individuals to use the results of their investigations in planning future actions, transferring and applying these results to other situations (Madsen, 1986). While research does not establish absolutes, it does enable one to suggest explanations and predictions that will hold up until more information is obtained in future investigations.

APPLYING THE RESEARCH ATTITUDE IN CLINICAL PRACTICE

Michel (1976) proposed that the development of the research attitude was perhaps the most important aspect of music therapy education: "Not only must students be able to continue to learn and grow in their field once formal education has been completed, but they must also know how to objectively evaluate their daily work with patients" (p. 113). The research attitude, then, with its

characteristic objective state of mind and structured plan of action that enables individuals to gather, analyze, critique, and evaluate information so they can use in planning future actions, is not something that should be foreign to music therapy clinicians. Rather, the characteristics of the research attitude are essential to effective clinical practice. This point can be illustrated further by comparing the steps followed in conducting an experimental research study with the procedures followed in developing, implement-

ing, and evaluating the effectiveness of music therapy treatment plans (see Table II).

Table II
PARALLELS BETWEEN STEPS IN IMPLEMENTING
RESEARCH STUDIES AND CLINICAL
TREATMENT PLANS

Research Studies	Clinical Treatment Plans
Statement of the research problem; purpose of the study	Statement of the client's problem; reason for treatment
Related literature	Consultation; related literature
Hypotheses; research questions	Specific treatment goals and/or objectives
Research design (including procedure and method of evaluation)	Treatment plan (including intervention strategy and method of evaluation)
	Results (observational data and whether or not client met goals/objectives)
Results (observational data and results of statistical tests)	Conclusions (continue, discontinue, or revise treatment plan)
Conclusions (accept or reject hypotheses)	Implications of results for current and future treatment plans and procedures
Discussion (generalizations, implications, suggestions for future research)	

The first step in the research process involves formulating a statement of the problem that is to be investigated. This is a natural step, for before researchers can conduct research, they must have something to find out about, a purpose for the study. Likewise, before clinicians can design treatment plans, they must determine that their clients have certain problems or needs that can be treated in music therapy sessions, a reason to begin music therapy intervention.

The second step in the research process is concerned with finding out more about the problem by learning what others have had to say about the same or similar problems. In experimental research, this information is usually obtained through a biblio-

graphic search and is reported formally in the "Related Literature" section of the research paper. To plan effective music therapy intervention strategies, music therapy clinicians also need to find out more about the problem they have defined as the target of therapy. This knowledge may be gained by continuing to observe the client or by reading reports in the client's records and talking with others who have observed or worked with the client. Clinicians may also consult with colleagues who have had extensive experience working with the particular client population in question or search the literature of music therapy and related fields to find out what types of approaches and treatment techniques others have used effectively with clients who have similar needs or problems. Many bibliographic sources (Eagle, 1976, 1978, 1982; Eagle & Miniter, 1984) and databases available through the internet or academic libraries (see listing of examples in "Passion for Research," 1998, p. 39) are now available to assist clinicians in this search for information.

The third step in the research process consists of narrowing down the general problem to something more specific that can be tested and evaluated. The information gained in the second step helps one determine more precisely what questions need to be asked or what answers must be sought. In experimental research, this third step involves the process of formulating hypotheses that state exactly what is to be investigated. In clinical practice, this third step involves the process of specifying what particular therapeutic goals and/or objectives the music therapy treatment procedures should help the client reach.

The next step in the research process involves determining ways to find an answer to the questions posed in the third step. Obviously, the more controlled one can make a situation, the more likely it will be that the answers one finds are the correct ones for the questions asked. In experimental research, this step is concerned with determining the research design, including components such as number and manner of selection of subjects, setting, materials and equipment, procedure, and evaluation techniques. In clinical practice, this step involves the process of determining what music therapy intervention strategies will be used to help the client meet the therapeutic goals, including consideration of components such as setting (group or individual treatment; specific way room is set up), materials and equipment to be used, specific implementation procedures, and method of evaluation that will be used to determine whether or not the client has

reached the goal.

The final steps in the research process involve reporting results and then drawing conclusions, generalizations, and/or implications from these results. Researchers do this by reporting the findings of their observations and statistical evaluations, accepting or rejecting their hypotheses based on these results, and proposing implications or generalizations from their findings. Music therapy clinicians go through a similar process when they report their observations of the client's behavior in music therapy sessions and, based on the client's responses and behavior, make determinations as to whether or not the client has reached the therapeutic goals or objective. These clinical results lead to conclusions as to the effectiveness of the treatment procedures used and decisions as to whether the treatment plan should be continued, discontinued, or revised. The results may also provide implications for revisions in the treatment technique or for intervention strategies that may be useful in future sessions with clients having the same or similar problems and needs.

While the preceding paragraphs focused on comparing the clinician's approach to developing, implementing, and evaluating music therapy intervention strategies with the steps of experimental research studies, similar parallels might also be drawn between music therapy clinical practice and other methods of quantitative or qualitative research. The point is that the same type of attitude that is important in conducting good research is also essential to effective clinical practice. Thus, the clinician already possesses some of the attitudes, skills, and knowledges necessary for doing quality research. The next section of this chapter focuses on ways clinicians can both use the research of others and conduct their own research in clinical settings.

USING AND DOING RESEARCH IN CLINICAL SETTINGS

If the profession of music therapy is to advance, develop, and be accepted as an important health and rehabilitation service, music therapists must learn to make research and research findings an integral part of everything they do (Smith, 1998). Research is essential both as a guide to practice and as tool to develop and support theory (Gaston, 1968b). Thus,

research is vital both to increasing knowledge about music therapy and to advancing music therapy clinical practice. It is essential, then, that music therapy clinicians (1) know how to *use* quality research, making appropriate applications and transfers to their particular clinical situation as they base their approaches on interventions, theories, and techniques that have been tested or verified by research, and (2) know how to *do* quality research that demonstrates the effectiveness and efficiency of unique or innovative strategies and applications they have discovered in their clinical work.

Music therapy clinicians *use* research when they read research reports and make transfers and applications to their clinical practice. If research in music education is seen as the means to better teaching and more successful learning (Colwell, 1990), research in music therapy might be seen as the means to better clinical practices and finding ways to help clients reach their therapeutic goals more efficiently and effectively. By reading published research, clinicians can learn about solutions to clinical problems that already been tested by formal research methods (Prickett, 1989; Shuler, 1990). By learning to make conscious use of research in their clinical practices, music therapists can grow professionally and discover ways of more effectively helping their clients. Although at first glance published research may not seem applicable to their clinical situations, as music therapy clinicians cultivate some knowledge of research terminology, analysis, and applications and learn to find ways of transferring research findings to their own situations and interests, they will find that much research will indeed have important clinical applications (Madsen, 1986; Taylor, 1987a).

Not only the researcher, but also the clinician, must be able to evaluate research, be aware of its limitations, and make potential appropriate parallels and applications (e.g., what techniques might be used and which should be avoided in particular situation; what procedures might make therapy more efficient and effective; what directions it suggests for the future). As Shuler (1990) noted: "A research study only provides information, and it is the reader – not the author – who draws the really important conclusions" (p. 38) as he/she considers the implications of the study for his/her particular clinical situation. Research data needs to be evaluated, clarified, and interpreted by the *user* (clinician) as well as by the researcher before being accepted, applied to practice, and used as a basis for clinical decisions (Colwell, 1990). The discussion sections of research reports may give clinicians ideas for potential applications, but it is ultimately the responsibility of the individual clinician to make

transfers and draw implications so that research will have greater meaning in his/her particular situation (Madsen, 1986; "Passion for Research," 1998).

Keeping abreast of current research and developments in the field, through reading and attending convention sessions about cutting-edge research and innovative practice, is an important part of professional behavior, something professionals in many fields do (Merrion, 1990, p. 24). Music therapists, too, will benefit from learning to become stronger and better-informed consumers of research and willing participants in the use and development of research within their area of practice. In addition to assisting clinicians in finding the most effective, efficient clinical strategies for helping their clients reach particular goals, intelligent and informed use of research can give them added credibility as they explain their clinical practices to other professionals, clients, administrators, and reimbursers (Prickett, 1995; Taylor, 1997).

> The degree to which music therapists can look other professionals, our clients, and our reimbursers straight in the eye when we talk about the viability of our clinical practices is directly related to the level of objective, documented research the we can cite. Research may be difficult, but the effort is worthwhile. (Prickett, 1995, p. 114)

As well as learning to use and apply the research of others, music therapy clinicians can also find ways to *do* research; i.e., to conduct their own research in clinical settings. Clinical and research papers published by clinicians, as well as educators and graduate students, are vital to continued development of systematic knowledge regarding music therapy clinical techniques and approaches (Braswell, Maranto, & Decuir, 1979b). Clinicians commonly develop clear, objective, and appropriate measures to test the effectiveness of clinical intervention strategies in the course of their clinical work in music therapy. When they take the time to (a) reflect on this data in relationship to other situations or other knowledge in the field of music therapy, (b) draw general or broader implications, applications, or conclusions, and (c) share these with others, they move from a *clinical process*, which involves action and reflection in relation to a particular client or situation, to a *research process*, which includes "an added perspective or meta reflection" (Bruscia, 1995a, p. 22) and seeks to apply, generalize, or transfer the findings to similar clients and contexts, thus increasing or modifying the general knowledge base in music therapy. As Aigen (1995e) noted, there is a type of natural progression from session notes to treatment summaries to in-depth case studies to research projects that analyze and compare the responses of many individual clients to music therapy procedures. By doing research in clinical settings, music therapy clinicians can improve their professional and clinical skills, determine which methods and procedures are most effective and efficient, and share their positive results "as sources of information and inspiration for others" (Rutkowski, 1996, p. 62).

Some forms of research, such as action research (Rutkowski, 1996), applied behavior analysis (Hanser, 1995), certain types of descriptive research (e.g., case studies, developmental studies, or interpretational research) (Aigen, 1995c; Lathom-Radocy & Radocy, 1995; Merrion, 1990; Wheeler, 1995) and some types of quantitative research (Aigen, 1995e; Forinash, 1995), may more easily coexist with the natural, day-to-day activities of music therapy

clinicians than some of the more formal, experimental methods. However, experimental studies can also be conducted in clinical settings, usually with some modifications that help balance clinical and research concerns and make *a priori* decisions to place clinical benefits above experimental concerns (Standley, 1992).

> Clinicians should not be discouraged from conducting research by the necessity to accommodate methodology to clinical priorities. . . . The impact of any new information on a developing field of study can be of great value since a body of research requires time to accumulate and is stimulated by a variety of factors. (Standley, 1992, p. 27)

Clinicians, then, should be encouraged to perform all kinds of research. Those who wish to do more formal studies may find it useful to collaborate or form partnerships with university professors (Shuler, 1990). The American Music Therapy Association's Research Committee also offers clinicians assistance and expertise in designing and reporting research studies.

IMPORTANCE OF REPORTING FINDINGS

Research may lead to new insights or discoveries for the individual researcher, but only when research is documented and disseminated (e.g., in journal articles, through conference presentations) does it have the ability to contribute to or modify existing knowledge or practice in the field of music therapy (Bruscia, 1995a). The body of knowledge in music therapy, like that of any profession, is contained within and dependent upon its literature (Braswell, Decuir, & Maranto, 1980). Therefore, music therapy clinicians, who have first-hand knowledge of the effectiveness or ineffectiveness of music therapy interventions with various populations, must take the time and make the effort to write up and report the knowledge and insights they gain from their clinical work and research if the knowledge base of music therapy is to be expanded.

Existing deficits will be ameliorated when a

concerted effort to communicate is made by the entire profession. . . . Music therapists in academic and clinical settings must therefore work together to resolve perceived deficiencies and shortcomings in the profession. (Braswell, Decuir, & Maranto, 1980, p. 147)

As was noted earlier in this chapter, many methods and approaches to research are available. Both descriptive and experimental methods, quantitative and qualitative approaches, increase music therapy's knowledge base. Moreover, "nothing is more scientific than to observe well and report accurately" (Gaston, 1968b, p. 230).

In addition to increasing the knowledge base of music therapy, published reports of clinical research findings may help generate new ideas for theories or more formal research studies that will then lead to improved or innovative clinical techniques and practices. "Sometimes the most stringent empirical research is derived from clinical innovation or exploratory endeavor" (Standley, 1992, p. 27). However, if these innovations or explorations are not shared with others through publications or conference presentations, they will have little impact on music therapy knowledge, research, or practice.

Published articles and research also provide an accessible, widely available database to help document the contributions of music therapy interventions and determine the cost effectiveness of music therapy treatment procedures (Furman, 1988, 1996). Thus, taking the time to report or publish clinical findings is essential to the growth and development of the profession.

SUMMARY

Since the earliest days of the modern music therapy profession, research has been seen as an essential element in establishing the therapeutic use of music as a viable treatment approach and in advancing knowledge and practice in music therapy. Although research and clinical practice may at times seem to have little in common, research can, in fact, be very important to practicing music therapy clinicians in several ways. Thus, an understanding of research techniques and methods is important to music therapy clinicians as well as music therapy researchers.

Research, or systematic inquiry, in music therapy can take many forms and be grouped or classified in several ways. When research is classified by *purpose*, it is often grouped into the two broad divisions of basic or applied research. Evaluation research, research and development, and action research are sometimes included in this grouping. Others classify research by *degree of formality*, as formal educational or therapeutic research, action research, or casual research. Research may also be classified by *topic*, as discipline, profession, or foundational research. One of the most common ways to classify research, however, is by *method*. Traditionally, research methods have been grouped into four main types: philosophical, historical, descriptive, and experimental. In recent years, research also has frequently been classified not so much by method as by the *general orientation or perspective* of the researcher (quantitative or qualitative). Quantitative research methods strive to quantify events or observations, focus on things that can be measured or counted, use numbers to describe data and report outcomes, and take a more objective approach. Qualitative methods, on the other hand, take a more subjective, humanistic, holistic approach and rely on detailed verbal descriptions of all aspects of an experience rather than measurements or numbers relating to isolated variables. It is important to realize that no research method or philosophy is inherently better than or superior to any other, and all methods or approaches have their own strengths and weaknesses in given situations.

The research attitude a certain way of thinking, a way of systematically investigating and studying phenomena to learn more about the world. It is characterized by "(1) an objective state of mind, (2) a structured mode of action, and (3) evaluation for future action" (Madsen & Madsen, 1978, p. 5). This attitude is as essential to effective clinical practice as it is to research. In fact, many parallels can be drawn between the steps the researcher follows in conducting experiments and the procedures the music therapy clinician follows in developing, implementing, and evaluating music therapy treatment plans.

Music therapy clinicians *use* research when they read research reports and make transfers and applications to their clinical work that lead them to discover new or better clinical techniques and approaches that help their clients reach therapeutic goals more efficiently and effectively. In addition, intelligent and informed use of research can give clinicians added credibility as they explain their clinical practices to other professionals, clients, administrators, and reimbursers. Music therapy clinicians may also at times *do* research that demonstrates the effectiveness and efficiency of unique or innovative strategies and applications they have discovered in their clinical work. Since the knowledge of music therapy, like that of any profession, is dependent upon its literature, music therapy clinicians can do much to aid the development of their profession by taking the time to report and publish the results of their clinical work. Only when they are documented and disseminated are research and clinical findings able to impact, add to, or modify music therapy knowledge, research, or practice.

QUESTIONS FOR THOUGHT AND DISCUSSION

1. List several ways research can be important for or helpful to music therapy clinicians.

2. List five different ways music therapy research can be classified and briefly describe the divisions in each classification. Which of these do you think would be most useful to music therapy clinicians? Why?

3. What are the three general characteristics of the research attitude? How is this attitude important to the practicing music therapy clinician as well as to the active researcher?

4. Describe some ways music therapy clinicians might *use* the research of others. How/why are these important?

5. Describe some ways music therapy clinicians might *do* research in clinical settings. Why/how is clinical research valuable to the profession?

6. Why is it vital to report and disseminate research and clinical findings? What are some ways this can be done?

SUGGESTIONS FOR FURTHER READING

Aigen, K. (1993). The music therapist as qualitative researcher. *Music Therapy, 12*(1), 16-39.

Aigen, K. (1998). Creativity in qualitative music therapy research. *Journal of Music Therapy, 35*(3), 150-175.

Bruscia, K. E. (1998). Standards of integrity for qualitative music therapy research. *Journal of Music Therapy, 35*(3), 176-200.

Colwell, R. (1990). Research findings: Shake well before using. *Music Educators Journal, 77*(3), 29-34.

Duerksen, G. L. (1968). The research process. In E. T. Gaston (Ed.), *Music in therapy* (pp. 409-424). New York: Macmillan.

Gay, L. R. (1981). *Educational research: Competencies for analysis and application* (2nd ed.). Columbus, OH: Charles E. Merrill.

George, W. E. (1968). Measuring and evaluating research. In E. T. Gaston (Ed.), *Music in therapy* (pp. 425-453). New York: Macmillan.

Gfeller, K., & Davis, W. B. (1992). The role of research in music therapy. In W. B. Davis, K. E. Gfeller, & M. H. Thaut, *An introduction to music therapy: Theory and practice* (pp. 302-351). Dubuque, IA: Wm. C. Brown.

Isaac, S., & Michael, W. B. (1971). *Handbook in research and evaluation.* San Diego, CA: EdITS.

Kenny, C. B. (1998). Embracing complexity: The creation of a comprehensive research culture in music therapy. *Journal of Music Therapy, 35*(3), 201-217.

Madsen, C. K. (1986). Research and music therapy: The necessity for transfer. *Journal of Music Therapy, 23*(2), 50-55.

Madsen, C. K., & Madsen, C. H., Jr. (1978). *Experimental research in music.* Raleigh, NC: Contemporary Publishing.

Ruud, E. (1998). Science as metacritique. *Journal of Music Therapy, 35*(3), 218-224.

Shuler, S. C. (1990). Solving instructional problems through research. *Music Educators Journal, 77*(3), 35-40.

Solomon, A. L., & Heller, G. N. (1982). Historical research in music therapy: An important avenue for studying the profession. *Journal of Music Therapy, 19*(3), 161-178.

Wheeler, B. L. (Ed.). (1995). *Music therapy research: Quantitative and qualitative perspectives.* Phoenixville, PA: Barcelona Publishers.

REFERENCES

Abeles, H. F. (1980). Responses to music. In D. A. Hodges (Ed.), *Handbook of music psychology* (pp. 105-140). Lawrence, KS: National Association for Music Therapy.

Abeles, H. F., & Chung, J. W. (1996). Responses to music. In D. A. Hodges (Ed.), *Handbook of music psychology* (2nd ed.) (pp. 285-342). San Antonio, TX: Institute for Music Research Press, The University of Texas at San Antonio.

Achterberg, J. (1985). *Imagery in healing: Shamanism and modern medicine.* Boston: New Science Library.

Adamek, M. S. (1996). In the beginning: A review of early special education services and legislative/regulatory activity affecting the teaching and placement of special learners. In B. L. Wilson (Ed.), *Models of music therapy interventions in school settings: From institution to inclusion* (pp. 3-12). Silver Spring, MD: National Association for Music Therapy.

Adamek, M. S., & Shiraishi, I. M. (1996). Music therapy with traumatic brain injured patients: Speech rehabilitation, intervention models, and assessment procedures. In C. E. Furman (Ed.), *Effectiveness of music therapy procedures: Documentation of research and clinical practice* (2nd ed.) (pp. 267-278). Silver Spring, MD: National Association for Music Therapy.

Adelman, E. J. (1985). Multimodal therapy and music therapy: Assessing and treating the whole person. *Music Therapy, 5*(1), 12-21.

Adreon, D. A. (1994, November). *Understanding autism: Implications for music therapy.* Paper presented at the 45th Annual Conference of the National Association for Music Therapy, Orlando, FL.

Aging Statistics. (1994). *ElderSong: The Music and Gerontology Newsletter, 8*(1), 1.

Aigen, K. (1990). Echoes of silence. *Music Therapy, 9*(1), 44-61.

Aigen, K. (1991). The voice of the forest: A conception of music for music therapy. *Music Therapy, 10*(1), 77-98.

Aigen, K. (1993). The music therapist as qualitative researcher. *Music Therapy, 12*(1), 16-39.

Aigen, K. (1994). "One voice" – The unification of AAMT and NAMT. *Tuning In: The Newsletter of the American Association for Music Therapy,* Fall 1994, pp. 1, 4-5.

Aigen, K. (1995a). An aesthetic foundation of clinical theory: An underlying basis of creative music therapy. In C. B. Kenny (Ed.), *Listening, playing, creating: Essays on the power of sound* (pp. 235-257). Albany, NY: State University of New York Press.

Aigen, K. (1995b). Cognitive and affective processes in music therapy with individuals with developmental delays: a preliminary model for contemporary Nordoff-Robbins practice. *Music Therapy, 13*(1), 13-46.

Aigen, K. (1995c). Interpretational research. In B. L. Wheeler (Ed.), *Music therapy research: Quantitative and qualitative perspectives* (pp. 329-364). Phoenixville, PA: Barcelona Publishers.

Aigen, K. (1995d). Philosophical inquiry. In B. L. Wheeler (Ed.), *Music therapy research: Quantitative and qualitative perspectives* (pp. 447-484). Phoenixville, PA: Barcelona Publishers.

Aigen, K. (1995e). Principles of qualitative research. In B. L. Wheeler (Ed.), *Music therapy research: Quantitative and qualitative perspectives* (pp. 283-311). Phoenixville, PA: Barcelona Publishers.

Aigen, K. (1998). Creativity in qualitative music therapy research. *Journal of Music Therapy, 35*(3), 150-175.

Albert, M. L., Sparks, R. W., & Helms, N. A. (1973). Melodic intonation therapy for aphasia. *Archives of Neurology, 29,* 130-131.

Alley, C. F. (1977). The effect of relaxation training to music on heart rate and verbal reports. *Dissertation Abstracts International, 37*(12-B), 6391.

Altrows, I. F., & Bryden, M. P. (1977). Temporal factors in the effects of masking noise on fluency of stutterers. *Journal of Communication Disorders, 10,* 315-329.

Altshuler, I. M. (1940). Rational music therapy of the mentally ill. In T. M. Finney (Ed.), *Volume of Proceedings, MTNA* (pp. 153-157). Pittsburgh: Arthur Rippl.

Altshuler, I. M. (1948). A psychiatrist's experience with music as a therapeutic agent. In D. Schullian & M. Schoen (Eds.), *Music and medicine* (pp. 266-281). New York: Henry Schuman.

Alvin, J. (1975). *Music therapy.* New York: Basic Books.

Alvin, J. (1978). *Music therapy for the autistic child.* London: Oxford University Press.

Alvin, J., & Warwick, A. (1991). *Music therapy for the autistic child* (2nd ed.). New York: Oxford University Press.

American Association for Music Therapy [AAMT]. (1993). *Introducing the American Association for Music Therapy* [brochure]. Valley Forge, PA: Author.

American Association for Music Therapy [AAMT]. (1994). *Membership Directory 1994.* Valley Forge, PA: Author.

American Association on Mental Retardation [AAMR]. (1992). *Mental retardation: Definition, classification, and systems of support* (9th ed.). Washington, D.C.: Author.

American Music Therapy Association [AMTA]. (1998). *AMTA Member Sourcebook 1998.* Silver Spring, MD: Author.

American Music Therapy Association [AMTA]. (n.d.). *Music therapy as a career* [brochure]. Silver Spring, MD: Author.

American Psychiatric Association [APA]. (1994). *Diagnostic and statistical manual of mental disorders* (4th ed.) [DSM-IV]. Washington, D.C.: Author.

American Speech and Hearing Association [ASHA]. (1980). *Speech and language disorders and the speech and language pathologist.* Washington, D.C.: Author.

Amir, D. (1990). A song is born: Discovering meaning in improvised songs through a phenomenological analysis of two music therapy sessions with a traumatic spinal-cord injured young adult. *Music Therapy, 9*(1), 62-81.

Anshel, A., & Kipper, D. A. (1988). The influence of group singing on trust and cooperation. *Journal of Music Therapy, 25*(3), 145-155.

Apel, W. (1972). *Harvard dictionary of music* (2nd ed.). Cambridge, MA: Harvard University Press.

Arnold, M. (1975). Music therapy in a transactional analysis setting. *Journal of Music Therapy, 12*(3), 104-120.

Arthritis Foundation. (1987). *Programs and services of the arthritis foundation.* Atlanta, GA: Author.

Atterbury, B. W. (1983a). A comparison of rhythm pattern perception and performance in normal and learning-disabled readers, age seven and eight. *Journal of Research in Music Education, 31*(4), 259-270.

Atterbury, B. W. (1983b). Success strategies for learning-disabled students. *Music Educators Journal, 69*(8), 29-31.

Atterbury, B. W. (1986). Success in the mainstream of general music. *Music Educators Journal, 72*(7), 34-36.

Atterbury, B. W. (1990). *Mainstreaming exceptional learners in music.* Englewood Cliffs, NJ: Prentice-Hall.

Autism Society of America. (1995). *What is autism?* [brochure]. Bethesda, MD: Author.

Ayres, B. R. (1987). The effects of a music stimulus environment versus regular cafeteria environment during therapeutic feeding. *Journal of Music Therapy, 24*(1), 14-26.

Bachman, M. L. (1991). *Dalcroze today: An education through and into music.* New York: Oxford University Press.

Bailey, L. M. (1983). The effects of live music versus tape-recorded music on hospitalized cancer patients. *Music Therapy, 3*(1), 17-28.

Bailey, L. M. (1984). The use of songs in music therapy with cancer patients and their families. *Music Therapy, 4*(1), 5-17.

Bain, L. J. (1991). *A parent's guide to attention deficit disorders.* New York: Delta.

Bang, C. (1980). A world of sound and music: Music therapy and musical speech therapy with hearing impaired and multiply handicapped children. *Journal of the British Association of Teachers of the Deaf, 4*(4). [Reprints available from Hohner, Inc., P.O. Box 15035, Richmond, VA 23227]

Barclay, M. W. (1987). A contribution to a theory of music therapy: Additional phenomenological perspectives on GestaltQualitat and transitional phenomena. *Journal of Music Therapy, 24*(4), 224-238.

Barker, L. W. (1991). The use of music and relaxation techniques to reduce pain of burn patients during daily debridement. In C. D. Maranto (Ed.), *Applications of music in medicine* (pp. 123-140). Washington, D.C.: National Association for Music Therapy.

Barker, V. L., & Brunk, B. (1991). The role of a creative arts group in the treatment of clients with traumatic brain injury. *Music Therapy Perspectives, 9,* 23-31.

Barna, V. (1993). Twilight years. *The Mesquite News* (Thursday, March 11, 1993), *110*(32), pp. 1A, 8A.

Barnard, R. I. (1953). The philosophy and theory of music therapy as an adjuvant therapy. In E. G. Gilliland (Ed.), *Music therapy 1952* (pp. 45-49). Lawrence, KS: Allen Press.

Barrickman, J. (1989). A developmental music therapy approach for preschool hospitalized children. *Music Therapy Perspectives, 7,* 10-16.

Bartlett, D. L. (1996). Physiological responses to music and sound stimuli. In D. A. Hodges (Ed.), *Handbook of music psychology* (2nd ed.) (pp. 343-385). San Antonio, TX: Institute for Music Research Press, The University of Texas at San Antonio.

Bartlett, D., Kaufman, D., & Smeltekop, R. (1993). The effects of music listening and perceived sensory experiences on the immune system as measured by interleukin-1 and control. *Journal of Music Therapy, 30*(4), 194-209.

Bartlett, J. C., & Snelus, P. (1980). Lifespan memory for popular songs. *American Journal of Psychology, 93*(3), 551-560.

Beckett, A. (1990). The effects of music on exercises as determined by physiological recovery heart rates and distance. *Journal of Music Therapy, 27*(3), 126-136.

Bednarz, L. F., & Nikkel, B. (1992). The role of music therapy in the treatment of young adults diagnosed with mental illness and substance abuse. *Music Therapy*

Perspectives, 10(1), 21-26.

Beggs, C. (1991). Life review with a palliative care patient. In K. E. Bruscia (Ed.), *Case studies in music therapy* (pp. 611-616). Phoenixville, PA: Barcelona Publishers.

Behrens, G. A. (1988). An objective approach to the expression of feelings. *Music Therapy Perspectives, 5*, 16-22.

Bellamy, T., & Sontag, E. (1973). Use of group contingent music to increase assembly line production rates of retarded students in a simulated sheltered workshop. *Journal of Music Therapy, 10*(3), 125-136.

Benenzon, R. O. (1981). *Music therapy manual.* Springfield, IL: Charles C Thomas.

Benenzon, R. O. (1982). *Music therapy in child psychosis.* Springfield, IL: Charles C Thomas.

Bennett, P. (1987). From Hungary to America: The evolution of education through music. *Music Educators Journal, 74*(1), 36-45, 60.

Berman, C. (1982, September). Dyslexia – adults can have it too. *Good Housekeeping*, p. 231.

Bernstorf, E. D., & Welsbacher, B. T. (1996). Helping students in the inclusive classroom. *Music Educators Journal, 82*(5), 21-29.

Berry, P., & Kirk, S. A. (1980). Issues in specific learning disabilities: Towards a data base for decision making. *The Exceptional Child, 27*(2), 115-125.

Birkenshaw-Fleming, L. (1993). *Music for all: Teaching music to people with special needs.* Toronto: Gordon V. Thompson.

Bitcon, C. H. (1976). *Alike and different: The clinical and educational use of Orff-Schulwerk.* Santa Ana, CA: Rosha Press.

Blacking, J. (1973). *How musical is man?* Seattle: University of Washington Press.

Blake, R. L., & Bishop, S. R. (1994). The Bonny method of Guided Imagery and Music (GIM) in the treatment of post-traumatic stress disorder (PTSD) with adults in the psychiatric setting. *Music Therapy Perspectives, 12*(2), 125-129.

Blissymbolics Communication Foundation. (1978). *Handbook of blissymbolics.* Toronto: Author.

Boldt, S. (1996). The effects of music therapy on motivation, psychological well-being, physical comfort, and exercise endurance of bone marrow transplant patients. *Journal of Music Therapy, 33*(3), 164-188.

Bolger, E. P., & Judson, M. A. (1984). The therapeutic value of singing. *New England Journal of Medicine, 311*, 1704.

Bonny, H. L. (1975). Music and consciousness. *Journal of Music Therapy, 12*(3), 121-135.

Bonny, H. L. (1978a). *Facilitating guided imagery and music sessions.* Baltimore, MD: ICM Publishing

Bonny, H. L. (1978b). *Guided imagery and music therapy: Past, present and future implications.* Baltimore, MD: ICM

Publishing.

Bonny, H. L. (1983). Music listening for intensive coronary care units: A pilot project. *Music Therapy, 3*(1), 4-16.

Bonny, H. L. (1986). Music and healing. *Music Therapy, 6A*(1), 3-12.

Bonny, H. L. (1989). Sound as symbol: Guided imagery and music in clinical practice. *Music Therapy Perspectives, 6*, 7-10.

Bonny, H. L. (1994). Twenty-one years later: A GIM update. *Music Therapy Perspectives, 12*(2), 70-74.

Bonny, H. L., & McCarron, N. (1984). Music as an adjunct to anesthesia in operative procedures. *Journal of the American Association of Nurse Anesthesiologists, 52*(February), 55-57.

Bonny, H. L., & Savary, L. M. (1973). *Music and your mind: Listening with a new consciousness.* New York: Harper & Row.

Bonny, H. L., & Savary, L. M. (1990). *Music and your mind: Listening with a new consciousness* (Rev. ed.). Barrytown, NY: Station Hill Press.

Boothroyd, A. (1980). Audiological considerations in music with the deaf. In C. Robbins & C. Robbins, *Music for the hearing impaired and other special groups: A resource manual and curriculum guide* (pp. 1-23). St. Louis: Magnamusic-Baton.

Borczon, R. M. (1995). Remembering Oklahoma City. *NAMT Notes*, Summer, 1995, pp. 1, 13-15.

Boswell, B., & Vidret, M. (1993). Rhythmic movement and music for adolescents with severe and profound disabilities. *Music Therapy Perspectives, 11*(1), 37-41.

Boswell, J. (1992). Human potential and lifelong learning. *Music Educators Journal, 79*(4), 38-40.

Bowers, J. (1998). Effects of an intergenerational choir for community-based seniors and college students on age-related attitudes. *Journal of Music Therapy, 35*(1), 2-18.

Bowles, C. L. (1991). Self-expressed adult music education interests and music experiences. *Journal of Research in Music Education, 39*(3), 191-205.

Boxberger, R. (1962). Historical bases for the use of music in therapy. In E. H. Schneider (Ed.), *Music therapy 1961* (pp. 125-166). Lawrence, KS: Allen Press.

Boxberger, R. (1963). A historical study of the National Association for Music Therapy. In E. H. Schneider (Ed.), *Music therapy 1962* (pp. 133-197). Lawrence, KS: Allen Press.

Boxill, E. H. (1985). *Music therapy for the developmentally disabled.* Rockville, MD: Aspen Systems.

Boxill, E. H. (1989). *Music therapy for living: The principle of normalization embodied in music therapy.* St. Louis: MMB Music.

Boyd, J. (1989). Problems and concerns with a diverse population. *Music Therapy Perspectives, 6*, 34-36.

Boyle, M. E. (1987). Music in operant procedures for the

comatose patient. In R. R. Pratt (Ed.), *The fourth international symposium on music: Rehabilitation and human well-being* (pp. 49-60). New York: University Press of America.

Boyle, M. E. (1989). Comatose and head injured patients: Applications for music in treatment. In M. H. M. Lee (Ed.), *Rehabilitation, music and human well-being* (pp. 137-148). St. Louis: MMB Music.

Braswell, C. (1968). Part IX. Development of music therapy in the community. In E. T. Gaston (Ed.), *Music in therapy* (pp. 345-406). New York: Macmillan.

Braswell, C., Decuir, A. & Jacobs, K. (1989). Job satisfaction among music therapists. *Journal of Music Therapy, 26*(1), 2-17.

Braswell, C., Decuir, A., & Maranto, C. D. (1980). Rating of entry level skills by music therapy clinicians, educators, and interns. *Journal of Music Therapy, 17*(3), 133-147.

Braswell, C., Maranto, C. D., & Decuir, A. (1979a). A survey of clinical practice in music therapy, part I: The institutions in which music therapists work and personal data. *Journal of Music Therapy, 16*(1), 2-16.

Braswell, C., Maranto, C. D., & Decuir, A. (1979b). A survey of clinical practice in music therapy, part II: Clinical practice, educational and clinical training. *Journal of Music Therapy, 16*(2), 50-69.

Brayton, E. R., & Conture, E. G. (1978). Effects of noise and rhythmic stimulation on the speech of stutters. *Journal of Speech and Hearing Research, 21*(2), 285-294.

Brewer, J. E. (1955). Music therapy for the mentally deficient. In E. T. Gaston (Ed.), *Music therapy 1954* (pp. 113-116). Lawrence, KS: Allen Press.

Brick, Sr. R. M. (1973). Eurhythmics: One aspect of audition. *Volta Review, 75*(3), 155-160.

Briggs, C. A. (1991). A model for understanding musical development. *Music Therapy, 10*(1), 1-21.

Bright, R. (1972). *Music in geriatric care.* New York: St. Martin's Press.

Bright, R. (1981). *Practical planning in music therapy for the aged.* Lynbrook, NY: Music-graphics.

Bright, R. (1986). *Grieving: A handbook for those who care.* St. Louis: MMB Music.

Bright, R. (1988). *Music therapy and the dementias: Improving the quality of life.* St. Louis: MMB Music.

Brodsky, W. (1989). Music therapy as an intervention for children with cancer in isolation rooms. *Music Therapy, 8*(1), 17-34.

Brodsky, W. (1991). A personal perspective of the power of music and mass communication, prior to and during the Gulf War Crisis in Israel: Implications for music therapy. *Music Therapy, 10*(1), 99-113.

Brodsky, W., & Sloboda, J. A. (1997). Clinical trial of a music generated vibrotactile therapeutic environment

for musicians: Main effects and outcome differences between therapy subgroups. *Journal of Music Therapy, 34*(1), 2-32.

Brody, J. E. (1982). Rock music fans suffer hearing loss, studies say. *Dallas Morning News* (Sunday, November 21), pp. 33AA, 40AA.

Brody, R. (1988). Tune and tone: Music can keep you upbeat about exercise. *Dallas Times Herald* (Friday, January 29), pp. E-1, E-10.

Brooks, D. M. (1989). Music therapy enhances treatment with adolescents. *Music Therapy Perspectives, 6,* 37-39.

Brotons, M. (1994a). Effects of performing conditions on music performance anxiety and performance quality. *Journal of Music Therapy, 31*(1), 63-81.

Brotons, M. (1994b). Preferences of Alzheimer's disease patients for music activities: Singing, instruments, dance/movement, games, and composition/improvisation. *Journal of Music Therapy, 31*(3), 220-233.

Brotons, M., Koger, S., & Pickett-Cooper, P. (1997). Music and dementias: A review of literature. *Journal of Music Therapy, 34*(4), 204-245.

Brotons, M., & Pickett-Cooper, P. (1996). The effects of music therapy intervention on agitation behaviors of Alzheimer's disease patients. *Journal of Music Therapy, 33*(1), 2-18.

Broucek, M. (1987). Beyond healing to "whole-ing": A voice for the deinstitutionalization of music therapy. *Music Therapy, 6*(2), 50-58.

Brown, C. J., Chen, A. C. N., & Dworkin, S. F. (1989). Music in the control of human pain. *Music Therapy, 8*(1), 47-60.

Bruhn, K., Cohen, D., Fletcher, R., McKinney, C., Smith, D. S., & Tims, F. C. (1996, November). *Music making and wellness: Strategic alliances between music therapists and the music products industry.* Paper presented at the 1996 Joint Conference of the National Association for Music Therapy and the American Association for Music Therapy, Nashville, TN.

Brunk, B. K. (1992, February). *Music therapy in physical medicine rehabilitation.* Seminar presented as part of the continuing education program of the Southwestern Region, National Association for Music Therapy, Dallas, TX.

Bruscia, K. E. (1986). Advanced competencies in music therapy. *Music Therapy, 6A*(1), 57-67.

Bruscia, K. E. (1987). *Improvisational models of music therapy.* Springfield, IL: Charles C Thomas.

Bruscia, K. E. (1989a). *Defining music therapy.* Spring City, PA: Spring House Books.

Bruscia, K. E. (1989b). The content of music therapy education at undergraduate and graduate levels. *Music Therapy Perspectives, 7,* 83-87.

Bruscia, K. E. (1989c). The practical side of improvisational music therapy. *Music Therapy Perspectives, 6,* 11-15.

Bruscia, K. E. (Ed.) (1991a). *Case studies in music therapy.* Phoenixville, PA: Barcelona Publishers.

Bruscia, K. E. (1991b). Embracing life with AIDS: Psychotherapy through guided imagery and music (GIM). In K. E. Bruscia (Ed.), *Case studies in music therapy* (pp. 581-602). Phoenixville, PA: Barcelona Publishers.

Bruscia, K. E. (1995a). The boundaries of music therapy research. In B. L. Wheeler (Ed.), *Music therapy research: Quantitative and qualitative perspectives* (pp. 17-27). Phoenixville, PA: Barcelona Publishers.

Bruscia, K. E. (1995b). Differences between quantitative and qualitative research paradigms: Implications for music therapy. In B. L. Wheeler (Ed.), *Music therapy research: Quantitative and qualitative perspectives* (pp. 65-76). Phoenixville, PA: Barcelona Publishers.

Bruscia, K. E. (1995c). Modes of consciousness in Guided Imagery and Music (GIM): A therapist's experience of the guiding process. In C. B. Kenny (Ed.), *Listening, playing, creating: Essays on the power of sound* (pp. 165-197). Albany, NY: State University of New York Press.

Bruscia, K. E. (1995d). Topics and questions in quantitative research. In B. L. Wheeler (Ed.), *Music therapy research: Quantitative and qualitative perspectives* (pp. 119-127). Phoenixville, PA: Barcelona Publishers.

Bruscia, K. E. (1995e). Topics, phenomena, and purposes in qualitative research. In B. L. Wheeler (Ed.), *Music therapy research: Quantitative and qualitative perspectives* (pp. 313-327). Phoenixville, PA: Barcelona Publishers.

Bruscia, K. E. (1998). Standards of integrity for qualitative music therapy research. *Journal of Music Therapy, 35*(3), 176-200.

Bruscia, K., Clair, A. A., Crowe, B., Farnan, L. A., Forinash, M., Hesser, B., Hughes, J. E., Selesky, E. C., Thomas, C. B., and Wright-Bower, L. M. (1998, November). *Plenary session: Envisioning music therapy education and training for the next millennium: The process of unification.* Paper presented at the Inaugural Conference of the American Music Therapy Association, Cleveland, OH.

Bruscia, K. E., Hesser, B., & Boxill, E. H. (1981). Essential competencies for the practice of music therapy. *Music Therapy, 1*(1), 43-49.

Bryant, D. R. (1987). A cognitive approach to therapy through music. *Journal of Music Therapy, 24*(1), 27-34.

Buday, E. M. (1995). The effects of signed and spoken words taught with music on sign and speech imitation by children with autism. *Journal of Music Therapy, 32*(3), 189-202.

Buechler, J. (1982). *Music therapy for handicapped children: Hearing impaired.* Washington, D.C.; National Association for Music Therapy.

Bumanis, A., & Yoder, J. W. (1987). Music and dance: Tools or reality orientation. In B. Karras (Ed.), *"You bring out the music in me": Music in nursing homes* (pp. 23-35). Binghamton, NY: Haworth Press.

Bunt, L., & Marston-Wyld, J. (1995). Where words fail music takes over: A collaborative study by a music therapist and a counselor in the context of cancer care. *Music Therapy Perspectives, 13*(1), 46-50.

Burleson, S. J., Center, D. B., & Reeves, H. (1989). The effect of background music on task performance in psychotic children. *Journal of Music Therapy, 26*(4), 198-205.

Burt, J. W. (1995). Distant thunder: Drumming with Vietnam veterans. *Music Therapy Perspectives, 13*(2), 110-113.

Butler, R. N. (1963). The life review: An interpretation of reminiscence in the aged. *Psychiatry, 26,* 65-76.

Caine, J. (1991). The effects of music on the selected stress behaviors, weight, caloric and formula intake, and length of hospital stay of premature and low birthweight infants in a newborn intensive care unit. *Journal of Music Therapy, 28*(4), 180-192.

Campbell, D. G. (1988). The cutting edge: Personal transformation with music. *Music Therapy, 7*(1), 38-50.

Campbell, D. G. (1991a). Imagery and the physiology of music. In D. Campbell (Ed.), *Music: Physician for times to come* (pp. 243-254). Wheaton, IL: Quest Books.

Campbell, D. G. (Ed.) (1991b). *Music: Physician for times to come.* Wheaton, IL: Quest Books.

Carle, I. L. (1982). Music therapy in a different key. *Music Therapy, 2*(1), 63-71.

Carruth, E. K. (1997). The effects of singing and the speed retrieval technique on improving face-name recognition in nursing home residents with memory loss. *Journal of Music Therapy, 34*(3), 165-186.

Carter, S. A. (1982). *Music therapy for handicapped children: Mentally retarded.* Washington, D.C.: National Association for Music Therapy.

Cassidy, J. W. (1992). Communication disorders: Effect on children's ability to label music characteristics. *Journal of Music Therapy, 29*(2), 113-124.

Cassidy, J. W., & Standley, J. M. (1995). The effect of music listening on physiological responses of premature infants. *Journal of Music Therapy, 32*(4), 208-227.

Cassity, M. D. (1976). The influence of a music therapy activity upon peer acceptance, group cohesiveness, and interpersonal relationships of adult psychiatric patients. *Journal of Music Therapy, 13*(2), 66-76.

Cassity, M. D. (1977). Nontraditional guitar techniques for the educable and trainable mentally retarded residents in music therapy activities. *Journal of Music Therapy, 14*(1), 39-42.

Cassity, M. D., & Cassity, J. E. (1991). *Psychiatric music therapy assessments and treatment employed in NAMT-*

approved clinical training facilities with adults, adolescents and children. Weatherford, OK: Authors.

Cassity, M. D., & Cassity, J. E. (1994a). *Multimodal psychiatric music therapy for adults, adolescents, and children.* St. Louis: MMB Music.

Cassity, M. D., & Cassity, J. E. (1994b). Psychiatric music\ therapy assessment and treatment in clinical training facilities with adults, adolescents and children. *Journal of Music Therapy, 31*(1), 2-30.

Cassity, M. D., & Theobold, K. A. K. (1990). Domestic violence: Assessments and treatments employed by music therapists. *Journal of Music Therapy, 27*(4), 179-194.

Castellano, J. A., & Wilson, B. L. (1970). The generalization of institute therapy to classroom behavior of an electively mute adolescent. *Journal of Music Therapy, 7*(4), 139-143.

Certification Board for Music Therapists. (1983, September-October). Music therapy certification information sheet. *NAMT Notes,* pp. 6, 8.

Certification Board for Music Therapists [CBMT]. (1991). *Recertification manual.* Tucson, AZ: Author.

Certification Board for Music Therapists [CBMT]. (1992). *Commonly asked questions about board certification and recertification.* Tucson, AZ: Author.

Certification Board for Music Therapists [CBMT]. (1997). *CBMT: The certification board for music therapists* [brochure]. Richmond, VA: Author.

Certification Board for Music Therapists [CBMT]. (1998a). *Certification board for music therapists code of professional practice* [brochure]. Richmond, VA: Author.

Certification Board for Music Therapists [CBMT]. (1998b). *Your music therapist is certified by the certification board for music therapists* [brochure]. Richmond, VA: Author.

Chance, P. (1986). Life after head injury. *Psychology Today, 20*(10), 62-69.

Chance, P. (1987). Music hath charms to soothe a throbbing head. *Psychology Today, 21*(2), 14.

Chapman, J. S. (1975). The relation between auditory stimulation of short gestation infants and their gross motor limb activity (Doctoral dissertation, New York University, 1974). *Dissertation Abstracts International, 36,* 1654B-1655B. (University Microfilms No. 75-21, 138)

Chavin, M. (1991). *The lost chord: Reaching the person with dementia through the power of music.* Mt. Airy, MD: ElderSong Publications.

Chavin, M. (1995). Can people with dementia learn? *ElderSong, 8*(4), 4-5.

Chesky, K. S., & Michel, D. E. (1991). The Music Vibration Table (MVT™): Developing a technology and conceptual model for pain relief. *Music Therapy Perspectives, 9,* 32-38.

Chetta, H. D. (1981). The effect of music and desensitization on preoperative anxiety in children. *Journal of Music Therapy, 18*(2), 74-87.

Children and Adults with Attention Deficit Disorders [CH.A.D.D]. (1995). *The disability named ADD: An overview of attention deficit disorders.* Plantation, FL: Author.

Chism, O. (1999). Classical: The thinking child's music. *Dallas Morning News* (Tuesday, January 12), pp. 5C, 4C.

Choi, B. C. (1997). Professional and patient attitudes about the relevance of music therapy as a treatment modality in NAMT-approved psychiatric hospitals. *Journal of Music Therapy, 34*(4), 277-292.

Christenberry, E. B. (1979). The use of music therapy with burn patients. *Journal of Music Therapy, 16*(3), 138-148.

Christie, M. E. (1995). The influence of a highly participatory peer on motivating group behaviors of lower functioning persons who have probable Alzheimer's type dementia: A feasibility study. *Music Therapy Perspectives, 13*(2), 87-90.

Claeys, M. S., Miller, A. C., Dalloul-Rampersad, R., & Kollar, M. (1989). The role of music and music therapy in the rehabilitation of traumatically brain injured clients. *Music Therapy Perspectives, 6,* 71-77.

Clair, A. A. (1990). The need for supervision to manage behavior in the elderly care home resident and the implications for music therapy practice. *Music Therapy Perspectives, 8,* 72-75.

Clair, A. A. (1991). Music therapy for a severely regressed person with a probable diagnosis of Alzheimer's disease. In K. Bruscia (Ed.), *Case studies in music therapy* (pp. 571-580). Phoenixville, PA: Barcelona Publishers.

Clair, A. A. (1996a). The effect of singing on alert responses in persons with late stage dementia. *Journal of Music Therapy, 33*(4), 234-247.

Clair, A. A. (1996b). *Therapeutic uses of music with older adults.* Baltimore: Health Professions Press.

Clair, A. A., & Bernstein, B. (1990). A comparison of singing, vibrotactile and nonvibrotactile instrumental playing responses in severely regressed persons with dementia of the Alzheimer's type. *Journal of Music Therapy, 27*(3), 119-125.

Clair, A. A., Bernstein, B., & Johnson, G. (1995). Rhythmic playing characteristics in persons with severe dementia, including those with probable Alzheimer's type. *Journal of Music Therapy, 32*(2), 113-131.

Clair, A. A., & Ebberts, A. G. (1997). The effects of music therapy on interactions between family caregivers and their care receivers with late stage dementia. *Journal of Music Therapy, 34*(3), 148-164.

Clair, A. A., & Heller, G. N. (1989). Willem Van de Wall (1887-1953): Organizer and innovator in music education and music therapy. *Journal of Research in Music Education, 37*(3), 165-178.

Clair, A. A., Tebb, S., & Bernstein, B. (1993). The effects of a socialization and music therapy intervention on self-esteem and loneliness in spouse caregivers of those diagnosed with dementia of the Alzheimer's type: A pilot study. *The American Journal of Alzheimer's Care and Related Disorders and Research,* Jan/Feb, pp. 24-32.

Clark, C., & Chadwick, D. (1979). *Clinically adapted instruments for the multiply handicapped.* Westford, MA: Modulations.

Clark, M., Gosnell, M., & Young, J. (1982). The bizarre riddle of MS. *Newsweek,* September 6, pp. 50-51.

Clark, M. E. (1986). Music therapy-assisted childbirth: A practical guide. *Music Therapy Perspectives, 5,* 23-27.

Clark, M. E., & Ficken, C. T. (1988). Music therapy in the new health care environment. *Music Therapy Perspectives, 5,* 23-27.

Clark, M. E., McCorkle, R. R., & Williams, S. B. (1981). Music therapy-assisted labor and delivery. *Journal of Music Therapy, 18*(2), 88-100.

Clarkson, G. (1991). Music therapy for a nonverbal autistic adult. In K. E. Bruscia (Ed.), *Case studies in music therapy* (pp. 373-385). Phoenixville, PA: Barcelona Publishers.

Clausman, R. J. (1980, April). *Special problems and needs of the profoundly and severely mentally retarded.* Paper presented at the 1980 Conference of the Great Lakes Regional Chapter of the National Association for Music Therapy, Fort Wayne, IN.

Clayton, L., & Morrison, J. (1992). *Coping with a learning disability.* New York: Rosen Publishing.

Clearwater, Y. (1985). A human place in outer space. *Psychology Today, 19*(7), 34-43.

Clendenon-Wallen, J. (1991). The use of music therapy to influence the self-confidence and self-esteem of adolescents who are sexually abused. *Music Therapy Perspectives, 9,* 73-81.

Cleveland Music School Settlement Music Therapy Department. (1985). *The music therapy levels system: A manual of principles and applications.* Cleveland, OH: The Cleveland Music School Settlement.

Clynes, M. (1977). *Sentics: The touch of emotions.* New York: Doubleday Anchor.

Clynes, M. (Ed.) (1982). *Music, mind and brain: The neuropsychology of music.* New York: Plenum Press.

Clynes, M. (1991). On music and healing. In D. Campbell (Ed.), *Music: Physician for times to come* (pp. 121-145). Wheaton, IL: Quest Books.

Coates, P. (1984). Sixty and still growing. *Music Educators Journal, 70*(9), 34-35.

Coates, P. (1987). "Is it functional?" A question for music therapists who work with the institutionalized mentally retarded. *Journal of Music Therapy, 24*(3), 170-175.

Codding, P. (1982). *Music therapy for handicapped children: Visually impaired.* Washington, D.C.: National Association for Music Therapy.

Codding, P. A. (1988). Music in the education/rehabilitation of visually disabled and multiply handicapped persons: A review of literature from 1946-1987. In C. E. Furman (Ed.), *Effectiveness of music therapy procedures: Documentation of research and clinical practice* (pp. 107-136). Washington, D. C.: National Association for Music Therapy.

Cohen, G. D. (1988). *The brain in human aging.* Springer Publishing.

Cohen, J. M. (1986). Rhythm and tempo in mania. *Music Therapy, 6A*(1), 13-29.

Cohen, N. S. (1988). The use of superimposed rhythm to decrease the rate of speech in a brain-damaged adolescent. *Journal of Music Therapy, 25*(2), 85-93.

Cohen, N. S. (1992). The effect of singing instruction on the speech production of neurologically impaired persons. *Journal of Music Therapy, 29*(2), 87-102.

Cohen, N. S. (1994). Speech and song: Implications for therapy. *Music Therapy Perspectives, 12*(1), 8-14.

Cohen, N. S. (1995). The effect of vocal instruction and Visi-Pitch™ feedback on the speech of persons with neurogenic communication disorders: Two case studies. *Music Therapy Perspectives, 13*(2), 70-75.

Cohen, N. S., & Ford, J. (1995). The effect of musical cues on the nonpurposive speech of persons with aphasia. *Journal of Music Therapy, 32*(1), 46-57.

Cohen, N. S., Hadsell, N. A., & Williams, S. L. (1997). The perceived applicability of applied music requirements in the vocational practices of professional music therapists. *Music Therapy Perspectives, 15*(2), 67-72.

Cohen, N. S., & Masse, R. (1993). The application of singing and rhythmic instruction as a therapeutic intervention for persons with neurogenic communication disorders. *Journal of Music Therapy, 30*(2), 81-99.

Coleman, K. A. (1996). Music therapy for learners with severe disabilities in a public school setting. In B. L. Wilson (Ed.), *Models of music therapy interventions in school settings: From institution to inclusion* (pp. 142-155). Silver Spring, MD: National Association for Music Therapy.

Coleman, K., McNairn, P., & Shioleno, C. (1995). *Quick tech magic: Music-based literacy activities.* Solana Beach, CA: Mayer-Johnson.

Colligan, K. G. (1987). Music therapy and hospice care. In B. Karras (Ed.), *"You bring out the music in me": Music in nursing homes* (pp. 103-122). Binghamton, NY: Haworth Press.

Collins, C. I. (1982, November). *The life and work of Ira M. Altshuler: Pioneer in music therapy.* Paper presented at the 33rd Annual Conference of the National Association for Music Therapy, Baltimore, MD.

Colwell, C. M. (1994). Therapeutic applications of music in the whole language kindergarten. *Journal of Music Therapy, 31*(4), 238-247.

Colwell, C. M. (1997). Music as a distraction and relaxation to reduce chronic pain and narcotic ingestion: A case study. *Music Therapy Perspectives, 15*(1), 24-31.

Colwell, R. (1990). Research findings: Shake well before using. *Music Educators Journal, 77*(3), 29-34.

Confrancesco, E. M. (1985). The effect of music therapy on hand grasp strength and functional task performance in stroke patients. *Journal of Music Therapy, 22*(3), 129-145.

Cooke, R. M. (1969). The use of music in play therapy. *Journal of Music Therapy, 6*(3), 66-75.

Cooper, N. (1985). Adult psychiatric patients. Concentration and communication skills: General hospital, psychiatric unit. In *The music therapy levels system: A manual of principles and applications* (pp. 37-43). Cleveland, OH: The Cleveland Music School Settlement.

Cordobes, T. K. (1997). Group songwriting as a method for developing group cohesion for HIV-seropositive adult patients with depression. *Journal of Music Therapy, 34*(1), 46-67.

Cordrey, C. (1994). *Hidden treasures: Music and memory activities for people with Alzheimer's.* Mt. Airy, MD: ElderSong.

Cormier, Sr. L. (1982). *Music therapy for handicapped children: Deaf-blind.* Washington, D. C.: National Association for Music Therapy.

Cowan, D. S. (1991). Music therapy in the surgical arena. *Music Therapy Perspectives, 9,* 42-45.

Cripe, F. F. (1986). Rock music as therapy for children with attention deficit disorder: An exploratory study. *Journal of Music Therapy, 23*(1), 30-37.

Crowe, B. (1985). Music therapy and physical medicine – expanding opportunities for employment. *Music Therapy Perspectives, 5*(1), 44-51.

Crowe, B. (1991). Music – the ultimate physician. In D. Campbell (Ed.), *Music: Physician for times to come* (pp. 111-120). Wheaton, IL: Quest Books.

Crowe, B., & Bruscia, K. (1999). Draft report of recommendations of the AMTA commission on education and clinical training. *Music Therapy Matters, 2*(1), 8-9.

Crowe, B., & Scovel, M. (1996). An overview of sound healing practices: Implications for the profession of music therapy. *Music Therapy Perspectives, 14*(1), 21-29.

Cummings, E., & Henry, W. E. (1961). *Growing old: The process of disengagement.* New York: Basic Books.

Cunningham, T. D., Jr. (1986). The effect of music volume on the frequency of vocalizations of institutionalized mentally retarded persons. *Journal of Music Therapy, 23*(4), 208-218.

Curtis, S. L. (1986). The effect of music on pain relief and relaxation of the terminally ill. *Journal of Music Therapy, 23*(1), 10-24.

Darrough, G. P. (1992). Making choral music with older adults. *Music Educators Journal, 79*(4), 27-29.

Darrow, A. A. (1985). Music for the deaf. *Music Educators Journal, 71*(6), 33-35.

Darrow, A. A. (1987a). Exploring the arts of sign and song. *Music Educators Journal, 74*(1), 32-35.

Darrow, A. A. (1987b). An investigative study: The effect of hearing impairment on musical aptitude. *Journal of Music Therapy, 24*(2), 88-96.

Darrow, A. A. (1989). Music therapy in the treatment of the hearing impaired. *Music Therapy Perspectives, 6,* 61-70.

Darrow, A. A. (1990). The effect of frequency adjustment on the vocal reproduction accuracy of hearing impaired children. *Journal of Music Therapy, 27*(1), 24-33.

Darrow, A. A. (1991). An assessment and comparison of hearing impaired children's preference for timbre and musical instruments. *Journal of Music Therapy, 28*(1), 48-59.

Darrow, A. A. (1992). The effect of vibrotactile stimuli via the SOMATRON™ on the identification of pitch change by hearing impaired children. *Journal of Music Therapy, 29*(2), 103-112.

Darrow, A. A. (1993). The role of music in deaf culture: Implications for music educators. *Journal of Research in Music Education, 41*(2), 93-110.

Darrow, A. A., & Cohen, N. (1991). The effect of programmed pitch practice and private instruction on the vocal reproduction accuracy of children with hearing impairments: Two case studies. *Music Therapy Perspectives, 9,* 61-65.

Darrow, A. A., & Gfeller, K. E. (1988). Music therapy with hearing-impaired children. In C. E. Furman (Ed.), *Effectiveness of music therapy procedures: Documentation of research and clinical practice* (pp. 137-174). Washington, D. C.: National Association for Music Therapy.

Darrow, A. A., & Gfeller, K. E. (1991). A study of public school music programs mainstreaming hearing impaired students. *Journal of Music Therapy, 28*(1), 23-39.

Darrow, A. A., & Gfeller, K. E. (1996). Music therapy with children who are deaf and hard-of-hearing. In C. E. Furman (Ed.), *Effectiveness of music therapy procedures: Documentation of research and clinical practice* (2nd ed.) (pp. 230-266). Silver Spring, MD: National Association for Music Therapy.

Darrow, A. A., & Goll, H. (1989). The effect of vibrotactile stimuli via the SOMATRON™ on the identification of rhythmic concepts by hearing impaired children. *Journal of Music Therapy, 26*(3), 115-124.

Darrow, A. A., & Heller, G. N. (1985). Early advocates of music education for the hearing impaired: William Wolcott Turner and David Ely Bartlett. *Journal of Research in Music Education, 33*(4), 269-279.

Darrow, A. A., Johnson, C. M., & Ollenberger, T. (1994).

The effect of participation in an intergenerational choir on teens' and older persons' cross-age attitudes. *Journal of Music Therapy, 31*(2), 119-134.

Darrow, A. A., & Schunk, H. A. (1996). Music therapy for learners who are deaf/hard-of-hearing. In B. L. Wilson (Ed.), *Models of music therapy interventions in school settings: From institution to inclusion* (pp. 200-223). Silver Spring, MD: National Association for Music Therapy.

Darrow, A. A., & Starmer, G. W. (1986). The effect of vocal training on the intonation and rate of hearing impaired children's speech: A pilot study. *Journal of Music Therapy, 23*(4), 194-201.

Davidson, J. B. (1980). Music and gerontology: a young endeavor. *Music Educators Journal, 66*(9), 27-31.

Davis, C. A. (1992). The effects of music and basic relaxation instruction on pain and anxiety of women undergoing in-office gynecological procedures. *Journal of Music Therapy, 29*(4), 202-216.

Davis, W. B. (1987). Music therapy in 19th century America. *Journal of Music Therapy, 24*(2), 76-87.

Davis, W. B. (1989). Music therapy in Victorian England: Frederick Kill Harford and the guild of St. Cecilia. *Music Therapy Perspectives, 7*, 17-22.

Davis, W. B. (1992a). Music therapy and elderly populations. In W. B. Davis, K. E. Gfeller, & M. H. Thaut, *An introduction to music therapy: Theory and practice* (pp. 133-163). Dubuque, IA: Wm. C. Brown.

Davis, W. B. (1992b). Music therapy for mentally retarded children and adults. In W. B. Davis, K. E. Gfeller, & M. H. Thaut, *An introduction to music therapy: Theory and practice* (pp. 67-92). Dubuque, IA: Wm. C. Brown.

Davis, W. B. (1992c). The music therapy treatment process. In W. B. Davis, K. E. Gfeller, & M. H. Thaut, *An introduction to music therapy: Theory and practice* (pp. 287-301). Dubuque, IA: Wm. C. Brown.

Davis, W. B. (1993). Keeping the dream alive: Profiles of three early twentieth century music therapists. *Journal of Music Therapy, 30*(1), 34-45.

Davis, W. B. (1996). An instruction course in the use and practice of musical therapy: the first handbook of music therapy clinical practice. *Journal of Music Therapy, 33*(1), 34-49.

Davis, W. B., & Gfeller, K. E. (1992). Music therapy: An historical perspective. In W. B. Davis, K. E. Gfeller, & M. H. Thaut, *An introduction to music therapy: Theory and practice* (pp. 16-37). Dubuque, IA: Wm. C. Brown.

Deaf people can hear music? (1980). *Florida Music Director, 34*(2), 17.

Del Olmo, F. (1998). Biomedicine brings hope for autism. *The Dallas Morning News* (Saturday, January 3), p. 25A.

DeMyer, M. K. (1974). *Parents and children in autism.* Washington, D.C.: V. H. Winston.

Denckla, M. B. (1990). The paradox of the gifted/impaired child. In F. R. Wilson and F. L. Roehmann (Eds.), *Music and child development: Biology of music making: Proceedings of the 1987 Denver Conference* (pp. 227-240). St. Louis: MMB Music.

Denenholz, B. (1959). Music as a tool of physical medicine. In E.H. Schneider (Ed.), *Music Therapy 1958* (pp. 67-84). Lawrence, KS: Allen Press.

Department of Health and Human Services. (1986). *Hocus-pocus as applied to arthritis* (HHS Publication No. (FDA) 85-1080). Rockville, MD: Author.

Dervan, N. (1982). Building Orff ensemble skills with mentally handicapped adolescents. *Music Educators Journal, 68*(8), 35-36.

Deschenes, B. (1990). Music therapy and the composer. *Music Therapy Perspectives, 8*, 85-87.

Dickens, G., & Sharpe, M. (1970). Music therapy in the setting of a psychotherapeutic centre. *British Journal of Medical Psychology, 43*(1), 83-94.

DiGiammarino, M. (1990). Functional music skills of persons with mental retardation. *Journal of Music Therapy, 27*(4), 209-220.

DiGiammarino, M. (1994). Functional music leisure skills for individuals with mental retardation. *Music Therapy Perspectives, 12*(1), 15-19.

Dileo, C. (1975). The use of a token economy program with mentally retarded persons in a music therapy setting. *Journal of Music Therapy, 12*(3), 155-160.

Ditson, R. (1961). A study of the effects of moderate background music on the behavior of cerebral palsied children. *Bulletin of the National Association for Music Therapy, 10*, 6.

Donnelly, M. (1991). Feeling the beat: Class helps deaf students make music. *Dallas Times Herald* (Saturday, April 13), p. A-21.

Dorow, L. (1976). Televised music lessons as educational reinforcement for correct mathematical responses with the educable mentally retarded. *Journal of Music Therapy, 13*(2), 77-86.

Douglass, D. (1985). *Accent on rhythm: Music activities for the aged* (3rd ed.). St. Louis: MMB Music.

Dowling, W. J., & Harwood, D. L. (1986). *Music cognition.* Orlando, FL: Academic Press.

Duerksen, G. (1968). The research process. In E. T. Gaston (Ed.), *Music in therapy* (pp. 409-424). New York: Macmillan.

Duerksen, G. (1978). *Music therapy: Using music to help others.* Unpublished paper, University of Kansas.

Dunn, B. (1995). A different beat: Music therapy in children's cardiac care. *Music Therapy Perspectives, 13*(1), 35-39.

Dvorkin, J. M. (1991). Individual music therapy for an adolescent with borderline personality disorder: An object relations approach. In K. E. Bruscia (Ed.), *Case studies in music therapy* (pp. 251-268). Phoenixville, PA: Barcelona Publishers.

Dworkis, J. L. (1994). Adult distractors: Attention deficit disorder affects grownups, too. *Dallas Morning News* (April 19), pp. 1C-2C.

Dychtwald, K. (1993). The age wave. *The Lutheran Witness, 112*(1), 2-5.

Dykman, R. A. (1979). In step with 94-142, two by two. *Music Educators Journal, 65* (5), 58-63.

Eagle, C. T., Jr. (Ed.). (1976). *Music therapy index* (Vol. 1). Lawrence, KS: National Association for Music Therapy.

Eagle, C. T., Jr. (Ed.). (1978). *Music psychology index* (Vol. 2). Denton, TX: Institute for Therapeutics Research.

Eagle, C. T., Jr. (Ed.). (1982). *Music therapy for handicapped individuals: An annotated and indexed bibliography.* Washington, D.C.: National Association for Music Therapy.

Eagle, C. T. (1991). Steps to a theory of quantum therapy. *Music Therapy Perspectives, 9,* 56-60.

Eagle, C. T., & Harsh, J. M. (1988). Elements of pain and music: The aio connection. *Music Therapy, 7*(1), 15-27.

Eagle, C. T., Jr., & Miniter, J. J. (Eds.). (1984). *Music psychology index* (Vol. 3). Phoenix, AZ: Oryx Press.

Early Childhood Intervention Council [ECIC]. (1992). *Policy and procedures manual.* Austin, TX: Author.

Eating to a slower beat may take bite out of appetite. (1991). *Dallas Times Herald* (Monday, June 3), p. D-1.

Edel, T. (1994). *Piano music for one hand.* Bloomington, IN: Indiana University Press.

Edelman, P. B. (1978). Juvenile corrections and the arts. In *The Healing Role of the Arts (Working papers – The Rockefeller Foundation)* (pp. 42-49). New York: The Rockefeller Foundation.

Edelstein, J. E. (1987). Musical options for upper limb amputees. In R. R. Pratt (Ed.), *The fourth international symposium on music: Rehabilitation and human well-being* (pp. 102-107). New York: University Press of America.

Edelstein, J. E. (1989). Musical options for upper limb amputees. In M. H. M. Lee (Ed.), *Rehabilitation, music and human well-being* (pp. 213-225). St. Louis: MMB Music.

Edgerton, C. D. (1990). Creative group songwriting. *Music Therapy Perspectives, 8,* 15-19.

Edgerton, C. L. (1994). The effect of improvisational music therapy on the communicative behaviors of autistic children. *Journal of Music Therapy, 31*(1), 31-62.

Edison, C. E., Jr. (1989). The effect of behavioral music therapy on the generalization of interpersonal skills from sessions to the classroom by emotionally handicapped middle school students. *Journal of Music Therapy, 26*(4), 206-221.

Edwards, D. (1976). *Peacebird.* Los Angeles: Franciscan Communications Center.

Edwards, E. M. (1975). Music and the hearing impaired. In R. M. Graham (Compiler), *Music for the exceptional child* (pp. 48-60). Reston, VA: Music Educators National Conference.

Edwards, M. C., Eagle, C. T., Pennebaker, J. W., & Tunks, T. W. (1991). Relationships among elements of music and physiological responses. In C. D. Maranto (Ed.), *Applications of music in medicine* (pp. 41-57). Washington, D.C.: National Association for Music Therapy.

Elliot, T. G., & McGahan, C. (1987). The power of music in prison. In R. R. Pratt (Ed.), *The fourth international symposium on music: Rehabilitation and human well-being* (pp. 170-175). New York: University Press of America.

Elliott, B. (1982). *Guide to the selection of musical instruments with respect to physical ability and disability.* St. Louis: Magnamusic-Baton.

Epstein, L., Hersen, M., & Hemphill, D. P. (1974). Music feedback in the treatment of tension headache: An experiment case study. *Journal of Behavior Therapy and Experimental Psychiatry, 5*(9), 59-63.

Erdonmez, D. (1991). Rehabilitation of piano performance skills following a left cerebral vascular accident. In K. E. Bruscia (Ed.), *Case studies in music therapy* (pp. 561-570). Phoenixville, PA: Barcelona Publishers.

Erikson, E. H. (1963). *Childhood and society.* New York: Norton.

Erikson, E. H. (1968). *Identity: Youth and crisis.* New York: Norton.

Erikson, E. H., Erikson, J. M., & Kivnick, H. Q. (1986). *Vital involvement in old age.* New York: W. W. Norton & Co.

Ernst, R. E., & Emmons, S. (1992). New horizons for senior adults. *Music Educators Journal, 79*(4), 30-34.

Euper, J. A. (1968). Early infantile autism. In E. T. Gaston (Ed.), *Music in Therapy* (pp. 181-190). New York: Macmillan.

Fagen, T. S. (1982). Music therapy in the treatment of anxiety and fear in terminal pediatric patients. *Music Therapy, 2*(1), 13-23.

Farbman, A. (1994). Opportunities for the music products industry in the 21st century: The emerging markets of people with disabilities and elderly persons. *Music Therapy Perspectives, 12*(2), 35-38.

Farnan, L. (1993). *FracTunes* – The 21st Century Light Organ. *Music Therapy Perspectives, 11*(2), 50-51.

Farnan, L. (1996). Music therapy for learners with severe disabilities in a residential setting. In B. L. Wilson (Ed.), *Models of music therapy interventions in school settings: From institution to inclusion* (pp. 113-126). Silver Spring, MD: National Association for Music Therapy.

Farnan, L., & Johnson, F. (1988a). *Everyone can move: Music and activities that promote movement and motor development.* New Berlin, WI: Jenson Publications.

Farnan, L., & Johnson, F. (1988b). *Music is for everyone: A handbook for providing music to people with special needs.* New Berlin, WI: Jenson Publications.

Feder, E., & Feder, B. (1981). *The expressive arts therapies.* Englewood Cliffs, NJ: Prentice-Hall.

Federal Register. (1977, Tuesday, August 23). *42*(163).

Fegers, B., Fricke, J. P., Minkenberg, H., & Moog, H. (1989). The use of the Fricke synthesizer in music education programs for severely physically handicapped students. In R. R. Pratt & H. Moog (Eds.), *First research seminar of the ISME commission on music therapy and music in special education: Proceedings of 1986; Bad Honnef, W. Germany* (pp. 69-84). St. Louis: MMB Music.

Feil, N. (1982). *Validation – the Feil method: How to help the disoriented old-old.* Cleveland, OH: Edward Feil Productions.

Feil, N. (1993). *The validation breakthrough: Simple techniques for communicating with people with "Alzheimer's-type dementia."* Baltimore: Health Professions Press.

Ficken, T. (1976). The use of songwriting in a psychiatric setting. *Journal of Music Therapy, 13*(4), 163-172.

Fischer, R. G. (1991). Original song drawings in the treatment of a developmentally disabled, autistic young man. In K. E. Bruscia (Ed.), *Case studies in music therapy* (pp. 359-371). Phoenixville, PA: Barcelona Publishers.

Fitzgerald-Cloutier, M. L. (1993). The use of music therapy to decrease wandering: An alternative to restraints. *Music Therapy Perspectives, 11*(1), 32-38.

Fles, M. (1995). Sound wave mirror. In C.B. Kenny (Ed.), *Listening, playing, creating: Essays on the power of sound* (pp. 87-90). Albany, NY: State University of New York Press.

Folts, M. (1977). Deaf children cannot play a musical instrument . . . can they? *The Volta Review, 77,* 453-456.

Ford, S. C. (1984). Music therapy for cerebral palsied children. *Music Therapy Perspectives, 1*(3), 8-13.

Ford, T. A. (1988). The effect of musical experiences and age on the ability of deaf children to discriminate pitch. *Journal of Music Therapy, 25*(1), 2-16.

Forinash, M. (1992). A phenomenological analysis of Nordoff-Robbins' approach to music therapy: The lived experience of clinical improvisation. *Music Therapy, 11*(1), 120-141.

Forinash, M. (1995). Phenomenological research. In B. L. Wheeler (Ed.), *Music therapy research: Quantitative and qualitative perspectives* (pp. 367-387). Phoenixville, PA: Barcelona Publishers.

Forinash, M., & Gonzalez, D. (1989). A phenomenological perspective of music therapy. *Music Therapy, 8*(1), 35-36.

Forinash, M., & Lee, C. (1998). Guest editorial. *Journal of Music Therapy, 35*(3), 142-149.

Fowler, R. S., Jr., & Fordyce, W. E. (1974). *Stroke: Why do they behave that way?* Seattle: Washington State Heart Association.

Freed, B. S. (1987). Songwriting with the chemically dependent. *Music Therapy Perspectives, 4,* 13-18.

Frego, R. J. D. (1995). Uniting the generations with music programs. *Music Educators Journal, 81*(6), 12-19, 55.

Friedlander, L. H. (1994). Group music psychotherapy in an inpatient psychiatric setting for children: a developmental approach. *Music Therapy Perspectives, 12*(2), 92-97.

Frisch, A. (1990). Symbol and structure: Music therapy for the adolescent psychiatric inpatient. *Music Therapy, 9*(1), 16-34.

Froehlich, M. A. R. (1984). A comparison of the effect of music therapy and medical play therapy on the verbalization behavior of pediatric patients. *Journal of Music Therapy, 21*(1), 2-15.

Froehlich, M. A. R. (Ed.). (1996). *Music therapy with hospitalized children: A creative arts child life approach.* Cherry Hill, NJ: Jeffrey Books.

Furman, C. E. (Ed.). (1988). *Effectiveness of music therapy procedures: Documentation of research and clinical practice.* Washington, D. C.: National Association for Music Therapy.

Furman, C. E. (Ed.). (1996). *Effectiveness of music therapy procedures: Documentation of research and clinical practice* (2nd ed.). Silver Spring, MD: National Association for Music Therapy.

Furman, C. E., Adamek, M. S., & Furman, A. G. (1991). Eminence of music therapy among music professions. *Music Therapy Perspectives, 9,* 39-41.

Furman, C. E., & Furman, A. G. (1988). Music therapy research with mental retardation: Analysis and clinical implications. In C. E. Furman (Ed.), E*ffectiveness of music therapy procedures: Documentation of research and clinical practice* (pp. 285-299). Washington, D.C.: National Association for Music Therapy.

Furman, C. E., & Furman, A. G. (1996). Uses of music therapy with people having mental retardation: An update of a previous analysis. In C. E. Furman (Ed.), *Effectiveness of music therapy procedures: Documentation of research and clinical practice* (2nd ed.) (pp. 279-296). Silver Spring, MD: National Association for Music Therapy.

Galloway, H. F., Jr. (1974). Stuttering and the myth of therapeutic singing. *Journal of Music Therapy, 11*(4), 202-207.

Galloway, H. F., Jr., & Bean, M. F. (1974). The effect of action songs on the development of body-image and body-part identification in hearing impaired preschool children. *Journal of Music Therapy, 11*(3), 125-134.

Gardner, H. (1983). *Frames of mind: The theory of multiple intelligences.* New York: Basic Books.

Gardner, W., Licklider, J. C. R., & Weisz, A. Z. (1960). Suppression of pain by sound. *Science, 132,* 32-33.

Gardstrom, S. C. (1987). Positive peer culture: A working definition for the music therapist. *Music Therapy*

Perspectives, 4, 19-23.

Gardstrom, S. C. (1996). Music therapy for juvenile offenders in a residential setting. In B. L. Wilson (Ed.), *Models of music therapy interventions in school settings: From institution to inclusion* (pp. 127-141). Silver Spring, MD: National Association for Music Therapy.

Garwood, E. C. (1988). The effect of contingent music in combination with bell pad on enuresis of a mentally retarded adult. *Journal of Music Therapy, 25*(2), 103-109.

Gaston, E. T. (1947). Functional aspects of music in hospitals. In H. N. Morgan (Ed.), *Music education source book* (pp. 205-207). Chicago: Music Educators National Conference.

Gaston, E. T. (1968a). Man and music. In E. T. Gaston (Ed.), *Music in therapy* (pp. 7-29). New York: Macmillan.

Gaston, E. T. (Ed.). (1968b). *Music in therapy.* New York: Macmillan.

Gay, L. R. (1981). *Educational research: Competencies for analysis and application* (2nd ed.). Columbus, OH: Charles E. Merrill.

Gervin, A. P. (1991). Music therapy compensatory techniques utilizing song lyrics during dressing to promote independence in the patient with a brain injury. *Music Therapy Perspectives, 9,* 87-90.

Gfeller, K. E. (1983). Musical mnemonics as an aid to retention with normal and learning disabled students. *Journal of Music Therapy, 20*(4), 179-189.

Gfeller, K. E. (1984). Prominent theories in learning disabilities and implications for music therapy methodology. *Music Therapy Perspectives, 2*(1), 9-13.

Gfeller, K. (1987a). Music therapy theory and practice as reflected in research literature. *Journal of Music Therapy, 25*(1), 28-43.

Gfeller, K. (1987b). Songwriting as a tool for reading and language remediation. *Music Therapy, 6*(2), 28-38.

Gfeller, K. (1988). Musical components and styles preferred by young adults for aerobic fitness activities. *Journal of Music Therapy, 25*(1), 28-43.

Gfeller, K. (1990). A cognitive-linguistic approach to language development for the preschool child with hearing impairment: Implications for music therapy practice. *Music Therapy Perspectives, 8,* 47-51.

Gfeller, K. (1992a). Music: A human phenomenon. In W. B. Davis, K. E. Gfeller, & M. H. Thaut, *An introduction to music therapy: Theory and practice* (pp. 38-64). Dubuque, IA: Wm. C. Brown.

Gfeller, K. (1992b). Music therapy in the treatment of learning disabilities. In W. B. Davis, K. E. Gfeller, & M. H. Thaut, *An introduction to music therapy: Theory and practice* (pp. 197-208). Dubuque, IA: Wm. C. Brown.

Gfeller, K. (1992c). Music therapy in the treatment of medical conditions. In W. B. Davis, K. E. Gfeller, & M. H. Thaut, *An introduction to music therapy: Theory and*

practice (pp. 234-250). Dubuque, IA: Wm. C. Brown.

Gfeller, K. (1992d). Music therapy in the treatment of sensory disorders. In W. B. Davis, K. E. Gfeller, & M. H. Thaut, *An introduction to music therapy: Theory and practice* (pp. 209-233). Dubuque, IA: Wm. C. Brown.

Gfeller, K. (1992e). The profession in a larger context. In W. B. Davis, K. E. Gfeller, & M. H. Thaut, *An introduction to music therapy: Theory and practice* (pp. 352-360). Dubuque, IA: Wm. C. Brown.

Gfeller, K., & Bauman, A. A. (1988). Assessment procedures for music therapy with hearing impaired children: language development. *Journal of Music Therapy, 25*(4), 192-205.

Gfeller, K., & Davis, W. B. (1992). The role of research in music therapy. In W. B. Davis, K. E. Gfeller, & M. H. Thaut, *An introduction to music therapy: Theory and practice* (pp. 302-351). Dubuque, IA: Wm. C. Brown.

Gfeller, K., & Hanson, N. (Eds.). (1995). *Music therapy programming for individuals with Alzheimer's disease and related disorders.* St. Louis: MMB Music.

Gfeller, K., Logan, H., & Walker, J. (1990). The effect of auditory distraction and suggestion on tolerance for dental restorations in adolescents and young adults. *Journal of Music Therapy, 27*(1), 13-23.

Gibbons, A. C. (1977). Popular music preferences of elderly people. *Journal of Music Therapy, 14*(4), 180-189.

Gibbons, A. C. (1982). Music aptitude profile scores in a noninstitutionalized, elderly population. *Journal of Research in Music Education, 30*(1), 23-29.

Gibbons, A. C. (1983a). Item analysis of the primary measures of music audiation in elderly care home residents. *Journal of Music Therapy, 20*(4), 201-210.

Gibbons, A. C. (1983b). Primary measures of music audiation scores in an institutionalized elderly population. *Journal of Music Therapy, 20*(1), 21-29.

Gibbons, A. C. (1985). Stop babying the elderly. *Music Educators Journal, 71*(7), 48-51.

Gibbons, A. C. (1988). A review of literature for music development/education and music therapy with the elderly. *Music Therapy Perspectives, 5,* 33-40.

Gibbons, A. C. (1989). Music therapy education/training at the University of Kansas. In R. R. Pratt & B. Hesser (Eds.), *Music therapy and music in special education: The international state of the art I (ISME Edition Number Three)* (pp. 101-128). St. Louis: MMB Music.

Gibbons, A. C., & McDougal, D. L. (1987). Music therapy in medical technology: Organ transplants. In R. R. Pratt (Ed.), *The fourth international symposium on music: Rehabilitation and human well-being* (pp. 61-72). New York: University Press of America.

Gilbert, J. P. (1977). Music therapy perspectives on death and dying. *Journal of Music Therapy, 14*(4), 165-171.

Gilbert, J. P. (1983). A comparison of motor music skills in non-handicapped and learning disabled children. *Journal of Research in Music Education, 31*(2), 147-155.

Gilbert, J. P. , & Beal, M. R. (1982). Preferences of elderly individuals for selected music education experiences. *Journal of Research in Music Education, 30*(4), 247-253.

Giles, M. M., Cogan, D., & Cox, C. (1991). A music and art program to promote emotional health in elementary school children. *Journal of Music Therapy, 28*(3), 135-148.

Gilliland, E. G. (1959). The mentally retarded. In E. H. Schneider (Ed.), *Music therapy 1958* (pp. 153-154). Lawrence, KS: Allen Press.

Gladfelter, N. D. (1996). Music therapy for learners with learning disabilities in a private day school. In B. L. Wilson (Ed.), *Models of music therapy interventions in school settings: From institution to inclusion* (pp. 184-199). Silver Spring, MD: National Association for Music Therapy.

Glassman, L. R. (1983). The talent show: Meeting the needs of the healthy elderly. *Music Therapy, 3*(1), 82-93.

Godley, C. A. S. (1987). The use of music in pain clinics. *Music Therapy Perspectives, 4*, 24-28.

Goetinck, S. (1996a). Arsenal of treatments presents tough choices. *The Dallas Morning News* (Monday, April 29), pp. 1F, 3F.

Goetinck, S. (1996b). Genes, environment both play major role. *The Dallas Morning News* (Monday, April 29), pp. 1F-3F.

Gold, M. (1982). Voice class without note reading: Training voices of students 55 and older. *Voice of the Lakes* (Newsletter of the Great Lakes Regional Chapter, National Association for Music Therapy), *26*(1), 31.

Goldberg, F. S. (1989). Music psychotherapy in acute psychiatric inpatient and private practice settings. *Music Therapy Perspectives, 6*, 40-43.

Goldberg, F. S. (1994). Guest editorial: Introduction to the special issue on psychiatric music therapy. Music *Therapy Perspectives, 12*(2), 67-69.

Goldberg, F. S., Hoss, T. M., & Chesna, T. (1988). Music and imagery as psychotherapy with a brain damaged patient: A case study. *Music Therapy Perspectives, 5*, 41-45.

Goldman, J. S. (1988). Toward a new consciousness of the sonic healing arts: The therapeutic use of sound for personal and planetary health and transformation. *Music Therapy, 7*(1), 28-33.

Gonzales, A. (1981, April). *Music therapy techniques to promote and enhance verbal and vocal responses in severe and profound developmentally handicapped clients.* Paper presented at the 1981 Conference of the Great Lakes Regional Chapter of the National Association for Music Therapy, Cleveland, OH.

Goodglass, H. (1963). Musical capacity after brain surgery. In E. H. Schneider (Ed.), *Music therapy 1962* (pp. 101-107). Lawrence, KS: Allen Press.

Goolsby, T. M., Jr., Frary, R. B., & Rogers, M. M. (1974).

bservation techniques in determination of the effects of background music upon verbalization of disadvantaged kindergarten children. *Journal of Music Therapy, 11*(1), 21-32.

Graham, R. M. (1974). The education of the music therapist. *College Music Symposium, 14*, 50-59.

Graham, R. M. (1975). Music education of emotionally disturbed children. In R. M. Graham (Compiler), *Music for the exceptional child* (pp. 111-129). Reston, VA: Music Educators National Conference.

Grandin, T. (1995). *Thinking in pictures.* New York: Doubleday.

Grandin, T., & Scarino, M. M. (1986). *Emergence: Labeled autistic.* Novato, CA: Arena Press.

Grant, R. E. (1989). Music therapy guidelines for developmentally disabled children. *Music Therapy Perspectives, 6*, 18-22.

Greenwald , M. A., & Salzberg, R. S. (1979). Vocal range assessment of geriatric clients. *Journal of Music Therapy, 16*(4), 172-177.

Gregoire, M. A., Hughes, J. E., Robbins, B. J., & Voorneveld, R. B. (1989). Music therapy with the gifted: A trial program. *Music Therapy Perspectives, 7*, 23-27.

Gresham, F. M., & Reschly, D. J. (1986). Social skill deficits and low peer acceptance of mainstreamed learning disabled children. *Learning Disability Quarterly, 9*, 23-32.

Griggs-Drane, E. R., & Wheeler, J. J. (1997). The use of functional assessment procedures and individualized schedules in the treatment of autism: Recommendations for music therapists. *Music Therapy Perspectives, 15*(2), 87-93.

Groene, R. W. (1993). Effectiveness of music therapy 1:1 interventions with individuals having senile dementia of the Alzheimer's type. *Journal of Music Therapy, 30*(3), 138-157.

Groeneweg, G., Stan, E. A., Celser, A., MacBeth, L, & Vrbancic, M. I. (1988). The effect of background music on the vocational behavior of mentally handicapped adults. *Journal of Music Therapy, 25*(3), 118-134.

Grout, D. J. (1973). *A history of western music* (2nd ed.). New York: W. W. Norton.

Gunsberg, A. (1988). Improvised musical play: A strategy for fostering social play between developmentally delayed and nondelayed preschool children. *Journal of Music Therapy, 25*(4), 178-191.

Gunsberg, A. (1991). A method for conducting improvised musical play with children both with and without developmental delays in preschool classrooms. *Music Therapy Perspectives, 9*, 46-51.

Guzzetta, C. E. (1991). Music therapy: Nursing the music of the soul. In D. Campbell (Ed.), *Music: Physician for times to come* (pp. 146-166). Wheaton, IL: Quest Books.

Gwyther, L. P. (1985). *Care of Alzheimer's patients: A manual for nursing home staff.* Washington, D.C., and Chicago, IL: American Health Care Association and Alzheimer's Disease and Related Disorders Association.

Haas, F., Pineda, H., & Axen, K. (1989). Music and respiration. In M. H. M. Lee (Ed.), *Rehabilitation, music and human well-being* (pp. 188-205). St. Louis: MMB Music.

Habboushe, F., & Maranto, C. D. (1991). Medical and psychological problems of musicians: An overview. In C. D. Maranto (Ed.), *Applications of music in medicine* (pp. 201-221). Washington, D.C.: National Association for Music Therapy.

Hackley, J. A. (September, 1973). Reality orientation brings patients back from confusion and apathy. *Modern Nursing Home.*

Hadsell, N. (1974). A sociological theory and approach to music therapy with adult psychiatric patients. *Journal of Music Therapy, 11*(3), 113-124.

Hadsell, N. A. (1989). Multivariate analyses of musicians' and nonmusicians' ratings of pre-categorized stimulative and sedative music. *Journal of Music Therapy, 26*(3), 106-114.

Hadsell, N. A. (1993). Levels of external structure in music therapy. *Music Therapy Perspectives, 11*(2), 61-65.

Hadsell, N. A., & Coleman, K. A. (1988). Rett syndrome: A challenge for music therapists. *Music Therapy Perspectives, 5*, 52-56.

Hager, M. (1983). Aging: Growing old actively. *Consumers Digest* (January/February 1983), pp. 21-23, 34.

Haines, J. H. (1989). The effects of music therapy on the self-esteem of emotionally disturbed adolescents. *Music Therapy, 8*(1), 78-91.

Halpern, S. (1978). *Tuning the human instrument.* Belmont, CA: Helpern Sounds.

Halpern, S. (1989). A new age of music in medicine. In M. H. M. Lee (Ed.), *Rehabilitation, music and human well-being* (pp. 82-100). St. Louis: MMB Music.

Hamel, P. M. (1979). *Through music to the self* (P. Lemesurier, Trans.). Boulder, CO: Shambala. (Original work published 1976)

Hamill, D. D., Leigh, J. E., McNutt, G., & Larson, S. C. (1981). A new definition of learning disabilities. *Learning Disability Quarterly, 4*, 336-342.

Hamilton, P., & Bailey, L. (1981, November). *The role of the healing arts in the care of the person with cancer.* Paper presented at the 32nd Annual Conference of the National Association for Music Therapy, Denver, CO.

Hammer, S. E. (1996). The effects of guided imagery through music on state and trait anxiety. *Journal of Music Therapy, 33*(1), 47-70.

Hanser, S. B. (1984). Music group psychotherapy: An evaluation model. *Music Therapy Perspectives, 1*(4), 14-16.

Hanser, S. B. (1985). Music therapy and stress reduction research. *Journal of Music Therapy, 22*(4), 193-206.

Hanser, S. B. (1987). *Music therapist's handbook.* St. Louis, MO: Warren H. Green.

Hanser, S. B. (1990). A music therapy strategy for depressed older adults in the community. *Journal of Applied Gerontology, 9*, 283-298.

Hanser, S. B. (1995). Applied behavior analysis. In B. L. Wheeler (Ed.), *Music therapy research: Quantitative and qualitative perspectives* (pp. 149-163). Phoenixville, PA: Barcelona Publishers.

Hanser, S. B., Larson, S. C., & O'Connell, A. S. (1983). The effect of music on relaxation of expectant mothers during labor. *Journal of Music Therapy, 20*(2), 50-58.

Hanser, S. B., & Wheeler, B. L. (1995). Experimental research. In B. L. Wheeler (Ed.), *Music therapy research: Quantitative and qualitative perspectives* (pp. 129-146). Phoenixville, PA: Barcelona Publishers.

Hanson, N., Gfeller, K., Woodworth, G., Swanson, E., & Garand, L. (1996). A comparison of the effectiveness of differing types and difficulty of music activities in programming for older adults with Alzheimer's disease and related disorders. *Journal of Music Therapy, 33*(2), 93-123.

Harris, C. S., Bradley, R. J., & Titus, S. K. (1992). A comparison of the effects of hard rock and easy listening on the frequency of observed inappropriate behaviors: Control of environmental antecedents in a large public area. *Journal of Music Therapy, 29*(1), 6-17.

Harvey, A. W. (1987). Utilizing music as a tool for healing. In R. R. Pratt (Ed.), *The fourth international symposium on music: Rehabilitation and human well-being* (pp. 73-87). New York: University Press of America.

Harvey, A. W. (1991). Music in attitudinal medicine. In D. Campbell (Ed.), *Music: Physician for times to come* (pp. 186-196). Wheaton, IL: Quest Books.

Havighurst, R. J. (1963). Successful aging. In R. H. Williams, C. Tibbitts, & W. Donahue (Eds.), *Processes of aging.* New York: Atherton Press.

The healing role of the arts (Working papers – The Rockefeller Foundation) (1978). New York: The Rockefeller Foundation.

Heaney, C. J. (1992). Evaluation of music therapy and other treatment modalities by adult psychiatric inpatients. *Journal of Music Therapy, 29*(2), 70-86.

Hedden, S. K. (1980a). The physical basis of music. In D. A. Hodges (Ed.), *Handbook of music psychology* (pp. 37-41). Lawrence, KS: National Association for Music Therapy.

Hedden, S. K. (1980b). Psychoacoustical parameters of music. In D. A. Hodges (Ed.), *Handbook of music psychology* (pp. 63-85). Lawrence, KS: National Association for Music Therapy.

Heidenreich, L. (n.d.). *Be active! Comprehensive eurhythmics:*

A video program of movement to music [brochure]. Milwaukee, WI: School Sisters of Notre Dame.

Heller, G. N. (1987). Ideas, initiatives, and implementations: Music therapy in America, 1789-1848. *Journal of Music Therapy, 24*(1), 35-46.

Henderson, S. M. (1983). Effects of a music therapy program upon awareness of mood in music, group cohesion, and self-esteem among hospitalized adolescent patients. *Journal of Music Therapy, 20*(1), 14-20.

Henry, D., Knoll, C. D., & Anderson, S. E. (1982). *Music works . . . A handbook for music therapists.* Stephenville, TX: Music Works.

Herlein, D. G. (1975). Music reading for the sightless: Braille notation. *Music Educators Journal, 62*(1), 42-45.

Herman, F. (1981, November), *"Hey! Look at me!"* Presentation at the 32nd Annual Conference of the National Association for Music Therapy, Denver, Co.

Herman, F. (1985). Music therapy for the young child with cerebral palsy who uses Blissymbols. *Music Therapy, 5*(1), 28-36.

Herman, F. (1991). The boy that nobody wanted: Creative experiences for a boy with severe emotional problems. In K. E. Bruscia (Ed.), *Case studies in music therapy* (pp. 99-108). Phoenixville, PA: Barcelona Publishers.

Hesser, B. (1995). The power of sound and music in therapy. In C. B. Kenny (Ed.), *Listening, playing, creating: Essays on the power of sound* (pp. 43-50). Albany, NY: State University of New York Press.

Hewett, F. M., & Forness, S. R. (1974). *Education of exceptional learners.* Boston: Allyn and Bacon.

Heyer, J. L., Downs, D. W., Kalloy, V., & Magdinec, M. (1986). Music conditioning before pure-tone screening of severely and profoundly mentally retarded adults. *Journal of Music Therapy, 23*(3), 142-156.

Hibben, J. (1984). Movement as musical expression in a music therapy setting. *Music Therapy, 4*(1), 91-97.

Hibben, J. (1991). Group music therapy with a classroom of 6-8 year old hyperactive-learning disabled children. In K. E. Bruscia (Ed.), *Case studies in music therapy* (pp. 175-189). Phoenixville, PA: Barcelona Publishers.

Hibben, J. (1992). Music therapy in the treatment of families with young children. *Music Therapy, 11*(1), 28-44.

Hodges, D. A. (1980). Neurophysiology and musical behavior. In D. A. Hodges (Ed.), *Handbook of music psychology* (pp. 195-223). Lawrence, KS: National Association for Music Therapy.

Hodges, D. A. (1996). Neuromusical research: A review of the literature. In D. A. Hodges (Ed.), *Handbook of music psychology* (2nd ed.) (pp. 197-284). San Antonio, TX: Institute for Music Research Press, The University of Texas at San Antonio.

Hodges, D. A., & Haack, P. A. (1996). The influence of music on human behavior. In D. A. Hodges (Ed.), *Handbook of music psychology* (2nd ed.) (pp. 469-555). San Antonio, TX: Institute for Music Research Press, The University of Texas at San Antonio.

Hoelzley, P. D. (1991). Reciprocal inhibition in music therapy: A case study involving wind instrument usage to attenuate fear, anxiety, and avoidance reactivity in a child with pervasive developmental disorder. *Music Therapy, 10*(1), 58-76.

Hoerning, K. (1982). A joyful sound. *Voice of the Lakes* (Newsletter of the Great Lakes Regional Chapter, National Association for Music Therapy), *26*(1), 32-33.

Hoffman, N. E. (1974). *Hear the music! A new approach to mental health.* Boynton Beach, FL: Star Publishing.

Hofmeister, G. L., & Cole, C. F. (1986, November). *The use of music in neuropsychological rehabilitation.* Paper presented at the 37th Annual Conference of the National Association for Music Therapy, Chicago, IL.

Hollander, F. M., & Juhrs, P. D. (1974). Orff-Schulwerk, an effective treatment tool with autistic children. *Journal of Music Therapy, 11*(1), 1-12.

Holloway, M. S. (1980). A comparison of passive and active music reinforcement to increase preacademic and motor skills in severely retarded children and adolescents. *Journal of Music Therapy, 17*(2), 58-69.

Horn, J. C., & Meer, J. (1987). The vintage years. *Psychology Today, 21*(5), 76-84, 88-90.

Hoskins, C. (1988). Use of music to increase verbal response and improve expressive language abilities of preschool language delayed children. *Journal of Music Therapy, 25*(2), 73-84.

Hospice web: A special kind of caring. (1999). Online, April 16, 1999. (Available http://teleport.com/hospice/index.html).

Howell, R. D., Flowers, P. J., & Wheaton, J. E. (1995). The effects of keyboard experiences on rhythmic responses on elementary school children with physical disabilities. *Journal of Music Therapy, 32*(2), 91-112.

Hughes, J. E., Robbins, B. J., McKenzie, B. A., & Robb, S. S. (1990). Integrating exceptional and nonexceptional young children through music play: A pilot program. *Music Therapy Perspectives, 8,* 52-56.

Humpal, M. E. (1990). Early intervention: The implications for music therapy. *Music Therapy Perspectives, 8,* 30-35.

Humpal, M. E. (1991). The effects of an integrated early childhood music program on social interaction among children with handicaps and their typical peers. *Journal of Music Therapy, 28*(3), 161-177.

Humpal, M. E., & Dimmick, J. A. (1995). Special learners in the music classroom. *Music Educators Journal, 81*(5), 21-23.

Hunter, B. C. (1994). Presidential perspectives: Reaching

out. *NAMT Notes,* July, 1994-September, 1994; pp. 1, 3.

Hurley, D. (1987). A sound mind in an unsound body. *Psychology Today 21*(8), 34-43.

Hurwitz, I., Wolff, P. H., Bortnick, B. D., & Kokas, K. (1975). Nonmusical effects of the Kodály music curriculum in primary grade children. *Journal of Learning Disabilities, 8*(3), 167-174.

Hylton, J. (1983). Music programs for the institutionalized elderly in a midwestern metropolitan area. *Journal of Music Therapy, 20*(4), 211-223.

International Rett Syndrome Association (1987). *What is Rett Syndrome?* Fort Washington, MD: Author.

Introducing the American Music Therapy Association. (1998). *Music Therapy Matters, 1*(1), 4.

Isaac, S., & Michael, W. B. (1971). *Handbook in research and evaluation.* San Diego: EdITS.

Isenberg-Grzeda, C. (1988). Music therapy assessment: A reflection of professional identity. *Journal of Music Therapy, 25*(3), 156-169.

Isenberg-Grzeda, C. (1995). The sound image: Music therapy in the treatment of the abused child. In C. B. Kenny (Ed.), *Listening, playing, creating: Essays on the power of sound* (pp. 137-149). Albany, NY: State University of New York Press.

Itoh, M., & Lee, M. H. M. (1989). Epidemiology of disability and music. In M. H. M. Lee (Ed.), *Rehabilitation, music, and human well-being* (pp. 13-31). St. Louis: MMB Music.

Jacobowitz, R. M. (1992). Music therapy in the short-term pediatric setting: Practical guideline for a limited time frame. *Music Therapy, 11*(1), 45-64.

Jacobs, A. (1987). Report on a project with autistic children at Indiana University. In R. R. Pratt (Ed.), *The fourth international symposium on music: Rehabilitation and human well-being* (pp. 157-164). New York: University Press of America.

Jacobson, S. (1987). All elderly people are not alike. *Dallas Times Herald* (Thursday, March 19), p. A-19.

James, M. R. (1986). Neurophysiological treatment of cerebral palsy: A case study. *Music Therapy Perspectives, 3,* 5-8.

James, M. R. (1987). Implications of selected social psychological theories on life-long skill generalization: Considerations for the music therapist. *Music Therapy Perspectives, 4,* 29-33.

James, M. R. (1988a). Music therapy and alcoholism: Part II--Treatment services. *Music Therapy Perspectives, 5,* 65-68.

James, M. R. (1988b). Music therapy values clarification: A positive influence on perceived locus of control. *Journal of Music Therapy, 25*(4), 206-215.

James, M. R., & Freed, B. S. (1989). A sequential model for developing group cohesion in music therapy. *Music Therapy Perspectives, 7,* 28-34.

Jaret, P. (1991). Turn down the racket. Readers Digest, November, pp. 153-156.

Jarvis, J. (1988). Guided imagery and music (GIM) as a primary psychotherapeutic approach. *Music Therapy Perspectives, 5,* 69-72.

Jellison, J. A. (1975). The effect of music on autonomic stress responses and verbal reports. In C. K. Madsen, R. D. Greer, & C. H. Madsen, Jr. (Eds.), *Research in music behavior: Modifying music behavior in the classroom* (pp. 206-219). New York: Teachers College Press.

Jellison, J. A., & Duke, R. A. (1994). The mental retardation label: Music teachers' expectations for children's social and music behaviors. *Journal of Music Therapy, 31*(3), 166-185.

Jellison, J. A., & Flowers, P. J. (1991). Talking about music: Interviews with disabled and nondisabled children. *Journal of Research in Music Education, 39*(4), 322-333.

Johnson, E. R. (1981). The role of objective and concrete feedback in self-concept treatment of juvenile delinquents in music therapy. *Journal of Music Therapy, 18*(3), 137-147.

Johnson, F. L. (1981). Music therapy for the multiply handicapped: A guide to references and resources. *Voice of the Lakes* (Newsletter of the Great Lakes Regional Chapter, National Association for Music Therapy), *25*(2), 20-22.

Johnson, F. L. (1996). Models of service delivery. In B. L. Wilson (Ed.), *Models of music therapy interventions in school settings: From institution to inclusion* (pp. 48-77). Silver Spring, MD: National Association for Music Therapy.

Johnson, J. M., & Phillips, L. L. (1971). Affecting the behavior of retarded children with music. *Music Educators Journal, 57*(7), 45-46.

Johnson, J. M., & Zinner, C. C. (1974). Stimulus fading and schedule learning in generalizing and maintaining behaviors. *Journal of Music Therapy, 11*(2), 84-96.

Johnson, R. E. (1981). E. Thayer Gaston: Leader in scientific thought on music in therapy and education. *Journal of Research in Music Education, 29*(4), 279-285.

Jonas, J. L. (1991). Preference of elderly music listeners residing in nursing homes for art music, traditional jazz, popular music of today, and country music. *Journal of Music Therapy, 28*(3), 149-160.

Jones, J. (1996, March). *Attention deficit disorder: a professional and personal perspective.* Paper presented at the Conference of the Southwestern Region of the National Association for Music Therapy, San Antonio, Texas.

Jones, R. E. (1986). Assessing developmental levels of mentally retarded students with the musical perception assessment of cognitive development. *Journal of Music Therapy, 23*(3), 166-173.

Jorgenson, H. (1974). The use of a contingent music activity to modify behaviors which interfere with learning. *Journal of Music Therapy, 11*(1), 41-46.

Josepha, Sr. M. (1964). Therapeutic value of instrumental performance for severely handicapped children. *Journal of Music Therapy, 1*(3), 73-79.

Josepha, Sr. M. (1968). Part III. Music therapy for physically disabled children and adults. In E. T. Gaston (Ed.), *Music in therapy* (pp. 97-171). New York: Macmillan.

Jung, C. (1956). *Symbols of transformation.* Princeton, NJ: Princeton University Press.

Justice, R. W. (1994). Music therapy interventions for people with eating disorders in an inpatient setting. *Music Therapy Perspectives, 12*(2), 104-110.

Kadaba, L. S. (1995). Shut in but not shut out: Senior citizens connect through teleconferencing. *The Dallas Morning News* (Friday, June 16), pp. 1C-2C.

Kanner, L. (1943). Autistic disturbances of affective contact. *Nervous Child, 2,* 217-250.

Kapla, P. S. (1975). Music and the hearing handicapped child. In R. M. Graham (Compiler), *Music for the exceptional child* (pp. 61-71). Reston, VA: Music Educators National Conference.

Kaplan, H. I., & Sadock, B. J. (1991). *Comprehensive glossary of psychiatry and psychology.* Baltimore, MD: Williams & Wilkins.

Karras, B. (1985). *Down memory lane: Topics and ideas for reminiscence groups.* Wheaton, MD: Circle Press.

Karras, B. (Ed.). (1987). *"You bring out the music in me": Music in nursing homes.* Binghamton, NY: Haworth Press.

Kaser, V. A. (1993). Musical expression of subconscious feelings: A clinical perspective. *Music Therapy Perspectives, 11*(1), 16-23.

Kastenbaum, R. (1979). A developmental-field approach to aging and its implications for practice. In D. P. Kent, R. Kastenbaum, & S. Sherwood (Eds.), *Research planning and action for the elderly: The power and potential of social science* (pp. 37-49). New York: Human Sciences Press.

Kauffman, J. M. (1977). *Characteristics of children's behavior disorders.* Columbus, OH: Charles E. Merrill.

Kay, L. (1996). Adult day care. *Correspondent, 94*(852), 22-23.

Kay, L. D. (1981). Music therapy activities for the severely and profoundly multiply handicapped child or adult. *Voice of the Lakes* (Newsletter of the Great Lakes Regional Chapter, National Association for Music Therapy), 25(2), 26-30.

Kay, L. D. (1998, November). *A beginner's guide to Gardner's multiple intelligences.* Paper presented at the Inaugural Conference of the American Music Therapy Association, Cleveland, OH.

Kearney, S., & Fussey, I. (1991). The use of adapted leisure materials to reinforce correct head positioning in a brain-injured adult. *Brain Injury, 5*(3), 295-302.

Kellmann, R. H. (1986). Developing music programs for older adults. *Music Educators Journal, 72*(5), 30-33.

Kemper, M. B. (1982). The use of music therapy to promote decision-making behavior among geriatric clients in nursing care facilities. *Voice of the Lakes* (Newsletter of the Great Lakes Regional Chapter, National Association for Music Therapy), 26(1), 18-25.

Kendall, J. (1986). Suzuki's mother tongue method. *Music Educators Journal, 72*(6), 47-50.

Kenny, C. B. (1982). *The mythic artery: The magic of music therapy.* Atascadero, CA: Ridgeview Publishing.

Kenny, C. B. (1998). Embracing complexity: The creation of a comprehensive research culture in music therapy. *Journal of Music Therapy, 35*(3), 201-217.

Kersten, F. (1981). Music as therapy for the visually impaired. *Music Educators Journal, 67*(7), 63-65.

Kersten, F. (1987). Human well-being of visually impaired students through accommodation in music classes for the sighted. In R. R. Pratt (Ed.), *The fourth international symposium on music: Rehabilitation and human well-being* (pp. 132-150). New York: University Press of America.

Kimbo Educational. (1995). *Kimbo Educational 1995 catalog.* Long Branch, NJ: Author.

Kivland, M. J. (1986). The use of music to increase self-esteem in a conduct-disordered adolescent. *Journal of Music Therapy, 23*(1), 25-29.

Knapp, R. A. (1980). A choir for total communication. *Music Educators Journal, 66*(6), 54-55.

Knox, R. A. (1994). Mozart's music fuels the brain. *Dallas Morning News* (Thursday, September 1), pp. 1C, 3C..

Korduba, O. M. (1975). Duplicated rhythm patterns between deaf and normal hearing children. *Journal of Music Therapy, 12*(3), 136-146.

Kovach, A. M. S. (1985). Shamanism and guided imagery and music: A comparison. *Journal of Music Therapy, 22*(3), 154-165.

Koza, J. E. (1990). Music instruction in the nineteenth century: Views from *Godey's Lady's Book,* 1830-1877. *Journal of Research in Music Education, 38*(4), 245-257.

Kramer, S. A. (1978). The effects of music as a cue in maintaining handwashing in preschool children. *Journal of Music Therapy, 15*(3), 136-144.

Kraus, T., & Galloway, H. (1982). Melodic intonation therapy with language delayed apraxic children. *Journal of Music Therapy, 19*(2), 102-133.

Krout, R. (1986a). *Music therapy in special education: Developing and maintaining social skills necessary for mainstreaming.* St. Louis: MMB Music.

Krout, R. (1986b). Use of a group token contingency with school-aged special education students to improve a music listening skill. *Music Therapy Perspectives, 3,* 13-16.

Krout, R. (1987). Music therapy with multi-handicapped students: Individualizing treatment within a group setting. *Journal of Music Therapy, 24*(1), 2-13.

Krout, R. (1992a). Integrating technology. *Music Therapy Perspectives, 10*(1), 8-9.

Krout, R. (1992b). Integrating technology, version 5.1. *Music Therapy Perspectives, 10*(2), 84-86.

Krout, R. (1995). Integrating technology. *Music Therapy Perspectives, 13*(1), 5-6.

Krout, R., Burnham, A. & Moorman, S. (1993). Computer and electronic music applications with students in special education: From program proposal to progress evaluation. *Music Therapy Perspectives, 10*(1), 8-9.

Krout, R. E., & Mason, M. (1988). Using computer and electronic music resources in clinical music therapy with behaviorally disordered students, 12 to 18 years old. *Music Therapy Perspectives, 5*, 114-118.

Kübler-Ross, E. (1969). *On death and dying.* New York: Macmillan.

Kübler-Ross, E. (1974). *Questions and answers on death and dying.* New York: Macmillan.

Landis, B., & Carder, P. (1972). *The eclectic curriculum in American music education; Contributions of Dalcroze, Kodály, and Orff.* Reston, VA: Music Educators National Conference.

Lane, D. L. (1991). The effect of a single music therapy session on hospitalized children as measured by salivary immunoglobin A, speech pause time, and a patient option Likert scale. *Pediatric Research, 29*(4, part 2), 11A.

Lane, D. L. (1994). Effects of music therapy on immune function of hospitalized patients. *Quality of Life – A Nursing Challenge, 3*(4), 74-80.

Langdon, G. S., Pearson, J., Stastny, P., & Thorning, H. (1989). The integration of music therapy into a treatment approach in the transition of adult psychiatric patients from institution to community. *Music Therapy, 8*(1), 92-107.

Langer, S. K. (1966). The cultural importance of the arts. *The Journal of Aesthetic Education,* Spring, pp. 5-12.

Larson, B. A. (1977). A comparison of singing ranges of mentally retarded and normal children with published songbooks used in singing activities. *Journal of Music Therapy, 14*(3), 139-143.

Lathom, W. (1961). The use of music with cerebral palsied children during activities involving physical control. *Bulletin of the National Association for Music Therapy, 10*, 10-16.

Lathom, W. (1968). The use of music therapy with retarded patients. In E. T. Gaston (Ed.), *Music in therapy* (pp. 66-77). New York: Macmillan.

Lathom, W. (1974). Application of Kodály concepts in music therapy. *Journal of Music Therapy, 11*(1), 13-20.

Lathom, W. (1980). An overview of music therapy. In *The use of the creative arts in therapy* (pp. 36-38). Washington, D.C.: American Psychiatric Association.

Lathom, W. (Ed.). (1981a). *Music therapy in the education of handicapped children and youth: A manual to conduct inservice training workshops for music educators, administrators, parents, and special educators* (Rev. ed.). Lawrence, KS: National Association for Music Therapy.

Lathom, W. (1981b). *The role of the music therapist in the education of severely and profoundly handicapped children and youth.* Lawrence, KS: National Association for Music Therapy.

Lathom, W. (1982). Survey of current functions of a music therapist. *Journal of Music Therapy, 19*(1), 2-27.

Lathom, W., & Eagle, C. T. (1982). Music for the severely handicapped. *Music Educators Journal, 68*(8), 30-31.

Lathom-Radocy, W. B., & Radocy, R. E. (1995). Descriptive quantitative research. In B. L. Wheeler (Ed.), *Music therapy research: Quantitative and qualitative perspectives* (pp. 165-181). Phoenixville, PA: Barcelona Publishers.

Lavine, R., Bucksbaum, M., & Poncy, M. (1976). Auditory analgesia: Somatosensory evoked response and subjective pain rating. *Psychophysiology, 13*(2), 140-148.

Lazarus, A. A. (1976). *Multimodal behavior therapy.* New York: Springer.

Lazarus, A. A. (1989). *The practice of multimodal therapy.* Baltimore: Johns Hopkins University Press.

Lazarus, L. W. (Ed.). (1988). *Essentials of geriatric psychiatry: A guide for health professionals.* New York: Springer Publishing.

Lefebvre, C. (1991). All her "yesterdays": An adolescent's search for a better today through music. In K. E. Bruscia (Ed.), *Case studies in music therapy* (pp. 219-230). Phoenixville, PA: Barcelona Publishers.

Lenhoff, H. M. (1998). Insights into the musical potential of cognitively impaired people diagnosed with Williams syndrome. *Music Therapy Perspectives, 16*(1), 33-36.

Leonhard, C. (1982). Humanizing music in a mechanized society. *Music Educators Journal, 68*(9), 23-24.

Levine-Gross, J., & Swartz, . (1982). The effects of music therapy on anxiety in chronically ill patients. *Music Therapy, 2*(1), 43-52.

Levinson, S., & Bruscia, K. (1985). Putting blind students in touch with music. *Music Educators Journal, 72*(2), 49.

Levis, L., & Lininger, L. (1994). *Increase the peace: A focused approach.* Austin & Buda, TX: Authors.

Lewis, C. B. (1985). *Aging: The health care challenge.* Philadelphia: F. A. Davis.

Liebman, S. S., & MacLaren, A. (1991). The effect of music and relaxation on third trimester anxiety in adolescent pregnancy. *Journal of Music Therapy, 28*(2), 89-100.

Lienhard, M. E. (1981, November). *Music therapy in a stress treatment program.* Paper presented at the 32nd Annual Conference of the National Association for Music Therapy, Denver, CO.

Life's work: What a hospice nurse does with her life is help people die. (1987). *Hippocrates, 1*(3), 54-61.

Lindberg, K. A. (1995). Songs of healing: Songwriting with an abused adolescent. *Music Therapy, 13*(1), 93-108.

Linderman, J., & Fridley, B. (1981, November). *Medical setting: Getting in and staying there.* Paper presented at the 32nd Annual Conference of the National Association for Music Therapy, Denver, CO.

Lipe, A. (1995). The use of music performance tasks in the assessment of cognitive functioning among older adults with dementia. *Journal of Music Therapy, 32*(3), 137-151.

Lipe, A. W. (1991). Using music therapy to enhance the quality of life in a client with Alzheimer's dementia: a case study. *Music Therapy Perspectives, 9*, 102-105.

Locsin, R. (1981). The effect of music on the pain of selected post-operative patients. *Journal of Advanced Nursing, 6*, 19-25.

Loewy, J. (1995). The musical stages of speech: A developmental model of pre-verbal sound making. *Music Therapy, 13*(1), 47-73.

Logan, K. (1996). Music is key to lifelong wellness. *Teaching Music, 3*(4), 42-43.

Logan, T. G., & Roberts, A. R. (1984). The effects of different types of relaxation music on tension level. *Journal of Music Therapy, 21*(4), 177-183.

Lorch, C. A., Lorch, V., Diefendorf, A.O., & Earl, P. W. (1994). Effect of stimulative and sedative music on systolic blood pressure, heart rate, and respiratory rate in premature infants. *Journal of Music Therapy, 31*(2), 105-118.

Lovejoy, F. H., & Estridge, D. (Eds.). (1987). *The new child health encyclopedia.* New York: Delacorte Press.

Lowe, J. C. (1973). Excitatory response to music as a reciprocal inhibitor. *Journal of Behavior Therapy and Experimental Psychiatry, 4*(3), 297-299.

Lucia, C. M. (1987). Toward developing a model of music therapy intervention in the rehabilitation of head trauma patients. *Music Therapy Perspectives, 4*, 34-39.

Luetje, V. M. (1989). Music therapy in crisis intervention. *Music Therapy Perspectives, 7*, 35-39.

MacNay, S. K. (1995). The influence of preferred music on the perceived exertion, mood, and time estimation scores of patients participating in a cardiac rehabilitation exercise program. *Music Therapy Perspectives, 13*(2), 91-96.

Madsen, C. K. (1981). *Music therapy: A behavioral guide for the mentally retarded.* Lawrence, KS: National Association for Music Therapy.

Madsen, C. K. (1986). Research and music therapy: The necessity for transfer. *Journal of Music Therapy, 23*(2), 50-55.

Madsen, C. K., Byrnes, S. R., Capperalla-Sheldon, D. A., & Brittin, R. V. (1993). Aesthetic response to music: Musicians versus nonmusicians. *Journal of Music Therapy, 30*(3), 174-191.

Madsen, C. K., & Madsen, C. H., Jr. (1978). *Experimental research in music.* Raleigh, NC: Contemporary Publishing.

Madsen, C. K., Michel, D. E., & Madsen, C. H., Jr. (1975). The use of music stimuli in teaching language discrimination with head start students. In C. K. Madsen, R. D. Greer, & C. H. Madsen, Jr. (Eds.), *Research in music behavior: Modifying music behavior in the classroom* (pp. 182-190). New York: Teachers College Press.

Madsen, S. A. (1991). The effect of music paired with and without gestures on the learning and transfer of new vocabulary: Experimenter-derived nonsense words. *Journal of Music Therapy, 28*(4), 222-230.

Mahlberg, M. (1973). Music therapy in the treatment of an autistic boy. *Journal of Music Therapy, 10*(4), 89-193.

Malone, A. B. (1996). The effects of live music on the distress of pediatric patients receiving intravenous starts, venipunctures, injections, and heal sticks. *Journal of Music Therapy, 33*(1), 19-33.

Mandel, S. E. (1988). Music therapy: A personal peri-surgical experience. *Music Therapy Perspectives, 5*, 109-110.

Mandel, S. E. (1991). Music therapy: A repeated personal peri-surgical experience. *Music Therapy Perspectives, 9*, 111-112.

Mandel, S. E. (1996). Music for wellness: Music therapy for stress management in a rehabilitation program. *Music Therapy Perspectives, 14*(1), 38-43.

Maranto, C. D. (1988). AIDS: Information and issues for music therapists. *Music Therapy Perspectives, 5*, 78-81.

Maranto, C. D. (Ed.) (1991). *Applications of music in medicine.* Washington, D.C.: National Association for Music Therapy.

Maranto, C. D. (Ed.) (1993a). *Music therapy: International perspectives.* Pipersville, PA: Jeffrey Books.

Maranto, C. D. (1993b). Music therapy in the United States of America. In C. D. Maranto (Ed.), *Music therapy: International perspectives* (pp. 605-662). Pipersville, PA: Jeffrey Books.

Maranto, C. D. (1996). Research in music and medicine: The state of the art. In M. A. R. Froehlich (Ed.), *Music therapy with hospitalized children: A creative arts child life approach* (pp. 39-66). Cherry Hill, NJ: Jeffrey Books.

Maranto, C. D., & Bruscia, K. E. (Eds.). (1987). *Perspectives on music therapy education and training.* Philadelphia: Temple University, Esther Boyer College of Music.

Maranto, C. D., & Bruscia, K. E. (1988). *Methods of teaching and training the music therapist.* Philadelphia: Temple University, Esther Boyer College of Music.

Marcus, D. (1995). Entering the world of tones. In C. B.

Kenny (Ed.), *Listening, playing, creating: Essays on the power of sound* (pp. 19-41). Albany, NY: State University of New York Press.

Market space. (1987). *Music Educators Journal, 73*(4), 11-12.

Marley, L. S. (1984). The use of music with hospitalized infants and toddlers: A descriptive study. *Journal of Music Therapy, 21*(3), 126-132.

Marsh, J., & Fitch, J. (1970). The effect of singing on the speech articulation of Negro disadvantaged children. *Journal of Music Therapy, 7*(3), 88-94.

Martin, J. A. (Ed.) (1989). *The next step forward: Music therapy with the terminally ill.* Bronx, NY: Calvary Hospital.

Martin, J. A. (1991). Music therapy at the end of a life. In K. E. Bruscia (Ed.), *Case studies in music therapy* (pp. 617-632). Phoenixville, PA: Barcelona Publishers.

Maslow, A. H. (1968). *Toward a psychology of being* (2nd ed.). New York: D. Van Nostrand.

Matteson, C. A. (1972). Finding the self in space: More than one handicap doesn't make less than one child. *Music Educators Journal, 58*(8), 63-65, 135.

Matthias, B. (1989). Breaking the sound barrier: Deaf use many methods to join hearing world. *Dallas Times Herald* (Monday, August 28), pp. B-1 & B-3.

Maultsby, M. C. (1977). Combining music therapy and rational behavior therapy. *Journal of Music Therapy, 14*(2), 89-97.

Maultsby, M. C. (1984). *Rational behavior therapy.* Englewood Cliffs, NJ: Prentice-Hall.

May, E. (1961). Music for deaf children. *Music Educators Journal, 47*(3), 39-40.

May, R. (1975). *The courage to create.* New York: W. W. Norton.

McCarthy, K. M. (1992). Stress management in the health care field: A pilot program for staff in a nursing home unit for patients with Alzheimer's disease. *Music Therapy Perspectives, 10*(2), 110-113.

McDonnell, L. (1984). Music therapy with trauma patients and their families on a pediatric service. *Music Therapy, 4*(1), 55-63.

McGinty, J. K. (1980). Survey of duties and responsibilities of current music therapy positions. *Journal of Music Therapy, 17*(3), 148-166.

McGuire, M. G., & Smeltekop, R. A. (1994a). The termination process in music therapy: Part I – Theory and clinical implications. *Music Therapy Perspectives, 12*(1), 20-27.

McGuire, M. G., & Smeltekop, R. A. (1994b). The termination process in music therapy: Part II – A model and clinical implications. *Music Therapy Perspectives, 12*(1), 28-34.

McKinney, C. H. (1990). Music therapy in obstetrics: A review. *Music Therapy Perspectives, 8*, 57-60.

McMaster, N. (1991). Reclaiming a positive identity: Music therapy in the aftermath of a stroke. In K. E. Bruscia (Ed.), *Case studies in music therapy* (pp. 547-559). Phoenixville, PA: Barcelona Publishers.

McNeil, C. (1995). *Alzheimer's disease: Unraveling the mystery.* Bethesda, MD: National Institute on Aging.

McRae, S. W. (1982). The Orff connection . . . reaching the special child. *Music Educators Journal, 68*(8), 32-34.

McReynolds, J. C. (1988). Helping visually impaired students succeed in band. *Music Educators Journal, 75*(1), 36-38.

Mead, V. H. (1986). More than mere movement: Dalcroze eurhythmics. *Music Educators Journal, 72*(6), 42-46.

Meer, J. (1985). Mental alertness and the good old days. *Psychology Today, 19*(3), 8.

Melzack, R., Weisz, A. Z., & Sprague, l. T. (1963). Strategems for controlling pain: Contributions of auditory stimulation and suggestion. *Experimental Neurology, 8*, 239-247.

Memory and aging [brochure]. (1987). Chicago, IL: Alzheimer's Disease and Related Disorders Association.

Mercer, C. D. (1987). *Students with learning disabilities* (3rd ed.). Columbus, OH: Merill Publishing.

Merriam, A. P. (1964). *The anthropology of music.* Evanston, IL: Northwestern University Press.

Merriam, S., & Cross, L. H. (1981). Aging, reminiscence, and life satisfaction. *Activities, Adaptation & Aging, 2*, 39-50.

Merrion, M. (1990). R & D for better teaching. *Music Educators Journal, 77*(3), 22-25.

Metzger, L. K. (1986). The selection of music for therapeutic use with adolescents and young adults in a psychiatric facility. *Music Therapy Perspectives, 3*, 20-24.

Metzler, R. K. (1974). The use of music as a reinforcer to increase imitative behavior in severely and profoundly retarded female residents. *Journal of Music Therapy, 11*(2), 97-110.

Metzler, R. K. (1982). Suzuki and therapy: Nurtured by love. *Voice of the Lakes* (Newsletter of the Great Lakes Regional Chapter, National Association for Music Therapy), *26*(2), 14-19.

Metzler, R. K., & Berman, T. (1991). Selected effects of sedative music on the anxiety of bronchoscopy patients. In C. D. Maranto (Ed.), *Applications of music in medicine* (pp. 163-178). Washington, D.C.: National Association for Music Therapy.

Michel, D. E. (1963). Music therapy in the southeastern United States. In E. H. Schneider (Ed.), *Music therapy 1962* (pp. 201-204). Lawrence, KS: Allen Press.

Michel, D. E. (1968). Music therapy in speech habilitation of cleft-palate children. In E. T. Gaston (Ed.), *Music in therapy* (pp. 162-166). New York: Macmillan.

Michel, D. E. (1971). Self-esteem and academic

achievement in black junior high school students: Effects of automated guitar instruction. *Council for Research in Music Education, Bulletin, 24*, 15-23.

Michel, D. E. (1976). *Music therapy: An introduction to therapy and special education through music.* Springfield, IL: Charles C Thomas.

Michel, D. E. (1981, November). *Music therapist role changes in the U.S.A. since 1946.* Paper presented at the 32nd Annual Conference of the National Association for Music Therapy, Denver, CO.

Michel, D. E. (1985). *Music therapy: An introduction, including music in special education* (2nd ed.). Springfield, IL: Charles C Thomas.

Michel, D. E., & Farrell, D. M. (1973). Music and self-esteem: Disadvantaged problem boys in an all-black elementary school. *Journal of Research in Music Education, 21*(1), 80-84.

Michel, D. E., & Jones, J. L. (1991). *Music for developing speech and language skills in children: A guide for parents and therapists.* St. Louis: MMB Music.

Michel, D. E., & May, N. H. (1974). The development of music therapy procedures with speech and language disorders. *Journal of Music Therapy, 11*(2), 74-80.

Millard, K. A. O., & Smith, J. M. (1989). The influence of group singing therapy on the behavior of Alzheimer's disease patients. *Journal of Music Therapy, 26*(2), 58-70.

Miller, B. F., & Keane, C. B. (1978). E*ncyclopedia and dictionary of medicine, nursing, and allied health* (2nd ed.). Philadelphia: W. B. Saunders.

Miller, E. B. (1994). Musical intervention in family therapy. *Music Therapy, 12*(2), 39-57.

Miller, K. J. (1979). *Treatment with music: A manual for allied health professionals.* Kalamazoo, MI: Western Michigan University Printing Department.

Miller, L. K., & Schyb, M. (1989). Facilitation and interference by background music. *Journal of Music Therapy, 26*(1), 42-54.

Miller, S. G. (1982). *Music therapy for handicapped children: Speech impaired.* Washington, D.C.: National Association for Music Therapy.

Miller, W. E. (1983). Research and family factors in aural rehabilitation of the elderly. *Activities, Adaptation, and Aging, 3*(4), 17-29.

Miluk-kolasa, B., Matejek, M., & Stupnicki, R. (1996). The effects of music listening on changes in selected physiological parameters in adult pre-surgical patients. *Journal of Music Therapy, 33*(3), 208-218.

Miorin, A. C., & Covault, M. L. (1979, April). *Nurturance therapy.* Paper presented at the 1979 Conference of the Great Lakes Regional Chapter of the National Association for Music Therapy, Kalamazoo, MI.

Mitchell, G. C. (1966). Bedtime music for psychotic children. *Nursing Mirror and Midwives Journal, 122*(20), 452.

Mitchell, R. L. (1978). Arts in the prisons. In *The healing role of the arts (Working papers – the Rockefeller Foundation)* (pp. 38-41). New York: The Rockefeller Foundation.

Montello, L., & Coons, E. E. (1998). Effects of active versus passive group music therapy on preadolescents with emotional, learning, and behavioral disorders. *Journal of Music Therapy, 35*(1), 49-67.

Monti, R. (1985). Music therapy in a therapeutic nursery. *Music Therapy, 5*(1), 22-27.

Moog, H. (1987). Playing instruments with the blind and severely visually handicapped. In R. R. Pratt (Ed.), *The fourth international symposium on music: Rehabilitation and human well-being* (pp. 151-156). New York: University Press of America.

Moore, R. S., Staum, M. J., & Brotons, M. (1992). Music preferences of the elderly: repertoire, vocal ranges, tempos, and accompaniments for singing. *Journal of Music Therapy, 29*(4), 236-252.

Moreno, J. (1988). Multicultural music therapy: The world music connection. *Journal of Music Therapy, 25*(1), 17-27.

Moreno, J. (1992). International perspectives. *Music Therapy Perspectives, 10*(2), 87-88.

Moreno, J. (1993). International perspectives. *Music Therapy Perspectives, 11*(2), 53-54.

Moreno, J. (1996). International perspectives. *Music Therapy Perspectives, 14*(2), 74-76.

Moreno, J., Brotons, M., Hairston, M., Hawley, T., Kiel, H., Michel, D., & Rohrbacher, M. (1990). International music therapy: A global perspective. *Music Therapy Perspectives, 8*, 41-46.

Morgan, E. (1975). Music – a weapon against anxiety: How music builds self-esteem in a psychiatric ward. *Music Educators Journal, 61*(5), 38-40, 87.

Morton, L. L., Kershner, J. R., & Siegel, L. S. (1990). The potential for therapeutic applications of music on problems related to memory and attention. *Journal of Music Therapy, 27*(4), 195-208.

Munro, S. (1984). *Music therapy in palliative/hospice care.* St. Louis: Magnamusic-Baton.

Munro, S. & Mount, B. (1978). Music therapy in palliative care. *Canadian Medical Association Journal, 119*, 1029-1034.

Murooka, H. (1975). *Lullaby from the womb.* Hollywood, CA: Capitol Records.

Murphy, M. E. (1992). Coping in the short term: The impact of acute care on music therapy practice. *Music Therapy, 11*(1), 99-119.

Music education linked to higher mathematics thinking. (1994). *Music Educators Journal, 81*(3), 15.

Muskatevc, L. C. (1967). The compleat therapist. *Journal of Music Therapy, 4*(4), 137-139.

Muslin, H. L. (1992). *The psychotherapy of the elderly self.* New

York: Brunner/Mazel.

Myers, D. E. (1991). Older adult learning: How important is achievement? *General Music Today, 4*(3), 30-31.

Myers, D. E. (1992). Teaching learners of all ages. *Music Educators Journal, 79*(4), 23-26.

Nagler, J. C. (1995). Toward the aesthetic lifeworld. *Music Therapy, 13*(1), 75-91.

Nagler, J. C., & Lee, M. H. M. (1989). Music therapy using computer music technology. In M. H. M. Lee (Ed.), *Rehabilitation, music and human well-being* (pp. 226-241). St. Louis: MMB Music.

National Association for Music Therapy [NAMT]. (1994a). *NAMT member sourcebook 1994*. Silver Spring, MD: Author.

National Association for Music Therapy [NAMT]. (1994b). Standards and procedures for academic program approval. *Music Therapy Perspectives, 12*(1), 39-50.

National Institute of Mental Health [NIMH]. (1993). *Learning disabilities*. Washington, D.C.: U.S. Government Printing Office.

National Osteoporosis Foundation. (1995). *Stand up to osteoporosis: Your guide to staying healthy and independent through prevention and treatment*. Washington, D.C.: Author.

National Paralysis Foundation. (n.d.). *Spinal victory*. Dallas, TX: Author.

Nelson, D. L., Anderson, V. G., & Gonzales, A. D. (1984). Music activities as therapy for children with autism and other pervasive developmental disorders. *Journal of Music Therapy, 21*(3), 100-116.

Nettl, B. (1956). *Music in primitive cultures*. Cambridge, MA: Harvard University Press.

Newcomer, P. L. (1980). *Understanding and teaching emotionally disturbed children*. Boston: Allyn & Bacon.

Newton, J., & Redmond, A. (1995, April). *A song in the night: Music in the spiritual/emotional care of hospitalized children and their families*. Paper presented at the Conference of the Southwestern Region of the National Association for Music Therapy, Irving, Texas.

Nicholas, M. J., & Gilbert, J. P. (1980). Research in music therapy: A survey of music therapists' attitudes and knowledges. *Journal of Music Therapy, 17*(4), 207-213.

Nocera, S. D. (1979). *Reaching the special learner through music*. Morristown, NJ: Silver Burdett.

Nolan, P. (1983). Insight therapy: GIM in a forensic psychiatric setting. *Music Therapy, 3*, 43-51.

Nolan, P. (1989). Music as a transitional object in the treatment of bulimia. *Music Therapy Perspectives, 6*, 49-51.

Nolan, P. (1994). The therapeutic response in improvisational music therapy: What goes on inside? *Music Therapy Perspectives, 12*(2), 84-91.

Nordoff, P., & Robbins, C. (1968). Improvised music as therapy for autistic children. In E. T. Gaston (Ed.), *Music in therapy* (pp. 191-195). New York: Macmillan.

Nordoff, P., & Robbins, C. (1971a). *Music therapy in special education*. New York: John Day.

Nordoff, P., & Robbins, C. (1971b). *Therapy in music for handicapped children*. London: Victor Gollancz Ltd.

Nordoff, P., & Robbins, C. (1977). *Creative music therapy*. New York: John Day.

Nowicki, A. L., & Trevisan, L. A. (1978). *Beyond the sound: A technical and philosophical approach to music therapy* (Rev. ed.). Porterville & Santa Barbara, CA: Nowicki/Trevisan.

O'Brien, N., & Goldstein, A. J. (1985). A systematic approach to developing a private practice in music therapy. *Music Therapy, 5*(1), 37-43.

O'Callaghan, C. C. (1996). Lyrical themes in songs written by palliative care patients. *Journal of Music Therapy, 33*(2), 74-92.

O'Callaghan, C. C. (1997). Therapeutic opportunities associated with the music when using songwriting in palliative care. *Music Therapy Perspectives, 15*(1), 32-38.

Oliver, S. (1989). Music therapy services of Arizona: An alternative approach to service provision. *Journal of Music Therapy, 26*(2), 95-99.

Olson, B. K. (1984). Player piano music as therapy for the elderly. *Journal of Music Therapy, 21*(1), 35-45.

Orff, G. (1980). *The Orff music therapy*. London: Schott & Co., Ltd.

Otten, J., & Shelley, F. D. (1977). *When your parents grow old*. New York: Signet.

Owens, L. D. (1979). The effects of music on the weight loss, crying, and physical movement newborns. *Journal of Music Therapy, 16*(2), 83-90.

Palisca, C. V. (1968). *Baroque music*. Englewood Cliffs, NJ: Prentice-Hall.

Palmer, M. D. (1977). Music therapy in a comprehensive program of treatment and rehabilitation for the geriatric resident. *Journal of Music Therapy, 14*(4), 190-197.

Palmer, M. (1985). Older adults are total people: music therapy with the elderly. In N. Weisberg & R. Wilder (Eds.), *Creative arts with older adults: A sourcebook* (pp. 103-111). NY: Human Sciences Press.

Palmer, M. (1989). Music therapy in gerontology: a review and a projection. *Music Therapy Perspectives, 6*, 52-56.

Palmer, M. F. (1953). *Musical stimuli in cerebral palsy, aphasia, and similar conditions*. In E. G. Gilliland (Ed.), Music therapy 1952 (pp. 162-168). Lawrence, KS: Allen Press.

Parente, A. B. (1989). Feeding the hungry soul: Music as therapeutic modality in the treatment of anorexia nervosa. *Music Therapy Perspectives, 6*, 44-48.

A passion for research (1998). *Teaching Music, 6*(2), 38-39, 56.

Paul, D. W. (1982). *Music therapy for handicapped children:*

motionally disturbed. Washington, D.C.: National Association for Music Therapy.

Pavlicevic, M., Trevarthen, C., & Duncan, J. (1994). Improvisational music therapy and the rehabilitation of persons suffering from chronic schizophrenia. *Journal of Music Therapy, 31*(2), 86-104.

Peach, S. C. (1984). Some implications for the clinical use of music facilitated imagery. *Journal of Music Therapy, 21*(1), 27-34.

Perez, M. (1989). Music, emotions, and hospitalized children: Some theoretical considerations. In M. H. M. Lee (Ed.), *Rehabilitation, music and human well-being* (pp. 242-252). St. Louis: MMB Music.

Peters, J. S. (1989). Music – A life-long coping mechanism. *Red River Valley* (Newsletter of the Southwestern Region, National Association for Music Therapy), Spring 1989, pp. 47-48.

Pfeifer, Sr. M. (1982). *Music therapy for handicapped children: Multi-handicapped.* Washington, D.C.: National Association for Music Therapy.

Pfeifer, Sr. M. (1989). A step in the right direction: Suggested strategies for implementing music therapy with the multihandicapped child. *Music Therapy Perspectives, 6,* 57-60.

Phipps, M. F. (1975). Music education for learning disabilities. In R. M. Graham (Compiler), *Music for the exceptional child* (pp. 130-135). Reston, VA: Music Educators National Conference.

Picture communication symbols combination book. (1994). Solana Beach, CA: Mayer-Johnson.

Pollack, N. J., & Namazi, K. H. (1992). The effect of music participation on the social behavior of Alzheimer's disease patients. *Journal of Music Therapy, 29*(1), 54-67.

Ponath, L. H., & Bitcon, C. H. (1972). A behavioral analysis of Orff-Schulwerk. *Journal of Music Therapy, 9*(2), 56-63.

Ponte, L. (1989). How noise can harm you. *Readers Digest,* March 1989, pp. 121-125.

Powers, M. D. (Ed.). (1989). *Children with autism.* Rockville, MD: Woodbine House.

Prange, P. (1990). Categories of music therapy at Judson retirement community. *Music Therapy Perspectives, 8,* 88-89.

Pratt, R. R. (1989). A brief history of music and medicine. In M. H. M. Lee (Ed.), *Rehabilitation, music and human well-being* (pp. 1-12). St. Louis: MMB Music.

Prazich, M. N. (1985). *A stroke patient's own story.* Danville, IL: Interstate Printers & Publishers.

Presti, G. M. (1984). A levels system approach to music therapy with severely behaviorally handicapped children in the public school system. *Journal of Music Therapy, 21*(3), 117-125.

Prickett, C. A. (1988). Music therapy for the aged. In C. E.

Furman (Ed.), *Effectiveness of music therapy procedures: Documentation of research and clinical practice* (pp. 285-299). Washington, D. C.: National Association for Music Therapy.

Prickett, C. A. (1989). A philosophy for music therapy. In R. R. Pratt & B. Hesser (Eds.), *Music therapy and music in special education: The international state of the art I* (ISME Edition Number Three) (pp. 98-100). St. Louis: MMB Music.

Prickett, C. A. (1995). Principles of quantitative research. In B. L. Wheeler (Ed.), *Music therapy research: Quantitative and qualitative perspectives* (pp. 97-117). Phoenixville, PA: Barcelona Publishers.

Prickett, C. A. (1996). Music therapy as a part of older people's lives. In C. E. Furman (Ed.), *Effectiveness of music therapy procedures: Documentation of research and clinical practice* (2nd ed.) (pp. 144-166). Silver Spring, MD: National Association for Music Therapy.

Prickett, C. A., & Moore, R. S. (1991). The use of music to aid memory of Alzheimer's patients. *Journal of Music Therapy, 28*(2), 101-110.

Priestley, M. (1975). *Music therapy in action.* London: Constable.

Priestley, M. (1985). *Music therapy in action* (2nd ed.). St. Louis: MMB Music.

Prueter, B. A., & Giles, M. M. (1981). The effect of music on acquisition of sign language by EMR children. *Voice of the Lakes* (Newsletter of the Great Lakes Regional Chapter, National Association for Music Therapy), *25*(1), 20-25.

Prueter, B. A., & Mezzano, J. (1973). Effects of background music upon initial counseling interactions. *Journal of Music Therapy, 10*(4), 205-212.

Pujol, K. K. (1994). The effect of vibrotactile stimulation, instrumentation, and precomposed melodies on physiological and behavioral responses of profoundly retarded children and adults. *Journal of Music Therapy, 31*(3), 186-205.

Purtilo, R. (1978). Health professional/patient interaction (2nd ed.). Philadelphia: W. B. Saunders.

Purvis, J., & Samet, S. (1976). *Music in developmental therapy: A curriculum guide.* Baltimore: University Park Press.

Radocy, R. E., & Boyle, J. D. (1988). *Psychological foundations of musical behavior* (2nd ed.). Springfield, IL: Charles C Thomas.

Ragland, Z., & Apprey, M. (1974). Community music therapy with adolescents. *Journal of Music Therapy, 11*(3), 147-155.

Redinbaugh, E. M. (1988). The use of music therapy in developing a communication system in a withdrawn, depressed older adult resident: a case study. *Music Therapy Perspectives, 5,* 82-85.

Reid, D. H., Hill, B. K., Rowers, R. J., & Montegar, C. A.

(1975). The use of contingent music in teaching social skills to a nonverbal, hyperactive boy. *Journal of Music Therapy, 12*(1), 2-18.

Remington, R. E., Foxen, T., & Hogg, J. (1977). Auditory reinforcement in profoundly retarded multiply handicapped children. *American Journal of Mental Deficiency, 82*(2), 299-304.

Reuer, B. (1996). Posturing for a changing world: Consulting as a career option. *Music Therapy Perspectives, 14*(1), 16-20.

Reynolds, B. J. (1982). Music therapy literature related to mental retardation. In S. A. Carter, *Music therapy for handicapped children: Mentally retarded* (pp. 34-48). Washington, D.C.: National Association for Music Therapy.

Richter, M. (1996). Savvy senior centers: Facilities for older people expand as boomers near retirement. *The Dallas Morning News* (Sunday, January 6), pp. C1-C2.

Rider, M. S. (1978). "The development of the Musical-Perception Assessment of Cognitive Development (M-PACD)." Unpublished master's thesis, Southern Methodist University, Dallas, TX.

Rider, M. S. (1981). The assessment of cognitive functioning level through musical perception. *Journal of Music Therapy, 18*(3), 110-119.

Rider, M. S. (1985). Entrainment mechanisms are involved in pain reduction, muscle relaxation, and music-mediated imagery. *Journal of Music Therapy, 22*(4), 183-192.

Rider, M. S. (1987). Music therapy: Therapy for debilitated musicians. *Music Therapy Perspectives, 4*, 40-42.

Rider, M., Mickey, C., Weldin, C., & Hawkinson, R. (1991). The effects of toning, listening, and singing on psychophysiological responses. In C. D. Maranto (Ed.), *Applications of music in medicine* (pp. 73-84). Washington, D.C.: National Association for Music Therapy.

Ridgway, R. W. (1983). A story – And a question. *Music Therapy Perspectives, 1*(2), 2-3.

Riegler, J. (1980). Comparison of a reality orientation program for geriatric patients with and without music. *Journal of Music Therapy, 17*(1), 26-33.

Rink, M. (1989). Music as a therapeutic aid for learning-disabled children with motor control problems. In R. R. Pratt & H. Moog (Eds.), *First research seminar of the ISME Commission on music therapy and music in special education: Proceedings of 1986; Bad Honnef, W. Germany* (pp. 93-107). St. Louis: MMB Music.

Ritholz, M. S., & Turry, A. (1994). The journey by train: Creative music therapy with a 17-year-old boy. *Music Therapy, 12*(2), 58-81.

Robb, S. L. (1996). Techniques in song writing: Restoring emotional and physical well-being in adolescents who have been traumatically injured. *Music Therapy Perspectives, 14*(1), 30-37.

Robb, S. L., Nichols, R. J., Rutan, R. L., Bishop, B. L., & Parker, J. C. (1995). The effects of music assisted relaxation on preoperative anxiety. *Journal of Music Therapy, 32*(1), 2-21.

Robbins, C., & Robbins, C. (1980). *Music for the hearing impaired and other special groups: A resource manual and curriculum guide.* St. Louis: Magnamusic-Baton.

Rogers, J. F. (1918). Music as medicine. *The Musical Quarterly, 4*(3), 365-375.

Rogers, L. (1968). Music therapy in a state hospital for crippled children. In E. T. Gaston (Ed.), *Music in therapy* (pp. 156-159). New York: Macmillan.

Rogers, A., & Fleming, P. L. (1981). Rhythm and melody in speech therapy for the neurologically impaired. *Music Therapy, 1*, 33-38.

Rorke, M. A. (1996). Music and the wounded of World War II. *Journal of Music Therapy, 33*(3), 189-207.

Rose, A. M., & Peterson, W. A. (1965). *Older people and their social world.* Philadelphia: F. A. Davis.

Roskam, K. S. (1979). Music therapy as an aid for increasing auditory awareness and improving reading skill. *Journal of Music Therapy, 16*(1), 31-42.

Rubin, B. J. (1973). Music therapy in an outreach station of the Milwaukee County Mental Health Center. *Journal of Music Therapy, 10*(4), 201-204.

Rubin, B. J. (1975). Music therapy in a community mental health program. *Journal of Music Therapy, 12*(2), 59-66.

Rudenberg, M. T. (1982). *Music therapy for handicapped children: Orthopedically handicapped.* Washington, D.C.: National Association for Music Therapy.

Rudenberg, M. T., & Royka, A. M. (1989). Promoting psychological adjustment in pediatric burn patients through music therapy and child life therapy. *Music Therapy Perspectives, 7*, 40-43.

Rutkowski, J. (1996). Conducting research in the music classroom. *Music Educators Journal, 82*(5), 42-44, 62.

Rutter, M., & Schopler, E. (Eds.). (1978). *Autism.* New York: Spectrum.

Ruud, E. (1980). *Music therapy and its relationship to current treatment theories* (Rev. Eng. ed.). St. Louis: Magnamusic-Baton.

Ruud, E. (1995). Improvisation as a liminal experience: Jazz and music therapy as modern "rites de passage." In C. B. Kenny (Ed.), *Listening, playing, creating: Essays on the power of sound* (pp. 91-117). Albany, NY: State University of New York Press.

Ruud, E. (1998). Science as metacritique. *Journal of Music Therapy, 35*(3), 218-224.

Sacks, O., & Tomaino, C. M. (1991). Music and neurological disorder. *The International Journal of Arts Medicine, 1*(1), 10-12.

Salas, J. (1990). Aesthetic experience in music therapy.

Music Therapy, 9(1), 1-15.

Salas, J., & Gonzalez, D. (1991). Like singing with a bird: Improvisational music therapy with a blind four-year-old. In K. E. Bruscia (Ed.), *Case studies in music therapy* (pp. 17-28). Phoenixville, PA: Barcelona Publishers.

Sandbank, G. (1989a). Music as a therapeutic resource for learning disabled children. In R. R. Pratt & H. Moog (Eds.), *First research seminar of the ISME Commission on music therapy and music in special education: Proceedings of 1986; Bad Honnef, W. Germany* (pp. 108-117). St. Louis: MMB Music.

Sandbank, G. (1989b). The right personality for the music therapist. In R. R. Pratt (Ed.), *Music therapy and music in special education: The international state of the art II* (ISME Edition Number Four) (pp. 87-93). St. Louis: MMB Music.

Sandness, M. I. (1991). Developmental sequence in music therapy groups: A review of theoretical models. *Music Therapy Perspectives, 9,* 66-72.

Sandness, M. I. (1995). The role of music therapy in physical rehabilitation programs. *Music Therapy Perspectives, 13*(2), 76-81.

Saperston, B. (1973). The use of music in establishing communication with an autistic mentally retarded child. *Journal of Music Therapy, 17*(4), 184-188.

Saperston, B. M. (1982). Case study: Timmy. In D. W. Paul, *Music therapy for handicapped children: Emotionally disturbed* (pp. 42-57). Washington, D. C.: National Association for Music Therapy.

Saperston, B. M. (1989). Music-Based Individualized Relaxation Training (MBIRT): A stress-reduction approach for the behaviorally disturbed mentally retarded. *Music Therapy Perspectives, 6,* 26-33.

Saperston, B., Chan, R., Morphew, C., & Carsrud, K. (1980). Music listening vs. juice as reinforcement for learning in profoundly mentally retarded individuals. *Journal of Music Therapy, 17*(4), 174-183.

Sarason, I. G., & Sarason, B. R. (1984). *Abnormal psychology: The problem of maladaptive behavior* (4th ed.). Englewood Cliffs, NJ: Prentice-Hall.

Scalenghe, R. (1984, November). *Music therapy with geriatric clients on an in-patient psychiatric unit.* Paper presented at the 35th Annual Conference of the National Association for Music Therapy, Albuquerque, NM.

Scartelli, J. P. (1982). The effect of sedative music on electromyographic biofeedback-assisted relaxation training of spastic cerebral palsied adults. *Journal of Music Therapy, 19*(4), 210-218.

Scartelli, J. P. (1984). The effect of EMG biofeedback and sedative music, EMG biofeedback only, and sedative music only on frontalis muscle relaxation ability. *Journal of Music Therapy, 21*(2), 67-78.

Scartelli, J. P. (1989). *Music and self-management methods.* St. Louis: MMB Music.

Scartelli, J. P. (1991). A rationale for subcortical involvement in human response to music. In C. D. Maranto (Ed.), *Applications of music in medicine* (pp. 29-40). Washington, D.C.: National Association for Music Therapy.

Scartelli, J. P., & Borling, J. E. (1986). The effects of sequenced versus simultaneous EMG biofeedback and sedative music on frontalis relaxation training. *Journal of Music Therapy, 23*(3), 157-165.

Schmidt, J. A. (1981). A special challenge: The profoundly retarded multiply handicapped. *Voice of the Lakes* (Newsletter of the Great Lakes Regional Chapter, National Association for Music Therapy), *25*(2), 23-25.

Schneider, C. W. (1961). The effects of Dalcroze eurhythmics upon the motor processes of schizophrenics. In E. H. Schneider (Ed.), *Music therapy 1960* (pp. 132-140). Lawrence, KS: Allen Press.

Schneider, E. H. (1954). The use of music with the brain damaged child. In M. Bing (Ed.), *Music therapy 1953* (pp. 95-98). Lawrence, KS: Allen Press.

Schneider, E. H. (1957). Relationships between musical experience and certain aspects of cerebral palsied children's performance on selected tasks. In E. T. Gaston (Ed.), *Music therapy 1956* (pp. 250-277). Lawrence, KS: Allen Press.

Schneider, E. H., Unkefer, R. F., & Gaston, E. T. (1968). Introduction. In E. T. Gaston (Ed.), *Music in therapy* (pp. 1-4). New York: Macmillan.

Schooler, K. K., & Estes, C. L. (1979). Differences between current gerontological theories: Implications for research methodology. In D. P. Kent, R. Kastenbaum, & S. Sherwood (Eds.), *Research planning and action for the elderly: The power and potential of social science* (pp. 107-116). New York: Human Sciences Press.

Schulberg, C. H. (1981). *The music therapy sourcebook: A collection of activities categorized and analyzed.* New York: Human Sciences Press.

Schullian, D. M., & Schoen, M. (Eds.). (1948). *Music and medicine.* New York: Henry Schuman.

Schulman, S. (1986). Facing the invisible handicap. *Psychology Today, 20*(2), 58-64.

Schuster, B. L. (1985). The effect of music listening on blood pressure fluctuations in adult hemodialysis patients. *Journal of Music Therapy, 22*(3), 146-153.

Schwankovsky, L. M., & Guthrie, P. T. (1982). *Music therapy for handicapped children: Other health impaired.* Washington, D.C.: National Association for Music Therapy.

Scott, C. (1958). *Music: Its secret influence throughout the ages.* New York: Samuel Weiser.

Scott, T. J. (1970). Use of music to reduce hyperactivity in children. *American Journal of Orthopsychiatry, 40*(4), 677-

680.

Scovel, M. A. (1990). Music therapy within the context of psychotherapeutic models. In R. F. Unkefer (Ed.), *Music therapy in the treatment of adults with mental disorders* (pp. 96-108). New York: Schirmer.

Sears, W. W. (1968). Processes in music therapy. In E. T. Gaston (Ed.), *Music in therapy* (pp. 30-44). New York: Macmillan.

Sekeles, C. (1989). Sounds and music in the treatment of hypotonis Down's syndrome children. In R. R. Pratt & H. Moog (Eds.), *First research seminar of the ISME Commission on music therapy and music in special education: Proceedings of 1986; Bad Honnef, W. Germany* (pp. 22-38). St. Louis: MMB Music.

Selm, M. E. (1991). Chronic pain: Three issues in treatment and implications for music therapy. *Music Therapy Perspectives, 9*, 91-97.

Shamrock, M. (1986). Orff Schulwerk: An integrated foundation. *Music Educators Journal, 72*(6), 51-55.

Shaw, J. P. (1988). The application of ragtime in music therapy with older adults. *Music Therapy Perspectives, 5*, 102-103.

Sheedy, P. (Autumn, 1995). Juvenile offenders get wired. *WaveRider Mental Notes*, pp. 3, 5.

Shehan, P. K. (1981). A comparison of medication strategies in paired associate learning for children with learning disabilities. *Journal of Music Therapy, 18*(3), 120-127.

Sheldon, D. A. (1997). The Illinois school for the deaf band: A historical perspective. *Journal of Research in Music Education, 45*(4), 580-600.

Shi-jing, L., Hui-ju, S., Guo, W., & Maranto, C. D. (1991). Music and medicine in China: The effects of music electro-acupuncture on cerebral hemiplegia. In C. D. Maranto (Ed.), *Applications of music in medicine* (pp. 191-199). Washington, D.C.: National Association for Music Therapy.

Shiraishi, I. M. (1997). A home-based music therapy program for multi-risk others. *Music Therapy Perspectives, 15*(1), 16-23.

Shively, C., & Henkin, L. (1986). Music and movement therapy with Alzheimer's victims. *Music Therapy Perspectives, 3*, 56-58.

Shoemark, H. (1991). The use of piano improvisation in developing interaction and participation in a blind boy with behavioral disturbances. In K. E. Bruscia (Ed.), *Case studies in music therapy* (pp. 29-38). Phoenixville, PA: Barcelona Publishers.

Short, A. E. (1991). The role of guided imagery and music in diagnosing physical illness or trauma. *Music Therapy, 10*(1), 22-45.

Short, A. E. (1992). Music and imagery with physically disabled elderly residents: A GIM adaptation. *Music Therapy, 11*(1), 65-98.

Shreffler, J. (1976). Music therapy and transactional analysis. *Voice of the Lakes* (Newsletter of the Great Lakes Regional Chapter, National Association for Music Therapy), *76*(3), 18-20.

Shuler, S. C. (1990). Solving instructional problems through research. *Music Educators Journal, 77*(3), 35-40.

Siegel, S. L., Cartwright, J. S., & Katy, E. (1986). Where's the research? *Journal of Music Therapy, 23*(1), 38-45.

Siegfried, T. (1997). Evidence from genes and brain reveals biology behind autism. *The Dallas Morning News* (Monday, December 15), p. 7D.

Siegfried, T., & Goetinck, S. (1996). Science gathers a growing body of physical clues to mental illness. *The Dallas Morning News* (Monday, April 29), pp. 1F, 6F, 8F.

Silber, F., & Hes, J. (1995). The use of songwriting with patients diagnosed with Alzheimer's disease. *Music Therapy Perspectives, 13*(1), 31-34.

Silverman, F. H. (1976). Long term impact of a miniature metronome on stuttering: An interim report, *Perceptual and Motor Skills, 42*, 13-22.

Skaggs, R. (1997a). *Finishing strong: Treating chemical addictions with music and imagery.* St. Louis: MMB Music.

Skaggs, R. (1997b). Music-centered creative arts in a sex offender treatment program for male juveniles. *Music Therapy Perspectives, 15*(2), 73-78.

Skaggs, R. (1997c). The Bonny method of guided imagery and music in the treatment of terminal illness: A private practice setting. *Music Therapy Perspectives, 15*(1), 39-44.

Skille, O. (1989). VibroAcoustic therapy. *Music Therapy, 8*(1), 61-66.

Slivka, H. H., & Magill, L. (1986). The conjoint use of social work and music therapy in working with children of cancer patients. *Music Therapy, 6A*(1), 30-40.

Slotoroff, C. (1994). Drumming technique for assertiveness and anger management in the short-term psychiatric setting for adult and adolescent survivors of trauma. *Music Therapy Perspectives, 12*(2), 111-116.

Smaligo, M. A. (1998). Resources for helping blind music students. *Music Educators Journal, 85*(2), 23-26, 45.

Smeltekop, R. A., & Houghton, B. A. (1990). Music therapy and psychopharmacology. In R. F. Unkefer (Ed.), *Music therapy in the treatment of adults with mental disorders* (pp. 109-125). New York: Schirmer.

Smith, B. B., & Knudson, L. A. (1995). *A song to set me free: A model for music therapy and music related activities for frail elderly and disabled adults.* Logan, UT: Sunshine Terrace Adult Day Center.

Smith, C. R., & Steinschneider, A. (1975). Differential effects of prenatal rhythmic stimulation on neonatal arousal states. *Child Development, 46*, 574-578.

Smith, D. S. (1989). Preferences for differentiated frequency loudness levels in older adult music listening.

Journal of Music Therapy, 26(1), 18-29.

Smith, D. S. (1990). Therapeutic treatment effectiveness as documented in the gerontology literature: implications for music therapy. *Music Therapy Perspectives, 8*, 36-40.

Smith, D. S. (1991). A comparison of group performance and song familiarity on cued recall tasks with older adults. *Journal of Music Therapy, 28*(1), 2-13.

Smith, D. S. (1998). Presidential perspectives: The family reunion. *Music Therapy Matters, 1*(4), 2, 13.

Smith, D. S., & Lipe, A. W. (1991). Music therapy practices in gerontology. *Journal of Music Therapy, 28*(4), 193-210.

Smith, E. D. (1972). *Handbook of aging.* New York: Barnes & Noble.

Smith, G. H. (1986). A comparison of the effects of three treatment interventions on cognitive functioning of Alzheimer's patients. *Music Therapy, 6A*(1), 41-56.

Smith, R. M., & Neisworth, J. T. (1975). *The exceptional child: A functional approach.* New York: McGraw-Hill.

Snell, A. M. (1996). Music therapy for learners with autism in a public school setting. In B. L. Wilson (Ed.), *Models of music therapy interventions in school settings: From institution to inclusion* (pp. 156-183). Silver Spring, MD: National Association for Music Therapy.

Solomon, A. L. (1980). Music in special education: Hearing and speech development. *Journal of Research in Music Education, 28*(4), 236-242.

Solomon, A. L. (1995). Historical research. In B. L. Wheeler (Ed.), *Music therapy research: Quantitative and qualitative perspectives* (pp. 487-501). Phoenixville, PA: Barcelona Publishers.

Solomon, A. L., & Heller, . N. (1982). Historical research in music therapy: An important avenue for studying the profession. *Journal of Music Therapy, 19*(3), 161-178.

Sparks, R., Helms, N., & Albert, M. (1974). Aphasia rehabilitation resulting from melodic intonation therapy. *Cortex, 10,* 303-316.

Sparks, R., & Holland, A. (1976). Melodic intonation therapy for aphasia. *Journal of Speech and Hearing Disorders, 41,* 287-297.

Special Committee on Aging. (1992). *Forever young: Music and aging. Hearing before the Special Committee on Aging, United States Senate, One hundred second Congress, first session, August 1, 1991* (Serial no. 102-9). Washington, D.C.: U.S. Government Printing Office.

Spencer, M. J. (1978). A case for the arts. In *The Healing Role of the Arts (Working papers – The Rockefeller Foundation)* (pp. 1-9). NY: The Rockefeller Foundation.

Spencer, S. L. (1988). The efficiency of instrumental and movement activities in developing mentally retarded adolescents' ability to follow directions. *Journal of Music Therapy, 25*(1), 44-50.

Spintge, R. (1989). The anxiolytic effects of music. In M. H. M. Lee (Ed.), *Rehabilitation, music and human well-being*

(pp. 82-100). St. Louis: MMB Music.

Spintge, R. (1991). The neurophysiology of emotion and its therapeutic applications in music therapy and music medicine. In C. D. Maranto (Ed.), *Applications of music in medicine* (pp. 59-72). Washington, D.C.: National Association for Music Therapy.

Spintge, R., & Droh, R. (1987). Effects of anxiolytic music on plasma levels of stress hormones in different medical specialties. In R. R. Pratt (Ed.), *The fourth international symposium on music: Rehabilitation and human well-being* (pp. 88-101). New York: University Press of America.

Spitzer, S. (1989). Computers and music therapy: An integrated approach. *Music Therapy Perspectives, 7,* 51-54.

Stambaugh, L. (1996). Special learners with special abilities. *Music Educators Journal, 83*(3), 19-23.

Standley, J. M. (1986). Music research in medical/dental treatment: Meta-analysis and clinical applications. *Journal of Music Therapy, 23*(2), 56-122.

Standley, J. M. (1991a). *Music techniques in therapy, counseling, and special education.* St. Louis: MMB Music.

Standley, J. M. (1991b). The role of music in pacification/stimulation of premature infants with low birthweights. *Music Therapy Perspectives, 9,* 19-25.

Standley, J. M. (1992). Clinical applications of music and chemotherapy: The effects on nausea and emesis. *Music Therapy Perspectives, 10*(1), 27-35.

Standley, J. M. (1996a). A meta-analysis on the effects of music as reinforcement for education/therapy objectives. *Journal of Research in Music Education, 44*(2), 105-133.

Standley, J. M. (1996b). Music in medical/dental treatment: An update of a prior meta-analysis. In C. E. Furman (Ed.), *Effectiveness of music therapy procedures: Documentation of research and clinical practice* (2nd ed.) (pp. 1-60). Silver Spring, MD: National Association for Music Therapy.

Standley, J. M., & Hughes, J. E. (1997). Evaluation of an early intervention music curriculum for enhancing prereading/writing skills. *Music Therapy Perspectives, 15*(2), 79-86.

Staum, M. J. (1987). Music notation to improve the speech prosody of hearing impaired children. *Journal of Music Therapy, 24*(3), 146-159.

Staum, M. J. (1988). Music for physical rehabilitation: An analysis of literature from 1950-1986 and applications for rehabilitation settings. In C. E. Furman (Ed.), *Effectiveness of music therapy procedures: Documentation of research and clinical practice* (pp. 65-104). Washington, D.C.: National Association for Music Therapy.

Staum, M. J. (1989). Music as motivation for language learning. In R. R. Pratt & H. Moog (Eds.), *First research seminar of the ISME Commission on music therapy and music in special education: Proceedings of 1986; Bad Honnef, W.*

Germany (pp. 62-68). St. Louis: MMB Music.

Staum, M. J. (1993). A music/nonmusic intervention with homeless children. *Journal of Music Therapy, 30*(4), 236-262.

Staum, M. J. (1996). Music for physical rehabilitation: An analysis of literature from 1950-1993 and applications for rehabilitation settings. In C. E. Furman (Ed.), *Effectiveness of music therapy procedures: Documentation of research and clinical practice* (2nd ed.) (pp. 61-105). Silver Spring, MD: National Association for Music Therapy.

Staum, M. J., & Brotons, M. (1992). The influence of auditory subliminals on behavior: A series of investigations. *Journal of Music Therapy, 29*(3),130-185.

Staum, M. J., & Brotons, M. (1995). Issues in music for children in a homeless shelter: Social objectives and choice of reinforcers. *Journal of Music Therapy, 32*(4), 248-264.

Staum, M. J., & Flowers, P. J. (1984). The use of simulated training and music lessons on teaching appropriate shopping skills to an autistic child. *Music Therapy Perspectives, 1*(3), 14-17.

Steele, A. L. (1968). Programmed use of music to alter uncooperative problem behavior. *Journal of Music Therapy, 5*(4), 103-107.

Steele, A. L. (1984). Music therapy for the learning disabled: Intervention and instruction. *Music Therapy Perspectives, 1*(3), 2-7.

Steele, P. H. (1987). Musical personality therapy and well-being. In R. R. Pratt (Ed.), *The fourth international symposium on music: Rehabilitation and human well-being* (pp. 27-36). New York: University Press of America.

Stein, A. M. (1991). Music to reduce anxiety during cesarean births. In C. D. Maranto (Ed.), *Applications of music in medicine* (pp. 179-190). Washington, D.C.: National Association for Music Therapy.

Steinke, W. R. (1991). The use of music, relaxation, and imagery in the management of post-surgical pain for scoliosis. In C. D. Maranto (Ed.), *Applications of music in medicine* (pp. 141-162). Washington, D.C.: National Association for Music Therapy.

Stevens, E., & Clark, F. (1969). Music therapy in the treatment of autistic children. *Journal of Music Therapy, 6*(4), 98-104.

Stratton, V. N., & Zalanowski, A. H. (1984). The relationship between music, degree of liking, and self-reported relaxation. *Journal of Music Therapy, 21*(4), 184-192.

Summer, L. (1981). Guided imagery and music with the elderly. *Music Therapy, 1*(1), 39-42.

Summer, L. (1988). *Guided imagery and music in the institutional setting.* St. Louis: MMB Music.

Summer, L. (1994). Considering classical music for use in psychiatric music therapy. *Music Therapy Perspectives,* 12(2), 130-133.

Summer, L. (1995). Unsound medicine. In C. B. Kenny (Ed.), *Listening, playing, creating: Essays on the power of sound* (pp. 59-64). Albany, NY: State University of New York Press.

Summer, L., & Summer, J. (1996). *Music: The new age elixir.* Amherst, NY: Prometheus Books.

Suzuki, S. (1969). *Nurtured by love: A new approach to education.* New York: Exposition Press.

Swaiko, N. (1974). The role and value of an eurhythmics program in a curriculum for deaf children. *American Annals of the Deaf, 119*(3), 321-324.

Swingler, T. (1994). Unlocking musicality: Using soundbeam as a new key to eloquence. In R. Krout, Integrating technology. *Music Therapy Perspectives, 12*(1), 4-5.

Talkington, L. W., & Hall, S. M. (1970). A musical application of Premack's hypothesis to low verbal retardates. *Journal of Music Therapy, 7*(3), 95-99.

Tanner, D. R., & O'Briant, R. M. (1980). Music can color a graying America. *Music Educators Journal, 67*(4), 28-30.

Taylor, D. B. (1969). Expressive emphasis in the treatment of intropunitive behavior. *Journal of Music Therapy, 6*(2), 41-43.

Taylor, D. B. (1973). Subject responses to precatagorized stimulative and sedative music. *Journal of Music Therapy, 10*(2), 86-92.

Taylor, D. B. (1981). Music in general hospital treatment from 1900 to 1950. *Journal of Music Therapy, 18*(2), 62-73.

Taylor, D. B. (1987a). A survey of professional music therapists concerning entry level competencies. *Journal of Music Therapy, 24*(3), 114-145.

Taylor, D. B. (1987b). The theoretical basis for the use of music with aphasic patients. In R. R. Pratt (Ed.), *The fourth international symposium on music: Rehabilitation and human well-being* (pp. 165-169). New York: University Press of America.

Taylor, D. B. (1988). Therapeutic musicians or musical physicians: The future is at stake. *Music Therapy Perspectives, 5*, 86-93.

Taylor, D. B. (1989). A neuroanatomical model for the use of music in the remediation of aphasic disorders. In M. H. M. Lee (Ed.), *Rehabilitation, music and human well-being* (pp. 168-178). St. Louis: MMB Music.

Taylor, D. B. (1990). Childhood sequential development of rhythm, melody and pitch. In F. R. Wilson and F. L. Roehmann (Eds.), *Music and child development: Biology of music making: Proceedings of the 1987 Denver Conference* (pp. 241-253). St. Louis: MMB Music.

Taylor, D. B. (1997). *Biomedical foundations of music as therapy.* St. Louis: MMB Music.

Taylor, J. A., Barry, N. H., & Walls, K. C. (1997). *Music and students at risk: Creative solutions for a national dilemma.*

Reston, VA: Music Educators National Conference.

Thaut, M. H. (1984). A music therapy treatment model for autistic children. *Music Therapy Perspectives, 1*(4), 7-13.

Thaut, M. H. (1987). A new challenge for music therapy: The correctional setting. *Music Therapy Perspectives, 4,* 44-50.

Thaut, M. H. (1989a). Music therapy, affect modification, and therapeutic change: Toward an integrative model. *Music Therapy Perspectives, 7,* 55-62.

Thaut, M. H. (1989b). The influence of music therapy interventions on self-rated changes in relaxation, affect, and thought in psychiatric prisoner-patients. *Journal of Music Therapy, 26*(3), 155-166.

Thaut, M. H. (1992a). Music therapy for the physically disabled child. In W. B. Davis, K. E. Gfeller, & M. H. Thaut, *An introduction to music therapy: Theory and practice* (pp. 164-179). Dubuque, IA: Wm. C. Brown.

Thaut, M. H. (1992b). Music therapy in correctional psychiatry. In W. B. Davis, K. E. Gfeller, & M. H. Thaut, *An introduction to music therapy: Theory and practice* (pp. 273-284). Dubuque, IA: Wm. C. Brown.

Thaut, M. H. (1992c). Music therapy in the rehabilitation of stroke and traumatic-brain-injured clients. In W. B. Davis, K. E. Gfeller, & M. H. Thaut, *An introduction to music therapy: Theory and practice* (pp. 251-272). Dubuque, IA: Wm. C. Brown.

Thaut, M. H. (1992d). Music therapy with autistic children. In W. B. Davis, K. E. Gfeller, & M. H. Thaut, *An introduction to music therapy: Theory and practice* (pp. 180-196). Dubuque, IA: Wm. C. Brown.

Thaut, M. H., & Davis, W. B. (1993). The influence of subject-selected versus experimenter-chosen music on affect, anxiety, and relaxation. *Journal of Music Therapy, 30*(4), 210-223.

Thaut, M. H., & Gfeller, K. E. (1992). Music therapy in the treatment of mental disorders. In W. B. Davis, K. E. Gfeller, & M. H. Thaut, *An introduction to music therapy: Theory and practice* (pp. 93-132). Dubuque, IA: Wm. C. Brown.

Thaut, M., Schleiffers, S., & Davis, W. (1991). Analysis of EMG activity in biceps and triceps muscle in an upper extremity gross motor task under the influence of auditory rhythm. *Journal of Music Therapy, 28*(2), 64-88.

Thaut, M. H., & Smeltekop, R. A. (1990). Psychosocial and neurophysiological aspects of music therapy interventions. In R. F. Unkefer (Ed.), *Music therapy in the treatment of adults with mental disorders* (pp. 85-87). New York: Schirmer.

Thomas, D. W., Heitman, R. J., & Alexander, T. (1997). The effects of music on bathing cooperation for residents with dementia. *Journal of Music Therapy, 34*(4), 246-259.

Thomas, L. (1974). *The lives of a cell: Notes of a biology watcher.* New York: Viking Press.

Thomas, M. W. (1976). Implications for music therapy as a treatment modality for the mentally ill deaf. *Voice of the Lakes* (Newsletter of the Great Lakes Regional Chapter, National Association for Music Therapy), *76*(1), 19-22.

Thompson, A. B., Arnold, J. C., and Murray, S. E. (1990). Music therapy assessment of the cerebrovascular accident patient. *Music Therapy Perspectives, 8,* 23-29.

Tims, F. (1981, November). *An American's experiences and music therapy work in a German hospital.* Paper presented at the 32nd Annual Conference of the National Association for Music Therapy, Denver, CO.

Tims, F. (1989). Experiential learning in the music therapy curriculum. *Music Therapy Perspectives, 7,* 91-92.

Toigo, D. A. (1992). Autism: Integrating a personal perspective with music therapy practice. *Music Therapy Perspectives, 10*(1), 13-20.

Tomaino, C. (1992). Medical problems of the elderly: Implications for music therapy assessment and intervention. In American Association for Music Therapy, *Proceedings booklet: "Body, Mind, Spirit: AAMT coming of age"* (pp. 220-227). U.S.A.: American Association for Music Therapy.

Tonchick, K. A. (1981). An introduction to Orff-Schulwerk: A philosophy and process of music for children. *Voice of the Lakes.* (Newsletter of the Great Lakes Regional Chapter, National Association for Music Therapy), *25*(3), 30-35.

Treder-Wolff, J. (1990). Affecting attitudes: Music therapy in addictions treatment. *Music Therapy Perspectives, 8,* 67-71.

Trevisan, L. A. (1978). A comparative study of scientific and spiritualistic perspectives of wholistic healing (via music and massage). In A. L. Nowicki and L. A. Trevisan, *Beyond the sound: A technical and philosophical approach to music therapy* (Rev. ed.) (pp. vii-xxii). Porterville & Santa Barbara, CA: Nowicki/Trevisan.

Tsao, C. C., Gordon, T. F., Maranto, C. D., Lerman, C., & Murasko, D. (1991). The effects of music and biological imagery on immune response (S-IgA). In C. D. Maranto (Ed.), *Applications of music in medicine* (pp. 85-121). Washington, D.C.: National Association for Music Therapy.

Tyson, F. (1959). The development of an out-patient music therapy referral service. In E. H. Schneider (Ed.), *Music therapy 1958* (pp. 129-134). Lawrence, KS: Allen Press.

Tyson, F. (1966). Music therapy in private practice – Three case histories. *Journal of Music Therapy, 3*(1), 8-18.

Tyson, F. (1981). *Psychiatric music therapy: Origins and development.* New York: Fred Weidner and Sons Printers.

Tyson, F. (1987). Analytically-oriented music therapy in a case of generalized anxiety disorder. *Music Therapy Perspectives, 4,* 51-55.

Underhill, K. K., & Harris, L. M. (1974). The effect of contingent music on establishing imitation in behaviorally disturbed retarded children. *Journal of Music Therapy, 11*(3), 156-166.

Unkefer, R. F. (1961). The music therapist. In E. H. Schneider (Ed.), *Music therapy 1960* (pp. 27-31). Lawrence, KS: Allen Press.

Unkefer, R. F. (Ed.). (1990). *Music therapy in the treatment of adults with mental disorders.* New York: Schirmer.

Vanderark, S., Newman, I., & Bell, S. (1983). The effects of music participation on quality of life of the elderly. *Music Therapy, 3*(1), 71-81.

Van de Wall, W. (1936). *Music in institutions.* New York: Russell Sage Foundation.

Van de Wall, W. (1944). Report on the survey. *National Music Council Bulletin, 5*, 9-13.

Van de Wall, W. (1946). *Music in hospitals.* New York: Russell Sage Foundation.

Van Riper, C. (1984). *Speech correction: An introduction to speech pathology and audiology.* Englewood Cliffs, NJ: Prentice Hall.

Velasquez, V. (1991). Beginning experience in piano performance for a girl with Down syndrome: A case study. *Music Therapy Perspectives, 9*, 82-86.

Ventre, M. E. (1994a). Guided Imagery and Music in process: The interweaving of the archetype of the mother, mandala, and music. *Music Therapy, 12*(2), 19-38.

Ventre, M. E. (1994b). Healing the wounds of childhood abuse: A Guided Imagery and Music case study. *Music Therapy Perspectives, 12*(2), 98-103.

Vescelius, E. A. (1918). Music and health. *The Musical Quarterly, 4*(3), 376-401.

Visiting Nurses Association of Dallas. (1981). *Home hospice* [brochure]. Dallas, TX: Author.

Wagner, M. J. (1975). Effect of music and biofeedback on alpha brain wave rhythms and attentiveness of musicians and non-musicians. *Journal of Research in Music Education, 23*(1), 3-13.

Walker, J. B. (1972). The use of music as an aid in developing functional speech in the institutionalized mentally retarded. *Journal of Music Therapy, 9*(1), 1-12.

Walls, K. C., Taylor, J. A., & Falzone, J. (1992). The effects of subliminal suggestions and music experience on the perception of tempo in music. *Journal of Music Therapy, 29*(3),186-197.

Walters, C. L. (1996). The psychological and physiological effects of vibrotactile stimulation, via a *Somatron,* on patients awaiting scheduled gynecological surgery. *Journal of Music Therapy, 33*(4), 261-287.

Warja, M. (1994). Sounds of music through the spiraling path of individuation: A Jungian approach to music psychotherapy. *Music Therapy Perspectives, 12*(2), 75-83.

Warner, J. D. (1981). Song and sign: The use of music in teaching sign language. *Voice of the Lakes* (Newsletter of the Great Lakes Regional Chapter, National Association for Music Therapy), *25*(1), 26-33.

Wasserman, N. M. (1972). Music therapy for the emotionally disturbed in a private hospital. *Journal of Music Therapy, 9*(2), 99-104.

Watson, D. (1979). Music as reinforcement in increasing spontaneous speech among autistic children. *Missouri Journal of Research in Music Education, 4*(3), 8-20.

Watts, T. D. (1980). Theories of aging: the difference in orientations. *Journal of Music Therapy, 17*(2), 84-89.

Weisberg, N. & Wilder, R. (1985). *Creative arts with older adults: A sourcebook.* New York: Human Sciences Press.

Weissman, J. A. (1983). Planned music activities to meet needs and treatment goals of aged individuals in long-term care facilities. *Music Therapy, 3*(1), 63-70.

Weitz, M. (1993). Beats of different drummers. *The Dallas Morning News* (September 5), pp. 1F, 4F.

Weldin, C., & Eagle, C. T. (1991). An historical overview of music medicine. In C. D. Maranto (Ed.), *Applications of music in medicine* (pp. 7-27). Washington, D.C.: National Association for Music Therapy.

Wells, K. E., & Helmus, N. (1968). Music therapy for severe speech disorders. In E. T. Gaston (Ed.), *Music in therapy* (pp. 159-162). New York: Macmillan.

Welsbacher, B. (1975). Music for the learning disabled. In R. M. Graham (Compiler), *Music for the exceptional child* (pp. 136-147). Reston, VA: Music Educators National Conference.

Wender, P. H., & Wender, E. H. (1978). *The hyperactive child and the learning disabled child.* New York: Crocon.

Wentworth, R. (1991). The effects of music an distracting noise on the productivity of workers with mental retardation. *Journal of Music Therapy, 28*(1), 40-47.

Werbner, N. (1966). The practice of music therapy with psychotic children. *Journal of Music Therapy 3*(1), 25-31.

Wesecky, A. (1986). Music therapy for children with Rett Syndrome. *Journal of Medical Genetics, 24*, 253-257.

West, T. M. (1994). Psychological issues in hospice music therapy. *Music Therapy Perspectives, 12*(2), 117-124.

Wexler, M. M. D. (1989). The use of song in grief therapy with Cibecue White Mountain Apaches. *Music Therapy Perspectives, 7*, 63-66.

Wheeler, B. (1981). The relationship between music therapy and theories of psychotherapy. *Music Therapy, 1*(1), 9-16.

Wheeler, B. (1983). A psychotherapeutic classification of music therapy practices: A continuum of procedures. *Music Therapy Perspectives, 1*(2), 8-12.

Wheeler, B. L. (1985). The relationship between musical and activity elements of music therapy sessions and client responses: An exploratory study. *Music Therapy,*

5(1), 52-60.

Wheeler, B. L. (1987). Levels of therapy: The classification of music therapy goals. *Music Therapy, 6*(2), 39-49.

Wheeler, B. L. (Ed.). (1995). *Music therapy research: Quantitative and qualitative perspectives.* Phoenixville, PA: Barcelona Publishers.

Wheeler, B. L., & Golden, S. (1987). NAMT and its Mid-Atlantic region: Changing together. *Music Therapy Perspectives, 4,* 56-63.

Whitcomb, J. B. (1992). Therapeutic interventions between dementia residents and their caregivers. In American Association for Music Therapy, *Proceedings booklet: "Body, Mind, Spirit: AAMT coming of age"* (pp. 147-150). U.S.A.: American Association for Music Therapy.

Whittall, J. (1991). Songs in palliative care: A spouse's last gift. In K. E. Bruscia (Ed.), *Case studies in music therapy* (pp. 603-610). Phoenixville, PA: Barcelona Publishers.

Whitwell, D. (1993). *Music as language: A new philosophy of music education.* Northridge, CA: WINDS.

Wigram, T. (1995). The psychological and physiological effects of low frequency sound and music. *Music Therapy Perspectives, 13*(1), 16-23.

Wilder, B. G. (1985). Singing bridges the gap. *Music Educators Journal, 71*(7), 34-36.

Williams, J. (1979). Music therapy and transactional analysis: Helping mothers and fathers develop their inner child. *Voice of the Lakes* (Newsletter of the Great Lakes Regional Chapter, National Association for Music Therapy), *23*(3), 21-23.

Wilson, B. L. (1990a). Assessment of adult psychiatric clients: The role of music therapy. In R. F. Unkefer (Ed.), *Music therapy in the treatment of adults with mental disorders* (pp. 126-144). New York: Schirmer.

Wilson, B. L. (1990b). Music therapy in hospital and community programs. In R. F. Unkefer (Ed.), *Music therapy in the treatment of adults with mental disorders* (pp. 88-95). New York: Schirmer.

Wilson, B. L. (Ed.) (1996). *Models of music therapy interventions in school settings: From institution to inclusion.* Silver Spring, MD: National Association for Music Therapy.

Wilson, C. V. (1976). The use of rock music as a reward in behavior therapy with children. *Journal of Music Therapy, 13*(1), 39-48.

Windwer, C. M. (1981). An ascending music stimulus program and hyperactive children. *Journal of Research in Music Education, 29*(3), 173-181.

Winn, T., Crowe, B. J., & Moreno, J. J. (1989). Shamanism and music therapy: ancient healing techniques in modern practice. *Music Therapy Perspectives, 7,* 67-71.

Winslow, G. A. (1986). Music therapy in the treatment of anxiety in hospitalized high-risk mothers. *Music Therapy Perspectives, 3,* 29-33.

Witt, A. E., & Steele, A.L. (1984). Music therapy for infant and parent: A case example. *Music Therapy Perspectives, 1*(4), 17-19.

Wolfe, D. (1978). Pain rehabilitation and music therapy. *Journal of Music Therapy, 15*(4), 162-178.

Wolfe, D. (1980). The effect of automated interrupted music on head posturing of cerebral palsied individuals. *Journal of Music Therapy, 17*(4), 184-206.

Wolfe, D. E. (1996). Group music therapy in acute mental health care: Meeting the demands of effectiveness. In C. E. Furman (Ed.), *Effectiveness of music therapy procedures: Documentation of research and clinical practice* (2nd ed.) (pp. 106-143). Silver Spring, MD: National Association for Music Therapy.

Wolfe, D. E., & Hom, C. (1993). Use of melodies as structural prompts for learning and retention of sequential verbal information by preschool students. *Journal of Music Therapy, 30*(2), 100-118.

Wolfe, D. E., & Stambaugh, S. (1993). Music analysis of Sesame Street: Implications for music therapy practice and research. *Journal of Music Therapy, 30*(4), 224-235.

Wolfe, J. R. (1983). The use of music in a group sensory training program for regressed geriatric patients. *Activities, Adaptation, and Aging, 3,* 49-62.

Wolfgram, B. J. (1978). Music therapy for retarded adults with psychotic overlay: A day treatment approach. *Journal of Music Therapy, 15*(4), 199-207.

Wolfgram, B. J. (1980). *Songs of life.* Sherman Oaks, CA: Alfred Publishing.

Wood, M. M., Graham, R. M., Swan, W. W., Purvis, J., Gigliotti, C., & Samet, S. (1974). *Developmental music therapy.* Lawrence, KS: National Association for Music Therapy.

Wooten, M. A. (1992). The effects of heavy metal music on affect shifts of adolescents in an inpatient psychiatric setting. *Music Therapy Perspectives, 10*(2), 93-98.

Worden, J. W. (1982). *Grief counseling and grief therapy – A handbook for the mental health practitioner.* New York: Springer Publishing.

World Health Organization (1964). *Constitution of the World Health Organization.* Geneva: World Health Organization.

Wylie, M. E. (1983). Eliciting vocal responses in severely and profoundly mentally handicapped subjects. *Journal of Music Therapy, 20*(4), 190-200.

Wylie, M. E. (1990). A comparison of the effects of old familiar songs, antique objects, historical summaries, and general questions on the reminiscence of nursing home residents. *Journal of Music Therapy, 27*(1), 2-12.

Wylie, M. E. (1996). A case study to promote hand use in children with Rett syndrome. *Music Therapy Perspectives, 14*(2), 83-86.

Wylie, M. E., & Blom, R. C. (1986). Guided imagery and

music with hospice patients. *Music Therapy Perspectives, 3,* 25-28.

Yairi, E. (1976). Effects of binaural and monaural noise on stuttering. *Journal of Auditory Research, 16,* 114-119.

Yalom, I. D. (1983). *Inpatient group psychotherapy.* New York: Basic Books.

York, E. (1994). The development of a quantitative music skills test for patients with Alzheimer's disease. *Journal of Music Therapy, 31*(4), 280-296.

Zamula, E. (1986). *Stroke: Fighting back against America's no. 3 killer* (HHS Publication No. (FDA) 86-1131). Rockville, MD: Department of Health and Human Services.

Zinar, R. (1987). *Music activities for special children.* West Nyack, NY: Parker Publishing.

Zoller, M. (1991). Use of music activities in speech-language therapy. *Language, Speech, and Hearing Services in Schools, 22,* 272-276.

AUTHOR INDEX

A

Abeles, H. F.: 49, 52, 57, 60

Achterberg, J.: 361

Adamek, M. S.: 2, 85, 103, 119, 135, 153, 172, 175, 182, 185, 187, 195, 267, 305, 306, 310, 316

Adelman, E. J.: 219, 241, 251, 373, 380

Adreon, D. A.: 194, 196-198, 203

Aigen, K.: 3, 40, 52, 57, 58, 69, 252, 380, 388, 407, 412-414, 419, 421

Albert, M. L.: 182, 310

Alley, C. F.: 254

Alley, J. M.: 78

Altrows, I. F.: 180

Altshuler, I. M.: 36, 37

Alvin, J.: 22-24, 26, 27, 31, 73, 96, 143, 168, 196-200, 202, 204, 207, 232, 308, 401

American Association for Music Therapy (AAMT): 13, 16, 39, 45, 410

American Association on Mental Retardation (AAMR): 79-85, 87, 90, 92, 94, 96, 265, 266

American Music Therapy Association (AMTA): 2, 7, 9, 12, 13, 15, 16, 18, 39-43, 45, 64-66, 69-71, 78, 86, 103, 119, 135, 154, 176, 196, 217, 244, 268, 280, 281, 305, 331, 360, 374, 410

American Psychiatric Association (APA): 79-81, 84, 98-102, 170-174, 189-191, 193, 194, 208-214, 237-241, 265, 266, 323-325

American Speech and Hearing Association (ASHA): 170-175

Amir, D.: 311, 313, 316

Anderson, S. E.: 41, 42

Anderson, V. G.: 191, 196-198, 200, 203, 204, 207

Anshel, A.: 377

Apel, W.: 21, 22

Apprey, M.: 231

Arnold, J. C.: 316

Arnold, M.: 402, 409

Arthritis Foundation: 148

Atterbury, B. W.: 84, 87, 93, 96, 98, 99, 101, 104-110, 112, 114, 115, 117, 126-128, 130, 132, 134, 135, 137, 140, 141, 143-146, 152, 153, 164-166, 168, 189-191, 194, 202, 214-216, 233, 236, 266, 268, 269, 272, 400

Autism Society of America: 189, 191

Axen, K.: 177, 185

Ayres, B. R.: 275

B

Bachman, M. L.: 137, 397, 398, 409

Bailey, L. M.: 232, 293, 360-367, 369, 371

Bailey, P.: 96

Bain, L. J.: 211, 212, 216

Bang, C.: 119, 121-123, 126, 127

Barclay, M. W.: 394

Barker, L. W.: 156. 291

Barker, V. L.: 162, 164, 165, 306, 311-313, 316

Barnard, R. I.: 6, 8

Barna, V.: 322

Barrickman, J.: 281, 286, 287

Barry, N. H.: 209, 236

Bartlett, D. L.: 29, 49, 51, 60, 292, 293, 379, 393

Bartlett, J. C.: 352

Bauman, A. A.: 116, 124, 125, 127, 130, 185

Beal, M. R.: 96, 332

Bean, M. F.: 124. 125

Beckett, A.: 7, 378, 379

Bednarz, L. F.: 258, 263

Beggs, C.: 362-367

Behrens, G. A.: 253

Bellamy, T.: 67, 86, 400

Benenzon, R. O.: 196, 199, 236, 398

Bennett, P.: 396, 397

Berman, C.: 102

Berman, T.: 292

Bernstein, B.: 333, 347

Bernstorf, E. D.: 112, 174, 187

Berry, P.: 101

Birkenshaw-Fleming, L.: 4, 5, 87, 93, 98, 101, 104, 105, 107-110, 112, 126-129, 132, 133, 137-141, 143, 152, 154, 160, 161, 163-166, 168, 189, 191, 194, 195, 205, 207, 232, 233, 274, 334

Bishop, S. R.: 255, 263, 391, 392, 405

Bitcon, C. H.: 394, 395, 409

Blacking, J.: 49, 50, 58

Blake, R. L.: 255, 263, 391, 392, 405

SUBJECT INDEX

A

Abused children or adolescents: 210, 211, 214
  music therapy interventions for: 222-224, 257, 404
Abusers of women and children
  music therapy interventions for: 259
Academic skills
  use of music to increase: 67, 76, 88-89, 106-107, 138, 164, 203, 228-229, 231, 274-275, 400 (*see also* Cognitive skills; Mental functioning)
Activities of daily living (ADLs)
  music therapy interventions for: 309, 343, 344
Adapting musical instruments: 90, 93, 156, 159-161, 163, 165, 167
Adjustment disorders: 219, 239
Advanced Certified Music Therapist (ACMT): 16, 17
Aesthetic enrichment
  music for: 57-58, 140-141, 153, 163, 177, 224, 230, 365, 379-380
Affective disorders: 219 (*see also* Mood disorders)
Africa
  music and healing in: 20
Age-associated memory impairment (AAMI): 326
Aged (*see* Elderly)
Ageism: 317
Aging process: 318-321
Aging, theories of: 326-328, 352
AIDS: 209, 356, 358, 360, 372
Alcoholism (*see* Substance abuse)
Allergies: 279
Alzheimer's disease: 320, 323-326, 330, 356
  music therapy interventions for: 261, 333, 344-349, 400
American Association for Music Therapy (AAMT): 13-17, 39, 40, 44, 410
  credentials awarded by: 16, 17
  education and training programs: 13-15
American Indians
  use of music for healing: 20-21
American Music Therapy Association (AMTA): 13-15, 18, 40-41, 44-45, 46, 410
  education and training programs: 13-15
American Sign Language (ASL): 117, 118, 174

Americans with Disabilities Act of 1990: 102 (*see also* Individuals with Disabilities Act)
Amputations: 150-151, 160, 161, 163, 166
Anderton, Margaret: 28, 34, 245
Anesthesia: 280
  music for: 282 (*see also* Pain reduction)
Anorexia: 210, 238, 241
  music therapy interventions for: 256-257
Antisocial personality disorders: 212, 238, 240
  music therapy interventions for: 259-261
Anxiety disorders: 209, 210, 212, 219, 237, 240, 320
  music therapy interventions for: 249, 254-256, 401, 406
Anxiety reduction: 280
  music therapy approaches for: 282, 284-293, 310, 364, 376, 393, 404 (*see also* Relaxation; Stress reduction; Stress treatment programs)
Aphasia: 98, 100, 172, 174, 304, 305
  music therapy interventions for: 182-185, 310
Apraxia: 172, 183, 304
Arabia
  music and healing in: 24
Arteriosclerosis: 319
Arthritis: 75, 148-149. 155. 156, 158, 160, 166, 294, 319
Arthrogryposis: 47, 166
Articulation disorders: 100, 171
  music therapy interventions for: 179-180
Asperger's disorder: 80, 189
Assessment: 2-4, 65, 197-198, 230, 232, 236, 246, 248, 250, 251, 262, 266, 281, 282, 287, 295, 296, 301, 304, 306, 314, 334, 337, 338. 344. 351. 360, 375, 394, 407, 412
Association for Music and Imagery (AMI): 392
Asthma: 279, 280
  music therapy interventions for: 288, 292, 393
At-risk children and adolescents: 7, 209-210, 214
  music therapy interventions for: 230-231, 400
Attending behaviors/Awareness
  use of music to increase: 73-74, 269-270, 347
    (*see also* Attention span; Reality orientation; Sensory stimulation/sensory training)
Attention-deficit disorders (ADD): 98, 100, 208, 211-212